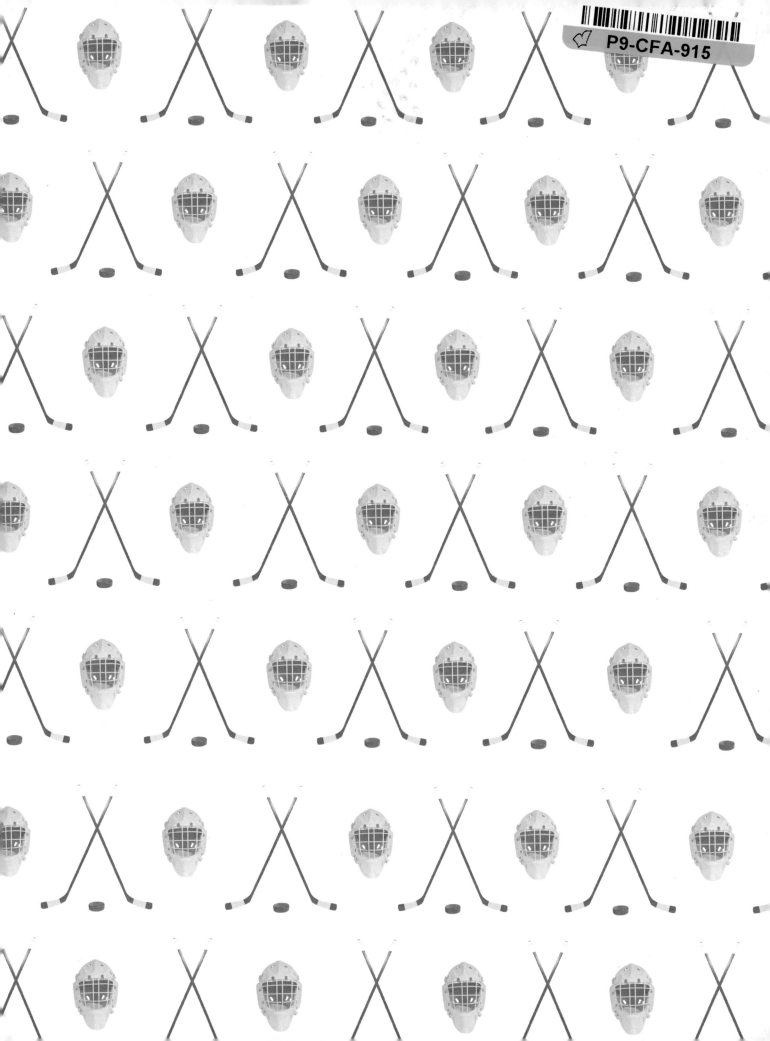

HOCKEY CHRONICLE

Year-by-Year History of the National Hockey League

Stan and Shirley Fischler
Morgan Hughes
Joseph Romain
James Duplacey

Publications International, Ltd.

Stan Fischler, the dean of North American hockey writers, has written more than 60 books in his distinguished career. He is the author of *Slapshot, Fischler's Illustrated History of Hockey, Bobby Orr and the Big, Bad Bruins,* and *Great Book of Hockey.* A professional hockey writer since 1954, Fischler has been published in *Sports Illustrated, The New York Times, The Hockey News,* and *Newsweek.* He has worked extensively in sports broadcasting, including pregame and postgame shows for SportsChannel.

Shirley Fischler has been writing about hockey since 1971 when she was assigned to cover the Stanley Cup playoffs by the *Kingston (Ontario) Whig-Standard.* For 15 years she hosted her show, "Young Side," on WABC radio in New York City, and she's been a frequent guest on television and radio. She has teamed with her husband on such books as *The Hockey Encyclopedia* and *The Best, The Worst, and Most Unusual in Sports.*

Morgan Hughes is the former editor of *Hockey Stars* and *Hockey Heroes* and has written about hockey for such national publications as *Goal, Hockey Scene,* and *Inside Sports.* He coauthored the *Hockey Almanac* and served as consultant for *Great Book of Hockey.* A freelance writer, he has also contributed to *The Sporting News, Village Voice,* and *Sport.*

Joseph Romain is the former librarian and associate curator of the Hockey Hall of Fame and Museum in Toronto. He is a freelance writer and library consultant who has written several hockey books, including *The Pictorial History of Hockey* and *Hockey Hall of Fame.*

James Duplacey has written numerous books concerning the history of hockey, including *Hockey Superstars: 1000 Point Players, Maple Leaf Magic,* and *Toronto Maples Leafs: Images of Glory.* He has served as curator of the Hockey Hall of Fame and Museum and managing editor of the *Official NHL Guide and Record Book.*

Editorial assistance provided by **Michael Sandrolini.**

Special thanks to **Ralph Dinger** for his photo research assistance.

ISBN: 0-7853-6307-6

Library of Congress Control Number: 2002105949

Front cover: Dave Sandford/Getty Images
Back cover: Scott Levy/Bruce Bennett Studios

Amateur Hockey Association of the United States: 409; **A/P World Wide Photos:** 65, 75, 97, 99, 103, 108, 109, 110, 111, 114, 116, 122, 123, 125, 127, 128, 129, 134, 139, 141, 144, 146, 147, 130, 231, 150, 151, 152, 153, 159, 162, 164, 170, 171, 176, 180, 183, 185, 187, 188, 189, 191, 194, 195, 200, 201, 207, 211, 212, 218, 222, 223, 224, 228, 229, 230, 234, 235, 236, 241, 242, 243, 246, 247, 249, 253, 254, 258, 261, 263, 266, 267, 271, 276, 277, 278, 284, 293, 294, 295, 296, 302, 303, 308, 320, 321, 328, 334, 352, 366, 376, 377, 386, 387, 396, 397, 401, 406, 416, 424, 426, 436, 442, 446, 453, 456, 466, 470, 476, 496, 501, 536; Hector Acevedo: 640; Paul Chiasson: 639; Jack Dempsey: 628; Kevork Djansezian: 638; David Duprey: 630, 641; Grant Halverson: 637, 640; Fred Jewell: 623, 631; Jay LaPrete: 624; Donna McWilliams: 620; Ottawa Sun-Jonathan Hayward: 618; Chris Putman: 639; Ryan Remiorz: 641; Tim Sharp: 621; Andrew Vaughan: 627; **Daniel S. Baliotti:** 363, 369; **Bruce Bennett Studios:** 8, 9, 10, 105, 120, 228, 242, 252, 253, 254, 266, 295, 300, 301, 303, 304, 309, 311, 313, 321, 324, 325, 326, 331, 332, 333, 334, 342, 343, 345, 346, 356, 357, 360, 363, 365, 366, 370, 372, 373, 374, 375, 376, 377, 379, 383, 384, 385, 387, 389, 390, 391, 392, 393, 394, 395, 396, 397, 399, 400, 401, 402, 403, 404, 405, 406, 407, 410, 411, 412, 413, 414, 415, 417, 419, 420, 421, 422, 423, 424, 425, 426, 427, 429, 430, 431, 432, 433, 434, 435, 436, 437, 439, 440, 441, 442, 443, 444, 445, 446, 447, 449, 450, 451, 452, 453, 454, 455, 456, 457, 459, 460, 461, 462, 463, 464, 465, 466, 467, 469, 470, 471, 472, 473, 474, 475, 476, 477, 479, 480, 481, 482, 483, 484, 485, 486, 487, 490, 491, 493, 494, 495, 496, 497, 499, 500, 501, 502, 503, 504, 505, 506, 507, 509, 510, 511, 512, 513, 514, 515, 516, 517, 519, 520, 521, 522, 523, 524, 526, 527, 530, 531, 532, 533, 534, 535, 536, 537, 538, 539, 541, 543, 544, 545, 546, 548, 549, 551, 565, 566, 568, 570, 571, 573, 574, 575, 578, 579, 580, 581, 584, 585, 586, 588, 589, 590, 591, 603, 604, 606, 614, 633, 634, 635, 636, 637, 639, 640; C. Andersen: 577, 580, 585, 589, 606; Bruce Bennett: 608, 614, 628, 634; M. Buckner: 619; M. Campanelli: 568; M. Desjardins: 574; Melchior DiGiacomo: 310, 312, 317, 318, 319, 323, 325, 327, 328, 329, 332, 335, 336, 337, 339, 340, 341, 342, 343, 345, 346, 349, 350, 351, 352, 353, 354, 355, 356, 357, 359, 361, 362, 363, 364, 365, 367, 373, 376, 382, 386, 392, 397, 406; Michael DiGirolamo: 525, 530, 543, 545; J. DiMaggio/J. Kalish: 371, 372, 373, 385, 391, 403; H. Dirocco: 605, 624; A. Foxall: 569, 575, 576; J.R. Giamundo: 532, 571, 583, 586, 605, 607, 619; Jim Gund: 548; M. Hicks: 576, 578, 581, 587; J. Johnson: 542; R. LaBerge: 584, 579; J. Leary: 11, 604, 609, 610; Scott A. Levy: 489, 515, 524, 529, 530, 531, 534, 539, 546, 547, 550, 551, 570; R. Lewis: 580, 581; Jon Margolis: 626; Andy Marlin: 626, 630; Brian McCormick: 569, 577; Jim McIsaac: 579, 584, 590, 605, 606, 607, 608, 609, 615, 616, 617, 618, 625, 626, 627, 635, 636, 637, 638; Brian Miller: 492, 495, 503, 511, 513, 522, 523; B. Monchamp: 567; Chris Pasatieri: 636; M. Rand: 546; L. Redkoles: 608; Steve Reyes: 520, 549; M. Roberts: 576; J. Russell: 616; D. Sandler: 534; J. Wiley: 544; Brian Winkler: 495, 506, 537, 542, 567, 587, 615, 617; Bill Wippert: 511; **David Bier Studios:** 257; **Boston Public Library:** 117, 127, 129, 141, 165, 193, 222, 241; **Herbert Brooks/University of Minnesota:** 355; **Canadian Amateur Hockey Association:** 41; **Colorado College:** 236; **Corbis:** 37, 49, 57, 109, 209, 213, 237, 243, 272, 278, 320, 364, 405; Shaun Best: 625; Jason Cohn: 625; Ron Martinez: 613; Tim Parker: 631; Reuters NewMedia Inc./Ray Stubblebine: 621; Tim Shaffer: 620; **Dan Diamond and Associates:** 89; **Stan Fischler Collection:** 51, 64, 73, 109, 113, 132, 145, 152, 158, 165, 181, 193, 194, 200, 206, 216, 240, 270, 283, 336, 342, 381; Bill Galloway Collection: 64, 169; Hockey Hall of Fame: 69; New York Rangers Fan Club: 255; Imperial Oil Turofsky Collection: 140; **Ernie Fitzsimmons Collection:** 73; **Getty Images:** Hasch Elsa: 620; Allsport USA: 610; Brian Bahr: 631; Nhan Chu: 624; Hasch Elsa: 610, 611; Harry How: 618; Ronald Martinez: 629; Donald Miralle: 614, 629; Jamie Squire: 627; **Hockey Hall of Fame and Museum:** 14, 15, 16, 17, 18, 19, 20, 21, 22, 23, 24, 25, 26, 27, 28, 29, 31, 32, 33, 35, 36, 37, 39, 40, 41, 43, 44, 45, 47, 48, 49, 52, 53, 55, 56, 57, 59, 60, 61, 63, 64, 65, 68, 71, 72, 76, 79, 80, 81, 83, 84, 85, 87, 88, 89, 91, 92, 95, 96, 97, 98, 99, 101, 102, 103, 104, 105, 107, 108, 110, 111, 114, 115, 116, 117, 119, 120, 121, 123, 126, 131, 132, 133, 134, 135, 137, 138, 139, 140, 144, 145, 146, 150, 152, 155, 156, 157, 158, 159, 161, 162, 163, 164, 165, 168, 169, 170, 171, 173, 174, 175, 177, 179, 180, 183, 186, 187, 192, 198, 199, 201, 203, 204, 205, 210, 211, 212, 213, 215, 216, 217, 218, 219, 221, 222, 224, 225, 227, 228, 229, 233, 234, 235, 239, 240, 245, 247, 248, 249, 251, 252, 253, 255, 258, 259, 260, 261, 267, 265, 269, 270, 271, 272, 273, 275, 276, 277, 279, 282, 283, 284, 285, 287, 288, 289, 290, 291, 294, 295, 296, 297, 299, 300, 301, 305, 307, 308, 309, 310, 312, 315, 316, 317, 324, 327, 335, 336, 340, 345, 347, 346, 350, 353, 360, 366, 371, 374, 380, 381, 390, 424; Alexandra Studio Photographers: 151, 168; David Bier Studios: 281; Michael Burns: 249; Kenneth Edmonds: 181; Bill Galloway: 143; Gorman Collection: 102; Imperial Oil Turofsky Collection: 67, 69, 77, 81, 105, 121, 147, 150, 153, 157, 174, 181, 182, 183, 186, 188, 189, 193, 195, 197, 204, 206, 219, 225, 231, 240, 259, 273; Doug MacLellan: 18, 69, 535, 547, 550; Pacific & Atlantic Photos, Inc.: 99; Frank Prazak: 291, 302, 304, 313; Public Archives, Canada: 22; Weekend Magazine: 211; Willis Collection: 93, 176; **The Ice Age:** 19; LaPresse: 207; **Doug McLatchy:** 237; **Tim Morse Photography:** 505; **National Hockey League:** 387; **Northern Michigan University:** 524; **Prince Albert Raider Hockey Club:** 465; **Saskatchewan Sports Hall of Fame and Museum:** 176; **University of Minnesota:** 182; **Wisconsin Men's Sports Information:** 445; Additional photography: Sam Griffith Studios.

CONTENTS

CONTENTS

CONTENTS

CONTENTS

The story of hockey in North America is one of athletes striving for excellence, doing what is necessary to succeed, toiling tirelessly to fulfill shared goals, sacrificing health and welfare to capture the holy grail of hockey, the precious Stanley Cup.

Many of the stories that make up the fabric of hockey are moving and inspirational—while others are almost too painful to bear. Hall of Fame coach and general manager Emil Francis once said: "Hockey is a slippery game. It's played on ice."

It is the objective of *Hockey Chronicle* to celebrate the talent and passion of the generations of players, coaches, managers, and visionaries who battled for secure footing in this slipperiest of sports. The book salutes the men—and women—who have guided hockey

Bobby Bauer, Woody Dumart, Milt Schmidt

from virtual "sideshow" status 100 years ago to its present position of prestige. (The 2002 Stanley Cup Finals between the Detroit Red Wings and Carolina were a huge ratings hit on network television.)

The history of hockey is replete with the inspiring work of such individuals as Jack Adams. Adams was GM of the NHL's Detroit Falcons (later renamed the Red Wings) during the Great Depression and often had to make ends meet with a very tight budget. One night during the 1932-33 season, Adams allowed a patron into Olympia Stadium in exchange for five bags of potatoes. "If the greatest star was made available to us for a dollar, ninety-eight," said Adams, "we couldn't have afforded him."

That anecdote illustrates the stark contrast between early-century hockey and the blockbuster sport of today. Though the essence of the game remains the same—six men and a puck—the financial state of the sport has changed dramatically. In fact, one could easily draw a line near the middle of the 20th century. The years 1900-45 were tough times, with hockey often limping along, with franchises coming and going, and wars interrupting the careers of superstars. However, from 1946 to the present, the great game has stabilized and steadily grown—beyond even the wildest dreams of its most daring visionaries.

Around 1900, seven years after Lord Stanley donated his famous chalice to the game of hockey, amateur and professional leagues began to pop up all over North America. There was the Eastern Canada Hockey Association (ECHA), the Federal Amateur Hockey League (FAHL), the Pacific Coast Hockey Association (PCHA), the Western Canadian Hockey League (WCHL), the National Hockey Association (NHA), and even the MPHL—the Maritime Professional Hockey League. Unfortunately, the cost of fielding teams and the difficulty of winter travel often forced teams as well as entire leagues to dissolve like snow in the springtime.

After the demise of the NHA in 1917, the new National Hockey League tried to make a go of it, fielding two teams in Montreal and one each in Toronto, Ottawa, and Quebec. But the early years proved to be quite the financial ordeal for some of the charter members. Quebec, afraid it would not survive the season, decided to sit out the year (and the next). An even bigger disaster struck on January 2, 1918, when the Montreal Arena burned to the ground, forcing the Wanderers to wander into oblivion. For that season and the next, the NHL was a paltry three-team league.

Business boomed in the 1920s, with new teams in Hamilton, Montreal, and Boston—followed by clubs in New York, Chicago, Detroit, and Pittsburgh. But the stock market crash of 1929 brought the league to its knees. During the Depression, the Pittsburgh Pirates relocated and became the Philadelphia Quakers, then became extinct. Ottawa moved to St. Louis, then closed up shop altogether. The Montreal Maroons couldn't make it out of the '30s, and the New York Americans, forced to compete in the same market as the 1928 Stanley Cup champion Rangers, also folded up the tent.

Six teams remained—Montreal, Toronto, Boston, Chicago, Detroit, and New York—and they would come to be known as the "Original Six." But World War II took a heavy toll on these franchises as well. A preponderance of stars, such as Bruins ace Milt Schmidt and Toronto's Turk Broda and Syl Apps, went off to battle, leaving managers to scramble to fill their rosters with comparative scrubs. Goalie Steve Buzinski's inability to stop the opposition earned him the nickname "The Puck Goes Inski." Fabled Rangers GM Lester Patrick said: "The situation was so bleak that it appeared the league would not open for the 1942-43 season."

Finally, with the conclusion of World War II in September 1945, hockey's long years of struggle came to an end. Wartime travel restrictions were lifted, old stars returned to their former clubs, and fans flocked to the stadiums with renewed enthusiasm. Rising stars, most notably Maurice "Rocket" Richard and Gordie Howe, thrilled old fans and lured new ones. The advent of television brought heroes to life, while a strengthening economy meant greater advertising revenue for the NHL owners.

Gordie Howe

The 1960s brought glory boys Bobby Hull, Jean Beliveau, and Frank Mahovlich. As the six-team NHL grew into a cash cow, cities throughout North America wanted in on the action. In 1967-68, in its single greatest moment of visionary growth, the league not only expanded, it doubled in size, adding the Pittsburgh Penguins, Philadelphia Flyers, Minnesota North Stars, St. Louis Blues, Los Angeles Kings, and Oakland Seals. The Buffalo Sabres and Vancouver Canucks hopped on the bandwagon in 1970-71, while the Atlanta Flames and the New York Islanders hitched on in 1972-73. The Washington Capitals and Kansas City Scouts debuted in 1974-75.

Around the same time, a rival league—the World Hockey Association—took root in 10 cities, raiding the NHL of some of its biggest names (Bobby Hull and Gordie Howe among them). Though many of its teams eventually relocated or disbanded, the WHA competed for hockey attention for seven years before four of its members—the Edmonton Oilers, Hartford Whalers, Winnipeg Jets, and Quebec Nordiques—were "invited" to join the NHL in a conciliatory merger.

The 1980s and 1990s gave the NHL community its greatest player of all-time as well as the promise of new horizons. But there were also some serious questions about the direction the game was taking as well as the ability of the league's presidential leadership.

Wayne Gretzky

Arriving in the NHL in 1979-80 as an 18-year-old phenomenon who didn't even have to shave yet, Wayne Gretzky took the Edmonton Oilers to four Stanley Cups in five years from 1984 to 1988. Moreover, he rewrote the record books in ways that almost certainly will never be equaled. After his stunning trade to Los Angeles in 1988, the Great One built the Kings into a contender and took them to the 1993 Stanley Cup Finals. His brilliance on the ice transformed California into a hockey mecca, turned Kings home games into the hardest ticket in town, and made the Great Western Forum "the place to be" if you were a sports fan in Tinseltown.

Indeed, Gretzky's influence was so great with youth throughout the West and Southwest that hockey suddenly discovered its long desired foothold in the geographic areas south of the Mason-Dixon line. Many hockey historians believe that without Gretzky, there would be no San Jose Sharks or Mighty Ducks of Anaheim.

It was during this period, while Major League Baseball and the NBA boomed, that the NHL became more determined than ever to find its launchpad to the 21st century—and its share of the public sports dollar. Poor leadership from the home office and lackluster marketing strategies were identified as chief problem areas. Thus, in February 1993, Gary Bettman—who had cut his management teeth alongside the NBA's David Stern—became the league's first "commissioner."

Martin Brodeur

After decades of perceived owner-serving presidents, the NHL had a new leadership model and a man at the helm who had a reputation for doing whatever was needed to improve the product. Bettman's regime took over with a vision toward guiding the sport to greater heights. Under his watch, the NHL oversaw the establishment of franchises in, of all places, Texas, Florida, Arizona, Tennessee, North Carolina, and Georgia. In Ohio, Bettman rubber-stamped the NHL's initiative to plant a team in Columbus. The Blue Jackets made their debut in 2000-01 and became an almost instant success.

Indeed, Bettman's courageous and Herculean efforts proved to be well worth it when the Florida Panthers, in only their third season of operation, went to the 1995 Stanley Cup Finals against Colorado...and again when the Dallas Stars captured the 1999 Stanley Cup...and yet again when the Carolina Hurricanes (formerly the Hartford Whalers) advanced to the 2002 Cup Finals. Bettman also made sure the NHL returned to the national airwaves by signing unprecedented TV contracts and mapping a course for an even rosier future.

It is the goal of this publication to capture the essence of each and every hockey season in the 20th and 21st centuries, the lean years as well as the fruitful ones. Each chapter (representing each season) opens with a feature story on the most important event of the year, while the rest of the chapter contains smaller articles on the other meaningful events of the campaign. Along the bottom of each page, a timeline details each significant moment of the year.

As you progress from the humble black-and-white photographs of the early days to the high-resolution photos of the 21st century, you'll see how drastically the game has changed. Back then, stars such as Rat Westwick and Moose Johnson pulled on scratchy wool sweaters and skated on frigid outdoor rinks banked by snow. Nowadays, rocket-powered skaters and fully armored goalies play in climate-controlled, state-of-the-art facilities, in a world of plastic, plexiglass, and vibrant, dazzling colors. Indeed, as much as it has remained the same over the course of time, the game of hockey—particularly at the NHL level—has steadily transformed and evolved.

Are today's stars better than the heroes of yesteryear? Probably. However, don't forget that the NHL's top goal-scorer every season is now presented with a trophy in the name of Rocket Richard. Today's players are dramatically bigger, measurably faster afoot, and more powerful in every facet. Yet today's skaters certainly owe a debt of gratitude to the game's pioneers, who—despite bankrupt teams, crumbling leagues, the Great Depression, and two world wars—plugged on and on, keeping the great sport of hockey alive for us to enjoy today, laying the groundwork so that future generations will continue to enjoy the sport. The *Hockey Chronicle* salutes each and every one of them.

The precise origin of hockey has remained a mystery to historians. Wide-ranging theories have pinpointed Montreal, Halifax, and Kingston as the most likely sites of "first games" in North America, but nothing has been proven. Likewise, the very first hockey leagues—primitive in nature and loosely formed—are just as difficult to isolate.

What is certain is this: As the game emerged from its shell, amateur groups organized in Quebec City, Kingston, Montreal, and Halifax starting in the late 1870s. Within a decade, hockey's popularity had grown so rapidly that amateur leagues sprouted on both sides of the 49th parallel.

Organized hockey took a giant stride forward in 1893. That year, Lord Stanley of Preston—Canada's governor general—offered a silver cup to be presented to the premier team in Canada. At first, only amateur teams battled for the coveted trophy because professional hockey was pretty much non-existent.

However, in 1904, a dentist in Houghton, Michigan, got the bright idea that play-for-pay hockey would interest the public more than the simon-pure variety. Dr. Jack Gibson obtained financial backing and organized

NHA, PCHA Emerge as Hockey's 'Big Two'

North America's first full-blown professional organization—the International Hockey League. It was an odd mix that included the Michigan towns of Houghton, Sault Ste. Marie, Portage Lake, and Laurium, as well as Pittsburgh and Sault Ste. Marie, Ontario.

Although the International League was short-lived, it proved to be a beacon that other hockey groups soon followed. As more and more pros ("ringers") seeped into the amateur ranks, the foremost amateur leagues read the handwriting and changed their positions. In 1908, the powerful Eastern Canada Amateur Hockey Association went the professional route, and soon it became clear to Stanley Cup trustees that the mug soon would be awarded to the

best pro teams and not the amateurs.

The most important of the new leagues was born in 1909. The National Hockey Association was organized with teams in Montreal, Renfrew, Cobalt, and Haileybury. Yet another pro league, the Canadian Hockey Association, was organized that same year. It granted franchises to teams in Ottawa, Quebec, and Montreal.

No less important was the westward move of the Patrick brothers, Frank and Lester, who organized the Pacific Coast Hockey Association in 1911. Its original clubs included New Westminster, Vancouver, and Victoria. The PCHA immediately signed marquee players like Newsy Lalonde, Hugh Lehman, and Harry Hyland.

Prior to World War I, the NHA and PCHA leaders agreed to organize a playoff between their top teams, the winner of which would take the Stanley Cup. In 1917, Seattle of the PCHA became the first American team to win Lord Stanley's bowl, indicating that pro hockey would become a significant money-maker on both sides of the border. The only question to be answered was, "Which league would rule the sport?"

1900

- Referee Fred Waghorne introduces the modern faceoff, dropping the puck between the players' sticks rather than placing it on the ice and risking injury.

- The Canadian Amateur Hockey League adopts use of the goal net.

- The Montreal Shamrocks go 7-1 to win the regular-season CAHL title.

- The Shamrocks claim this year's Stanley Cup. The Cup, donated by Lord Stanley of Preston in 1893, is awarded each year to the champion of amateur Canadian hockey.

- To attain the Stanley Cup, the Shamrocks defeat Winnipeg two games to one, then outscore Halifax 21-2 in a two-game, total-goals series.

- Shamrocks ace Harry Trihey scores 12 goals in five playoff games during the Stanley Cup "challenge."

In 1892, Lord Stanley of Preston, the Governor General of Canada,
decided to donate a trophy to honor the best amateur hockey team in Canada.
Captain Charles Colville, an aide to Lord Stanley, purchased this gold-lined
silver cup on a trip to England, spending 10 guineas (slightly less than $50).
The Montreal Victorias reigned as Stanley Cup champions from 1895-99, but the
Montreal Shamrocks ruled in 1899 and 1900.

1901

• The Ottawa Senators win the CAHL regular-season title with a 7-0 record, but they fail to make it to the Stanley Cup Finals.

• Russell Bowie of the Montreal Victorias leads the CAHL with 24 goals.

• Ottawa goalie Bouse Hutton leads the CAHL with a 2.90 goals-against average.

• The Stanley Cup challenge features the Montreal Shamrocks and the Winnipeg Victorias—which the Vics win two games to none.

• Future Montreal Canadiens star Aurel Joliat is born on August 29, 1901, in Ottawa, Ontario.

• The Intercollegiate Hockey League is formed in the United States. Members include Columbia, Dartmouth, Harvard, Princeton, and Yale.

Waghorne the First to Drop the Puck

Prior to 1900, a faceoff began when the puck was placed on the ice by the ref, who then had to make certain each center was lined up correctly. However, this often led to sticks in tender areas of the ref's anatomy. Thankfully, referee Fred Waghorne debuted a new method in 1900. He simply dropped the puck, "allowing them to do as they darn well pleased," he said. The new faceoff method was eventually adopted.

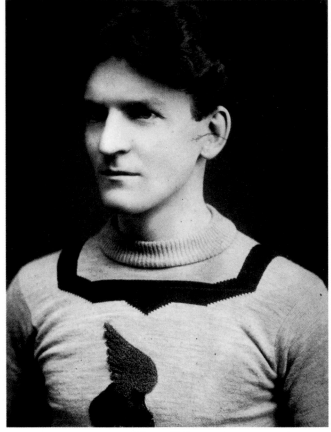

Harry Trihey

Fred Waghorne

Talented Trihey Powers Montreal

Henry J. (Harry) Trihey was captain of the Montreal Shamrocks for their two Stanley Cup wins in 1899 and 1900. Trihey was known as a powerhouse on the lacrosse field and the football field as well as on the ice. He took the notion of the three-man line seriously in a time when hockey was a seven-man game. Under Trihey's captainship, the rover was not a footloose forward; he was truly a roving player.

1902

- Winnipeg defends its 1901 Stanley Cup in January 1902, defeating the Toronto Wellingtons in two games.

- The Montreal AAA club wins the CAHL regular-season title with a 6-2 record, ahead of second-place Ottawa (5-3).

- Art Hooper of the AAAs leads the league in goals (17), scoring nine against the Montreal Shamrocks on January 5, 1902.

- The Montreal AAAs defeat Winnipeg in three games to win the 1902 Stanley Cup.

- Player Jack Gibson leaves amateur hockey and opens a dentistry practice in Michigan. He will eventually reenter hockey as the first professional owner.

- Future Montreal Canadiens star Howie Morenz is born on June 21, 1902, in Mitchell, Ontario.

Russell Bowie

Bowie Averages a Hat-Trick a Game

On February 20, 1901, Russell Bowie of the Montreal Victorias scored seven goals in a game and was well positioned to dominate the CAHL. He finished the season with 24 goals, 14 more than his nearest rival. His entire career was played with the Montreal Victorias, where he averaged almost three goals per game.

Gibson Banned for Accepting $1

As an amateur in Berlin, Ontario, Jack Gibson—along with his teammates—accepted a silver dollar as a token of the town's appreciation for their league championship in 1902. The league brass frowned upon the gift and banned all the players from amateur play. Gibson's response came in 1905, when he organized the first pro ice hockey league.

Hockey History Buffs Indulge in The Trail

This fine red-leather edition of *The Trail of the Stanley Cup* was the property of Clarence Campbell, longtime president of the NHL. The three-volume collection, written by Charles L. Coleman, covers the years 1893 (the first year of the Stanley Cup) through 1967 and is considered the most important chronicle of the history of the game.

The Trail of the Stanley Cup

Jack Gibson

1903

- Ottawa and Winnipeg tie for the CAHL regular-season title (6-2).

- The famed Ottawa Silver Seven team features Art Moore and Harvey Pulford on defense, and a forward line of Dave Gilmour, Suddy Gilmour, Billy Gilmour, and superstar Frank McGee.

- Russell Bowie scores 22 goals for the Montreal Victorias, including seven against Quebec on January 10 and six against the Montreal Shamrocks two weeks later.

- Frank McGee of Ottawa is second in goals (14), scoring five against Winnipeg on February 7, 1903.

- The Montreal AAAs defend their 1902 Stanley Cup in February 1903, as they defeat the Winnipeg Victorias in four games.

- The Ottawa Silver Seven wins the 1903 Stanley Cup by defeating the Montreal Victorias and the Rat Portage Thistles.

One-Eyed McGee Nets Three a Game

Frank McGee

Frank McGee starred on the famed Ottawa Silver Seven from 1903-06, potting 14 goals in six games in 1903. A center and rover (rover was the seventh position), McGee was a lightning-fast skater who could stick-handle and shoot with the very best of them. McGee, who averaged nearly three goals a game during his playing days, had sight in just one eye. In 1916, he was killed in France during World War I.

Ottawa Hockey Club

Ottawa Grabs Cup, Won't Give It Up

The Ottawa Hockey Club, which would come to be known as the Silver Seven, began its quest for dynasty status in 1903. The Silver Seven won the Stanley Cup in March 1903 and hung on to it until December 1906, defeating nine challengers along the way. The Montreal Victorias and Rat Portage Thistles both fell prey to the dynastic seven in '03. Ottawa Hall of Famers included Frank McGee, Harvey Pulford, Harry Westwick, Billy Gilmour, and J.B. Hutton.

Wheelers Enjoy Stanley Cup Joyride

The Montreal Winged Wheelers owned the Stanley Cup for a year, winning it from the Winnipeg Victorias in March 1902 and losing it to the Ottawa Silver Seven in March 1903. Montreal was captained by Dickie Boon (center, wearing hat), a crafty poke-checker with tremendous speed. The logo of the team, the winged wheel, was resurrected many years later when James Norris, an alumnus of the team, formed the Detroit Red Wings.

Montreal Winged Wheelers

1904

- The Federal Amateur Hockey League is formed. Teams include the Ottawa Senators, the Montreal Wanderers, the Capitals, the Nationals, and a club in Cornwall.

- Quebec wins the CAHL title with a 7-1 record, while the Montreal Wanderers are 6-0 in the FAHL.

- The Montreal Victorias' Russell Bowie leads the CAHL in goals (27).

- Blair Russell of the Montreal Victorias scores seven goals against the Montreal Shamrocks on January 2, 1904, while Quebec's Herb Jordan strafes the Shams with eight goals on January 19.

- In the playoffs, Ottawa defeats the Winnipeg Rowing Club and then Toronto of the Ontario league.

- Ottawa's playoff series with the Wanderers is canceled after a Game 1 tie, as teams can't decide where the tie game should be replayed. Ottawa then beats Brandon to retain the Cup.

Paddy Moran

Moran's Stand-Up Routine Is a Hit

Except for a one-year stint for Haileybury of the NHA, goalie Paddy Moran played his hockey in Quebec from 1902-17. In 1904, he powered his Bulldogs to a 7-1 regular-season record, best in the CAHL. Moran was known as a stand-up goalie who frequently used his stick to paddle away enemy shots. Paddy led Quebec to Stanley Cups in 1912 and '13 and was elected to the Hall of Fame in 1958.

Harvey Pulford

Pulford Captains the Dynastic Seven

The Jim Thorpe of Canada, Harvey Pulford starred on his country's best football and lacrosse teams and was also an outstanding light-heavyweight boxer. His greatest feats, though, came on the ice, as this dominating blueliner served as captain of the dynastic Ottawa Silver Seven. Pulford and his mates defeated three Stanley Cup challengers in 1904: the Winnipeg Rowing Club in January, the Toronto Marlboros in February, and Brandon in March.

1905

• The Montreal Victorias win the CAHL title with a 9-1 record, edging Quebec (8-2). The Ottawa Senators take the FAHL (7-1).

• Russell Bowie scores a CAHL-high 26 goals for the Victorias, while Frank McGee leads the FAHL with 17 goals.

• Former amateur player Jack Gibson organizes the International Hockey League, the game's first pro league.

• The IHL has teams in the Michigan cities of Portage Lake, Laurium, Houghton, and Sault Ste. Marie, as well as in Pittsburgh and Sault Ste. Marie, Ontario.

• The Ottawa Silver Seven meets Dawson City (which has traveled more than 4,000 miles) in the Stanley Cup challenge.

• In Game 2 against Dawson City, Frank McGee scores 14 goals as Ottawa wins 23-2. Ottawa later beats Rat Portage to retain the Stanley Cup.

Ottawa Watches Challengers Drop Like Flies

This confident Ottawa crew had reason to appear a little cocky, as it continued to knock off all challengers for the Stanley Cup including clubbings of Dawson City and Rat Portage in 1905. The club was known as the Silver "Seven" because, in their day, seven men played at one time, with the extra man being a rover. It's unknown where "Silver" derived from, but it might as well have referred to Lord Stanley's silver bowl.

Ottawa Silver Seven

McGee Scores 14 vs. Dawson City

In January 1905, Dawson City challenged the Ottawa Silver Seven for the Stanley Cup. It was significant because the Yukon Territory team had to travel 4,000 miles (by dogsled, ship, and train) at a cost of $3,000 to get to Ottawa—only to be thoroughly humiliated. Ottawa crushed Dawson City 9-2 in Game 1 and then massacred the Yukon Nuggets 23-2 in Game 2. Frank McGee went into a goal-happy frenzy in Game 2, tickling the twine 14 times.

Frank McGee

Tommy Smith

Smith Packs His Suitcase, Racks Up Goals

It's hard to summarize the career of Tommy Smith, a 5'4" goal-scorer who played for at least 10 teams in his career. While skating for the Ottawa Vics in 1906, Smith led the FAHL with 12 goals (including eight in a game). In future years, he would be the leading goal-scorer in the OPHL (1908-09) and the NHA (1910-11, 1913-14, 1914-15). Smith, one of 13 children, is a member of the Hockey Hall of Fame, as is his brother Alf.

1906

• The CAHL combines with Ottawa and the Montreal Wanderers to form the Eastern Canada Amateur Hockey Association. Ottawa and the Wanderers tie for first place at 9-1.

• Smiths Falls takes the FAHL title with a 7-0 mark, thanks to goalie Percy LeSueur (1.9 GAA).

• Ottawa's Harry Smith leads the ECAHA in goals (38), including an eight-goal explosion against the Montreal Shamrocks on February 17.

• Tommy Smith of the FAHL's Ottawa Vics leads his league in goals (12), thanks to an eight-goal game against Brockville on February 23.

• Ottawa defends its 1905 Stanley Cup in February 1906. The Silver Seven beat Queens University in two games, by a combined 28-14, before beating Smiths Falls in two straight.

• The Montreal Wanderers win the 1906 Cup in March by beating Ottawa 12-10 in a two-game series.

Montreal Wanderers

Wanderers End Ottawa's Dynasty

In March 1906, the Silver Seven's stranglehold on the Stanley Cup was finally broken. It was the Montreal Wanderers who yanked it from their grasp, beating Ottawa 12-10 in a total-goals series. Over the next 2½ years, the Wanderers would dominate the game, playing eight challenge matches for the Cup and losing only one series, that being to the Kenora Thistles. Lester Patrick and Moose Johnson were among the big names on the Wanderers squad.

Team from Rat Portage Wins Cup

The Kenora Thistles, a star-studded team out of the backwater of Rat Portage, Ontario, challenged the Montreal Wanderers for the Stanley Cup in January 1907. In this incredible series, in which 11 of the 15 participants would wind up in the Hall of Fame, the Thistles prevailed by scores of 4-2 and 8-6. The Wanderers, however, took the Cup back from Kenora two months later. Ringer Art Ross and the unstoppable Tom Phillips shined for the Thistles.

Russell Nets More Than Four Goals a Game

To say that Ernie Russell of the Montreal Wanderers had a good year in 1906-07 is a little like saying the Titanic had a rough ride across the Atlantic. The bottom line is that he scored an ECAHA-high 42 goals in the nine-game season. A closer look at the scoring exposes the following: twice he scored five goals, once he scored six, and twice he scored eight! It's no wonder that the Wanderers went 10-0 during the season and won the Stanley Cup.

Ernie Russell

Kenora Thistles

• In a Stanley Cup challenge in December 1906, the Montreal Wanderers beat New Glasgow 17-5 in a two-game series.

• The Montreal Wanderers win the ECAHA title with a 10-0 record, while the Ottawa Montagnards top the FAHL with an 8-1 mark.

• Ernie Russell leads the ECAHA in goals (42), thanks to two eight-goal games against the Montreal Shamrocks and a six-goaler vs. Quebec.

• Cornwall's Owen McCourt leads the FAHL in goals with 16, including seven vs. Morrisburg in February.

• Owen McCourt is killed when Ottawa's Charles Masson hits him in the head. Masson is charged with manslaughter but is acquitted.

• The Wanderers lose twice to Kenora before it's determined that Kenora is using ringers. In a rematch, Montreal beats Kenora to win the Stanley Cup.

Marty Walsh

Walsh's 28 Goals Lead the OPHL

Marty Walsh skated for the Ottawa Senators in 1908 and tied for the ECAHA lead with 28 goals. Two years earlier, Walsh had played against Ottawa when his Queens University team challenged for the Cup.

Lalonde Stars in Numerous Leagues

Newsy Lalonde, who would eventually lead the NHL in scoring, led the OPHL in goals with 29 in 1907-08. Lalonde played in a seemingly endless number of leagues, including the FAHL, MHL, OPHL, NHA, PCHA, WCHL, and NHL.

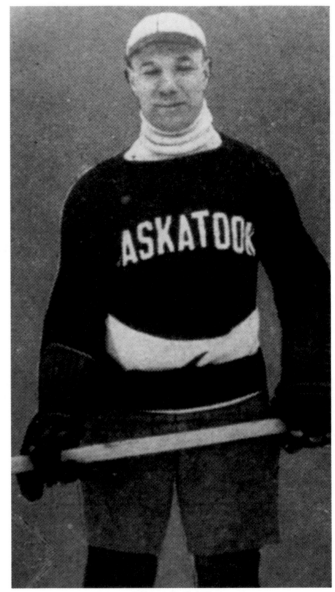

Newsy Lalonde

1907-08

• The Montreal Wanderers repeat as ECAHA champs (8-2), while Toronto wins the Ontario Professional Hockey League title with a 10-2 record.

• Ottawa's Marty Walsh ties Russell Bowie of the Montreal Victorias for the ECAHA goal title (28).

• Marty Walsh has the ECAHA's biggest game, a seven-goal outburst against the Montreal Wanderers.

• Newsy Lalonde, a future NHL superstar, leads the OPHL with 29 goals, including eight in a game against Brantford.

• The Wanderers defeat three challengers for the Stanley Cup. They first trounce the Ottawa Victorias in a total-goals playoff 22-4.

• The Wanderers dispatch the Winnipeg Maple Leafs 20-8 in two games and Toronto 6-4 in one game to retain the Stanley Cup.

Ottawa Senators

Billy Gilmour

Ottawa Wins the ECHA, and the Cup

The Ottawa Hockey Club sat and stewed while the Montreal Wanderers dominated Stanley Cup play from 1906-08. Because of a rule change, however, the winner in the ECHA in 1908-09 would automatically receive the Cup. Ottawa won the title, and thus the Cup, by virtue of its 10-2 record, one game better than Montreal (9-3). This new Ottawa team, the Senators, featured Hall of Famers Percy LeSueur, Cyclone Taylor, Billy Gilmour, Marty Walsh, and Bruce Stuart.

Billy Gilmour Claims Cup After Cup

The Gilmour brothers—Billy, Suddy, and Dave—all played for the Ottawa Silver Seven when they won the Stanley Cup in 1903. In 1904, Dave left the team and the game, leaving Billy and Suddy to defend the Cup and the family name. Suddy left the team following the 1904 Cup win, but Billy went on to play several more seasons, winning the Stanley Cup with the Silver Seven in 1905 and '06 and nabbing the mug again with the 1909 Ottawa Senators.

1908-09

- In December 1908, the Montreal Wanderers meet their fourth Stanley Cup challenger of the calendar year. They beat Edmonton in two games.

- No longer an all-amateur league, the Eastern Canada Amateur Hockey Association is renamed the Eastern Canada Hockey Association.

- The ECHA is down to four teams. The Ottawa Senators win the regular-season title with a 10-2 record, ahead of the Montreal Wanderers (9-3).

- Brantford and Galt tie atop the OPHL with 10-4 records. The title is decided by a one-game playoff, which is won by Galt 7-1.

- Ottawa's Marty Walsh leads the ECHA in goals with 38. Brantford's Tommy Smith tops the OPHL (33).

- The Ottawa Senators are awarded the Stanley Cup by virtue of their ECHA title. The Winnipeg Shamrocks hope to challenge Ottawa, but arrangements to meet can't be made.

Montreal Wanderers

Wanderers Beat Berlin, Win Cup

The Montreal Wanderers of 1910 were a powerhouse team with a host of future Hall of Famers in the lineup. Among them were Jimmy Gardner, Jack Marshall, Ernie Russell, and Dickie Boone. As champions of the new NHA, the Wanderers took possession of the Stanley Cup, and they promptly defended it against the Berlin, Ontario, team of the "Trolley League." The one-game, winner-take-all match was won by the Wanderers by a score of 7-3.

Renfrew Hockey Club

Pitre's the First to Sign with Canadiens

Of all the teams currently in the NHL, only one dates as far back as 1909-10: the Montreal Canadiens. The Canadiens, one of the NHA's original teams in 1909-10, would roll right into the NHL in 1917-18. The first player ever to sign with the Canadiens was Didier Pitre, a fast skater with tremendous potential. Newsy Lalonde and future Habs owner Joe Cattarinich also skated for this club.

Didier Pitre

NHA Is Born; Renfrew Inks Big Stars

The 1909-10 season saw the birth of the National Hockey Association, a precursor to the NHL. The NHA's original members included the Montreal Wanderers, Montreal Canadiens, Cobalt, Haileybury, and Renfrew. Renfrew's owners, who were silver barons in Northern Ontario, spent big money to land big stars. Cyclone Taylor signed for $5,000 while the Patrick brothers (Lester and Frank) reportedly received $3,000 each. Newsy Lalonde also played for Renfrew.

1909-10

- The ECHA becomes the CHA, which includes Ottawa, Quebec, All-Montreal, the Montreal Shamrocks, and the Nationals.

- The National Hockey Association debuts with teams in Renfrew, Cobalt, Haileybury, and Montreal (the Wanderers and the Canadiens).

- In January 1910, the CHA gives up its efforts. Two of its teams, Ottawa and the Shamrocks, join the NHA.

- The Wanderers win the NHA race with an 11-1 mark. Newsy Lalonde, who plays for both the Wanderers and Renfrew, leads the NHA with 38 goals, including nine in a game.

- Ottawa defends its 1909 Stanley Cup in January 1910 by defeating both Galt (15-4) and Edmonton (21-11) in total-goals series.

- In March, after the NHA season is over, the Wanderers meet OPHL champion Berlin for the 1910 Stanley Cup. The Wanderers win 7-3.

Ottawa Senators

Walsh's 50 Goals Lead Ottawa to Cup

When the chaos of the 1910-11 season came to a close, the Ottawa Senators were on the top of the pile. They won the NHA with a 13-3 record and then clubbed both Galt (by the score of 7-4) and Port Arthur (13-4) to win the Stanley Cup. Marty Walsh (first row, far left) led the way with 37 goals in the regular season and a whopping 13 tallies in the two Stanley Cup games. Ottawa's Dubby Kerr scored 32 goals in the regular campaign.

Hall Not as Bad as You'd Think

Bad Joe Hall, one of the nastiest defensemen of his day, joined the Quebec Bulldogs in 1910-11. Hall, who was born in England, began his hockey career in 1904 and played on numerous teams until his death in 1919. Quebec teammate Joe Malone said of Bad Joe: "He wasn't mean, despite what a lot of people said about him, (but) he certainly liked to deal out a heavy check."

Joe Hall

Ross Likes to Mix It Up

Montreal Wanderers defenseman Art Ross was not quite as demure as one would gather from this photo. In February 1911, Ross knocked out Quebec's Eddie Oatman, triggering a brawl that was broken up by police. Ross was quite a rabble-rouser in his playing days. In February 1915, he and Minnie McGiffen got into such a heated brawl during a game that cops came in and arrested them.

Art Ross

1910-11

- The Haileybury and Cobalt teams merge and become the Quebec Bulldogs. Meanwhile, the lowly Montreal Shamrocks drop out of the NHA.

- Newsy Lalonde joins the Montreal Canadiens, and future star Georges Vezina makes his debut for the Habs.

- On February 25, Wanderers defender Art Ross knocks Eddie Oatman of Quebec cold, inciting a brawl that requires police intervention.

- Ottawa (13-3) finishes first in the NHA, as Ottawa's Marty Walsh leads the league in goals (37).

- In Stanley Cup action, Galt (OPHL champ) beats Port Hope (Eastern Ontario League champ) while Port Arthur (New Ontario League) tops Prince Albert (Saskatchewan League).

- Ottawa routs Galt 7-4 and Port Arthur 13-4 to win the Cup. Marty Walsh scores 10 against Port Arthur.

Patrick Bros. Strike Gold on the West Coast

Frank Patrick, along with his brother Lester, is one of the most important figures in the history of pro hockey. In 1911, the Patrick brothers began a hockey empire on the west coast of Canada and the United States. The Pacific Coast Hockey Association reigned for 13 years on the sunshine coast and was a formidable rival to the NHA and NHL. Frank was among the leading players, coaches, managers, and owners of the circuit.

O'Brien Trophy

O'Brien Trophy Not Quite the Stanley Cup

The O'Brien Trophy, perhaps the most elaborate of hockey prizes, was named after the O'Brien family of Renfrew, Ontario. The O'Briens operated the NHA and instituted this trophy as emblematic of the league's championship. Their stated goal was to make this award the most important trophy in the game. It was an ambitious goal indeed, considering that the Stanley Cup was—and is to this day—the most coveted trophy in all of sports.

Frank Patrick

Moncton Victorias

Bulldogs Chew Up Moncton

The Moncton Victorias challenged the NHA champion Quebec Bulldogs for the Stanley Cup in March 1912. Ironically, four of the seven members of the Moncton, New Brunswick, team had played for Galt (OPHL) a year earlier. But just as Galt was trounced in its Stanley Cup game, so too was Moncton. Quebec beat the Tommy Smith-led club by scores of 9-3 and 8-0.

1911-12

- Renfrew drops out of the NHA and two teams from Toronto are added. The O'Brien Cup—named for NHA founder Ambrose O'Brien—becomes the NHA's championship trophy.

- The NHA switches to six-man hockey, as it eliminates the "rover" position.

- The Wanderers' Ernie Johnson and Harry Hyland are branded as "outlaws" for jumping to New Westminster of the new Pacific Coast Hockey Association.

- Quebec (10-8) wins the NHA. Ottawa's Skene Ronan leads in goals with 35.

- New Westminster (9-6) takes the PCHA title, as Vancouver's Newsy Lalonde leads in scoring (27 goals).

- Moncton (Maritime Professional Hockey League champion) challenges Quebec for the Stanley Cup, but Jack McDonald scores nine goals in two games as Quebec wins the series 17-3.

Victoria Senators

Phantom Joe Explodes for 43 Goals

Joe Malone was not exactly new to the game, but his first explosive goal-scoring season came in 1912-13 with the Quebec Bulldogs. The 23-year-old poured in 43 goals in 20 NHA contests, including seven in a game against Toronto. When the Bulldogs played Sydney that spring in a Stanley Cup series, Malone potted nine goals in one game. Malone was so swift on the ice that he earned the nickname "Phantom Joe."

Joe Malone

Victoria Wins All But the Cup

The NHA's Quebec Bulldogs retained the Stanley Cup in 1912-13 by trouncing a Maritime squad from Sydney, Nova Scotia. Following that series, Quebec accepted an exhibition challenge against the PCHA champs, the Victoria Senators. Thank goodness for Quebec that the Cup wasn't on the line, as Victoria won two of the three games in handy fashion. From 1914 through 1926, the champion of the East would face the champion of the West for the Stanley Cup.

Quebec's the Top Dog in the NHA

The Quebec Bulldogs dominated the NHA in 1912-13. They went 16-4 and showed their superiority in scoring (112) and defending (75). The loop's top two goal-scorers were Quebec's Joe Malone (front row, center) and Tommy Smith (front row, far left), while Bulldog defenders Joe Hall (front row, third from right) and Harry Mummery (front row, far right) were the two most feared men on the ice. It's also doubtful that anyone had a tougher mascot.

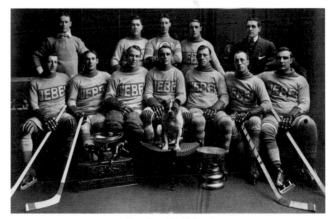

Quebec Bulldogs

1912-13

• Scoring star Harry Hyland reenters the NHA (with the Wanderers) after just one year in the PCHA, and the Canadiens reacquire Newsy Lalonde from Vancouver.

• Ottawa debuts a pair of future Hall of Famers—Punch Broadbent and goalie Clint Benedict.

• Quebec (16-4) takes first place in the NHA, as the Bulldogs' Joe Malone leads the league in goals (43). Harry Hyland scores eight goals in one game against Quebec.

• Victoria wins the PCHA title, as Tom Dunderdale wins the scoring race (27 goals).

• Quebec challenges Sydney for the Stanley Cup. Joe Malone scores nine goals in Game 1 as the Bulldogs breeze to a 20-5 total-goals victory.

• In an exhibition series, Quebec loses two out of three games to Victoria of the PCHA. It's a preview of Stanley Cup challenges to come.

Puck from 1914 Finals

Toronto Claims Its First-Ever Stanley Cup

The city of Toronto did not cherish a Stanley Cup until 1914, when the Toronto Blueshirts (NHA) used this puck to beat the Victoria Cougars (PCHA) for the coveted mug. The Blueshirts' road to the Cup wasn't easy. After finishing the 1913-14 NHA season tied with the Montreal Canadiens, Toronto had to defeat them in a two-game, total-goals series—which they did, 6-2. Three days later, Victoria arrived for a five-game series, which Toronto swept in three.

Baker Shows Americans Can Play Too

One of the greatest players before World War I was Hobey Baker, an American. Born in Pennsylvania, Baker learned to skate effortlessly and stick-handle with finesse. At Princeton, he captained his team to two intercollegiate titles. In the 1914 Ross Cup series against the Montreal Stars, he led his amateur St. Nicholas (New York City) team to victory, causing one wag to write: "Uncle Sam has the cheek to develop a first-class hockey player... who wasn't born in Montreal!"

Hobey Baker

Tommy Dunderdale

Dunderdale Leads PCHA in Scoring

Tommy Dunderdale left the National Hockey Association in 1912 to play on the West Coast for the Victoria Cougars of the Pacific Coast Hockey Association. He stayed with the Western loop until his retirement in 1924. While he was there, he managed to score more goals than any player in the Pacific Coast league, finding the mark 228 times in 291 games. He scored 23 goals for PCHA-champion Victoria in 1913-14.

1913-14

- In the NHA, goalies are not allowed to leave their feet to make saves—and risk penalties for doing so. Also, assists are recorded for the first time.

- The NHA and PCHA come to terms on a Stanley Cup series format to decide hockey's overall champion.

- The Canadiens and Toronto tie for the NHA title (13-7). Quebec's Tommy Smith wins the scoring race (39 goals, including nine in a game).

- The Canadiens' Didier Pitre and Toronto's Frank Nighbor jump to the PCHA. Victoria repeats as PCHA champ.

- Toronto beats the Canadiens 6-2 in a total-goals playoff. Jack Walker scores a hat-trick in Game 2.

- Victoria travels east to face Toronto for the Stanley Cup. Toronto wins three straight in the best-of-five format, as Roy "Minnie" McGiffen scores a critical O.T. goal in Game 2.

Vancouver Millionaires

Ross Tries to Kick Off a New League

Art Ross has sometimes been called the Alan Eagleson of his day. In 1914, with rumors of a new league forming in the East, Ross was suspended from the NHA for allegedly tampering with players under contract. He was apparently promising high salaries in the new league. Ross defended his right to deal with contracted players and, though the new league never got off the ground, Ross was allowed back into the NHA.

Art Ross

Millionaires Give PCHA Its First Cup

In 1914-15, the Stanley Cup series was played on the home ice of the PCHA for the first time. The Ottawa Senators, champions of the NHA, boarded a train and headed to Vancouver. But in a stunning rout, the Millionaires swept the series by scores of 6-2, 8-3, and 12-3, giving the PCHA its first Stanley Cup. Hall of Famers Cyclone Taylor, Frank Nighbor, Hugh Lehman, Mickey Mackay, and player/manager Frank Patrick starred for Vancouver.

Smith Scores Wherever He Plays

Tommy Smith had a heck of a year in 1914-15 despite being shuffled around. A regular with the Quebec Bulldogs, he was shipped to the Ontarios prior to the season opener. Halfway through the season, Quebec ace Joe Malone sprained his ankle and Smith went back to Quebec for the balance of the year. Nevertheless, Smith led the NHA in goals with 39 in 19 games.

Tommy Smith

1914-15

• Emmett Quinn is voted the new president of the NHA, while player Art Ross is temporarily banished from hockey for allegedly negotiating with players to form a new league.

• Ottawa and the Wanderers tie for first place (14-6), as Ottawa's Clint Benedict has the best GAA (3.30).

• Tommy Smith, splitting the year between Quebec and Ontario, leads the NHA in goals (39).

• Vancouver wins the PCHA title behind goalie Hugh Lehman and the league-best scoring of Mickey Mackay (34 goals).

• Ottawa beats the Wanderers 4-1 in the NHA playoffs before taking on Vancouver for the Stanley Cup.

• After trouncing Ottawa 6-2 and 8-3 in the first two games, the Vancouver Millionaires rout the Senators 12-3 in Game 3 to win the Stanley Cup.

Newsy Lalonde

Hot-Tempered Lalonde Leads NHA in Goals

Edouard "Newsy" Lalonde, who won the NHA scoring title in 1915-16 with 31 goals for the Montreal Canadiens, was also one of the nastiest players of his day. During one game in 1912-13, Lalonde slammed Montreal Wanderer Odie Cleghorn into the boards with such force that Odie's teammate and brother, Sprague, charged across the rink and smashed Newsy across the forehead with his stick. The blow just barely missed Lalonde's eye.

Didier Pitre

Cannonball Shoots Habs to the Cup

Didier "Cannonball" Pitre, the first man ever to sign with the Montreal Canadiens, also led them to their first-ever Stanley Cup. Thanks to a line of Pitre, Newsy Lalonde, and Jack Laviolette, the Canadiens roared to the 1915-16 NHA title (going 16-7) and then beat the Portland Rosebuds in the first Stanley Cup series to go five games. Pitre scored a hat-trick in Game 3 of the low-scoring series thanks to his famous "cannonball" shot.

Cyclone Taylor

Taylor Scores 'Em Frontward and Backward

Fred "Cyclone" Taylor, a multi-talented star for the Vancouver Millionaires from 1912-21, potted six in a game in the 1915-16 season. Several years earlier, while playing for Renfrew, Taylor brashly announced that he would skate backward through the entire Ottawa Senators squad and score a goal. It is on record that Taylor did, in fact, skate backward for "about five yards" before lifting a blistering backhander into the Ottawa cage.

1915-16

- The Wanderers' Sprague Cleghorn is lost for the year after a collision with Toronto's Ken Randall. Canadiens ace Skene Ronan is arrested for assaulting Toronto's Alf Skinner.

- The Canadiens (16-7) pace the NHA, thanks to the league-high scoring of Newsy Lalonde (31 goals).

- The PCHA adds a fourth team—the Seattle Metropolitans, featuring Frank Foyston. But Portland (13-5) wins the league title on the goaltending of Tom Murray (2.80 GAA).

- On February 1, 1916, Cyclone Taylor and Lloyd Cook of Vancouver each score six goals against Victoria.

- The Canadiens face Portland in a Stanley Cup series that goes five games. Montreal's Didier Pitre scores a hat-trick in Game 3, and Portland's Fred Harris does the same in Game 4.

- The Canadiens win their first Cup, as Goldie Prodgers scores the winner in a 2-1 Game 5 nail-biter.

228th Battalion

Army Unit Fields Team in the NHA

In a game where fighting is as commonplace as scoring, it is reasonable that an army unit should figure somewhere in its history. In 1916-17, the 228th Battalion had so many former hockey players among its ranks that it was able to field a team in the NHA, although it had to withdraw after 10 games when the men were shipped overseas. Goldie Prodgers, Eddie Oatman, and Hall of Famer George McNamara skated for the 228th team.

Seattle Metropolitans

Ottawa's Nighbor Bangs In 41 Goals

Ottawa's Frank Nighbor tied Joe Malone for the NHA scoring title in 1916-17, as he spanked in 41 goals in just 19 games. Nighbor, known as the "Flying Dutchman," had turned pro in 1913 and joined the Ottawa club in 1915. There he remained until 1929, dazzling fans with his scoring, his stick-handling, and his famous poke-checks. He won four Stanley Cups with Ottawa and became the initial winner of both the Hart Trophy and the Lady Byng Trophy.

Frank Nighbor

Seattle Wins the States' First Cup

The first United States city to hoist a Stanley Cup was—surprise!—Seattle. The Metropolitans claimed the prize in 1917 after winning the PCHA title and then beating the Montreal Canadiens in the Stanley Cup series. The Mets featured Hall of Famers Jack Walker, Frank Foyston, and Hap Holmes (goalie), plus Bernie Morris (who scored 14 goals in the Cup series) and manager Pete Muldoon (of the famed "Muldoon's Curse").

1916-17

• World War I depletes the rosters of several teams and inspires the formation of a new NHA member, the 228th Battalion team. However, the 228th is soon ordered overseas and leaves after 10 games.

• Frank Robinson assumes the NHA presidency, as Emmett Quinn resigns.

• Quebec's Joe Malone and Ottawa's Frank Nighbor top the NHA with 41 goals apiece. Malone rings up eight goals against the Wanderers.

• Seattle wins the PCHA title on Harry Holmes' outstanding goaltending. Vancouver's Gordon Roberts wins the scoring title with 43 goals.

• The Canadiens (first-half champs) beat Ottawa (second-half champs) in the NHA playoffs, 7-6 on total goals.

• The Habs travel to Seattle and take Game 1 of the Stanley Cup series 8-4. Seattle wins the remaining games—6-1, 4-1, and 9-1—as Bernie Morris scores 14 times in four games.

DISGRUNTLED NHA OWNERS ESTABLISH THE NHL

As World War I exploded toward a climax on European battlefields, a more dignified war was taking place on ice rinks and in hockey boardrooms. The goal was to establish dominance over the professional game. Lester and Frank Patrick had done so in the West with their Pacific Coast Hockey Association, but a free-for-all of sorts was developing in the East, home of Canada's two largest cities, Toronto and Montreal.

Clashes over control of the National Hockey Association grew increasingly fierce, mostly because of one individual, Edward J. Livingstone. Regarded as the George Steinbrenner of his day, Livingstone managed to antagonize every one of his fellow owners. By 1917, they decided that they had had enough. But how to get rid of Livingstone? That was the question.

Livingstone had been a franchise-holder in Toronto and, therefore, was a legitimate NHA member. The solution of his foes was subtraction by addition. Livingstone was eliminated as an owner simply by the creation of a new league.

The coup d'etat was executed in November 1917 during a meeting at the Windsor Hotel in Montreal. All of the top pro teams—Ottawa Senators, Quebec Bulldogs, Montreal Canadiens, Montreal Wanderers, and Toronto Arenas—were represented. Livingstone, though, was kept from the meeting.

When the participants finally emerged from the smoke-filled room, they had created a brand-new entity, the National Hockey League, with only Quebec taking a temporary sabbatical. Thus, the new NHL embraced Ottawa, Montreal (Wanderers, Canadiens), and Toronto. NHA secretary Frank Calder was named president of the new circuit and it was off and running.

Many of the world's best players graced the new league's rosters. The Wanderers had the immortal Bert Lindsay (father of Hall of Famer Ted) in goal and such aces as Sprague and Odie Cleghorn. The Canadiens were led by Joe Malone and Joe Hall, with Newsy Lalonde the player/manager. Toronto's best included Reg Noble, Corbett Denneny, and Harry Meeking, while Ottawa boasted Cy Denneny, Jack Darragh, and Eddie Gerard.

Unfortunately, the Wanderers never made it through the season, as fire leveled the Montreal Arena on January 2, 1918. Wanderers owner Sam Lichtenhein attempted to borrow players from other squads, but when they refused to help, he withdrew his club from the NHL.

With a three-team league, the NHL barely survived its maiden season. Nevertheless, it did reach the finish line and the Toronto Arenas became the first NHL club to qualify for Stanley Cup play, hosting a series with Vancouver of the PCHA. Five games later, the NHL had its first Cup winner. Toronto defeated Vancouver three games to two, thanks to the outstanding play of Corbett Denneny, one of the new league's first stars.

The triumph notwithstanding, the NHL still was treading on thin fiscal ice. It now was a question of how long the baby circuit could survive with only three teams. The next season, 1918-19, would hold the answer.

1917-18

- The National Hockey League is created after squabbling among owners led to the demise of the National Hockey Association.

- The NHL's first franchises go to Ottawa (Senators), Toronto (Arenas), and Montreal (with two teams, the Canadiens and Wanderers).

- Former NHA owner Eddie Livingstone, much disliked by peers, is banned from participating in the NHL.

- Although granted a franchise, Quebec chooses not to participate until the 1918-19 season.

- Frank Calder, former secretary/treasurer of the NHA, is elected as the NHL's first president.

- On December 19, 1917, the NHL begins its 22-game schedule. The Wanderers' Harry Hyland scores five goals on opening night.

When Frank Calder was called upon to lead the new National Hockey League, he was no stranger to first-division hockey. As secretary of the NHA, he was really the rightful heir to the new throne. With delicate maneuvering, he was able to steer the new league through some pretty tough times. In the first year alone, the Quebec franchise decided to suspend operations and the Montreal Arena burned down, causing the Wanderers to fold.

• Joe Malone, a former Quebec star, switches to the Canadiens. He registers three five-goal games on the year, including five on opening night.

• Joe Malone, the game's first superstar, wins the NHL's scoring title with 44 goals in 20 games.

• Montreal Arena, home of both the Wanderers and Canadiens, burns down on January 2, 1918. Wanderers owner Sam Lichtenhein pulls his team out of the NHL after only six games (1-5).

• The Canadiens decide to continue their season. They'll play in the tiny Jubilee rink, which seats only 3,250.

• The NHL adopts a rule allowing goalies to leave their feet. It abolishes the $2 fine previously assessed in the NHA for "flopping."

• Ottawa goalie Clint Benedict is the man who instigates the new flopping rule, since he ignored the old rule so often.

Arenas: First NHL Team to Hoist the Cup

On March 30, 1918, the Toronto Arenas became the first NHL team to capture the Stanley Cup—an ironic turn of events since the Toronto franchise was a last-minute addition to the new league. Led by the steady goaltending of Hap Holmes (bottom row, middle) and the slick scoring skills of Alf Skinner (middle row, second from right), the Arenas downed PCHA champion Vancouver in a tightly contested five-game battle.

Toronto Arenas

Cyclone Taylor's Stick

Cyclone Scores with Fancy Stick

Perhaps the most talented player in the PCHA in 1917-18 season was Fred "Cyclone" Taylor, who led all marksmen with 32 goals in 18 games. The secrets of Taylor's success were his blinding speed, his agility, and his unique hockey stick. The stick featured a curve in the shaft, rather than the blade, giving him better maneuverability in stick-handling past thick-necked defensemen.

1917-18

- The Canadiens, winners of the first half of the season's split schedule, go on to finish 13-9-0.

- The Arenas, winners of the second-half title, finish at 13-9-0.

- Ottawa finishes third in the standings with a record of 9-13-0.

- The Arenas defeat Montreal for the NHL title in a two-game, total-goals series, 10-7.

- Ottawa's Cy Denneny finishes second to Joe Malone in regular-season scoring with 36 goals. Reg Noble leads Toronto with 28 goals, third in the NHL.

- Canadiens goalie Georges Vezina leads the league in wins (13) and goals-against (3.93).

- Elmer Lach, a future scoring star with the Montreal Canadiens, is born in Nokomis, Saskatchewan, on January 22, 1918.

Vezina's Tops Among Goalie Threesome

Georges Vezina led NHL crease cops with a 3.93 GAA in 1917-18. Nicknamed the "Chicoutimi Cucumber" because of his cool demeanor, Vezina recorded a shutout on February 18—one of only two the league saw all year. Still, you had to be something special to tend goal in the NHL in 1917-18, as there were only three full-time goalie positions available. Toronto netminder Hap Holmes and Ottawa's Clint Benedict were, like Vezina, future Hall of Famers.

Cy Denneny

Georges Vezina

Malone Knocks Home 44—Or 2.20 Per Game

When the Canadiens' Joe Malone scored 44 goals in 20 games in 1917-18, he established a 2.2 goals-per-game average—the highest per-game mark in NHL history. To equal this feat in an 84-game schedule would require 185 goals on the season! Phantom Joe tallied five goals in a game three times, victimizing goalies Hap Holmes (once) and Clint Benedict (twice).

Joe Malone

Denneny Pots 36 in 22 Games

Though small in stature, Cy Denneny of the Ottawa Senators mixed brains and brawn to become one of the NHL's finest marksmen. In 1917-18, he netted goals in 12 consecutive games. He finished second in the scoring race with 36 goals in 22 games, though the Senators finished with a 9-13-0 record. Eddie Gerard and Jack Darragh—a holdover from Ottawa's Stanley Cup team of 1911—aided the Ottawa scoring cause.

• Future Bruins star Milt Schmidt is born in Kitchener, Ontario, on March 5, 1918.

• The PCHA is reduced to three teams (Seattle, Vancouver, and Portland). In a tight PCHA race, Seattle wins the regular-season title, edging Vancouver by two games.

• Vancouver's Fred "Cyclone" Taylor leads the PCHA in goals (32).

• Vancouver defeats Seattle 3-2 in a two-game, total-goals playoff and will face Toronto for the Stanley Cup.

• The first four games of the Stanley Cup series are high-scoring affairs.

Toronto wins the first and third games 5-3 and 6-3, while Vancouver wins the other two games 6-4 and 8-1.

• On March 30, 1918, Toronto becomes the first NHL Stanley Cup winner. The Arenas win Game 5 2-1 on a third-period goal by Corbett Denneny.

When the NHL launched its second season, bittersweet feelings were sweeping North America. Both Americans and Canadians jubilantly hailed the end of World War I with the Armistice in November 1918; but simultaneously, they grew increasingly apprehensive about an influenza epidemic that already had engulfed Europe and now was spreading from Halifax to Victoria. Little did anyone realize that one of its victims would be the 1919 Stanley Cup playoffs and—on a personal note—one of hockey's best players.

The Spanish flu was not a main concern when the playoffs began. Seattle had won the Pacific Coast Hockey Association title, eliminating Vancouver in a two-game, total-goals series 7-5. NHL champion Montreal took the transcontinental train to Seattle, where the Stanley Cup Finals would take place at the home of the Metropolitans.

Playing before a partisan home crowd, the Metropolitans demolished Montreal 7-0 in the opening game. But the Canadiens rebounded in Game 2 with a 4-2 win. Seattle then beat Montreal goalie Georges Vezina seven times again in Game 3, winning 7-2.

Remarkably, Game 4 ended in a 0-0 tie after 20 minutes of

FLU BUG KILLS HALL, CANCELS STANLEY CUP

overtime. NHL historian Charles L. Coleman described the contest as "the greatest match ever played on the Pacific Coast." Among other highlights, the game featured the unusually robust play of Canadiens hit man Joe Hall and Seattle enforcer Cully Wilson. By this time, the series had captured the imagination of all of Canada and the Northwest U.S. Game 5 provided even more thrills, as the Habs rebounded from a three-goal deficit to even the count 3-3, thanks to two goals by Newsy Lalonde and another by Jack McDonald.

Everyone in the rink was aware of the worldwide flu epidemic and the fact that there were some objections to such large public gatherings. No less ominous was the behavior of some players who

appeared more exhausted than usual.

When the game went into overtime, Canadiens forwards Lalonde and Didier Pitre switched to defense and performed admirably in front of goalie Vezina. Finally, at 15:57 of the first sudden-death period, Odie Cleghorn beat Seattle goalie Hap Holmes for the winning goal.

With the series tied at 2-2-1, the Stanley Cup was up for grabs. But a decision was not forthcoming. Well before the fifth game had ended, Canadiens star Joe Hall was rushed to the hospital, suffering from the dreaded influenza. In addition, Billy Couture, Jack McDonald, Newsy Lalonde, and Louis Berlinquette also were bedridden, along with Montreal manager George Kennedy. The latter suggested that the series be continued with Victoria players substituting for the ailing Canadiens, but the Metropolitans refused the offer. Other suggestions for a resumption of the series were refused.

On April 5, 1919, less than a week after he had dragged his pain-racked body off the ice, Hall died in a Seattle hospital. The 1919 Stanley Cup Finals were canceled—the only time such a development has ever occurred.

1918-19

- Quebec's franchise fails to state its intentions for the 1918-19 season, and so the NHL remains a three-team league for another year.

- To speed the game's action, the NHL adds two bluelines and permits forward passing between the two bluelines.

- The NHL also institutes new rules prohibiting substitutions for penalized players: three minutes for minors, five for majors, and no substitution for players assessed match penalties.

- New statistics are introduced. Assists are tracked (along with goals) to compose scoring totals.

- The Canadiens (10-8-0 overall), capture the first half of the regular-season title.

- The Senators, with seven victories in their last eight games, win the second-half championship. They go 12-6-0 overall.

The year 1919 was a bad one for sports all around. Not only was the World Series blackened by the Black Sox, but the Stanley Cup Finals were canceled because of an influenza epidemic. With the series tied 2-2-1 (Game 4 was a 0-0 tie), players from both the Montreal Canadiens and Seattle Metropolitans were hospitalized because of the Spanish flu. Montreal's Joe Hall died from the illness and no Stanley Cup was awarded.

• The defending-champion Arenas suffer the sophomore jinx and fall to last place in the standings (5-13-0).

• Montreal's Newsy Lalonde leads the NHL in scoring (21-9-30).

• Montreal's Odie Cleghorn, in his first NHL season, is runner-up in the scoring race on the strength of his 23 goals and 29 points.

• Ottawa's Clint Benedict leads the NHL in wins (12) and GAA (2.94).

• Joe Hall, the Canadiens' big, bad defenseman, leads the league in penalty minutes (85).

• In the rival PCHA, the Portland franchise suspends operations while Lester Patrick's Victoria Aristocrats resume play.

• The PCHA adopts a "deferred" penalty rule, ensuring six men and a goalie on the ice at all times.

Holmes Finds a Home in Seattle

Harry "Hap" Holmes made his Seattle teammates very happy during the 1918-19 season, leading all PCHA goaltenders with a 2.3 GAA. Holmes, an NHL goalie a year earlier, wore this distinctive Seattle jersey with pride. Hap helped the Mets defeat Vancouver in the 1919 playoffs, allowing only two goals in two games. He also went "mano a mano" with Georges Vezina in Game 4 of the Cup Finals, as each pitched shutouts for 80 minutes.

Harry Holmes' Jersey

Odie Cleghorn

Cleghorn Bangs His Way to 32 Goals

One of the roughest hockey players to ever lace up skates, Odie Cleghorn had his finest season in 1918-19, scoring 23 goals for the Montreal Canadiens. Cleghorn didn't let up in the postseason, scoring seven times against Ottawa in the NHL playoffs and two more against Seattle in the Stanley Cup Finals. Odie and brother Sprague, both products of a rough neighborhood, were once described as a "disgrace to the game" by referee Lou Marsh.

1918-19

- Vancouver wins the PCHA regular-season title, and Cyclone Taylor leads in goals (23).

- Seattle's Cully Wilson, a known tough guy, breaks the jaw of Vancouver's Mickey MacKay, squelching the Millionaires' playoff chances.

- The Seattle Metropolitans, with Hap Holmes in goal, take the PCHA title and earn the right to face the NHL champion.

- The NHL playoff between Montreal and Ottawa is a best-of-seven series. The Habs win four games to one, with Newsy Lalonde scoring five goals in one game. They'll face Seattle for the Stanley Cup.

- Seattle wins Games 1 and 3 of the Cup Series, 7-0 and 7-2, but Montreal wins Game 2 4-2.

- Goalies Georges Vezina (Montreal) and Hap Holmes (Seattle) pitch

U.S. Star Baker Dies in Plane Crash

The hockey world lost one of its greatest stars when Pennsylvania native Hobart "Hobey" Baker was killed in France while testing a fighter plane on December 21, 1918. Baker had retained his amateur status throughout his career, refusing all offers to turn pro. Renowned for his stick-handling, skating, and on-ice leadership, Baker led St. Nicholas to the Ross Cup in 1914 and Princeton to two intercollegiate titles. He was 27 when he died.

Clint Benedict

Benedict Goes From Worst to First in Nets

Goalie Clint Benedict, playing for Ottawa in 1918-19, led the NHL in both victories (12) and GAA (2.94). It was a huge turnaround for Benedict, who a year earlier had posted a league-worst 5.18 GAA for Ottawa. The turnaround proved permanent, as Benedict would go on to lead the NHL in goals-against for five straight years. Hall of Fame defensemen Sprague Cleghorn and Eddie Gerard helped Clint keep the puck out of the net.

"HOBEY" BAKER MEETS DEATH IN FRANCE

Killed in Airplane Crash Near Toul, France

FORMER PRINCETON STAR

Captain Hobart A. H. Baker, the famous Princeton athlete, known in his college days as "Hobey" Baker, an aviator in the American army in France, has been killed in the fall of his plane. News of his death was received yesterday by his friend, Percy Pyne.

Mr. Pyne received a cable message from Paris signed "Inglehart," a member of Baker's air squadron, which said that Captain Baker had been killed in an airplane acident, and requested that his family be notified.

Hobey Baker's Obituary

Newsy Lalonde

Lalonde Nets Five Goals in Playoff Game

After leading the NHL in scoring in 1918-19 (21-9-30), the Canadiens' Newsy Lalonde exploded for five goals in one playoff game against Ottawa. Over the course of Lalonde's checkered career, he played for teams in Cornwall, Portage, Toronto, Montreal, Renfrew, Vancouver, Saskatoon, and New York. Despite the heavy traveling, he is regarded by many as the finest hockey player of the first quarter of the century.

---

shutouts for 80 minutes in Game 4 of the Stanley Cup Finals. The game is declared a 0-0 draw.

• The fifth game of the Stanley Cup Finals sees the Canadiens win 4-3 on Jack McDonald's overtime goal. The series is tied 2-2-1.

• In the middle of Game 5, Montreal's Joe Hall is taken to the hospital, sick with the influenza that is plaguing the nation.

• Before the Stanley Cup can be decided with a sixth game, many players from both teams are hospitalized with influenza.

• On April 1, 1919, the playoffs are canceled. For the only time in its history, the Stanley Cup is not awarded.

• On April 5, 1919, less than a week after falling sick, Joe Hall dies in a hospital.

JOE MALONE: HOCKEY'S ANSWER TO BABE RUTH

If the NHL was to survive its post-natal crises, it would require mass public acceptance. In the wake of the notorious Black Sox scandal, Major League Baseball thrived because of the emergence of Babe Ruth as a national hero in the early 1920s. At almost the same time, the National Hockey League was blessed with a hero of its own, Joe Malone.

Like Ruth, Malone had established his roots in the previous decade, starring for the Quebec Bulldogs in the National Hockey Association. When Quebec suspended its operations, the strikingly handsome Malone was acquired by the Montreal Canadiens, for whom he scored 44 goals in 20 games in 1917-18. Malone survived the influenza epidemic and would have re-signed with Les Canadiens after the 1918-19 season. However, the Bulldogs rejoined the NHL in 1919-20 and reclaimed Malone, along with other former Quebec players such as Harry Mummery, Jack McDonald, and Tom Smith.

Quebec iced a dreadful team in 1919-20, going 4-20-0 and coughing up nearly twice as many goals as it scored. But Malone performed nobly, virtually carrying the Bulldogs on his shoulders. Skating against the Toronto St. Patricks one night, Malone scored an astonishing seven goals—an NHL record that has never been equaled. Malone's scoring prowess inspired headlines across Canada and provided the three-year-old league with a superstar on which to pin its publicity.

Many observers consider Malone the greatest natural goal-scorer ever. "He might have been the most prolific scorer of all time if they had played more games in those days," said Frank Selke Sr., the former Canadiens manager who remembered Malone as a young professional. "It was amazing the way Joe used to get himself in position to score. In that respect, his style was similar to Gordie Howe's. Joe was no Howie Morenz as far as speed was concerned, but he was a clean player like Dave Keon and Frank Boucher. On the other hand, Joe never took a backward step from anybody."

Malone's deft play won him the nickname "Phantom Joe." Wrote historian Charles Coleman: "Malone was a tricky stick-handler, deceptive skater, and always a clean, sportsmanlike player. He stood out in an era that was featured by rough play."

Naturally, Malone never obtained as much media ballyhoo as Ruth garnered for his baseball exploits. For all his skills, Joe lacked the Babe's bombast and Ruth's proclivity for permissiveness. And, of course, baseball was a more established and popular sport at the time.

But just as Ruth had the knack for delivering baseball's most exciting moment—the home run—so Malone manufactured the most galvanic feat in hockey—the big goal. In 1919-20, he won his second scoring title in three years, tallying 39 red ones and 45 points. He punctuated his performance with a six-goal performance against Ottawa on the final night of the season. As one newsman observed, "Imagine what Joe Malone would have done if he had played for a good team."

1919-20

- The dormant Quebec Bulldogs finally become operational, thus expanding the NHL to four teams.

- The Toronto Arenas change their nickname to the St. Patricks.

- On January 10, 1920, Canadiens center Newsy Lalonde scores six times against Toronto to help Montreal to a 14-7 victory. The 21 goals set an NHL record that will remain untouched for 66 years.

- On January 31, 1920, Quebec's Joe Malone sets the all-time NHL record for goals in a game when he nets seven against Toronto in a 10-6 win.

- On February 21, the St. Pats host the Ottawa Senators before a record crowd of 8,500—a sign of good things to come for the NHL.

- On March 3, 1920, the Canadiens humiliate Quebec 16-3, setting the all-time NHL record for goals in a game.

On January 31, 1920, Quebec's Joe Malone did what no other NHL player has ever done. He scored seven goals in one game, creating nightmares for Toronto goalie Ivan Mitchell. Malone led the league in goals with 39 in 24 games, tallying 43 percent of the Bulldogs' red lights. In his NHL career, Phantom Joe pumped in 146 goals in 125 games, a pace that Rocket Richard, Wayne Gretzky, and Mario Lemieux never even approached.

• On March 6, 1920, Toronto St. Pats winger Mickey Roach knocks five goals past Quebec goalie Frank Brophy en route to an 11-2 win.

• On March 10, 1920, Joe Malone scores six goals against Ottawa. Quebec wins 10-4.

• Ottawa's record of 19-5-0 is good enough for the regular-season title. Quebec goes 4-20-0, yielding an all-time NHL record 7.38 goals a game.

• Quebec center Joe Malone captures the scoring title with 39 goals and 48 points in 24 games.

• Hot on Malone's heels in the scoring race is Newsy Lalonde, who finishes the season with 36 goals and 42 points.

• Playmaker Corb Denneny of the Toronto St. Patricks leads the NHL in assists with 12.

Canadian Olympic Team

Canadians Wow the World at Olympic Games

The Canadian Olympic team made its first international appearance at the 1920 Olympic Games in Antwerp, Belgium. Ice hockey made its Olympic debut at these games, and the Canadian side was represented by the Winnipeg Falcons, winners of the Allan Cup in 1920. Managed by W.A. Hewitt and featuring Frank Frederickson, Canada won all three of its games by a combined score of 29-1.

Lester Patrick

Patrick Rules the Roost in PCHA

Lester Patrick continued to patrol the blueline for the Victoria Cougars in 1919-20. Patrick, whose innovations include the bluelines, jersey numbers, and the modern arena, scored two goals on the year. He may not have been a scoring champ, but he played for, coached, managed, and owned the team. As the head of the PCHA, he also okayed the use of adding ringer Bernie Morris to the Seattle lineup when the Mets played Ottawa in the Stanley Cup Finals.

1919-20

• Toronto's Cully Wilson, a rugged right winger who was banned from the PCHA for his "aggressive play," leads the NHL with 79 PIM.

• Ottawa's Clint Benedict leads the NHL in wins (19) and GAA (2.67). He's the only goalie in the league to record any shutouts, and he has five.

• Because the Senators win both halves of the season's split schedule, there are no NHL playoffs.

• Seattle wins the PCHA's regular-season title and then knocks off Vancouver in the playoffs. Seattle will thus meet Ottawa in the Stanley Cup Finals.

• Seattle is aided in the Finals by a ringer, as the Mets lure winger Bernie Morris out of retirement and insert him into the lineup.

• Because their color scheme too closely resembles Seattle's colors, the Senators agree to switch to white sweaters for the Finals.

Darragh's Hat-Trick Helps Ottawa Win Cup

Jack Darragh played his entire career in his home-town of Ottawa. Known for his smooth stride and mechanical style of play, he was one of the dominant players of his day. In 1919-20, he scored a respectable 22 goals in 22 games for the Senators. He topped off the season with a Stanley Cup championship, scoring three goals in the decisive Game 5 of the Finals. Four years later, at the age of 34, Darragh died of a sudden heart attack.

Frank Foyston

Foyston Knocks Home 26 to Lead the PCHA

Frank Foyston was no stranger to success. A member of the 1914 Stanley Cup champion Toronto Blueshirts and the 1917 champion Seattle Metropolitans, Foyston was an established star. In 1919-20, however, he finally accomplished the one feat that had eluded his grasp, as he won the PCHA scoring title for the first time with 26 goals. He also notched three double-goal games in the Cup Finals, although the Mets fell to Ottawa in five games.

Memorial Cup

Amateurs Get a Cup of Their Own

The Stanley Cup had once been the trophy awarded exclusively to Canadian amateur teams. But with professionals now skating for the mug, a new trophy needed to be forged for the amateurs. The Memorial Cup, which debuted in 1919-20, would be contested by amateur junior teams in Canada. Impressively, the Cup is still a coveted prize. The very first Memorial Cup was won by the Toronto Canoe Club, which was apparently as slick on the ice as it was in the water.

Jack Darragh

- Ottawa takes Game 1 of the Finals 3-2, as Jack Darragh scores the winner with four minutes to go.

- In Game 2, Ottawa's Clint Benedict records a shutout and Jack Darragh notches another game-winning goal as the Senators win 3-0.

- Playing by NHL rules in Game 3, Seattle scores a 3-1 victory. Frank Foyston notches his third two-goal game of the Finals in Game 4, as Seattle wins 5-2 to tie the series.

- Jack Darragh scores a hat-trick in Game 5 of the Finals, as Ottawa wins 6-1 and claims the Stanley Cup.

- In amateur competition, the first Memorial Cup (which will come to symbolize excellence in Canadian junior hockey) is captured by the Toronto Canoe Club.

- Ice hockey debuts in the Olympics—at the Summer Games—and Canada emerges with the gold medal.

GOLD DUST TWINS SPARK OTTAWA TO ANOTHER CUP

Any talk of early hockey dynasties usually centers around the Canadian capital. The Ottawa Silver Seven captured four straight Stanley Cups after the turn of the century and, in the years surrounding 1920, the Ottawa Senators staked their claim as the NHL's first dynasty. In 1918-19, the Senators posted a league-best 12-6-0 record. A year later, they finished atop the NHL once more with a 19-5-0 mark and subsequently demolished Seattle in the Stanley Cup Finals.

Ottawa's domination was based on shrewd management and a rich talent source in the nearby Ottawa Valley, which sent many a star to the NHL. During the 1920-21 season, Ottawa featured an enviable lineup. Clint Benedict reigned as the league's finest goaltender, and such forwards as Cy Denneny, Jack Darragh, and Frank Nighbor ranked among the world's best. Eddie Gerard and Sprague Cleghorn were acclaimed as two of the top defensemen of their day.

Denneny was one of the best left wingers in the NHL's first epoch. A rough-and-tumble player despite his small stature, Denneny was sometimes cast into the enforcer's role when looking out for smaller, mild-mannered linemates. The rugged Harry Broadbent was a tough cop on the beat as well, and when this duo was paired together, they were gleefully referred to as the "Gold Dust Twins" by the delirious Senator faithful.

Darragh was a steady, unspectacular, and unselfish player who skated in Ottawa for 13 seasons. Though never a big star, Jack tallied amazingly consistent goal totals and frequently came up big in the playoffs. Gerard was one of the NHL's most versatile players, skating on defense or at forward with equal brilliance.

Cleghorn was as tough as they came. "He was a product of a rough neighborhood," said the late Bobby Hewitson, "where everything you got you had to fight for. And he played hockey the same way."

During the 1920-21 season, the Senators immediately asserted their strength in an impressive manner, winning their first five games. They finished in second place at 14-10-0, but knocked off first-place Toronto in the playoffs. Ottawa's Benedict blanked Toronto twice, qualifying the Senators for the Stanley Cup, which they would defend against the Vancouver Millionaires. The best-of-five series would prove a litmus test for Ottawa's dynastic claims.

Undaunted by the Senators' reputation, the Millionaires played Ottawa even through four games, three of which were decided by a single goal. The climactic fifth game was played in front of a hostile Vancouver audience, but the Senators rallied from a 1-0 first-period deficit to tie the count in the second. Then, just minutes later, Denneny sent a pass to Darragh, who converted it for the winning goal.

Ottawa thus won its eighth Stanley Cup, including two out of four since the NHL was organized. A year later, Ottawa led the NHL with a 14-8-2 mark. Few could dispute the Senators' claim to dynastic status.

1920-21

• The Quebec Bulldogs are sold to Percy Thompson of Hamilton, Ontario, prior to the start of the season. Their name is changed to the Hamilton Tigers.

• Babe Dye goes from the Toronto St. Pats to Hamilton and Billy Couture moves from the Montreal Canadiens to the Tigers—to help the new team become competitive.

• On December 22, Hamilton pounds Montreal 5-0, as Babe Dye scores a pair of goals against Georges Vezina.

• Toronto immediately reclaims Babe Dye from Hamilton after his scoring outburst. They instead send Mickey Roach to the Tigers.

• In Hamilton, the Tigers finish last in the league with a 6-18 record.

• Ottawa's 8-2 record wins them the first-half title, while the Toronto St.

The Ottawa Senators needed every one of their superstars to hold off
Vancouver in the 1921 Stanley Cup Finals. Ottawa prevailed in the maximum
five games, and each game was decided by just one goal. Ten of the Senators pictured
are in the Hockey Hall of Fame: Sprague Cleghorn, Eddie Gerard, George Boucher,
Harry Broadbent, Jack Darragh, Clint Benedict, Cy Denneny, Frank Nighbor, Frank
Ahearn, and Tommy Gorman.

Pats earn a playoff berth with a 10-4 record over the second half.

• On January 26, 1921, Corbett Denneny, Toronto's top left winger, nets six goals against Hamilton.

• Not to be outdone by his brother, Cy Denneny—Ottawa's leading scorer—scores six goals against Hamilton on March 7, 1921.

• Montreal's Newsy Lalonde scores five times in a 10-5 St. Patrick's Day rout of the Tigers.

• Though he's just third in goals (33) and fourth overall in assists (eight),

Newsy Lalonde takes the scoring title with 41 total points.

• Toronto's Babe Dye wins the goal-scoring title with 35.

• Ottawa's Cy Denneny finishes second in the NHL in goals (34) and points (39).

Harry Cameron

Newsy Lalonde

Babe Dye

Cameron Curves In 18 from the Blueline

Harry Cameron proved he was the finest defenseman in the NHL during 1920-21, as he netted a healthy 18 goals for the Toronto St. Patricks. A rough competitor who came to the St. Pats from the Montreal Canadiens, Cameron's fierce presence along the bluelines vaulted the Pats into a first-place finish. Cameron was one of the first NHL players to curve his shots—without altering the blade of his stick.

Once Again, Lalonde Leads in Scoring

In 1920-21, the Canadiens' Newsy Lalonde enjoyed another goal-happy season. In the 24 regular-season games, he scored 33 goals and added eight assists for a league-leading 41 points. This was the second time Lalonde captured the scoring title, having won the prize in 1919. This was also the last big NHL season for the aging vet. After a poor 1921-22 campaign, he was traded to Saskatoon of the WCHL for Aurel Joliat.

Twice-Traded Dye Leads in Goals

Babe Dye had every excuse for a bad year in 1920-21. His Toronto squad traded him to Hamilton early in the season, and after one game he was bounced back to the Hog Town club. The uncertainty should have rattled the young scoring ace, but he had his finest season ever, scoring for Toronto in 11 straight games and leading the NHL with 35 goals in 24 games. Purely a goal-scorer, Dye recorded just two assists on the year—fewest ever for a 30-goal scorer.

1920-21

- Clint Benedict once again is a stalwart in goal for Ottawa, leading the NHL in wins (14) and GAA (3.13) for the second straight year.

- In a two-game, total-goals playoff matchup, Ottawa cruises past Toronto, 5-0 and 2-0. Goalie Clint Benedict stars for the Senators.

- In the PCHA, the Vancouver Millionaires are back atop the regular-season standings, edging Seattle by a half-game.

- On March 4, 1921, Seattle and Victoria play to a triple-overtime 4-4 tie, as Victoria's Moose Johnson is honored.

- Vancouver and Seattle meet in a one-sided playoff, as the Millionaires trounce their rivals 13-2 over two games.

- In Game 1 of the Stanley Cup Finals, 11,000 fans pack Vancouver's arena to watch the Millionaires beat Ottawa 2-1.

Moose Johnson

Cy Denneny's Skates

Denneny Comes Up Short Again

Pictured are the humble skates of Cy Denneny, who starred on left wing for the Cup champion Ottawa Senators in 1920-21. It wouldn't have been surprising if Denneny skated in peach-colored pumps, as he was a perennial "bridesmaid" when it came to scoring. Six times Denneny finished second in the NHL scoring race, winning the title only in 1923-24. Cy was second fiddle in 1920-21, as he mustered 39 points but fell two short of Newsy Lalonde's total.

Johnson Carries a Big Stick

On March 4, 1921, the Victoria Aristocrats held a "Moose Johnson Night," honoring their veteran defenseman. Johnson, who won four Stanley Cups with the Montreal Wanderers in the early 1900s, played on several teams until his retirement in 1922. Moose was a big man who also used a big stick. That combination gave him a reach of 99 inches, reputedly the longest in hockey. When Johnson retired, his stick was given a proper burial.

• The Senators win Game 2 of the Finals, as Punch Broadbent breaks a 3-3 tie with less than four minutes to play.

• Ottawa wins Game 3 3-2, as rough-house defenseman Sprague Cleghorn scores the winner.

• Vancouver's Alf Skinner scores twice and Bill Cook knocks home the game-winning goal as the Millionaires take Game 4 of the Stanley Cup Finals 3-2.

• Alf Skinner stakes Vancouver to a 1-0 lead early in Game 5, but Jack Darragh—hero of the 1919-20

playoffs—scores the tying and winning goals to help Ottawa win its second straight Stanley Cup.

• Jack Darragh leads all playoff competitors in goals (five) and points (five), while teammate Clint Benedict posts a 1.71 playoff GAA.

HOCKEY'S A HIT IN THE WEST, ALBEIT BRIEFLY

Professional hockey gathered tremendous momentum during the post-World War I period, especially in Western Canada and Northwestern United States. The boom began with Frank and Lester Patrick's creation of the Pacific Coast Hockey Association and the development of arenas in Vancouver, Seattle, Portland, Spokane, and Victoria.

The success was enhanced by the emergence of stars such as high-scoring Bernie Morris of the Seattle Metropolitans and Cyclone Taylor of the Vancouver Millionaires—not to mention the innovative creations of the Patricks. Among other things, the brothers originated the penalty shot and were the first to put numbers on jerseys.

Meanwhile, hockey grew substantially in the Canadian prairies, as former railway stations developed into major cities. In 1921, a new association of teams—the Western Canada Hockey League—was organized with franchises granted to Calgary, Edmonton, Saskatoon, and Regina. As expected, the WCHL immediately lured a spate of excellent players, many of whom would eventually star in the NHL.

The Edmonton Eskimos featured Hal Winkler in goal and Bullet Joe Simpson on defense, as well as high-scoring Duke Keats on the forward line. Calgary's Tigers boasted a superb defense in Mervyn "Red" Dutton and Herb Gardiner.

Saskatoon's lineup included one of the finest right wings of all time, Bill Cook, as well as former NHLer Rusty Crawford and veteran goalie Sammy Hebert. The Regina Capitals iced an excellent squad headed by sharp-shooting Dick Irvin, Charles McVeigh, and stick-handling genius George Hay.

In its first season, 1921-22, the WCHL took dead aim at the Stanley Cup, challenging both the PCHA and NHL for the trophy. Three WCHL teams—Edmonton, Regina, and Calgary—battled for league supremacy, with the Eskimos winning the regular-season crown. The only WCHL team that didn't flourish was Saskatoon. By February, attendance in Saskatoon was so bad that the team was moved to Moose Jaw.

Regina wound up the victor in the WCHL playoffs, thus earning the right to meet the PCHA champ, Vancouver. Vancouver emerged from the two-game, total-goals series with a 5-2 victory. The Millionaires next met the NHL champ, Toronto, in the best-of-five Stanley Cup Finals, which the Ontarians won three games to two.

Western hockey flourished, but only for a short time. Its arenas were primitive compared to those being erected in the East, and the towns were too small to compete over the long haul with such cities as Toronto and Montreal. The beginning of the end came when American promoters exploited pro hockey. A huge new arena was blueprinted for New York City (Madison Square Garden) and similar rinks were built or were in the planning stages for Boston, Pittsburgh, and Chicago. Big Eastern money lured the stars away from the prairies—and ultimately the Pacific Coast—and thus put an end to the Western hockey boom.

1921-22

- On August 4, 1921, Maurice Richard is born in Montreal.

- An NHL rule change eliminates the split-season schedule and institutes a playoff between the top two finishing teams. Also, the NHL reduces minor penalties from three minutes to two and puts a 20-minute limit on overtime.

- The Western Canada Hockey League begins operations in Calgary, Regina, Saskatoon, and Edmonton.

- Edmonton's Duke Keats leads the WCHL in scoring.

- Montreal Canadiens owner George Kennedy dies, leaving his widow to sell the team to Joe Cattarinich and Leo Dandurand for $10,000.

- In a bizarre move, Sprague Cleghorn—a former Montreal Wanderer—is reclaimed by the NHL, assigned to struggling Hamilton, and promptly traded to the Montreal Canadiens.

The Western Canada Hockey League was formed in 1921-22, and one of the freshman loops' young stars was Bullet Joe Simpson. It was said that Simpson, who patrolled the blueline for the Edmonton Eskimos, could skate like the North Wind itself. Simpson, who would help the Eskimos to two WCHL championships, was glad to be playing at all. He was wounded twice while fighting during World War I.

• Sprague Cleghorn doesn't come to the Habs cheaply, as Montreal sends Harry Mummery, Amos Arbour, and Cully Wilson to Hamilton for Sprague.

• On January 14, 1921, Sprague and Odie Cleghorn each score four goals against Hamilton.

• The Canadiens' Newsy Lalonde leaves the team in a dispute with the Canadiens' owners.

• NHL President Frank Calder mediates the dispute between Newsy Lalonde and his bosses. Lalonde returns to the Habs after a four-game absence.

• In Ottawa, the Senators are powered by Punch Broadbent, who scores in 16 straight games, setting an all-time NHL record. He leads the league in goals (32) and points (46).

• The Senators win the regular-season title with 14 wins in 24 games.

Pats Get Help from Gerard

The Toronto St. Patricks won their first Stanley Cup in 1922 by defeating Vancouver in a thrilling five-game series. It's interesting to note that Toronto lost defenseman Harry Cameron to injury during the series but got permission from Vancouver to replace him with Ottawa star Eddie Gerard. However, after one game of Eddie's puck-hawking and bodychecks, Vancouver gave thumbs down to Gerard's stand-in act.

Toronto St. Patricks

Montreal Canadiens

Cleghorns Epitomize Rugged Habs

The 1921-22 Montreal Canadiens, now under new ownership, were a rough-and-tumble assembly. Third in the four-team NHL, they had little to boast about. The single league leader on the squad was Sprague Cleghorn, who led all sinners with 63 minutes in the cooler. His brother Odie, also known for his ability to intimidate, stood fifth in the goal-scoring competition with 21 tallies.

1921-22

- Ottawa leads the league in both goals (106) and fewest goals against (84).

- The St. Pats, still led by the powerhouse line of Reg Noble centering Corb Denneny and Babe Dye, face Ottawa in a two-game, total-goals playoff matchup.

- The St. Pats eke out a 5-4 victory over Ottawa in Game 1 of the playoffs, then hold on for a scoreless tie in Game 2 to earn a berth in the Stanley Cup Finals.

- The PCHA institutes the penalty shot, awarded to a player who is tripped on a clear breakaway.

- Seattle rides the scoring of Frank Foyston and Jim Riley to win the regular-season PCHA championship.

- The Victoria Aristocrats see the debut of boss Lester Patrick in goal after their regular netminder, Norm Fowler, is suspended for brawling.

Hugh Lehman

Lehman Leads Vancouver to Cup Finals

When the Patrick brothers opened up the West to professional hockey, Hugh Lehman was one of the Eastern stars they brought along. Lehman was an outstanding goaltender and a great student of the game. Old Eagle Eyes played for the New Westminster Royals for three seasons and was sent to the Vancouver Millionaires in 1914. In 1921-22, Lehman carried Vancouver to the Stanley Cup Finals, although they lost to the Toronto St. Pats.

Punch Broadbent

Punch Scores in 16 Straight Games

Ottawa's Punch Broadbent saved up his energy and gave his mates a Christmas present they wouldn't soon forget. Broadbent scored a goal on December 24, 1921, and continued to pot goals for 16 straight games, setting an NHL record that has never been equalled. Joe Malone, with goals in 14 straight in 1917-18, is the one man who has come closest. Broadbent scored 25 times during his streak and finished the year with a league-high 32 goals.

Babe Dye

Megastar Dye Powers Pats to the Cup

Before signing with the Toronto St. Pats, Babe Dye had been a star with the Toronto Argonauts football team, and he was offered $25,000 to play with the Philadelphia Athletics baseball club. He broke into the St. Pats' lineup in 1919-20 and the following year captured the goal-scoring title. In 1921-22 he was second in goals (30), but this time he led his team to the Stanley Cup, scoring four goals in Game 5 of the Finals.

• Vancouver wins the PCHA playoffs after shutting out Seattle twice.

• The Vancouver Millionaires beat Regina of the WCHL for a berth in the Cup Finals against Toronto.

• Toronto loses Game 1 of the Finals 4-3, as Vancouver's Jack Adams scores his third goal of the game with just 3:30 left in the third period.

• Babe Dye, Toronto's classy left winger, scores early in O.T. of Game 2 to pull the St. Pats even in the Finals. However, Hugh Lehman registers another shutout, giving Vancouver the third game 3-0.

• Toronto goalie John Roach tosses a shutout of his own in Game 4 of the Finals, beating Vancouver 6-0.

• Babe Dye, who leads all playoff scorers with 11 goals, bangs four goals past Hugh Lehman as the St. Pats skate to a 5-1 Game 5 victory and their second Stanley Cup.

BENEDICT, DYE PUT FANNIES IN THE SEATS

Still in its infancy in the early 1920s, the NHL longed for marquee attractions to fill its arenas. In 1922-23, two men pushed their way to the forefront. One, Clint Benedict, could stop the puck better than any of his contemporaries, while the other, Babe Dye, could fire it better than anyone else.

Benedict's career spanned 18 years, during which he won three Stanley Cups with the Ottawa Senators and one with the Montreal Maroons. In addition, he forced a rewrite of the rule book. During the World War I era, goaltenders were penalized for dropping to the ice to make a save. Benedict defied the rule and received so many penalties that officials deleted it. Thereafter, puck-blocking from any angle, including the ice level, was allowed.

After Ottawa moved into the NHL, Benedict led the Senators to Cup wins in 1920, 1921, and 1923. The 1922-23 season in particular showed Benedict at his best. He paced Ottawa to a first-place finish in the NHL's regular season. In the NHL playoffs, he outdueled Canadiens goalie Georges Vezina, winning the two-game, total-goals series 3-2. In the best-of-three Stanley Cup Finals, Benedict bested Edmonton 2-1 and 1-0.

Statistically, Benedict outshined the more-famous Vezina. Both played regularly from 1917-18 through 1924-25, but Benedict had a 3.01 GAA and 21 shutouts during that time while Vezina posted a 3.35 G.A. mark and 13 shutouts. Benedict was also the first major-league goalie to wear facial protection. In 1929-30 while playing for the Maroons, Benedict was struck in the face by a Howie Morenz shot. He then donned a leather mask in a game to protect his broken nose.

Benedict's ascent in goal was matched on offense by a power shooter from Toronto. Babe Dye could shoot the puck faster than anyone who preceded him on the NHL stage. Babe played much bigger than his 5'8", 150-pound frame, and his dashing good looks merely added to his charisma.

Dye made his NHL debut in 1919-20 with the Toronto St. Patricks. As a rookie, he made an unfavorable impression on teammates with his cockiness, and his playing time was limited. But Dye busted out of the gate as a sophomore, leading the league with 35 goals. He finished second in red lights in 1921-22 (30) and added a whopping nine tallies in the 1922 playoffs.

In 1922-23, Dye led the NHL in scoring for the first time. Playing in 22 games, Dye recorded 26 goals and 11 assists for 37 points, six more than runner-up Cy Denneny. Although he was not known for his dynamic speed, Dye compensated with extraordinary stick-handling ability and a wrist shot (there were no slapshots in those days) of extraordinary speed.

The one-two combination of a spectacular goalie and a galvanic shooter helped the NHL spread the hockey gospel even further. The glamour of the game was becoming as important as its more prosaic elements, and for that, the owners could thank Benedict and Dye.

1922-23

• Newsy Lalonde's feud with the bosses in Montreal results in his exile to Saskatoon (WCHL) for diminutive Aurel Joliat, a future Hall of Famer.

• Joe Malone, his career on the downswing, is traded by Hamilton to Montreal for Bert Corbeau and Edmond Bouchard.

• Not about to stand "pat" after their Stanley Cup title, the St. Pats ship Corbett Denneny to Vancouver for playoff scoring hero Jack Adams in the first interleague transaction.

• For the first time ever, the unique sounds of NHL hockey are broadcast live over radio airwaves. Foster Hewitt, sitting in a glass booth at Toronto's Mutual Street Arena, does the play-by-play.

• On opening night, Toronto's Babe Dye—the playoff scoring champ of the previous year—picks up where he left off with a five-goal game against Montreal's Georges Vezina.

No one could shoot the puck with more accuracy than Toronto's Cecil "Babe" Dye, one of the NHL's first superstars. In 1922-23, the Babe led the league in goals for the second time in three seasons, netting 26 in 22 games. A tricky stick-handler with a bullet shot, Dye opened the 1922-23 season by blowing five pucks past Canadiens stopper Georges Vezina. In the two years previous, Dye had orchestrated two separate 11-game goal-scoring streaks.

• The Ottawa Senators, whose top line features Cy Denneny, Frank Nighbor, and Punch Broadbent, win the regular-season title with 14 wins. They go undefeated at home.

• Clint Benedict, Ottawa's puck-stopper extraordinaire, wins his fifth straight G.A. title with a 2.25 mark.

• Babe Dye, the dynamic St. Pats scorer, leads the NHL in goals (26) and points (37).

• Billy Boucher, Montreal's scrappy right winger, is second in the NHL in goals (23), fourth in points (27), and first in penalty minutes (52).

• Edmond Bouchard of Hamilton leads the NHL in assists (12), but his Tigers win just six times.

• Ottawa wins its two-game, total-goals playoff matchup with the Canadiens. The Senators outscore the Habs 3-2.

George Boucher

Ottawa Senators

Boucher Tops Blueliners in Scoring

By 1922-23, George Boucher had been playing defense for six NHL seasons and had two Stanley Cups under his belt. His 15 goals in 1922-23 led all NHL backliners and were a career high for this future Hall of Famer. His Stanley Cup ring for 1923 would prove to be one of a set of four, all with the Ottawa Senators. Boucher was once considered a great halfback while playing for the Ottawa Rough Riders.

Gerard Leads Ottawa to Another Cup

After relinquishing their crown to the Toronto St. Pats in 1922, the Ottawa Senators regained the Stanley Cup in 1923 by beating Edmonton 2-1 and 1-0 in the Finals. Senators Cy Denneny and Punch Broadbent scored the winning goals, while Clint Benedict starred in nets. Captain Eddie Gerard, who played the last game with a separated shoulder, would never skate again in the NHL. The defenseman retired with four Stanley Cups to his credit.

1922-23

- Montreal owner Leo Dandurand suspends Sprague Cleghorn and Billy Couture before Game 2 of the playoffs as a result of their attacks on Ottawa players in Game 1.

- As a player/coach in Saskatoon, Newsy Lalonde leads the WCHL in scoring but his club finishes last.

- Edmonton wins the regular-season WCHL title and dispatches Regina in the playoffs.

- The PCHA adopts a six-man format, eliminating the rover.

- Victoria's Frank Frederickson leads the PCHA in scoring (41 goals).

- The newly renamed Vancouver Maroons defeat Seattle (yet again) in the PCHA playoffs. Vancouver next faces Ottawa in another round of playoffs.

- Ottawa nips Vancouver in Game 1 of their playoff matchup 1-0, as Punch Broadbent scores the game-

Foster Hewitt

"Duke" Keats

Duke Keats

Keats Captains the Eskimos to Cup Finals

Although he had no royal blood in his veins, Gordon "Duke" Keats was the king of Edmonton during the 1922-23 season. Keats joined the Eskimos in 1921-22, their inaugural year in the WCHL, and was promptly named team captain. In 1922-23, he led the league with 24 goals, directed the Eskimos to the WCHL title, and helped them win a spot in the Stanley Cup Finals. There, they managed just one goal against Ottawa and lost in two games.

Hewitt and Hockey Hit the Airwaves

The fame of Foster Hewitt spanned more than 50 years. He was a rank amateur on the ice, but in the broadcast booth he was the unrivaled champion of the rink. On March 22, 1923, Hewitt called the play-by-play for one of the first hockey broadcasts ever, at Toronto's Mutual Street Arena. He would go on to broadcast thousands of games and would remain in the radio business until 1981.

Frederickson's 41 Pace PCHA

A disciplined, intelligent hockey player, Frank Frederickson was the PCHA scoring leader in 1922-23 with 41 goals. The big Icelander first caught people's attention in 1920, when he led his amateur Winnipeg Falcons team to the Olympic gold medal. Playing for Lester Patrick's Victoria Cougars in 1925, Frederickson won the Stanley Cup.

Frank Frederickson

winner. However, Vancouver wins Game 2 4-1, as the Senators suffer injuries to Clint Benedict, Eddie Gerard, and Cy Denney.

• The Senators recover from their injuries and reform their attack. They dispatch the upstart Maroons with victories in the next two games, 3-2 and 5-1, to take the best-of-five series three games to one.

• The Senators next face Edmonton for the Stanley Cup. The Finals are switched to a best-of-three format.

• Ottawa wins Game 1 of the Finals 2-1, as Cy Denney beats Eskimo goalie Hal Winkler in O.T. In Game 2, Punch Broadbent scores the only goal of the game to clinch the Stanley Cup for the Senators.

• Ottawa's Clint Benedict has a GAA of 1.30 in postseason play. He surrenders just 10 goals in eight games.

Through its formative years, organized hockey had become notorious for its robust, often vicious, quality. One reason for this was the frontier spirit in Western Canada. Hockey sprouted in dozens of rough-and-tumble prairie towns where lawlessness was as common as the autumn frost. As a result, bloodshed on ice was not uncommon, and some of the early stars—such as Bad Joe Hall and Sprague Cleghorn—were as renowned for their wood-chopping as their scoring prowess.

It wasn't until the post-World War I era that a scintillatingly clean player made a big impact. The skater in question was Frank "Dutch" Nighbor, a native of Pembroke, Ontario, who cut his puck teeth with the Toronto Arenas (NHA) and Vancouver Millionaires (PCHA). Nighbor achieved genuine stardom when he signed with the Ottawa Senators.

"He was a great checker, either poking the puck from an opponent's stick as he came head-on or hooking it from him as he attempted to go by," said Frank Boucher, who played against Nighbor and became his most famous disciple. "I learned that

NICE GUY NIGHBOR WINS THE FIRST HART

Nighbor had spliced an additional eight inches to the handle of his stick, giving him a terrific reach in poking or hooking the puck. And it was perfectly legal because the rules specified only that sticks must not exceed three inches in width at any point, making no reference to length."

Nighbor was far from a wimp; it was just that he militantly refused to be suckered into fighting. In his mind, fisticuffs were not part of the game. "Of all the hockey players I saw," said Boucher, "nobody was more scarred about the face than Frank Nighbor. Newsy Lalonde would rip his stick into Nighbor's face, yet I don't recall him ever hitting back."

Turning the other cheek did not hinder Nighbor's production. In 1923-24, Dr. David A. Hart

presented the Hart Trophy to the NHL for the league's most valuable player. Nighbor won the trophy, edging out his less discreet foe, Cleghorn.

The Senators became known as the "Super Six" with Nighbor centering Cy Denneny and either Jack Darragh or Harry Broadbent. In that role, as one critic noted, Nighbor became "the NHL's best all-round player." According to *The Trail of the Stanley Cup,* "It was hard for his admirers to make up their minds at which he was best, offence or defence."

Nighbor's extraordinarily clean play combined with superior skills eventually caught the eye of Lady Byng, wife of Canada's governor general, who frequented Senators games in Ottawa. Lady Byng was so taken by Nighbor's exemplary play that she decided to present a trophy "to the player judged to have exhibited the best type of sportsmanship and gentlemanly conduct combined with a high standard of playing ability." Nighbor won the first Lady Byng Trophy in 1924-25 and took it again in 1925-26. The prestige of the trophy and the lofty status of Nighbor gave new dignity to cleanly played hockey.

1923-24

- After the Cleghorn/Couture episode of the previous year, the NHL redefines actionable match fouls, assesses new fines, and mandates presidential review for possible further punishment.

- The game's first individual trophy is introduced when Dr. David Hart,

father of Canadiens coach Cecil Hart, dedicates the Hart Trophy for the NHL's most valuable player.

- The Ottawa Senators take the regular-season title with 16 wins.

- Cy Denneny, the Senators' veteran left winger, snaps home a league-high

22 goals in 21 games and wins the scoring title with 23 points.

- Billy Boucher, Montreal's chippy right winger, finishes second overall in scoring with 22 points (16 goals).

- Ottawa's George Boucher's 19 points are tops among all NHL backliners.

In 1923-24, when the Hart family donated a trophy to be awarded
to the most valuable player in the league, they didn't have to look far for the
logical first recipient. Ottawa's Frank Nighbor was a smooth, calculated skater.
He didn't have the flash of Montreal's Howie Morenz, or the scoring
power of Aurel Joliat or Cy Denneny, but his ease on the ice and his obvious
talent made him the clear choice for the Hart.

• Montreal introduces a new offensive genius when it adds Howie Morenz to its top line, between Aurel Joliat and Billy Boucher.

• Georges Vezina, playing in his seventh season for Montreal, wins his first G.A. title with a near-microscopic mark of 2.00.

• Despite finishing with just 13 points (10 goals among them), Ottawa's Frank Nighbor is voted the league's most valuable player and is the first recipient of the Hart Trophy.

• Early in the year, the Canadiens' Sprague Cleghorn sits out a one-game suspension after deliberately injuring

Ottawa's Cy Denneny and Lionel Hitchman in separate incidents.

• In the WCHL, Saskatoon's Bill Cook—a future NHL star—scores 26 goals and wins the scoring title.

• Calgary wins the four-team race for regular-season honors in the WCHL.

Canadian Olympic Team

Georges Vezina's Skates

Canada Blows Out Olympic Foes

The Allan Cup champion Toronto Granites represented Canada in the 1924 Winter Olympics and, boy, did they put on a show. In its five games, Canada slaughtered Switzerland 33-0, Czechoslovakia 30-0, Sweden 22-0, Great Britain 19-2, and the U.S. 6-1. Frank Rankin (bottom row, far right) coached this mighty club while Harry Watson (bottom row, second from left) led the assault with 30 goals.

Vezina's GAA as Petite as His Feet

Pictured are the tiny skates of the Canadiens' Georges Vezina, the diminutive goalie with the minuscule GAAs. Vezina led the NHL with a 2.00 GAA in 1923-24, then yielded just six goals in six postseason games to lead Montreal to the Stanley Cup.

1923-24

- Regina finishes second in the WCHL and will face Calgary in a two-game, total-goals playoff.

- Mickey MacKay, the Vancouver Maroons' top producer, wins the PCHA scoring title on the strength of his 23 goals.

- The Maroons finish second and will take on regular-season champion Seattle for PCHA bragging rights.

- After Montreal beats Ottawa in the NHL playoffs on the strength of the Joliat-Morenz-Boucher line, Habs owner Leo Dandurand proclaims his team defender of the Stanley Cup.

- Leo Dandurand further insists that the two Western leagues stage a playoff, the winner to face his Habs for the Cup. He will not get his way, as all three league champions will go at it in the playoffs.

- In the first stage of playoffs, Calgary defeats Regina for the

Montreal Canadiens

MacKay Snaps In 23 Goals to Lead PCHA

When Mickey MacKay signed on as a professional hockey player in 1914, it was with the PCHA's Vancouver Millionaires. He exceeded all expectations and topped all goal-scorers in the loop, with 34 goals in only 17 games. In 1923-24, MacKay again led the PCHA in goals, with 23 markers. Nicknamed the "Wee Scot," MacKay was a charismatic player who befuddled goalics with his quick breakaways and in-close shooting ability.

Star-Studded Canadiens Win 'World' Title

Despite boasting such immortals as Howie Morenz, Aurel Joliet, and goalie Georges Vezina, the Montreal Canadiens finished a modest 13-11-0 in 1923-24. Nevertheless, the Habs defeated first-place Ottawa in a one-game playoff and then knocked off Western champs Vancouver and Calgary to win the Stanley Cup. The globes on the Canadiens' jerseys, which they unveiled prior to the 1924-25 season, signified their "world" championship.

Cy Denneny

Denneny's 22 Goals Lead League

Cy Denneny, the veteran leader of the Ottawa Senators, captured the NHL's scoring title in 1923-24, tallying 22 goals and one assist. Denneny appeared in only 21 games during the season because he was speared by Canadiens defenseman Sprague Cleghorn. Although it was suggested that Cleghorn was going out of his way to deliberately injure Ottawa players, the NHL decided not to suspend him.

Mickey MacKay

WCHL title. Meanwhile, Vancouver dispatches Seattle to win the PCHA crown.

• In the second stage of playoffs, Calgary and Vancouver face each other, with Calgary winning and earning a bye in the upcoming NHL portion of the playoffs.

• The Vancouver Maroons are no match for the Montreal Canadiens, losing the semifinals in two games, 3-2 and 2-1.

• The Canadiens crush Calgary in the Finals, beating them 6-1 in the opening game on the strength of a Howie Morenz hat-trick.

• Georges Vezina shuts out Calgary in the second game of the Finals, while Howie Morenz, Aurel Joliat, and Billy Boucher each score in a 3-0 Cup-clinching victory.

• For the second straight Olympics, Canada wins the hockey gold medal and the U.S. takes the silver.

HOCKEY 1924-25 CHRONICLE

THE NHL WELCOMES ITS FIRST U.S. TEAM

It wasn't easy at first, but the NHL survived its early growing pains. And by its seventh season, it had attracted the attention of several American promoters. U.S. hockey already had proven a big hit on the amateur level and at the universities, and the United States already had its first ice legend, Hobey Baker. Baker had starred for Princeton University before losing his life in a post-World War I plane crash.

By the early 1920s, Bostonians had taken hockey to their hearts, and it was only a matter of time before some cash baron decided to buy an NHL franchise and bring it to Beantown. The lucky tycoon was Charles F. Adams, a New England grocery magnate who watched the 1924 Stanley Cup playoffs in Montreal and came away convinced that big-league hockey couldn't miss in the United States.

"After my dad went to Montreal, he was sold on the NHL," said his son, Weston Adams Jr., who later became Bruins president. "When he returned home, he told us this was the greatest hockey he had ever seen. He wouldn't be happy until he had a franchise. It was Montreal that got us started."

Adams was supported by sportsmen Tom Duggan, Frank Sullivan, and Russ Layton. After being granted a new NHL franchise for Boston, Adams enlisted the aid of Arthur Ross, a star defenseman with Ottawa and the Montreal Wanderers in the old NHA. Immediately after his arrival in Boston, Ross went about the business of signing players for the new club. On December 1, 1924, the Boston Bruins became the first U.S. team to skate in the NHL.

Other potential American entries closely watched the birth and growth of the Bruins. Artistically, the Bruins were hardly encouraging, as their goalies—led by Charlie Stewart—couldn't guard against an onslaught of shots. Offensively, little-known Jimmy Herberts led the meager attack with just 22

points. Boston opened with a win over the Montreal Maroons—the year's other expansion team—and then proceeded to lose 11 consecutive games.

The expansion Bruins struggled greatly, finishing the season at 6-24-0, eight points behind the rookie Maroons. Boston scored just 49 goals and gave up 119. The club featured future stars like Lionel Hitchman and past stars like Alf Skinner, but no present stars. "We had three teams that year," said Weston Adams Jr. "One coming, one going, and one playing."

Even though the Bruins won only six games, they had won the hearts of Boston. The NHL's "American experiment" turned out to be a roaring success. Charles Adams was besieged with calls from other U.S.-based promoters, and soon applications poured in from other American cities. With the completion of New York's Madison Square Garden, a bid came from a Manhattan-based syndicate—while another was received from Pittsburgh. Unquestionably, hockey in the USA was here to stay, and the NHL's first great expansion boom was just around the corner.

1924-25

- After seven years of successful operation as a four-team league, the NHL expands to six teams.

- Donat Raymond and Thomas Strachan are awarded a franchise in Montreal—the Maroons. The owners immediately go after some big names to stock their lineup.

- Charles Adams pays the requisite $15,000 fee and takes control of the Boston Bruins. The Bruins become the first U.S. team in the NHL.

- The season is expanded from 24 games to 30, which will lead to player insurrection during the later stages of the campaign.

- A year after the Hart Trophy is introduced, the NHL adds the Lady Byng Trophy for sportsmanship and accomplishment. It is named for the wife of the Canadian governor general, Baron Byng.

- Longtime Toronto hero Reg Noble ends up in a Montreal Maroons

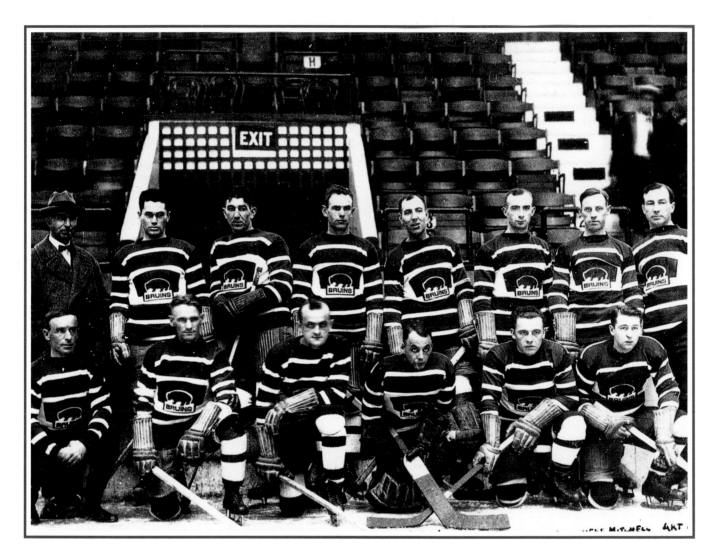

In 1924-25, the NHL expanded from four teams to six, adding
the Boston Bruins and the Montreal Maroons. The Bruins had a color scheme
of brown and yellow because owner Charles F. Adams (top row, far left)
owned the Brookside Stores, whose colors were brown and yellow. Boston,
managed by Art Ross (top row, far right) and featuring many former World Hockey
League players, went 6-24-0 in 1924-25.

jersey, as do former Ottawa goalie Clint Benedict and scoring ace Punch Broadbent.

• After four terrible seasons, Hamilton emerges to win 19 games and beat Toronto by one point in the regular-season standings.

• On December 5, 1924, Red Green scores five of his 19 goals against Toronto's John Roach in a 10-3 Hamilton victory.

• On December 22, 1924, Toronto's Babe Dye victimizes Boston goalie Charlic Stewart for five goals as the St. Pats roll to a 10-2 win.

• On January 7, 1925, Maroons right wing Punch Broadbent beats Hamilton goalie Jake Forbes for five goals.

• Toronto's Babe Dye leads the NHL in both goals (38) and points (44).

• Young Canadiens star Aurel Joliat is second in goals (29).

Lady Byng Trophy

Lady Byng Rewards Good Sportsmanship

Governors general have a tradition of influencing Canada's favorite sports. The Stanley Cup and the Grey Cup (football) were both donated by governors general. Lady Byng, the wife of Governor General Lord Byng, donated this fine trophy in 1924 to be given to the NHL player who best exhibited both sportsman-like conduct and a high level of play. The first winner was Ottawa's Frank Nighbor.

Hamilton Tigers

Ticked-Off Tigers Go on Strike

In 1924-25, a team went on strike for the first time in NHL history. The Hamilton Tigers, led by Hart Trophy winner Billy Burch (20 goals), finished in first place with a 19-10-1 record. However, they refused to participate in the playoffs without receiving the playoff pay they felt was their due. NHL President Frank Calder suspended the team and its players and awarded their playoff berth to third-place Montreal.

Joliat Magnificent in Montreal

The 1924-25 season witnessed the emergence of the Mighty Atom, 136 pounds of dynamite named Aurel Joliat. Although he had been in the NHL for two years, Joliat made his presence felt like never before, scoring a career-high 29 goals. Teamed with the great Howie Morenz, these two speedsters epitomized the Canadiens' Flying Frenchmen. Joliat and Morenz skated together for 11 consecutive years, winning a combined four Hart Trophies.

Aurel Joliat

1924-25

- Ottawa's Cy Denneny finishes first in assists (15) and second in points (42).

- Canadien Georges Vezina wins his second straight G.A. title (1.87).

- Ottawa rookie Alex Connell sets an NHL record with seven shutouts.

- Though his team wins the regular-season title, Hamilton's Red Green calls a wildcat strike, claiming his contract is for 24 games and insisting that he and his mates receive extra money for playoffs.

- NHL President Frank Calder rejects Red Green's strike argument, sus-pends the entire Tigers club, and declares a playoff between second-place Toronto and third-place Canadiens.

- In the West, the PCHA suffers financial woes. When Seattle shuts down operations, the league is finished.

Victoria Cougars

Stanley Cup Moves West to Victoria

The Stanley Cup returned to Western Canada in 1925 for the first time in 10 years. The WCHL's Victoria Cougars shocked the Montreal Canadiens with a three-games-to-one triumph in the Stanley Cup showdown. In the decisive fourth game, Victoria's Frank Frederickson (top row, third from right) scored a pair of goals and Hap Holmes (top row, third from left) shut down the attack of Les Glorieux for a convincing 6-1 thrashing.

Rookie Connell Sets Shutout Mark

Alex Connell, the "Ottawa Fireman," put out a few blazes for the Senators during the 1924-25 season. Though just a rookie, the confident Connell set an NHL record with seven shutouts while recording a splendid 2.20 goals-against average. Brought in to replace the great Clint Benedict, Connell became an instant favorite among Ottawa fans for his acrobatic saves and genial personality.

Habs Reign as Champs of the World

After the Montreal Canadiens captured the Stanley Cup in 1924, they commissioned special jerseys for their players to wear in 1924-25. Although they were world champs in 1924, they were not able to defend their global title in 1924-25. In fact, the Habs—who finished third in the NHL with a 17-11-2 record— made the playoffs only because the first-place Hamilton Tigers were banned from the postseason.

Canadiens Jersey

Alex Connell

- Former PCHA teams Vancouver and Victoria join the WCHL, which adopts a regular-season and playoff format identical to the NHL's.

- Calgary wins the regular-season WCHL title, and a playoff bye. Saskatoon and Victoria battle in the semifinals.

- The Victoria Cougars beat Saskatoon on total goals (6-4), then upset Calgary with a 3-1 total-goals victory (a 1-1 tie and a 2-0 win).

- The Canadiens advance to the Stanley Cup Finals with a pair of wins over Toronto, 3-2 and 2-0. They'll take on Victoria.

- Hap Holmes outduels Georges Vezina in goal as the Cougars shock the Habs in four games to win the Stanley Cup (5-2, 3-1, 2-4, 6-1).

- Ottawa's Frank Nighbor takes the inaugural Lady Byng Trophy, while Hamilton's Billy Burch wins the Hart Trophy as the league's MVP.

HOCKEY HITS BROADWAY— AND WITH RAVE REVIEWS

As significant as the Bruins' debut in Boston may have been, NHL barons understood that they would not really make it big in the U.S. until they scored on Broadway. Interestingly, the road to New York hockey began in Hamilton, Ontario. And it was driven by, of all people, a Prohibition bootlegger.

At the end of the 1924-25 season, Red Green of the Hamilton Tigers, complaining that the extension of the regular season from 24 to 30 games should include a pay raise, led the Tigers on a walkout. Unable to handle the situation in Hamilton, NHL President Frank Calder agreed on a sale of the team and its relocation to New York.

Curiously, a Canadian-born newspaperman covering sports in New York City inspired Big Bill Dwyer to launch the Americans. William McBeth, a sportswriter from Windsor, Ontario, believed that if hockey could be properly staged in Manhattan, it would be an instant hit. McBeth initially had his listeners and his backers, but he lacked one item—a major-league arena.

The city of New York did have one arena to house the sport, Madison Square Garden, which had been built in Manhattan in the early 1920s. The new Garden wasn't perfectly suited for ice hockey, since it was built primarily for prize-fighting and lacked adequate sight lines for the Canadian game. However, the Garden contained 15,000 seats and enough good ones to satisfy even the most discriminating fans. Still, the owners of Madison Square Garden weren't interested in buying an NHL franchise, so McBeth had to go elsewhere for money.

His choice was Dwyer, a character among characters in that era of wonderful nonsense. A native New Yorker, the pot-bellied Dwyer grew up in the area around the new Garden, living the life of a quasi-Dead End Kid. He did a short stretch in prison and bounced around the West Side of Manhattan until Prohibition arrived. He became rich as a bootlegger and decided to invest his money in the New York Americans. The Americans ended up playing their games in Madison Square Garden.

With Tommy Gorman as manager, the Amerks premiered in the Garden on December 15, 1925. In spite of the team's 3-1 loss to the Montreal Canadiens that night, owner Dwyer nonetheless broke out the champagne at game's end.

Billy Burch, with 22 goals in that first year, headed a roster that included such talent as brothers Shorty and Red Green and defensemen Alex McKinnon and Bullet Joe Simpson. The Americans finished their first season with a record of 12-20-4.

Though they didn't make the playoffs, the Amerks had become a hit on Broadway. They so frequently filled Madison Square Garden that the arena owners decided that they too should own a hockey team. They applied for a second New York franchise, which would become the Rangers. Bringing the NHL to Broadway turned out to be one of the league's best moves.

1925-26

- The Hamilton Tigers are purchased by reputed New York City bootlegger Big Bill Dwyer for $75,000.

- Renamed the New York Americans, the former Tigers are housed in Madison Square Garden, where they draw 17,000 fans for opening night.

- The NHL expands to seven teams, as the Pittsburgh Pirates join the party. Former Canadiens star Odie Cleghorn serves as player/coach.

- Rule changes include: delayed penalties to ensure four skaters on the ice at all times; no more than two players are allowed to remain behind the blueline after the puck leaves the defensive zone; and a faceoff results from excessive puck-ragging.

- The regular-season schedule grows from 30 games to 36.

- Tragedy strikes as the Canadiens' Georges Vezina collapses on opening

The New York Americans finished in fifth place in 1925-26, their freshman NHL year. The members of the class were more or less the same assembly that finished first the previous season as the Hamilton Tigers. Among the fraternity were coach Newsy Lalonde, Billy Burch, Bullet Joe Simpson, and Mickey Roach. The Americans never matched the heights of their Hamilton heritage and sadly became a home for aging hockey stars.

night and is diagnosed with tuberculosis. The goalie great will die four months later.

• On December 26, 1925, the Americans and Pirates combine for a record 141 shots on goal. New York (73 shots) wins 3-1.

• The Maroons vault to second place in their second NHL season.

• Maroons rookie Nels Stewart leads the league in goals (34) and points (42). He also wins the Hart Trophy.

• Boston sophomore Carson Cooper is second with 28 goals, though his

Bruins—with Art Ross at the helm—finish no better than fourth.

• The Ottawa Senators (24-8-4) capture their sixth regular-season title. Alex Connell leads the NHL in wins (24) and GAA (1.17), posting an unheard-of 15 shutouts.

Alex Connell

Connell Stars Behind Plate, Between Pipes

Alex Connell was not much of a hockey man early on. His athletic skills were varied, but mostly he was a baseball player. He played catcher in the Interprovincial League, and was also a member of Ottawa's Eastern Canada lacrosse championship teams in the 1920s. In 1925-26, his second season as Ottawa's first-string goalie, he registered an amazing 15 shutouts as well as a 1.17 GAA. He won 24 of his 36 games.

Stewart Wins Scoring Title as NHL Frosh

He was quite simply the finest rookie to ever lace on blades in the NHL. Nels "Ol' Poison" Stewart joined the Montreal Maroons in 1925-26 and led the entire league in both goals (34) and scoring (42). He also won the Hart Trophy. With all guns blazing, Stewart led the Maroons' charge through the playoffs, scoring six goals in eight games as the Maroons knocked off Pittsburgh, Ottawa, and Victoria to win the Stanley Cup. Stewart, a future Hall of Famer, would eventually become the first NHLer to score 300 goals.

Nels Stewart

Georges Vezina

Vezina Dies of Tuberculosis

Georges Vezina spent his entire life playing hockey. As a boy in Chicoutimi, Quebec, it is said that he was always the first to arrive at the rink and the last to leave. Signed as a member of the Montreal Canadiens in 1910, he played in every game over the next 15 years, never once allowing a substitute to fill in between the pipes. Vezina developed chest pains in 1925 and died of tuberculosis on March 24, 1926. He was 39.

1925-26

- Pittsburgh is surprisingly competitive in its inaugural campaign, finishing third. Pirates rookie Roy Worters finishes with a 1.94 GAA and seven shutouts.

- Without Georges Vezina, the Habs fall to last place, just behind the struggling Toronto St. Pats.

- The NHL sees its first 100-minute penalty leader. Actually, five skaters finish above the century mark, led by Toronto's Bert Corbeau (121).

- Ottawa's Frank Nighbor leads the NHL in assists (13) en route to his second Lady Byng Trophy.

- As regular-season champs, the Senators earn a playoff bye. The second-place Maroons dispatch third-place Pittsburgh in a two-game, total-goals series, 6-4.

- The Maroons shock heavily favored Ottawa in the NHL playoffs. Former Senators goalie Clint Benedict blanks

Montreal Maroons

Maroons Need Two Years to Win First Cup

The expansion Montreal Maroons were not expected to be competitive for some time. However, thanks to the scoring touch of rookies Nels Stewart (34 goals) and Babe Siebert (16), the Maroons ascended to the NHL throne in only their second year, 1925-26. Stewart and Siebert mixed with such veterans as Reg Noble, Dunc Munro, Punch Broadbent, and Clint Benedict to give the English-speaking Montrealers their first Stanley Cup.

Americans Skate in the Garden

The demise of the NHL's Hamilton franchise gave rise to the second NHL team in the United States. The New York Americans emerged in 1925-26, and they played their games in the new Madison Square Garden at the corner of Madison Square and 26th Street in the Big Apple. The Garden, which seated 13,000 for hockey, would also be the home of the NHL's Rangers beginning in 1926-27.

Madison Square Garden

his former mates 1-0 in the second game. Montreal will face the WCHL champ in the Stanley Cup Finals.

• The Western Canada Hockey League is on its last legs. Regina moves to Portland and "Canada" is dropped from the league title. This will be the league's final year.

• Edmonton takes the regular-season WHL title but fails to reach the Stanley Cup Finals. Victoria, the third-place finisher, upsets Saskatoon and Edmonton for the right to defend its Cup title.

• The best-of-five Finals features brilliant goaltending from the

Maroons' Clint Benedict, who records 3-0 shutouts in Games 1 and 2. In Game 3, Victoria's Frank Frederickson scores late to win it 3-2.

• Montreal clinches the Cup with a 2-0 victory in Game 4. Nels Stewart scores both goals and Clint Benedict notches his fourth playoff shutout.

NEW YORK'S BOUCHER CLICKS WITH THE COOKS

The disbanding of the PCHA and WCHL benefitted many NHL teams, but none more so than the New York Rangers, a new team that joined the league in 1926-27. From the Western circuits, the Rangers obtained Frank Boucher and one of pro hockey's most famous brother acts, Bill and Bun Cook.

Boucher, a center and a protege of the clean-playing Frank Nighbor, was a stick-handling marvel. Wrote Montreal hockey columnist Dink Carroll: "He would take the puck away from the enemy with the guile and smoothness of a con man picking the pockets of yokels at a country fair, then whisk it past the enemy goaltender or slip it to Bill or Bun."

Bill Cook, one of hockey's all-time best right wings, and Bun, a superior left wing, melded perfectly with Boucher. "Bill, Bunny, and I clicked as a line from the beginning," said Boucher. "We never put diagrams on paper. Somehow, just in describing our ideas, we'd all grasp it. Bill would do most of the talking. He'd say, 'Now look, when I want that puck I'll yell for it, and you get that damn puck to me when I yell. Don't look up to

see where I am; just put it there and I'll be there.'"

The "drop pass," which became a standard NHL play (and is to this day) was invented by Bun Cook and executed by himself, Bill, and Boucher to perfection. "As soon as Bunny crossed the other team's blueline," said Boucher, "he faked a shot, drawing a defenseman to him. Then he left the puck for me coming in fast behind him. If the defenseman turned to cover Bun, I carried the puck on in. If he came for me, I slid it past him to Bun circling behind. And if both defensemen came for us, leaving Bill open, I'd flip the pass across to him."

They moved with the grace of figure skaters and passed the puck with radar-like accuracy. Bill was

the crackerjack shot, Bun had the brawn, and Boucher had all the class in the world. The presence of the troika in the lineup assured the expansion Rangers of box-office success in a town that already had a popular team, the Americans.

Because NHL clubs in that era maintained extremely small rosters, it was not uncommon for players to remain on the ice for up to 60 minutes a game. Thus, the Cooks and Boucher were able to weave their magic all night long. And while there had been innumerable set lines before, none came close to bewitching the public in the manner of this trio.

Thanks to Boucher and the Cooks, the 1926-27 Rangers finished first in the American Division (25-13-6), an unheard-of achievement for an expansion team. Bill Cook led the NHL in scoring (33-4-37), tallying eight more goals than anyone else.

Boucher and the Cooks formed the NHL's first power line, one that remained intact through the 1935-36 season. In that time, the trio played on two Stanley Cup winners (1927-28 and 1932-33) and were acknowledged as one of the greatest and most durable triumvirates in hockey history.

1926-27

- New York receives its second NHL franchise in two years as the New York Rangers arrive on the scene.

- The Rangers are joined by two more teams, the Chicago Black Hawks and Detroit Cougars (formerly the Victoria Cougars of the WHL), expanding the NHL to 10 teams.

- The NHL divides into two divisions, Canadian and American, and lengthens the schedule to 44 games.

- The demise of the Western hockey leagues results in the Stanley Cup coming under the exclusive control of the NHL.

- Conn Smythe, who was instrumental in assembling the Rangers, is fired before the season because of a management dispute.

- On February 14, 1927, the Toronto St. Pats are sold to Hugh Aird and Conn Smythe. Their nickname is changed to the Maple Leafs.

The NHL added teams in Detroit, Chicago, and New York in 1926-27.
The New York franchise was the property of a Southerner, Tex Rickard, and people
soon called the team Tex's Rangers. Pictured here are (front row, left to right)
Bill Cook, Frank Boucher, Ching Johnson, and coach Lester Patrick as well
as (back row, left to right) Murray Murdoch, H. Westerby, and Bun Cook. This
talented unit won the American Division in its inaugural season.

• Star players from the defunct Western leagues proliferate the NHL. Eddie Shore joins the Bruins, Bill and Bun Cook sign on with the Rangers, and Frank Foyston and Frank Frederickson go to Detroit.

• Lester Patrick, a maverick in the West, returns to the East. He takes over the Rangers and will lead them to dominance in their early years.

• Bill Cook, the speedy right winger who plays with brother Bun and center Frank Boucher on the Rangers' top line, wins the goal-scoring title as well as the points race (33-4-37).

• Fellow first-year NHLer Dick Irvin, who cruises the left wing with Mickey MacKay and Babe Dye in Chicago, leads the league in assists (18) and is second in total points (36).

• Herb Gardiner, in his first year with the Habs, is a mountain of strength on defense and wins the Hart Trophy.

Senators Hoist Their Last Cup

The Ottawa Senators, boasting such stars as Cy Denneny, Alex Connell, Hec Kilrea, Frank Nighbor, and George Boucher, won their last Stanley Cup in 1927. The '27 Finals were historic in a couple of ways: It was the last time Ottawa appeared in a Cup series, and it was the first time that two NHL teams faced off in the decisive match. Games 1 and 3 were washed out because of bad ice conditions, but Ottawa won Games 2 and 4 to win the silver bowl.

Ottawa Senators

Detroit Cougars

Former WHL Stars Migrate to Detroit

When the Western Hockey League collapsed in 1926, most of the Victoria Cougars found a new home in the Motor City. The new franchise was called the Detroit Cougars and featured such stars as Frank Foyston (front row, second from left), Frank Frederickson (back row, fifth from right), and Hap Holmes (back row, second from right). The Cougars, though, had little bite, finishing in the cellar of the newly created American Division.

1926-27

• Still going strong, the Ottawa Senators survive the infusion of talent and remain atop the standings, taking the Canadian Division with 30 wins in 44 games.

• Alex Connell, Ottawa's brick wall in goal, tallies 30 wins, 13 shutouts, and a 1.57 GAA.

• Canadien George Hainsworth, who replaces Georges Vezina, is the first recipient of the Vezina Trophy, given to the goalie on the team that allows the fewest goals. Hainsworth records 14 shutouts.

• Maroons goalie Clint Benedict leads the NHL in GAA (1.51).

• The first-year Rangers ride the goaltending of Lorne Chabot (1.56 GAA, 10 shutouts) and the scoring of Frank Boucher and the Cook brothers to a first-place finish in the American Division.

• The New York Americans, playing in the Canadian Division, finish

Herb Gardiner

Wise, Old Gardiner Named MVP

His entry in the *Hockey Encyclopedia* shows the Canadiens' Herb Gardiner as a 35-year-old rookie in 1926-27 who scored just six goals and 12 points. As is so often the case, the stats miss the point entirely. Gardiner was a natural athlete who, when he joined the NHL in 1926-27, was already a seasoned hockey man. He had played with the Winnipeg Vics as early as 1908. Gardiner's veteran leadership was so great that he earned the 1926-27 Hart Trophy.

Cook's an Instant Star in New York

When Bill Cook entered the NHL for the 1926-27 season, he was a ready-made star for the expansion New York Rangers. Three times a scoring champion with the Saskatoon Sheiks of the WCHL, Cook was used to the limelight, if not the bright lights of Broadway. In his rookie season with the Rangers, he fired in 33 goals and added four assists to lead the league in both goals and scoring.

Vezina Trophy

Vezina Trophy Honors NHL's Best Netminder

Soon after the untimely death of Georges Vezina in March 1926, Canadiens owners Leo Dandurand, Louis Letourneau, and Joe Cattarinich presented the Vezina Trophy to the NHL. From 1926-27 through 1980-81, the prize was awarded to the goaltender(s) on the team that allowed the fewest goals during the season. Ironically, Vezina's replacement in the cage, George Hainsworth, was the first winner of the Vezina Trophy.

Bill Cook

Toronto Club Renamed the Maple Leafs

A new love affair began in Toronto on February 14, 1926. Conn Smythe, business tycoon and hockey man, purchased the NHL's Toronto St. Patricks and renamed them the Toronto Maple Leafs. For Smythe, a true patriot, the maple leaf was a proud symbol. It had been worn by soldiers and would one day be stitched into the Canadian flag. The Toronto club, however, had little to be proud of in 1926-27, as it finished last in the Canadian Division.

Maple Leafs Symbol

fourth, but Billy Burch (19 goals) wins the Lady Byng Trophy.

• In the playoffs, the Bruins trounce Chicago in the total-goals preliminary round, then knock off the Rangers.

• The Canadiens nip the Maroons but fall to Ottawa in the next round.

• With the score tied 0-0 after two O.T. periods, Game 1 of the Finals is called off due to bad ice in Boston. Ottawa tops the Bruins 3-1 in Game 2.

• Game 3 of the Finals is tied 1-1 after one overtime period when the match is called off, again due to deteriorating ice conditions (this time in the Ottawa arena).

• Cy Denneny scores twice in Game 4, leading Ottawa to a 3-1 Cup-clinching victory. It's the Senators' last Stanley Cup victory.

RANGERS WIN CUP AS OLD MAN PATRICK STARS IN NET

In the long annals of professional hockey, there have been many instances where goaltenders have been hurt and unlikely replacements rushed in to plug the gap. But the granddaddy of all such episodes—and by far the most stirring—involved New York Rangers coach/manager Lester Patrick in the 1928 Stanley Cup Finals.

It was Game 2, with the Montreal Maroons leading the series one-up. The entire final round had to be played in Montreal because the Barnum & Bailey Circus was firmly camped in the Rangers' home at Madison Square Garden. After a scoreless first period in Game 2, Montreal center Nels Stewart fired a blast that impacted Rangers goalie Lorne Chabot right above the eye. Chabot could not continue.

Without a spare goalie, Patrick requested that Alex Connell—the Ottawa Senators' netminder who happened to be sitting in the stands—be loaned to New York for the duration of the game, but the Maroons denied Patrick's request. Furthermore, NHL President Frank Calder informed Patrick that he had 10 minutes to find a suitable replacement before the game would be considered a forfeit. With time running out,

Patrick astonished the onlookers by choosing himself to play goal, a position he had never played in his life.

"We thought at first that it was just a mild injury to Chabot's eye," said Patrick. "Some of the boys said, 'Lester, you go in there.' But I said, no, I didn't want to. However, they persisted, so I donned Chabot's uniform, skates, and what-have-you and everything fit like a glove—except the skates. I took care of that by putting on an extra pair of socks."

The presence of the 44-year-old replacing the capable Chabot caused an eruption of laughter from the Forum crowd, but they were soon silenced as the Rangers built a human wall in front of Patrick. When necessary, Patrick performed superbly, stopping 15

of the Maroons' 16 shots and preserving a 1-1 tie at the end of regulation.

"Lester was an inspiration to the rest of us," said Frank Boucher, "although his antics were somewhat overdrawn. 'Let them shoot!' he'd cry. Just as loudly from behind our bench came the voice of (temporary Rangers coach) Odie Cleghorn. 'For God's sake, don't let them shoot!'"

With seven-plus minutes to go in O.T., the puck skittered behind the Maroons' goal and was snared by Rangers defenseman Ching Johnson. Boucher was stationed in front of the net and yelled for the pass. "Ching pushed the puck to me," Boucher recalled, "and I sent it into the net." The time was 7:05 and the Rangers had scored an improbable victory.

For Game 3, Patrick used goalie Joe Miller, whom he borrowed from the New York Americans. Montreal won the third game 2-1, but the Rangers were undaunted. Miller posted a 1-0 shutout in Game 4 and New York took a 2-1 victory in Game 5, thus clinching the series. Had it not been for Patrick, Montreal would have taken the second game—and probably the Cup as well.

1927-28

- In the interest of encouraging offensive play, rules are adopted to allow forward passes in the defensive and neutral zones.

- A goal net designed by Art Ross, with a double-curved back and flax netting (to better catch pucks), is adopted for use in the NHL.

- In Chicago, the season begins with the dismissal of coach Pete Muldoon, whose first-year Hawks had finished in third place in 1926-27.

- Pete Muldoon is so upset by his firing that he affixes a "hex" on the entire Chicago franchise, saying it will never win an NHL title. His prophecy

will come to be known as the Curse of Muldoon.

- Barney Stanley is hired to coach the Hawks and they drop to the cellar with a 7-34-3 record. Their two home wins are the fewest ever by an NHL team.

The patriarch of hockey's Royal Family was Lester Patrick, who won his first Stanley Cup in 1906 with the Montreal Wanderers. In 1926-27, as the manager/coach of the New York Rangers, he donned the blades again, appearing in one game as a blueliner. Later, in Game 2 of the 1928 Cup Finals, he filled in for injured goalie Lorne Chabot. Patrick did so magnificently, allowing only one goal in the Rangers' 2-1 overtime victory over the Maroons.

• The Canadiens, with Howie Morenz, Aurel Joliat, and Art Gagne spearheading the attack, win the Canadian Division with a record of 26-11-7.

• Habs goalie George Hainsworth allows just 48 goals in 44 games, finishing with a league-high 26 wins,

a 1.09 GAA, and 13 shutouts. He earns the Vezina Trophy.

• Hal Winkler's 1.59 GAA is the best in the American Division, as his Bruins capture the division title.

• Ottawa's Alex Connell strings together an amazing six straight

shutouts—more than 440 minutes of scoreless hockey—en route to his outstanding 1.30 GAA.

• Frank Boucher, the class of the Rangers, wins the first of his seven Lady Byng Trophies. His club finishes second in the American Division.

Ross Finishes First, Designs New Goal Net

When grocery magnate Charles F. Adams put NHL hockey on the Boston market, he hired Art Ross to stock the shelves. Ross reigned as manager and sometimes-coach of the Bruins for 30 years, signing such stars as Bill Cowley, Cooney Weiland, and Milt Schmidt. Ross, who coached Boston to a first-place finish in the American Division in 1927-28, also saw the NHL adopt his goal net that season. You'd recognize the design: It's the same one still in use today.

Olympic Games

George Hainsworth

Hainsworth Is as Tiny as His GAA

At 5'6" and 150 pounds, George Hainsworth had an uphill battle to make it in the big leagues. In his rookie year, though, he took the Vezina Trophy as the league's most effective stopper. In 1927-28, he repeated the Vezina win with a 1.05 GAA and 13 shutouts. He led his Canadiens to the best record in the league (26-11-7), but they were upset by their rival Maroons in the semifinals.

It's Canada 38, Foes 0 at Olympic Games

The Canadian Olympic team captured its third straight gold medal at the 1928 Olympic Games in St. Moritz, Switzerland. Represented by the Toronto Varsity Grads, the Canadians didn't allow a goal in their three-game championship round, routing Sweden 11-0, Great Britain 14-0, and Switzerland 13-0. Conn Smythe, owner/manager of the Maple Leafs, hand-picked the Grads but had to bow to business pressures and stay home.

Art Ross

1927-28

- Montreal's Howie Morenz becomes the first NHLer ever to eclipse the 50-point mark, finishing the season with 33 goals, 18 assists, and 51 points. He nabs the Hart Trophy.

- In the playoffs, the American Division pits the Rangers against third-place Pittsburgh, while the Canadian Division sees the Maroons and Senators battle.

- The two first-place division winners, the Canadiens and Bruins, receive first-round playoff byes.

- The Rangers (6-4) and Maroons (3-1) win their total-goals series.

- In the semifinals, the Maroons top the Canadiens in total goals, 3-2.

- The Rangers upset Boston with a 1-1 tie and a 4-1 shellacking to earn a berth in the Stanley Cup Finals.

- The Maroons win Game 1 of the Finals 2-0, but a bizarre episode

Morenz a Lot Better Than He Thinks He Is

In 1923, when a young Howie Morenz was called up to honor a contract with the Montreal Canadiens, he wired back stating that he could not come to Montreal because he wasn't good enough to play for the big club. Wily owner Leo Dandurand wired back stating that if Morenz wasn't in uniform by Monday morning, he'd sue. Howie took the train to Montreal and never looked back. In 1927-28, he led the league in goals (33), assists (18), and points (51).

Muldoon Puts a Hex on the Hawks

Pete Muldoon, who had coached Chicago to a respectable 19-22-3 record in 1926-27 (their first NHL season), was fired by owner Frederic McLaughlin at the start of 1927-28. So outraged was Muldoon that he stormed out of McLaughlin's office and boomed, "You'll see. I'll make sure you never win an NHL title!" Hauntingly, the Black Hawks would go a full 40 years before winning a regular-season title. Chicagoans blamed the dry spell on the "Curse of Muldoon."

Boucher Wins Byng, Scores Cup Winner

Frank Boucher may not look like a gentle man here, but his record of good sportsmanship and clean play is unmatched in the history of the game. He won seven Lady Byng Trophies in his career, the first coming in 1927-28 after he scored 35 points while spending just 15 minutes in the penalty box. Boucher also starred in the 1928 Finals. He scored two goals in the decisive Game 5 as the Rangers nipped the Maroons 2-1 to claim the Stanley Cup.

Howie Morenz

Pete Muldoon

Frank Boucher

occurs in Game 2. Lester Patrick, coach of the Rangers, is forced to play goal after Lorne Chabot is hit in the eye by a Nels Stewart shot.

• Lester Patrick sparks the Rangers to a 2-1 victory in Game 2 of the Finals. Frank Boucher wins it with a goal in overtime.

• The Maroons take Game 3 of the Finals 2-1, as the Rangers stick Joe Miller—borrowed from the New York Americans—in goal.

• Game 4 of the Finals goes to the Rangers, as sub Joe Miller records a 1-0 shutout.

• The Rangers' Frank Boucher scores twice in Game 5 as the Rangers win 2-1 and nab their first Stanley Cup.

• On March 31, 1928, Gordie Howe is born in Floral, Saskatchewan.

• Canada skates off with its third straight Olympic hockey gold medal.

Through the latter part of the Roaring '20s, the NHL was blessed with superstar forwards (such as Howie Morenz and Bill Cook) and glittering goaltenders (like George Hainsworth and Lorne Chabot). But a truly magnetic defenseman didn't surface until Eddie Shore was auctioned off by the failing Pacific Coast Hockey Association and reported to the Bruins in 1926.

Shore was brash beyond belief and had a thirst for mayhem. In his second NHL season, 1927-28, Shore set a penalty record with 165 minutes' worth of fouls. Shore's boisterousness was immediately transferred to the Boston crowd, until it was impossible to determine which was the catalyst for mania—the frenetic Bruins audience or the player, Shore.

Shore was downright vicious on the ice, flattening foes with some of the hardest body crunches known to hockey. Moreover, he was indestructible. Shore once broke three ribs in a game in New York. The damage was so severe that the Bruins left him in the care of a physician and hopped on a train for a game in Montreal. Meanwhile, Eddie stumbled to his hotel's lobby and hailed a cab for

ROUGH-AND-READY SHORE TERRORIZES NHL FOES

Grand Central Station, where he had purchased a ticket for the late train to Montreal. He arrived in time for the game with the Canadiens and wound up playing. He scored two goals and added an assist to boot.

In Shore's day, it was an unwritten rule that defensemen remain at or near their blueline instead of launching offensive rushes. But Shore broke the rule constantly. He took advantage of his great skating strides and managed to tally 12 goals and seven assists in 1928-29, placing sixth in scoring in the American Division. Shore's scoring exploits continued through the 1930s, a decade in which he won four Hart Trophies.

But his scoring ability never overshadowed his defensive work, which covered the spectrum.

Shore could poke-check and hook-check with extreme finesse, and body-check with consummate ferocity.

"Shore's abnormally long stride built up a momentum that carried him down the ice with frightening speed," said writer/editor Ed Fitzgerald. "His chilling disregard for personal safety enabled him to maintain peak speed to a point well beyond the limit dared by lesser men. The result was that he came up consistently with plays that other stars were lucky to duplicate once in a lifetime."

Shore, who teamed with defenseman Lionel Hitchman, became truly dominating during the 1928-29 season, during which the Bruins amassed a 13-game undefeated string. His defensive work enabled Boston's rookie goaltender, Cecil "Tiny" Thompson, to produce a dozen shutouts and a 1.18 goals-against average.

The Shore-Hitchman-Thompson combination orchestrated a first-place finish in the NHL's American Division. After knocking off the powerful Canadiens in the playoffs, the Bruins then ousted the Rangers in two games, 2-0 and 2-1, for Boston's first Stanley Cup.

1928-29

• The NHL now permits forward passing in the defensive and neutral zones and into the attacking zone from the neutral zone. However, forward passing is still not allowed in the offensive zone.

• A minor penalty will now be assessed to any player who delays the

game by passing the puck into his own defensive zone.

• Regulation ties will now result in a 10-minute, non-sudden-death overtime period.

• All the offensive rule changes cannot steal the thunder from

Canadiens goalie George Hainsworth. He records 22 shutouts, a mark that has never been approached. His 0.98 GAA is also the greatest ever.

• The Canadiens roar to the top of the Canadian Division with a record of 22-7-15. Montreal loses just three road games—an NHL mark.

Eddie Shore was known as the toughest man on skates. He wasn't particularly vicious; he was just absolutely single-minded. If you got in his way, he would hurt you. Shore was a defenseman, though he scored with ease. In 1928-29, he tied for second in scoring on the Bruins while maintaining a very tight defense. The Bruins finished first in the American Division and won the Stanley Cup, largely on the back of the remarkable Shore.

• The Americans finish nine points behind Montreal thanks to Roy Worters' 1.21 GAA and 13 shutouts. Worters wins the Hart Trophy.

• Toronto finds a new phenom in Ace Bailey. The speedy winger leads the NHL in goals (22) and points (32).

• Chicago sets an all-time NHL record by being shut out in eight straight games.

• The Canadiens, with much assistance from George Hainsworth, piece together a 17-game unbeaten streak that takes them through January and February.

• Detroit's Carson Cooper leads the American Division in scoring with just 27 points (18 goals).

• New York Ranger center Frank Boucher leads the NHL in assists (16) and captures his second Lady Byng Trophy.

Tiny Thompson

Thompson's Out of Sight in Playoffs

Although his nickname was "Tiny," rookie Cecil Thompson came up big for the Bruins in 1928-29, leading the league with 26 victories and posting a 1.18 GAA. Boston manager Art Ross claimed that he signed Thompson without ever having seen him play. The 23-year-old rookie made good on the Bruins' investment by going undefeated in the 1929 playoffs, allowing only three goals in five games.

Roy Worters

Worters Tosses Shutouts, Wins Hart

Roy "Shrimp" Worters joined the New York Americans in 1928 and quickly established himself as one of the league's best netminders. It was quite an honor considering the mind-blowing numbers put up by goalies George Hainsworth and Tiny Thompson. With a 1.21 GAA and 13 shutouts, Worters won the year's Hart Trophy.

George Hainsworth

Hainsworth: 0.98 GAA, 22 Shutouts

In 1928-29, the Year of the Goalie, one netminder stood above all others. The Canadiens' George Hainsworth allowed only 43 goals and recorded an astounding 22 shutouts. His 0.98 GAA remains the greatest NHL mark of all time, while his 22 goose eggs are seven more than anyone else has ever recorded. The Canadiens won 22 games, lost seven, and tied 15—many of which were 0-0 stalemates.

1928-29

- Chicago's Charlie Gardiner posts a 1.93 GAA, yet his record is 7-29-8.

- Rookie goalie Cecil Thompson leads the NHL in victories (26) as Boston wins the American Division.

- The Rangers trade Lorne Chabot to the Maple Leafs and install John Roach as their goalie. Roach helps New York to a second-place finish behind Boston with a 1.48 GAA.

- The playoffs begin with a new format. The first-, second-, and third-place teams from each division face their opposite number in the other division.

- In the opening round of playoffs, Toronto and Detroit (third-place finishers in their respective divisions) play a two-game, total-goals series. The Maple Leafs win 7-2.

- The New York Americans and New York Rangers meet in a hometown clash. The teams fight to a scoreless

Ace Bailey

Bill Cook, Frank Boucher, Bun Cook

Bread Liners Find A Way to Score

Rangers Bill Cook, Frank Boucher, and Bun Cook all reached double digits in goals in 1928-29—quite an achievement in a season that saw teams score at a goal-and-a-half-per-game rate. Boucher, known as "Raffles" due to his creative on-ice playmaking, led the league with 16 assists. Hauntingly, this threesome was known as the Bread Line, a sight that would become quite common in North America after the stock market crash of '29.

Bailey's the Leafs' New Scoring Ace

Ace Bailey was the trump card in the Toronto forward line. The Leafs' deck wasn't yet stacked with talent, but Bailey and linemates Andy Blair and Dan Cox were an impressive unit. In 1928-29, Bailey led all league scorers with 22 goals and 32 points, finishing runner-up for the Hart Trophy. A versatile skater, Bailey also took turns on defense, where he teamed with Hap Day to form an explosive backline duo.

tie in Game 1 and the Rangers win it in double overtime of Game 2.

• Montreal and Boston square off in the third opening-round series—a best-of-five matchup—and the Bruins sweep the Habs with a pair of 1-0 wins and a decisive 3-2 win.

• The Rangers next face Toronto in Round 2. Boston awaits to meet the winner in the Stanley Cup Finals, which will be a best-of-three format.

• The best-of-three semifinals goes to New York in thrilling fashion. The Rangers dispatch the Maple Leafs 1-0 and 2-1 in overtime.

• Boston's Tiny Thompson shuts out the Rangers in the first game of the Finals, as Dit Clapper and Dutch Gainor score for the Bruins.

• Boston's Bill Carson breaks a 1-1 tie at 18:02 of the third period to win Game 2 of the Finals. The Bruins thus win their first-ever Stanley Cup.

BRUINS GO 38-5-1, BUT THE HABS SIP CHAMPAGNE

In the late 1920s, the Boston Bruins were renowned for their formidable defense, led by goalie Tiny Thompson and defenseman Eddie Shore. If the Bruins could beef up their attacking units, many thought, they would really be in business.

This was accomplished with a vengeance in the 1929-30 campaign, thanks to the managerial genius of Art Ross. Ross fused a forward line comprised of right wing Aubrey "Dit" Clapper, center Ralph "Cooney" Weiland, and left wing Norman "Dutch" Gainor, and they became instant terrors. The "Dynamite Trio," as the line became known, was spearheaded by Weiland, who garnered an NHL-record 73 points (43 goals, 30 assists). Weiland had more than doubled the statistics of Toronto's Ace Bailey, who led the league in scoring the previous year with 32 points.

The 1929-30 Bruins posted a record of 38-5-1—the greatest mark the NHL has ever seen. What made their performance more impressive was the exceptionally high quality of opposition. The Rangers (Cook brothers-Boucher), Canadiens (Morenz-Joliat), and Maroons (Nels Stewart) each had formidable teams from goal-tending on out, but the Bruins were still far better than anyone else. At one point, the Bean-towners won 14 games in a row.

Not only did Weiland lead the league in scoring, but Clapper finished second in goals (41) and third in points (61). Eddie Shore kicked his game up another notch, while goalie Tiny Thompson won his first Vezina Trophy thanks to a GAA of 2.23. He was now being compared with such accomplished contemporaries as George Hainsworth and Roy "Shrimp" Worters.

Despite their powerhouse regular-season performance—and a thrashing of the Maroons in the playoffs—Boston fell in the Stanley Cup Finals to the Canadiens. The Bruins were clearly better than the Habs, but the Finals in those days were merely a best-of-three affair. Anything could happen in such a short series, as the Bruins found out.

When the Cup Finals opened at Boston Garden on April 1, 1930, the Bruins were without Gainor. His loss was sorely felt, as the Canadiens shut out Boston 3-0. Surprisingly, the Habs' scoring was opened by Albert "Battleship" Leduc, who had tallied only six goals all season.

The second game was played at the Montreal Forum, and Gainor returned to the Bruins' lineup. Boston manager Art Ross was hoping that his crack defense of Lionel Hitchman and Shore would thwart the Canadiens, while Clapper and Co. would provide the scoring. But it wasn't to be.

Inspired by the home crowd, Les Canadiens jumped to a 3-0 lead, thanks largely to Morenz and Pit Lepine. Shore ignited a Bruins comeback, pulling Boston to within a goal of a tie. As the clock ticked down, a Boston goal by Weiland was disallowed because he kicked it in. The Habs prevailed 4-3 and swept the Bruins in the series in two games. The very next year, the Stanley Cup Finals were extended to a best-of-five series.

1929-30

- The Detroit Cougars, who joined the NHL in 1926-27, change their name to the Falcons.

- A new NHL rule allows forward passing in all zones, while another rule permits players to kick the puck—although not into the goal. Also, goalies may no longer "freeze" the puck; they must clear it immediately after a save.

- High-sticking penalties are introduced, as the league tries to reduce its inherent violence.

- An "off-side" rule is written. It prohibits an attacking player from preceding the puck into the enemy's zone.

- The NHL's scoring skyrockets from 642 goals in 1928-29 to 1,301 goals in 1929-30.

- The Bruins win the American Division by 30 points over Chicago.

Boston's 1929-30 squad read like a "Who's Who" of pro hockey. They boasted two 40-goal scorers (Cooney Weiland and Dit Clapper), the league's toughest defensemen (Eddie Shore and Lionel Hitchman), and hockey's steadiest goaltender (Tiny Thompson). They were unstoppable in the regular season, winning 38 games, 15 more than any other team. Their joyride came to an end in the Stanley Cup Finals, where they were quickly ousted by Montreal.

Their 38-5-1 record is the greatest NHL mark of all time, and their 14-game winning streak—and 20-game home winning streak—set NHL records.

• Ralph "Cooney" Weiland sparks the Bruins with a record-setting 43-goal, 73-point season.

• The Rangers' Frank Boucher tallies a record 36 assists and wins his third straight Lady Byng Trophy.

• Struck in the face by a Howie Morenz shot, Maroons goalie Clint Benedict sets a precedent when he dons a leather mask in a game to protect his broken nose.

• On December 14, 1929, Montreal's Pit Lepine erupts for five goals against Ottawa's Alex Connell.

• On December 19, 1929, Pittsburgh's Johnny McKinnon and Toronto's Hap Day make history when the two defensemen each notch four goals in the same game.

Clint Benedict

Benedict Does as He Pleases, Dons a Mask

In the late 1910s, when goalies were required to remain on their feet to make a save, Clint Benedict refused to conform to the league rule. He continually flopped to the ice, forcing the league to change its rule and allow netminders to drop and stop. As a result, goalies took their fair share of pucks and sticks to the face. After breaking his nose for the third time on the season in 1929-30, Benedict created a leather mask and wore it for a couple of games.

Pirates Fare as Badly as the Economy

The fortunes of America's steel-making industry collapsed with the rest of the industrial world in 1929. In Pittsburgh, the weight was shared by the hockey club. The Pittsburgh Pirates, one of hockey's most futile organizations, endured a horrific 5-36-3 season, setting NHL records for most goals allowed (185) and fewest victories in a 44-game season. After the 1929-30 campaign, the Pirates packed it in and moved across the state to Philadelphia.

Pittsburgh Pirates

Hap Day

Day Dumps Pill Biz, Stars in NHL

Hap Day didn't have to play professional hockey. He would have been just as content to issue remedies from behind the counter of his Toronto pharmacy. However, Conn Smythe had bigger plans for the talented Day and made him the Leafs' first captain—and the leader of the team's defensive corps. From his dispensary on the blueline, Day led all Toronto rearguards in 1929-30 with seven goals—including four in one game.

1929-30

- On March 18, 1930, Montreal center Howie Morenz lights the lamp five times against the New York Americans.

- Tight defense is not totally absent, as Boston's Tiny Thompson leads all goalies in wins (38) and GAA (2.23).

- The Maroons' Nels Stewart tallies 39 goals and 55 points and carries his club to a first-place finish in the regular season. He's awarded the Hart Trophy, his second.

- The playoffs match the Canadiens and Black Hawks (second-place finishers in their respective divisions)

and the Rangers and Senators (third-place finishers) in total-goals series.

- The Habs shut out Chicago 1-0 in the first game, then extend the second game to triple overtime. With the score 2-2, the game is called at 11:43 of the third O.T., giving Montreal the series three goals to two.

Nels Stewart

Forgotten Stewart Pumps In 39 Goals

Sadly, the name Nels Stewart is too often a forgotten one. Ol' Poison, as he was known, played a rugged 15 years with the Montreal Maroons, Boston Bruins, and New York Americans. In 1929-30 with the Maroons, Stewart scored 39 goals and added 16 assists in his 44 games, leading his team to first place in the Canadian Division. The Maroons, however, were overpowered by the Bruins in the first round of playoffs.

Dit Clapper

Clapper Makes Noise, Bangs In 41

Coming off a Stanley Cup championship season, Dit Clapper had the best year of his long and admirable career in 1929-30. Clapper had scored only nine goals in 1928-29 and was never known as a high scorer. But the taste of winning made him hunger for more, and he potted 41 goals and earned 20 assists in 1929-30. The Bruins finished at the top of the American Division but were stopped cold by Montreal's George Hainsworth in the Finals.

Cooney Weiland

Weiland Pots Nearly a Goal Per Game

After George Hainsworth racked up 22 shutouts in 1928-29, the NHL introduced forward-passing rules, making the job of puck-stopping just that much harder. No one took more advantage of the new edicts than Boston's Cooney Weiland, who scored an NHL-record 43 goals in 44 games in 1929-30. Weiland and his Beantown teammates dominated the NHL, scoring a league-high 179 goals while allowing a league-low 98.

- The Rangers easily skate past Ottawa, winning 5-2 in the second match after Game 1 ended 1-1.

- In the playoff meeting of division winners, Boston beats the Maroons three games to one. The Bruins await the winner of the Canadiens-Rangers series.

- Game 1 between the Canadiens and Rangers goes to quadruple overtime. Montreal's Gus Rivers beats John Roach after nearly seven periods of heart-stopping hockey.

- The Rangers are spent in Game 2, as Montreal beats them 2-0 to clinch a berth in the Finals.

- Riding high on emotion, the Habs shut down the Bruins' powerful offense, winning the first game of the Finals 3-0.

- The Habs clinch the Stanley Cup with a 4-3 victory in Game 2, as Howie Morenz scores the winner at 17:50 of the second period.

Early in 1930, most hockey analysts predicted that the Boston Bruins would become the NHL's first post-expansion dynasty. Their Stanley Cup victory in 1929 and regular-season runaway a year later suggested an endless skein of championships—that is, until the Montreal Canadiens quickly disposed of them in the 1930 Stanley Cup Finals.

The Habs' ascension was based on the maturation of several key players, but none was more critical to the Canadiens than Howie Morenz, also known as the "Stratford Flash." Although not a French-Canadian (his roots were traced to Switzerland), Morenz epitomized the elan of the Montreal team. Of all the "Flying Frenchmen," Morenz flew highest and fastest of all.

"The kid's *too* fast," said one observer. "He'll burn himself out." "He's the hardest player in the league to stop," said Boston Bruins defenseman Eddie Shore. "Howie comes at you with such speed that it's almost impossible to block him with a body-check. When he hits you, he usually comes off a lot better than the defenseman."

Morenz's linemates were no less threatening. Tiny left wing Aurel

FLYING FRENCHMEN SOAR TO STANLEY CUP

Joliat could not be intimidated. He compensated for his small stature with a vast repertoire of stick-handling maneuvers and pirouettes. "He transported the world of ballet to the hockey arena," said one admirer.

Right wing Johnny "Black Cat" Gagnon—nicknamed for his swarthy complexion, jet black hair, darting moves, and natural puck sense—joined the Canadiens in 1930-31. Guarding the nets was veteran goaltender George Hainsworth, who had won three Vezina Trophies and remained in mint condition despite his advanced age.

The addition of Gagnon on the Morenz line seemed to rejuvenate the aging Joliat. "Aurel always used to get the puck and pass it to me," said Gagnon, "and then I'd pass it to him. We had the same

stick-handling style and I always knew what kind of moves he'd make. As soon as he hit the blueline, he'd throw me a pass behind his back."

Morenz won the 1930-31 scoring crown (28-23-51) and also annexed the Hart Trophy. Joliat tied for 10th in the league in scoring (35 points), while Gagnon contributed 25. Les Canadiens finished in first place (26-10-8) and battled the rival Bruins in the playoffs. The series went the full allotment of games, with Montreal squeaking by with a 3-2 win in Game 5. That victory sent the Canadiens to the Stanley Cup Finals against the Chicago Black Hawks.

The Joliat-Gagnon connection was primarily responsible for Montreal's Stanley Cup victory. Although the Canadiens won the first game 2-1, they lost heart-breakers in Game 2 (double overtime) and Game 3 (triple overtime).

The Canadiens took Game 4 4-2, tying the best-of-five round at two games apiece. In the final match, Joliat sent a pass that put Gagnon in the clear for a 1-0 lead. Morenz scored late in the game, giving Montreal a 2-0 victory and its second straight Stanley Cup.

1930-31

- After fourth- and fifth-place finishes, the struggling Pittsburgh Pirates relocate to Philadelphia and change their name to the Quakers.

- The NHL introduces the use of a four-sided scoreboard clock in some arenas, and it sanctions the use of farm teams by several NHL clubs.

- According to legend, Toronto manager Conn Smythe bets on a long-shot horse to raise money to pry King Clancy from Ottawa. He wins and Clancy becomes a Leaf.

- The Habs' Howie Morenz wins his second scoring title with 51 points. He also nabs his second Hart Trophy.

- Toronto sophomore Charlie Conacher leads the league in goals with 31. Ranger Bill Cook has 30.

- Toronto center Joe Primeau, playing between Busher Jackson and Ace Bailey, notches a league-high 32 assists.

He was not the first superstar in hockey, but in the early 1930s Howie Morenz was the biggest. Known as the Mitchell Meteor, the Stratford Streak, and even the Babe Ruth of Hockey, Morenz was a whirling dervish on the pond. His teammate, Aurel Joliat, once said that he could play three games in one night if he was playing beside the great Howie Morenz. In 1930-31, Morenz led the league in scoring (28-23-51) and won the Hart Trophy.

• Detroit's talented second-year center Ebbie Goodfellow finishes second in the points race (48).

• Maroons center Nels Stewart sets an all-time NHL record when he scores two goals just four seconds apart on January 3, 1931, in a 5-3 win over Boston.

• Americans goaltender Roy Worters earns his first Vezina Trophy, as New York gives up the fewest goals in the league (74).

• The Lady Byng Trophy is presented to Frank Boucher of the Rangers for the fourth straight season.

• In an attempt to promote hockey during the Depression, the NHL introduces its first All-Star team.

• The initial All-Star squad consists of Montreal's Howie Morenz at center with his regular linemate Aurel Joliat on the left side and New York Ranger Bill Cook on the right.

Four-Sided Clock

Philadelphia Quakers

Philadelphians Run Quakers Out of Town

There have been many bad hockey teams in the history of the NHL, but the Philadelphia Quakers of 1930-31 were likely the worst team of all time. With a threadbare lineup and a porous defense, the Quakers went 4-36-4 and were outscored 184-76. Not even the City of Brotherly Love could embrace these unlovable losers, and the one-year blunder team was ridden out of town, never to return.

NHL Unveils Its New Four-Sided Clock

Hockey is played between two opposing teams, but each team has another player to factor into their game: the time clock. Beginning in the 1930-31 season, fans, players, and officials were able to "stay in the game" from any angle in the arena, watching the seconds tick away on all four sides of this mammoth marvel.

King Clancy

Smythe Signs a Star—With a Sense of Humor

Conn Smythe knew that if the Leafs were to blossom into Stanley Cup champions, he needed power, speed, and the luck of the Irish. He found all three in Frank "King" Clancy. Despite the bad economic times, Smythe was able to find a ransom to bring the King to Hog Town in 1930-31. Clancy, a two-time Stanley Cup winner with Ottawa whose talent was matched only by his wit, earned a berth on the NHL's First All-Star Team, which debuted in 1930-31.

1930-31

- The first All-Star defensemen are Boston's Eddie Shore and Toronto's King Clancy. Chicago's Charlie Gardiner is selected as the goalie.

- Boston's Eddie Shore leads all backliners in scoring (31 points) and is second overall in PIM (108).

- Black Hawks goaltender Charlie Gardiner leads the NHL with a dozen shutouts.

- Chicago (second in the American Division) outscores Toronto (second in the Canadian Division) 4-3 in their two-game, total-goals series.

- The Rangers (third in the American) trounce the Maroons (third in the Canadian) 8-1 in their series.

- In the best-of-five semifinals between the Canadiens and Bruins, each team posts an overtime victory and enters Game 5 tied at two games apiece.

Conacher Rifles In a League-High 31

Many of the Conacher clan skated for NHL teams, but only Charlie, the Big Bomber, shoved and scored his way into the Hockey Hall of Fame. As the trigger man on the Leafs' famed Kid Line, Charlie led all NHL sharpshooters in goals in 1930-31, blasting 31 pucks over, under, and through NHL goaltenders. He and his Kid Line teammates, Joe Primeau and Busher Jackson, were poised to become hockey's best forward unit.

Charlie Conacher

Wentworth Burns Habs in Cup

Cy Wentworth was not a big man—5'9" and 170 pounds—but he stood his ground behind the Black Hawks' blueline. Dick Irvin, who coached the Hawks in 1930-31, was a big fan of Wentworth, who helped Chicago register the fewest goals against in the American Division. Irvin likely gave Wentworth a bear hug after Game 3 of the 1931 Finals, as Cy beat Canadiens goalie George Hainsworth in triple overtime to win the game.

George Hainsworth, Roy Worters

NHL Goalies Share a Common Bond

In a world where every man they met waved a stick in their faces, NHL goaltenders had little peace of mind. In the 1930s, goalies were not only expected to play every game, they were expected to perform regardless of being cut, stitched, kicked, or broken. Despite the rigorous demands, goalies Roy Worters and George Hainsworth took their licks and kept on kicking. Worters won the Vezina Trophy in 1930-31; Hainsworth won it three times previously.

Cy Wentworth

• Montreal's George Hainsworth outduels Boston's Tiny Thompson in the decisive fifth game, as the Canadiens skate to a 3-2 overtime victory in Montreal.

• The Canadiens beat Chicago 2-1 in Game 1 of the Finals, as Pit Lepine notches the winner. Game 2 goes to double overtime before Chicago's Johnny Gottselig snaps a 1-1 tie.

• Game 3 goes to 13:50 of triple overtime, tied 2-2, before Chicago's Cy Wentworth nets a winner.

• Despite leading 2-1 in the third period with the championship in sight, the Hawks fizzle and let the Habs score three unanswered goals. Montreal wins 4-2 and sends the series to a fifth game.

• The Hawks have no ammunition left, as the Canadiens win Game 5 2-0 and hoist their second straight Stanley Cup.

SMYTHE'S HORSE COMES IN; LEAFS WIN THE CUP

Conn Smythe was a much-decorated World War I hero who later propelled the University of Toronto hockey clubs to championships in the early 1920s. It was in 1927, however, that he entered the public eye. On February 14, 1927, Smythe (along with Hugh Aird) purchased the NHL's Toronto St. Patricks. At his new post, Smythe would become one of the most powerful men in the National League over the next 30 years.

Immediately after purchasing the Toronto team, Smythe changed its name to the Maple Leafs. It was too late to salvage the 1926-27 season (the Leafs were destined for the cellar), so Smythe turned his thoughts to long-term results. He created a five-year plan that he thought would vault the Leafs to the top.

Smythe traded for many players including King Clancy, an Ottawa Senators defenseman who came to Toronto in 1930 via a racetrack bet. Apparently, Smythe's horse was running at Woodbine Racetrack with odds of 100-1 against. Yet Smythe put his bankroll on his horse and cheered him on to an astonishing victory. With his winnings, he bought Clancy from Ottawa for $35,000

and threw in two extra players. Clancy turned out to be worth the hefty price.

By the 1931-32 season, Smythe's Leafs were led by the Kid Line, comprised of right wing Charlie Conacher (age 22), left wing Busher Jackson (20), and center Joe Primeau (25). The three youngsters dominated the league's scoring charts, with Jackson finishing on top with 53 points (on 28 goals). Primeau finished second in points and led the league in assists (37), while Conacher placed fourth in scoring and tied for first in goals (34).

Complementing Smythe's splendid sextet was the continent's most spectacular new arena, Maple Leaf Gardens. Work on the Gardens began just five months before the start of the 1931-32 season, but, amazingly, it was

completed by Opening Day. The arena immediately became to hockey what Yankee Stadium was to baseball.

Toronto finished the 1931-32 season with a 23-18-7 record, placing second in the Canadian Division. The Leafs entered the playoffs and met Chicago in a two-game, total-goals series that opened in the Windy City. Behind Charlie Gardiner's air-tight goaltending, the Black Hawks stifled the Leafs 2-0 in Game 1. In the second game, however, Toronto blew out Chicago 6-0 and advanced to the semifinals, where they met the Montreal Maroons.

Against the Maroons, the Leafs were again in trouble. They trailed Montreal 3-2 in Game 2 before Hap Day tied the score late in the third period. The Leafs' Bob Gracie then won the match in overtime, putting Toronto in the Finals against the Rangers.

The Leafs' Kid Line dominated New York in the Finals. They swept the Rangers with the tennis-like scores of 6-4, 6-2, 6-4 and skated off with the Stanley Cup. Smythe had said he needed five years to build a winner and, sure enough, five years is what it took.

1931-32

- The Ottawa Senators, once a proud franchise, are forced to fold their tents for a season, as dwindling attendance threatens financial doom.

- The Philadelphia Quakers, who suffered through a 4-36-4 season after transferring from Pittsburgh, disband prior to the season.

- The eight-team league continues its divisional format but extends the schedule to 48 games in an attempt to generate income.

- On November 12, 1931, Conn Smythe proudly opens the Maple Leaf Gardens at the corner of Carlton and Church Streets in downtown Toronto.

- On January 19, 1932, Toronto's Charlie Conacher scores five goals against the Americans in an 11-3 drubbing.

- Toronto's Charlie Conacher ties the Rangers' Bill Cook for the goal-scoring crown with 34.

For most of his life, Conn Smythe was a leader of men. Even back in the 1920s, Smythe led a team to the Allan Cup and another to the Olympic gold medal. Smythe spent countless hours on cold, wooden arena benches watching hockey players from coast to coast, and the Maple Leafs were the result of his astute observation and shrewd personal relations. In 1932, Smythe's star-studded team led the league in goals on the way to the Stanley Cup.

• Leafs center Joe Primeau leads the league in assists with 37, setting a new league mark, and finishes second overall in points with 50.

• Busher Jackson, the third member of Toronto's Kid Line, leads the league in scoring with 53 points.

• Montreal's flashy Howie Morenz finishes third in points (24-25-49) and leads the Habs to a first-place finish in the Canadian Division. He's awarded his third Hart Trophy.

• Joe Primean cops the Lady Byng, thus ending Frank Boucher's four-year stranglehold on the prize.

• Chicago's Charlie Gardiner leads the NHL in GAA (1.92) and also wins the Vezina Trophy.

• One year after capturing the Vezina Trophy, Americans goalie Roy Worters leads the league in losses (20) as the Amerks fall to the Canadian Division basement.

Bill Cook, Frank Boucher, Bun Cook

Bread Line Cooks Up 34 Goals

The recipe for the Bread Line was written in the cold kitchens of the old Western Hockey League. That's where Bill Cook, Bun Cook, and Frank Boucher learned how to play the game. More often than not, the spotlight shone on Boucher, the playmaker of the trio. In 1931-32, however, it was Bill Cook who took the bows. He tied for the league lead in goals with 34 and earned a spot on the First All-Star Team.

Maple Leaf Gardens

Maple Leaf Gardens Opens for Business

Conn Smythe had a dream of a hockey empire in his home-town of Toronto. He was clever, rich, and influential, and he wanted an arena that would properly house the hand-picked team he had assembled. Despite an extra-ordinarily tight construction schedule, Smythe and his labor force—who received shares in the new company as payment for their work—completed Maple Leaf Gardens in time for Opening Night on November 12, 1931.

1931-32

- The Rangers win the American Division regular-season title with a 23-17-8 record, as the once-powerful Bruins fall to last place.

- In the first round of playoffs, Toronto and Chicago (the second-place finishers) meet and the Hawks win the first game 2-0. However, the Leafs win the series with a 6-0 victory in Game 2.

- In the battle of third-place teams, the Maroons outscore Detroit 3-1 in their two-game, total-goals series.

- The Rangers and Canadiens meet in a best-of-five semifinal series. Montreal wins Game 1, but the Rangers take Game 2 in triple O.T. New York's Bun Cook scores with 28 seconds left in the sixth period for a 4-3 win.

- New York goalie John Roach shuts the Canadiens down in Game 3 (2-0). The Rangers earn a ticket to the Finals with a 5-2 win in Game 4.

Chuck Gardiner

Gardiner Best at Guarding the Goalcage

Chicago's Chuck Gardiner probably looked longingly at this artist's recreation of the Hawks' goaltender. The artist made sure to include a bruised forehead, but he was kind enough to give Gardiner a narrow cage to protect. Though Gardiner had to play his game between regulation-size goalposts, he was able to keep the puck out with more efficiency than any goalie of his day. In 1931-32, he registered a 1.92 GAA and won the Vezina Trophy.

Conacher's Scoring Helps Leafs Win Cup

In 1931-32, the Maple Leafs reached the Stanley Cup Finals for the first time in their young history. Their opponents were the New York Rangers, matching the Kid Line against the Bread Line. Youth was served in this series, as the Leafs—propelled by Kid Liner Charlie Conacher—sliced up the Rangers in three straight games. Conacher, who fired in a career-high 34 goals in the regular season, added six more timely markers in the playoffs.

Charlie Conacher

Joe Primeau

Gentleman Primeau Nabs the Byng

The pivot of the Kid Line was a smooth-skating centerman named Joe Primeau. He was an expert at avoiding checks and slipping the puck to one of his sharpshooting linemates. Primeau, who led the league in assists in 1931-32 with 37, was better known by his nickname "Gentleman Joe." In the spring of '32, he was awarded the Lady Byng Trophy as the player who combined high skill with gentlemanly play.

• Toronto wins its semifinal series with the Maroons thanks to an overtime goal in Game 2. The Leafs take momentum and confidence into the Finals.

• The Rangers, apparently exhausted from their trials against Montreal, drop Game 1 of the Finals 6-4, as

Toronto's Busher Jackson scores a hat-trick.

• King Clancy scores twice for the Maple Leafs in Game 2 as the Rangers' defense fails again. Toronto wins 6-2.

• Despite two-goal performances by Frank Boucher and Bun Cook, the

Rangers lose Game 3, again surrendering six goals to the powerful Toronto offense. The Maple Leafs thus win their third Stanley Cup.

• For the fourth straight Olympics, Canada takes the gold medal in hockey. The U.S. again takes home the silver.

COOK LINE, AITKENHEAD POWER THE RANGERS

After his club's defeat in the 1932 Stanley Cup Finals, Rangers manager Lester Patrick made two key moves that would eventually turn the Blueshirts into champions again. First, he acquired Babe Siebert from the Montreal Maroons and put him on a line with Art Somers and Cecil Dillon. Secondly, he replaced goaltender John Ross Roach with Andy Aitkenhead. "Aitkenhead," said teammate Frank Boucher, "was an acrobatic young man who sometimes wore a tweed cap when he played goal."

Of the original Rangers, the two most significant losses were goalie Lorne Chabot and defenseman Taffy Abel. Patrick traded Chabot after Lorne's eye injury in the 1928 playoffs, mistakenly believing that Chabot was puck-shy. Patrick discarded Abel because of his weight problem.

Despite the additions and subtractions, New York's 1928 championship nucleus was intact. Veterans Boucher, Bill and Bun Cook, Ching Johnson, and Murray Murdoch led the way. "My philosophy for winning is simple," Patrick explained. "I look for the leaders. Then I let them lead. I give my last instructions in the dressing room just before the game, then I sit and let them think about whatever they like."

The Cook-Boucher-Cook line continued to rank among the NHL's best. Bill, who had tied for the league lead in goals in 1931-32, captured the NHL scoring championship in 1932-33. Bun and Boucher also finished among the league's top 10 scorers.

In the playoffs, the Rangers knocked off both the Canadiens and Red Wings and were set to meet Toronto again in the Stanley Cup Finals. Prior to the Stanley Cup series, though, the Rangers got a break from an unexpected source—the Boston Bruins. A night before the Finals were to begin, the Bruins and Leafs played the final game of their series. Toronto won 1-0 but only after 4:46 of the sixth overtime period. The Leafs didn't reach their train until 3 a.m. and had to face New York the next night.

"We won the opener 5-1 and the Leafs never fully recovered," Boucher recalled. In addition to Aitkenhead's world-class goaltending and the Rangers' balanced offense, the New Yorkers were fortified by an outstanding defensive corps that included Johnson, Earl Seibert, Ott Heller, and Doug Brennan. They beat Toronto 3-1 in Game 2, lost Game 3 3-2, and battled Toronto to a 0-0 tie through regulation of Game 4.

Near the 7:30 mark of Game 4's first overtime, the Rangers began a line change. Bun Cook skated to the bench and was replaced by Butch Keeling. Bill Cook and Boucher also were heading for the bench when Keeling suddenly fired a rink-wide pass to Bill Cook.

"Bill took the pass in full stride at the Toronto blueline along the right-wing boards and cut quickly toward the goal," recalled Boucher. "He could see a wide opening at Lorne Chabot's right as he moved in and fired for the hole."

Cook beat the Leaf goalie at 7:33, giving the Rangers their second Stanley Cup in their seven-year history.

1932-33

- Following a one-year hiatus, the Ottawa Senators resume operations.

- The league mandates that if a goalie is called for a penalty, a teammate can serve the time for him.

- Prior to the start of the season, the NHL experiences another "mini-strike" when a salary cap is placed at $70,000 per team—and $7,500 for the highest paid player.

- NHL President Frank Calder receives permission by ownership to suspend the strikers, but he does not. Before the season begins, the protesters return to their teams.

- Player changes are prevalent. In one of the biggest moves, the Rangers sell star goalie John Roach to Detroit for $11,000.

- Boston goalie Tiny Thompson ties John Roach for the league lead in victories (25) and also wins the GAA race (1.83).

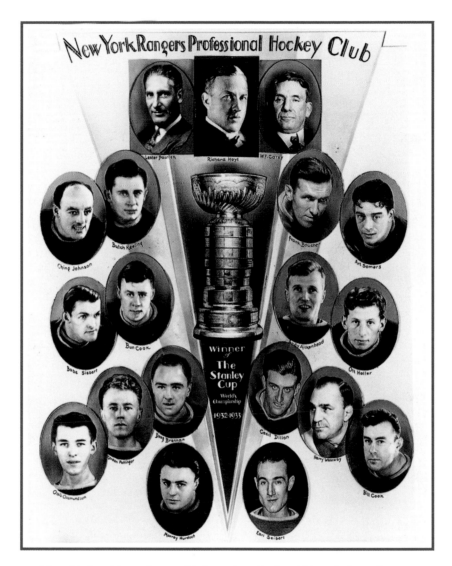

New York celebrated a world championship in 1933 and, for a change,
it wasn't the Yankees. Hockey's Rangers joined the victory parade, avenging their loss
to the Leafs in 1932 with a four-game victory over Toronto in the '33 Stanley Cup
Finals. New York featured five future Hall of Famers: Ching Johnson,
Frank Boucher, Babe Siebert, Bill Cook, and coach Lester Patrick. Cook scored
the Cup-winning goal in overtime of Game 4.

• The Bruins rebound from a last-place finish in 1931-32 to finish atop the American Division.

• The Falcons, with Jack Adams at the helm, tie Boston (25-15-8).

• Toronto wins the hotly contested Canadian Division with a record of 24-18-6. The Montreal Maroons finish second.

• Ranger sniper Bill Cook leads the league in goals (28) and points (50).

• Ranger Frank Boucher wins the assists race (28) and retakes the Lady Byng Trophy (his fifth).

• Busher Jackson, Toronto's gifted left winger, is second overall in goals (27) and points (44).

• Baldy Northcott leads the surprising Maroons in scoring (22-21-43).

• Tiny Aurel Joliat leads the Habs in scoring (18-21-39).

Frank Calder, NHL Officials

Calder Copes with Depression

The Depression was sinking its teeth into the NHL in 1932-33, causing league president Frank Calder (second from left) some sleepless nights. In order to keep expenses down, Calder instituted a salary cap of $70,000 for each team—a move that angered players, who protested with a brief strike before the season. Ottawa joined the league in 1932-33, but the franchise would last only two years because of low funds.

Rearguard Shore Wins MVP Award

In 1932-33, Eddie Shore was hockey in Boston. He played every game like it was his last and set the pace for the style of hockey in Beantown for years to come. The league's best rushing backliner terrorized enemy forwards as well as goalies, especially in 1932-33 when he notched a career-high 35 points. The league awarded Shore the Hart Trophy (his first of four), making him the first blueliner to win the coveted silverware.

Eddie Shore

Jackson's 'Nothing But a Busher'

Toronto's Busher Jackson, who finished second in the NHL in goals (27) and points (44) in 1932-33, was a big-city kid with an attitude early in his career. In fact, Toronto equipment man Tim Daly took umbrage with the youngster's attitude. When, as a raw rookie, Jackson complained about the quality of lumber he was carrying on the ice, Daly—who had seen bush-league boasters before—hit him with a name that stuck: "Kid, you ain't nothin' but a Busher."

Busher Jackson

1932-33

- Howie Morenz, the Canadiens' 30-year-old legend, is beginning to fade, scoring just 14 goals in 46 games.

- Eddie Shore, unanimously viewed as the game's greatest backliner, earns the Hart Trophy. It's the first time a defenseman wins the coveted award.

- The Bruins (thanks largely to Eddie Shore) give up the fewest goals (88), earning Tiny Thompson the Vezina Trophy.

- The NHL comes out with its first Rookie of the Year Award. (However, it's still four years before the first Calder Trophy is introduced.)

- Detroit's Carl Voss, a talented center who started the year with the Rangers, is named the NHL's first Rookie of the Year.

- In the playoffs, Detroit beats the Maroons 5-2 in their two-game, total-goals series.

Tiny Thompson

Thompson's Big Year Ends in Heartbreak

After a subpar year, Tiny Thompson regained his goaltending crown in 1932-33 by leading all crease cops in wins (25), GAA (1.83), and shutouts (11). On April 3, 1933, Thompson played the greatest game of his career. In the decisive Game 5 of the Stanley Cup semifinals, Thompson stopped all comers for 164 minutes and 46 seconds before falling to Toronto in a painful 1-0 loss. It was the longest NHL game ever played at that point.

Conacher Uses Mitts on Ice, in Ring

Lionel Conacher could play a lacrosse game in the morning, tackle a football game before supper, and win a hockey game at night—and still be ready for a prize fight by morning. Conacher, whose hockey mitts are pictured here, was voted Canada's Athlete of the Half-Century. The Big Train skated in the NHL for 12 seasons, highlighted by a 28-point year for the Maroons in 1932-33. Later in life, he won a seat in the Canadian Parliament.

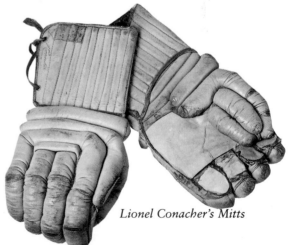

Lionel Conacher's Mitts

- The Rangers edge the Canadiens 8-5. New York then knocks off Detroit in the semifinals.

- Toronto and Boston, winners of their respective divisions, play a thrilling five-game series. Four of the games go to overtime; Game 5 goes to six overtime periods.

- On April 3, 1933, the Bruins and Leafs play 164:45 of scoreless hockey. Toronto's Ken Doraty beats Tiny Thompson at 4:46 of the sixth O.T.

- The Finals are anticlimactic, as Cecil Dillon and the Rangers easily handle the Leafs. New York prevails by scores of 5-1, 3-1, 2-3, and 1-0.

- Bill Cook's O.T. goal in Game 4 wins the Cup for New York. Cecil Dillon leads with eight goals and 10 points.

- The United States wins the World Hockey Championship, ending Canada's string of six straight victories.

Although the Chicago Black Hawks had been members of the NHL since 1926, they had, for the most part, been an artistic failure. They hadn't won a Stanley Cup in their first seven seasons, and in 1932-33 they went 16-20-12.

This dismal trend was reversed in 1933-34 under the leadership of charismatic coach/manager Tommy Gorman and the goaltending of Charlie Gardiner. The Hawks posted a 20-17-11 record, largely because they yielded the fewest goals in the league (83). Gardiner's goaltending had reached new degrees of perfection. He posted a stunning 1.73 goals-against average and racked up 10 shutouts. In 14 other games, he permitted just one goal in each.

But astute Gardiner watchers perceived something unusual about the goalie's deportment: He had become intolerant of mistakes. Unknown to everyone, Gardiner was suffering from a chronic tonsil infection that may have affected him emotionally. Winning the Stanley Cup became an obsession with him.

Gardiner's Hawks did make it to the Stanley Cup Finals. In the playoffs, they knocked off the Canadiens 4-3 in a total-goals series, and then beat the Maroons

DYING GARDINER LEADS HAWKS TO THE CUP

6-2 in another total-goals affair. That put Chicago in the Finals against the favored Red Wings, whose firepower included Ebbie Goodfellow, Larry Aurie, and Cooney Weiland.

The best-of-five series opened in Detroit, and the Black Hawks won the first game 2-1 in double overtime. In the second, also at Detroit's Olympia Stadium, the Hawks ran away with the game 4-1. As the teams returned to Chicago for Game 3, the experts had conceded the Stanley Cup to the Black Hawks.

But little did they know how bad Gardiner was feeling. His body was racked with pain. Captain Lionel Conacher and Tommy Gorman realized they had a weary and tormented player. "He's bad," said Gorman, turning to Conacher in the dressing room

before the teams took the ice.

Gardiner took command for two periods, but when the final buzzer sounded Detroit had won the game 5-2. "Look," Gardiner said to his depressed teammates, "all I want is one goal next game. Just one goal and I'll take care of the other guys."

As he took his place in the goalcrease on April 10, 1934, Gardiner's body was already numb with fatigue. But for two periods, the game remained scoreless. In the third, Detroit captured the momentum and seemed poised to break the 0-0 deadlock, but Gardiner's flailing arms and jabbing legs held them at bay. Gardiner weakened as the contest went through the first overtime and into the second.

Despite his fatigue, the courageous goalie was true to his word. He held Detroit scoreless halfway through the second overtime. At the 10-minute mark, Chicago's Mush March moved into Detroit territory and unleashed a shot at Wilf Cude. Before the goalkeeper could move, the puck sailed past him and the red light flashed. The Black Hawks had won their first Stanley Cup. Less than two months later, Gardiner died in a Winnipeg hospital.

1933-34

• To further enhance scoring, the league mandates that only three players (including the goalie) may occupy the defensive zone.

• For the first time ever, visible time clocks are required in all of the NHL's arenas.

• The NHL changes its on-ice officiating format. Two referees replace the one-referee, one-linesman system.

• The Detroit franchise, in serious financial straits, is purchased by James Norris Sr. Norris, a former amateur hockey star with Montreal's

famed Winged Wheelers, renames his squad the Red Wings.

• The Red Wings' top line of Cooney Weiland centering Herbie Lewis and Larry Aurie leads them to their best season ever. They win the American Division for the first time.

A star at the start of the 1930s, Chicago's Charlie Gardiner got even better in the next three seasons—although nobody realized he was suffering from a chronic tonsil infection, a disease that had begun to cause uremic convulsions. He still managed to play all 48 games in 1933-34, recording a stunning 1.73 GAA. Though terribly ill, Gardiner starred in the Cup Finals, posting a double-overtime shutout in the decisive Game 4. He died two months later.

• Detroit's John Sorrell nets 21 goals. That ties him for fourth in the league with Boston's Nels Stewart.

• The Maple Leafs and Canadiens strike a blockbuster deal. Goalie George Hainsworth goes to Toronto while puck-stopper Lorne Chabot heads to Montreal.

• The Maple Leafs win the Canadian Division with a record of 26-13-9. The Canadiens finish second, 11 points back.

• The Black Hawks give up the fewest goals, earning Charlie Gardiner his second Vezina Trophy in what will be his last NHL season.

• The Rangers, the defending Stanley Cup champions, fall to third place, though Cecil Dillon ties for fourth in scoring with 39 points.

• Boston's Marty Barry finishes second in goals (27) for the last-place Bruins and ties Ranger Cecil Dillon for fourth overall in scoring (39).

Chicago Black Hawks

Hawks Filled with Famous Names

The Stanley Cup champion Black Hawks of 1933-34 featured a lot of famous surnames, but some of these guys aren't who you might think. Pictured are Jack Leswick (not Tony), Lionel Conacher (not Charlie), Paul Thompson (not Tiny), Tom Cook (not Bill or Bun), and Clarence Abel (not Sid). Team president Frederic McLaughlin was the man who fired coach Pete Muldoon in 1927, sparking the famous Curse of Muldoon.

Big Bomber Nets a League-High 32

As the right winger for the most famous line in hockey, the Kid Line, Toronto's Charlie Conacher was the most feared shooter in the NHL in 1933-34, leading the league in both goals (32) and points (52). The Big Bomber made the First All-Star Team for the first of three consecutive years. However, despite scoring five points in five Cup semifinal games, Conacher couldn't carry the Leafs past the Red Wings, who nipped Toronto three games to two.

Charlie Conacher

• With 52 points in 42 games, Leafs right winger Charlie Conacher wins his first NHL scoring title. He also grabs his third goal-scoring title (32) in four years.

• Toronto's King Clancy emerges as the NHL's most productive defenseman (28 points).

• Red Horner, Toronto's tough defenseman, is the most penalized player (146 minutes). Chicago's Lionel Conacher finishes a distant second (87).

• Detroit goalie Wilf Cude leads the NHL in GAA (1.57).

• Chicago's Charlie Gardiner tops the league in shutouts with 10.

• Toronto's George Hainsworth leads the league in victories with 26.

• On December 12, 1933, Boston's Eddie Shore nearly kills Toronto star Ace Bailey in a vicious, unprovoked

Clancy a Star Among Stars in Toronto

King Clancy was an institution at Maple Leaf Gardens in Toronto. The affable Irishman was more than just a joker; he was a superstar among some of the greatest ever to play. The Leafs he played with in 1933-34 included the Kid Line of Jackson, Primeau, and Conacher as well as Hap Day, Ace Bailey, and goalie George Hainsworth. Clancy's 28 points led all NHL defensemen, and the Leafs finished first in the Canadian Division.

Ace Bailey

King Clancy

Boston's Barry Outscores His Famous Mates

Marty Barry played center for the last-place Boston Bruins of 1933-34. A Quebec City boy, Barry had been playing in the NHL since 1927 and always scored his share of goals. In 1933-34, he outscored team leaders Nels Stewart and Dit Clapper, chalking up 27 goals (second in the league) and a dozen assists for 39 points. This was his best season to date, and he would continue to post big numbers for the remainder of the decade.

Marty Barry

Bailey Nearly Killed by Shore Check

On December 12, 1933, the NHL was shaken when Toronto star Ace Bailey was nearly killed after a vicious check from behind by Bruins defenseman Eddie Shore—who mistakenly thought Bailey had tripped him. Bailey suffered a fractured skull and was close to death for two weeks. Although Bailey survived, he never played hockey again. Shore was slapped with a suspension, while the league staged a benefit game for Bailey and his family.

attack. Shore blindsides Bailey, who flips backward and lands on his head.

• For two weeks, Ace Bailey hovers near death after his attack by Eddie Shore, who is suspended by the league. Bailey will recover from his head injury but will never play again.

• On February 14, 1934, the league stages its first All-Star Game—between Toronto and an NHL "All-Star" team—as a fund-raiser for Ace Bailey. Toronto wins 7-3.

• In the playoffs, the American Division's second-place Black Hawks take on the Canadian Division's

second-place Canadiens. Chicago wins 4-3 on total goals.

• The third-place finishers (New York Rangers and Montreal Maroons) play to a 0-0 tie in Game 1 before Montreal prevails in the deciding game 2-1.

Detroit Red Wings

Detroiters Get a New Nickname

After years of playing second-division hockey, the Detroit franchise got a needed infusion of cash and hockey know-how when James Norris purchased the team in 1933. Norris had played with Montreal's AAA team, long known as the Winged Wheelers. To this day, the Detroit Red Wings carry the emblem of the winged wheel on their chests. The 1933-34 team motored its way to a first-place finish in the American Division with a 24-14-10 record.

Aurel Joliat

Tiny Joliat Wins League's Biggest Award

Sometimes a player's contribution to the game cannot be measured in statistics. In 1933-34, Aurel Joliat finished just eighth in the league in scoring with 37 points. However, when Howie Morenz succumbed to an ankle injury, Joliat assumed the reins of the Canadiens and guided the team to a second-place finish. The 5'6", 135-pound Joliat shook off numerous aches and pains to lead his team and was awarded the Hart Trophy.

March Scores Cup Winner in O.T.

Goaltender Charlie Gardiner may have carried the Black Hawks to the 1934 Stanley Cup, but credit right winger Mush March with a big assist. March was not a big scorer, but his consistent hard work and his playmaking ability kept the Hawks within range, as they finished second in the American Division. Marsh was also a hero of the playoffs, whacking home the Cup-winning goal at 10:50 of double overtime in the fourth and final game.

Mush March

1933-34

- The Black Hawks meet the Maroons in the semifinals. The Hawks prevail 6-2 in a two-game, total-goals series.

- The Maple Leafs and Red Wings face each other in a best-of-five semifinals. Detroit wins Game 1 in O.T. 2-1, then trounces the Leafs 6-3 in the second game.

- The Maple Leafs, with their backs to the wall, tie the semifinal series with wins in Games 3 and 4, outscoring the Wings 8-2 in the process.

- The Red Wings hold Toronto's Kid Line (Busher Jackson, Joe Primeau, and Charlie Conacher) in check to win Game 5 by the score of 1-0.

- Chicago nips Detroit 2-1 in Game 1 of the Finals, as Paul Thompson scores in double overtime.

- Chicago wins Game 2 of the Finals 4-1, but Detroit wins Game 3 5-2.

- Game 4 remains scoreless until 10:05 of double overtime, when

Ace Bailey, Eddie Shore

Toronto Maple Leafs

Bailey and Shore Bury the Hatchet

The last time these two men met, they were not smiling. Ace Bailey and Eddie Shore might have gone to their graves as sworn enemies, considering the circumstances earlier in the season, but all seems to have been forgiven here on March 6, 1934, where the two met in Boston to show the world that the hatchet had been buried. The irony here is to see Shore wearing a helmet; headgear would have saved Ace's career.

Norris the King of NHL Boardrooms

James Norris

They call Gordie Howe "Mr. Hockey." If one were looking around NHL boardrooms for candidates for the title, the name James Norris would be near the top of the list. Norris bought the NHL's Detroit Falcons in 1932, renamed them the Red Wings, and owned the team until his death in 1952. At one time, Norris and his family controlled Detroit's Olympia Stadium, Chicago Stadium, and New York's Madison Square Garden.

Toronto's Train Derailed in Playoffs

The Maple Leafs took the express track through the 1933-34 season, winning a league-high 26 games and scoring 57 more goals than any other team. Once again, Charlie Conacher led the way with 32 goals while linemate Gentleman Joe Primeau paced the loop with 32 helpers. Despite all their firepower, the Leafs lost a five-game struggle with the Red Wings in the semifinals and limped home to Hog Town without Lord Stanley's vaunted mug.

Mush March scores for the Hawks to give them their first Stanley Cup.

• Red Wing Larry Aurie is the leading playoff scorer with 10 points.

• Doc Romnes leads the Black Hawks in playoff scoring with two goals and nine points. Charlie Gardiner,

Chicago's brilliant goaltender, has a 1.50 playoff GAA.

• Montreal Canadien Aurel Joliat, third in the league in goals with 22, is bestowed the Hart Trophy.

• Russ Blinco of the Maroons is named Rookie of the Year.

• Frank Boucher, the Rangers' leading scorer, wins his sixth Lady Byng Trophy in seven years.

• Two months after winning the Stanley Cup, Chicago goalie Charlie Gardiner dies of a brain hemorrhage at age 29.

MAROONS SHINE BRIGHT BEFORE FADING OUT

In the bilingual metropolis of Montreal, it was perfectly natural for both the French- and English-speaking natives to each have a team of their own. Les Canadiens were first, representing the francophones. In 1924, businessman Jimmy Strachan organized a team for the English rooters and called them the Maroons.

The Maroons-Canadiens rivalry was intense, with the Forum rocking every time the English and French teams clashed. The Maroons won the Stanley Cup in 1926 and remained one of the NHL's most competitive teams for the next few years, although they didn't win another Cup. In 1934-35, however, manager Tommy Gorman blended a group of first-class veterans with standout youngsters, and it turned out to be a wonderful mix.

Veteran Lionel Conacher, who had helped body-check the Chicago Black Hawks to the 1934 Stanley Cup, was acquired by Montreal a few months later. Conacher anchored a rock-solid defense that included Stew Evans, Allen Shields, and Cy Wentworth. Behind them was Alex Connell, a 10-year veteran who had previously starred for Ottawa, Detroit, and Ottawa again.

Scoring was well-distributed among such solid forwards as Baldy Northcott, Herb Cain, Bob Gracie, Russ Blinco, and Earl Robinson, who led the team with 35 points. Nobody on the Maroons finished among the league's top ten, however.

The Maroons played tough hockey and occasionally were involved in tumultuous games. On January 22, 1935, they clashed with the Bruins at Boston Garden. A near riot erupted after Boston's Eddie Shore flattened Montreal's Jimmy Ward, who was hospitalized with a severe concussion. Lionel Conacher knocked out Boston's Nels Stewart with a punch later in the game, and Conacher became involved in a battle with several Bruins fans. In another game, the New York Americans' Red

Dutton used his stick to whack the hand of the Maroons' Hooley Smith. Dutton skated to the Montreal bench and apologized, but Smith responded by knocking out Dutton with a left hook.

Although they finished second in the Canadian Division in 1934-35, the Maroons jelled at playoff time. In the opening round, Connell played some of the best goal of his life, shutting out defending-champion Chicago in two straight games. The Maroons then disposed of the Rangers in two games and reached the Finals against the Leafs.

The Torontonians never stood a chance. The Maroons nipped them 3-2 in Game 1 on Dave Trottier's overtime goal, and then shredded the Leafs 3-1 and 4-1 to win their second Stanley Cup.

Nobody knew it at the time, but that championship marked the beginning of the end for the proud Montreal franchise. The Great Depression was wrecking the Canadian economy, and both the Canadiens and Maroons were suffering at the gate. The Maroons remained strong the following two seasons, but they plummeted to the cellar in 1937-38. The Maroons folded in the summer of 1938, ending a brief but glorious life in the NHL.

1934-35

• The NHL adopts the use of a penalty shot, awarded to any player who is tripped and prevented from a clear shot on goal. The penalty shot is to be taken from within a 10-foot circle 38 feet from the goal.

• The struggling Ottawa franchise, strapped for financing, transfers to St.

Louis. The team's new name is the St. Louis Eagles.

• A huge trade sees Canadiens stars Howie Morenz and Lorne Chabot sent to Chicago for Lionel Conacher, Roger Jenkins, and Leroy Goldsworthy. The Hawks need goalie Chabot because of the death of Charlie Gardiner.

• The Cup-defending Black Hawks fire manager/coach Tommy Gorman, who takes over the Maroons.

• Alex Connell, the former star goalie for Ottawa who sat out the 1933-34 season, takes over the puck-stopping chores for the Maroons.

The Maple Leafs and Montreal Maroons met in the Finals for the first time in 1934-35. The Maroons had resurrected goaltender Alex Connell from the New York Americans and he responded by leading Montreal past Chicago and the Rangers in the playoffs. In the Finals, he allowed only four goals in three games as the Maroons swept the Leafs in three straight. Montreal's Baldy Northcott led all postseason scorers with four goals.

• The Toronto Maple Leafs, still powered by the Kid Line, win the Canadian Division by nine points over the Maroons.

• Charlie Conacher, the Leafs' talented left winger, wins his second straight scoring title (57 points).

• A new star is on the horizon, as Detroit's Syd Howe finishes second in total points with 47.

• Detroit's Larry Aurie, the playoff scoring leader the previous year, is right behind teammate Syd Howe with 46 points.

• The Americans' Art Chapman and the Rangers' Frank Boucher top the NHL charts in assists with 34 and 32, respectively.

• Rangers sniper Cecil Dillon is second in the NHL in goals, as he powers in 25.

Stanley Cup Presentation

Champion Maroons on the Way Out

Although the Maroons were crowned Cup champions in 1934-35, their franchise was on its last legs. Shortly after NHL President Frank Calder (center) presented the bowl to G.M. Tommy Gorman (shaking hands), it became clear that Montreal could not support two hockey teams. The Maroons survived for three more years on the ice, but the league kept the franchise on the books for the next 12 years, hoping against hope that they would find a wealthy backer to buy the team.

Fans Love Russian-Born Schriner

Dave "Sweeney" Schriner of the New York Americans was the first NHL star to hail from the icy climes of Russia. Born in Siberia in 1911, Schriner was the most celebrated freshman in the NHL in 1934-35, collecting 18 goals and 22 assists and winning Rookie of the Year honors. After a fine minor-league career with the Syracuse Stars, Schriner was promoted to the NHL and became an instant crowd favorite at Madison Square Garden.

Sweeney Schriner

1934-35

- Toronto's Red Horner leads the league in penalty minutes (125).

- Scottish-born scrapper Irv Frew, a 5'9" defenseman for St. Louis, is second in PIM with 89.

- The Boston Bruins rebound from a last-place finish in 1933-34 to capture the American Division title. They finish a point ahead of Chicago.

- Marty Barry leads the Bruins' balanced attack, notching 20 goals and 40 points.

- Boston's Eddie Shore, a year after nearly killing Toronto's Ace Bailey, is the highest scoring defenseman in the league (33 points).

- The defending-champion Black Hawks play the tightest defense, allowing just 88 goals in 48 games. Chicago's Lorne Chabot tops the league in GAA with a 1.83 mark.

Lorne Chabot

Chabot Hits His Peak in Chicago

Lorne Chabot began his NHL career with the Rangers, where he proved to be a tough competitor. In Toronto, where he played from 1928-29 through 1932-33, he continued to turn away shooters with his steady, reliable service. After his one season with the Canadiens, he moved to Chicago, where in 1933-34 he turned in his single Vezina Trophy-winning season. Chabot won 26 games, eight being shutouts, and finished the season with a 1.83 GAA.

Eddie Shore

'Strong Boy' Shore Cops Second Hart

Known to Beantown hockey fanatics as the Boston Strong Boy, Eddie Shore won his second career Hart Trophy as the NHL's MVP in 1934-35, appearing in all 48 games while compiling seven goals and 26 assists. A marvel with the puck and a demon with his fists, Shore was the backbone of the Bruins franchise, often controlling the pace of the game from his office on the blue-line.

Kid Liners Power NHL's Best Offense

Pictured is the Maple Leafs' Kid Line, one of the most famous threesomes in NHL history. Charlie Conacher, the Big Bomber, delivered right on target during the 1934-35 season. He paced the NHL in goals (36) and points (57), leading the Leafs to a first-place finish in the Canadian Division. The line scored 68 of Toronto's league-high 157 goals, as Busher Jackson found the net 22 times and playmaker Joe Primeau flipped in 10.

Charlie Conacher, Joe Primeau, Busher Jackson

• Maroons goalie Alex Connell, a veteran of 11 NHL seasons, finishes with nine shutouts and the second-best GAA (1.92).

• Maple Leafs goalie George Hainsworth again leads the NHL in victories (30).

• In Chicago, the sad demise of Howie Morenz is evident in his production—eight goals in 48 games.

• Detroit defenseman Ralph "Scotty" Bowman records the first-ever successful penalty shot, as he beats the Maroons' Alex Connell.

• St. Louis boss Eddie Gerard is fired after 13 games, replaced by former NHL star George Boucher.

• On November 20, 1934, Toronto's Busher Jackson scores four third-period goals, as the Leafs beat St. Louis 5-2.

Aurie Stars on Up-And-Down Wings

In 1934-35, Larry Aurie played in Detroit on a line with Herbie Lewis and Cooney Weiland. This was not a bell-ringer of a season for the Red Wings, as they finished in last place in the American Division. Actually, the mid-1930s were a confusing time for the Wings, as they finished first, last, first, first, and last in consecutive years. Aurie had a strong 1934-35 season, finishing third in the league in points with 46.

Larry Aurie

Horner Means Bad News for Foes

The NHL's bad boy of the 1930s was Toronto's Red Horner, who "won" the third of his eight straight penalty crowns in 1934-35. As a youth, Horner delivered the news as Conn Smythe's paper boy, and he constantly begged the Leafs' manager for a tryout. Smythe gave him a spot with the farm club and Horner soon made the jump to the big club. His job was to keep opponents from crossing into the Leaf zone, and he handled the task with authority.

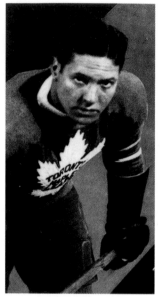

Red Horner

St. Louis Eagles

Eagles Fly for One Year, Then Go Under

The NHL had a new look for the 1934-35 season. One of the league's proudest franchises, the Ottawa Senators, collapsed under the burden of the Depression. The franchise was transferred to St. Louis for 1934-35 and was called the Eagles. Frank Finnigan, Joe Lamb, Bill Cowley, and Carl Voss were among the stars who flew for the Eagles, but they finished 11-31-6 and folded themselves after the season.

1934-35

- In the opening round of playoffs, the Black Hawks meet the Maroons and the Rangers face the Canadiens.

- The Black Hawks are held scoreless by Alex Connell over two games, as the Maroons win 1-0 on Baldy Northcott's O.T. goal in Game 2.

- The Rangers win a 6-5 total-goals shootout, winning 2-1 and tying 4-4 to advance past the Habs.

- In Game 1 of their semifinal matchup, the Maroons beat the Rangers 2-1. The teams skate to a 3-3 tie in Game 2, meaning the Maroons win the total-goals series 5-4.

- Toronto and Boston (division champs) play a best-of-five series. The Leafs dominate the Bruins, winning three games to one.

- In Game 1 of the Stanley Cup Finals, the Maroons win 3-2 thanks to an overtime goal by Dave Trottier. Montreal's Russ Blinco scores the

Baldy Northcott

Northcott Scores Lone Goal in Semis

A native of Calgary, Lawrence "Baldy" Northcott first suited up with the Montreal Maroons in 1929-30. Northcott led the team in scoring in 1932-33, connecting for 22 goals and 43 points. A clever stick-handler and a deadly marksman, Baldy was the hero of Montreal's 1935 semifinals series against Chicago. His overtime goal in Game 2 was the only tally of the two-game, total-goals series.

Alex Connell

Goalie Connell Puts Out the Fire

Alex Connell was known as the Ottawa Fireman, not only for his ability to put out the fire on the ice (he starred for eight years in Ottawa), but also because he worked for the Ottawa Fire Department. Many thought Connell was washed up by 1934, but that fall Maroons G.M. Tommy Gorman signed him up, and he backstopped the team to the Stanley Cup title. He posted nine shutouts during the season and went undefeated with a 1.14 GAA in the playoffs.

Frank Boucher

Boucher Takes Home the Lady Byng—Literally

It's often said that such-and-such hockey player "wins" a trophy, but in reality he only has his name inscribed on the award; he doesn't get to keep it. Frank Boucher, however, won the Lady Byng Trophy so many times—copping No. 7 in 1935—that the NHL decided to just give him the darned thing. They forged a new Lady Byng Trophy the following year. The 1934-35 season marked the last time the Cook-Boucher-Cook line would be a dominant force.

game-winner in Game 2, as the Maroons top the Leafs 3-1.

• The Maroons take Game 3 4-1 to sweep the Maple Leafs and win their last Stanley Cup. Baldy Northcott, the leading playoff scorer, scores the game-winning goal.

• In postseason awards, the NHL honors New York American winger Dave "Sweeney" Schriner (40 points) as its Rookie of the Year.

• Chicago goalie Lorne Chabot, in his first year with the Hawks, wins the Vezina Trophy.

• New York Ranger center Frank Boucher is presented with the Lady Byng Trophy for the seventh time. The NHL actually gives him the trophy to keep.

• Despite his reputation and mean streak, Boston's Eddie Shore is awarded his second Hart Trophy.

WINGS AND MAROONS GO TO SEXTUPLE OVERTIME

Nothing in sports can match the heart-thumping excitement of overtime hockey, as every rush, every shot can mean sudden death for one team, sudden victory for the other. The greatest nail-biter of all took place on March 24, 1936, at the Montreal Forum. It was the first game of the semifinals matchup between the hosting Maroons and the visiting Detroit Red Wings.

Led by Hooley Smith, Baldy Northcott, and Jimmy Ward, the Maroons presented one of the most formidable attacks in the league. Detroit, however, was also strong up front. The Red Wings' first line of Marty Barry, Herbie Lewis, and Larry Aurie was enjoying a splendid season, with Barry winning the scoring championship in the American Division.

Despite the notable scorers on both teams, three periods of play elapsed without either club scoring a goal. This meant sudden-death overtime; the first team to score would win the game. Since both teams were getting strong goaltending, there was reason to suspect that the overtime might take awhile. But it lasted more than just awhile; it took pretty much all night.

The respective goaltenders, Norm Smith for Detroit and Lorne Chabot of the Maroons, brilliantly repulsed all shots through five consecutive sudden-death periods. Four minutes and 46 seconds after the ninth overall period began, the teams broke the NHL record for the longest game, set by Toronto and Boston in 1933. Still, well into the sixth sudden-death session of this game, there was no end in sight.

The veterans of both teams were fatigued beyond recovery. It was essential to employ the players with the most stamina; and naturally, those with even a smidgen of energy remaining were the little-used younger skaters. One of them was Modere "Mud" Bruneteau, who a season earlier had played for the Wings' minor-league team. During the 1935-36 regular season, he had mustered only two points. At age 21, he was the youngest man in the longest game.

Red Wings coach Jack Adams believed that Bruneteau now had the most energy left. "At 2:25 a.m.," said Adams, "I looked along our bench for the strongest legs, and I scrambled the lines to send out Syd Howe, Hec Kilrea, and Bruneteau."

Just after the 16th minute of the sixth overtime, Bruneteau surrounded the puck in the Detroit zone and passed it to Kilrea. They challenged the Montreal defense, Kilrea faking a return pass and then sliding it across the blueline. Bruneteau cut behind the Detroit defense, retrieved the puck, and fired it past the falling Chabot. The puck stuck in the twine and didn't even fall to the ice.

There was a dispute when the goal judge neglected to flash his red light, but referee Nels Stewart arbitrated. "You're bloody right it's a goal!" Stewart announced, and put up his hand as a signal. After a complete game and 116 minutes and 30 seconds of overtime, the Detroit Red Wings had defeated the Montreal Maroons 1-0.

1935-36

- The league loses one team, the St. Louis Eagles, due to financial difficulties. Eagles players are dispersed around the league.

- The Bruins pluck budding superstar Bill Cowley from the Eagles, while the Americans salvage Carl Voss.

- Bill Beveridge, last year's NHL loss leader (31) with St. Louis, takes over for Maroons goalie Lorne Chabot.

- Detroit prevails in the American Division with a 24-16-8 record. The other three teams in the Division—Boston, Chicago, and the Rangers—each finish six points behind.

- The Maroons (22-16-10) take the Canadian Division, edging Toronto by two points.

- The Canadiens finish the season at 11-26-11. Their horrible record brings an NHL ruling granting the Habs first rights to all French Canadian players for three years.

The Red Wings rookie who defeated the Maroons in Game 1 of the 1936 Stanley Cup semifinals was known to his mother as Modere, but in Detroit they called him Mud. At the 16:30 mark of overtime No. 6, Mud Bruneteau scored his first NHL playoff goal, ending the longest game in NHL history. Thanks to Bruneteau, the Wings went on to sweep Montreal in three games before raking the Maple Leafs aside in the Stanley Cup Finals.

• Six of the NHL teams finish with winning records, as the Canadiens and Americans absorb the losses.

• New York American Sweeney Schriner wins the scoring title (45 points) in just his second NHL season.

• Charlie Conacher, replaced on Toronto's top line by tiny Pep Kelly, still ties for the NHL lead in goals (23). Leafs center Billy Thoms also knocks home 23.

• Art Chapman, who centers Sweeney Schriner's line for the Americans, tops the charts with 28 assists.

• Detroit's Marty Barry, traded by Boston for Cooney Weiland, finishes second in the league in total points with 40.

• Goalie Norm Smith, a former Maroons starter, leads the Red Wings with his NHL-best 24 wins.

Red Horner

Horner Stews in the Box for 167 Minutes

Red "The Paper Boy" Horner delivered bad news to foes in 1935-36. Big Red spent 167 minutes in the sin bin, setting a new record for NHL outlaws. Although Horner spent a lot of time cooling his heels, he was always known as a clean, aggressive player. Hall of Fame goaltenders George Hainsworth and Turk Broda owed much of their fame to Horner's rock-solid defense.

Art Chapman

Chapman Leads NHL in Assists

A clever stick-handler and pinpoint passer, Art Chapman led the NHL for the second straight year in assists during the 1935-36 campaign. He set up 28 goals, many of them by linemate Sweeney Schriner. Originally a member of the Boston Bruins, Chapman came to the Americans in a trade midway through the 1933-34 season. In 1934-35, Chapman registered a league-leading 34 assists and a career-high 43 points.

Shore Dons a Helmet, Wins MVP Award

In 1933-34, following the famed "Bailey-Shore incident," every member of the Bruins was given a leather helmet. Many of them left the headgear in the dressing room, but Eddie Shore was a quick study and wore the protection off and on over the balance of his career. Critics felt he had lost his edge, that the helmet signified a loss of courage, but none of them dared say it to his face. In 1935-36, Shore won his second Hart Trophy.

Eddie Shore

1935-36

- The Hawks' trio of Doc Romnes, Paul Thompson, and Mush March notches 113 points.

- The Maroons' Baldy Northcott, Hooley Smith, and Jimmy Ward finish with 105 points for the Canadian Division champs.

- Toronto tough guy Red Horner sets an NHL record with 167 PIM.

- Black Hawk Paul Thompson ties Detroit's Marty Barry for second overall in points (40).

- The Maple Leafs' offense leads the NHL in goals with 126.

- Boston's defense (led by Eddie Shore) and goaltending (Tiny Thompson) allow just 83 goals.

- Tiny Thompson leads the league in GAA (1.71) and shutouts (10). Thompson becomes the first goalie to record an assist when Babe Siebert converts his pass into a goal.

Mike Karakas

Thompson Paces Punchless Hawks

Chicago had really no scoring stars prior to World War II (when the Bentley brothers came along). In fact, Paul Thompson (right) became the first Black Hawk to score 40 points in a season, hitting the number exactly in 1935-36, the club's 10th year of existence. Thompson's 40 points tied him for second in the league.

Sweeney Schriner

Karakas Keeps His GAA Below 2.00

It isn't easy replacing a legend, but that was the daunting task facing Chicago's Mike Karakas as he prepared for the 1935-36 season. A native of Aurora, Minnesota, the rookie goaltender was given the No. 1 goaltending job after Lorne Chabot suffered a serious injury before the season. In his first season facing NHL marksmen, Karakas was voted the league's best rookie, registering nine shutouts and a sparkling 1.92 goals-against average.

Carl Voss, Paul Thompson

Schriner's the Pride of the Amerks

One year after capturing the NHL's Rookie of the Year Award, the Americans' Dave "Sweeney" Schriner won his first scoring title in 1935-36 with 19 goals and 26 assists. Schriner, the first Americans player to lead the league in scoring, also became the first Amerk to make the NHL's First All-Star Team, which debuted in 1930-31. The next American to crack the exclusive team would be Tom Anderson in 1941-42, the club's last year of existence.

• Boston's Babe Siebert and the Americans' Joe Jerwa top all NHL backliners with 21 goals.

• Howie Morenz joins another team—the Rangers.

• The opening round of playoffs features a shootout between Toronto and Boston. The Leafs take the two-game, total-goals series 8-6 after losing 3-0 in Game 1.

• The New York Americans win their total-goals series against the Black Hawks 7-5, thanks to a 3-0 victory in Game 1.

• The respective division champs—the Red Wings and Maroons—play a best-of-five series. The longest game in history unfolds in Game 1, which goes to 16:30 of the sixth O.T.

• Red Wing rookie Mud Bruneteau wins the NHL's longest game, as he beats the Maroons' Lorne Chabot.

Thoms Comes Out of Nowhere to Score 23

In his three previous seasons with the Maple Leafs, Bill Thoms was never noted for his goal-scoring skills. An excellent forechecker with speed and skill, Thoms had only 20 career goals as he took to the ice for the 1935-36 season. However, Thoms exploded offensively for the Leafs in his fourth NHL campaign, scoring 23 times to tie for the league lead in goals with teammate Charlie Conacher.

Great Britain Olympic Team

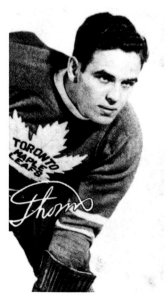

Bill Thoms

Tiny Thompson

'British' Team Wins Olympic Gold

In 1936, Great Britain won the Olympic gold medal for ice hockey. In Britain, it was heralded as a major national achievement. After all, they had displaced the Canadians, who had dominated international hockey since the beginning of international play. In Canada, however, the win was snickered upon. All of the team's important players were Canadians who had become naturalized Brits, brought in to buttress the emerging British semi-pro leagues.

Tiny Skates Off with His Third Vezina

Cecil "Tiny" Thompson came up big for the Boston Bruins during the 1935-36 season, leading all NHL goaltenders with 10 shutouts and a miserly 1.71 goals-against average. Thompson, who made his NHL debut in 1928-29, captured his third Vezina Trophy in 1935-36 by allowing only 82 goals in 48 games. Unfortunately, he coughed up eight goals in two games during the playoffs as the Bruins were quickly eliminated by the Maroons.

1935-36

- Detroit's Norm Smith skates off with a 1-0 shutout in the marathon game. He plays 176:30 without allowing a goal.

- Norm Smith shines again in Game 2, beating the Maroons 3-0. His 248 minutes of shutout hockey is an all-time playoff record.

- Detroit goes to the Finals for the second time after beating the Maroons 2-1 in Game 3.

- In the other semifinal, the Leafs beat the Americans in three games.

- Detroit soars past Toronto in the first two games of the Finals. The

Wings win 3-1 in Game 1 and 9-4 in Game 2.

- The courageous Maple Leafs beat Detroit 4-3 in Game 3, as Buzz Boll scores in overtime.

- The Wings claim Game 4 of the Finals 3-2, as Pete Kelly scores the

Norm Smith

Smith Records 176-Minute Shutout

One of the NHL's steadiest goaltenders, Detroit's Norm Smith had his finest season in 1935-36, leading the league in minutes (3,030) and victories (24). Smith, who made his NHL debut with the Montreal Maroons during the 1931-32 campaign, appeared in 25 games for the Wings in 1934-35. In Game 1 of the 1936 semifinals, Smith shut out the Maroons for a record 176 minutes before Detroit won in the sixth O.T.

Red Wings' Barry Nets Cup Winner

In a blockbuster trade prior to the 1935-36 season, the Red Wings acquired Marty Barry from the Bruins for Cooney Weiland. Barry, who had reached the 20-goal plateau in five straight seasons, was an instant star in Detroit, leading all Red Wing scorers with 21 goals. In the fourth game of the Stanley Cup Finals against Toronto, Barry's second-period goal gave the Wings a lead they would never surrender, as Detroit went on to win its first Stanley Cup.

Marty Barry

game-winning goal. Detroit thus wins its first-ever Stanley Cup.

• Toronto has three players atop the playoff scoring chart—Buzz Boll, Billy Thoms, and Joe Primeau.

• Johnny Sorrell's seven playoff points lead Detroit.

• Though his Black Hawks are first-round playoff losers, Chicago goalie Mike Karakas is named the NHL's Rookie of the Year.

• Doc Romnes, the slick playmaker for Chicago, wins the Lady Byng Trophy.

• Boston's Eddie Shore wins his third Hart Trophy in four years. The Bruins' Tiny Thompson captures the Vezina Trophy, his third.

• Great Britain wins its first and only Olympic gold medal in ice hockey. After four straight golds, Canada settles for the silver.

THOUSANDS MOURN LOSS OF MORENZ, DEAD AT 34

Once the darling of the Montreal Canadiens, Howie Morenz began to lose favor at the Forum in 1933-34, when his speed and points were on the decline. Morenz, an aging 32, was traded to Chicago at the end of the year, and for the next two seasons he struggled with the Black Hawks and New York Rangers. New York's Lester Patrick was happy to return him to the Canadiens for the 1936-37 season.

Wearing the bleu, blanc, et rouge once more proved to be a tonic for Morenz. True, he had lost some of his old getaway power, but he was reunited with his old buddies, Johnny Gagnon and Aurel Joliat, and every so often he'd bring the Forum crowd to its feet with an exquisite Morenz rush.

He was doing just that on the night of January 28, 1937, at the Forum when Chicago defenseman Earl Seibert body-checked him, sending Morenz hurtling feet first into the endboards. It wasn't a normal spill. When his skate rammed into the wood, a "snap" could be heard around the rink and Morenz crumpled in excruciating pain. The crowd leaped to its feet in fear.

Howie was rushed to the hospital with a badly broken leg, and many speculated whether he would ever return to play again. Once in the hospital, the 34-year-old Morenz began brooding about his fate. Instead of recuperating, he suffered a nervous breakdown. Then he developed heart trouble.

Nobody is quite sure what transpired in the hospital to bring about the utter deterioration of Howie's condition. One theory has it that he was overwhelmed by friends who filled his room with flowers, books, and candy. "The hospital," said one visitor, "looked like Times Square on a Saturday night. The continual stream of visitors tired him."

Perhaps too late, hospital officials forbade all but Howie's immediate family from visiting him. Then, early on March 8, 1937, Morenz was given a complete checkup, and it appeared as though he was rallying. It was a deceptive analysis. A few hours later, Howarth William Morenz was dead.

The funeral service for Morenz was held at center ice of the Forum, where thousands filed silently past his bier. Montreal journalist Andy O'Brien, of *Weekend Magazine,* was there at the time and recalled the scene.

"Outside," said O'Brien, "the crowd was so great, we of the press had to enter through the boiler room on Closse Street. As I walked below the north end, profound silence left an impression of emptiness; but at the promenade, I stopped at breathless awe. The rink was jammed to the rafters with fans standing motionless with heads bared."

The NHL paid a tribute to Morenz on November 2, 1937, by sanctioning an All-Star Game at the Forum. The game pitted the Canadiens and Maroons against a blue-ribbon NHL squad, with the All-Stars winning 6-5 and the proceeds given to the Morenz family. Howie's uniform was presented to his son, Howie Morenz Jr., who would eventually become a professional hockey player like his father.

1936-37

- The NHL takes stewardship of the New York Americans franchise, which is in deep financial trouble.

- The NHL introduces the Calder Trophy, which will honor the league's rookie of the year. It is named after NHL President Frank Calder.

- An era ends in Toronto, as the great Joe Primeau, age 30, retires after eight NHL seasons.

- The Rangers enter the season without Bun Cook, thus ending the long reign of the Bill Cook-Frank Boucher-Bun Cook line.

- The Rangers ice a new "brother" act—Neil and Mac Colville.

- The Habs rescue Howie Morenz from exile, reuniting him with Aurel Joliat and Johnny Gagnon.

- The Red Wings repeat as American Division champs, going 25-14-9. The

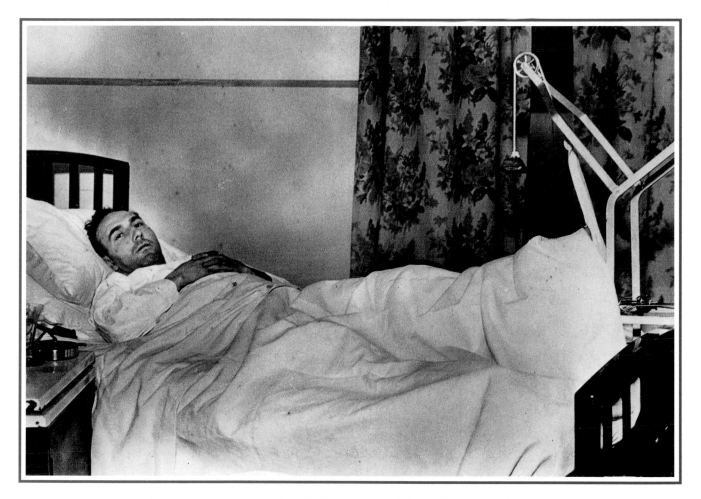

Howie Morenz may not have had the speed and flash of his earlier days, but he was back in Montreal in 1936-37 and regained the hearts of his old fans. The crowd went silent in January, though, when he crashed into the endboards, shattering his leg and bringing his declining career to an abrupt end. While in the hospital, Morenz suffered a nervous breakdown as well as heart trouble and died in his hospital bed at the age of 34.

powerful Wings club leads the NHL in goals scored (128) and fewest allowed (102).

• The sophomore jinx strikes Chicago goalie Mike Karakas. The 1935-36 Rookie of the Year leads the league in losses (27).

• The Black Hawks, three years removed from a Stanley Cup, finish out of the playoffs.

• The Maple Leafs replace legendary George Hainsworth with 21-year-old rookie Turk Broda, who will go on to enjoy years of playoff glory.

• Cecil Hart takes over as coach of the Habs, replacing Syl Mantha. He leads his club to first place in the Canadian Division (24-18-6).

• At age 34, Nels Stewart scores 20 goals in 30 games for the Americans. He finishes with 23 tallies and a share of the league goal-scoring lead.

1930s Fans Peer Through Wire Fences

Hockey had a distinctly different look and sound in the 1930s. Fans were protected by a wire-mesh fence that screamed and rattled with the sound of a wayward shot or a grimacing defenseman running an opposing forward into the metal diamonds. The ice was a misty gray, unmarked except for two bluelines and a goal line. There was no center red marker to define the neutral zone and the goalcrease was as big as the man in the peaked cap could dare to keep clear.

Toronto Maple Leafs vs. New York Americans

Calder Trophy

Norm Smith

Calder Trophy Honors Best Rookie

A new piece of silverware appeared on the NHL awards table in the 1936-37 season. Although the league had been recognizing its outstanding rookie since the 1932-33 season, it wasn't until the 1936-37 campaign that NHL President Frank Calder donated a trophy in his name to be awarded to the league's best newcomer. Syl Apps of the Maple Leafs was the first rookie to have his name engraved on the new trophy.

Smith Earns Vezina, Then Busts Elbow

Following his breakthrough season in 1935-36, Norm Smith continued his masterful play for the Red Wings in 1936-37, capturing the Vezina Trophy after leading the league with six shutouts and a 2.13 goals-against average. However, in the 1937 playoffs, he suffered a severe elbow injury in a game against the Canadiens and was forced to sit out most of the best-of-five final series against the Rangers.

1936-37

- Detroit sniper Larry Aurie shares the NHL lead in goals (23) despite a season-ending broken ankle.

- The Americans' Sweeney Schriner wins his second straight scoring championship (46 points) despite finishing fourth in goals (21) and third in assists.

- Toronto rookie Syl Apps—Joe Primeau's replacement—leads the NHL in assists (29) and comes within one point of the scoring title (45).

- Butch Keeling, the Rangers' 11-year veteran, has his best year ever (22 goals).

- Red Wing center Marty Barry is second in assists (27) and third in points (44).

- Bob Gracie leads the Maroons in scoring with 36 points.

- Detroit's Norm Smith extends his mastery of the league, winning the

Larry Aurie

Syl Apps

Pole-Vaulter Apps Cops the First Calder

Syl Apps made his debut with the Maple Leafs during an exhibition series following the 1935-36 season. That summer, he traveled to Berlin, Germany, where he represented Canada in the Olympic pole-vaulting competition and finished a respectable sixth. Once back in his wintery homeland, Apps launched his NHL career by notching 45 points and winning the first Calder Trophy as the NHL rookie of the year.

Ol' Poison Skates Toward 300 Mark

Pictured are the ice skates of Nels Stewart, who in 1936-37 reigned as the No. 1 scorer in NHL history. Despite splitting the season with Boston and the New York Americans, Ol' Poison tied for the league's goal-scoring title with Detroit's Larry Aurie as each netted 23. In 1937-38, Stewart became the first NHLer to score 300 goals, and two years later he retired with 324 career tallies.

Aurie's 23 Goals Lead the League

As the trigger man on one of the NHL's most acclaimed forward units, Larry Aurie was right on target during the 1936-37 season. Teamed with centerman Marty Barry and left winger Herbie Lewis, Aurie tied for the NHL lead in goals with 23. It was the first time in his career that he had reached the 20-goal plateau, and his excellent production propelled the Red Wings to their second straight Stanley Cup title.

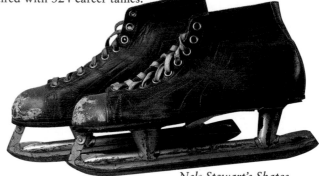

Nels Stewart's Skates

G.A. title (2.13). Norm Smith ties Boston's Tiny Thompson for the league lead in shutouts (six).

• Rangers goalie Dave Kerr has the second-stingiest GAA (2.19).

• Red Horner slams his way to a fifth penalty crown (124 minutes).

• On January 28, 1937, Howie Morenz is checked from behind by Chicago's Earl Seibert. Morenz's skate gets stuck and his leg is badly broken.

• Slow to heal and distressed over his deteriorating condition, Morenz dies suddenly of heart failure on March 8, 1937, at the age of 34.

• The funeral services for Howie Morenz draw a packed house at the Montreal Forum. Thousands more linger outside.

• The playoffs undergo a change in format, as teams play best-of-three series instead of total-goals series in the first round.

Marty Barry

Kerr Tosses Four Shutouts in Playoffs

In his third season with the Rangers, Davey Kerr led the Broadway Blues to the 1937 Stanley Cup Finals with one of the most outstanding displays of goaltending in the history of the franchise. Although the Rangers had a losing record during the season, Kerr registered four shutouts in nine playoff games. He led all postseason goalies with six wins, four shutouts, and a goals-against average of 1.11.

Davey Kerr

Barry's Two Goals Give Wings the Cup

Marty Barry was the offensive catalyst for the Red Wings during the 1937 playoffs. Barry led all postseason scorers in goals (four), assists (seven), and points (11) as the Red Wings defended their Stanley Cup crown. In the fifth and deciding game of the 1937 Finals against the Rangers, Barry scored the Cup winner in the first period and later added an insurance marker as Detroit prevailed 3-0.

Babe Siebert

Siebert Pulls Habs Out of the Doldrums

One of the NHL's most respected on-ice leaders, Albert Charles "Babe" Siebert joined the faltering Canadiens in 1936 and led the team from the NHL basement to the top of the Canadian Division in one season. An 11-year veteran and expert tactician, Siebert helped the Canadiens overcome the death of Howie Morenz and remain focused on their drive to first place. Siebert was justly awarded the Hart Trophy as the NHL's MVP.

1936-37

• The Maroons and Bruins (second-place division finishers) battle to a third game, which is won by Montreal 4-1.

• In the battle of third-place finishers, the Rangers sweep the Maple Leafs in two straight games.

• In the semifinals, the Rangers oust the Maroons with a pair of shutouts, 1-0 and 4-0. New York goalie Dave Kerr stars in goal.

• Detroit and the Canadiens, the division champs, battle in a best-of-five format. The Red Wings win the first two games.

• The emotionally wrought Habs tie their semifinal series with a pair of high-pressure wins.

• The fifth game between Detroit and Montreal is tied 1-1 after regulation. It goes to triple overtime before Detroit's Hec Kilrea beats Wilf Cude to send the Red Wings to the Finals.

Backup Robertson Saves the Day

In an emergency situation, the Red Wings turned to Earl Robertson in 1937. After Detroit goaltender Norm Smith was injured in Game 1 of the Finals against the Rangers, the Wings replaced him with Robertson, who had no NHL experience. Nevertheless, Robertson won Game 2, lost Game 3 1-0, pitched a shutout in Game 4, and won Game 5 3-0 to clinch the Cup for Detroit. Though he never played for the Wings again, Robertson toiled several years with the Americans.

Frank Calder, Jack Adams

Earl Robertson

Adams Hoists Second Straight Cup

Detroit coach Jolly Jack Adams smiles after receiving the 1937 Stanley Cup from NHL President Frank Calder. Adams, who won the Cup as a player with the Toronto Arenas in 1918, was given the job of designing a new model for the Motor City team in 1927-28. Despite three different names and countless ownership shifts, the Red Wings rose to NHL supremacy in 1935-36 and again in 1936-37, becoming the first American team to win consecutive Cups.

• Red Wings goalie Norm Smith is injured in Game 1 of the Finals against the Rangers. Detroit sends untested Earl Robertson into goal. He loses 5-1.

• With Earl Robertson still in goal, Detroit wins Game 2 of the Cup Finals 4-2.

• Detroit and New York trade 1-0 wins in Games 3 and 4, as goalies Dave Kerr (four playoff shutouts) and Earl Robertson steal the show.

• In Game 5, Earl Robertson blanks the Rangers 3-0, giving the Red Wings their second consecutive Stanley Cup.

• Toronto's Syl Apps wins the Calder Trophy as rookie of the year.

• The Canadiens' Babe Siebert (28 points) wins the Hart Trophy.

• The Lady Byng Trophy goes to Detroit's Marty Barry, while teammate Norm Smith wins the Vezina.

HAWKS PULL GOALIE OFF THE STREET, WIN CUP

One of the most incredible Stanley Cup playoff upsets of all time came from an American-ized Chicago Black Hawks squad in 1937-38. The Black Hawks were never thought to be serious contenders for the Stanley Cup. In fact, some thought their chances were 100-1 against.

The Hawks finished the regular season with a dismal 14-25-9 record, which placed them third in the American Division. They lost their first game of the playoffs 6-4 to the Canadiens, but then stunned Les Habs with a 4-0 victory. Game 3 was tied 2-2 in overtime when Black Hawk Lou Trudel fired the key shot. The puck glanced off teammate Paul Thompson and into Montreal's net, sending the Black Hawks to the semifinals against the New York Americans.

The favored Americans shut the Hawks down in the opening game, beating them 3-1 at Madison Square Garden. A loss in Game 2 would have eliminated the Black Hawks, but they managed to pull it out in double overtime 1-0, thanks to a goal from rookie Cully Dahlstrom. In the decisive Game 3, the Hawks prevailed in another thriller, 3-2, as Chicago's Doc Romnes knocked in the winner. Despite a

losing record, the Black Hawks were off to meet the Maple Leafs in the Stanley Cup Finals.

Toronto was a clear-cut favorite over Chicago, especially since Black Hawks star goaltender Mike Karakas had suffered a broken toe in the final game of the semis and could not dress for the Finals. Chicago coach Bill Stewart requested permission to use Rangers goalie Dave Kerr, but Toronto owner Conn Smythe rejected the idea. The Hawks, now desperate for a goaltender, literally pulled some guy off the street. They found Alfie Moore (who had some experience with the New York Americans) in a Toronto tavern on the afternoon of Game 1 and signed him to a contract.

Amazingly, Moore rejected virtually everything the Leafs shot

at him, as Chicago defeated Toronto 3-1 at Maple Leaf Gardens. For Game 2, Chicago decided to test yet another minor-leaguer, but Paul Goodman was a bad choice. Toronto won the game 5-1, as Gordie Drillon and George Parsons each scored twice for the Leafs.

It became clear that if the Hawks were to knock off Toronto, they needed the services of star goalie Karakas. At last, the Chicago trainer outfitted Karakas with a special shoe to protect his toe. He suited up for Game 3 and the Hawks went on to win 2-1, with Doc Romnes and Carl Voss providing the Chicago goals. The Hawks needed one more big win from Karakas, and he provided it in Game 4. The Hawks prevailed 4-1 and skated off with the Stanley Cup.

Few could believe that Chicago had won the series. In fact, NHL President Frank Calder, expecting the Maple Leafs to take the Cup, had already shipped the mug to Toronto. The series was also notable for another reason. Many of the Stanley Cup winners—plus coach Stewart—were born in the United States. Black Hawks owner Frederic McLaughlin, himself an American, couldn't have been more proud.

1937-38

- The NHL adopts a rule calling for a faceoff to ensue when the puck is shot from the defensive side of center past the offensive goal line (icing).

- Penalty shots will be awarded if anyone but the goalie falls on the puck within 10 feet of the goal.

- The league stages its second All-Star Game on November 2, 1937. It's a fund-raiser for the family of Howie Morenz, who died the previous March.

- The Maroons prepare for their final NHL season. First-year coach King Clancy is behind the bench.

- The Chicago Black Hawks hire their 13th coach in 12 years—Bill Stewart.

- The Bruins assemble the famed Kraut Line with Milt Schmidt, Bobby Bauer, and Woody Dumart.

- The Bruins (30-11-7) win their division by seven points over the

Alfie Moore (right, posing with Turk Broda) was a career minor-leaguer who spent 1937-38 with the New York Americans' farm squad in Pittsburgh. He was enjoying a pint at a Toronto tavern one April afternoon when he was asked if he wanted to play goal for Chicago in the opening game of the 1938 Stanley Cup Finals. Moore replaced an injured Mike Karakas, and although he allowed a goal on the first shot he faced, he stoned Toronto the rest of the way in a 3-1 Chicago victory.

Rangers and by 30 points over third-place Chicago (which will find its redemption in the playoffs).

• Toronto (24-15-9) beats the Americans and Canadiens (who tie for second) by 12 points in the Canadian Division.

• The Bruins, with the league's tightest defense, give up just 89 goals in 48 games.

• Toronto, with the line of Syl Apps, Busher Jackson, and Gordie Drillon, boasts the league's most prolific offense (151 goals).

• Toronto's sophomore sensation, Gordie Drillon, leads the league in goals (26) en route to his first scoring championship (52 points).

• Syl Apps, the up-and-coming Toronto superstar, leads the NHL in assists (29).

All-Star Game Held to Aid Morenz Family

Benefit Game Jersey

Not since the Ace Bailey benefit game in 1934 had NHL All-Stars faced each other in competition. But in November 1937, the NHL commissioned an All-Star Game between a combined Montreal Canadiens/ Maroons team and a group of stars from the remaining teams in an effort to raise money for the Morenz family. The contest, which marked the final on-ice appearance of defenseman King Clancy, went to the NHL All-Stars, who beat the Montrealers 6-5.

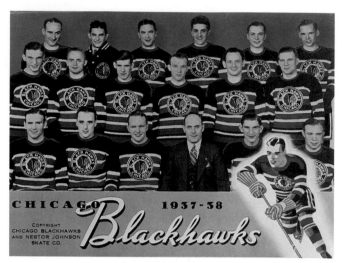

Chicago Black Hawks

A Hodge-Podge of Hawks Wins Cup

The 1937-38 Black Hawks were coached by a baseball umpire, owned by a man who attempted to compile an all-American roster, and led by a player who had never scored over 20 goals in a season. However, coach Bill Stewart (bottom row, in suit), owner Frederic McLaughlin, and leading scorer Paul Thompson (top row, third from left) combined to bring the Windy City its second Stanley Cup of the decade, as the Hawks shocked Toronto in the Finals.

Rangers Feature a Trio of Patricks

When Murray "Muzz" Patrick arrived in a Rangers uniform in 1937-38, he was united with brother Lynn and father Lester. Muzz played only one game that year, but he drew two assists. Lynn made his debut three years earlier, and in 1937-38 he had his first big year with 15 goals and 19 assists. Lester Patrick, coach of the Rangers since 1926-27, guided the New Yorkers into the playoffs for the 11th time in 12 years in 1937-38.

Lynn, Lester, and Muzz Patrick

1937-38

- The Rangers feature a trio of Patricks. Lester is the coach/G.M. while his sons, Lynn and newcomer Muzz, are players.

- Maroons goalie Bill Beveridge loses 30 games, while Boston's Tiny Thompson wins 30.

- A year after winning the Stanley Cup, the Detroit Red Wings fall to fourth in their four-team division.

- Chicago's Paul Thompson is third in the league in scoring (44 points) behind Maple Leafs Gord Drillon (52) and Syl Apps (50).

- Maroons winger Georges Mantha has a career year. He's second in the NHL in goals (23) and fourth in points (42).

- Habs winger Toe Blake combines with Paul Haynes for 30 goals and 68 points, while Aurel Joliat slips to six goals in this his last season.

Bobby Bauer, Milt Schmidt, Woody Dumart

Kraut Liners Are Top Dogs in Beantown

The 1937-38 season marked the birth of Boston's famed Kraut Line. Bobby Bauer, Milt Schmidt, and Woody Dumart were given the moniker in reference to their hometown of Kitchener, a German community in Southern Ontario. In their first year together, the Kitchener Kids combined for 46 goals and 88 points. With the three youngsters leading the way, the Bruins ascended to the top of the league with a 30-11-7 record.

Sophomore Apps Leads in Assists

The Calder Trophy winner in 1937, Toronto's Syl Apps had another outstanding season in 1937-38, collecting 21 goals and a league-leading 29 assists. Apps and linemate Gord Drillon fed off one another, as Drillon finished first and Apps second in league scoring. Besides competing in the pole-vault in the 1936 Olympics, Apps was also an excellent football player at McMaster University in Hamilton.

Syl Apps

Drillon's Tops in Scoring

Toronto's Gordie Drillon, an import from the Maritime provinces, led the league in scoring in 1937-38. The sophomore skater registered 26 goals and 52 points to edge teammate Syl Apps in the scoring parade. Noted for having the most accurate shot in the NHL, Drillon had starred in New Brunswick before making his debut in Maple Leaf Gardens. Drillon made his first appearance in the Leafs' blue and white in 1936-37.

Gordie Drillon

- Boston's Tiny Thompson leads the league with a "tiny" 1.85 GAA.

- Toronto's Red Horner is the league's highest-scoring backliner (24 points) and most penalized (92 PIM).

- The Rangers have four skaters—Art Coulter (90), Ott Heller (68), Joe Cooper (57), and Babe Pratt (56)— among the top five penalty leaders.

- Rangers goalie Dave Kerr leads the NHL in shutouts (eight) and finishes second in GAA (2.00).

- Earl Robertson, the Stanley Cup hero of the previous year for Detroit, turns in a 2.31 GAA for the Americans. He'll mind the net for New York for the duration of the franchise.

- Sweeney Schriner, a former scoring champ, scores 21 goals (tied for fourth overall) but falls out of the scoring race.

Tiny Thompson

Thompson Still Ranks No. 1 in Nets

Tiny Thompson poses for photographers prior to the start of the Bruins' 1938 semifinal series with Toronto. Already recognized as one of the NHL's all-time great netminders, Thompson captured his fourth career Vezina Trophy in 1937-38, leading the league in wins (30) and goals-against average (1.85). The Leafs bested the venerable Thompson on this night, winning 1-0 on a goal by George Parsons in double overtime.

Bill Stewart

Stewart Leads Lowly Hawks to Title

Chicago coach Bill Stewart has his eyes on the prize after his team defeated the Maple Leafs to win the Stanley Cup in 1938. Stewart, who doubled as a baseball umpire in the off-season, became the first American-born coach to win the Cup. The Black Hawks downed the Montreal Canadiens, the New York Americans, and the Leafs to win their second mug. Chicago's 14-25-9 regular-season record remains the worst ever for an NHL Cup winner.

Eddie Shore

Shore Takes Aim at Fourth Hart Trophy

Eddie Shore added another piece of silverware to his trophy shelf in 1937-38, winning his NHL-record fourth Hart Trophy as league MVP. Shore's gritty and determined play along the Bruins' blueline vaulted the team into the top spot in the NHL with a 30-11-7 record. Led by Shore, the Bruins paced the league in goals against, allowing only 89 tallies in the 48-game season. Offensively, Shore potted just three goals.

1937-38

- In the opening round of playoffs, the Hawks beat the Canadiens, winning Game 3 3-2 in O.T.

- The quarterfinal matchup between the Americans and Rangers also goes to O.T. of Game 3. The Amerks' Lorne Carr beats Dave Kerr in triple overtime for a 3-2 victory.

- In the semifinals, the Hawks dispatch the Americans in three games. Chicago wins the second game 1-0 on a double-overtime goal by rookie ace Cully Dahlstrom.

- The Maple Leafs and Bruins enter a thrill-a-minute, best-of-five semifinal series with two excellent goalies—

Turk Broda and Tiny Thompson, respectively.

- The Leafs sweep the Bruins in the semis, outscoring Boston by one goal in each game. The Leafs win Game 1 on George Parson's double-overtime goal, and they take Game 3 on Gord Drillon's O.T. goal.

Stanley Cup Quarterfinals

King Clancy

New York Teams Meet in Playoffs

The New York Americans and New York Rangers faced each other in the playoffs only twice in their histories, the final time coming in the opening round of the 1938 playoffs. In this photo, Nels Stewart of the Americans (far right) celebrates his third-period, game-tying goal in the decisive Game 3. The Americans won the game, and the series, on a goal by Lorne Carr at the 40-second mark of the third overtime period.

The End Is Near for Clancy, Maroons

Frank "King" Clancy (wearing hat) watches the Montreal Canadiens battle the crosstown Maroons during the 1937-38 season. Clancy was appointed as the Maroons' coach at the start of the season, but he lasted only 18 games. At the end of the season, the Maroons folded operations.

• The underdog Black Hawks stun Toronto in the first game of the Finals 3-1. Johnny Gottselig scores a pair and sub goalie Alfie Moore stars for injured Mike Karakas.

• Chicago uses another sub goalie, Paul Goodman, in Game 2 of the Finals, but he loses 5-1.

• Mike Karakas returns to nets for Game 3 of the Finals. He stops everything but Syl Apps' first-period goal, as Chicago wins 2-1.

• The Hawks beat the Leafs in Game 4 of the Finals 4-1, as Carl Voss scores the winning goal. The Hawks thus win their second Stanley Cup.

• Eddie Shore recaptures the Hart Trophy, his fourth. Teammate Tiny Thompson wins the Vezina.

• Chicago's Cully Dahlstrom skates off with the Calder Trophy.

• Gordie Drillon, the scoring champ, also wins the Lady Byng Trophy.

SUDDEN-DEATH HILL NETS THREE IN OVERTIME

The first NHL player to score three sudden-death playoff goals in a career was Mel Hill—and he scored them all in one series. Hill, a 25-year-old forward for the Boston Bruins, wielded his legendary magic in the 1939 playoffs.

During the season, the Bruins finished first (36-10-2) in the American Division, a full 16 points ahead of the second-place Rangers. In the playoffs, it was expected that either center Bill Cowley or the Kraut Line (Milt Schmidt, Bobby Bauer, and Woody Dumart) would lead the attack. Instead, the 1939 playoffs belonged to the little-known Hill.

During the regular season, Hill had been an unobtrusive right wing on the Bruins' third line, scoring only 10 goals. Apparently, he was saving it all up for Boston's semifinal matchup with the Rangers. The best-of-seven series opened at Madison Square Garden, and after three normal periods the teams had battled to a 1-1 tie. No one could muster a goal through the first overtime—or the second.

By this time, the Rangers' strategy had become apparent to Boston coach Art Ross. New York, it seemed, was determined to stifle Cowley's scoring chances with some blanket checking while keeping a watchful eye on high-scoring left wing Roy Conacher as well. A few seconds before the third overtime, Ross summoned Cowley to his side. "We've got to fool them," he told Cowley. "They're watching Conacher so carefully, it would be better to feed Hill."

It took nearly an entire overtime period before Cowley could convert Ross' advice into action. Finally, at about 19:20 of the third overtime, Cowley spotted Hill camped in front of New York goalie Dave Kerr. Hill shot, and at 1:10 a.m. the Bruins won the game.

Game 2 moved to Boston, and after three periods the teams were tied 2-2. At the eight-minute mark of the first overtime, Cowley charged the Rangers' defense and dropped the puck back to Hill, who proved a hero once again. Hill fired it in from 40 feet and the Bruins rejoiced with another sudden victory. The Bruins took their momentum back home, where they cruised to a 4-1 victory in Game 3.

The Rangers, however, refused to roll over and startled the Bruins with three straight victories, sending the series to the decisive encounter. Game 7 was yet another heart-thumper, as the teams went all the way to the third overtime tied at 1-1.

Eight minutes into the third O.T., Boston's Conacher received a pass from defenseman Eddie Shore and hammered a drive. Rangers goalie Bert Gardiner gloved the puck and flipped it into the corner, expecting his defenseman to retrieve it. Instead, Cowley got there first, spotted Hill, and fed him the puck. Gardiner moved to stop Mel's shot, but he was too late. The puck was in and the Bruins had won the series, four games to three.

In the Stanley Cup Finals, Boston breezed past Toronto four games to one. As for young Mel, he became known forever as "Sudden Death" Hill.

1938-39

- The NHL's penalty-shot ruling is changed, as shooters are now allowed to skate in on the goalie.

- The NHL's two-referee system is abandoned, as the league returns to the old one-referee, one-linesman system.

- On June 22, 1938, the Montreal Maroons announce they are withdrawing from the NHL due to financial problems.

- The NHL outlines per diem expenses for players at $5.00 per man for food and $2.50 per man for hotels.

- The seven-team NHL ends the divisional format and allows six teams to qualify for the Stanley Cup playoffs.

- Ironically, the defending-champion Black Hawks are the only team not to make the playoffs.

New York Rangers goaltender Bert Gardiner forces himself to
share a smile with Boston's Mel Hill following the conclusion of the Boston-New
York semifinal series of 1939. Hill earned the nickname "Sudden Death" after
scoring three overtime goals in the series. Hill nailed the overtime winners in
Games 1, 2, and 7 of the semifinals—the last two against Gardiner—in one of
the greatest playoff performances in NHL history.

• Although they won the Stanley Cup under coach Bill Stewart, the Black Hawks fire Stewart after an 8-10-3 start.

• The powerful Boston Bruins go 36-10-2 and finish 16 points ahead of the second-place Rangers.

• The Bruins unveil a new offensive weapon: rookie left winger Roy Conacher, who skates on the top line with Bill Cowley and Mel Hill.

• Roy Conacher, a strapping 22-year-old, achieves a sensational feat. He leads the NHL in goals (26) as a rookie.

• Playmaking wizard Bill Cowley of Boston leads the league in assists (34) and is third in scoring (42).

• The Montreal Canadiens struggle through a 15-24-9 season but capture the final playoff berth, as they finish seven points ahead of Chicago.

Mac Colville, Neil Colville, Alex Shibicky

Colville-Shibicky Line Sparks Rangers

While Washington offered America a New Deal to pull the country out of the Depression, the Rangers' new deal was a trio of fresh skaters who replaced the aging Bread Line. The line of Neil Colville, Mac Colville, and Alex Shibicky—each in their fourth NHL season—combined for 49 goals and 98 points in 1938-39 as the Rangers finished second in the new seven-team NHL. Shibicky topped the threesome with 24 goals, while Neil led in points with 37.

Toe Blake

Mr. Zero Posts 12 Goose Eggs

One of the greatest goaltenders in NHL history made his first appearance between the pipes in 1938-39. Frank "Mr. Zero" Brimsek led all netminders with 33 wins, 10 shutouts, and a stingy 1.58 GAA. He was even more spectacular in the playoffs, where he won eight games in leading the Bruins to their second Stanley Cup title. Brimsek earned his nickname by posting six shutouts in Boston's first 12 games of the season.

Frank Brimsek

Blake Leads in Scoring, Cops the Hart

Hector "Toe" Blake was one of the lone bright lights for the 15-24-9 Canadiens during the 1938-39 season. In only his third full season in the league, Blake led all NHL sharp-shooters with 47 points and also captured the Hart Trophy—a rarity for a young player on a bad team. Blake, who started his NHL career with the Montreal Maroons, was acquired by the Habs in 1935-36 and quickly became one of the team's best young stars.

1938-39

• Habs left winger Toe Blake wins the scoring title with 47 points.

• Sweeney Schriner leads the New York Americans to a fourth-place finish with 44 points (second overall).

• Playing on a line with Neil and Mac Colville, Rangers left winger Alex

Shibicky bags 24 goals (tying him for second overall with Toe Blake).

• The Rangers' "top" trio of Alex Shibicky and the Colvilles (49 goals, 98 points) is outscored by teammates Phil Watson, Bryan Hextall, and Dutch Hiller (45 goals, 101 points).

• The Bruins debut Frank Brimsek in goal after Tiny Thompson is injured.

• Frank Brimsek, a 23-year-old Minnesotan, leads the NHL in wins (33), GAA (1.58), and shutouts (10).

• During one stretch, Frank Brimsek plays 231:54 minutes of shutout

Frank Calder, Art Ross, Eddie Shore, Weston Adams

Disgruntled Shore Signs for $7,000

When Boston superstar Eddie Shore threatened to sit out the 1938-39 season because of a contract dispute with the Bruins' front office, NHL chief Frank Calder intervened and convinced the four-time Hart Trophy winner to sign on the dotted line for $7,000. Watching the proceedings are (left to right) Calder, Boston manager and coach Art Ross, Shore, and Bruins President Weston Adams.

Jimmy Fowler, Red Horner

Cup-Winner Stewart Gets the Thumb

Rarely is a coach fired just months after winning the Stanley Cup, but such was the case of Chicago Black Hawks coach Bill Stewart, who was given the ziggy after starting the 1938-39 season 8-10-3. At least he had a second job to fall back on. Stewart, a baseball umpire during the summer, is seen here donning the tools of the trade prior to an exhibition game between the Boston Red Sox and Boston Braves.

Bill Stewart

Toronto's Horner Still No Angel

The perennial leader of the "penalty race," Red Horner spent only 85 minutes in purgatory in 1938-39. Though he had come a long way down since he registered his career-high 167 minutes in 1935-36, he was still able to lead the sinners to the furnace this season. Paired with Jimmy Fowler on the Leafs' defensive squad, the two are seen here, dressed as gents and ready for a night on the town.

hockey, breaking the record set by his predecessor, Tiny Thompson (224:47). Brimsek is nicknamed "Mr. Zero."

• Tiny Thompson is not out of work long. He's purchased by Detroit after the Bruins cast him aside.

• Rangers goalie Dave Kerr turns in a 2.19 GAA and 26 victories.

• Toronto's burly netminder, Turk Broda, records eight shutouts (second to Frank Brimsek).

• Montreal's slick Paul Haynes is second in the league in assists (33).

• Toronto's Red Horner, the reigning bad boy of the NHL, "wins" his seventh straight penalty crown (85 PIM), though he has new competition from Ranger Muzz Patrick (72 PIM).

• Future Hall of Famer Bobby Hull is born on January 3, 1939, in Pointe Anne, Ontario.

Conacher: First Rook to Lead NHL in Goals

Roy Conacher

Boston's Roy Conacher was the NHL's sharpest rookie shooter in 1938-39, becoming the first freshman ever to lead the league in goals after piling 26 pucks past enemy goalies during the 48-game campaign. Conacher continued to produce for the Bruins in the playoffs, collecting six goals. Included was the Stanley Cup winner in Game 5 of the Finals against Toronto, as the Bruins won their second championship.

Americans Net Nothing vs. Leafs

Turk Broda of the Maple Leafs sprawls to make a save on New York Americans star Nels Stewart. In their best-of-three playoff series in 1939, the Americans mustered zero goals against Toronto as the Turk pitched a pair of shutouts. Broda, nicknamed Turk because his face was as freckled as a turkey egg, beat Detroit in the semifinals but was outshined by a red-hot Frank Brimsek of the Bruins in the Finals.

Bill Cowley

Cowley Sticks It to Rangers in Semifinals

Boston's multi-talented centerman Bill Cowley adds another layer of tape to his stick prior to Game 1 of the Boston-New York Rangers semifinal on March 21, 1939. The extra effort paid off for Cowley, who scored the tying goal and set up the game winner in Boston's 2-1 overtime victory over the Rangers. The Bruins won the series in seven games, while Cowley led all postseason scorers with three goals and 11 assists.

Stanley Cup Quarterfinals

- The playoff system is reformed. The Bruins (No. 1) and Rangers (No. 2) earn first-round byes. Toronto (No. 3) plays the Americans (No. 4), and the Wings (No. 5) play Montreal (No. 6).

- Toronto sweeps the Americans (4-0 and 2-0) in their best-of-three series.

- Detroit outlasts Montreal in their quarterfinal series, thanks to a 1-0 overtime victory in Game 3 on Marty Barry's goal.

- Toronto and Detroit play a best-of-three semifinal series. Toronto wins Game 3 on Gordie Drillon's winner in overtime.

- The Bruins and Rangers play the first seven-game playoff series since 1918-19. Four games go to O.T.

- Boston beats the Rangers 2-1 in Game 1, as Mel Hill scores with 35 seconds left in triple overtime. The Bruins win Game 2 3-2 when Hill again scores, at 8:24 of the first O.T.

Bruins Yield 12 Goals in 'Nine' Games

The first-ever seven-game NHL playoff series, between the Bruins and Rangers in 1939, was actually more like nine games, as the teams played 133 minutes of overtime (the equivalent of 2.2 games). It's not surprising the Rangers scored only 12 goals during the affair considering they had to penetrate a wall of defenseman Eddie Shore (on knees) and goalie Frank Brimsek, both future Hall of Famers.

Stanley Cup Semifinals

Stanley Cup Celebration

Beantowners Sup with the Stanley Cup

Members of the 1938-39 Bruins join family, friends, and members of the media for a celebration of the team's Stanley Cup championship. In the first-ever best-of-seven Stanley Cup Finals, the Beantowners downed the Maple Leafs in five games to return Lord Stanley's ceremonial chalice to Boston for the second time in franchise history. Bill Cowley, with 14 postseason points, and Frank Brimsek, with a GAA of 1.50, were the playoff heroes for the Bruins.

• Boston takes Game 3 before the Rangers stave off elimination with three straight wins. Game 5 is tied at 1-1 until 17:19 of O.T., when Rangers rookie Clint Smith wins it.

• The Bruins eliminate the Rangers in Game 7, as Mel Hill scores in the third overtime to snap a 1-1 tie.

• The Stanley Cup Finals are anticlimactic, as Boston rolls to a four-games-to-one victory over Toronto. The Bruins win by scores of 2-1, 2-3, 3-1, 2-0, and 3-1.

• Bruins goalie Frank Brimsek, brilliant in the semis, is unbeatable in the Finals, allowing just six goals.

• Frank Brimsek becomes the first person to win both the Vezina Trophy and the Calder Trophy.

• The Rangers' Clint Smith skates off with the Lady Byng Trophy.

• Montreal's Toe Blake, the scoring champ, captures the Hart Trophy.

The New York Rangers, who had not won a Stanley Cup since 1933, underwent a startling front-office change before the 1939-40 season. Lester Patrick, who had coached the club since its inception in 1926, turned the reins over to his former star center, Frank Boucher.

Skeptics doubted that the mild-mannered Boucher could whip the Blueshirts into winners, but Frank had plenty of raw material with which to work—especially forwards Phil Watson, Bryan Hextall, and Neil Colville. The Rangers were also strong in goal with Dave Kerr, who would claim the 1939-40 Vezina Trophy.

New York finished the regular season at 27-11-10, three points behind first-place Boston. But the tide turned quickly in the playoffs, as the New Yorkers beat the Bostonians four games to two behind Kerr's stellar goaltending. Kerr shut out the high-scoring Bruins three times despite a Boston team that featured such stars as Milt Schmidt, Bobby Bauer, Woody Dumart, and goalie Frank Brimsek. "It's the second-best team I had ever seen," said Boucher. The best was the Bruins team that won the Stanley Cup the year before.

MAPLE LEAFS, CIRCUS CAN'T STOP THE RANGERS

That series win sent New York to the Stanley Cup Finals against Toronto. Because the Ringling Brothers Circus already had been booked into Madison Square Garden, the Rangers could play only the first two games of the Finals at home. All the remaining games would be slated for Maple Leaf Gardens.

Facing this schedule imbalance, the Rangers knew they had to win both games at New York. Undaunted, Boucher's Blueshirts opened with a 2-1 win at home on Alf Pike's sudden-death goal. They also won Game 2, 6-2, thanks to Bryan Hextall's hat-trick.

The move to Maple Leaf Gardens helped Toronto gain a 2-1 win in Game 3 and a 3-0 victory in Game 4. Neither team seemed destined to win Game 5,

as it rolled into one overtime and then another. Finally, at 11:43 of the second sudden-death session, low-scoring Rangers defenseman Muzz Patrick took a pass from Neil Colville and beat goalie Turk Broda. New York was now just a win away from the Stanley Cup.

Game 6 appeared to be all Toronto's as the Leafs built a 2-0 lead after two periods. It was then that manager Patrick entered the dressing room. "Well, boys," he said, "you've had your fun. Now let's get down to business. I've made arrangements for a victory party in the Tudor Room of the Royal York (Hotel). I'll see you there. Don't let me down."

The Rangers responded in the third period, as Colville and Pike rifled home goals two minutes apart. The game entered sudden-death overtime but was over soon after.

The overtime was only two minutes old when the line of Hextall, Watson, and Dutch Hiller charged into the enemy zone. Hiller got the puck to Watson, who shoveled a pass to Hextall. At 2:07, Hextall blasted the rubber past goalie Broda. Despite playing the last four games on the road, the Rangers were Stanley Cup champions.

1939-40

- The NHL adopts a rule concerning a substitute who replaces a goalie who's serving a penalty. The sub may not don any goaltending equipment other than a goalie's stick and gloves.

- The league's third All-Star Game is staged on October 29, 1939, to raise funds for the family of Canadiens

hero and coach Babe Siebert, who drowned in the off-season.

- The war in Europe begins. It will soon take its toll on the NHL, as players will enlist for military duty.

- Cooney Weiland, 35, replaces Art Ross as coach of the Bruins.

- The Rangers hire former star Frank Boucher as coach in what will be deemed a brilliant move.

- In a blockbuster deal, the Leafs acquire Sweeney Schriner from the Amerks for Busher Jackson, Murray Armstrong, ex-Black Hawk Doc Romnes, and Buzz Boll.

The Rangers of 1939-40 were a family business. The Patrick clan had
Lester in the front office, Muzz on defense, and Lynn on the forward line. The
Colville brothers, Mac and Neil, combined for 59 points. The Rangers were
wonderfully successful in their first 14 years, making the playoffs 13 times and
winning three Stanley Cups. Few would have guessed that they would go 50-plus
years without hoisting another silver mug.

- The Bruins have the best line in hockey, as the Kraut Line combines for 61 goals and 138 points.

- The Kraut Line—Woody Dumart, Milt Schmidt, and Bobby Bauer—features the NHL's newest scoring champion as Schmidt finishes with 52 points.

- Because of the conflict in Europe, the Kraut Line is renamed the Kitchener Kids.

- The Bruins boast the NHL's top four scorers: Milt Schmidt (52 points), Bobby Bauer (43), Woody Dumart (43), and Bill Cowley (40).

- Milt Schmidt leads the league in assists (30) and ties Woody Dumart for second in goals (22).

- Rangers right winger Bryan Hextall captures the goal-scoring title (24).

- Bryan Hextall's center, Phil Watson, is second in the NHL in assists (28).

Dumart a Main Cog in the Bruin Machine

As the sharp-shooting left winger on the Bruins' famed Kraut Line, Woodrow "Woody" Dumart scored 43 points in 1939-40, tying him with linemate Bob Bauer for second in the league. Who did they trail in the scoring race? Their other linemate, Milt Schmidt, who topped the NHL with 52 points. Dumart was a smooth skater who kept himself out of trouble on the ice, spending only 16 minutes in the penalty box during the season.

Frank Boucher

Coach Boucher Takes Rangers All the Way

After 12 years as the front-line centerman for the New York Rangers, Frank Boucher stepped behind the bench for the 1939-40 season, replacing the famed Lester Patrick as coach. Boucher, of course, knew this Rangers club inside out, and his insight helped the team to a 27-11-10 record, second best in the NHL. In the playoffs, Boucher's squad motored past the Bruins and the Maple Leafs to bring the third Stanley Cup to New York City.

Woody Dumart

Smallish Schmidt Leads in Scoring

When Milt Schmidt tried out for the Maple Leafs in the mid-1930s, Conn Smythe dismissed him as being too small to play in the NHL. Luckily for Boston fans, Art Ross had no such prejudice and signed the cagey centerman for the Beantown team. In 1939-40, Schmidt paced the league in assists (30) and points (52), leading the league in scoring for the first time. Schmidt also set a personal high with 22 goals during the 48-game campaign.

Milt Schmidt

- Toronto's Gord Drillon ties Boston's Bill Cowley for fourth in points (40).

- Herb Cain, the flashy Bruins winger, ties Toronto's Gord Drillon for fourth overall in goals (21).

- Rangers goalie Dave Kerr wins the GAA race with a 1.60 mark, as the New York squad surrenders the fewest goals in the league (77).

- The Bruins win the regular-season title with powerful offense (170 goals) and 31 victories.

- Boston sophomore Frank Brimsek goes 31-12-5 with six shutouts.

- Chicago gives last year's playoff stand-in Paul Goodman a shot, and he goes 16-10-5 with a 2.00 GAA.

- Toe Blake leads the last-place Canadiens in scoring (17-19-36).

- After 14 years in Boston, Eddie Shore is sold to the Americans.

Bill Cowley

Cowley One of Many High-Scoring Bruins

The NHL's assist leader in 1938-39, Bill Cowley finished tied for fourth in the league in points in 1939-40, with 13 goals and 27 assists. If it weren't for Boston's high-scoring first-string line of Schmidt, Dumart, and Bauer, Cowley would have tied for the league scoring title with Gord Drillon. Cowley, who led all postseason scorers with 14 points in 1939, managed only one point in six playoff games in 1940.

Hextall Leads in Goals, Wins Cup

Boston may have had four of the top five scorers in the NHL in 1939-40, but the Rangers' Bryan Hextall led everybody with 24 goals. Hextall fired in four more during the playoffs, including three goals in Game 2 of the Finals. He also knocked in the Cup winner in Game 6. With the finale tied 2-2 in overtime, Hextall beat Toronto goalie Turk Broda at the 2:07 mark to give the Rangers the coveted silver bowl.

Bryan Hextall

- Eddie Shore retires and becomes owner/coach of the American Hockey League's Springfield Indians.

- Detroit's brilliant Ebbie Goodfellow leads all backliners in goals (11).

- Four NHL backliners—Dit Clapper and Bill Hollett (Boston), Ebbie Goodfellow (Detroit), and Charlie Conacher (Americans)—score 28 points.

- Red Horner, Toronto's nasty defenseman, leads the league in penalty minutes (87) for the eighth and final time.

- Toronto's third-place finish rests on the shoulders of goalie Turk Broda, who posts a 2.30 GAA and records four shutouts.

- The Red Wings suffer their third losing record in a row, finishing 16-26-6 (fifth place).

Turk Broda

Broda Loses, Wins Back His Job

In 1939-40, veteran Turk Broda suffered his first slump, causing Conn Smythe to call on rookie Phil Stein to fill the gap. In his first outing, Stein fought Detroit to a 2-2 tie and won a spot on the lineup card while Broda regrouped on the bench. In the pre-game warmup before his next start, Stein took a shot off the forehead, forcing Broda to stand in for his stand-in. Turk regained his form and Stein never played in the NHL again.

Eddie Shore, Cooney Weiland

Shore Tries to Play on Two Teams

Eddie Shore greets new Bruins coach Cooney Weiland prior to an exhibition game between the Bruins and the Springfield Indians. Shore bought the minor-league Springfield team and tried to cram two professional hockey seasons into one winter by playing for both teams. The Boston hierarchy was not impressed by Shore's shenanigans. They dealt the future Hall of Famer to the NHL's old-folks home, the New York Americans.

Ebbie Goodfellow

Goodfellow Stars at His New Position

A versatile centerman for the early part of his career, Ebbie Goodfellow was moved to defense in the mid-1930s. In 1939-40, he proved he was still hot with the stick, leading all rearguards in goals with 11. Ebenezer Goodfellow was as good as his name, and a natural leader of men. He wore the captain's jersey for the Red Wings for five seasons and earned an NHL First All-Star Team nomination in 1939-40.

1939-40

- Red Dutton's New York Americans outdistance the Canadiens by nine points for the last playoff spot.

- The Maple Leafs (No. 3) quickly dispatch the Black Hawks (No. 4) in the quarterfinals, beating them 3-2 in overtime and 2-1.

- The Red Wings oust the Amerks in a tightly fought best-of-three series, winning Game 1 in O.T. and taking the decisive third game 3-1.

- Toronto sweeps Detroit in the semifinals, as Turk Broda beats the Wings 2-1 and 3-1.

- The first-place Bruins and second-place Rangers meet in a best-of-seven rematch of their 1939 playoff war.

- After trailing Boston two games to one, the Rangers reel off three straight wins to advance to the Finals. Rangers goalie Dave Kerr pitches shutouts in Games 1, 4, and 5.

Oshawa Generals

Generals Win Another Memorial Cup

The Oshawa Generals became the first team to win consecutive Memorial Cup titles, going all the way in both 1938-39 and 1939-40. One of their stars was defenseman Frank Eddolls (front row, third from right), who would eventually play for the NHL's Canadiens and Rangers.

Montreal's Siebert Dies at Age 35

NHL fans endured another tragedy when Canadiens veteran Babe Siebert drowned prior to the 1939-40 season. Siebert had recently been named coach of the Montreal team. The NHL staged a benefit All-Star Game to raise funds for Siebert's family.

Babe Siebert

• The Rangers take Game 1 of the Finals 2-1, as Alfie Pike scores at 15:30 of overtime.

• After absorbing a 6-2 beating in Game 2, the Leafs rebound and tie the Finals with 2-1 and 3-0 wins over New York.

• The Rangers win Game 5 of the Finals 2-1, as Muzz Patrick scores in the second overtime.

• On April 13, 1940, the Rangers win their third Stanley Cup, as Bryan Hextall breaks a 2-2 tie at 2:07 of overtime.

• Detroit defenseman Ebbie Goodfellow wins the Hart Trophy, while Boston's Bobby Bauer captures the Lady Byng.

• Ranger Dave Kerr claims the Vezina Trophy, while rookie teammate Kilby MacDonald cops the Calder.

THREAT OF WORLD WAR LOOMS OVER THE NHL

The guns that signaled the start of World War II went off in September 1939, when Nazi hordes invaded Poland. Within days, the British Commonwealth began mobilization. From those dark days until the summer of 1945, the perils of war consumed the thoughts of all the world's people. The sport of hockey became insignificant.

NHL players didn't become directly involved in the war effort until 1940. Hitler was preparing for an invasion of England, and England's Royal Air Force needed help. At that point, Canada was called upon to supply able-bodied men.

NHL President Frank Calder knew that if the war extended beyond 1941, it could have dire effects on professional hockey. Already, there was talk that the league might have to suspend operations if parliamentarians in Ottawa decided that hockey was impeding the war effort. However, the NHL owners were given a mandate to continue operations from both the Canadian and American governments as long as they were able to ice enough teams. "Somehow," recalled Bruins manager Art Ross, "we were able to find enough players. But it wasn't easy."

The Bruins would lose their entire Kraut Line to the Royal Canadian Air Force—but not until after the 1941-42 season. Each of the triumvirate remained in 1940-41, with the only change being the line's name. "Kraut Line" was too politically sensitive, so Milt Schmidt, Bobby Bauer, and Woody Dumart instead became the Kitchener Kids, since they were all from Kitchener, Ontario.

Because the United States was not yet directly involved in the war, a state of normalcy prevailed among four of the five American teams—Detroit, Chicago, Boston, and the Rangers. Only one, the New York Americans, experienced problems.

The Amerks, managed by former defenseman Mervyn "Red" Dutton, were hurting both artistically and financially despite talented young defenseman Pat "Boxcar" Egan and up-and-coming goalie Chuck "Bonnie Prince Charlie" Rayner. New York finished the season in the cellar with a record of 8-29-11.

Boston was the class of the league. With the kids from Kitchener—as well as NHL scoring champ Bill Cowley and star goalie Frank Brimsek—the Bruins went 27-8-13, which included a 23-game undefeated streak. Boston needed seven games to get past Toronto in the semis, but they then broomed Detroit in four games in the Finals.

There was little jubilation, however, since the dark days of war loomed ahead. That spring, Japan was expanding its territorial claims in the Pacific, and Germany was primed for an invasion of the Soviet Union. As the teams dispersed at season's end, players wondered whether they'd see each other before the end of the war.

Muzz Patrick of the Rangers already had made it clear that he was enlisting, as had Kilby MacDonald. One thing was for sure: The National Hockey League was ready for war.

1940-41

- The NHL mandates the use of between-periods ice flooding to improve the quality of the league's ice surfaces.

- Future Rangers star Jean Ratelle is born on October 3, 1940, in Lac St. Jean, Quebec.

- Dick Irvin, who coached the Leafs to a third-place finish in 1939-40, leaves Toronto for Montreal. Hap Day, who skated for Toronto for 13 years, takes over as Leafs coach.

- The Canadiens debut a pair of highly touted rookie forwards—Elmer Lach and Johnny Quilty.

- The Red Wings install Johnny Mowers in goal, as Tiny Thompson retires after 12 NHL seasons.

- The struggling Americans debut future star Chuck Rayner in goal.

- John Mariucci, a legend of Minnesota amateur hockey, jumps

Leafs manager Conn Smythe (in jersey) loved a knuckle-dusting
hockey match, and when it came to fighting that mattered, he answered the call
of national duty. Smythe represented Canada in two world wars and strongly
encouraged his players to trade in their team uniforms for the khaki Maple Leaf
of their country. Despite the fact that many players joined the service, his Leafs
stayed an upper-division team throughout the war.

from the University of Minnesota to the Black Hawks.

• The Bentley brothers—Max and Doug, from Delisle, Saskatchewan—power the Black Hawks' offense.

• The Rangers' fiery Phil Watson and the Black Hawks' Joe Cooper engage in a bloody, stick-swinging brawl that leaves Watson cut and dazed.

• On the strength of their league-leading offense (168 goals), the Bruins capture their fourth consecutive regular-season title. They finish at 27-8-13.

• Toronto, once a devastating scoring machine, takes second in the standings with the NHL's stingiest defense (99 goals against).

• The Maple Leafs, with Turk Broda in goal, lead the NHL in victories (28) but trail Boston by five points in the final standings.

Bauer Captures the Lady Byng

Boston's Bobby Bauer received his second Lady Byng Trophy as the league's most gentlemanly player in 1940-41, amassing 39 points while spending only two minutes in the penalty box. The Bauer family was legendary in Kitchener, Ontario. Bobby's brother David was a top prospect in the Leafs organization, and their father designed a line of ice skates that would soon be worn by most of the game's top players.

Bobby Bauer

Bryan Hextall

Hextall's the Best at Right Wing

Bryan Hextall retained his goal-scoring crown in 1940-41, leading all NHL snipers with 26 red lights. A first-team All-Star in 1939-40, Hextall was honored again in 1940-41, earning the right wing spot on the NHL's dream team. His Rangers dropped down a peg in 1940-41, finishing fourth with a 21-19-8 record. Although they scored their share of goals, the defense allowed 48 more tallies than it did during the 1939-40 season.

Sweeney Schriner

Schriner Worth the Price of Four Players

One of Conn Smythe's shrewdest moves was trading four players to the New York Americans for that team's top star, David "Sweeney" Schriner. A two-time NHL scoring champion in the 1930s, Schriner joined the Leafs in 1939-40; by 1940-41, he was the team's leading sharp-shooter with 24 goals. To obtain Schriner, Toronto gave the Amerks Murray Armstrong, Buzz Boll, Doc Romnes, and the last remaining member of the Kid Line—Busher Jackson.

1940-41

- Wally Stanowski, a Leafs backliner, wows the crowds with his length-of-the-ice rushes.

- Boston's Bill Cowley sets new NHL records for assists (45) and points (62) and wins his first and only scoring title.

- Bryan Hextall, the Rangers' talented right winger, wins his second straight goal-scoring title (26).

- Boston's Roy Conacher, beneficiary of Bill Cowley's expert playmaking, ties for second in the league in goals with 24.

- Maple Leafs left winger Sweeney Schriner, coming off an 11-goal season, bounces back with 24, tying him for second overall.

- Boston's Frank Brimsek and Detroit's Johnny Mowers tie for second in GAA (2.13) behind Turk Broda (2.06).

Lynn Patrick, Dorothea Davis

Howe Does the Dirty Work, Scores a Lot

Syd Howe did a tour of the hockey circuit before coming to the Red Wings during the 1934-35 season. After stints in Ottawa, Philadelphia, and the hockey backwater of St. Louis, Syd found his way to the Motor City. Howe exhibited the hard-working spirit of the Olympia Stadium faithful, playing the corners, digging for the puck, and delivering timely body-checks. In 1940-41, he compiled 44 points to lead all Red Wing shooters.

Syd Howe

Patrick Scores 44, Weds a Model

Lynn Patrick was a model hockey player and Dorothea Davis was a model, so it seems only natural that they became one of hockey's most glamorous couples. On April 8, 1939, they were married at the Marble Collegiate Church in New York. In 1940-41, Patrick had the first big season of his career, tying for the team lead in points, with 20 goals and 24 assists, while playing on the potent Patrick-Watson-Hextall line.

Irvin Asked to Rebuild Canadiens

After nine seasons behind the bench in Toronto, and seven trips to the Stanley Cup Finals, Dick Irvin brought his formidable know-how to St. Catherine Street to become the coach of the rebuilding Canadiens. Coach Pit Lepine, who sat in during the 1939-40 season after the death of Babe Siebert, stepped aside to allow Irvin to come aboard. Irvin would turn the Canadiens into a super-power by 1943-44.

Dick Irvin

- The Stanley Cup champion Rangers struggle to a 21-19-8 record and a fourth-place finish.

- The retirement of Red Horner, Toronto's belligerent defenseman, opens the door for a new penalty king—Detroit's Jimmy Orlando (99 PIM).

- On March 4, 1941, the Bruins unleash a record 83 shots on goal in a 3-2 victory over Chicago.

- Five NHLers—Syl Apps and Gord Drillon (Maple Leafs), Bryan Hextall and Lynn Patrick (Rangers), and Syd Howe (Red Wings)—tie for runner-up in the points race (44).

- Detroit (No. 3) and the Rangers (No. 4) meet in the Stanley Cup quarterfinals, with the Red Wings taking the decisive third game 3-2.

- Chicago (No. 5) and Montreal (No. 6) clash in the other Stanley Cup quarterfinal. The Hawks win the decisive third game 3-2.

No Doubt: Broda's Tops in the League

Turk Broda established himself as hockey's finest netminder in 1940-41, allowing 99 goals in 48 games for a sparkling goals-against average of 2.06. Broda led the league in victories with 28 and tied for second with four shutouts. He earned his first Vezina Trophy and was selected to the NHL's First All-Star Team. In the semifinal play-off against Boston, he held the Bruins to two goals or less in five of the seven games.

Left Winger Conacher Nets Two Dozen

A long line of Conachers have worn NHL jerseys. They all have had three things in common: they could skate, they could fight, and they could score. Roy Conacher was no exception. In 1940-41, playing left wing, Conacher led the Bruins with 24 goals, as center Bill Cowley set him up with perfect passes. In the long march to the Stanley Cup, he helped the Bruins bring the mug home, collecting six points in 11 playoff games.

Bill Cowley

Cowley Racks Up a Record 45 Assists

In 1940-41, nothing could keep Bill Cowley from the puck. He galloped from end to end, digging across the line and sending pucks to the free man. Cowboy Bill set a new NHL record for assists with 45 while winning the NHL scoring title with 62 points. In the postseason, however, Cowley was forced to watch his teammates win the Stanley Cup from the sidelines, as a knee injury limited him to only two games.

Turk Broda

Roy Conacher

1940-41

• The Red Wings win Game 1 of their semifinals with Chicago 3-1, then sweep the Hawks on Gus Giesebrecht's winner in overtime.

• The Bruins and Maple Leafs go to seven games in the semis. Toronto takes control of the series in Game 5 when Pete Langelle beats Frank

Brimsek, putting the Leafs up three games to two.

• Boston's outstanding defense shines in Games 6 and 7. The Bruins beat the Leafs 2-1 in both games.

• In the Finals, the heavily favored Bruins roll past the Wings. Bruin Pat

McCreavy pots the winner in Game 1 as Boston wins 3-2.

• In Game 2 of the Finals, Terry Reardon and Roy Conacher score for Boston to win the game 2-1.

• Milt Schmidt breaks up a 2-2 tie in the second period of Game 3, and Art

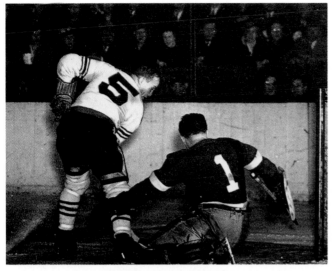

Mowers Stymies Hawks in Semis

On March 30, 1941, the Red Wings defeated the Black Hawks 2-1 in overtime (on a goal by Gus Giesebrecht) to reach the Stanley Cup Finals for the first time since 1937. Johnny Mowers (#1) was a key reason, making numerous stops like this one against Mush March (#5). Along the road to the Finals, Mowers allowed only eight goals in five games. He continued his fine play against Boston in the championship round.

Stanley Cup Semifinals

Boston Bruins

Boston First to Go 4-0 in Cup Finals

The Bruins returned to the winner's circle in 1941 with a four-game victory over the Red Wings in the Finals. After surviving a tough seven-game semifinal against the Maple Leafs, the Bruins cruised through the Finals, completing the first best-of-seven sweep in NHL history. Eddie Wiseman (front row, far right) led all marksmen during the postseason with six goals, including the insurance marker in Boston's 3-1 win in the Cup-clinching game.

Jackson adds insurance, as the Bruins take a three-games-to-none lead in the Finals.

• The Bruins win Game 4 3-1 to become the first team to pull off a four-game sweep in the Stanley Cup Finals.

• Milt Schmidt, the Bruins' "center" of attraction, is the top playoff scorer with five goals and 11 points.

• Bill Cowley, on the strength of his record-breaking scoring performance, skates off with his first of two Hart Trophies.

• Montreal rookie Johnny Quilty (18 goals, 34 points to lead the Habs) earns the Calder Trophy.

• Turk Broda, the burly Leafs goalie, wins the Vezina Trophy.

• Boston's Bobby Bauer takes his second straight Lady Byng Trophy.

LEAFS PULL OFF THE ULTIMATE COMEBACK

In the history of major-league sports, only once has a team overcome a three-games-to-none deficit in the final series to win the league championship. It happened in the NHL, and it happened in the spring of 1942. The Maple Leafs emerged as the jubilant victors, the Red Wings the tragic losers.

Detroit reached the 1942 Stanley Cup Finals despite a regular-season record of 19-25-4. Toronto (27-18-3) was the clear favorite, but that was before Wings coach Jack Adams devised a strategy that fooled his Toronto counterpart, Hap Day. In an era when teams traditionally carried the puck over the enemy blueline, Adams scrapped that plan and ordered his players to, instead, simply shoot the puck into the corners and then outskate their foes to the rubber. It was a stroke of genius.

As Adams had hoped, the radical strategy took the Leafs by surprise. In Game 1 of the Finals, the faster Red Wings continually beat the Leafs to the puck and crafted a 3-2 win at Maple Leaf Gardens. They followed that with a 4-2 victory at Toronto and then won 5-2 at Olympia Stadium for a seemingly insurmountable three-games-to-none lead.

Toronto's embattled coach responded with two dramatically courageous changes. He benched his best scorer, Gordie Drillon, and replaced him with fourth-line forward Don Metz. Also, ace defenseman Bucko McDonald was scratched in favor of untried rookie defenseman Ernie Dickens.

The newcomers provided a welcome tonic in Game 4. After falling behind 2-0, the Leafs rallied for a 4-3 win with Metz setting up the winning goal. Late in the game, Adams—who was incensed at penalties the Wings had received—accosted referee Mel Harwood. As a result of the fracas, Adams was suspended for the remainder of the series by NHL President Frank Calder.

Galvanized by the turnabout, the Leafs rebounded smartly in Game 5, back at home. This time, Metz produced a hat-trick and added two assists en route to a 9-3 Maple Leaf rout. Detroit had the home-ice advantage in Game 6, but Toronto's Turk Broda blanked the reeling Wings 3-0. The series was now knotted up, with Game 7 set for Maple Leaf Gardens.

In the finale, Detroit opened the scoring with a goal by Syd Howe. Sensing victory, the Wings tightened their defense and preserved the lead through the second period and into the third. But their defensive strategy was disrupted by a two-minute tripping penalty early in the period. The Maple Leafs' Sweeney Schriner converted on the power play to tie the score 1-1. Toronto took advantage of its momentum, scoring less than two minutes later on a goal by Pete Langelle.

Frantic now that they were behind, the Wings plunged headlong into the Maple Leaf zone with little concern for defense. But Toronto capitalized on Detroit's offensive obsession and surged ahead, as Schriner knocked in another goal. When the bell sounded, Toronto rejoiced with a 3-1 victory, signaling the greatest comeback in hockey history.

1941-42

- The NHL adopts a split minor/major policy on penalty shots. The minor penalty allows a 28-foot "free" shot; the major penalty allows the player to skate in on the goalie.

- The league adds a second linesman to each game; each contest now has one referee and two linesmen.

- Future Hall of Famer Rod Gilbert is born on July 1, 1941, in Montreal.

- Prior to the season's start, the New York Americans change their name to the Brooklyn Americans, even though they play in Manhattan's Madison Square Garden.

- Rangers goalie Dave Kerr retires after 11 seasons with 203 career wins and a 2.17 G.A. average.

- Goalie Sugar Jim Henry, a star for the senior-league Regina Rangers, is promoted. He replaces the retired Dave Kerr.

After winning Games 4, 5, and 6 of the 1942 Finals, the Maple Leafs were brimming with confidence. Toronto trailed Detroit 1-0 after two periods of Game 7, but during intermission Sweeney Schriner (right) looked up to manager Conn Smythe and said, "What'cha worried about, boss? We'll get'cha a couple of goals." Sure enough, the Leafs stormed back, scoring three times in the third period to win the game 3-1 and the series four games to three.

• Despite the Japanese attack on Pearl Harbor on December 7, 1941, no NHL games are canceled.

• The Bruins' lineup is depleted when Milt Schmidt, Bobby Bauer, and Woody Dumart join the RCAF (Royal Canadian Air Force).

• Rangers left winger Lynn Patrick leads the league in goals with 32 and is second overall in points (54).

• Rangers playmaker Phil Watson tops the NHL in assists (37).

• The Rangers' Bryan Hextall wins his only scoring championship with 24 goals (second overall), 32 assists (second), and 56 points.

• Boston's Roy Conacher and Red Hamill (who was traded by Boston to Chicago early in the year) tie Bryan Hextall for second overall in goals with 24.

Frank Brimsek

Goals Are Up But Brimsek Stars in Net

Frank "Mr. Zero" Brimsek saw his goals-against average soar in 1941-42, yet his 2.45 GAA was still the lowest in the NHL. With many of hockey's best players overseas, the NHL saw more goals being scored around the league. For the first time since 1929-30, every team scored at least 100 goals. Brimsek was able to post only three "zeroes," but he was still good enough to win his second Vezina Trophy.

Bryan Hextall

Hextall Part of Powerful Rangers Line

In 1941-42, the NHL was a single-division loop and the Rangers were at the top of the standings. Bryan Hextall played on the Rangers' line that brought them to the top of the hill. Left winger Lynn Patrick scored more goals (32) than any shooter, centerman Phil Watson earned the greatest number of assists in the league (37), and Hextall, right winger on the line, led all NHL scorers with 56 points.

Kraut Liners Join the RCAF

The 1941-42 season saw the end of an era in Boston. The famed Kraut Line of Milt Schmidt, Woody Dumart, and Bobby Bauer played 36 games for Art Ross before answering a higher call. All three joined the Royal Canadian Air Force, where they kept their hockey skills sharp by playing in Ottawa, where their camp was based. With this super trio, the Ottawa RCAF team captured the Allan Cup, emblematic of the senior hockey championship of Canada.

Bobby Bauer, Milt Schmidt, Woody Dumart

1941-42

• Sid Abel, the Red Wings' up-and-coming new star, finishes third in the NHL in assists (31) and tied for fifth in points (49).

• Detroit left wing Don Grosso is third in the NHL in points (53) and fourth in assists (30).

• The Rangers have three players—Bryan Hextall (first), Lynn Patrick (second), and Phil Watson (fourth)—among the top NHL scorers.

• The Americans don't win much, but rugged defender Pat Egan ensures they aren't pushed around, as he wins the penalty crown with 124 PIM.

• Without their top line, the Bruins fall to third, but goalie Frank Brimsek wins the GAA title (2.45).

• Rookie Rangers goalie Sugar Jim Henry leads the league in wins (29), as the Rangers take first place with a 29-17-2 record.

Brooklyn Americans

Lester Patrick, Jim Henry

Rookie Henry Leads in Wins

Rangers manager Lester Patrick congratulates his netminder, Sugar Jim Henry, on his first big-league shutout on March 8, 1942. Henry held the Leafs scoreless in the 2-0 tilt. Henry finished his rookie season with a league-leading 29 wins, two shutouts, and a 2.98 GAA. The 21-year-old goaltender helped his team to the top of the NHL standings and into the playoffs, where he registered a 2.17 average.

Amerks Fold; NHL Down to Six Clubs

The New York Americans renamed themselves the Brooklyn Americans for the 1941-42 season. The financially desperate franchise was peppered with new and former stars, including Harry Watson (third from left), Mel "Sudden Death" Hill (eighth from left), and Charlie Rayner (kneeling). The Amerks went 16-29-3 and suspended operations after the season. The NHL thus became a six-team league, and would remain so for the next quarter-century.

Watson Leads the League in Helpers

For the first time in their history, the Rangers finished atop the NHL standings in 1941-42. One of the main reasons was the play of veteran centerman Phil Watson, who led all NHL set-up artists with 37 assists—and also added 15 goals. When the going got rough, he was a handy man to have around. He spent 58 minutes in penance but rarely went to the "confessional" alone, usually taking an opposing sinner in with him.

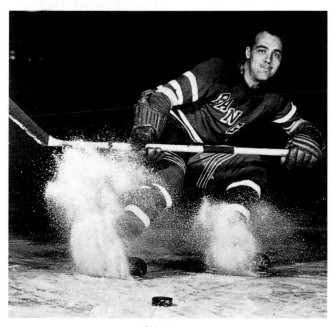

Phil Watson

- Toronto finishes in second place, three points out of first. Turk Broda, Toronto's stalwart in goal, is second in GAA (2.83) and leads the league in shutouts (six).

- Future Bruins star Phil Esposito is born on February 20, 1942, in Sault Ste. Marie, Ontario.

- In the playoffs, third-place Boston eliminates fourth-place Chicago in three games.

- The fifth-place Red Wings oust the sixth-place Habs in three games.

- Detroit sweeps Boston in their best-of-three semifinal series.

- Toronto wins the first two games of their best-of-seven semifinal series against the favored Rangers.

- The Rangers bounce back to win Game 3 of the semis on Jim Henry's 3-0 shutout, but Toronto wins two of the next three to stun the Rangers in six games.

Anderson Wins Hart Trophy, Loses His Job

The performance of Tom "Cowboy" Anderson was the only bright spot for the Brooklyn Americans during the 1941-42 season. The veteran defenseman delivered 12 goals and 29 assists for the cellar-dwelling Americans, earning the Scotland native the Hart Trophy. When the Amerks franchise folded at the conclusion of 1941-42, the 31-year-old Anderson found himself without an NHL employer and opted to finish his career in the American Hockey League.

Tom Anderson

Stanley Cup Quarterfinals

Bruins Beat Hawks in Quarterfinals

From 1938-39 through 1941-42, the NHL featured seven teams—and six of them made the playoffs. This photo captures the action of the 1942 quarterfinals between Boston and Chicago. Des Smith (not seen here) beats Hawks goaltender Sam LoPresti in sudden-death of Game 1 to give the Bruins a huge edge in the best-of-three quickie series. Chicago won the next game 4-0 but was eliminated in the third game 3-2. Boston went on to the semifinals, where it lost to Detroit.

Jack Adams

Adams Blows His Stack During Finals

The turning point in the 1942 Finals came at the conclusion of Game 4. Detroit was leading the game 3-2 when referee Mel Harwood made a couple of bad calls against the Wings. The Leafs stormed back to win the game 4-3, and Detroit coach Jack Adams stormed onto the ice and abused Harwood verbally and physically. Adams was suspended for the rest of the series and the Leafs went on to win the Cup. Harwood never refereed in the NHL again.

1941-42

- The Finals pit the Leafs against the Red Wings in what will be an historic series.

- Don Grosso scores the winners in Game 1 (3-2) and Game 2 (4-2) of the Finals as the Wings win in Toronto.

- The Wings cruise past the Leafs 5-2 in Game 3 of the Finals, giving Detroit a commanding three-game lead.

- After Carl Liscombe puts Detroit up 3-2 in the third period of Game 4, Syl Apps and Nick Metz score as Toronto averts elimination.

- Following Game 4 of the Finals, Detroit coach Jack Adams storms the ice and attacks referee Mel Harwood, whom Adams feels called a lousy game.

- League President Frank Calder suspends Adams indefinitely for his attack on referee Mel Harwood.

Former Stars Help Out the War Effort

Bun Cook, Frank Boucher, and Bill Cook (the three on the left) reunite for a charity game at Boston Garden on February 6, 1942. With many NHLers overseas, exhibition games featuring former stars were a profitable way to raise funds and awareness for the battles in Europe and the Pacific. On this evening, Boucher, coach of the Rangers, and Bun Cook, manager of the Providence Reds, stepped from behind the bench to dazzle their fans once again.

Bun Cook, Frank Boucher, Bill Cook

Langelle Nets Cup Winner in Game 7

Pete Langelle was a spare part on the very powerful Maple Leafs team of 1941-42. Langelle wasn't a member of the team's first-string line or the second-string unit, but he ended up scoring one of the biggest goals in team history. After winning Games 4, 5, and 6 of the Cup Finals against Detroit, Toronto was tied 1-1 in the third period of Game 7. Langelle scored at the 9:43 mark to clinch the Cup for the Leafs.

Pete Langelle

- The Leafs' offense explodes in Game 5 of the Finals. Don Metz scores a hat-trick as Toronto routs Detroit 9-3.

- Game 6 of the Finals features the brilliant goaltending of Turk Broda, who records a 3-0 shutout.

- In the third period of Game 7, the Leafs' Pete Langelle beats Johnny Mowers for the Cup-winning goal. Toronto wins 3-1.

- Toronto becomes the only team ever to overcome a three-game deficit in the Finals to win the Stanley Cup.

- Postseason awards go to Boston's Frank Brimsek (Vezina), Toronto's Syl Apps (Lady Byng), and Rangers rookie Grant Warwick (Calder).

- Tom "Cowboy" Anderson, the lone bright star in the Amerks' disastrous season, captures the Hart Trophy.

WORLD WAR NEARLY WIPES OUT NHL ROSTERS

By the spring of 1942, World War II was blazing from the Atlantic to the Pacific, and NHL rosters had been severely depleted by armed forces enlistments. "The situation was so bleak," said New York Rangers manager Lester Patrick, "that it appeared the league would not operate in the 1942-43 season."

However, in late summer 1942, the Canadian government advised the NHL owners to continue operating for the duration of the war. Still, it was hard to fill the rosters since players fit for military duty were urged to enlist, and they did so in droves. "They took the youngest and single guys first," said Jack Church of the Maple Leafs. "By 1942, a lot of NHL players started getting called."

No team was hurt more by the recruiting drive than the Rangers, who had finished first the previous season. The Rangers lost goalie Sugar Jim Henry to the armed forces and, when training camp opened in Winnipeg, the team didn't have a single goaltender on its roster. This inspired manager Lester Patrick to send an SOS to scouts all over Canada: "Send me a goaltender, any goaltender."

By opening night, the Blueshirts finally did dredge up a puck-stopper, but they had to reach all the way down to the Swift Current (Saskatchewan) Intermediates for Steve Buzinski. Steve was so bad that he soon earned the nickname Steve Buzinski "The Puck Goesinski." The Rangers ran through a string of hapless goalies—from Lionel Bouvrette to Bill Beveridge to Jimmy Franks—but none of them could cut it. As a result, the Blueshirts finished in last place, 11-31-8.

You almost got the feeling that the armed forces had better hockey players than the NHL. In fact, the U.S. Coast Guard organized a team of hockey pros called the Cutters at Curtis Bay in Maryland. The team featured All-Star Bruins goalie Frank Brimsek, Rangers captain Art Coulter, crack Black Hawks defenseman Johnny Mariucci, and Red Wings defenseman Alex Motter.

Despite the drop in quality, NHL games still had a unique allure to them. Fans became fascinated with ersatz wartime replacements such as Reg Bentley, older brother of Chicago Black Hawks stars Doug and Max Bentley. Reg played 11 games alongside his brothers before packing it in as a major-leaguer. Meanwhile, brother Doug led the league in scoring with 73 points.

The Red Wings, having lost fewer players to the armed forces than most clubs, reigned as the league's best team. Syd Howe powered the offense, while Johnny Mowers shined in goal. In the semifinals, the Wings dusted off the Maple Leafs four games to two. And in the Finals, Detroit swept the Bruins (who had lost their entire Kraut Line to the RCAF), with Mowers tossing shutouts in the final two affairs.

Despite the diluted NHL product, people were flocking to the games. "The public will support hockey," concluded *Montreal Gazette* columnist Dink Carroll, "as long as there are games to watch."

1942-43

- The NHL suspends regular-season overtime to better meet wartime train schedules.

- Teams are limited to 14 players. The 12-player minimum is abolished.

- The financially strapped Americans fold, leaving the NHL with six teams (four to make the playoffs). The league will remain a six-team league for the next quarter-century.

- The regular-season schedule is expanded by two games, to 50.

- NHL President Frank Calder dies of a heart attack. Former Americans boss Red Dutton takes over. Former NHL referee Clarence Campbell—Calder's designee as his successor—waits in the wings.

- Military service in Europe and the Pacific continues to ravage NHL lineups.

In the wartime years, many of the league's best players joined the armed forces. Before heading overseas, most players were stationed at boot camps around Canada, learning their new jobs and waiting for the call to Europe. In Ottawa, the RCAF Flyers boasted the Kraut Line of Bauer, Dumart, and Schmidt and captured the Allan Cup in 1941-42. In 1942-43, another armed forces team, the Ottawa Commandos, won Canada's senior hockey title.

• On January 14, 1943, Montreal's Alex Smart tallies four points (including three goals) in his first NHL game, setting a record.

• On January 28, 1943, Chicago's Max Bentley ties an NHL record when he scores four goals in one period.

• On February 6, 1943, Montreal's Ray Getliffe records the league's first five-goal game in 11 years when he beats up on goalie Frank Brimsek and the Bruins. The Habs win 8-3.

• While the line of Elmer Lach, Toe Blake, and Joe Benoit dominates the scoring, the Habs break in a new talent—right winger Maurice "Rocket" Richard.

• Doug Bentley, Chicago's scrappy left winger, bangs home a league-high 33 goals.

• Doug Bentley also wins the scoring title (73 points).

Gaye Stewart

World War II Takes Its Toll on the NHL

Toronto manager Conn Smythe liked to see his men in uniform. Here, he congratulates big Syl Apps on his new job with the Canadian fighting team as Leafs coach Hap Day (between them) looks on. The war really began to sink its teeth into the NHL in 1942-43. Overtime was discontinued because of wartime restrictions on train travel. Also, NHL rosters were trimmed from 15 players to 14.

Syl Apps, Conn Smythe

Stewart's the First Flying Fort to Star

The rebuilding Maple Leafs found a fresh new face in Gaye Stewart, who led all rookies in 1942-43 with 24 goals and 47 points to capture the Calder Trophy. Stewart, from Fort William, Ontario, was teamed with another rookie from the same town, Norman "Bud" Poile, who compiled 35 points. Amazingly, a third native of Fort William, Gus Bodnar, joined the Leafs in 1943-44, and the Flying Forts Line was born.

Earl Seibert, Art Weibe, Bob Carse, Red Hamill

Hawks' Hamill Prepared to Join Service

Red Hamill (right) says goodbye to his teammates as he leaves the Hawks' dressing room on February 7, 1943, to report for his military service examination in Toronto. Saying goodbye to him are (left to right) Earl Seibert, Art Wiebe, and Bob Carse. Wiebe is holding Hamill's jersey, promising to save it for Hamill's return. Hamill ended up finishing the season with the Hawks, but he spent the next two years in the service.

1942-43

- Boston's Bill Cowley leads the NHL in assists (45). He's second behind Doug Bentley with 72 points.

- Chicago's Max Bentley, kid brother of linemate Doug, is second in the NHL in assists (44) and third in points (70).

- Playing for a new team, Gord Drillon scores 28 goals—third overall in the NHL—for the Canadiens.

- Chicago's Red Hamill pots 28 goals, tying him for third in the league.

- Buddy O'Connor, Montreal's sophomore sensation, is third in

assists (43), ahead of Toronto's Billy Taylor (42).

- The Rangers suffer a collapse without Sugar Jim Henry in goal, as they fall to last place (11-31-8).

- Rangers goalie Steve Buzinski posts a 6.11 GAA in nine games and earns

Reggie, Max, and Doug Bentley

Bentley Bros. Play Together in Windy City

Denizens of the Chicago Stadium were treated to a rare lineup in 1942-43. This is the All-Bentley Team, with Max at center, Doug on right wing, and the oldest of the Bentley trio, Reg, playing on the left wing. Reggie Bentley, six years older than Max and two years older than Doug, played only one year in the NHL. In his single season, he played in 11 games and notched one goal and a pair of assists for a career total of three points.

Dutton Named NHL President

When Big Bill Dwyer's son, Big Bill Jr., took over the New York Americans franchise from his dad, he moved Mervyn "Red" Dutton to the bench to coach the ailing franchise. That was in 1935. In 1942-43, Dutton was out of a job, with the Americans ceasing operations. As a consolation prize, Dutton was given the job of NHL president. He replaced Frank Calder, who died February 4, 1943.

Red Dutton

Getliffe Beats Brimsek Five Times

After six years of modest scoring, Ray Getliffe picked up the pace during the war years of 1942-43 (18-28-46) and 1943-44 (28-25-53). On February 6, 1943, he enjoyed 60 minutes of glory. Getliffe became the first NHLer since 1932 to score five goals in a game. He did it against a Hall of Fame goalie too—Boston's Frank Brimsek.

Ray Getliffe

the nickname Steve Buzinski "The Puck Goesinski."

• Bryan Hextall, the Rangers' gifted right winger, continues to score well (27-32-59).

• Detroit's Jimmy Orlando takes the penalty title (99 minutes) but is

bloodied in a stick fight with Toronto rookie Gaye Stewart.

• Detroit wins the regular-season title (25-14-11).

• Red Wings goalie Johnny Mowers leads the NHL in victories (25), shutouts (six), and GAA (2.47).

• The Bruins, thanks to Bill Cowley and Frank Brimsek, finish in second place (24-17-9).

• Toronto (third place) and Montreal (fourth place) take the final two playoff positions, as Chicago and the Rangers are shut out.

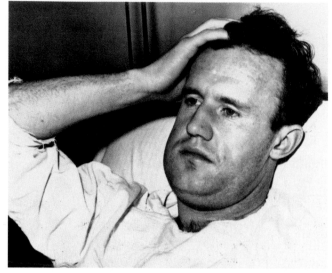

Bill Cowley

Steve Buzinski

Goaltender Buzinski Lets Puck Go Inski

Goaltender Steve Buzinski may not have had the greatest career in hockey, but this Ranger anomaly may have had the greatest nickname in the game. They called him "Steve Buzinski, The Puck Goesinski" on account of his less-than-stellar play in 1942-43. Buzinski played 560 minutes of NHL hockey and posted a horrific 6.11 GAA. On one occasion, he went to clear the puck and accidentally slipped it into his own net.

Ailing Cowley Bounces Back

In 1941-42, Cowboy Bill Cowley suffered a compound fracture on the lower right jaw during a game against Detroit. He missed much of the season as a result. The following year, Cowley rebounded with the most productive season of his career. The Bruins' centerman played in 48 matches, scored 27 goals, and bested all skaters in assists with 45. Cowley's 72 points were one off the league lead of 73, produced by Doug Bentley.

Goalie Mowers Mows 'Em Down

The 1942-43 season was not the end of the line for Red Wings goaltender Johnny Mowers, but it was his last stand as a first-line backstop in the NHL. In 1941-42, Mowers had the dubious distinction of losing more games than any other goaltender, with 19 wins and 25 losses. In 1942-43, he turned this around, winning more games than anyone, with 25, and topping his season with a 2.20 playoff average, a Vezina Trophy, and the Stanley Cup.

Johnny Mowers

1942-43

- Game 2 of the Detroit-Toronto series extends to quadruple O.T. before 20-year-old Maple Leaf Jack McLean beats Johnny Mowers for the winner.

- With the series deadlocked after four games, the Red Wings shut down Toronto with a pair of wins, taking

Game 5 4-2 and clinching the series on Adam Brown's overtime goal in Game 6.

- The Bruins, still without their top players, play with guts and determination to beat Montreal four games to one.

- Three of Boston's semifinal wins are in O.T., as Don Gallinger, Busher Jackson, and Ab DeMarco victimize Montreal goalie Paul Bibeault.

- The Stanley Cup Finals are anticlimactic, as the powerful Red Wings sweep Boston in four games.

McLean Ends Marathon Game

Jackie McLean skated his way through the ranks of amateur and minor-league hockey to find himself the Leafs' most promising rookie forward in 1942-43. In his 27 appearances, the fewest among Leafs forward men, McLean found the net nine times and helped his fellows for eight more. His biggest goal came in the semifinals against Detroit, when he scored at the 10:18 mark of the fourth overtime. It ended the third-longest game in NHL history.

Stanley Cup Finals

Wings Sweep Bruins in Cup Finals

Detroit goalie Johnny Mowers leaves his cage to smother a long shot from Boston's Jack Crawford (not in picture) in the first period of the third game of the 1943 Finals. Boston's Don Gallinger (#11) and Detroit's Jack Stewart (#2) scramble for a rebound. Mowers gave up five goals in the first two games of the series and shut the Bruins out for the next two. The Wings swept the series for their only Stanley Cup of the decade.

Jackie McLean

• Detroit wins Game 1 of the Finals 6-2, thanks to a hat-trick by Mud Bruneteau. The Wings beat Boston in Game 2 4-3.

• Johnny Mowers records shutouts in Games 3 and 4 of the Finals, winning 4-0 and 2-0. The Wings skate off with their third Stanley Cup.

• Carl Liscombe, Detroit's talented left winger, leads all playoff scorers with 14 points.

• Bill Cowley, the year's assist leader, is awarded the Hart Trophy.

• Detroit goalie Johnny Mowers wins the Vezina Trophy.

• Toronto winger Gaye Stewart (24 goals, 47 points) captures the Calder Trophy. Max Bentley, whose brother took the scoring title, is honored with the Lady Byng Trophy.

• Future goalie great Tony Esposito is born on April 23, 1943, in Sault Ste. Marie, Ontario.

MONTREAL'S PUNCH LINE HAS THE LAST LAUGH

They were called the Punch Line, but there was nothing funny about their play. The trio of Rocket Richard, Elmer Lach, and Toe Blake terrorized opponents, especially in the mid-1940s when the Canadiens featured perhaps the most dominating teams in hockey history.

Because of his elan and flamboyant goal-scoring, Richard inevitably obtained the most attention, but Blake made the trio tick. "He was the line's spark-plug," said hockey historian William Roche, "and its anchor."

The triumvirate first played together in 1943-44. Before the season, Montreal coach Dick Irvin had realized that his young right wing, Richard, was capable of spectacular production if aligned with the proper linemates. Irvin had theorized that the hard-nosed Lach was the ideal center for Richard, but he wasn't sure about left wing. He finally decided that Blake would be worthy of an experiment on the unit, and in no time the line was made for keeps.

Originally nicknamed the Mad Dog Line, the trio was more appropriately renamed the Punch Line. Fortified by this powerful unit—as well as a stellar defense and the goal work of rookie Bill

Durnan (who finished with a 2.18 GAA)—the Canadiens opened the 1943-44 season like gangbusters. By midseason, they had a dizzying record of 20-2-3 and were a full 13 points ahead of second-place Toronto.

Montreal finished the season at 38-5-7 and was expected to romp in the playoffs. Toronto stunned Montreal in the opening round by beating them 3-1 in Game 1, but that just served as a wake-up call. In Game 2, the Rocket turned on the juice, scoring all five Montreal goals in a 5-1 rout. The last time a player had scored five or more goals in a Stanley Cup match was in 1917, when Seattle's Bernie Morris netted six against Les Canadiens. The Leafs closely guarded Richard in Game 3, but Glen Harmon and

Ray Getliffe knocked home goals in the 2-1 Montreal win.

From that point on, the Canadiens juggernaut couldn't be contained. Montreal won Game 4 4-1 at Maple Leaf Gardens, then wrapped up the series in Toronto with a devastating 11-0 romp. The Canadiens moved on to the Stanley Cup Finals to play the Black Hawks, who had dispatched Detroit in five semifinal games.

Montreal jumped all over the Hawks, beating them 5-1 in the first game and 3-1 in the second, with Richard scoring all three goals. In Chicago for Game 3, the Hawks moved to a 2-1 lead in the third period, but Mike McMahon and Phil Watson scored for Montreal to fashion a 3-2 victory and an insurmountable lead in the series.

The Canadiens took Game 4 on an overtime goal by Blake, who already had four assists in the game. The Habs took the series in four games and were Stanley Cup champions for the first time in 13 years—mostly because of Richard and the Punch Line. Montreal would be just as devastating in 1944-45, with the team going 38-8-4 and the Punch Liners finishing 1-2-3 in scoring.

1943-44

- The "modern age" of hockey begins, as the NHL introduces the center red line to speed up the game and reduce off-sides.

- Delayed penalties are instituted. Action is not stopped until the "guilty" team touches the puck.

- While other teams are weakened by the war, the Montreal Canadiens emerge as a new power.

- Montreal goes 38-5-7 and doesn't lose a game at home. The Habs have the league's best offense (234 goals) and easily the best defense (109 goals against).

- The Paul Bibeault experiment ends, as the Habs go with gifted rookie Bill Durnan in goal.

- In Montreal, the Habs replace Joe Benoit on the right side of Elmer Lach and Toe Blake with upcoming superstar Maurice Richard. In his first full NHL season, Richard nets 32.

Early in the 1943-44 season, Montreal coach Dick Irvin put a feisty young sophomore named Maurice Richard (left) on a line with veterans Toe Blake (right) and Elmer Lach (center), and the legendary Punch Line was born. Richard, who missed most of 1942-43 with injuries, exploded for 32 goals, while Blake and Lach added 26 and 24 goals, respectively. Paced by the new line's scoring "punch," the Canadiens finished with an incredible 38-5-7 record.

• Montreal's trio of Elmer Lach, Toe Blake, and Maurice Richard is dubbed the Punch Line.

• The Rangers, without many of their better players, remain mired in last place. They finish 6-39-5—their worst record of all time.

• Rangers coach Frank Boucher, age 42, attempts a comeback. He plays 15 games and notches 14 points.

• Goalie Tubby McAuley, an NHL rookie, loses all 39 Rangers games and posts a horrific 6.20 GAA. The Rangers' 6.20 GAA is the league's highest since 1919-20.

• Though they can't afford the loss in talent, the Rangers "lend" Phil Watson to the Habs for the entire season.

• On October 30, 1943, Gus Bodnar scores the fastest goal ever by a rookie in his first NHL game when he scores 15 seconds into Toronto's win over New York.

Durnan Signs with Habs, Stars in Net

Montreal unveiled a new goaltender in 1943-44, 28-year-old rookie Bill Durnan. Although the Habs had wanted Durnan to turn pro for many years, he was content to play senior hockey in the Montreal area. In 1943-44, with a lucrative contract in his pocket, Durnan became the NHL's best goalie, leading the league in wins (38) and GAA (2.18) and claiming the Vezina Trophy. In the playoffs, Durnan went 8-1 as Montreal marched to the Stanley Cup.

Cain Scores 82 to Set an NHL Record

Herb Cain poses with Bruins manager Art Ross and teammate Bobby Bauer in a prewar photo. Cain, who had played for the Maroons and Canadiens before joining the Bruins in 1939, scored 82 points in 1943-44 to shatter the NHL record. Ironically, he had never scored more than 36 points in any previous season. Despite Cain's super performance, the Bruins finished out of the postseason hunt, finishing fifth with a 19-26-5 mark.

Herb Cain, Art Ross, Bobby Bauer

Bill Durnan

Gus Bodnar

Rookie Bodnar Scores in an Instant

Gus Bodnar was expected to make a contribution to the Maple Leafs in 1943-44, but no one predicted he would make his presence felt so darn quickly. Fifteen seconds into his first NHL shift, Bodnar slipped a wrist shot behind Rangers goaltender Ken McAuley to set a record for the fastest goal by a rookie in his first game. Bodnar went on to capture the Calder Trophy, collecting 22 goals and 40 assists.

1943-44

- On January 23, 1944, Detroit routs the Rangers 15-0, setting the all-time NHL record for the most lopsided victory.

- On February 3, 1944, Detroit's Syd Howe scores six goals in a 12-2 drubbing of the Rangers. It's the NHL's first six-goal game in 23 years.

- Herb Cain, Boston's 31-year-old left winger, wins the scoring title with a record 82 points—46 points better than his previous best season.

- Doug Bentley, Chicago's port-side sniper, is the game's most prolific goal-scorer (38).

- Ex-Ranger Clint Smith, the center on Doug Bentley's line in Chicago, leads the NHL in assists (49).

- Detroit's Carl Liscombe, Boston's Herb Cain, and Toronto's Lorne Carr tie for second in the NHL in goals with 36 apiece.

New Red Line Marks Birth of Modern Era

The NHL unveiled a new rule in 1943-44 that would dramatically affect the way the game would be played. The league introduced the center red line, which opened the game to forward passing from zone to zone and blue-line to blueline. The new rule transformed the sport from a stick-handling game to more of a passing game, which rewarded teams adept at rapid transition from defense to offense. Opening up the passing lanes marked the beginning of hockey's modern era.

Red Line

Turk Broda

Broda One of Many Stars to Fight in War

By the 1943-44 season, many of the NHL's greatest stars were serving overseas in the armed forces. Toronto lost Turk Broda (right), Syl Apps, Sweeney Schriner, and Gaye Stewart. Boston lost the entire Kraut Line. The Rangers were the hardest hit, losing most of their front-line players. The franchise considered folding but hung on despite a record of 6-39-5 in 1943-44.

• Mud Bruneteau has a career year, scoring 35 goals for the Red Wings.

• Toronto's attack is spearheaded by Lorne Carr (74 points).

• Toronto's Babe Pratt sets a new standard for offensive defensemen with 17 goals and 57 points.

• The Maple Leafs, who finish third overall, debut a young center with a big future—Teeder Kennedy.

• Montreal's Elmer Lach finishes fifth in the league in points (72).

• Mike McMahon, Montreal's scrappy 5'8" defenseman, leads the NHL in penalty minutes (99), edging Boston's Pat Egan (95) by a pair of minors.

• Bill Durnan, the Habs' rookie goalie, leads the league in victories (38) and GAA (2.18) in what is a sign of things to come.

Clint Smith

Smith Sets a New Standard for Assists

Clint Smith played a respectable, if not stellar, seven years in New York with the Rangers, winning his one and only Stanley Cup in 1939-40. In 1943-44, Smith sailed out of his doldrums, recording an NHL-record 49 assists and 23 goals for 72 points. Moreover, he helped left winger Doug Bentley win the goal-scoring race. For his outstanding play, and his four minutes in the sin bin, Smith won the Lady Byng Trophy.

Tubby McAuley

Tubby's as Bad as It Gets in Nets

During the war years, the Rangers were having real trouble finding a plumber to back up their able defensive squad of Ott Heller and Bucko McDonald. After the fiasco of 1942-43, they gave the nod to Ken "Tubby" McAuley in 1943-44. McAuley didn't give the Madison Square faithful much to cheer about, however, allowing 310 goals in the 50-game season (6.20 GAA) and leading his club into the NHL's dark cellar.

Doug Bentley

Doug Bentley Holds Up the Family Name

As the only Bentley in the Chicago lineup for 1943-44, Doug Bentley had a family tradition to uphold. He did so with the flair expected of Saskatchewan's No. 1 son, tallying a league-high 38 goals and 39 assists for a total of 77 points—plus 12 in the playoffs. His brother Max was in the service in 1943-44 and 1944-45. However, the two teamed up again in 1945-46 and put on a terrific show, combining for over 100 points.

1943-44

- Toronto's Paul Bibeault leads the league in shutouts (five).

- Toronto and Chicago sew up the last two playoff berths, as Boston and the Rangers slip from contention.

- Toronto stuns Montreal with a 3-1 victory in Game 1 of the semifinals.

It's the first home loss of the season for the Canadiens.

- The Habs beat the Leafs in Game 2 5-1, as Maurice Richard amazingly scores all five Montreal goals. The Canadiens go on to take the remaining three games of the series.

- Not only do the Black Hawks upset Detroit in their semifinal series, but they do so in five games.

- The Finals are never in question, as the Canadiens reel off four straight wins to sweep past the Hawks and celebrate their first Cup in 13 years.

League Gets a Good Look at Richard

A very young Maurice Richard gives us a glimpse of the face all goaltenders of his time feared the most. In his rookie season, 1942-43, a hobbled Richard collected 11 points in 16 games. In 1943-44, his injuries healed, he scored 32 goals and assisted on 22 more. Rocket really took off in the postseason. In just nine playoff games, he collected 12 goals and 17 points, the highest playoff points total of his career.

Pratt Scores Big, Wins Hart Trophy

Babe Pratt had one of his finest seasons in 1943-44. Pratt was known to play the odds on and off the rink; he liked to gamble. Off the ice, it was cards and ponies. On the ice, it was leaving the defense unattended as he swooped up ice to try his luck against NHL goaltenders. In 1943-44, he found the mark 17 times and registered 40 assists, a defensive record that would stand for 21 years. Pratt was honored with the year's Hart Trophy.

Howe Scores Six Goals in One Game

Detroit is known for producing automobiles and hockey stars named Howe. In 1943-44, Syd Howe did something that Gordie and Marty never did. On February 3, 1944, Howe scored six goals as Detroit shellacked the Rangers 12-2. Sure, the goals came against Tubby McAuley, one of the worst goalies in NHL history, but Howe was the only NHLer between 1921 and 1967 to net a half-dozen in a game.

Maurice Richard

Babe Pratt

Syd Howe

- Toe Blake, Maurice Richard, and Phil Watson fire game-winners in the first three games of the Finals, as Montreal wins by scores of 5-1, 3-1, and 3-2.

- Montreal clinches the Cup with a 5-4 overtime win in Game 4. Toe Blake converts a pass from Butch

Bouchard and beats Mike Karakas at 9:12 of the extra session.

- Maurice Richard's 12 postseason goals are the most in the playoffs since Newsy Lalonde's 17 in 1919.

- Toe Blake's 18 playoff points match Newsy Lalonde's record feat of 1919.

- Babe Pratt, Toronto's ace defenseman, captures the Hart Trophy. Chicago's Clint Smith earns his second Lady Byng Trophy.

- Montreal rookie Bill Durnan is awarded the Vezina Trophy. Gus Bodnar of the Leafs captures the Calder Trophy.

ULCERS KEEPS HIS COOL, LEADS LEAFS TO THE CUP

In NHL annals, there never was a more incongruous player than Frank McCool. The Maple Leafs puck-stopper for 1944-45 was a tall, skinny Albertan who appeared eminently suited for the job of librarian or bank clerk, but not goaltender. Moreover, McCool was hardly cool under pressure. In fact, this nervous Nellie was afflicted by a chronic case of ulcers and needed frequent infusions of milk to steady his stomach.

"Every game was a life-and-death struggle for Frank," remembered Leafs publicist Ed Fitkin. "He sipped milk in the dressing room between periods, and there were times when he took sick during a game. But one thing about him, he'd never quit."

Toronto turned to "Ulcers" McCool in 1944-45 because regular goaltender Turk Broda was serving his military duty. McCool was an average NHL goalie during the regular season, posting a 3.22 GAA. And though he earned the Calder Trophy, experts believed that he would be Toronto's Achilles' heel in the postseason.

In the opening round, Toronto was forced to face the powerful Canadiens, who had gone 38-8-4 during the season. Ulcers notwithstanding, McCool performed brilliantly in Game 1, matching Habs goalie Bill Durnan save for save. The game was tied 0-0 late in the third period when Toronto's Ted Kennedy avoided overtime with a backhand goal with 22 seconds left. McCool had scored a shutout in his first playoff game and—proving his performance was not a fluke—came back two nights later to stun the Canadiens once more, winning 3-2.

After Montreal won the third game 4-1, Gus Bodnar's overtime goal in Game 4 gave the Leafs a 3-1 series lead. Montreal got one back, dominating the Leafs 10-3 in Game 5, but Toronto rebounded and defeated the Habs in six games, completing one of the most gigantic upsets in NHL history. After the sixth game, the trembling McCool bubbled, "Somebody get me a glass of milk before I pass out."

The Leafs advanced to face the Red Wings, who had finished the regular season 15 points ahead of them. Many in the Toronto camp wondered whether McCool's ulcers could stand the pressure of the Stanley Cup Finals.

To the astonishment of everyone, McCool staked the Maple Leafs to three consecutive shutouts—1-0, 2-0, and 1-0. Finally, after 188 minutes and 35 seconds without a Detroit score, McCool gave up a goal early in Game 4, which Detroit captured by a count of 5-3. The Wings proceeded to win Game 5 2-0. Though Game 6 was a scoreless affair through regulation, Ed Bruneteau beat McCool at 14:16 of overtime.

In the final game, McCool experienced more stomach aches. He exited to the dressing room for an antacid, then returned in mint condition while the teams battled through the third period tied 1-1. Late in the game, Toronto defenseman Babe Pratt hammered in a power-play goal. McCool hung on for a 2-1 victory, ending the most nerve-racking—but most rewarding—year of his life.

1944-45

• The NHL's attempts to improve scoring lead to dramatic results.

• In Montreal, a legend grows as Maurice "Rocket" Richard scores at an unheard of goal-per-game rate.

• On December 28, 1944, Montreal's Maurice Richard sets an NHL record with eight points in one game. He burns Detroit for five goals and three assists in a 9-1 blowout.

• On January 21, 1945, the Bruins score four goals within a minute and 20 seconds in a 14-3 rout of the Rangers.

• Montreal again dominates the league, going 38-8-4 and outdistancing second-place Detroit by 13 points.

• The Red Wings initiate Ted Lindsay, a scrappy winger who skates with Syd Howe and Mud Bruneteau on the Wings' top line.

Maple Leafs Babe Pratt (left) and Frank McCool (right) spend some quality time with a pair of youngsters. McCool played only two seasons of NHL hockey, but in the first of those, in 1944-45, he set an example for would-be goalies, registering a 3.22 GAA and winning the Calder Trophy. McCool, nicknamed "Ulcers" because of his terrible jitters on the ice, was as cool as the Chicoutimi Cucumber in the 1945 Finals, tossing back-to-back-to-back shutouts.

• The Maple Leafs finish a distant third, 28 points off the pace.

• Chicago, with Doug and Max Bentley serving military duty, stumbles to a fifth-place finish.

• The members of Montreal's Punch Line finish 1-2-3 in NHL scoring.

• Montreal's Elmer Lach, the savvy center who feeds Maurice Richard, sets an NHL record for assists (54) and leads the league in scoring (80).

• Rocket Richard records the NHL's first 50-goal season, scoring 50 goals in 50 games. He also finishes second in the league in points (73).

• Montreal's Toe Blake ties for second in the NHL in goals (29) and finishes third in points (67).

• Toronto's Teeder Kennedy ties Toe Blake for second in goals (29).

• Chicago's Bill Mosienko, a future hero for the Hawks, nets 28 goals.

Billy Taylor, Gaye Stewart, Syl Apps, Bud Poile

War Vets Hope the NHL Will Take Them Back

Four members of the Maple Leafs who fought in World War II were Billy Taylor, Gaye Stewart, Syl Apps, and Bud Poile. Among the worries that these brave soldiers faced was the concern that their on-ice jobs would be gone when they returned form the war. Although many of the stars found their old roster spots waiting for them, many others had simply grown too old to compete against the younger legs that had replaced them.

Kennedy's the Leader of the Leafs

Maple Leafs center Ted "Teeder" Kennedy entered his third season of NHL play in 1944-45. Kennedy was becoming one of the team's leaders, marshalling his defensemen, keeping the linesmen honest, and ensuring that the focus remained on the opposition. As an on-ice and off-ice leader of the team, it was fitting that he would show the boys how it was done, leading the team in points with 54.

Ted Kennedy

Hollett Leads Backliners in Scoring

Over the course of his 11-year NHL career, Flash Hollett had proved he was no slouch. Traded from Boston to Detroit in 1944, he was on the verge of entering his golden years. In 1944-45, Hollett sparked the Red Wings' defense. He scored a flashy 20 goals, more than any other backliner had ever scored, and tied Babe Pratt for the defensemen lead with 41 points.

Flash Hollett

1944-45

- Boston's indefatigable Bill Cowley continues to produce, finishing second overall in assists (40) and fourth in points (65).

- The Leafs install a new goalie, Frank McCool, as Turk Broda serves his military duty.

- The Red Wings, who used four goalies in 1943-44, rely most heavily on 18-year-old Harry "Apple Cheeks" Lumley.

- Chicago and the Rangers struggle to avoid the cellar. Mike Karakas loses a league-high 29 games for the Hawks.

- Rangers goalie Tubby McAuley follows a 6.20-GAA performance of last year with a still-disastrous 4.94 mark. This will be his last year in the league.

- Thanks largely to Montreal's tough defense, goalie Bill Durnan leads the league with a 2.42 GAA.

Maurice Richard, Toe Blake

Blake Lights the Lamp 29 Times

Toe Blake, the Old Lamplighter, relaxes with Canadiens linemate Maurice Richard. Blake, who started his career with the Montreal Maroons, had his finest season in 1938-39, when he captured both the Art Ross and Hart Trophies while skating for the Habs. In 1944-45, he collected a career-high 67 points with 29 goals and 38 assists. The Habs' captain since 1940, Blake was renowned for his consistent and intelligent style of play.

Lach Helps Richard Reach Magical Mark

When Maurice Richard broke the ice, becoming the first person to score 50 goals in 50 games in 1944-45, it had repercussions throughout the Montreal lineup. In order for Richard to scratch this new mark in the record books, somebody had to be feeding him the puck. That somebody was Elmer Lach. The centerman recorded 54 assists, a new NHL record, and tallied 80 points, good enough to lead the league. Linemate Toe Blake finished third in the league in scoring.

Elmer Lach

Jack Adams, Harry Lumley

Teenage Apple Cheeks Stars in Wings' Goal

Although there was a scarcity of players at every position during the war, there was a virtual goaltending famine in the mid-1940s. The Red Wings were forced to employ 17-year-old Harry Lumley between the pipes during the 1943-44 campaign. However, young Apple Cheeks was not out of place in a big-league uniform. In 1944-45, he earned Detroit's No. 1 goaltending job and posted a 2.21 postseason GAA as the Wings fell one game short of the Stanley Cup.

• Toronto rookie Frank McCool ties Chicago's Mike Karakas for the league lead in shutouts with four.

• Boston's Pat Egan leads the league in penalty minutes with 86.

• Joe Carveth leads Detroit with 54 points, one more than Syd Howe.

• Toronto's Babe Pratt and Detroit's Flash Hollett top NHL defensemen with 41 points apiece. Hollett is tops with 20 goals; he's the first defenseman ever to score 20.

• The Stanley Cup playoffs begin with a huge upset, as Toronto shocks the Canadiens in six semifinal games. The Leafs win twice—in Montreal—before the Canadiens win a game.

• Toronto takes a three-games-to-one lead over Montreal with a dramatic overtime victory in Game 4. Gus Bodnar pots the winning goal at the 12:36 mark.

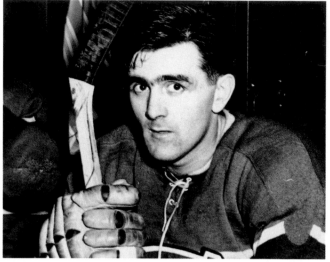

Maurice Richard

Mosienko Is Penalty-Free, Wins the Byng

The feisty Bill Mosienko played his entire career with the Black Hawks. The 5'8" right winger first made his mark in 1943-44, when he scored 32 goals. In 1944-45, before the famed Pony Line of Mosienko and the Bentley brothers was formed, Mosienko scored 54 points and remarkably spent no time in the penalty box. For his production and good behavior, he was awarded the Lady Byng Trophy.

Bill Mosienko

Richard Nets 50 Goals in 50 Games

Maurice "Rocket" Richard was as serious a competitor as the game has ever produced. At 5'10" he was not a big man, except where it counted: in the slot and in the winner's circle. Once the Rocket got it in his mind that he would put the puck into the net, heaven help anybody who got in his way. In 1944-45, he was fixated on the numbers game. He slammed in 50 goals in 50 regular-season matches, plus six more in his six playoff games.

Boxcar Spends Lots of Time in Box

When Pat Egan moved from Detroit to Boston, he brought some lumber with him. In his first full season with the Bruins, 1944-45, Egan lived up to his reputation as a tough guy, leading all bad boys with 86 minutes in the penalty box. Boxcar Egan, as he was known, was unable to derail his former Red Wings in the semifinal round, as Detroit prevailed in seven games. Egan played for four NHL teams in 11 years, but he never sipped Stanley Cup champagne.

Pat Egan

1944-45

- Montreal erupts for 10 goals in Game 5 of the semis, but the Leafs win Game 6 and advance.

- In the other semifinal series, the Red Wings take seven games to get past Boston, as each team posts strong wins on the road.

- The Stanley Cup Finals are a rematch of the 1942 Finals, when Toronto overcame a three-games-to-none disadvantage to stun Detroit.

- The Leafs win the first three Finals games by scores of 1-0, 2-0, and 1-0 as Frank McCool is unbelievable in

nets. Sweeney Schriner, Ted Kennedy, and Gus Bodnar score the winners.

- In a reversal of the 1942 Finals, the Red Wings fight back and tie the series.

- Detroit wins Game 4 of the Finals 5-3, then takes Game 5 2-0 thanks to Harry Lumley's shutout.

Pratt Scores Cup Winner in Game 7

In the 1940s, the Maple Leafs were never to be counted out of the running. In 1944-45, they finished third in the NHL. In the playoffs, however, Babe Pratt and the defensive squad held the high-scoring Habs in check and disposed of them in six games. In the tight final series with the Red Wings, Pratt netted the winner at 12:14 of the third period of the seventh game, giving the Leafs the Cup.

Babe Pratt

Carveth's 11 Playoff Points Lead League

As a minor-league prospect with the Detroit Pontiacs and Indianapolis Capitols, Jumpin' Joe Carveth showed considerable potential, and he delivered on that promise for the Red Wings during the 1944-45 season. Carveth tallied 26 goals and 28 assists during the regular season and a league-leading 11 points in the playoffs. Although the Wings dropped a seven-game decision to the Maple Leafs, Carveth scored key goals in two of Detroit's three victories.

Joe Carveth

Toronto Maple Leafs

Leafs' Win Over Habs a Real Stunner

Toronto captured the Stanley Cup in 1944-45 thanks to the efforts of rookie goalie Frank McCool (back row, second from left) and the scoring prowess of Ted Kennedy (middle row, fourth from left). The shocker came in the Stanley Cup semifinals, when the Leafs (24-22-4 on the year) upset the powerful Canadiens (38-8-4). Toronto was outscored 21-15 in the series but still won in six games.

• Game 6 of the Finals is scoreless after regulation, but the Wings break the deadlock at 14:16 of O.T. Eddie Bruneteau, whose older brother (Mud) scored the goal to end the longest game ever, nets the winner.

• The Leafs respond with a tense 2-1 victory in Game 7. Babe Pratt scores

the winner and Toronto captures its fourth Stanley Cup.

• Teeder Kennedy leads Toronto and all playoff scorers in goals with seven.

• Detroit's Joe Carveth is the postseason scoring champ (11 points).

• The Canadiens' Elmer Lach, the center on the Punch Line, captures the Hart Trophy. Teammate Bill Durnan again runs away with the Vezina Trophy.

• Frank McCool nabs the Calder Trophy while Chicago's Bill Mosienko wins the Lady Byng.

RETURNING WAR VETS FALL FLAT ON THE ICE

World War II ended during the summer of 1945, and by the opening of NHL training camps in September, many key players had returned from the service to rejoin their teams. The Rangers had been the hardest hit club by far, as they had lost much of their first-place 1942 squad to the armed forces. They finished last for three straight seasons (1942-43, 1943-44, 1944-45) and eagerly awaited their returning stars.

"When we went to camp," said coach Frank Boucher, "we had six of the soldiers back—Alf Pike, Neil and Mac Colville, Alex Shibicky, and the two Patricks, Muzz and Lynn. But it soon became apparent that most of them could not regain the skills that had made the Rangers soar."

Indeed, most of the NHL's returning stars had lost their touch when they returned. The Rangers also suffered the loss of captain and All-Star defenseman Art Coulter, who retired after serving in the U.S. Coast Guard. As a result, the Rangers finished last again in 1945-46 with a 13-28-9 record.

Bruins goalie Frank Brimsek returned to Boston from his Coast Guard stint but, like the returning Rangers, didn't display the same skills as before. The same could be said for Kraut Liners Bobby Bauer and Woody Dumart—although their center, Milt Schmidt, returned to his pre-war level of excellence. Toronto goalie Turk Broda still retained his youthful skills, but he returned too late in 1945-46 to help the Leafs, who finished out of the playoffs.

By contrast, the Canadiens' post-war regeneration suffered least. Many of their stars—Maurice Richard, Bill Durnan, Toe Blake, etc.—had not gone to war, and they entered the 1945-46 campaign without missing a beat. Durnan was still the world's best goalie, Richard the most dangerous scorer, and Emile "Butch" Bouchard the best defenseman.

Several critics, among them Boston Bruins manager Art Ross, had branded the Canadiens as "strictly a wartime club," but Richard and company maintained their superiority even after the war. As historian Ricky Black noted, "The Canadiens were capable of winning hockey games, war or no war."

Les Habs, led by their Punch Line, continued their explosive attack. Coach Dick Irvin employed a "fire wagon" style of hockey that pushed the Canadiens to first place and on a joyride through the playoffs. They swept Chicago in the opening round and rapidly dispatched the Bruins in the Stanley Cup Finals four games to one.

Fans flocked to the arenas in 1945-46, thanks to such magnetic attractions as Chicago's Max Bentley, who won the scoring title (31-30-61) as well as the Hart Trophy. Though many of the returning stars had lost a step, soothsayers predicted good times ahead for the NHL. After all, if the league could survive a decade of depression and five years of world war, then the succeeding years should be exciting and profitable. As it turned out, their predictions were right on target.

1945-46

- Applications for NHL franchises are filed in Philadelphia, Los Angeles, and San Francisco.

- The Philadelphia Arena Company of the American Hockey League seeks a court injunction prohibiting operation of an NHL franchise in their market.

- The Hall of Fame, 16 years before the completion of its building, names 14 inductees.

- Among the initial Hall of Fame inductees are Hobey Baker, Chuck Gardiner, Georges Vezina, Howie Morenz, Art Ross, Frank McGee, and Lord Stanley of Preston.

- In Boston, Art Ross steps down as coach and is replaced by Dit Clapper.

- Chicago's Max Bentley returns from the military in time for the season.

- Bruins goalie Frank Brimsek returns to the NHL after spending two years in the service.

Boston's Kitchener Kids returned to the fold during the 1945-46 season.
Although it took a little time for the "Krauts" to regain their skating legs and
timing, they were firing on all cylinders by the end of the campaign. Woody
Dumart had the finest year of the trio, clicking for 22 goals and 12 assists. With
Milt Schmidt (center), Bobby Bauer (left), and Dumart (right) bolstering the offense,
the Bruins climbed to second place with a 24-17-8 mark.

- Boston's Kraut Line—Milt Schmidt, Bobby Bauer, and Woody Dumart— returns to the NHL after three long years in the RCAF.

- The Rangers reunite Neil and Mac Colville with Alex Shibicky, but the war years have taken their toll and the line fails.

- The Maple Leafs are bolstered by the return of Syl Apps, Gaye Stewart, and Don Metz from military duty.

- Babe Pratt, Toronto's former Hart Trophy winner, is suspended for nine games after admitting to placing bets on hockey games.

- Coach Dick Irvin guides the Montreal Canadiens to another regular-season title (28-17-5). They give up the fewest goals in the league for the third straight year.

- The Bruins, with a rejuvenated lineup, climb from fourth place to second place.

Clapper Coaches, Mans the Blueline

After coaching the Bruins off and on since their inception, Art Ross stepped aside for good in 1945-46, handing the coaching reins to Dit Clapper (center), who continued to take a semi-regular shift for the Beantowners. Clapper suited up for his 19th season in 1945-46. Once one of the league's top forwards, Dit joined Eddie Shore on the Boston blueline in 1937-38, enabling him to contribute for another nine seasons.

Dit Clapper

Alex Shibicky

Shibicky, Blueshirts Stumble Along

Despite the return of Alex Shibicky and Neil and Mac Colville, the Rangers continued to struggle in 1945-46. Shibicky played in only 33 games, managing a mere 10 goals and 15 points. Although the Rangers remained deep in the NHL basement, there was reason for optimism. Edgar Laprade won the Calder Trophy, Chuck Rayner was acquired to stabilize the goaltending, and left winger Tony Leswick showed great promise.

Goalie Durnan Catches with Either Hand

Bill Durnan wasn't only the most outstanding goalie of the mid-1940s, he was also one of the most unusual. Durnan was ambidextrous, meaning he could shoot and catch with either hand. This way he could confuse the opposition and always have his catching glove protecting the wide side of the net. Durnan, whose symmetrical gloves are pictured here, won his third straight Vezina Trophy in 1945-46.

Bill Durnan's Gloves

1945-46

- Chicago's Pony Line—Max and Doug Bentley with Bill Mosienko—helps the Hawks lead the NHL in goals (200).

- Gaye Stewart leads the NHL in goals with 37 and is second in scoring with 52 points.

- Montreal center Elmer Lach is the league leader in assists (34) for the second straight year.

- The Black Hawks' Max Bentley is second overall in both goals (30) and assists (31). He wins the points title with 61.

- Montreal's Toe Blake is third in goals (29). Blake ties Chicago's Clint Smith for third place in the points race (50).

- Maurice Richard finishes fifth in points (27-21-48) one year after his historic 50-goal season.

Jack Stewart

Blake Adds Byng to Trophy Case

Today, the name Toe Blake evokes an image of a thick-set winning coach behind the Canadiens bench. In the 1930s and 1940s, Blake was known as one of the most successful left wingers in the game. In 1938-39, Blake won the Hart Trophy and also led the league in scoring. In 1945-46, Blake added the Lady Byng Trophy to his mantle by scoring 50 points—third in the league—and receiving only one penalty.

Toe Blake

Stewart Takes the Law into His Own Hands

Black Jack Stewart was an enforcement specialist for Detroit. It was said that whatever injustices got past the officials would be taken care of by Stewart. The problem for Stewart, however, was that his own brand of lawmaking often cost him lay-up time in the sin bin. In 1945-46, he led all penitents with 73 minutes in purgatory. Incidentally, Stewart remains the last penalty leader to tally fewer than 100 minutes.

Max Bentley

Bentley Rides High on the New Pony Line

Chicago's Max Bentley had a lot to smile about in 1945-46. Along with his brother Doug and right winger Bill Mosienko, he had established the Pony Line, Chicago's response to the old Kid Line in Toronto. The Ponies collected 149 points over the season, with Max—centerman for the trio—finishing second in the league in goals with 31 and first overall in scoring with 61 points. Chicago led the league in goals for the first time in 19 years.

- Montreal's Bill Durnan captures the GAA title (2.60).

- Black Jack Stewart, Detroit's nasty backliner, leads the NHL in penalty minutes with 73.

- In Detroit, left wing Adam Brown leads the team in points with just 31.

- The sixth-place Rangers introduce a new full-time goalie, former Americans netminder Chuck Rayner, but he leads the league in losses (21).

- The Rangers' only bright spot is rookie Edgar Laprade, their second-best scorer (34 points).

- One year after winning the Stanley Cup, the Maple Leafs finish in fifth place and out of the playoffs.

- With last year's playoff disaster still in their memories, the Canadiens blow out the Black Hawks in the semifinals. Montreal outscores Chicago 26-7 in a four-game sweep.

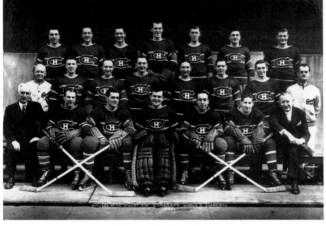

Montreal Canadiens

This Year's Habs Won't Be Denied

For the third year running, the Canadiens finished atop the NHL in 1945-46. In their two previous postseason outings, they had come home empty-handed, but this season was different. Maurice Richard, who slumped to 27 goals during the season, pumped in seven during the playoffs. Linemates Elmer Lach (17 points) and Toe Blake (13 points) helped Montreal blow out its playoff opponents, Chicago and Boston, by a combined score of 45-20.

Conn Smythe, Red Dutton, Babe Pratt

NHL Forgives Pratt for His Sins

Toronto manager Conn Smythe and Merv "Red" Dutton close the book on Babe Pratt's "lifetime" suspension for being involved with gamblers. Pratt admitted in 1945-46 to having dealt with gamblers, putting small bets on games he would later play in. Since, as Pratt claimed, the bets were small—and always paid him to win—the Board of Governors relented, allowing Pratt to reenter the league only a few games after his expulsion.

Stewart's 37 Goals Wasted in Toronto

While Montreal's Maurice Richard was suffering from goal-scoring amnesia in 1945-46, Toronto's Gaye Stewart was taking up where the Rocket left off. Stewart, playing on a line with Billy Taylor and Lorne Carr, scored 37 goals, first among NHL sharpshooters. His team, however, finished fifth in the six-team league, as sophomore goalie Frank McCool floundered in his second tour of duty.

Gaye Stewart

1945-46

- Second-place Boston has little trouble with the Red Wings, winning their semifinal series in five games.

- Game 5 of the Bruins-Red Wings semifinals goes to overtime before Don Gallinger clinches the series for Boston.

- Game 1 of the Finals goes to overtime before Montreal's Maurice Richard beats Frank Brimsek at 9:08 to give the Habs a 4-3 victory.

- Down 2-1 in Game 2 of the Finals, the Canadiens tie the game on Butch Bouchard's third-period goal and win on Jim Peters' O.T. goal at 16:55.

- In a relative blowout, Montreal wins Game 3 of the Finals 4-2, as the Canadiens' Kenny Mosdell scores twice.

- With their backs to the wall, the Bruins win Game 4 of the Finals 3-2 in overtime. Former Hab Terry Reardon scores at 15:13 of O.T.

Boston Bruins

Bruins Feeling Good After Beating Wings

Bruins manager Art Ross (extreme left) looks confident as his team arrives back in Boston after taking the Red Wings in Games 3 and 4 of the 1946 Cup semi-finals. Back in Beantown, the Bruins managed to squeak out a 4-3 overtime win to eliminate the Wings, but they would have to face the high-scoring Canadiens in the Finals. Ross and the Bruins managed to win just one game against the Habs, who boasted too much firepower.

Toronto Maple Leafs vs. New York Rangers

Aging Leafs Not What They Used to Be

Many of the Leafs' stars who had served overseas returned for the 1945-46 season, but even the efforts of Syl Apps (white jersey) couldn't revive the falling Leafs. Toronto fell from the Stanley Cup pent-house to the NHL outhouse, finishing in fifth place. Conn Smythe, still recovering from serious wounds suffered during battle, dumped many of Toronto's older legs—including Billy Taylor, Sweeney Schriner, and Lorne Carr—after the season.

• Elmer Lach and Dutch Hiller combine for two goals and five points as the Canadiens trounce Boston 6-3 in Game 5. Montreal thus wins its sixth Stanley Cup.

• Montreal's Elmer Lach is the playoff scoring leader with 17 points.

• The Canadiens' Toe Blake and Maurice Richard top the playoff charts with seven goals apiece.

• For his heroic post-war perfor-mance in the NHL, top scorer Max Bentley is presented with the Hart Trophy.

• Montreal's Toe Blake, a hero of the playoffs, skates off with the Lady Byng Trophy.

• Bill Durnan wins his third straight Vezina Trophy for the Habs.

• Rangers center Edgar Laprade captures the Calder Trophy.

GOALIES FEAR THE WRATH OF ROCKET RICHARD

By October 1946, all NHL players who had served in World War II had returned to their teams. And for the first time since the beginning of the war, the league opened a season in a relative state of normalcy. Having won two Stanley Cups in the previous three years, Montreal's Canadiens were the team to beat—and the man to stop was Maurice "Rocket" Richard.

"He can shoot from any angle," said Boston goalie Frank Brimsek. "You can play him for a shot to the upper corner and the Rocket wheels and fires a backhander to the near, lower part of the net."

Richard was the ultimate scorer. He not only owned all the offensive tools, but he also burned with an intensity that put fear in the hearts of goaltenders, who could actually see the desire on his face. "When he skated in on the net," said Hall of Fame goaltender Glenn Hall, "the Rocket's eyes would shine like a pair of searchlights. It was awesome to see him coming at you."

Richard had scored 50 goals during the 50-game 1944-45 season and continued to be the league's most intimidating shooter through 1946-47, when he scored 45 goals. To defuse the Rocket, teams employed a variety of tactics, many illegal. The Rangers' Tony Leswick and Detroit's Ted Lindsay constantly harassed Richard with insults and high sticks.

Toronto's Bill Ezinicki and Vic Lynn tried elbows and butt-ends to distract the Rocket. But Richard was an excellent boxer, and he occasionally punched out his assailants. During a game a couple years earlier, he twice kayoed Rangers defenseman Bob Dill—a former Golden Gloves boxer—in penalty box bouts. But too often, officials failed to penalize Richard's tormentors, causing the Rocket to lash out at officials both on and off the ice.

"Maurice became more and more frustrated," said Canadiens manager Frank Selke Sr. "It was only a matter of time before he would really explode."

The most damaging eruption took place after Montreal had finished first (34-16-10) and disposed of Boston in the opening playoff round. The Habs entered the Finals against the impudent Maple Leafs, who—in the first two games—rocked the Rocket with illegal assaults. In Game 2, Richard no longer could subdue his anger and viciously retaliated against Ezinicki and Lynn with high sticks, cutting both about the head. NHL President Clarence Campbell slapped Richard with a $250 fine and a one-game suspension.

The sentence, stiff for the day, traumatized the entire Canadiens team, and they proceeded to lose Game 3. When Richard returned for Game 4, he was uncharacteristically subdued and the Leafs won again, giving them a 3-1 lead in games.

Richard finally exploded for two goals and a Montreal win in the fifth game, but it was too little and too late. Toronto suffocated him in the sixth and final meeting, winning 2-1 in what was a major Cup upset. The Canadiens might have won the series had the Rocket's temper not gotten the best of him.

1946-47

- Based on informal hand gestures originated by Hall of Fame referee Bill Chadwick, the NHL adopts official signals to indicate penalties.

- The NHL mandates that linesmen from neutral cities be hired for every game.

- Red Dutton, who has served as NHL president following the death of Frank Calder in 1942, retires. The NHL installs a new president, former referee Clarence Campbell.

- Montreal announces the retirement of general manager Tommy Gorman, who is replaced by Frank Selke.

- The league announces it will dish out $1,000 to each trophy winner and each member of the All-Star team.

- The NHL's regular-season schedule is expanded from 50 games to 60 games.

In 1946-47, Montreal's Maurice Richard regained his power as a goal-scoring devil. With Elmer Lach laid up for much of the season, Buddy O'Connor filled in at center, shoveling pucks across to the Rocket who put them to good use. With strong goaltenders working across the NHL, Richard was hard-pressed to repeat his record 50-in-50 season, but he managed 45 goals in the 60-game campaign and added six more in the playoffs.

• The Montreal Canadiens capture their fourth straight regular-season title with a 34-16-10 record.

• The second-place Toronto Maple Leafs lead the league in goals (209) thanks to Ted Kennedy (28), Howie Meeker (27), and Syl Apps (25).

• Chicago falls from third place to sixth, losing 37 games despite Max Bentley's second scoring title.

• Chicago's Max Bentley is fourth in goals (29), second in assists (43), and first overall in points (72), edging Montreal's Maurice Richard by a point.

• After an "off" year, Montreal's Rocket Richard is first in goals (45).

• Boston's Bobby Bauer and Detroit's Roy Conacher tie for second in the league in goals (30).

• Detroit's Billy Taylor leads the league with a career-high 46 assists.

Chadwick's Hand Signals Adopted

Referee Bill Chadwick nails Canadiens forward Murph Chamberlain (#12) for an infraction during this Montreal-Toronto game. Chadwick was the first on-ice official to develop hand signals to indicate what penalty he was calling. With the hand signals, both the players and the fans knew immediately what call had been made. The NHL made such signals official for the 1946-47 season.

Bill Chadwick

Clarence Campbell

Campbell Appointed as NHL President

The NHL appointed a new president on September 5, 1946, when it hired Rhodes scholar Clarence S. Campbell to oversee the league's operations. Campbell was no stranger to hockey action since he was a former NHL referee. Campbell, who played hockey at Oxford with political luminaries Lester Pearson and Roland Mitchner, replaced Red Dutton, who had been temporarily serving as president since the death of Frank Calder in 1943.

Ted Kennedy

Teeder Leads Leafs, Scores Cup Winner

It started early in the 1946-47 season. Once, during a break in the action at Maple Leaf Gardens, a booming voice bellowed, "C'mon Teeeederrrr." It became the team's rallying cry. The "Teeder" in question was Ted Kennedy, who led the team in goals (28) and assists (32) in 1946-47. Kennedy was a quietly confident leader who was as classy as he was productive. He sealed his hero's status by scoring the Cup-winning goal on April 19, 1947.

1946-47

- The Red Wings debut a right winger from Saskatchewan named Gordie Howe.

- A feud between Montreal and Toronto erupts after Leafs winger Don Metz knocks Habs center Elmer Lach to the ice. Lach suffers a fractured skull, which ends his season.

- The Bruins finish in third place. The Kraut Liners—Woody Dumart, Milt Schmidt, and Bobby Bauer—combine for 81 goals and 168 points.

- Montreal's Bill Durnan leads the league in GAA (2.30) for the fourth straight year.

- Turk Broda, back in place as the Leafs' only netminder, is second in GAA (2.87) and shutouts (four).

- The Rangers finish out of the playoffs again, but goalie Chuck Rayner leads the league in shutouts with five.

Leafs Loaded with Famers

Toronto won its sixth Stanley Cup title in 1946-47, completing an impressive rebuilding job by manager Conn Smythe. Gaye Stewart, who led the NHL in goals in 1945-46, sits front row, far left. Next to him, left to right, are Hall of Famers Ted Kennedy, Smythe, Hap Day, and Syl Apps. Fellow Hall of Famers Harry Watson and Turk Broda stand behind Day and Apps.

Bill Durnan

Durnan Stops Pucks with Either Hand

In 1946-47, for the fourth year running, Bill Durnan won more games than any other NHL netminder (34) and registered the lowest average (2.30 GAA). Aside from captaining the team in 1947-48 (he remains the last goaltender to do so), Durnan had another idiosyncrasy: he was ambidextrous. He wore two catching gloves and no blocker.

Toronto Maple Leafs

• On January 8, 1947, Toronto's Howie Meeker sets an NHL rookie record with five goals in a 10-6 win over Chicago.

• On March 16, 1947, Detroit's Billy Taylor sets an NHL record with seven assists in a 10-4 win over Chicago.

• Toronto defeats Detroit 3-2 in Game 1 of their playoff series, as Howie Meeker wins it with an overtime goal. The Wings roar back in Game 2, winning 9-1.

• The Leafs bounce back with three straight wins, outscoring the Wings 14-3, to advance to the Finals.

• In the other playoff series, Montreal wins the first two games—the second on an O.T. goal by Ken Mosdell—before Boston prevails in Game 3.

• Montreal's awesome offense overwhelms Boston in Game 4, 5-1. John Quilty scores in double O.T. of Game 5 to put Montreal in the Finals.

Bentley Edges Rocket for Scoring Title

Despite finishing 16 goals behind Maurice Richard (45 to 29), Chicago's Max Bentley won the NHL scoring title in 1946-47, edging the Rocket 72 to 71. Nevertheless, Bentley would be traded to Toronto at the end of the season, making him one of just two players in NHL history to change teams after winning a scoring title. Joe Malone had moved from Quebec to the Montreal Canadiens after winning his 1919-20 scoring championship.

Howie Meeker

Max Bentley

Elmer Suffers 'Lach Jaw,' Cracked Skull

Elmer Lach was plagued by injury in 1946-47, slowing down what was looking like a repeat of his scoring-championship season of 1945-46. With a broken jaw bone, Lach had to suffer the endless jokes about his "Lach Jaw"—until being taken out of play entirely by a fractured skull. In the 31 games Lach did manage to play, he scored a very respectable 30 points, giving notice that he was still a shooter to be reckoned with.

Elmer Lach

Meeker, Not Howe, Wins the Calder

In 1946-47, Gordie Howe, the man who would become known as Mr. Hockey, made his debut in the NHL. One of the few awards Howe would not collect was the one he missed this year—the Calder Trophy. That's because another newcomer was shooting and scoring his way into the record books. Toronto's Howie Meeker fired 27 goals and added 18 assists for a freshman total of 45 points. For his efforts, Meeker was awarded the Calder as the NHL's rookie of the year.

1946-47

- The blowouts continue in the Finals, as Montreal stuffs Toronto 6-0 in Game 1.

- The Maple Leafs rebound from their Game 1 loss with a 4-0 victory in Game 2, as Turk Broda records a shutout.

- Maurice Richard is ejected from Game 2 for stick-swinging and is suspended for one game by NHL boss Clarence Campbell.

- In Toronto for Game 3, the Maple Leafs claim an easy 4-2 victory to go up two games to one.

- Montreal's Glen Harmon and Toronto's Harry Watson trade first-period goals in Game 4. The contest remains tied until 16:36 of overtime, when Syl Apps wins it for the Leafs.

- Their backs to the wall, the Habs take Game 5 3-1 on Maurice Richard's two goals.

Stanley Cup Semifinals

Leafs Oust Wings in Five Semi Games

Toronto's Wally Stanowski, Howie Meeker, Sid Smith, and Bill Barilko (left to right) circle a fallen Red Wing during the 1947 Stanley Cup semifinals. The Maple Leafs downed the Wings in five games to reach the Finals for the fourth time in the decade, despite being bombed 9-1 in Game 2 of the semis. Embarrassed by the blowout, the Leafs rebounded to win the next three games by the scores of 4-1, 4-1, and 6-1.

Stanley Cup Finals

Riled Leafs Come Back to Whip the Habs

After the Canadiens blanked the Maple Leafs 6-0 in the first game of the 1947 Finals, Habs goalie Bill Durnan (right) asked a nearby reporter, "How did these guys even make the playoffs?" When that statement hit the morning papers, it provided all the incentive the Leafs would need. Toronto won four of the next five games, completely shutting down the Habs by allowing only seven goals in the five matches.

- Buddy O'Connor scores at 25 seconds of Game 6 to give the Habs the early lead. However, Toronto's Vic Lynn and Teeder Kennedy score to give the Leafs a 2-1 win. The Leafs capture their sixth Stanley Cup.

- Maurice Richard leads all playoff scorers with six goals and 11 points.

- Maurice Richard captures his first Hart Trophy. Amazingly, it's the only one he'll ever win.

- Montreal's Bill Durnan grabs his fourth straight Vezina Trophy.

- Boston's Bobby Bauer wins his third Lady Byng Trophy.

- Toronto's Howie Meeker captures the Calder Trophy, beating out runner-up Jimmy Conacher of Detroit.

- The World Hockey Championships resume for the first time in eight years. Czechoslovakia, not Canada, winds up with the gold medal.

BENTLEY PUSHES THE LEAFS TO NEW HEIGHTS

When the Toronto Maple Leafs beat the Montreal Canadiens for the 1946-47 Stanley Cup, it was regarded as a fluke victory. Leafs owner Conn Smythe was well aware of the criticism and was determined to build a stronger, deeper team.

"We had two great centers in Syl Apps and Ted Kennedy," said Smythe. "If we could get one more, our strength down the middle would make us the best."

To achieve that goal, Smythe took an enormous gamble. He traded the youthful and talented Flying Forts Line of Bud Poile, Gaye Stewart, and Gus Bodnar—as well as highly regarded defenseman Bob Goldham and 1942 Cup hero Ernie Dickens—to Chicago. In return, he received 1946-47 scoring champion Max Bentley and minor-leaguer Cy Thomas. At the time, it was considered the biggest trade in hockey history. And the deal did precisely what Smythe had hoped, turning the Maple Leafs into a perfectly balanced hockey machine.

Turk Broda was the Vezina-winning goalie thanks to a talented, mean-spirited defense that protected him. Backliners Garth Boesch, Bill Barilko, Gus Mortson, Jim Thomson, and Wally Stanowski blended together perfectly—as did the three forward lines: Bill Ezinicki-Apps-Harry Watson, Howie Meeker-Kennedy-Vic Lynn, and Nick Metz-Bentley-Joe Klukay.

"It was the best Toronto team I ever had," said Smythe, who had operated the Leafs since 1927. "Bentley gave us strength down the center and was the final piece of the puzzle."

Max played some of his greatest hockey for the Maple Leafs, but he wasn't on the ice alone. Captain Apps was at the top of his game and goalie Broda never made more clutch saves. Ezinicki was belting everyone in sight, and the Kennedy line developed into one of the most exciting units since the days of Primeau, Jackson, and Conacher.

Moreover, another youngster, Barilko, had arrived in 1946-47 to give the Leafs some zip. Only 19 years old at the time, Barilko had been playing for the Hollywood Wolves of the old Pacific Coast League. Smythe phoned coach Tommy Anderson for a report on Barilko. "He's pretty green," said Anderson, "but he's a big boy, not afraid of anyone. And he learns fast."

Barilko learned fast, and by the 1947-48 season he had developed a "snake-hips" body-check that put the fear of God into opponents. Elmer Lach of the Canadiens said: "Barilko is the hardest hitter in the league. When he hits you, he hurts you."

Toronto finished the 1947-48 season in first place (32-15-13), and their success was no longer considered a fluke. The Leafs flew past Boston in the semifinals four games to one, and then steam-rolled the Red Wings in the Finals.

The Wings were no match for Smythe's greatest team. With the three lines clicking and Broda deflecting the rubber, Toronto broomed Detroit in four straight, humiliating the Wings 7-2 in the finale. With two straight Cups, the Maple Leafs were on their way to becoming a dynasty.

1947-48

- The league introduces several measures, including awarding goals and penalty shots and assessing major penalties, to eliminate stick throwing.

- Future Canadiens goalie Ken Dryden is born on August 8, 1947, in Hamilton, Ontario.

- Art Ross donates the Art Ross Trophy to the NHL. It will be awarded annually to the NHL's scoring leader.

- The first "annual" All-Star Game is held on October 13, 1947. The Leafs, defending Cup champs, lose to the NHL team of All-Stars 4-3.

- In a seven-player blockbuster trade, Toronto acquires Max Bentley from Chicago (with Cy Thomas) for Gus Bodnar, Gaye Stewart, Bud Poile, Bob Goldham, and Ernie Dickens.

- In a move they will regret, the Habs trade Buddy O'Connor, a sleek center, to the Rangers.

Doug Bentley laughs with brother Max shortly after Max was traded to the Maple Leafs in November 1947. Although the Leafs had two front-line centermen in Syl Apps and Ted Kennedy, Conn Smythe realized that there was room for a third, especially if that third was one of the NHL's top scorers. Smythe sent five players to Chicago to acquire the younger Bentley, who was known as the "Dipsy Doodle Dandy from Delisle (Saskatchewan)."

• Buddy O'Connor teams with Rangers Phil Watson and Bryan Hextall, and the trio notches 115 points. New York finishes in fourth place.

• Montreal suffers the loss of Toe Blake. He breaks his ankle in January, ending his career at age 35.

• As Toe Blake's career ends, the Habs watch the emergence of a new star—rookie defenseman Doug Harvey.

• With so many changes, the Habs fall out of the playoffs for the first time in eight years.

• Detroit's fiery Ted Lindsay emerges as a scoring ace, notching a league-high 33 goals.

• The Red Wings put together a new front line—Ted Lindsay, Sid Abel, and Gordie Howe. The Motor City trio is dubbed the "Production Line."

New Art Ross Trophy Honors Scoring Champ

Art Ross Trophy

Although the NHL had been recognizing its scoring leader since 1918, it was not until the 1947-48 season that a trophy was established to reward the highest point-getter in the league. Art Ross, the general manager and long-time coach of the Boston Bruins who invented the puck and net used in the NHL, donated a trophy bearing his own name to be awarded to the player who led the league in points during the regular season.

Traded Maple Leafs, Black Hawks

Seven Swap Jerseys in Bentley Trade

The seven players involved in the "trade of the century" were (top row, left to right) Max Bentley, Bob Goldham, Ernie Dickens, and Cy Thomas and (bottom row, left to right) Bud Poile, Gus Bodnar, and Gaye Stewart. The Leafs traded their entire "Flying Forts" line—Poile, Bodnar, and Stewart—to obtain two-time scoring champion Bentley as well as Thomas. Thomas played only eight games with the Leafs before ending up in the "Where are they now?" file.

RCAF Players Win Olympic Gold

In 1948, Canada sent members of the Royal Canadian Air Force to compete in the St. Moritz Winter Olympics. The squad went 7-0-1 and edged Czechoslovakia for the gold medal. More impressively, Canada outscored its opponents 69-5. Coach Frank Boucher II (second row, second from right) was the son of the famous Ranger star. None of these players, however, went on to stardom in the NHL.

Canadian Olympic Team

- New York's Billy Taylor is suspended for life for betting on games. Don Gallinger, Taylor's teammate with the Bruins, is also suspended for gambling.

- Playing without his brother Max, Chicago's Doug Bentley leads the NHL in assists with 37.

- Montreal's Elmer Lach captures his second scoring title (61 points). He thus wins the first Art Ross Trophy.

- Toronto catapults to first place in the standings with a record of 32-15-13. Behind goalie Turk Broda (2.38 GAA), the Leafs boast the tightest defense in the NHL.

- With their Production Line—Ted Lindsay-Sid Abel-Gordie Howe—the Red Wings finish second to Toronto with a record of 30-18-12.

- Detroit's Harry Lumley is another key to the Wings' success, as he tallies seven shutouts.

NHL's First All-Star Team

O'Connor Cops Both the Hart and Lady Byng

The Canadiens sent pint-sized Buddy O'Connor (5'7", 145 pounds) to New York following the 1946-47 season. In 1947-48, O'Connor gave the Habs something to think about. He played in all 60 games and averaged one point per game, scoring 24 goals and notching 36 assists. MVP voters were impressed enough to award him the Hart Trophy. Morcover, O'Connor won the Lady Byng after spending just eight minutes in the box.

Buddy O'Connor

League Stages First All-Star Game

Clarence Campbell (third from right) honors the league's First All-Star Team for 1947-48 (left to right): coach Tommy Ivan, Jack Stewart, Elmer Lach, Bill Quackenbush, Turk Broda, Maurice Richard, and Ted Lindsay. All except Lach played in the first official All-Star Game in the fall of 1947. The All-Stars beat the Cup champion Leafs 4-3, with proceeds going to the players' pension fund.

Lach Wins the First Art Ross Trophy

Lester Patrick, Elmer Lach, and Art Ross celebrate the awarding of the first Art Ross Trophy to Montreal's Lach, the scoring champ of 1947-48 (30-31-61). Lach is wearing a special brace to protect a broken jaw, which would keep him out of 24 games in 1948-49.

Lester Patrick, Elmer Lach, Art Ross

• Frank Brimsek has a losing record in Boston (23-24-13), but still the Bruins edge New York for third place.

• Buddy O'Connor finishes his first year in New York with 36 assists (second overall) and 60 points (second).

• The mercurial Rocket Richard follows his 45-goal season with 28 (third best in the league).

• In the playoffs, Toronto defeats Boston in Game 1 on Nick Metz's overtime winner, then takes Games 2 and 3.

• The Bruins muster a 3-2 win in Game 4 of the semis, but Toronto wins Game 5 by the same score and advances to the Finals.

• Detroit needs six games to defeat the Rangers in their semifinals matchup. The Wings win the last two games 3-1 and 4-2 to advance.

Michigan Wolverines

Wolverines Win the First NCAA Title

The National Collegiate Athletic Association staged its first championship hockey tournament in 1948 and the University of Michigan came out the victor, beating Dartmouth 8-4 in the title game. The Wolverines' roster was comprised of seven American players and eight Canadians, including Torontonian Al Renfrew (front row, center). In 1964, Renfrew would coach the Wolverines to their seventh NCAA title—a record that has never been matched.

Gordie Howe, Sid Abel, Ted Lindsay

Production Line Debuts in Motor City

The fabled Production Line debuted in Detroit in 1947-48, and the three teammates quickly became a smooth-running machine. Ted Lindsay was a rambunctious competitor with a lightning-fast wrist shot, Sid Abel was the team captain with a veteran's savvy, and Gordie Howe was the blossoming newcomer who could shoot from the right or left side with equal dexterity. In 1947-48, the trio combined for 63 goals and 124 points, but the best was yet to come.

1947-48

- In the Stanley Cup Finals, Toronto explodes for three first-period goals and wins Game 1 5-3.

- Max Bentley scores a pair of goals—including the winner—as the Maple Leafs take Game 2 of the Finals 4-2.

- In Game 3, Toronto's Harry Watson scores at 19:42 of the second period—and Vic Lynn adds insurance late—as Turk Broda shuts out Detroit's powerful attack 2-0.

- Discouraged and outclassed, the Red Wings give up seven goals in the fourth game of the Finals and score

just two. Toronto thus completes the sweep and skates off with its second straight Stanley Cup.

- Toronto's Teeder Kennedy leads all playoff scorers with 14 points.

- Rangers center Buddy O'Connor becomes the first NHLer ever to win

Beantowners, Leafs Battle in the Garden

Boston police escort Toronto goalie Turk Broda onto the ice prior to Game 4 of the 1948 semifinals. Police were prepared for any Beantown shenanigans for April Fools' Day, 1948. The previous game between these perennial rivals saw Maple Leafs Bill Barilko, Garth Boesch, and coach Hap Day jumped by rowdy fans following an on-ice brawl. Even Boston's own Pete Babando was attacked by the rowdy Bruins fans. Toronto won the series in five games.

Stanley Cup Finals

Leafs Down the Wings, Hoist the Cup

The Toronto juggernaut continued to roll in the 1948 Finals against Detroit. The Leafs outscored the Red Wings 18-7 in the four-game sweep, returning the Stanley Cup to Maple Leaf Gardens for the fourth time in the decade. Ted Kennedy (in front of net) led all playoff scorers with 14 points (eight goals). Leafs goalie Turk Broda recorded the only postseason shutout, blanking the Wings 2-0 in Game 3 of the Finals.

Turk Broda

Stanley Cup Semifinals

Leafs Crush Boston in NHL Semis

Toronto defeated Boston 5-4 in the opening game of the 1948 semifinals. With hard-working forecheckers such as Bill Ezinicki (far left) and Syl Apps (captain), the Leafs tied the game at 4-4 late in the final frame. Toronto, capitalizing on this shift in momentum, pounded Bruins netminder Frank Brimsek with 17 shots in the overtime. Nick Metz scored at 17:03 of the extra session, sparking the Leafs to an easy five-game series triumph.

both the Hart Trophy and the Lady Byng Trophy in the same year.

• Toronto's Turk Broda captures his second Vezina Trophy.

• Detroit's Jim McFadden, who tallied 24 goals and 48 points, is voted the game's top rookie.

• Dit Clapper, Aurel Joliat, Frank Nighbor, Lester Patrick, Eddie Shore, Cyclone Taylor, and Frank Calder are named to the Hockey Hall of Fame.

• Future star defenseman Bobby Orr is born on March 20, 1948, in Parry Sound, Ontario.

• The first Olympics in 12 years are held, and Canada captures the gold medal.

• The first NCAA Division I hockey tournament begins. Michigan wins the title by defeating Dartmouth 8-4 in the finals. Dartmouth forward Joe Riley is named the tourney's MVP.

WINGS, HABS, AND LEAFS ALL DROP THE GLOVES

Having won two consecutive Stanley Cups, Toronto had established itself as the team to beat in 1948-49, despite the premature retirement of captain Syl Apps. Determined to win a third straight Cup, Leaf boss Conn Smythe laid down a rule for his skaters: "If you can't beat 'em in the alley, you can't beat 'em on the ice." As a result, some white-hot rivalries developed between the Leafs and other clubs, particularly the Red Wings and Canadiens.

On New Year's Night, 1949, Canadiens defenseman Ken Reardon took a few machete-like swings with his stick at the head of Toronto center Cal Gardner, who quickly retaliated. The bout cost each player $250 and a one-game suspension.

In an issue of *Sport* magazine, Reardon vowed an escalation of the war. "I'm going to see that Gardner gets a mouthful of stitches," vowed Reardon. "I may have to wait a long time, but I'll get even." NHL President Clarence Campbell issued a $1,000 bond warning to Reardon; if he attacked Gardner again, he would blow the bond.

The Red Wings also nurtured a big-time hate for Toronto, having lost to the Leafs in two straight

playoffs. Leafs right winger Bill Ezinicki and Detroit left wing Ted Lindsay carried a running feud through the season, and even Detroit goalie Harry Lumley and Toronto netminder Turk Broda engaged in a post-game bout at center ice.

Meanwhile, the Red Wings-Canadiens confrontations continued to sizzle throughout the regular season. Maurice Richard was the prime object of the Wings' disaffection. Detroit's Sid Abel zeroed in on the Rocket whenever possible, and young Gordie Howe hassled Richard at every turn. A powerful club, the Motor City sextet took the regular-season title (34-19-7) and collided with the Canadiens in the first round of the Stanley Cup playoffs.

In the opening playoff game, the Red Wings literally struck the first blow when defenseman Black Jack Stewart broke Montreal center Elmer Lach's jaw with a controversial body-check. The Habs cried foul. "Elmer doesn't carry the puck in his teeth," said Montreal coach Dick Irvin, "but that's where they've been checking him." Irvin's objections went for naught, as Detroit won the series in seven games.

Detroit met Toronto in the Finals and thus had its chance for revenge. But the Leafs' heavy hitters—led by Ezinicki and Bashin' Bill Barilko—neutralized the Detroiters in a manner that left critics astonished. Despite finishing 18 points behind the Wings in the regular season, the Leafs took the first two games in Detroit and then claimed a pair of 3-1 victories in the Gardens. Intense motivation was a mighty factor, as the Leafs simply outworked Jack Adams' club.

With the second sweep, Toronto became the first NHL team to win three straight Stanley Cups. However, the Red Wings and Canadiens weren't about to tip their hats to the dynastic Maple Leafs. The bitter rivalries would pick up again in the fall of '49.

1948-49

- The two-time defending-champion Toronto Maple Leafs begin the season without Syl Apps and Nick Metz, who have retired.

- In a game between Montreal and Toronto, Habs defenseman Ken Reardon and Toronto center Cal Gardner engage in a vicious stick fight.

- Conn Smythe, owner of the Leafs, sends coach Hap Day to Montreal to "buy" Maurice Richard. Day comes up empty.

- The Red Wings, boasting the Production Line of Ted Lindsay, Sid Abel, and Gordie Howe, win the regular-season title (34-19-7).

- Powered by the line of Kenny Smith, Paul Ronty, and Johnny Peirson (62 goals, 132 points), the Bruins finish in second place, nine points behind Detroit.

- Montreal's Bill Durnan leads the league in GAA (2.10) and shutouts (10), as the Habs finish third.

In the northern reaches of the NHL, the late 1940s saw tremendous rivalries. The most intense of these involved some of the biggest names in hockey. Maurice Richard is remembered today for his scoring outbursts, but in his own day he was better known and feared for his temper. Here, he thumps Terry Sawchuk over the head with his stick. A meeting involving Detroit, Montreal, or Toronto was often marred by stick-swinging, fisticuffs, and the letting of blood.

• Coach Charlie Conacher can't get Chicago into the playoffs. The Black Hawks finish in fifth place, out of the playoffs for the third straight year.

• Roy Conacher, the Hawks' superb left winger, wins the NHL scoring title with 68 points, beating linemate Doug Bentley by two points.

• Chicago's Doug Bentley wins the league assists title (43), one more than linemate Roy Conacher.

• Sid Abel, Detroit's ace playmaker, surprises a few people when he leads the league in goals (28) and ties for third in points (54).

• Scottish-born Jimmy Conacher, traded from Detroit to Chicago, ties teammate Roy Conacher and Toronto's Harry Watson for second overall in goals (26).

• Red Wings sniper Ted Lindsay ties for second in goals (26) and ties for third in points (54).

Lach Suffers More Injuries

Montreal's great Elmer Lach was the defending scoring champion when the 1948-49 season opened. However, in a December 11 game against the Black Hawks, Lach collided with Chicago defenseman Bob Goldham and suffered a badly broken jaw. In Game 1 of the 1949 semifinals, he re-injured the jaw, forcing him to miss the remainder of the playoffs. Just two years earlier, Lach had sustained a broken cheekbone and a fractured skull.

Forum Sports Magazine

Bill Durnan, Turk Broda

Sid Abel

Sid's More Than Able; Named MVP

Sid Abel, Detroit's veteran centerman, had the finest season of his long career in 1948-49. Teamed with Gordie Howe on his right side and the rambunctious Terrible Ted Lindsay on his left, Abel led all NHL snipers with 28 goals. Abel, who had never reached the 20-goal mark in his career, tied Lindsay for third in the league in scoring and was awarded the Hart Trophy as the league's most valuable player.

Once Again, Durnan's the Best in Nets

Two of the game's greatest goaltenders, Bill Durnan and Turk Broda, greet each other after one of their many on-ice battles. Durnan, who didn't make the NHL until the age of 28, was the dominant goalie in the league in his first four seasons, winning the Vezina Trophy each year. After surrendering the award to Broda in 1947-48, Durnan regained the crown in 1948-49 with his finest season, recording 10 shutouts and a miserly 2.10 GAA.

1948-49

- Toronto's Wild Bill Ezinicki leads the NHL in penalty minutes (145).

- Montreal boasts three players among the top five penalty leaders: Murph Chamberlain (111 PIM), Maurice Richard (110), and Ken Reardon (103).

- Much of Maurice Richard's penalty time comes from his personal feud with Rangers left winger Tony Leswick, the NHL's premier "pest."

- Buddy O'Connor, the NHL's MVP a year earlier, notches just 35 points in 46 games for the Rangers.

- After a 6-11-6 start, the Rangers dismiss coach Frank Boucher and hand the job to Lynn Patrick, but the club falls to sixth place with an 18-31-11 record.

- Boston meets Toronto in the first round of playoffs, while Detroit takes on Montreal.

Not-So-Famous Conacher Has Heck of a Year

James Conacher may not have been a blood relative of the famous Conachers of Cabbagetown, but in 1948-49 he performed like one. When he was traded from Detroit to Chicago, where he joined Roy Conacher, James accepted the job as the Black Hawks' lamplighter, scoring 26 goals and tying Roy for second in the league's goal-scoring race.

James Conacher

Black Hawks' Conacher Wins Scoring Title

Roy Gordon Conacher finally settled down in Chicago in 1948-49. After five years in Boston, he had been shifted to Detroit for the 1946-47 season and to the Windy City for 1947-48. In his second season with the Hawks, Conacher finished second in the league in goals with 26 and second in the loop in assists with 42. His combined points total of 68 was No. 1 in the league.

Roy Conacher

Even in Down Year, Richard Makes News

Maurice Richard slides into the boards in a game against Toronto. Despite a poor year in 1948-49, Richard made headlines when the Leafs attempted to acquire him, but came up empty. Montreal G.M. Frank Selke Sr. said of Richard: "No player in the history of the National League was as great an offensive threat as Rocket Richard from the blueline in. His dark eyes would glow like embers as he bore down on the opposing netminder. I remember the Rocket."

Toronto Maple Leafs vs. Montreal Canadiens

- The defending-champion Leafs show their mettle, dispatching the Bruins in five games.

- Boston's only playoff win comes in Game 3, when Woody Dumart unlocks a 4-4 tie at 16:14 of overtime to beat Toronto.

- The war between Detroit and Montreal lasts seven games. Game 1 stretches to triple O.T. before Max McNab wins it for the Red Wings.

- During Game 1, Montreal's Elmer Lach is sidelined with a broken jaw after a run-in with Detroit's surly Black Jack Stewart.

- Montreal exacts a measure of revenge in Game 2 when tiny Gerry Plamondon, an obscure winger, beats Harry Lumley in O.T. to give the Habs a 4-3 win.

- After taking the series lead with a 3-2 victory in Game 3, the Habs drop the next two by the same 3-1 score.

Bentley Stars on Offensive-Minded Hawks

The Black Hawks had no trouble scoring in 1948-49. Besides Art Ross Trophy winner Roy Conacher, the team featured the league's No. 2 scorer in Doug Bentley, who netted 23 goals and led the league with 43 assists. Unfortunately, bad defense led to a 21-31-8 record. In fact, Chicago featured the worst defense in the league each year from 1946-47 through 1951-52. Famous goalies such as Emile Francis, Jim Henry, Frank Brimsek, and Harry Lumley couldn't get it done.

Doug Bentley

Hap Day

Day Tries to Buy Richard

In 1948-49, Toronto manager Conn Smythe sent coach Hap Day to Montreal with instructions to obtain Maurice Richard's contract. "Maple Leaf Gardens has never been close with a buck," said Day, "and I have explicit instructions to meet any price mentioned for Richard's services." Montreal manager Frank Selke, however, turned Day away. "All the money in Toronto wouldn't buy him," said Selke.

Ezinicki Is a Real Tough Guy

Wild Bill Ezinicki hailed from the North End of Winnipeg, Manitoba. Anyone who has spent time in Winnipeg's North End will understand the ease with which Ezinicki filled the "tough guy" role. In 1948-49, Wild Bill earned his name and his salary, spending 145 minutes in the penalty box in only 52 games, an achievement unmatched by any other league bad boy of his day.

Bill Ezinicki

1948-49

- Montreal takes Game 6 3-1, but the Red Wings—on home ice for Game 7—eke out a 3-1 victory of their own to advance to the Stanley Cup Finals.

- Toronto wins Game 1 of the Finals 3-2, as scrappy left winger Joe Klukay scores at 17:31 of the first extra session.

- Toronto's Turk Broda—one of the NHL's first recognized "money" goalies—allows one goal in each of the next three games of the Finals.

- Game 2 features a hat-trick from Maple Leafs winger Sid Smith, as Toronto wins 3-1.

- Toronto burns Detroit with three second-period goals to again win 3-1.

- Cal Gardner scores the game-winning goal in Game 4 of the Finals, as Toronto wins yet another 3-1 affair. The Leafs thus sweep the Red Wings for the Stanley Cup.

Pentti Lund

Blueshirts Sign a Finn, Finish Last

When the New York Rangers brought in their secret weapon from Finland, they expected that Pentti Lund would have the key to the team's future. He may have brought the talent to win the 1949 Calder Trophy, but the only key he seemed to bring them was the key to the cellar door. Lund tallied 14 goals and 16 assists for a total of 30 points, but the Rangers as a team had serious trouble scoring and finished the year with an 18-31-11 record.

Stanley Cup Finals

Leafs Blow Past Wings in Cup Finals

Ignoring the pile of players fighting for position in the Detroit crease, Toronto Maple Leaf captain Ted Kennedy (far right) fires a shot at Detroit's Harry Lumley during the 1949 Stanley Cup Finals. With Kennedy setting the table for teammates Sid Smith and Fleming Mackell, the Leafs set an NHL record with their third straight Stanley Cup title, downing the Red Wings in four straight games, the last three by identical 3-1 scores.

- Toronto becomes the first team to win three straight Stanley Cups since the Ottawa Silver Seven in 1902-06.

- Gordie Howe is the leading playoff scorer (8-3-11).

- Sid Abel captures his only Hart Trophy, edging Montreal's Bill Durnan.

- Bill Durnan cops his fifth Vezina Trophy in the last six years.

- Detroit defenseman Bill Quackenbush nabs the Lady Byng Trophy.

- In a dismal season of failure, the Rangers' lone bright spot is Finnish rookie Pentti Lund, who's voted the game's outstanding freshman.

- Boston College wins the NCAA hockey crown, nipping Dartmouth 4-3 in the finals. Dartmouth goalie Dick Desmond is named the tournament's MVP.

Having won three consecutive Stanley Cups, the Maple Leafs took aim at an unprecedented fourth straight title in 1949-50. Coach Hap Day and manager Conn Smythe detected two obstacles on the horizon. One was the rapidly improving Red Wings and the other was complacency, which accompanies many championship teams. Conn was worried that the Leafs were becoming fat, both physically and mentally.

Smythe's fears were confirmed early in the fall of 1949, when the Leafs opened their campaign with the vigor of a pricked balloon. Smythe studied his slumping club throughout November. Finally, on November 30, Smythe began what became known as hockey's "Battle of the Bulge." Although Smythe singled out only a few players for his blasts, the primary target of his ire was his longtime goaltender, Walter "Turk" Broda.

Smythe demanded that his players reduce their weight to specified limits. Broda, who weighed 197 pounds, was ordered to lop off seven. Smythe promptly called up reserve goalie Gil Mayer from his farm team in Pittsburgh. This was the supreme insult to Broda, who—except for a World War II stint in the service—had

PUDGY BRODA PREVAILS IN THE BATTLE OF THE BULGE

played virtually every game during his 12 seasons in Toronto. It was Tuesday and Smythe was giving Turk until Saturday to fulfill the demand.

After one day of severe dieting, Broda trimmed his weight from 197 to 193, but he couldn't get much lower than that. Then Smythe dropped another bombshell. He sent five players and cash to Cleveland of the American Hockey League for tall, 23-year-old goalie Al Rollins.

It was clear that Rollins was a direct challenge to Broda and that Turk had better shape up—pronto! With that in mind, a well-known nutritionist advised that the way to lose weight was by willpower. "Overweight," he told the rotund goalie, "is caused solely by eating more food than is needed."

The climax of the week-long calorie crusade finally arrived on Saturday afternoon when, one by one, the penitent Leafs stepped on the scales under Smythe's watchful eye. Harry Watson, Garth Boesch, Vic Lynn, Sid Smith, and Howie Meeker all weighed in under the limit. Finally, it was Broda's turn.

Turk moved forward and gingerly placed his feet on the platform. The numbers finally settled—just under 190 pounds. He had made the cut! If Turk was delighted, Smythe was doubly enthused because he regarded his goaltender with paternal affection. Broda and the Maple Leafs celebrated later that night with a 2-0 victory over the Rangers.

The 35-year-old Broda went on to enjoy his best season in years, posting a 2.45 GAA and a career-high nine shutouts. But although Turk and the Leafs had won the Battle of the Bulge, they lost a much more important battle—their semifinals confrontation with the Wings. Despite Broda's trim 1.43 GAA, Toronto lost to Detroit in seven games. The Wings then knocked off New York in the Finals and began to stake their claim as hockey's next dynasty.

1949-50

- In a rule change, goaltenders will no longer have to face a penalty shot if they commit a major penalty. Instead, they will be represented in the penalty box by a teammate.

- The NHL season is expanded to 70 games.

- Future Philadelphia Flyers great Bobby Clarke is born on August 13, 1949, in Flin Flon, Manitoba.

- Detroit goes 37-19-14, beating out Montreal by 11 points.

- The Red Wings lead the NHL with 229 goals. The members of the

powerful Production Line finish first, second, and third in the league in scoring.

- Detroit left winger Ted Lindsay leads the NHL in assists (55) en route to his first and only scoring championship (78 points).

After trimming the fat in Conn Smythe's famous Battle of the Bulge in December 1949, goalie Turk Broda went on to have a heck of a year. In the regular season, Broda chalked up 30 wins and nine shutouts. In the playoffs, he continued his stingy netminding against the Red Wings. In the seven-game series, Broda won three games with shutouts and lost two in sudden-death overtime. His 1.42 GAA in the playoffs put him atop the goaltending statistics.

• Red Wings center Sid Abel is third in goals (34), third in assists (35), and second in points (69).

• Detroit's Gordie Howe is second in goals (35) and third in points (68).

• Maurice Richard is back atop the goal-scoring chart (43) after a dismal 20-goal performance in 1948-49. He also finishes fourth in points (65).

• Chicago's diminutive Metro Prystai leads the Hawks in goals (29) and finishes fourth in the league.

• The Hawks are second in goals (203) but have the worst defense in the NHL (244 goals against). They finish last for the third time in four years.

• Despite their poor finish under the command of George Boucher, the Bruins boast the league's second-best assist-maker, Paul Ronty (36).

Lumley Takes the Wings All the Way

Harry Lumley was the youngest goaltender in NHL history when he made his debut at the age of 17 during the 1943-44 season. Six years later, he led the Red Wings to the Stanley Cup championship with eight wins and three shutouts during the 1950 postseason schedule. One of those victories was a 1-0 overtime win over Toronto in Game 7 of the semifinals. Detroit and Lumley did it the hard way, stretching both series to their seven-game limit.

Harry Lumley

Chuck Rayner

Goalie Rayner Wins the Hart

Chuck "Bonnie Prince Charlie" Rayner dazzled Rangers fans in 1949-50 with his stellar work in net. He posted a 2.62 GAA and became the first goaltender since 1928-29 to win the Hart Trophy. Rayner was a roaming goalie who often skated up ice in an attempt to score. He was never able to turn the trick in regular play, but he was known to bend the hemp in exhibition games against some of the best minor-league teams on the continent.

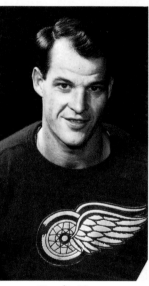
Gordie Howe

Howe's 35 Goals Fuel the Wings

Gordie Howe finally arrived as an NHL star during the 1949-50 season. While he scored just 35 goals in his first three seasons, Howe netted 35 exactly in 1949-50. He finished third in the league in scoring (68 points) behind linemates Ted Lindsay and Sid Abel and second in goals to Rocket Richard. Detroit's Production Line powered the Wings to a league-best 37-19-14 record and a Stanley Cup title.

1949-50

- Bill Durnan leads the league in GAA (2.20) for the sixth time in the last seven years.

- Harry Lumley matches the Red Wings' potent offense with sterling goaltending, finishing with the most wins (33), the second-best GAA (2.35), and seven shutouts.

- Turk Broda overcomes a weight problem to hold onto his job in Toronto. He then leads the NHL in shutouts (nine) and finishes third in GAA (2.48).

- Under coach Lynn Patrick, the Rangers climb back into the playoffs with a fourth-place finish.

- Toronto's third-place finish is fueled by Sid Smith (45 points) and Ted Kennedy (44).

- The Wings and Maple Leafs meet in the first round of the playoffs. In Game 1, Gordie Howe misses a check on Ted Kennedy and crashes into the boards, fracturing his skull.

Edgar Laprade

Good-Natured Laprade Wins the Lady Byng

The Lady Byng Trophy is given to the player who shows a very high level of sportsmanship combined with outstanding play. In 1949-50, the Lady Byng was given to Edgar Laprade, who played on a Rangers line with Tony Leswick and Dunc Fisher. Laprade scored 22 goals, a career high, and 44 points, a team high. More significantly, he spent only two minutes in the penalty box and showed an almost unnatural good spirit both on and off the ice.

Bill Durnan, Maurice Richard

Durnan Wins Vezina, Then Retires

Maurice Richard does his best to elicit a laugh from the usually stoic Bill Durnan before an important game against the Maple Leafs. Durnan was the NHL's outstanding goaltender in 1949-50, winning his sixth Vezina Trophy in seven seasons, a remarkable achievement for a goalie who never wanted to play professional hockey. Shortly after this photo was taken, Durnan announced his retirement, citing frayed nerves as the major reason he was hanging up the pads.

Paul Ronty

Ronty Leads Bruins with 59 Points

Paul Ronty continued to develop into a front-line forward during the 1949-50 season, registering his second consecutive 20-goal campaign for the Bruins. After a breakthrough 20-goal, 49-point season in 1948-49, Ronty increased his totals to 23 goals and 59 points in the 1949-50 campaign. Ronty was the leading scorer for the fifth-place Bruins, and his 36 assists were the second-highest total in the league.

• Detroit and Toronto trade victories over the first six games, as tensions run high. Game 4 goes to double overtime before Detroit's Leo Reise scores 38 seconds into the second extra period.

• Game 7 is tied 0-0 after regulation, but Detroit's Leo Reise pots his second O.T. winner of the series to send the Wings to the Finals.

• In the other semifinal series, the Rangers ride the brilliant goaltending of Chuck Rayner to shock the Montreal Canadiens in five games. New York's 4-1 victory in Game 5 sends them to the Finals.

• New York takes a 1-0 lead in Game 1 of the Finals, but Detroit rallies with four unanswered goals and wins the game 4-1.

• Chuck Rayner holds the Wings' offense in check in Game 2 and Edgar Laprade scores twice for New York, as the Rangers win 3-1.

Howe Injured, Hovers Near Death

In Game 1 of the 1950 semifinals between the Maple Leafs and Red Wings, Detroit's Gordie Howe suffered a serious injury when he collided with Toronto's Ted Kennedy and hit his head on the boards. The talented right winger underwent a series of delicate brain operations and hovered near death for two days. Howe made a remarkable recovery and so did his teammates. They won Game 7 1-0 on an overtime goal by Leo Reise.

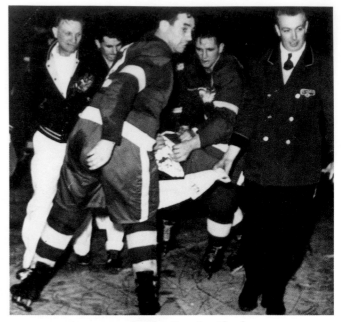

Stanley Cup Semifinals

Maurice Richard

Fiery Rocket Lights It Up 43 Times

One of the most intense competitors to play any sport, Rocket Richard led the NHL in goals for the third time in his career during the 1949-50 season, drilling home 43 goals in 70 games for the Canadiens. Many goaltenders have stated that the most frightening aspect of facing Richard was encountering the unrelenting fire in the Rocket's eyes, a red glare that made him the NHL's most feared marksman.

Pete Babando

Babando Pots Cup Winner in Double O.T.

The Red Wings traded for Pete Babando before the 1949-50 season and got rid of him after the campaign. However, in the Stanley Cup Finals, he ended up scoring the biggest goal in franchise history. With Game 7 tied 3-3 in double overtime, Babando beat New York goalie Chuck Rayner at the 8:31 mark to send Olympia Stadium into a frenzy.

1949-50

- Detroit's strapping Doc Couture scores what proves to be the winner in Game 3, as Harry Lumley shuts out the Rangers 4-0.

- In Game 4 of the Finals, New York's Don Raleigh scores at 8:34 of O.T. to break up a 3-3 game.

- In Game 5, the Rangers play Detroit tightly and take a 1-1 game into overtime. Once more, it is Don Raleigh who wins it, giving New York the series edge.

- The Rangers score early in the third period of Game 6 for a 4-3 lead, but they cannot hold off Detroit. Ted Lindsay and Sid Abel score to win it 5-4 and force Game 7.

- Game 7 goes to the second overtime tied 3-3. Detroit's Pete Babando winds up the hero, as he beats goalie Chuck Rayner and wins the Cup for the Wings.

Wings' D Clamps Down on Rangers

Detroit defenders Harry Lumley (goalie) and Black Jack Stewart (middle) were both key performers in Detroit's seven-game victory over the Rangers in the 1950 Finals. Lumley posted three shutouts in the postseason while recording a goals-against average of 2.00. Stewart, a mainstay on the Red Wings' defense since 1938, had the finest playoff series of his career, contributing five points while playing his usual tight-fisted style along the blueline.

Stanley Cup Finals

Wings Work Overtime to Win the Cup

Sid Abel proudly displays the Stanley Cup after the Red Wings downed the Rangers in the 1950 Stanley Cup Finals. The Wings fought back from a 3-2 deficit in games to win Game 7 on a goal in double overtime by Pete Babando. The Rangers, forced to play the entire championship round on the road because the circus was visiting Madison Square Garden, won Games 4 and 5 in overtime before losing the final two matches to the Red Wings.

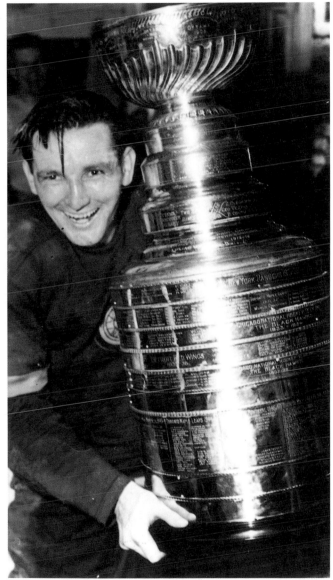

Sid Abel

- Gordie Howe, out of the hospital after suffering a fractured skull, joins his mates on ice as Detroit hoists its fourth Stanley Cup.

- The Hart Trophy goes to Rangers goalie Chuck Rayner, who edges Toronto's Ted Kennedy.

- Edgar Laprade, the savvy Rangers center, wins his one and only Lady Byng Trophy.

- Bill Durnan claims his sixth and final Vezina Trophy.

- Boston goalie Jack Gelineau earns the Calder Trophy.

- Colorado College wins the NCAA title by walloping Boston University 13-4 in the finals. Boston goalie Ralph Bevins is named tourney MVP.

- The first intraleague draft is held on April 30, 1950. Clubs are allowed to protect 30 players, with remaining players available for $25,000 each.

As the 1951 playoffs began, NHL fans envisioned a Stanley Cup Finals meeting between rivals Detroit and Toronto. After all, the Red Wings had become the first NHL team to ever reach 100 points (44-13-13), while Conn Smythe's Leafs had finished just six points back. However, the Wings-Leafs matchup would never happen. Instead, Toronto and Montreal would hook up in the Finals—a series that would become the most nail-biting of all time.

Toronto reached the Finals by dusting off the Bruins in the semis, while Montreal made it by stunning the Wings in their playoff matchup. Rocket Richard was the hero, as he scored in quadruple overtime in Game 1 and triple O.T. in Game 2.

The Canadiens, who finished 25-30-15 during the season, seemingly needed another dose of luck to beat the Leafs. As the Finals unfolded, however, Smythe was the one who had the leprechauns on his side. The series opened at Maple Leaf Gardens, and Game 1 entered overtime tied 2-2. At 5:51 of the extra session, Toronto's Sid Smith beat goalie Gerry McNeil to give the Leafs a one-game edge. "It was," wrote

BARILKO'S THE HERO IN ALL-O.T. FINALE

Jim Vilpond of the *Toronto Globe and Mail,* "as fast and exciting a hockey game as has been seen here this season."

Game 2 also went into overtime tied 2-2, but this time Richard emerged as the hero, as he beat Turk Broda at 2:55. In the third game, the Rocket put Montreal into the lead only to have Smith tie the score at 1-1. For the third straight game, the clubs went into overtime—although this time there was one difference: Toronto coach Joe Primeau had benched Broda in favor of the younger Al Rollins.

The move paid off handsomely. Three times within the first four minutes of overtime, the Canadiens pierced the Toronto defense, and each time Rollins was equal to the occasion. Finally, Toronto's Tod Sloan slipped a

pass to Ted Kennedy, who beat McNeil at 4:47.

Never in Stanley Cup history had there been four consecutive overtime games, but that record was about to be broken at the Montreal Forum. A goal by the Canadiens' Elmer Lach tied the game at 2-2, setting up the record-breaking extra session. At 5:15, Toronto's Harry Watson found the net to give the Leafs their third sudden-death victory.

It seemed impossible that five straight games of the Cup Finals would enter O.T., and with the Habs nursing a 2-1 lead late in the game, it appeared Montreal would break the spell. However, Max Bentley—playing the most intense hockey of his life—set up Sloan with 32 seconds remaining, assuring a fifth straight O.T.

Like all the overtimes, this one ended quickly, as the Leafs' Bill Barilko scored at 2:53 of the extra session to end the all-overtime series. As one could imagine, bedlam reigned in the Maple Leaf dressing room. "We just out-Irished them," said a beaming Smythe, who was holding a telegram of congratulations from a Father H. Murphy. "See what I mean?" he added. "Pure Irish luck."

1950-51

- The NHL rules that each team must provide an emergency goaltender for every game, for use by either team, in case of injury or illness.

- The Hall of Fame inducts nine new members—among them Newsy Lalonde and Joe Malone—bringing the number of inductees to 35.

- Before the season begins, Detroit trades Harry Lumley, Al Dewsbury, Don Morrison, and Pete Babando to Chicago. Chicago sends Gaye Stewart, Metro Prystai, and Jim Henry to Detroit.

- Jim Henry doesn't play a single game for the Wings as Terry

Sawchuk, a sensational 21-year-old rookie, becomes Detroit's regular goalie.

- In Toronto, another goalie prospect makes headlines as Al Rollins usurps Turk Broda as the Leafs' No. 1 puck-stopper.

The story of Bill Barilko (pictured being hoisted) is one of ultimate triumph and tragedy. In Game 5 of the 1951 Finals, Barilko dove for a loose puck at the 2:53 mark of overtime and backhanded the rubber past Montreal's Gerry McNeil. The goal won the Stanley Cup for Toronto and made the uncelebrated backliner a household name. He made headlines again three months later when his airplane disappeared on a fishing trip to Northern Ontario. He was never seen alive again.

- In Montreal, goalie Gerry McNeil takes over after the retirement of legend Bill Durnan.

- NHL President Clarence Campbell fines Maurice Richard $500 for attacking referee Hugh McLean in a New York hotel lobby.

- The Red Wings win the regular-season title. They go 44-13-13 and beat out Toronto by six points.

- Gordie Howe, fully recovered from his fractured skull, captures the NHL's "triple crown." He leads the league in goals (43), assists (43), and points (a record 86).

- Montreal's Rocket Richard finishes with 42 goals, one shy of Gordie Howe's league-high mark, but is 20 points behind as the runner-up for total points.

- Toronto's Tod Sloan (31) and Sid Smith (30) are a distant third and fourth in the goal-scoring race.

Terry Sawchuk

Rookie Sawchuk Wins a Record 44

The Detroit Red Wings had a rich minor-league system. One of their greatest prospects was goaltender Terry Sawchuk, who had already captured the rookie-of-the-year award in the AHL and the USHL. In 1950-51, he was ready for prime time, and he completed his triple crown by winning the Calder Trophy as the NHL's best freshman. Sawchuk won an NHL-record 44 games in his rookie season while compiling 11 shutouts and a 1.99 GAA.

Howe Comes Back with a Vengeance

After suffering a serious head injury during the 1950 playoffs, Gordie Howe wore a helmet for part of the 1950-51 campaign, making him one of the few NHL players to wear the head protection during the season. The helmet seemed to give Howe added confidence, and he rebounded to lead the NHL in goals (43), assists (43), and points (86). The Saskatchewan native won the first of his four straight Art Ross Trophies.

Milt Schmidt

Schmidt's Still Proving Smythe Wrong

Milt Schmidt had one of his finest years in 1950-51, collecting 61 points in 62 games. Schmidt had tried out for the Maple Leafs in the early 1930s but was turned away by Conn Smythe because of his small size. However, Schmidt kept maturing, eventually becoming a solid 5'11", 180-pounder. In the mid-1940s, Smythe dispatched Frank Selke to Boston in an attempt to purchase the crafty Schmidt, but Bruins manager Art Ross turned Selke away.

Gordie Howe

1950-51

- Ted Kennedy (43) ties Gordie Howe's assist mark, while Maple Leaf mate Max Bentley (41) gives Toronto two of the three best assist men.

- Sid Abel, the centerman on the famed Production Line, ties Milt Schmidt and Ted Kennedy for fourth place in total points (61).

- Toronto's new goalie, Al Rollins, leads the NHL in GAA (1.77).

- Terry Sawchuk leads the league in wins (44) and has a 1.99 GAA.

- Ted Lindsay is fined $300 and suspended three games for a stick fight with Boston's Bill Ezinicki.

- The Red Wings' Red Kelly leads all NHL blueliners with 54 points, three shy of Babe Pratt's league record for a defenseman.

- The playoffs pit Detroit against Montreal and Toronto against Boston.

Carl Pelanger, Hugh McLean

McLean's Call Angers Richard

NHL on-ice official Hugh McLean aroused the temper of Maurice Richard during a Montreal-Boston matchup in 1950-51. McLean failed to call a penalty late in the game on a play where the Rocket was tripped and cut. Richard ran into McLean the following morning in a hotel lobby, grabbed the arbitrator by the tie, and threatened to punch him before cooler heads prevailed. Richard was fined $500 and McLean never refereed in the NHL again.

Al Rollins

Rollins Posts 1.77 Average

In 1950-51, the Maple Leafs promoted a young goal-tender named Al Rollins from their USHL farm team in Kansas City to share goal-tending duties with incumbent Turk Broda. Rollins went on to post a league-leading 1.77 goals-against average—the best mark between 1940 and 1972—and earned the Vezina Trophy. The Leafs' unique tandem of Rollins and Broda was the first two-goaltender system to be implemented in the NHL.

- The Leafs outscore the Bruins 17-5 and take the semifinal series 4-1.

- Game 2 of the semis is suspended because of a local Toronto curfew and the game is declared a tie. However, Toronto reels off four straight wins, holding the Bruins to just two goals.

- In a stunning upset, the third-place Montreal Canadiens skate past Detroit in six semifinal games.

- Game 1 of the semis is tied at 2-2 until Montreal's Maurice Richard beats Terry Sawchuk at 1:09 of the fourth O.T.

- Game 2 is scoreless through five full periods, as Terry Sawchuk and Gerry McNeil put on a goaltending clinic. But Maurice Richard again nets the winner, this time at 2:20 of triple O.T.

- Detroit bounces back with a pair of wins in Montreal, 2-0 in Game 3 and 4-1 in Game 4.

Dr. David Tracy, New York Rangers

Hypnotist Can't Help Rangers

Ever since they lost an inordinate number of stars to the war effort in 1942, the Rangers wallowed in a funk they couldn't escape. In a publicity stunt in 1950, the team hired Dr. David Tracy to hypnotize the players into playing better. Here, he casts his spell on (left to right) Tony Leswick, Ed Slowinski, Chuck Rayner, and Edgar Laprade. Unfortunately, the Blueshirts finished 20-29-21 in 1950-51 and wouldn't reach the .500 mark until 1955-56.

Rocket Pots 42, Nearly Wins the Hart

Montreal right winger Maurice Richard (center) trips up Chicago's Vic Stasiuk (left) in action between the Canadiens and Black Hawks on November 9, 1950. Richard reached the 40-goal plateau for the fourth time in his marvelous career in 1950-51, burying 42 shots behind enemy goaltenders in 65 games. The rambunctious Rocket also earned his eighth consecutive postseason All-Star nomination and finished runner-up for the Hart Trophy.

Red Kelly

Kelly Scores Big, Claims the Lady Byng

Leonard "Red" Kelly established himself as one of the NHL's greatest defensemen during the 1950-51 season, leading all rearguards in scoring with 17 goals and 37 assists. The likable redhead, a cool customer on and off the ice, spent only 24 minutes in the penalty box during the season and was awarded the Lady Byng Trophy. Kelly, a second-team All-Star in 1950, earned his first berth on the NHL's First All-Star Team in 1951.

Vic Stasiuk, Maurice Richard, Gerry McNeil

1950-51

- The Habs play road warriors at Olympia Stadium in Detroit, beating the Red Wings 5-2 in Game 5.

- On home ice, Montreal completes the unlikely upset, tipping the powerful Wings 3-2 to advance to the Stanley Cup Finals.

- The Finals between Canada's two rivals—Montreal and Toronto—feature five O.T. games in a row.

- Toronto wins Game 1 3-2 when Sid Smith scores at 5:51 of overtime.

- Montreal wins Game 2 3-2, as Maurice Richard collects his third

O.T. winner of the playoffs, beating Turk Broda at 2:55 of overtime.

- Toronto's Ted Kennedy beats Gerry McNeil at 4:47 of O.T. to win Game 3 2-1. The Leafs' Harry Watson scores in Game 4 at 5:15 of O.T, giving Toronto a 3-2 win.

McNeil Wins Marathon Game

Montreal goaltender Gerry McNeil sprawls to swipe a rebound away during the opening game of the 1951 Montreal-Detroit semifinal series. The game required 61 minutes of overtime before Rocket Richard stole the puck from Red Wings defenseman Leo Reise and fired it past Terry Sawchuk to give the Canadiens the series lead. The Habs went on to capture the best-of-seven set in six games.

Stanley Cup Semifinals

Semifinal Game Played to a Draw

Boston's Pete Horeck stares down Bill Barilko (#5) during Game 2 of their 1951 Stanley Cup semifinal game in Toronto. This happened to be the first tie game in the playoffs since the NHL dropped the two-game, total-goals format in 1936-37. After four periods, the score was tied 1-1. As the teams prepared for the second overtime period, city officials—enforcing a midnight curfew—blew the whistle on the extended game, sending fans home without a winner.

Stanley Cup Semifinals

Barilko Nets Cup Winner in O.T.

For the only time in NHL history, every game of the 1951 Finals went into overtime. It was a matchup between two classic teams, the Canadiens of Richard, Lach, and Bouchard against the Leafs' Kennedy, Broda, and Bentley. Toronto won the series in five games on overtime goals from Sid Smith, Teeder Kennedy, Harry Watson, and (pictured here) Bill Barilko. These were the only overtime goals any of these players would ever score.

Stanley Cup Finals

- The Habs hold a 2-1 lead late in the third period of Game 5 when Toronto's Tod Sloan scores to tie it up with 32 seconds left on the clock.

- Leafs defenseman Bill Barilko scores at 2:53 of O.T. in Game 5. The goal ends the all-overtime Finals and gives Toronto the Cup.

- Boston's Milt Schmidt (61 points) is awarded the Hart Trophy.

- Detroit's Red Kelly captures his first of four Lady Byng Trophies.

- Toronto rookie Al Rollins wins the Vezina Trophy, but Detroit goalie Terry Sawchuk captures the Calder.

- The Cup-winning goal is the last ever scored by Bill Barilko, as he dies shortly after the playoffs in an airplane crash at age 24.

- Michigan wins its second NCAA hockey championship with a 7-1 rout of Brown. Still, Brown goalie Ed Whiston is named tourney MVP.

PRODUCTION LINE CRANKS OUT A STANLEY CUP

Ever since the Red Wings' 1950 Stanley Cup win, the Motor City Six ranked as the NHL's premier team. Their power extended from goal (Terry Sawchuk) to defense (Red Kelly) to offense, where a remarkable trio propelled Jack Adams' club to new heights.

The Production Line—comprised of right wing Gordie Howe, left wing Ted Lindsay, and center Sid Abel—tormented foes with an assortment of weaponry. Abel had the savvy, while Lindsay and Howe blended style and aggression that intimidated their opponents. The result was four straight first-place finishes from 1948-49 through 1951-52.

Abel, a Red Wing since 1938, captured the Hart Trophy in 1949. Although he never won a scoring title, Abel garnered 34 goals in 1949-50, third in the league. Among Sid's many assets were a mean streak and the strength with which to back it up.

Lindsay's blazing competitive spirit made him one of the toughest and most feared skaters in the NHL. Ted accumulated over 760 stitches on his person, all mementos from the various battles he waged on the ice. The stitches earned him the moniker Scarface, although he was also known as Terrible Ted and Tempestuous Ted.

Ted was a little guy (5'8", 163 pounds), and he resented players who thought they could take advantage of his small stature. He would not be intimidated. "Okay, so I was cocky," he admitted. "I had the idea that I had to beat up everyone in the league, and I'm still not convinced it wasn't a good idea. Probably I'd do it the same way if I did it all over again. That's the way I am."

The most gifted of the trio was Howe, who possessed extra-ordinary strength in a body that measured 6'1", 200 pounds. Howe's armament was the most formidable the game has known. "His shot was uncanny," said goalie Glenn Hall, "because it would come at the net in so many different ways." Unique among superstars, Howe was an ambidextrous stick-handler. He could deliver a remarkably accurate shot with so fluid a motion that goalies frequently failed to see the puck leave Gordie's stick.

The Production Line reached its peak in 1951-52, when the Wings finished 44-14-12. Howe led the league in both goals (47) and points (86) and captured his first of six Hart Trophies. Lindsay finished second in the league in scoring with 69 points.

In the playoffs, the Red Wings steamrolled over the defending-champion Maple Leafs, flattening them in four straight games. The Richard-led Canadiens were expected to provide an obstacle in the Finals, but the power of the Production Line—as well as the stellar netminding of Sawchuk—overwhelmed the Habs. Detroit broomed Montreal in four, giving the Wings an 8-0 playoff record.

The original Production Line ended that spring, as the aging Abel was sold in the off-season to the Chicago Black Hawks. However, talented Alex Delvecchio took over Abel's spot in 1952-53, and the new Production Line continued on, as strong as ever.

1951-52

- The NHL rules that visiting teams will wear basic white jerseys during games, while the home teams will wear colored jerseys.

- The goalcrease is enlarged from 3 × 7 feet to 4 × 8 feet, and the faceoff circles are expanded from a 10-foot radius to a 15-foot radius.

- Future Canadiens star Guy Lafleur is born on September 20, 1951, in Thurso, Quebec.

- The Red Wings post the best record in the NHL for the fourth straight year (44-14-12). They finish 22 points ahead of second-place Montreal.

- Detroit scores the most goals in the NHL (215) and yields the fewest (133).

- Detroit's Gordie Howe wins his second straight scoring title with 86 points. His 47 goals are 16 more than runner-up Bill Mosienko of Chicago.

Detroit is known for production, and so it was with their famous on-ice
line of Gordie Howe (left), Sid Abel (center), and Terrible Ted Lindsay
(right). The Production Line was running at full output during the 1951-52 season.
The Red Wings finished first for the fourth consecutive year with a league-leading
215 goals and a league-low 133 goals against. Howe captured his second straight
scoring title with 47 red lights and 39 assists.

• Montreal's Elmer Lach rebounds
from a poor season and leads the
NHL in assists (50).

• The feud between Gordie Howe and
Maurice Richard is suspended, as
Richard suffers through an injury-
plagued season.

• Detroit's Ted Lindsay is second in
the NHL in points (69).

• Don Raleigh, the Rangers' slick
center, is second in the NHL in assists
(42) and fourth in points (61).

• On March 23, 1952, Chicago's Bill
Mosienko sets an NHL record by

scoring three goals in 21 seconds. He
scores at 6:09, 6:20, and 6:30 of the
third period as Chicago beats New
York 7-6.

• In Montreal, a hard-shooting right
winger named Bernie Geoffrion rips
30 goals (tied for third in the league)
in his first full season.

Sugar Jim Leads Bruins to Playoffs

The Boston Bruins, led by Milt Schmidt (center) and Red Sullivan (far left), made their second consecutive appearance in the playoffs in 1951-52. The Bruins, who finished in fourth place with a 25-29-16 record, featured a new goaltender in Sugar Jim Henry (far right), who hadn't played in the NHL since 1949. Sugar Jim appeared in all 70 games for the Bruins, registering seven sweet shutouts and an excellent 2.51 GAA.

Boston Bruins

Canadians Storm to Olympic Gold

The Edmonton Mercurys represented Canada at the 1952 Olympic Games in Oslo, Norway. The team of amateurs blazed through the Olympic tournament by going undefeated in eight games, the only blemish being a 3-3 tie with the United States. The team remained in Europe after the Olympics and completed a series of 50 exhibition games against European squads. The Canadian team was victorious in an astounding 45 of those games.

Canadian Olympic Team

1951-52

- Maurice Richard misses 22 games and still ties Toronto's Sid Smith for fifth in goals (27).

- The Canadiens add rookie left winger Dickie Moore to the Richard-Lach unit—and with outstanding results.

- The Rangers, who replace coach Neil Colville with Bill Cook, introduce rookie right winger Wally Hergesheimer. He nets 26 goals.

- The fourth-place Bruins are paced by the scoring of Milt Schmidt and Johnny Peirson (50 points apiece).

- Boston replaces Jack Gelineau in goal with Sugar Jim Henry, back in the NHL after a two-year hiatus.

- Terry Sawchuk, Detroit's superb netminder, wins 44 games for the second year in a row and records the NHL's best GAA (1.90).

Maurice Richard, Bernie Geoffrion

Geoffrion Introduces the Slapshot

The 1951-52 season saw the arrival of a new star in Montreal. Bernie "Boom Boom" Geoffrion captured the Calder Trophy with 30 goals and 54 points. Geoffrion introduced a new offensive weapon that earned him his unique nickname. Many laughed at his new "slap" shot until he began slapping pucks over, under, and through enemy goaltenders. Geoffrion's new way of firing the puck soon became standard practice around the league.

Mosienko Nets Three Goals in 21 Seconds

Princess Elizabeth, Ted Kennedy

Kennedy Bows to the Future Queen

Canada is a constitutional monarchy, so it was a tremendous honor for Leafs captain Ted Kennedy to meet the future Head of State, Princess Elizabeth, on October 13, 1951. The Princess and her husband Philip, the Duke of Edinburgh, were treated to a 20-minute afternoon exhibition game staged in honor of the royal visitors. The Leafs were hit hard with reality that evening, however, as the visiting Black Hawks came in and dumped Toronto 3-1.

Bill Mosienko

The final game of the 1951-52 season was not expected to create much fanfare, as both the Rangers and the Black Hawks were already out of the playoff picture. Nevertheless, Chicago's Bill Mosienko put his name in the record books. Mosienko scored three third-period goals in an NHL-record 21 seconds. The Ranger goalie was Lorne Anderson, who never played in an NHL rink again.

- Toronto goalie Turk Broda plays only one game in this his last season. Al Rollins plays full-time.

- The playoffs feature Detroit vs. Toronto and Montreal vs. Boston.

- Montreal and Boston engage in a war of wills, as the Habs outscore

Boston 9-1 in the first two games before the Bruins win the next three.

- Game 6 of the semis goes to double O.T. before Montreal's Paul Masnick beats Jim Henry.

- Game 7 in Montreal starts badly for the Habs, as Maurice Richard is

knocked unconscious in a first-period collision.

- Maurice Richard, still dazed from his earlier injury, breaks a 1-1 tie late in Game 7. He skates the puck through the entire Bruins team and scores one of the most famous playoff goals ever.

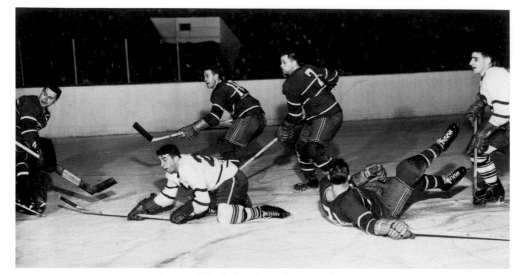

Toronto Maple Leafs vs. Montreal Canadiens

Smith Scores 27, Claims the Lady Byng

A new star rose to the rafters in Maple Leaf Gardens during the 1951-52 season. Sid Smith (far right), who led the AHL in scoring with 55 goals and 112 points in 1948-49, was the top Leaf shooter with 27 goals and 57 points in 1951-52. A gentleman on and off the ice, Smith was awarded the season's Lady Byng Trophy as the league's most productive nice guy. He spent only six minutes in the penalty box.

Lach Tallies a League-High 50 Assists

One of the most productive set-up artists in the history of the Canadiens, Elmer Lach led all NHL players with 50 assists during the 1951-52 season. A two-time NHL scoring leader in the 1940s, Lach struggled in the early part of the 1950s when injuries and poor production threatened his status as the pivot man on the famed Punch Line. However, he rebounded in 1951-52 to register 65 points, his highest total since 1944-45.

Elmer Lach

Sawchuk Posts Four Shutouts in Playoffs

After a regular season in which he led all goaltenders in virtually every statistical category, Terry Sawchuk continued to amaze right through the 1953 post-season. The Red Wings won eight consecutive games in the playoffs and did not allow a single goal on home ice. Sawchuk registered eight wins, four shutouts, and a GAA of 0.63 as Detroit motored past Toronto and Montreal to take the Cup.

Terry Sawchuk

1951-52

• In the other semifinals, Detroit sweeps Toronto in four games. The Wings have nine days off to rest up for their Finals meeting with Montreal.

• Detroit romps over the battered Canadiens in the Finals, sweeping Montreal in four games, Detroit

goalie Terry Sawchuk allows just two goals in the series.

• The Wings take Game 1 3-1. Ted Lindsay records the game-winner in Game 2, as Detroit prevails 2-1.

• In Game 3 of the Finals, Gordie Howe's first-period goal is all goalie

Terry Sawchuk needs, as the Red Wings win 3-0.

• Detroit's Metro Prystai scores twice in Game 4 as Sawchuk blanks the Habs again, 3-0. After going 8-0 in the playoffs, the Wings skate off with the Stanley Cup.

Dazed Rocket Scores Series-Winning Goal

In one of the most famous moments in hockey history, a bloodied but unbowed Maurice Richard accepts congratulations from Boston goaltender Jim Henry, who was playing despite two black eyes and a broken nose. In Game 7 of the 1952 Bruins-Montreal semifinal, Richard suffered a head injury that rendered him semi-conscious. In the game's waning moments, however, Richard took to the ice and skated through the entire Bruins team to score the series-winning goal.

Jim Henry, Maurice Richard

Stanley Cup Finals

Terry Sawchuk, Sid Abel

Wings Cap Off Their Best Year Ever

Red Wing captain Sid Abel shares a Cup and a smile with playoff hero Terry Sawchuk. The 1952 playoffs were a stroll in the park for the Wings. Not only did they go 8-0, but they were absolutely perfect at home, recording four shutouts in four games. This was probably the best Red Wings team of all time. They won the regular-season championship by 22 points and their superstars—Abel, Sawchuk, Gordie Howe, Ted Lindsay, and Red Kelly—were all in their prime.

Wings Bring Habs to Their Knees

Montreal defenseman Bud MacPherson drops to his knees in an attempt to block this shot from a Detroit attacker during action in Game 4 of the 1952 Stanley Cup Finals. Detroit's Johnny Wilson (#17) and Montreal's Billy Reay (#14) converge around Gerry McNeil, awaiting a possible rebound. Although McNeil allowed only 11 goals in the series, the Canadiens fell in four straight games to the powerhouse Red Wings.

- Terry Sawchuk ends the playoffs with four shutouts and an unheard-of GAA of 0.63.

- The Vezina Trophy goes to Terry Sawchuk, who helped his cause with 12 regular-season shutouts. Al Rollins is runner-up.

- Gordie Howe captures his first of six Hart Trophies. Elmer Lach is runner-up.

- Toronto's Sid Smith is awarded the Lady Byng Trophy.

- Bernie Geoffrion is awarded the Calder Trophy.

- Canada wins the Olympic hockey gold medal, while the United States takes the silver.

- Michigan wins its second straight NCAA hockey title with a 4-1 win over Colorado College. Nevertheless, Colorado goalie Ken Kinsley is named tourney MVP.

BRUINS GO AIRBORNE TO SHOOT DOWN THE WINGS

In April 1953, the Red Wings fully expected to extend their eight-game playoff winning streak, which they orchestrated a year before. The Detroiters not only had the most superstars (Gordie Howe, Ted Lindsay, Terry Sawchuk), but their second-liners were equally superb.

Marty Pavelich and Glen Skov ranked among the all-time best defensive forwards, while Marcel Pronovost and Bob Goldham rated among the NHL's best blueliners. Then there was Red Kelly, the game's No. 1 defenseman and winner of the year's Lady Byng Trophy for clean play and competence.

Nobody came close to Detroit in the regular-season race, which deflected attention toward a race of another kind. Howe took dead aim at Maurice Richard's record of 50 goals in a season, and though Howe fell just short, he still led the league in goals (49), assists (46), and points (a record 95), thus capturing his second career "triple crown."

Detroit's playoff opponent, Boston, seemed like easy fodder. The Bruins plugged their net with goalie Jim Henry, who was considered too old to stop Detroit. Boston's defense was mediocre, and its famous forwards, Milt Schmidt and Woody Dumart, were well past their prime. "Everyone expected an easy Detroit win," said Rangers manager Frank Boucher. "Maybe even a four-game sweep."

The opening game reinforced Boucher's point. Playing before their home crowd at Olympia Stadium, the Red Wings trashed Boston 7-0. But in the second game, the Bruins thoroughly outskated and outshot the Red Wings. The Eddie Sandford-Fleming Mackell-Johnny Peirson line began clicking, and Detroit's Production Line was thoroughly nullified by Schmidt, Dumart, and Joe Klukay. Boston won 5-3.

The third contest, played at the Boston Garden, was tied 1-1 after three periods. When the overtime began, the teams warily pawed at each other, accenting defense. Boston was using two rookie defensemen, Bob Armstrong and Warren Godfrey, but they played flawlessly. If the Bruins were to win, though, they had to beat Sawchuk, and the word was he could be beaten most easily by a high shot.

In the 12th minute of overtime, winger Jack McIntyre went into orbit for the Bruins. He hurled over the Detroit blueline and flicked his wrists. The puck took off like a jet leaving the runway and eluded the transfixed Sawchuk at 12:29.

Game 4 was played on Howe's birthday, but the Bruins were the ones who did the celebrating. Dumart shadowed Howe with unaccustomed efficiency, and Boston ran off with a 6-2 win. The Wings finally broke free in Game 5 with a 6-4 victory at home, but the Bruins earned their way into the Finals by winning Game 6 4-2 at Boston Garden.

The upset-minded Bruins took aim at Montreal in the Finals, but the Canadiens emerged victorious, taking the decisive Game 5 1-0 on an overtime goal by Elmer Lach. As for the Wings, they'd be back on top in 1953-54—and this time, they wouldn't be denied.

1952-53

- The Hockey Hall of Fame inducts five new members, including Moose Johnson, Mickey MacKay, and Bill Cook.

- Cleveland applies for an NHL franchise prior to the season, but the request is refused.

- The Red Wings break up the Production Line when they sell Sid Abel to Chicago, where he becomes player/coach.

- Detroit installs Alex Delvecchio at center between Gordie Howe and Ted Lindsay and the Production Line is back, never missing a beat.

- Detroit wins the regular-season title with a record of 36-16-18, 15 points better than second-place Montreal.

- Boston and Chicago finish tied for third with 69 points in 70 games.

- Toronto misses the playoffs for only the third time in 23 years, while the

Using tight checking and outstanding goaltending, the Bruins shocked the
Red Wings in the 1953 Cup semifinals. The Bruins, who finished 21 points behind
the first-place Wings, threw a defensive blanket over Detroit star Gordie Howe,
limiting him to only two goals in the series. With Sugar Jim Henry (pictured)
providing sweet goaltending, the Bruins rebounded from a 7-0 thrashing in
the opening game to down the Wings in six.

Rangers sit home for the third time in three years.

• Gordie Howe leads the league in goals, assists, and points. His 95 points are a new NHL record.

• Once viewed as untouchable, Maurice Richard's 50-goal season is challenged by Gordie Howe, who finishes with 49.

• Alex Delvecchio, promoted to the Production Line, finishes second in the league in assists (43).

• Ted Lindsay is runner-up to Gordie Howe in total points (71). Lindsay is also second in the league in penalty minutes (111).

• The NHL crowns a new penalty king—the Canadiens' tenacious Rocket Richard (112 minutes).

• Boston's Fleming Mackell leads his club in goals (27) and points (44).

Plante's Debut a Big Success

Jacques Plante made his first NHL appearance in 1952-53, allowing only four goals in three regular-season games. During the playoffs, coach Dick Irvin surprisingly gave Plante four starts. Plante thanked him by winning three games, allowing only seven goals. Plante's key performance came in the semifinals against Chicago, with the Habs down three games to two. Plante blanked the Hawks 3-0 to force a seventh game, which Montreal also won.

Jacques Plante

Kelly Still the Best Blueliner

Red Kelly continued to be the NHL's dominant defenseman during the 1952-53 season, leading all league blueliners with 46 points (19 goals and 27 assists). Kelly, who went overseas in the off-season to provide moral support to Canadian and American troops serving in the Korean War, received his second Lady Byng Trophy in 1952-53. He deserved it after receiving only four minor penalties over the course of the 70-game schedule.

Red Kelly

Barons Want to Play for the Cup

In 1952-53, the AHL's Cleveland Barons issued a Stanley Cup challenge to the NHL brass. Their challenge was denied for two reasons: Cleveland had not yet even captured the title of its own league, and the NHL did not consider the Barons, or the AHL, to be of major-league caliber. Big names on the Barons included coach Bun Cook (front row, third from right), Johnny Bower (front row, fourth from left), and Fred Shero (middle row, fifth from left).

Cleveland Barons

1952-53

- Wally Hergesheimer, tied with Alex Delvecchio for fourth in points (59), is among New York's few bright spots.

- The Red Wings debut another brilliant young goalie, Glenn Hall. Terry Sawchuk, however, remains Detroit's No. 1 man, winning 32 games and posting a league-leading 1.90 GAA.

- The Hawks and Leafs swap goalies, as Al Rollins moves to Chicago and Harry Lumley heads to Toronto.

- Harry Lumley leads the league in losses (30) for the third year in a row.

However, he also ties for the league lead in shutouts (10).

- Chuck Rayner, the Rangers' 32-year-old goalie, loses his job to rookie Gump Worsley.

- Detroit's Red Kelly leads all defensemen with 46 points.

Vic Lynn, Al Rollins, Gus Mortson

Lindsay's the Best at Left Wing

Ted Lindsay celebrates his 200th career goal with coach Tommy Ivan after Detroit's 5-2 win over the Rangers on December 21, 1952. The 25th player in league history to score 200 goals, Lindsay went on have one of his strongest NHL campaigns, collecting 32 goals and 39 assists for the second-highest points total in the league. The unruly left winger was rewarded for his excellent season by being named to the NHL's First All-Star Team.

Detroit Red Wings vs. Montreal Canadiens

Rollins Nearly Wins the Hart

Toronto's Al Rollins was traded to Chicago just before the 1952-53 season began. A playoff hero for the Leafs in 1951, Rollins solidified Chicago's last line of defense, winning 27 games, registering six shutouts, and finishing runner-up to Gordie Howe for the Hart Trophy. With former Leafs Vic Lynn and Mortson at his side, Rollins was never homesick for his old Toronto teammates.

Tommy Ivan, Ted Lindsay

Howe Falls a Goal Short of 50

In 1944-45, Maurice Richard scored 50 goals, a feat many pundits said would never be equaled. Only eight seasons later, Gordie Howe entered the final game of the season with 49 goals. Ironically, that game was against Richard and the Canadiens. The Rocket and his teammates threw a blanket over Howe, never allowing him the opportunity to equal Richard's sacred mark. Howe finished the season with 49 goals and an NHL-record 95 points.

• On November 8, 1952, Rocket Richard scores his 325th goal, overtaking Nels Stewart for the all-time lead. In the same game, teammate Elmer Lach notches his 200th goal.

• In March 1953, the AHL's Cleveland Barons announce they want

to challenge the upcoming NHL champion for the Stanley Cup. The NHL governors do not accept the challenge.

• The Stanley Cup playoffs feature Detroit vs. Boston and Montreal vs. Chicago.

• When the Red Wings trounce the Bruins 7-0 in Game 1, experts begin planning a parade in Motown.

• The Bruins storm back and win the next three games against Detroit, outscoring the Red Wings 13-6 to put them on the brink of elimination.

Geoffrion Weds Morenz's Daughter

Montreal's Bernie Geoffrion poses with his wife Marlene on their honeymoon during the spring of 1953. Geoffrion, while displaying his revolutionary slapshot, netted 22 goals in 1952-53 and added six more in the playoffs. Marlene, the daughter of former Canadiens superstar Howie Morenz, is seen exchanging American money for Canadian cash.

Romeo Moreau, Bernie Geoffrion, Marlene Geoffrion

Abel Becomes Hawks' Player/Coach

An era came to a close in Detroit when team captain Sid Abel left the team to become the playing coach of the lowly Black Hawks in 1952-53. Abel boosted the Hawks' confidence and the club climbed from the NHL basement to fourth place with a 27-28-15 record. The Black Hawks shocked the hockey world in the playoffs by taking a 3-2 lead in games in the 1953 semifinals against the Canadiens before bowing to the eventual Stanley Cup champions.

Sid Abel (right)

Sandford Comes Alive in Playoffs

A versatile performer who was adept at playing all three forward positions, Ed Sandford was a fan favorite in Boston, especially during the 1952-53 season. Never noted as a goal-scorer, Sandford was switched to center just prior to the 1953 playoffs and he responded by playing the best hockey of his career. In the postseason, Sandford led all NHL marksmen in goals (eight) and points (11) as the Bruins made it to the Stanley Cup Finals.

Eddie Sandford

1952-53

• Detroit briefly revives in Game 5, outscoring Boston 6-4, but the end comes three nights later when the Bruins advance with a 4-2 victory.

• In its first playoff in seven years, Chicago plays valiantly. After dropping two against Montreal, the Hawks win three straight.

• Canadiens rookie Jacques Plante shuts out Chicago 3-0 in Game 6. Montreal cruises 4-1 in Game 7 to advance to the Finals.

• Montreal and Boston split the first two games of the Finals, with the Habs winning 4-2 in Game 1 and the Bruins prevailing 4-1 in Game 2.

• Montreal's Gerry McNeil, back in goal, blanks Boston 3-0 in Game 3.

• Maurice Richard's hat-trick in Game 4 stakes the Habs to a 7-3 win and a three-games-to-one lead.

• Game 5 is scoreless through regulation, thanks to goalies Gerry

Montreal Canadiens

Good Defense Helps Habs Win Cup

The Stanley Cup champion Canadiens pose with hockey's Holy Grail after defeating the Bruins to win their sixth NHL championship in 1953. Outstanding goaltending and an unmovable defense—anchored by Butch Bouchard, Doug Harvey, and Tom Johnson—were the keys to the Habs' victory. The first seven players in the first row (Jacques Plante, Maurice Richard, Elmer Lach, Bert Olmstead, Dick Irvin, Frank Selke, and Bernie Geoffrion—left to right) are in the Hockey Hall of Fame.

Rocket, Habs Beat Bruins in Finals

Maurice Richard slips the puck past Boston's Sugar Jim Henry in Game 1 of the 1953 Stanley Cup Finals, helping the Habs to a 4-2 victory. The Canadiens, paced by the Rocket's four goals, captured the Stanley Cup in five games. Elmer Lach scored the last postseason goal of his illustrious career in overtime during the fifth and deciding contest, giving the Canadiens a 1-0 victory and the Stanley Cup.

Stanley Cup Finals

McNeil and Sugar Jim Henry. But Elmer Lach scores at 1:22 of O.T. to win the Cup for Montreal.

• Boston's Eddie Sandford is the postseason scoring leader (8-3-11).

• Goalie Jacques Plante turns in a 1.75 playoff GAA.

• Detroit's Gordie Howe takes his second straight Hart Trophy. Chicago goalie Al Rollins is runner-up.

• Terry Sawchuk wins the second of his four Vezina Trophies, while teammate Red Kelly cops the Lady Byng.

• The Calder Trophy goes to Rangers goalie Gump Worsley.

• Michigan claims its third straight NCAA hockey championship, trouncing Minnesota 7-3 in the title game. Wolverine forward John Matchefts is named tourney MVP.

WINGS NEED LUCKY SHOT TO BEAT THE MIGHTY HABS

The two marquee teams of 1953-54 were clearly the Red Wings and Canadiens. Success was becoming old hat for the Wings, as they were cruising toward their sixth straight regular-season title. But the Canadiens, the 1952-53 Cup champs, were on the threshold of greatness. Throughout the season, fans envisioned a Montreal-Detroit matchup in the Finals.

The Habs were becoming loaded with superstars. Bernie Geoffrion, who won the Calder Trophy in 1952, had mastered the new slapshot, and rookie Jean Beliveau joined him at center after lengthy contract negotiations. Dickie Moore was fast becoming the NHL's best left wing, and Maurice Richard never looked better on the right side.

Beliveau, the newest kid on the block, was the antithesis of Richard, Geoffrion, and Moore. His long strides indicated that he was not really trying very hard, and—unlike his volcanic teammates—he displayed no thirst for violence. Unfortunately, the gentile Beliveau became an easy target for opponents. They roughed him up so much during his rookie year that he missed 26 games due to injuries.

Despite his distaste for the rough stuff, Beliveau was a heck of a talent. His stick-handling ability suggested that he had an invisible string linking the puck to his stick blade, and his shot was hard and accurate. "The playing of Beliveau," commented Canadian novelist Hugh MacLennan, "is poetry in action."

Of course, the Red Wings weren't lacking in the superstar department. In 1953-54, Detroit's classy Red Kelly became the first winner of the Norris Trophy as the NHL's best defenseman. Kelly also won the Lady Byng Trophy for the second straight year, a feat unprecedented for a backliner.

Gordie Howe maintained his offensive excellence, leading the league in scoring (33-48-81) for the fourth straight year. Detroit's overall balance enabled the Red Wings to once again take first place (37-19-14), seven points ahead of Montreal. A Canadiens-Red Wings Final did indeed come to pass, as Detroit ousted Toronto and Montreal bested Boston in the semifinals.

In the Stanley Cup Finals, Montreal coach Dick Irvin started young goalie Jacques Plante. But when Detroit took a three-games-to-one lead, Irvin yanked Plante in favor of Gerry McNeil. The veteran played the best goal of his life, beating Detroit 1-0 and 4-1 to tie the championship series at three. Appropriately, Game 7 at Olympia Stadium went down to the wire. The game was tied 1-1 and then entered overtime. The score remained deadlocked through the 4:25 mark when the Wings invaded Canadiens territory.

Detroit's Tony Leswick released a soft, easily playable shot. McNeil was preparing to catch the puck when his ace defenseman, Doug Harvey, reached up to deflect it into the corner. Harvey, a top baseball fielder, ironically got only a piece of the rubber. It bounced off Harvey's glove, took a right turn past McNeil, and flew into the net at 4:29. On this freakiest of freak shots, Detroit had won its third Stanley Cup in five years.

1953-54

• A new award is established—the James Norris Trophy—for the league's best defenseman. It's named after the former owner of the Red Wings.

• The NHL's intraleague draft structure is revised, allowing teams to protect 20 (instead of 30) players.

The claiming price is reduced from $25,000 to $15,000 per player.

• Future Islanders star Denis Potvin is born on October 29, 1953, in Ottawa, Ontario.

• The lowly Rangers make headlines with a series of roster moves, beginning with their decision to demote 1952-53 Calder Trophy winner Gump Worsley to the minor leagues.

• Goalie Johnny Bower, a career minor-leaguer, debuts with the Rangers at 29 years of age.

Members of the Red Wings gather around goaltender Terry Sawchuk after beating Montreal in the 1954 Stanley Cup Finals. The Wings rolled up a three-games-to-one lead in the series only to have the Habs roar back with 1-0 and 4-1 victories. The seventh game was settled in overtime when Montreal defenseman Doug Harvey knocked the puck into his own net attempting to corral a shot by Detroit's Tony Leswick, giving the Red Wings the Stanley Cup.

• New York G.M. Frank Boucher signs Max Bentley, the two-time scoring champ, to run the power play.

• Against the advice of all the experts, Rangers boss Frank Boucher inks Camille Henry, a 135-pound left winger, to an NHL contract.

• The Red Wings capture their sixth straight regular-season title, going 37-19-14.

• The Canadiens finish in second place, seven points back of the Red Wings. They lead the league with 195 goals.

• Toronto finishes in third place, thanks to Harry Lumley's league-leading 1.86 GAA and 13 shutouts.

• The Black Hawks are back in the basement, going 12-51-7 and scoring just 133 goals. The Rangers miss the playoffs for the fifth time in six years.

Norris Trophy

Norris Trophy Honors NHL's Best Blueliner

After years of lobbying for an award saluting the league's best defenseman, the NHL introduced the James Norris Memorial Trophy in 1953. Presented to the league by the four children of former Detroit Red Wings owner James Norris, the silverware is awarded "to the defense player who demonstrates throughout the season the greatest all-round ability in the position." Fittingly, the first winner of the trophy was Red Wings defenseman Red Kelly.

Camille Henry

Eel Slithers Way to Calder Trophy

The Rangers featured a new star during the 1953-54 season. Camille "The Eel" Henry won the Calder Trophy as the NHL's best newcomer, counting 24 goals and 15 assists for the Broadway Blues. Blessed with explosive speed and clever instincts, Henry was an instant crowd favorite at Madison Square Garden. Although he stood only 5'8" and weighed 150 pounds, Henry survived the rough going to finish second on the team in goals.

Harry Lumley

Lumley Comes of Age, Wins Vezina Trophy

Harry Lumley was known as "Apple Cheeks" when he first entered the NHL as a 17-year-old. In 1953-54, an older, mature Lumley was the league's best goaltender, racking up a Toronto-record 13 shutouts and leading the league in GAA with a lowly mark of 1.86. Lumley's outstanding work between the pipes earned him the Vezina Trophy. It was the only time in his distinguished career that he took home the silverware as the league's top netminder.

1953-54

- Gordie Howe captures an unprecedented fourth straight scoring crown with 81 points. He also leads the league in assists (48).

- Montreal's Maurice Richard leads the NHL in goals (37) for the fourth time.

- Bernie Geoffrion, playing in the shadow of the aging Rocket Richard, is third in the NHL in goals (29).

- Ted Lindsay, Detroit's fiery left winger, is fifth in goals (26), third in assists (36), third in points (62), and third in penalty minutes (110).

- On October 5, 1953, Detroit rookie center Earl Reibel records four assists in his first NHL game, setting an NHL record.

- On January 9, 1954, Montreal's Bert Olmstead collects eight points (four goals) in a 12-1 win over Chicago.

Rocket Blasts 37 Goals to Lead NHL

For the first time in four seasons, Maurice "Rocket" Richard won the goal-scoring crown, blasting 37 pucks past NHL goaltenders during the 1953-54 campaign. The Canadiens' offensive catalyst, who led the NHL in goals for the fourth time in his career, also found himself on top in penalty time as well, spending 112 minutes in the box. Richard faltered in the playoffs, however, recording only three goals and no assists in 11 games.

Max and Doug Bentley

Bentleys Play Together in New York

One of the greatest brother combinations in NHL history was reunited in 1953-54, when Max and Doug Bentley joined the Rangers for their final skate around the NHL. Max was purchased by New York following the 1952-53 campaign, and he convinced Doug to come out of retirement and join the Rangers. Both performed admirably in their final season, with Max collecting 32 points in 57 games and Doug adding 12 points in his 20-game stint on Broadway.

Maurice Richard

Bert Olmstead

Olmstead Posts Eight Points in One Game

Montreal's Bert Olmstead was a smooth-skating winger with exceptional playmaking skills. On January 4, 1954, Olmstead placed his name in the NHL record books by becoming the first NHL player since Maurice Richard in 1944 to collect eight points in a single game. Olmstead scored four goals and set up four others in a 12-1 victory over Chicago.

• Just after New Year's Day, the Rangers talk former NHL superstar Doug Bentley into joining his brother Max in a comeback attempt.

• On January 21, 1954, Doug Bentley ends his 18-month retirement, scoring in his first game as a Ranger.

• The playoffs feature Detroit against Toronto and the Habs against Boston.

• Little drama accompanies the semifinals, as the Red Wings whip the Leafs in five games.

• In Game 5, the Red Wings and Leafs end regulation tied at 3-3. The

Wings win it in double O.T. on a goal by Ted Lindsay.

• The Canadiens sail through a four-game sweep of the Bruins, outscoring their rivals 16-4.

• In the Finals, Detroit and Montreal trade 3-1 wins in the first two games.

Norris Winner Kelly Spends Time in Korea

A global conflict exploded in Asia during the early 1950s when the Korean War erupted in North and South Korea. Numerous NHL players, such as 1953-54 Norris Trophy winner Red Kelly (top right), traveled to Korea to entertain the troops and deliver some well-needed encouragement. Kelly scored a career-high five goals during the 1954 playoffs, helping the Red Wings to their third Cup of the decade.

Korean War

Gordie Howe

Rollins Leads in Losses but Wins the Hart

Not much went right for the Black Hawks during the 1953-54 season, as the team fell into the NHL basement. Perhaps the only bright spot for the Hawks was veteran goaltender Al Rollins, who withstood Chicago's porous defense and performed admirably. Even though his 47 losses and 3.23 GAA were by far the worst marks in the league, he was recognized for his talent and courage and was awarded the Hart Trophy.

Al Rollins

Howe Scores Goals from Either Side

Gordie Howe captured his fourth straight Art Ross Trophy in 1953-54 by leading all NHL skaters in assists (48) and points (81). Howe, who came within a single goal of 50 in 1952-53, was a dazzling stick-handler with pinpoint accuracy on his rocketing wrist shots. He was equally adept at firing the puck from the left side as he was from the right, which allowed him to fool enemy defenders and confuse even the best NHL goaltenders.

1953-54

- Detroit thrashes Montreal 5-2 in Game 3.

- The Habs, with two excellent goalies (Gerry McNeil and Jacques Plante), are outdone by Detroit puck-stopper Terry Sawchuk, who wins Game 4 of the Finals 2-0.

- Facing elimination, Gerry McNeil slams the door on Detroit. All-Star center Kenny Mosdell scores at 5:45 of O.T. to give the Habs a 1-0 victory.

- Montreal wins Game 6 of the Finals 4-1, thanks to two goals by Busher Curry.

- Game 7 is tied on goals by Busher Curry (Montreal) and Red Kelly (Detroit) when regulation ends. The next goal wins the Cup.

- The Wings' Tony Leswick finds the back of the Montreal net at 4:29 of O.T. to win the Stanley Cup for Detroit, its third in five years.

Soviets Win Their First World Title

The Soviet Union National Team made its first appearance on the international hockey scene in the world championships of 1954 and surprised the hockey world by winning the gold medal. The Soviets defeated the Canadian representatives, the East York Lyndhursts, 7-2 in the gold-medal game. The Soviets, led by Vsevelod Bobrov and Vladimir Zabrodsky, went undefeated in the seven-game tourney to capture their first international hockey title.

Soviet National Team

Wings Thwart the Leafs in Semifinals

Detroit goaltender Terry Sawchuk slides across the crease in an attempt to rob Toronto's Ted Kennedy during action in the 1954 semifinals. Kennedy's shot dribbled wide of the post, enabling Detroit to escape with a narrow 2-1 victory in the March 30 contest. Although Sid Smith (#8) and Tod Sloan (#15) seem to have command of the slot, it was the Red Wings who controlled the series, dropping the Leafs in five games.

Stanley Cup Semifinals

• Even though Chicago gave up 60 more goals than any other team in the league, goalie Al Rollins is awarded the Hart Trophy.

• Detroit defenseman Red Kelly takes his third Lady Byng Trophy in four years. He also wins the first Norris Trophy.

• Toronto goalie Harry Lumley captures the Vezina Trophy for the only time in his 16-year career. Terry Sawchuk is runner-up.

• Despite his tiny frame, Camille Henry scores 24 rookie goals and wins the Calder Trophy.

• Rensselaer Polytechnic Institute wins the NCAA championship, beating Minnesota 5-4 in overtime in the finals. RPI forward Abbie Moore is named tourney MVP.

• The Soviet Union wins the hockey world championship—its first of many such titles.

Maurice "Rocket" Richard, regarded as the Babe Ruth of hockey, was a galvanic power forward, one who could score from virtually any angle. "He once beat me carrying not one but two defensemen on his back," said Black Hawks goalie Emile Francis.

Yet for all his prowess, Richard had never won a scoring championship. This rankled the Rocket because he believed he had been unfairly deprived of the title by inept refereeing. In 1954-55, though, Richard was rocketing toward his greatest scoring season ever. Concurrently, his Canadiens were challenging the Red Wings for the regular-season title.

With the season winding down, the Canadiens skated against the Bruins at Boston Garden. The game was typically rough and, at one point, Richard and Bruins defenseman Hal Laycoe went at it. The Rocket took exception to linesman Cliff Thompson's one-sided intervention and floored the official. Richard was ejected from the game, and NHL President Clarence Campbell ordered a hearing two days later.

Campbell and Richard had often clashed in the past. The Rocket was convinced that the

ROCKET'S SUSPENSION SPARKS RIOTS IN MONTREAL

president relied on the advice of the league's power brokers. Often, those power brokers—especially Toronto's Conn Smythe—had insisted that Richard be severely punished. For his throw-down of Thompson, Campbell suspended Richard for the final three games of the season and for the entire playoffs.

News of the harsh suspension quickly spread across Montreal, leaving the populace in a state of rage and rebellion. That night, the Habs were to play the Red Wings in a game that would decide first place.

Despite his suspension, the Rocket arrived at the rink that night—as did Campbell, who had been warned by police not to attend. The president entered the arena after the game had started. The fans, observing his entrance, pelted him with fruits and

vegetables. One spectator ran up to Campbell and punched him. Then out of nowhere, a tear-gas bomb exploded near ice level.

Richard and his wife ran for safety and found sanctuary in the Forum clinic. To Richard's amazement, Campbell was also there. Richard was warned to not even speak to Campbell, and Campbell was soon led out of the Forum through a back door.

When Richard returned home that night, he heard on the news about the violence that was raging outside the Forum. Soon afterward, manager Frank Selke urged Richard to go on radio and TV to calm the citizens. Richard agreed, and he told his fans that he deserved the suspension, even though he believed it shouldn't have been so severe. With that, the rioting subsided.

The incomplete game was forfeited to the Wings, who wound up finishing two points ahead of Montreal in the standings. Moreover, Montreal's Bernie Geoffrion overtook Richard in the scoring race, beating him 75 to 74. Les Habs ended up reaching the Finals, but they were defeated by Detroit in seven games. Had Richard not been suspended, the result likely would have been reversed.

1954-55

- The NHL begins the practice of maintaining an "out-of-town" scoreboard at each arena.

- The NHL rules for the first time that referees and linesmen are to wear the now-familiar "zebra-striped" shirts.

- Teams begin to wear colored sweaters at home and white sweaters on the road.

- In Detroit, Tommy Ivan steps down as coach after seven outstanding years. He's replaced by Jimmy Skinner.

- After a 10-14-6 start, the Bruins install recently retired Milt Schmidt behind the bench.

- Sid Abel is fired as coach of Chicago after a disastrous 1953-54 season. Frank Eddolls, a former NHL defenseman, takes over.

In one of the darkest moments in NHL history, a fan attacks NHL President Clarence Campbell at the Montreal Forum on March 17, 1955. Campbell, who had just suspended Canadiens star Rocket Richard for the duration of the regular season and playoffs, endured the wrath of the Montreal fans, who felt his actions were unwarranted. This game was eventually forfeited to Detroit and a riot ensued on the streets of Montreal that caused millions of dollars in damage.

- Canadiens goalie Gerry McNeil retires at age 28, leaving the door wide open for Jacques Plante.

- The Red Wings win the regular-season title for the seventh straight time—an all-time record. Their 42-17-11 mark is just two points better than Montreal's.

- Montreal leads the league in goals (228). It features the NHL's top three goal-scorers and scoring leaders.

- Bernie Geoffrion, who scores five times in a game against the Rangers, ties Maurice Richard for the league lead in goals (38). Teammate Jean Beliveau finishes with 37.

- Bernie Geoffrion leads the NHL with 75 points, while Rocket Richard tallies 74 points and Jean Beliveau garners 73.

- Bert Olmstead makes an art of wrestling loose pucks out of corners to set up his linemates. He leads the NHL in assists (48).

Ivan Moves from Detroit to Chicago

In a shocking move, Detroit's Tommy Ivan resigned as coach of the Red Wings prior to the 1954-55 season. Ivan, who had directed the Wings to six first-place finishes and three Stanley Cup titles in his seven years behind the bench, left Detroit to take on general manager duties with the sadsack Black Hawks. Despite Ivan's involvement, the Hawks finished out of the playoffs for the eighth time in the past decade.

Tommy Ivan

Hal Laycoe, Jimmy Carter

Laycoe Preps for Battle with Richard

Boston defenseman Hal Laycoe, the only player in the NHL to wear glasses during the 1954-55 season, discusses the sweet science of boxing with lightweight champ Jimmy Carter. Laycoe would need all the advice Carter could offer when he battled Montreal's Maurice Richard. A former teammate of Richard, Laycoe's celebrated clash with the Rocket occurred near the end of the season and resulted in Richard being suspended for the duration of the schedule.

Maurice Richard

Rocket Works Himself into a Tizzy

Maurice Richard often confessed he couldn't remember many of the goals he scored during his illustrious career because he worked himself into a frenzy on the ice, all in an effort to win. That frantic behavior backfired on the Canadiens' superstar when he attacked linesman Cliff Thompson in a game against Boston near the end of the 1954-55 season. His subsequent suspension cost him his last real chance at a scoring championship.

1954-55

- Dutch Reibel leads the Red Wings' attack (66 points, four ahead of Gordie Howe) and is the NHL's fourth-best scorer.

- Danny Lewicki (29-24-53) and Andy Bathgate (20-20-40) lead the fifth-place Rangers.

- Toronto goalie Harry Lumley has the NHL's best GAA (1.94) for the second straight year.

- Detroit's Terry Sawchuk, the wall of misery for NHL shooters, wins 40 games and is honored with his third Vezina Trophy.

- Gump Worsley retakes his starting job as the Rangers' No. 1 goalie, but he leads the league in losses (33).

- With Jim Henry's playing days dwindling, the Bruins rely on 21-year-old goaltender John Henderson as a stop-gap.

Rocket Fans Boo Boom Boom

Throughout much of the 1954-55 season, Bernie Geoffrion and teammate Maurice Richard were engaged in a friendly competition for the scoring title. However, after the Rocket was suspended for the season with three games remaining, Geoffrion was able to surpass Richard to win his first Art Ross Trophy with 75 points. Richard was viewed as a hockey icon in Quebec, and Geoffrion was booed by his own fans for "stealing" the scoring title away from the Rocket.

Detroit Red Wings

Bernie Geoffrion

Detroit Beats Habs for Season Title

Detroit's Terry Sawchuk (center) is given a victory ride by elated teammates after the Red Wings captured their seventh consecutive NHL regular-season title in 1955. The Wings, who were engaged in a neck-and-neck battle with the Canadiens through most of the season, finally salted away the title with a 6-0 shutout over the Habs in the last game of the season. Marcel Pronovost (left) and Vic Stasiuk (right) give Sawchuk a lift.

Harvey's 43 Assists Set a New Record

Montreal's Doug Harvey had perhaps his finest NHL season in 1954-55, establishing a league record for assists by a defenseman. He set up his teammates for 43 goals while setting a career high with 49 points. A smooth skater with outstanding skills and speed, Harvey became the second NHL blueliner to win the Norris Trophy. He had finished runner-up to Red Kelly the previous season.

Doug Harvey

• Canadiens defenseman Doug Harvey finishes second in the league in assists (43) and breaks Babe Pratt's record for assists by a backliner.

• Rocket Richard becomes entangled in a brawl with Boston's Hal Laycoe, who cut Richard with his stick.

• Maurice Richard's attempts to avenge his attack by Hal Laycoe result in linesman (and former Boston Bruin) Cliff Thompson using excessive force.

• The scuffle between linesman Cliff Thompson and Rocket Richard results in NHL President Clarence

Campbell suspending Richard for the rest of the regular season and playoffs.

• On March 17, 1955, a riot breaks out at the Montreal Forum during a Habs-Red Wings game, as fans attack Clarence Campbell in protest over his suspension of Rocket Richard.

Alex Delvecchio

Delvecchio Saves the Best for Last

Popular Detroit centerman Alex Delvecchio, nicknamed "Fats," feasted on post-season goaltenders during the Red Wings' successful defense of their Stanley Cup title in 1955. After a season in which he scored only 17 goals, Delvecchio rebounded in the postseason to find the mark seven times. In one of his best playoff performances, Delvecchio scored a pair of goals in Detroit's 3-1 win in Game 7 of the Finals against Montreal.

Earl Reibel, Gordie Howe

Reibel, Howe Score Big in Playoffs

Earl "Dutch" Reibel and Gordie Howe share a smile after the Red Wings defeated the Canadiens to win the 1955 Stanley Cup. Howe set an NHL postseason record with 20 points, while Reibel contributed the finest playoff performance of his career. A gifted centerman who pivoted the Production Line with Howe and Ted Lindsay, Dutch fired five goals and added seven assists to boost the Motowners into the Stanley Cup winner's circle.

Ted Kennedy

Teeder Retires After Earning Hart

Ted Kennedy peers pensively at his famed No. 9 jersey after announcing his retirement in 1955. Kennedy, who would soon be named the league's Hart Trophy winner, decided to hang up the blades after the Red Wings swept the Maple Leafs from the 1955 semifinals in straight games. Nevertheless, Kennedy was in his old form during the best-of-seven set, scoring or assisting on four of the six goals the Leafs managed in the series.

1954-55

- Because of his suspension, Rocket Richard finishes one point out of a scoring title.

- Detroit faces Toronto in the semifinals, while Montreal hosts Boston.

- Playing without Maurice Richard—their heart and soul—the Canadiens still wallop Boston, outscoring the Bruins 16-9 in a five-game triumph.

- Detroit's mastery of the Maple Leafs continues, as the Red Wings sweep Toronto in four games.

- In the Finals, Montreal scores to take a 2-1 lead in the third period of Game 1, but Detroit responds with three late goals and wins 4-2.

- In Game 2 of the Finals, Montreal is stunned by a four-goal performance by Ted Lindsay, losing 7-1.

- The Habs bounce back with a pair of wins at home, 4-2 and 5-3.

Stanley Cup Semifinals

Wings Crush Leafs Again in Semifinals

In 1954-55, for the fourth time in the decade, the Red Wings eliminated the Maple Leafs in the semifinals, this time sweeping the Leafs in four straight games. Terry Sawchuk, seen here stalling Sid Smith's goal-scoring attempt during Detroit's 2-1 win in Game 3, allowed only six goals in the series. It was another case of sweet vindication for the Red Wings, who were swept in the Stanley Cup Finals by the Leafs in 1948 and 1949.

Wings Enjoy Fourth Cup of the Decade

G.M. Jack Adams hugs Terry Sawchuk following Detroit's seven-game victory over Montreal in the 1955 Stanley Cup Finals. The Wings, who swept Toronto in the semifinals, opened a quick two-game lead over Montreal only to see the Habs tie the series after four games. In the seventh match, Alex Delvecchio's two goals were the margin of difference as the Wings won their fourth Cup of the decade by a 3-1 score.

Jack Adams, Terry Sawchuk

- Detroit and Montreal trade home-ice victories, with the Wings prevailing 5-1 in Game 5 and the Canadiens winning 6-3 in Game 6.

- Detroit wins the decisive Game 7 3-1, as Alex Delvecchio scores twice. Detroit thus wins its fourth Stanley Cup in six years.

- Gordie Howe, who scored the winner in Game 7, sets a new playoff record with 20 points.

- Toronto's Ted Kennedy, on the verge of retiring, wins the Hart Trophy. Teammate Sid Smith receives the Lady Byng Trophy.

- Chicago's Ed Litzenberger (51 points) captures the Calder Trophy. Montreal's Doug Harvey wins the Norris Trophy as top defenseman.

- Michigan wins its fifth NCAA title, beating Colorado College in the finals. Colorado's Phil Hilton is tourney MVP.

The art of goaltending has been evolving since 1918, when Clint Benedict's penchant for dropping to the ice forced a rule change. But never in hockey history has there been a net-minder who revolutionized his profession so dramatically and so quickly as Jacques "Jake the Snake" Plante.

In his spare time, Plante had a hobby of knitting toques, the French-Canadian wool caps worn by his ancestors. On the ice, he was a cocky competitor who displayed a bizarre goaltending style. Plante believed he could aid his defensemen by roaming out of his cage to retrieve pucks that skidded behind his net—which in his day was a strict taboo.

Plante introduced his style as a rookie in the spring of 1953, when the Canadiens were engaged in a thrilling semifinal against Chicago. Montreal coach Dick Irvin had been relying mostly on veteran goaltender Gerry McNeil, but with his team down three games to two he inserted his inexperienced, experimental rookie in the net.

It was a bold move indeed, but the confident Plante was up to the challenge. He stopped the Black Hawks cold, shutting them out

WANDERING PLANTE LEADS HABS TO STANLEY CUP

3-0. Montreal then won the seventh game and cruised past Boston to win the Stanley Cup. In four playoff games, Plante posted a 1.75 goals-against average.

Plante remained a backup in 1953-54, but when called upon he was brilliantly effective—and certainly eccentric. The Snake occasionally enraged opposing fans with his scrambles behind the net for the puck. One time, the play backfired on him. He missed the disk, and an opponent retrieved it and shoved the rubber into the cage.

Nevertheless, by the 1955-56 campaign, Plante had become the best in the business. "Starting that season," said coach Toe Blake, "for five years Jacques was the greatest goalie the league has ever seen."

Plante's goaltending in 1955-56

was as exquisite as the Canadiens' offensive attack. With coach Blake orchestrating his club to perfection, the Canadiens romped to the regular-season title, going 45-15-10 and finishing 24 points ahead of second-place Detroit. Four of the top seven scorers were Canadiens, and Jean Beliveau, Maurice Richard, Doug Harvey, and Plante were named to the First All-Star Team. Plante's 1.86 GAA earned him the Vezina Trophy—his first of five straight and sixth overall—while Harvey captured the Norris Trophy and Beliveau claimed the Hart.

Plante maintained his level of excellence in the playoffs, as the Habs cake-walked past the Rangers in the semis and Detroit in the Finals. Montreal beat each team in five games, with Plante posting a sterling 1.80 playoff GAA.

Plante's extraordinary success inspired other goaltenders to mimic his unique style. And in November 1959, Jacques became a trend-setter once again, as he became the first NHL goaltender to wear a mask. Fellow goalies soon donned face protectors of their own, and by the late 1960s goalie masks became standard equipment.

1955-56

- On June 3, 1955, Detroit trades Terry Sawchuk, Vic Stasiuk, Marcel Bonin, and Lorne Davis to Boston for Gilles Boisvert, Real Chevrefils, Norm Corcoran, Warren Godfrey, and Ed Sandford.

- The Wings send Tony Leswick, Glen Skov, Johnny Wilson, and Benny Woit

to Chicago for Dave Creighton, Bucky Hollingworth, and Jerry Toppazzini.

- The Red Wings trade Real Chevrefils and Jerry Toppazzini to Boston for Murray Costello and Lorne Ferguson.

- On August 18, Detroit ships Dave Creighton and Bronco Horvath to New York for Billy Dea and Aggie Kukulowicz.

- Eight games into the season, the Wings reacquire Metro Prystai from Chicago for Ed Sandford.

In 1955-56, Toe Blake (left) was appointed head coach of the
Canadiens and led his former mates to the Stanley Cup championship.
He couldn't have done it without goalie Jacques Plante (right), who posted the
stingiest full-season goals-against average (1.86) of his extraordinary career.
Montreal allowed just 131 goals during the regular season, the fewest allowed
by any NHL team during the second half of the 20th Century.

• In Montreal, the long reign of coach Dick Irvin ends when the 15-year bench boss leaves to rebuild the struggling Black Hawks. Former star left winger Toe Blake assumes command of the Habs' bench.

• The Rangers kick coach Muzz Patrick "upstairs" to take over as general manager. Phil Watson, who played with the Rangers for 12 years, becomes head coach.

• Detroit's seven-year string of first-place finishes ends, as Montreal goes 45-15-10 and beats the second-place Wings by 24 points.

• Jean Beliveau, the latest Montreal superstar, leads the NHL in both goals (47) and points (88).

• Bert Olmstead of Montreal leads the league in assists (56).

• Red Wing Gordie Howe finishes second in the NHL in points (79).

Fontinato Breaks 200-PIM Barrier

In the 1950s, ice rinks were battle grounds. Fierce team loyalties governed the players' conduct both on the ice and off. One of the game's roughest competitors was Leapin' Louie Fontinato (left, under restraint), who in 1955-56 became the first NHLer to spend over 200 minutes in the sin bin. Fontinato was not just a one-dimensional player, he was also a solid defenseman who contributed 18 points to the Rangers' attack in 1955-56.

New York Rangers vs. Detroit Red Wings

Jean Beliveau

Beliveau Soars to Top of the Charts

Jean Beliveau fully lived up to his huge billing in 1955-56, his third NHL season. The Canadiens star paced the league in both goals (47) and points (88) after finishing third in each category as a sophomore. He also proved to be a rambunctious antagonist, spending 143 minutes in the box. His performance on the ice earned him the Art Ross Trophy as leading scorer and the Hart Trophy.

Bathgate Gives Hope to Ranger Fans

The late 1940s and most of the 1950s were dismal times for the Rangers. The team missed the playoffs in 11 of 13 seasons from 1943 through 1955. However, a bright light appeared with the emergence of Andy Bathgate. In only his second full NHL season, the talented playmaker finished the 1955-56 campaign with a team-leading 66 points.

Andy Bathgate

1955-56

- Gordie Howe and Maurice Richard tie for second overall in goals (38).

- Toronto center Tod Sloan notches 37 goals, fourth best in the NHL.

- Rangers right winger Andy Bathgate, another successful proponent of the slapshot, is second in the

league in assists (47). New York defenseman Bill Gadsby chalks up 42 assists (third best).

- Vic Stasiuk, acquired from Detroit with Terry Sawchuk, plays on Boston's top line (with Cal Gardner and Johnny Peirson) and leads the club in scoring (37 points).

- The Habs' Jacques Plante emerges as the NHL's top goalie, as he leads the league in wins (42) and GAA (1.86).

- Terry Sawchuk, who helped the Red Wings to three Stanley Cups, suffers a huge reversal with Boston, leading the NHL in losses (33).

Terry Sawchuk

Trade to Boston Ticks Off Sawchuk

The hockey world was shocked on June 3, 1955, when Detroit traded the world's best goalie, Terry Sawchuk, to Boston. Sawchuk, who had led the Wings to three Stanley Cup titles in five years, appeared in 68 games for Boston and led the league in losses with 33. Sawchuk was not pleased with the deal and showed a feisty side that had never surfaced before on the ice. He led all goaltenders in penalty time, accumulating 20 minutes of purgatory penance.

Sloan Scores 37, Takes a Breather

Toronto forward Tod Sloan takes a well-deserved breather away from the ice. Sloan was one of the few bright spots for the Leafs during the 1955-56 campaign, scoring a career-high 37 goals and leading the team with 66 points, the highest totals of his career. Although not very big, Sloan was an aggressive center who wasn't afraid to roam into the corners to dig out loose pucks or stand in the slot awaiting rebounds.

Tod Sloan

Detroit Red Wings vs. Chicago Black Hawks

Hall's Every Bit as Good as Sawchuk

Although Jack Adams was criticized heavily for the Terry Sawchuk trade, he had a marvelous young rookie waiting in the "Wings." Glenn Hall (pictured thwarting Chicago's Eric Nesterenko) won the Calder Trophy in 1955-56, leading all netminders with 12 shutouts. He appeared in all 70 games for Detroit, compiling a 30-24-16 record with a 2.11 GAA. Hall eventually earned the nickname "Mr. Goalie" for his consistent play between the pipes.

• Detroit rookie Glenn Hall leads the NHL in shutouts (12).

• The Canadiens debut rookie forward Henri Richard, Maurice Richard's kid brother. The smaller Henri is nicknamed the "Pocket Rocket."

• On November 5, 1955, Jean Beliveau scores three goals in 44 seconds—all on the power play. It's the second-fastest hat-trick in NHL history.

• The Rangers end their playoff drought with a third-place finish. They feature a snarling sophomore

defenseman, Lou Fontinato, who sets a new penalty-minute record (202).

• The playoffs feature Montreal against the Rangers and Detroit vs. Toronto.

• Montreal dispatches the Rangers in five games, outscoring them 24-9.

Toronto Marlboros

Marlies Win Another Cup

The Toronto Marlboros captured their second consecutive Memorial Cup during the 1955-56 season. Coached by former Maple Leaf great Walter "Turk" Broda (front row, fourth from right), the Marlies featured a number of outstanding NHL prospects, including Bob Pulford, Bob Nevin, and Al MacNeil. The Marlies motored past the Montreal Jr. Canadiens and the Regina Pats to win the Memorial Cup.

Soviets Beat Canada, Win Olympic Gold

Canadian forward Billy Colvin, a member of the Kitchener-Waterloo Dutchmen, attempts to center the puck past the outstretched stick of Soviet defender Ivan Tregubov during the 1956 Olympic Games in Italy. The Soviets, who had won the world championship in their first appearance on the international scene in 1954, beat the U.S. 4-0 and Canada 2-0 in the medal rounds to win the Olympic gold. The U.S. beat Canada for the silver.

Olympic Games

1955-56

- The Red Wings eliminate Toronto in five games. Only Game 3 goes to O.T., but Detroit's Ted Lindsay wins it at 4:22 of the first extra session.

- The Finals match the Canadiens and Red Wings for the fourth time in five years—with the Canadiens still looking for a way to win.

- Montreal's Jean Beliveau scores a pair in Game 1, as the Habs overcome a 4-2 Detroit lead to win 6-4. Montreal breezes to a 5-1 win in Game 2.

- Detroit's Ted Lindsay breaks up a 1-1 tie in Game 3 of the Finals, as Detroit wins 3-1. However, Jacques

Plante shuts out the Red Wings in Game 4 3-0.

- Montreal's Maurice Richard scores the Cup-clinching goal in Game 5, as the Canadiens win 3-1.

- Jean Beliveau's 12 goals and 19 points lead all playoff scorers.

Once Again, Wings Roll Over Toronto

Toronto forward Ron Stewart escapes the grasp of Detroit defender Red Kelly (#4) only to have his breakaway opportunity snuffed out by goaltender Glenn Hall during the fourth game of the 1956 semifinals. Although the Leafs escaped with a 2-0 victory on this evening, the Wings won the next game to advance to the Finals.

Stanley Cup Semifinals

Habs Finally Figure Out the Wings

Emile "Butch" Bouchard accepts the Stanley Cup after the Canadiens defeated the Red Wings in five games to avenge their seven-game losses to the Motowners in 1954 and 1955. Jean Beliveau was the offensive catalyst for the Habs, connecting for 12 goals in 10 playoff games. It was also a sweet moment for coach Toe Blake, who led the team to the Cup in his first season behind the bench.

Detroit Can't Handle Plante and Beliveau

The Canadiens gained a measure of revenge against the Red Wings in the 1956 Stanley Cup Finals, ending Detroit's two-year reign as NHL champion. Paced by Jacques Plante (1.80 playoff GAA) and Jean Beliveau, the Habs clipped the Wings in five games to win their second Stanley Cup of the decade. Beliveau was the catalyst for Montreal as he scored 12 postseason goals, the most in the Stanley Cup playoffs since 1919.

Jacques Plante

Stanley Cup Celebration

- Jean Beliveau wins the Hart Trophy. Teammate Jacques Plante cops his first Vezina Trophy, an honor he'll enjoy six more times in his career.

- Dutch Reibel, the Wings' second-leading scorer (56 points), wins the Lady Byng Trophy.

- Detroit's Glenn Hall, the Vezina runner-up, wins the Calder Trophy.

- Canadien Doug Harvey wins the second of his seven Norris Trophies.

- The Toronto Marlboros win their second straight Memorial Cup.

- The Soviet Union claims its first-ever Olympic hockey gold medal. The United States takes the silver.

- Michigan wins its all-time best sixth NCAA title, beating Michigan Tech 7-5 in the finals. Wolverines Goalie Lorne Howes is tourney MVP.

PLAYERS, SON CHALLENGE THE POWER OF SMYTHE

Although he was never NHL president, Maple Leafs boss Conn Smythe wielded as much behind-the-scenes power as any individual. But Smythe was falling out of favor in Toronto in 1956-57 because of his slowly sinking hockey club. And on the league front, Smythe and his fellow owners were being taken on by a newly formed players' union. The ultimate insult to Smythe was that his team captain, Jim Thomson, was among the union leaders.

The idea for organizing a players' association developed at the 1956 NHL All-Star Game, held in October in Montreal. Detroit ace Ted Lindsay enlisted Thomson, Montreal's Doug Harvey, Chicago's Gus Mortson, the Rangers' Bill Gadsby, and the Bruins' Fernie Flaman. The NHL Players' Association was formally unveiled on February 11, 1957; and instantly the Smythe-led owners declared war.

Smythe branded Thomson a "traitor" and then ordered every one of his players in for a third degree. Other teams did likewise, but the new NHLPA wouldn't go away. Smythe mounted pressure, benching Thomson while ordering G.M. Hap Day to leave him home for the team's final road trip.

Meanwhile, the mutinous Maple Leaf Gardens situation worsened. Day, who had been Smythe's ally since the late 1920s, became an outcast when he obliquely backed the union. Smythe turned on Day as well as coach Howie Meeker. "My legs have been cut out from under me," said Day.

The Maple Leaf mutiny resulted in Day's departure and the eventual—albeit temporary—elevation of Meeker from coach to general manager. The Leafs had an awful season (21-34-15) and nothing was going well for Smythe. In fact, he was being eased out of his team leadership by his equally irascible son, Stafford, who enjoyed challenging his father as much as Conn relished taking on the union.

"The people my father respects," said Stafford, "are those who stand up to him and fight. After I learned to do this, he respected me, but we had plenty of scraps."

Conn Smythe's stooge, NHL President Clarence Campbell, joined the anti-union battle, warning NHLPA members that he would "terminate" their pension contract if they misbehaved. Though concerned about Campbell's threat, the players and their attorney, Milton Mound, pushed forward, and their campaign eventually survived the season and ran into 1957-58.

However, the NHLPA fallout was severe. After the season, Detroit banished Lindsay to Chicago, while Smythe also shipped Thomson to the last-place Black Hawks. "I didn't want anyone telling us what we had to do," Smythe asserted. Montreal wasn't too happy with Harvey either, but after he helped the Canadiens to the Stanley Cup in April, he was spared.

Although the players attempted to maintain solidarity, defections among their ranks eventually undermined their strength. The players' first union died in 1957-58, and the players would have to wait more than a decade for a truly successful players' association.

1956-57

- Due to the overwhelming success of the Canadiens' power play, the NHL amends the penalty rule. A penalized player may now return to the ice if the opponent scores a power-play goal.

- In October 1956, a group of NHL players—led by Detroit star Ted Lindsay—meets at the All-Star Game and plants the seeds for an NHL players' association.

- King Clancy is replaced behind the Toronto bench by Howie Meeker.

- After a third straight sixth-place finish, Black Hawks coach Dick Irvin resigns due to poor health. General manager Tommy Ivan takes over as coach.

- Jimmy Skinner's Red Wings retake first place in the regular season. They finish 38-20-12 and edge the Canadiens by six points.

Following the conclusion of the 1956-57 season, there was a changing of the guard at Maple Leaf Gardens. Conn Smythe (left) handed over control of the team to his son, Stafford (right). The younger Smythe and his six partners, known collectively as the "Silver Seven," ran the team by committee. The other members of the Maple Leaf gold mine were Harold Ballard, John Bassett, George Mara, George Amell, George Gardiner, and Bill Hatch.

• Montreal boasts the league's top offense (210 goals) as well as the stingiest defense (155 goals against).

• Detroit's fabled Production Line features a new center, Norm Ullman.

• Detroit's Gordie Howe leads the league in goals (44) and points (89).

• Detroit's tenacious Ted Lindsay leads the NHL in assists (55) and is second in points (85).

• Montreal's Maurice Richard is replaced by Boom Boom Geoffrion on the Canadiens' top line, which includes Jean Beliveau and Bert Olmstead.

• Despite his demotion, Rocket Richard ties Jean Beliveau for the team lead in goals (33), good enough for second in the NHL.

• Ed Litzenberger is fourth overall in goals (32) and fifth in points (64) for the last-place Black Hawks.

Jean Beliveau

Beliveau's Becoming the Habs' Leader

Jean Beliveau was the complete hockey player: a crafty centerman, an accurate passer, and a deadly shooter. In 1956-57, Big Jean finished second in goals (33) to Gordie Howe and second in assists (51) to Ted Lindsay. He showed remarkable poise for a player in only his third full NHL season and was already becoming a leader among his Montreal teammates. In the postseason, Beliveau collected a dozen points in helping the Habs to the Stanley Cup.

Real Chevrefils

Chevrefils Knocks In 31 for Bruins

A respected defensive forward who spent his first four seasons in Boston, Real Chevrefils was traded to the Red Wings in the blockbuster deal that sent Terry Sawchuk to the Bruins in June 1955. However, after only 38 games in Motown, Chevrefils was on the move again, this time back to Boston. Apparently happy to be home, Chevrefils caught fire in 1956-57, scoring 31 goals and helping the Bruins reach the Stanley Cup Finals.

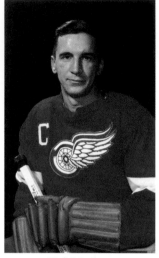

Ted Lindsay

Terrible Ted Leads League in Helpers

He was known as Terrible Ted, but to Detroit fans he was Mr. Wonderful. Lindsay had been a regular with the Motor City squad since 1945, and in 1956-57 he had one of the finest years of his remarkable career. He led all NHL scorers with 55 assists while scoring an even 30 goals. Although the Wings bowed out of the playoffs after five semifinal games against Boston, Lindsay had a hand in six of the 14 goals scored against the Bruins.

1956-57

- Andy Bathgate sets a Ranger team record when he finishes with 77 points (fourth in the NHL).

- The third-place Bruins suffer through a tumultuous year, with star netminder Terry Sawchuk playing erratically in goal.

- Don McKenney is the Bruins' top scorer (60 points).

- Montreal's Doug Harvey (50 points) and Ranger Bill Gadsby (41) pace all NHL defenders in scoring.

- Detroit sophomore Glenn Hall leads the NHL in wins (38).

- The Canadiens' Jacques Plante wins the GAA title (2.02). He also leads the league in shutouts (nine).

- Harry Lumley's one-year retirement opens the door for Ed Chadwick, who plays all 70 games for the Leafs but wins just 21 games.

Maurice Richard, Toe Blake, Jean Beliveau

Richard Nets 33 in Last Big Year

The 1956-57 season was to be the last great campaign for Maurice Richard. At the age of 35, Richard was beginning to show the signs of wear, but he still found the strength to score 33 goals and 62 points in 63 games. With former linemate Toe Blake behind the bench and a youthful Jean Beliveau centering the play, Richard saved his best work for the playoffs, potting eight goals as the Habs won their second straight Stanley Cup.

Litzenberger Registers 64 Points

Ed Litzenberger had the finest year of his young career in 1956-57, counting 32 goals and 32 assists for the Hawks. Litzenberger was originally the property of the Canadiens, but the Habs dispatched him to Chicago in late 1954 in an effort to help the floundering Black Hawks. Litzenberger set an NHL record in the 1954-55 season by appearing in 73 games during a 70-game schedule, playing 29 games for Montreal and 44 for the Hawks.

Ed Litzenberger

Minor-League Vet Hebenton Wins the Byng

A hard-working veteran who spent six years in the minors before finally making his mark in the NHL with the Rangers, Andy Hebenton was awarded the Lady Byng Trophy in 1956-57 after compiling 21 goals, 23 assists, and only 10 minutes in penalties. In his rookie campaign of 1955-56, Hebenton became an instant crowd favorite while producing 24 goals. Hebenton was a rather mature 26 years old when he entered the NHL.

Andy Hebenton

- Al Rollins, a former league MVP, absorbs all 39 losses for the desperate Black Hawks.

- Chicago's Gus Mortson (147 PIM) edges Rangers defenseman Lou Fontinato (139 minutes) for the penalty title.

- Boston's Real Chevrefils makes the top five in goals (31).

- Future New York Islanders star Mike Bossy is born on January 22, 1957, in Montreal.

- The playoffs feature Detroit vs. Boston and Montreal vs. the Rangers.

- The Bruins upset the Red Wings in five games. Detroit wins Game 2 7-2, but Boston wins four close ones to advance.

- Montreal ousts the Rangers in five semifinal games, as New York's only triumph is a 4-3 O.T. win in Game 2.

Gordie's the Scoring King Once Again

After allowing Bernie Geoffrion and Jean Beliveau to steal away his scoring-leader crown in 1955 and 1956, Gordie Howe returned to the throne in 1956-57, dominating all NHL marksmen with 44 goals and 89 points. Shortly after capturing his fifth Art Ross Trophy, Howe added his third Hart Trophy to his mantelpiece, edging out Beliveau for the award. In the playoffs, Howe scored or assisted on seven of Detroit's 14 postseason goals.

Colorado College Tigers

C.C. Tigers Score 13 in Title Game

The Colorado College Tigers won their second NCAA hockey championship in 1956-57 with a 13-6 victory over the Michigan Wolverines in the finals. It was historically significant because this was (and remains) the highest-scoring championship game in NCAA history. The star of Colorado was William "Red" Hay (front row, fourth from right), a highly prized prospect who was invited to join the Canadiens at training camp prior to the 1957-58 season.

Gordie Howe

Stanley Cup Semifinals

Habs Hold Off the Rangers in Semis

Camille "The Eel" Henry (left) tries to slide a shot past Montreal goaltender Jacques Plante in Game 2 of the Rangers-Canadiens semifinals encounter in 1957. The Blues, making only their third postseason appearance of the decade, won this game in overtime on a goal by Andy Hebenton, but they dropped the next three contests as the Habs motored into the championship round for the seventh straight season.

• With Don Simmons in goal for ailing Terry Sawchuk, the Bruins fall 5-1 in Game 1 of the Finals, as Rocket Richard scores four goals.

• Habs goalie Jacques Plante pitches a shutout in Game 2, as Jean Beliveau's second-period goal is the only score of the 1-0 game.

• Bernie Geoffrion scores twice in the first period of Game 3. Montreal goes on to beat Boston 4-2. The Bruins rally on home ice with a 2-0 victory in Game 4, as Fleming Mackell scores both goals.

• Montreal's Dickie Moore scores 14 seconds into the second period of

Game 5. It turns out to be the Cup-clinching goal, as Montreal rolls to a 5-1 victory.

• Bernie Geoffrion leads all playoff scorers with 18 points.

• Gordie Howe, the Art Ross Trophy winner as scoring champ, claims the

Stanley Cup Finals

Plante Shuts Down Bruins in Finals

The Bruins were surprise participants in the 1957 Stanley Cup Finals, having upset the Red Wings in five games in the semis. In the Finals, the Canadiens—paced by Rocket Richard's four goals in the opening game and Jacques Plante's stellar goaltending—easily dispatched the upstart Bruins in five games. Here, Plante celebrates his 1-0 victory over the Beantowners in Game 2 of the series. The Bruins couldn't score more than two goals in any game against Plante.

Champion Habs Are Big News

Maurice Richard and Canadiens coach Hector "Toe" Blake grace the cover of *Sport Revue* following the Habs' five-game victory over the Bruins. The Rocket, whose regular-season output dipped to 33 goals, redeemed himself in the postseason. The newly appointed Montreal captain registered 11 points in the playoffs as the Canadiens captured their second straight Stanley Cup crown. Blake won eight Stanley Cups in his 13 years as Montreal's coach.

Sport Revue

Hart Trophy as well. Jean Beliveau is the runner-up.

• Jacques Plante captures his second straight Vezina Trophy.

• Andy Hebenton, the Rangers' classy right winger, wins the Lady Byng Trophy.

• Boston's Larry Regan, a diminutive right winger who scored 14 of his 41 career goals as a rookie, wins the Calder Trophy over Toronto freshman goalie Ed Chadwick.

• Montreal's Doug Harvey wins the third of his seven Norris Trophies as the NHL's foremost defenseman.

• Colorado College ends Michigan's hockey dynasty for good, crushing the Wolverines 13-6 in the NCAA finals. Colorado's Bob McCusker is voted the tourney MVP.

• In Canadian amateur hockey, the Flin Flon (Manitoba) Bombers win the Memorial Cup.

Having won their second straight Stanley Cup in the spring of 1957, the Canadiens now sought to tie the Maple Leafs' record of three consecutive championships. There was no reason to think they would be thwarted, although captain Maurice Richard was now 36 and gradually slipping into a lower gear.

"With each passing year," said the Rocket, "it became harder and harder for me. But my linemates kept me going. My brother Henri was such a speedy skater that I had to work hard to keep up with him. And Dickie Moore on the left was a terrific competitor, and he could score too."

Indeed, Moore was one of the greatest of all Canadiens, even though he was often over-shadowed by the flamboyant Rocket, the boisterous Boom Boom Geoffrion, and the gracefully majestic Jean Beliveau. Moore combined outstanding skills with great tenacity to lead the NHL in scoring in both 1957-58 and 1958-59.

During Montreal's record run of five straight Stanley Cups—from 1956 through 1960—Moore was the key "swing-man." Whenever Geoffrion, Beliveau, or Richard were sidelined, Dickie

MOORE LEADS IN SCORING DESPITE BROKEN HAND

pinch-hit on their line and, almost always, the line would get hot. "When Maurice Richard and Doug Harvey faded," said former Canadien Ken Reardon, "I expected Dickie to take over as leader of the team, and he did."

Moore wasn't afraid to mix it up either. He often feuded with the feared Ted Lindsay, which was like walking unarmed into the den of a tiger. "I loved to beat those Wings more than any other club," Moore said. "They had been so high and mighty for years. It always felt good to whip 'em."

Hobbled by injuries, Moore remained a disappointment until 1955-56. He scored 50 points that year, but more importantly he played a full 70-game schedule for the first time. From then on, he zoomed off like a space rocket

and hit his own personal moon when he won the scoring title in 1957-58.

Typically, Dickie had to clear a cumbersome hurdle to win that title. Moore, Andy Bathgate, and Henri Richard were locked in a tight race for the scoring lead. Then Dickie broke his left wrist. Montreal's management feared he would be lost for the season, but Moore had other ideas. "How about putting a cast on my arm?" he suggested. "Let me take care of the rest."

Sure enough, when the Canadiens faced off in their next game, there was Moore on the ice, handcuffed with a bulky plaster cast on his left arm. Gone was the freedom to stick-handle and the possibility of flicking a wrist shot, but nothing dampened Dickie's spirit. He played in every game, tallying 36 goals and 84 points.

The powerful Canadiens finished the season at 43-17-10, 19 points better than anyone else. In the playoffs, Montreal blew out the Wings in the semis and then flew past the Bruins in the Finals. Rocket Richard, Geoffrion, Beliveau, and, of course, Dickie Moore, fueled Montreal's playoff attack, and the Canadiens skated off with their third consecutive Stanley Cup.

1957-58

- After two bad years with Terry Sawchuk in goal, the Bruins send him back to Detroit for Johnny Bucyk.

- The Red Wings trade Glenn Hall and legend Ted Lindsay to Chicago for Johnny Wilson, Hank Bassen, Forbes Kennedy, and Bill Preston.

- Red Wing Johnny Wilson is the new left winger on the Production Line, with Gordie Howe and Alex Delvecchio.

- Willie O'Ree, the first black man to play in the NHL, is signed by the Bruins. He plays just two games.

- Maurice Richard scores his 500th career goal on October 19, 1957, against Glenn Hall of Chicago.

- Detroit replaces coach Jimmy Skinner with former star center Sid Abel.

- Johnny Bucyk joins Bronco Horvath and Vic Stasiuk on the Bruins' Uke

Although Dickie Moore had been a member of the Canadiens since 1951-52, it was not until his fourth full season that he delivered on the promise he had shown as a junior player. In 1957-58, he earned a spot on a line with the Richard brothers and responded with a career year. He led all NHL snipers with 36 goals and 84 points. Impressively, he spent the last few weeks of the season wearing a cast to protect a broken wrist.

Line, as Boston slides back a notch to fourth place.

• The Chicago lineup is renewed by goalie Glenn Hall and a rookie left winger named Bobby Hull. Still, the Black Hawks miss the playoffs for the 11th time in 12 years.

• The Canadiens overcome serious injuries to remain first overall. They go 43-17-10 and edge second-place New York by 19 points.

• Dickie Moore, en route to his first scoring championship, breaks his right wrist and plays the last month of the season with a cast.

• During a practice session in midseason, Boom Boom Geoffrion collides with a teammate and suffers a ruptured bowel.

• Last rites are given to Bernie Geoffrion by a Roman Catholic priest, but he survives his injury after major stomach surgery.

Blueliner Gadsby Knows How to Score

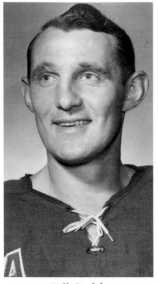

Bill Gadsby

In the 1950s, New York's Bill Gadsby was one of the NHL's few rushing defensemen. Although most of the media attention was focused on Red Kelly and Doug Harvey, Gadsby was the only rearguard besides Kelly to finish among the top 10 scorers during the decade, tying for ninth in 1955-56 with 51 points. In 1957-58, Gadsby led all NHL blueliners with 14 goals and 46 points as the Rangers rose to second place, their highest finish since 1942.

Maurice Richard, Henri Richard, Dickie Moore

Ted Lindsay

Pocket Rocket Leads in Assists

Since 1955-56, Henri Richard had skated in the shadow of his powerful sibling, the Rocket. In 1957-58, he came into his own, leading the league in assists with 52 and collecting 80 points. Though not as feisty as his brother, the Pocket Rocket could take care of himself in any tussle. Teamed on a line with Rocket and Dickie Moore, the trio combined for 198 points, helping the Habs to a first-place finish.

Lindsay Banished to Chicago

During the 1956-57 season, Ted Lindsay and a group of fellow NHLers attempted to form the first players union. Clarence Campbell and the NHL owners would have no part of collective bargaining in their money machines. Lindsay's punishment was swift and severe. After 13 seasons in Detroit, he was exiled to Chicago, the league's worst team.

1957-58

• The Canadiens have the top scoring offense (250 goals) and the toughest defense (158 goals against).

• Montreal's Jacques Plante leads in shutouts (nine) and GAA (2.11).

• Dickie Moore leads the NHL in goals (36) and points (84), while Habs teammate Henri Richard leads the league in assists (52) and finishes second in points (80).

• The Rangers, who climb all the way up to second despite feuding with bombastic coach Phil Watson, see Andy Bathgate set a new team record with 78 points (third in the league).

• Gordie Howe is second in the NHL in goals (33) and places fourth in points (77).

• Rangers goalie Lorne "Gump" Worsley has the second-best GAA (2.32), while Glenn Hall has seven shutouts for the Black Hawks (second).

Howe Puts Up More Big Numbers

Gordie Howe congratulates Maurice Richard after the Canadiens swept the Red Wings in the 1958 semifinals. Howe, who surrendered his scoring crown to Montreal's Dickie Moore, still had an excellent season, collecting a team-leading 33 goals and 77 points to finish fourth in the scoring parade. In the playoffs, the Canadiens constantly assigned their best checkers to cover Howe, limiting him to only one goal in the four-game series.

O'Ree Breaks the NHL's Color Barrier

In 1957-58, Willie O'Ree was called up to play two games for the big club in Boston. A quick and fruitless trip to the NHL is normally nothing to remember, but in the case of O'Ree, the moment was historic. O'Ree, born in Fredericton, New Brunswick, was the first black man to play hockey in the major league. He returned to the Bruins in 1960, when he played a full season and recorded 14 points.

Bernie Geoffrion

Geoffrion Recovers from Ruptured Bowel

During a morning practice on January 28, 1958, Bernie Geoffrion collapsed at the Montreal Forum and was rushed to the hospital with a ruptured bowel. The Canadiens star was in critical condition for 48 hours following emergency surgery, and while he pulled through for a complete recovery, he was out of action for 28 games. However, as he had done the previous season, the Boomer rebounded to have an excellent playoff round, scoring six goals in 10 games.

Maurice Richard, Gordie Howe

Willie O'Ree

- Ranger Bill Gadsby leads all defensemen in scoring (46 points).

- New York's Lou Fontinato captures his second penalty-minute title in three years (152 PIM).

- The playoffs feature Montreal vs. Detroit and New York vs. Boston.

- The Rangers win Game 1 of the semis 5-3 before the Bruins even the series with Jerry Toppazzini's overtime goal in Game 2.

- The Bruins hammer New York 5-0 in Game 3 and outscore the Rangers 14-3 in Games 5 and 6. They advance to the Finals.

- The Red Wings are no match for Montreal, as the Habs outscore Detroit 13-2 in the first two games.

- Detroit plays Montreal closer in Game 3 but loses in O.T. on Andre Pronovost's winner. The Habs win Game 4 4-3 to return to the Finals.

Stanley Cup Semifinals

Bruins, Circus Do In Rangers

Andy Bathgate (right) prepares to pass the puck out from behind the Bruins' net during Game 3 of the 1958 semifinals. Boston defenders Allan Stanley (#10), Don Simmons (goalie), and Leo Boivin (left) were able to shut down the Rangers on this evening, blanking the Broadway Blues 5-0. Boston went on to eliminate the Rangers in six games, the last four of them played in Boston because the circus was making its annual pilgrimage to Madison Square Garden.

Habs Crush Wings in Cup Semis

An era came to a close in Detroit following the 1957-58 semifinal series. So swift and so powerful was the attack of Montreal and Maurice Richard (right) that the Detroit organization was shaken to the core. In the opening round of the playoffs, Gordie Howe (left) and Detroit dropped 8-1 and 5-1 decisions in the Montreal Forum. Although the games were closer on home ice at the Olympia, the Wings could manage only six goals in the Habs' four-game sweep.

Fleming Mackell

Mackell's 19 Playoff Points Lead League

Fleming Mackell gives a few pointers to his son Mike during a pre-game skate at Boston Garden. Mike would have been wise to listen to his father, for the elder Mackell excelled during the 1957-58 season, notching 20 goals and 40 assists. In the playoffs, Mackell was the Bruins' main offensive weapon, discharging five goals and 14 assists to head all postseason skaters with 19 points. It was his best NHL season by far.

Stanley Cup Semifinals

1957-58

- Montreal's Bernie Geoffrion, who makes a dramatic recovery from near-fatal stomach surgery, scores early in Game 1 of the Finals. Dickie Moore scores another and the Habs beat Boston 2-1.

- Boston bombs Montreal 5-2 in Game 2, but Jacques Plante shuts out the Beantowners 3-0 in Game 3. The three goals come from Maurice Richard (two) and Henri Richard.

- The Bruins take Game 4 3-1, but Montreal wins Game 5 3-2 thanks to Maurice Richard's sixth career playoff overtime goal (an all-time record).

- Bernie Geoffrion scores a pair of goals in Game 6 as the Habs win 5-3 and capture their third straight Stanley Cup—and ninth overall.

- Maurice Richard leads all playoff performers in goals (11), but Boston's Fleming Mackell tops all postseason competitors in points (19).

Habs Flatten Beantowners in Cup Finals

Stanley Cup Finals

Boston's Johnny Bucyk (#9) squashes Montreal's Doug Harvey, while Bronco Horvath and Jean Guy Talbot (far left) search for the puck, during the 1958 Stanley Cup Finals. Although the Bruins gave the Canadiens a brave battle, the overpowering Habs were too much for the Bostonians. The turning point in the series came in Game 5, when Maurice Richard scored in overtime to leave the Habs a single win away from the title.

Beliveau and Richard Hoist Another Cup

Two of the heroes of Montreal's six-game Stanley Cup victory over Boston share the spotlight after the conclusion of the series. Maurice Richard scored the overtime winner in Game 5 and Jean Beliveau collected a goal and an assist in the clinching game. The Canadiens became only the second NHL club to win three straight Stanley Cups, tying the mark set by the Maple Leafs from 1947-49.

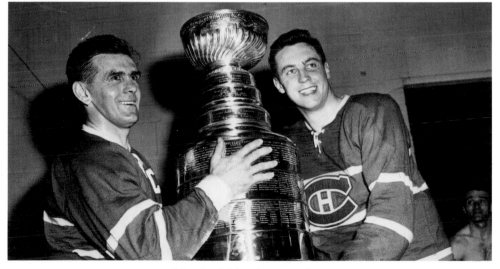

Maurice Richard, Jean Beliveau

• Gordie Howe wins his fourth Hart Trophy, edging Andy Bathgate.

• Jacques Plante claims his third straight Vezina Trophy.

• Camille Henry, the Rangers' tiny winger, wins the Lady Byng Trophy.

• Toronto's Frank Mahovlich (20 goals, 36 points) wins the Calder Trophy, beating out Chicago's Bobby Hull.

• Montreal's Doug Harvey wins his fourth straight Norris Trophy, finishing second among NHL defenders with 41 points.

• Denver University defeats North Dakota in the finals 6-2 to win the NCAA hockey championship. Denver forward Murray Massier is voted tourney MVP.

• In Canadian junior hockey, the Ottawa-Hull Junior Canadiens capture the Memorial Cup.

LEAFS CATCH FIRE IN MARCH, BURN THE RANGERS

In August 1951, 13½ games behind the league-leading Brooklyn Dodgers, the New York Giants launched a big push that eventually landed them the National League pennant. Hockey never had experienced a late-season comeback quite like that—at least not until 1958-59, when the Toronto Maple Leafs came out of nowhere to earn a playoff berth and reach the Stanley Cup Finals.

This was a season in which the Canadiens were shooting for their fourth straight Stanley Cup and would easily finish first. The Canadiens were so consistently strong that fans looked to other teams for story lines, and they finally found the best of all in Toronto.

The Maple Leafs, who entered 1958-59 with few expectations, were under the tutelage of new coach Punch Imlach. Some thought Toronto could finish ahead of the reeling Red Wings; but for the Leafs to make the playoffs, some other team would really have to go in the tank. No one expected that that team would be New York, which had finished in second place a year earlier.

Coached by the tempestuous Phil Watson, the Rangers were aiming for second place again until dissension—caused primarily by Watson—eroded the team's spirit. The Rangers started to wobble early in March, although they were still way ahead of the Leafs—nine points ahead on March 11 and seven points up on March 14.

On Saturday, March 14, New York had its chance to polish off Toronto, as Watson brought his Rangers to Maple Leaf Gardens for the first of a home-and-home series with the Leafs. A New York victory on Saturday night would give the Rangers a nine-point bulge over Toronto, and with four games remaining on their schedule, the Leafs could never make up the difference.

Then it happened. Toronto won home-and-home games with the Rangers and moved relentlessly to the final night of the season, by which time the Leafs needed a win in Detroit coupled with a Rangers loss in New York to take the playoff berth. Sure enough, the Rangers blew a lead and lost to Montreal 4-2, while Imlach's Maple Leafs rallied from a two-goal deficit to defeat the Red Wings 6-4.

"Even a week before the season ended, you could have got a hundred-to-one against us even making the playoffs," recalled Imlach. "I remember hearing later that Conn Smythe had said to somebody on Toronto's hockey committee, 'What did you get, did you get a coach or did you get a madman?' This because I'm saying, 'We're gonna make it, we're gonna make it.' They got a madman, all right, but they didn't know it at the time."

Toronto's magic continued against Boston in the playoffs, as the Leafs won two overtime games and then—in the decisive seventh game in Boston—nipped the Bruins 3-2. The fun ended quickly in the Stanley Cup Finals, as the Canadiens whipped the Leafs in five games. Still, the Habs couldn't erase the memories of Toronto's late-season run—one of the most amazing in NHL history.

1958-59

- The Hall of Fame inducts 22 new members, including Frank Boucher, King Clancy, Sprague Cleghorn, Alex Connell, Red Dutton, Frank Foyston, Ching Johnson, and Conn Smythe.

- Toronto signs 34-year-old goalie Johnny Bower, a career minor-leaguer who spent some time with the Rangers. The Leafs also acquire defenseman Allan Stanley from Boston and Bert Olmstead from Montreal.

- Montreal continues to dominate the NHL. The Canadiens go 39-18-13 to beat out second-place Boston by 18 points.

- The Canadiens boast the league's best offense (258 goals) and best defense (158 goals against).

- Habs winger Dickie Moore sets an NHL scoring record with 96 points (41 goals and a league-leading 55 assists).

The battle for the last playoff spot in the 1958-59 season was between
the Toronto Maple Leafs and the New York Rangers. Punch Imlach, who now
was not only the coach of the Leafs but the general manager as well, predicted a
fourth-place finish for the Toronto team. His youthful squad made good on
his prognostication, winning five of its last six games to squeeze past
the Rangers by a single point.

- Jean Beliveau finishes first in goals (45) and second in points (91).

- Andy Bathgate tallies 40 goals and 88 points—new Rangers records—but the team stumbles to fifth place.

- Three players—Jean Beliveau, Gordie Howe, and Rangers defenseman Bill Gadsby—tie for third in assists (46) behind Dickie Moore (55) and Andy Bathgate (48).

- Black Hawk Ed Litzenberger ties for fourth with 33 goals (along with New York's Andy Hebenton) and finishes fifth in points (77).

- Montreal's Jacques Plante again leads the NHL in wins (38), shutouts (nine), and GAA (2.16).

- Toronto's Johnny Bower, who many thought was over the hill, turns in the NHL's second-best goals-against average (2.74).

Johnson, Not Harvey, Wins Norris Trophy

It was no surprise that the Norris Trophy remained in Montreal in 1958-59, but a few eyebrows were raised when Tom Johnson supplanted teammate Doug Harvey as the league's best defenseman. Johnson reached double figures in goals (10) for the first time in his career and patrolled the Habs blueline in his usual consistent fashion. Harvey, who slumped to 20 points, had to settle for a spot on the Second All-Star Team.

Toe Blake, Jacques Plante

Tom Johnson

Moore's 96 Points Set a New Record

As the defending Art Ross Trophy winner, all eyes were on Montreal's Dickie Moore to defend the scoring crown he won in 1958. Incredibly, Moore exceeded all expectations. He not only captured his second straight scoring title, but he also established a new NHL single-season record for points. Moore led the NHL in assists (55) and points (96) to eclipse the mark of 95 set by Gordie Howe in 1953.

Dickie Moore

Blake Has the League's Best Goalie

It was no secret that Montreal coach Toe Blake and All-Star goaltender Jacques Plante rarely saw eye-to-eye. Nevertheless, Blake knew that there was no better netminder in the league than the crafty Plante. In 1958-59, Plante led the league in victories (38), shutouts (nine), and GAA (2.16). He also won the Vezina Trophy and led the Canadiens to the Stanley Cup Finals for the ninth consecutive year.

1958-59

- Chicago's Ted Lindsay notches 58 points and leads the league in penalty minutes (184).

- The Rangers boast three players among the top five penalty leaders— Lou Fontinato (149 PIM), 5'9" winger Jim Bartlett (118), and rookie Eddie Shack (109).

- New York's Bill Gadsby leads all defensemen with 51 points.

- Boston finishes second thanks to Don McKenney (62 points), Vic Stasiuk (60), and John Bucyk (60).

- Chicago finishes in third place despite a losing record (28-29-13).

Still, the Hawks make the playoffs for the first time in six years.

- Toronto closes the season strong to surpass the slumping Rangers and earn the final playoff spot.

- The Red Wings, two years after finishing atop the standings, fall to

Aging Bower Finally Hits the Big Time

Although Johnny Bower had seen some NHL action, he was a career minor-leaguer who was resigned to spend the balance of his hockey days on the "Greyhound circuit." However, Toronto's new brain trust, under the sharp eye of Punch Imlach, signed the venerable 34-year-old "China Wall" and gave him one last shot at the big time. Bower responded by leading the Leafs into the playoffs in 1958-59 for the first time in three seasons.

Johnny Bower

Don McKenney

Team-Conscious Delvecchio Wins the Lady Byng

One of the few highlights for the Red Wings in 1958-59 was Alex Delvecchio. The steady forward sacrificed some of his offensive totals to concentrate on special teams for the last-place Motowners—in addition to taking a regular tour of duty on the Production Line. Delvecchio had 19 goals and 35 assists and spent only six minutes in the penalty box to earn the Lady Byng Trophy.

Alex Delvecchio

McKenney's 62 Points Power Bruins

A steady, confident center with excellent defensive skills, Don McKenney had one of his best seasons in 1958-59, topping all Boston skaters with 32 goals and 62 points. McKenney's production and leadership at center gave the Bruins two potent forward units, the Uke Line and the trio of McKenney, Gerald Toppazzini, and Fleming Mackell. In the playoffs, McKenney was his usual consistent self, collecting seven points in the team's seven-game loss to Toronto.

---

sixth, as Terry Sawchuk leads the NHL in losses (36).

• The playoffs feature Montreal vs. Chicago and Toronto vs. Boston.

• Boston wins the first two games of its semifinal series at home, beating Toronto 5-1 and 4-2.

• The Leafs win Game 3 of their semifinal series when Gerry Ehman scores at 5:02 of overtime to break up a 2-2 tie.

• Toronto triumphs in Game 4, as sophomore sensation Frank Mahovlich scores 11:21 into O.T. to win it 3-2.

• Boston drops Game 5 of the semifinals 4-1 before beating the Leafs in Game 6 5-4.

• Poised to win the series on home ice, the Bruins are stunned when Toronto hands them a 3-2 loss in the decisive seventh game.

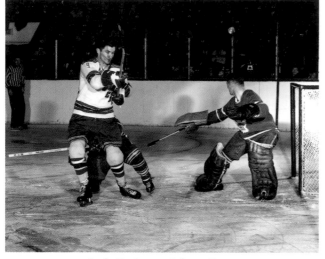

Andy Bathgate, Johnny Bower

Bathgate Captures the Hart Trophy

In New York, all eyes were on Andy Bathgate, who had slowly matured into one of the league's top players. In 1958-59, Bathgate finished third in goals and second in assists for a career-high 88 points. His dynamic play earned him the Hart Trophy. Although such great right wingers as Maurice Richard and Gordie Howe were still skating and scoring, Bathgate got the nod on the NHL's First All-Star Team.

Gentleman Jean Pours In 45 Goals

After an injury-plagued 1957-58 season, Montreal's Jean Beliveau returned to the top of the goal-scoring parade in 1958-59, slipping 45 shots past NHL goaltenders. Beliveau added 46 helpers for a career-high 91 points. The classy Beliveau also tempered his irascible on-ice style, spending more time making plays than making enemies. As a result, he spent only 67 minutes in the penalty box, down from 143 in 1955-56.

Jean Beliveau

1958-59

- In their semifinal against Chicago, the Canadiens win the first two.

- The courageous Black Hawks fight back with home-ice wins in Game 3 and Game 4.

- The Canadiens take the next two semifinal games, 5-2 and 5-4, to advance to the Finals for the ninth straight year.

- Montreal's Marcel Bonin breaks a 3-3 tie in the third period of Game 1 of the Finals, as the Habs win 5-3.

- The Habs win Game 2 3-1, as Claude Provost scores twice.

- The Leafs gain a brief glimmer of hope when Dick Duff scores at 10:06 of overtime to win Game 3 3-2.

- Bernie Geoffrion scores the game-winning goal and records two assists as Montreal takes Game 4 of the Finals 3-2.

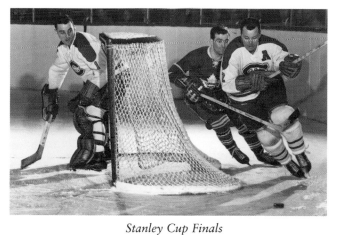

Stanley Cup Finals

Duff's Goal Biggest Since Barilko's

Dick Duff, seen here battling Montreal defenseman Doug Harvey, scored an important goal in the rebirth of the Toronto franchise. Ever since the death of playoff hero Bill Barilko, the Leafs had struggled. In 1958-59, they made the Finals for only the second time in the decade. In Game 3, Duff took a pass from George Armstrong and scored the winner in overtime to give the Leafs their first win in the Finals since Barilko's infamous goal in 1951.

Stanley Cup Finals

Leafs Fall to Veteran Habs

After defeating Boston in seven tough games in the semifinals, the Leafs met the Canadiens in the championship round. The Leafs had youth and energy, but the Habs had seasoned veterans like goalie Jacques Plante. Montreal dispatched the Leafs in five games, limiting Toronto to three goals or fewer each game.

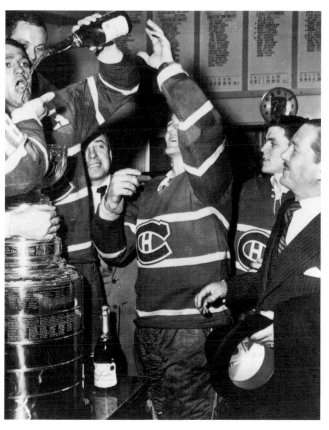

Stanley Cup Celebration

Once Again, Habs Sip Champagne

Bernie Geoffrion (left) tastes the bubbly as the Canadiens celebrate their five-game series win over the Maple Leafs in the 1959 Finals. There were concerns that the Canadiens were becoming old and complacent, but the veteran squad proved the cynics wrong by setting an NHL record with their fourth consecutive Stanley Cup victory. Senator Hartford Molson (far right), an owner of the famous beer company, bought the Habs in 1957.

• Bernie Geoffrion scores twice more in Game 5, as the Canadiens win 5-3 and claim their fourth straight Cup.

• Montreal's Dickie Moore leads all playoff performers with 17 points, while teammate Marcel Bonin is tops with 10 goals.

• New York's Andy Bathgate wins the Hart Trophy, while Gordie Howe finishes runner-up.

• Detroit's Alex Delvecchio earns the Lady Byng (54 points, six PIM).

• Montreal's Jacques Plante wins his fourth straight Vezina Trophy.

• Canadien Tom Johnson wins the Norris Trophy, while teammate Ralph Backstrom grabs the Calder.

• North Dakota beats Michigan State 4-3 in overtime to claim the NCAA hockey championship. Fighting Sioux forward Reg Morelli is named tourney MVP.

To opposing general managers, it seemed virtually impossible to halt the Montreal juggernaut. Having won a fourth straight Stanley Cup in 1959, Habs manager Frank Selke did some minor re-tooling but still retained his basic championship cast. "I saw the great, old Cup-winning Canadiens teams of the early '30s, with Howie Morenz and Aurel Joliat," said Rangers G.M. Muzz Patrick, "but there's no comparing that team with this one. This Montreal team is many, many times better."

There were challengers, to be sure. The Black Hawks' rebuilding program was paying rich dividends, especially Bobby Hull, who tallied 81 points in 1959-60 to end Dickie Moore's two-year reign as scoring champion. Chicago also received superb netminding from Glenn "Mr. Goalie" Hall and top-notch defense out of the Pierre Pilote-Elmer Vasko combination.

But the Hawks and other challengers lacked Montreal's awesome depth. A total of eight future Hall of Famers dotted the Montreal roster, including Maurice and Henri Richard, Boom Boom Geoffrion, Jean Beliveau, Dickie Moore, Doug Harvey, Tom Johnson, and

STAR-STUDDED CANADIENS MAKE IT FIVE IN A ROW

Jacques Plante. With that collection of superstar talent, the Canadiens finished the season at 40-18-12.

What glitches the Canadiens encountered seemed minor, except for one personality feud. Coach Toe Blake and goalie Plante battled during the first month of the season over Plante's insistence on wearing a facemask during practice. Blake argued that the mask would make his goalie less effective during games, but Plante insisted that the mask was essential and, furthermore, would someday be standard equipment.

The conflict came to a head on November 1, 1959, at Madison Square Garden, when a shot struck Plante's unprotected face. The goalie crumpled to the ice, blood spurting from his wound. Plante was quickly sewn up with

seven stitches, but he refused to return to the game unless he was permitted to wear his mask. Blake reluctantly agreed.

Not a whit puck-shy, Plante played sensationally to beat the Rangers 3-1. Blake had hoped Plante would then discard his new protective covering, but Jacques insisted on using it again. The goalie permanently won his case for the mask by reeling off 10 straight games without defeat.

Punch Imlach's Maple Leafs loomed as a potential threat to Montreal after Toronto obtained defenseman Red Kelly from Detroit and then converted him to center. The Kelly trade loomed large, as Toronto finished in second place and then ousted Detroit in a six-game semifinal. The Canadiens, though, still seemed invincible, as they whisked away Chicago in four semifinal games.

Imlach tried every available stratagem in the Finals, including the heavy-checking game, but to no avail. Montreal orchestrated another four-game sweep and skated off with the Stanley Cup. The Canadiens merely confirmed what everyone had known already: This was the greatest team the hockey world had ever seen.

1959-60

- The Hall of Fame names three new inductees—Jack Adams, Cy Denneny, and Tiny Thompson—bringing the total number of members to 67.

- The NHL passes a new rule prohibiting players from leaving the bench to join a fight on the ice.

- Maurice Richard, at age 38, prepares for his final NHL season.

- On November 1, 1959, an Andy Bathgate slapshot cuts the face of Montreal goalie Jacques Plante.

- After receiving repairs for a seven-stitch cut, Jacques Plante returns to

the ice wearing a mask. Plante goes on to become the first goalie to regularly wear a mask.

- The Rangers, who carry on a personality feud with coach Phil Watson, lose nine of their first 15 games. Watson is then fired and replaced by Alf Pike.

The 1960 Stanley Cup Finals marked the conclusion of the greatest period in Montreal Canadiens history. The Habs appeared in their 10th consecutive Finals series, winning their sixth Stanley Cup within that span. The secrets of the Canadiens' success were opportunistic scoring and steadfast defense, led by five-time Norris Trophy winner Doug Harvey (center) and five-time Vezina Trophy recipient Jacques Plante (right).

• The Canadiens, once again the pride of the NHL offensively (255 goals) and defensively (178), finish in first place (40-18-12), 13 points ahead of second-place Toronto.

• The NHL crowns a new scoring king, as third-year pro Bobby Hull of the Black Hawks notches 81 points,

one more than Boston's Bronco Horvath.

• Bobby Hull ties Bronco Horvath for the league lead in goals (39).

• Boston's Don McKenney leads the NHL in assists with 49.

• Montreal's Jean Beliveau (34), New York's Dean Prentice (32), and Canadiens Henri Richard and Bernie Geoffrion (30 each) round out the top five goal-scorers.

• Ranger Andy Bathgate notches 48 assists and ties Jean Beliveau for third in points (74).

NHL Brass Cracks Down on Violence

In 1959-60, the league began to curb the extent of fisticuffs around the rinks. Many spectators didn't mind a good dust-up from time to time, but bench-clearing brawls not only delayed the games but were dangerous to the on-ice combatants. (Lou Fontinato, right, feels the pain here.) In this season, the NHL introduced rules and severe fines to prevent players from leaving their benches to enter altercations.

NHL Violence

Gordie Howe, Johnny Bower, Frank Selke Jr.

Captain Howe Claims the Hart

Gordie Howe had long been the on-ice leader for the Red Wings, but he was hesitant to accept the position of team captain. However, in the 1958-59 season, he donned the "C" for the first time and, of course, proved himself worthy of the honor. In the 1959-60 season, he captured the Hart Trophy, even though he tied for fifth in the league in scoring and his team finished with a losing record.

Pilote Among NHL's Best on Defense

Pierre Pilote completed his fourth full season in a Black Hawks uniform in 1959-60. A solid defenseman with fine offensive skills, Pilote proved himself to be a durable iron man, never missing a game in five straight campaigns. In 1959-60, he led all NHL defensemen with seven goals and 38 assists. Pilote's play along the Chicago blueline procured him a position on the NHL's Second All-Star Team.

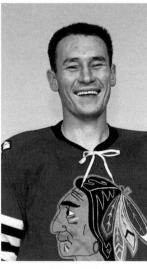

Pierre Pilote

1959-60

• Jacques Plante, playing with a mask despite the objections of his coach, Toe Blake, leads the NHL in wins (40) and GAA (2.54).

• Glenn Hall, the emerging superstar in Chicago's nets, absorbs a league-high 29 losses, but the Hawks finish third and make the playoffs.

• Carl Brewer, Toronto's hard-hitting sophomore defenseman, leads the NHL in penalty minutes (150), beating out Lou Fontinato (137).

• The Black Hawks, with an ever-improving roster, debut an ill-tempered, Czech-born centerman destined for greatness—Stan Mikita.

• Pierre Pilote, a veteran defenseman for Chicago, leads all NHL backliners in points (45).

• The New York Rangers show off a "novelty"—American-born goalie Jack McCartan, hero of Team USA in the 1960 Olympics.

Plante Dons a Facemask

Jacques Plante changed the face of goaltending forever in 1959-60. On November 1, 1959—ironically one day after Halloween—Plante took a shot in the face from Andy Bathgate. After several minutes in the infirmary, he reappeared sporting a crude fiberglass mask. Although his coach, Toe Blake, didn't want him to wear the protection, Plante refused to continue without it and went on a lengthy winning streak. With Plante's success, hockey history was made.

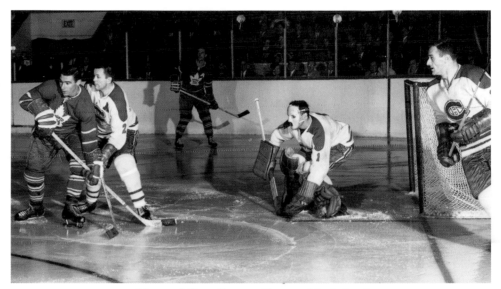

Montreal Canadiens vs. Toronto Maple Leafs

Bronco Horvath

Horvath Falls Just Short in Scoring Race

In a heated 1960 scoring race, Boston's Bronco Horvath battled to the wire with Chicago's Bobby Hull before falling one point shy. Horvath entered the last game of the season, ironically against the Hawks, with a one-point lead over Hull, but the Golden Jet rallied for a pair of points to win the title. As a consolation, Horvath set an NHL record with a 22-game point-scoring streak on his way to accumulating 39 goals and 41 assists.

Bobby Hull

Hull Jets to the Top of the Scoring Chart

The 1959-60 campaign heralded the arrival of one of the modern era's greatest stars. Bobby Hull, the Golden Jet, had been in the league since 1957-58, but in this season he took off. He tied for the league lead in goals with 39 and led in points with 81 to win his first Art Ross Trophy. Hull was called the Golden Jet not only because of his blond locks but also because of his explosive speed and ability to strike on target.

• The playoffs feature Montreal vs. Chicago and Toronto vs. Detroit.

• Detroit beats Toronto 2-1 in Game 1 at Maple Leaf Gardens. Toronto rebounds to win the next two games, including a triple-overtime affair in Game 3, with Frank Mahovlich scoring the winning goal.

• Detroit wins Game 4 of the semifinals on Gerry Melnyk's goal at 1:54 of the first sudden-death period.

• The Maple Leafs eliminate Detroit with a pair of wins, 5-4 and 4-2.

• The Canadiens sweep Chicago in four games, winning the first two

contests by 4-3 scores. Defenseman Doug Harvey scores in overtime to win Game 2.

• Jacques Plante records a pair of shutouts, 4-0 and 2-0, to send the Habs to the Finals for the 10th straight year.

Olympic Games

Team USA Wins the Gold at Squaw Valley

In 1960, the Olympic Winter Games were held in North America at Squaw Valley, California. The American team was expected to be competitive, but no one expected it to win the gold medal. However, with goaltender Jack McCartan, the Christian brothers, and a young Tommy Williams, the U.S. team went a perfect 7-0-0, including a 2-1 victory over Canada, to win its first Olympic gold medal in ice hockey competition.

Jack McCartan

McCartan Enjoys a Bit of Stardom

A hero of the 1960 Olympics was goaltender Jack McCartan, who immediately signed with the New York Rangers and appeared in four games near the end of the season. McCartan was tremendous in his brief tour of duty, winning two games, tying one, and compiling a goals-against average of 1.75. McCartan floundered in his second year, however, posting a bloated 4.91 goals-against average in seven games. He never played in the NHL again.

1959-60

- Montreal beats Toronto 4-2 in Game 1 of the Finals.

- Dickie Moore and Marcel Bonin score in the first six minutes of Game 2, and Montreal goes on to win 2-1.

- Montreal builds a 3-0 lead halfway through Game 3, and Maurice

Richard scores the last playoff goal of his career, as Montreal wins 5-2.

- The Maple Leafs are discouraged and inefficient in Game 4, unable to solve Jacques Plante. He registers a 4-0 shutout to give Montreal its second straight sweep in the playoffs.

- On April 14, 1960, the Canadiens hoist their all-time record fifth straight Stanley Cup, concluding the greatest dynasty the game has ever known.

- Henri Richard and Boom Boom Geoffrion lead all playoff scorers with 12 points each.

Phil Watson

Stanley Cup Semifinals

O.T. Win Helps Leafs Beat Wings in Semis

Two of the leading men of their time, Gordie Howe and Johnny Bower, meet in the 1960 semifinals. The key game in this series was a triple-overtime duel in Game 3 in Detroit. Toronto's Frank Mahovlich slipped the puck past Terry Sawchuk at the three-minute mark of the third overtime period to give the Leafs a hard-earned 5-4 victory. Although Detroit tied the series with an over-time win of its own, the Leafs won the series in six games.

Watson Suffers Ulcers After Losses Mount

There was considerable surprise in the summer of 1959 when Rangers coach Phil Watson was given a vote of confidence by management despite losing six of the last seven games in 1958-59 to miss the playoffs by a single point. When the Blues stumbled early in 1959-60, winning only three of their first 15 games, Watson was hospitalized after a severe ulcer attack. Alf Pike was brought in to relieve Watson, who never returned behind the bench in New York.

Rocket Accepts Stanley Cup, Then Retires

Although they were bitter enemies, NHL President Clarence Campbell and Maurice Richard manage to smile as the 1960 Stanley Cup is presented to the Canadiens' team captain. In training camp the following year, after Richard scored a hat-trick in a game, he left the ice and took off his skates for the final time. He announced his retirement moments later, and the career of hockey's greatest offensive weapon passed into legend.

Clarence Campbell, Maurice Richard

- Gordie Howe (73 points) captures his fifth Hart Trophy, beating out scoring champ Bobby Hull.

- Boston's Don McKenney wins the Lady Byng Trophy.

- Chicago's Billy Hay, a linemate of Bobby Hull, is voted the Calder Trophy based on his 18 goals and 55 points.

- Montreal's Doug Harvey retakes his place as the NHL's top defender, winning his fifth Norris Trophy.

- For the first time ever, the United States wins the Olympic hockey gold medal, beating Canada (silver) and the Soviet Union (bronze).

- Denver beats Michigan Tech 5-3 in the finals of the NCAA hockey tournament. The tourney MVP award is divided among Tech's Lou Angotti and Boston University's Bob Marquis and Barry Urbanski.

BELLIGERENT HAWKS BEAT THE LIFE OUT OF MONTREAL

Though Montreal lost Maurice Richard to retirement in 1960-61, the Canadiens seemed as strong as ever—at least on the surface. Winners of 40 games in 1959-60, the Habs recorded 41 victories in 1960-61. Bernie Geoffrion equaled Richard's feat of 50 goals in a season, led the league in scoring (95), and captured the Hart Trophy. Moreover, Doug Harvey's defensive excellence earned him another Norris Trophy.

However, the Habs never could replace the Rocket's leadership, which led to a debilitating internal problem. Geoffrion, the club's senior superstar, passionately wanted the captaincy and made his displeasure public when teammate Jean Beliveau got the captain's "C." Majestic as he was, Beliveau lacked Richard's fire, and this vital missing element would ultimately cost the Canadiens in the playoffs.

The Habs were challenged by two increasingly powerful clubs: the Black Hawks, sparked by young scorers Stan Mikita and Bobby Hull, and the Maple Leafs, led by Frank Mahovlich (48 goals) and goalie Johnny Bower. At one point, the Leafs looked good enough to finish first.

Toronto had a six-point lead on Montreal early in March, but the Habs rampaged in the final weeks while Punch Imlach's skaters— especially Mahovlich—faded. The Canadiens finished with 92 points, two more than the Leafs. But the big push enervated the defending champs, who were targeting a sixth straight Stanley Cup title.

It was the Canadiens' misfortune to encounter a vigorous Chicago club in the opening playoff round. Windy City coach Rudy Pilous had analyzed the Montrealers and divined a simple but perfect plan: punish Montreal's superstars at every turn. The bigger, more belligerent Chicagoans— particularly Reg Fleming, Jack Evans, and Pierre Pilote—reduced the Habs to a crawl.

Black and blue, the Canadiens limped out of the playoffs in six games, their extraordinary five-Cup run at an end. The Black Hawks, who had not won a Stanley Cup in 23 years, then mopped up the Red Wings in six games behind Glenn Hall's masterful goaltending.

After the final playoff game, the Chicago dressing room was hauntingly quiet. Only an occasional whoop seared the air, while the Stanley Cup was placed on a rubbing table in the middle of the room. Fleming had an explanation. "I guess it's been so long for most of these guys," he said, "that they just don't know how to celebrate."

Slumped in a corner, almost hidden by a rack of overcoats, was Hall. His voice was almost inaudible. "I'm a tired hockey player," said the sad-eyed goalie who had played in 82 consecutive games. "Too tired to scream, but awfully enthused about the whole thing."

The Black Hawks may have been the quietest and driest Cup winners hockey has known, for nobody was drenched with beer and nobody popped a champagne cork. "There's no champagne," said jubilant owner Jim Norris. "I didn't order any. I was afraid of jinxing the boys."

1960-61

- The Canadian National Exhibition, the City of Toronto, and the NHL reach agreement on the construction of a Hall of Fame building on the CNE grounds in Toronto.

- The Hall of Fame names four new inductees—George Boucher, Sylvio Mantha, Frank Selke, and Jack Walker—bringing the total number of members to 71.

- The Maple Leafs, who acquired Red Kelly from Detroit in late 1959-60, move the defenseman to center.

- Vic Stasiuk, traded from Boston to Detroit for Murray Oliver, joins Gordie Howe and Alex Delvecchio on the Wings' top line.

- On November 27, 1960, Gordie Howe scores his 1,000th point.

- On January 16, 1961, Chicago goalie Glenn Hall plays his 500th straight game, including playoffs.

Glenn Hall played 18 seasons of NHL hockey and won many awards for his brilliance in nets, but his only Stanley Cup victory came in 1961, when the Black Hawks captured the title with a six-game conquest of the Red Wings. Hall led all playoff goalies in wins (eight), shutouts (two), and GAA (2.25). In the semifinals against Montreal, he held the Habs scoreless through Games 5 and 6 (both 3-0 victories), enabling Chicago to advance to the Finals.

• Just as in 1959-60, Montreal finishes first, Toronto second, Chicago third, and Detroit fourth. The Canadiens go 41-19-10 to edge the Maple Leafs by two points.

• Montreal leads the NHL in scoring for the eighth straight year (254 goals).

• Montreal's Bernie Geoffrion finishes the season with 50 goals, becoming just the second player ever to do so. He leads the NHL in both goals and points (95).

• Toronto's Frank Mahovlich finishes second in goals (48).

• Montreal's Jean Beliveau is first in the league in assists (58) and second in points (90).

• Toronto's Frank Mahovlich (84 points), Ranger Andy Bathgate (77), and Gordie Howe (72) round out the top five scorers.

Boom Boom's the Second to Net 50

Bernie Geoffrion, playing in his 11th NHL season, won his second scoring title in 1960-61 and became only the second man in league history to record 50 goals in a season—following in the footsteps of his former teammate, Maurice Richard. On March 16, 1961, before a delirious Forum crowd, the 30-year-old Geoffrion beat Toronto goalie Cesare Maniago for his final goal of the year (he went scoreless in two more games).

Bernie Geoffrion

Pierre Pilote

Pilote Plays D, Fights, and Scores

Chicago defenseman Pierre Pilote was at his fighting best during the 1960-61 campaign, his fifth full season in the league. After leading the league in penalty minutes (165), the 29-year-old blueliner went on a scoring rampage during the playoffs, notching 12 assists and sharing the overall scoring lead with Detroit's Gordie Howe (15 points). With Pilote's leadership, the Black Hawks won the Cup.

Habs Boss Blake Loses His Cool

Montreal entered the 1961 Stanley Cup playoffs as five-time defending champs in search of an unprecedented sixth straight title. At the helm was their fiery genius coach, Toe Blake, bench boss of their five previous Cups. Following a Game 3 triple-overtime loss to Chicago in the opening round, Blake attacked referee Dalton McArthur, whom Blake felt overlooked several calls against his players. Toe was later fined $2,000 by the NHL.

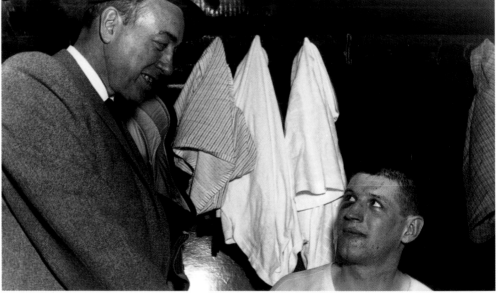

Toe Blake (left)

1960-61

- Andy Bathgate leads the Rangers in scoring for the sixth straight year, with 29 goals and 77 points, but the team fails to make the playoffs.

- The Bruins put 22-year-old rookie Bruce Gamble in goal and finish sixth, losing 42 of 70 games.

- Toronto's Johnny Bower, getting better and better at age 36, leads the league in GAA (2.50).

- Chicago's Pierre Pilote leads the league in penalty minutes (165 PIM), while teammate Reggie Fleming is second (145).

- Wayne Gretzky is born on January 26, 1961, in Brantford, Ontario.

- The playoffs feature Montreal vs. Chicago and Detroit vs. Toronto.

- The Leafs defeat the Wings in Game 1 of the semifinals 3-2, as George Armstrong scores in double overtime.

Johnny Bower

36-Year-Old Bower Wins First Vezina

Johnny Bower's journey to the Hall of Fame was fraught with setbacks and hurdles. After tying for the NHL lead in minutes played as a rookie on the 1953-54 Rangers, Bower was exiled to the minors for three years and then left unprotected in the 1958 draft. The Leafs grabbed him and brought him back to the NHL. By 1960-61, the 36-year-old goalie reached his peak, leading the NHL in wins (33) and GAA (2.50) and winning the Vezina Trophy.

Kelly Excels in New City, New Position

After more than a dozen years wearing a Red Wings sweater, future Hall of Famer Red Kelly was traded to Toronto at the end of the 1959-60 season for Marc Reaume. The former Norris Trophy-winning defenseman switched to center and, in 1960-61, scored 20 goals (his best to date) and notched 50 assists as the playmaker for wingers Frank Mahovlich (48 goals) and Bob Nevin (21 goals). Kelly won his fourth Lady Byng Trophy as a tribute to his sportsmanship.

Red Kelly

Glenn Hall

Hall Does It All, Plays in 500 Straight

The 1960-61 campaign was a personal showcase for Black Hawks goalie Glenn Hall. On January 16, 1961, the future Hall of Famer played in his unprecedented 500th consecutive game. He led the league with six shutouts, was third overall in goals-against average (2.57), and was the runner-up to Toronto's Johnny Bower for the Vezina Trophy. Hall was brilliant in the playoffs, winning eight games in 12 outings with a 2.25 GAA and a pair of shutouts.

- After dropping the opener, the Red Wings defeat Toronto in each of the next four games, as Terry Sawchuk shines in goal.

- The Canadiens, seeking their sixth straight Cup, trounce the Black Hawks 6-2 in their semifinals opener.

- The Black Hawks upset the Habs 4-3 in Game 2 at Montreal. Chicago then wins Game 3 2-1 at home on Murray Balfour's triple-overtime winner.

- Following Game 3, Montreal coach Toe Blake attacks referee Dalton McArthur and is fined $2,000.

- Montreal evens the series with a 5-2 win in Game 4, but Glenn Hall tallies a pair of 3-0 shutouts in Games 5 and 6 to eliminate the defending champs.

- Chicago and Detroit meet in the Stanley Cup Finals for the first time since 1934.

Gretzky Born in Little Town of Brantford

Wayne Gretzky's Skates, Bronzed Feet

Far from the bruising chaos of the NHL, in the smallish town of Brantford, Ontario, Wayne Gretzky was born on January 26, 1961. By age three, he was already an adroit skater. By the time he was nine, he was playing with (and beating) teenagers. An avid fan of Detroit legend Gordie Howe, young Wayne donned the No. 9 jersey that would eventually turn into his famous 99. His first pair of skates and a bronze casting of his feet sit in the Hockey Hall of Fame.

Bobby Hull, Gordie Howe

Frank Mahovlich

Mahovlich Thrills Fans, Nets 48

Frank Mahovlich was the "Big M" in Toronto not only with his teammates, whom he led in scoring in 1960-61 with 48 goals and 84 points, but also with fans. He's shown here signing autographs in the Maple Leafs' locker room. Just 22 years old and playing in his fourth full NHL season, Mahovlich was the league's third-leading scorer in 1960-61 and was second overall in goals, trailing only Montreal's Bernie Geoffrion (who scored 50).

Howe's the First to Score 1,000

Known as Mr. Hockey to his face and Mr. Elbows behind his back, Gordie Howe (pictured with Chicago's dynamic winger, Bobby Hull) pioneered new territory for NHL scorers during the 1960-61 season. On November 27, 1960, during a 2-0 win over the visiting Maple Leafs, Howe notched an assist and became the first player in NHL history to reach the 1,000-point plateau. Hull joined him 11 years later as just the fifth NHLer to record 1,000 points.

1960-61

- Chicago beats Detroit 3-2 in Game 1 of the Finals.

- Detroit wins Game 2 3-1 and Chicago prevails by the same score in Game 3. The Wings take Game 4 2-1.

- Chicago's powerhouse offense erupts in Game 5. Stan Mikita and Murray Balfour each score twice in Chicago's 6-3 triumph.

- Five different Hawks beat Wings goalie Hank Bassen for a 5-1 Cup-clinching win in Game 6. The Black Hawks raise their first Stanley Cup since 1938.

- Chicago's Pierre Pilote shares the playoff scoring title with Detroit's Gordie Howe (15 points).

- Montreal's Bernie Geoffrion—recipient of the Art Ross Trophy—wins the Hart Trophy, edging Toronto goalie Johnny Bower.

Sawchuk Shuts Down Leafs in Cup Semis

In the 1961 semifinals, the Maple Leafs took on their arch-rival Red Wings, who were represented in goal by the brilliant Terry Sawchuk (pictured applying a kick save to Eddie Shack's in-tight shot on goal). The Leafs won the first game, but the Wings allowed just five goals through the next four as Detroit continued its domination of the Leafs with a five-game triumph.

Stanley Cup Semifinals

Balfour Nets O.T. Winner in Cup Semis

Murray Balfour played 41 playoff games with the Black Hawks, but lit the red light just nine times. One of those postseason tallies made the history books. On March 26, 1961, during the Hawks' opening-round series against Montreal, Balfour scored at 12:12 of triple overtime against Jacques Plante, giving Chicago a 2-1 win and a lead in their series, which they eventually won in six games en route to a Stanley Cup title.

Bobby Hull

Hull, Hawks End Stanley Cup Drought

Bobby Hull shares a moment of joy with fans as the Windy City Six edged closer to their first Cup in 23 years. The Hawks, who hadn't made the Finals since 1944 and had failed to make the playoff action 12 times since then, took six games to oust the Red Wings. Hull was Chicago's second-leading playoff scorer (14 points) and assisted Ab McDonald's Cup-clinching score at 18:47 of the second period in Game 6.

Murray Balfour

• Red Kelly, a three-time Lady Byng Trophy winner with Detroit, wins his first Lady Byng with the Leafs.

• Johnny Bower wins the Vezina Trophy—his first—ending the five-year reign of Montreal goalie Jacques Plante.

• Dave Keon (with 20 rookie goals) beats out Toronto teammate Bob Nevin (21 goals) for the Calder.

• Montreal's Doug Harvey, the top scoring defenseman in the NHL (39 points), wins his sixth Norris Trophy in seven years.

• Denver wins its second straight NCAA championship, routing St. Lawrence 12-2 in the finals. Denver's Bill Masterton is the tourney's MVP.

• Future star defenseman Paul Coffey is born on June 1, 1961, in Weston, Ontario.

LEAFS PACK PLENTY OF PUNCH, SIP FROM CUP

If the charismatic Punch Imlach wasn't the most dominant off-ice NHL personality of the 1960s, he was certainly right up there. Toronto originally hired Imlach in the late 1950s as an assistant general manager, but he took over as coach in 1959-60 and guided the Leafs to the Finals in his first two seasons.

The 1960-61 Leafs were impressive, going 39-19-12. However, they were upset in the semifinals by Detroit, largely because young Leafs such as forwards Dave Keon, Bob Nevin, and Eddie Shack had yet to fully acclimate to Imlach's system.

In 1961-62, though, all the pieces were in place for a championship team. Besides the aforementioned trio, Punch had a neck-ribbed defense that mixed smart veterans like Allan Stanley and Tim Horton with aggressive youngsters Carl Brewer and Bob Baun. Bert Olmstead, the best corner man in hockey, still had his legs, while Frank Mahovlich was an All-Star at left wing. Ancient Johnny Bower still shined in goal. From top to bottom, there was not a weak link in the chain.

The Leafs had plenty of injuries in 1961-62, but they overcame each one in a race that featured three top clubs: the defending-champion Black Hawks, the proud Canadiens, and Imlach's Torontonians. Although the Habs finished first (42-14-14), Imlach was unconcerned. "We were ready for the playoffs," Punch said.

The Canadiens appeared just as ready after beating Chicago in their first two playoff games. However, Chicago stunned the Habs with four straight victories to advance. Meanwhile, Toronto had its hands full with New York after the Rangers rallied to tie the series at two apiece. But the Leafs' double-overtime win in Game 5 opened the gates, and they triumphed in six games to reach the Finals.

Toronto took the first two Finals games at home, but the bruising Black Hawks bashed their way to two victories in Chicago. "Some people figured we were through, that we wouldn't win another game against them," said Imlach. "But we had something left—including a whole team of players who didn't scare."

Sure enough, Toronto won Game 5 8-4 and then returned to Chicago Stadium for one of the toughest Cup Final games ever played. It was 0-0 well into the third period before Bobby Hull put the Hawks ahead 1-0. The crowd delayed the game for 10 precious minutes with a hail of celebratory debris. However, the premature demonstration cost the home club its momentum and the lead, as Bob Nevin scored almost immediately after the faceoff. Toronto then took its first Stanley Cup in 11 years on Dick Duff's gamer a few minutes later.

"When the game was over," Imlach recalled, "Bert Olmstead was so tired that he couldn't get off the bench. So I had to lean close to him to hear what he said. He told me, 'It's been a long haul, Punch.'"

For the Leafs, though, it was only the beginning of another hockey dynasty. Punch Imlach's club would successfully defend the Stanley Cup in 1963, and again in 1964.

1961-62

- The NHL rules that penalty shots will now be taken by the player against whom the foul is committed—rather than a designee.

- The Hockey Hall of Fame officially opens in Toronto on August 21, 1961.

- The Hall of Fame names 17 inductees, including Syl Apps, Charlie Conacher, Hap Day, George Hainsworth, Joe Hall, Maurice Richard, and Milt Schmidt.

- Harold Ballard, Stafford Smythe (son of Conn Smythe), and John Bassett purchase controlling interest in Maple Leaf Gardens en route to taking over the team.

- New York fires Alf Pike after two losing years and installs ex-Habs star Doug Harvey as player/coach.

- The Canadiens win the regular-season title for the fifth year in a row,

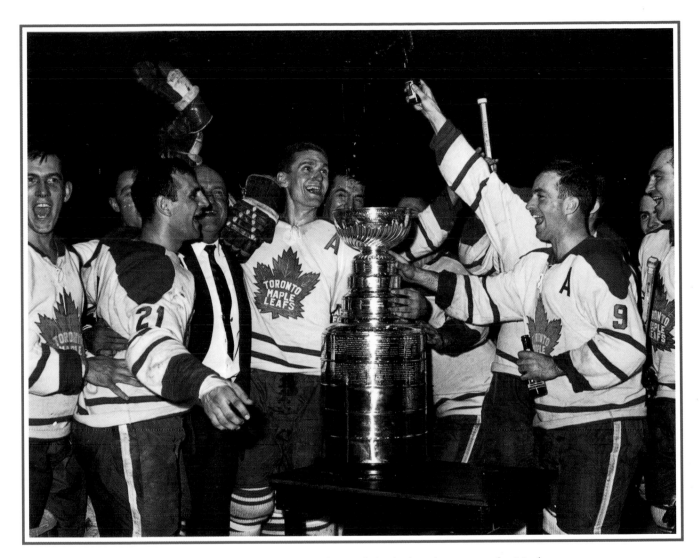

After two unsuccessful trips to the Finals in the last three years, the Maple Leafs finally sipped champagne from the silver Stanley Cup when, on April 22, 1962, they capped off the 1961-62 season with a six-game victory over reigning champion Chicago. Several Leafs gather around the coveted trophy for a moment of celebration, including Dick Duff (#9), who scored the Cup-winning goal.

going 42-14-14. Toronto finishes second for the third straight year.

• The Habs' attack—led by Claude Provost (33 goals), Gilles Tremblay (32), and Ralph Backstrom (27)—leads the NHL in goals (259) for the ninth consecutive year.

• Chicago's Bobby Hull leads the league with 50 goals, becoming the third player in NHL history to hit the number exactly.

• New York's Andy Bathgate paces the NHL in assists (56) and ties Bobby Hull for the league lead in points (84).

• Three players—Detroit's Gordie Howe, Toronto's Frank Mahovlich, and Montreal's Claude Provost—tie for second in goals (33).

• Stan Mikita, the Black Hawks' newest superstar center, is second in assists (52) and ties Gordie Howe for third in points (77).

Talbot Tops Rearguards in Scoring

Jean Guy Talbot

Jean Guy Talbot played 17 seasons in the NHL (13 with Montreal), and while he never won an award, he retired in 1971 with his name on seven Stanley Cups. In 1961-62, the husky defenseman reached a career high in points (47), tops among all backliners in the league. His 42 assists were the sixth best in the NHL. Unfortunately for Talbot, ex-Montreal defenseman Doug Harvey (a Ranger in 1961-62) annexed his seventh Norris Trophy as Talbot was among the runners-up.

Hockey Hall of Fame

Hall of Fame Throws Open Its Doors

On August 26, 1961, Canadian Prime Minister John Diefenbaker officially opened the Hockey Hall of Fame in Toronto. On the site of the Canadian National Exhibition, the building featured the flags of all six NHL teams. The late James D. Norris was credited with being among the most ardent supporters of a hockey shrine, and—along with Toronto hockey genius Conn Smythe—did much of the preliminary work to ensure financial support was in place.

Gordie Howe, Jean Beliveau

Howe Pots His 500th Career Goal

In a tale of teams going in opposite directions, the 1961-62 Red Wings—led by the unrivaled Gordie Howe—finished out of the playoffs while Jean Beliveau led the Canadiens to a first-place finish. On March 14, 1962, during a 3-2 loss at New York, Howe scored a goal and joined Beliveau's former teammate, Maurice Richard, as just the second player in NHL history to record 500 career goals. Beliveau would become the fourth man to turn the trick, in 1971.

1961-62

• Billy Hay, who centers Bobby Hull's line in Chicago, ties teammate Stan Mikita for second in the NHL in assists (52).

• Jacques Plante leads the NHL in victories (42) and goals-against average (2.37).

• Chicago's Glenn Hall leads the league in shutouts (nine) and is third in GAA (2.66).

• Montreal's Jean Guy Talbot, who replaces Doug Harvey as the Habs' top defender, leads all NHL backliners with 47 points.

• In his new role as Montreal's enforcer, Lou Fontinato captures his third penalty title (167 PIM). He's followed by Boston rookie Terrible Ted Green (116).

• Red Kelly runs for office in the Canadian Parliament—and wins. He also scores 22 goals for the Leafs.

Montreal Canadiens vs. Toronto Maple Leafs

Healthy Plante Regains the Vezina Trophy

Montreal goalie Jacques Plante, who missed much of the 1960-61 season due to a knee injury, was back in nets for the Habs in 1961-62, leading the league in wins (42) and goals-against average (2.37) as his team returned to the top of the standings. Plante (shown standing his ground against Toronto's Frank Mahovlich while Habs defenseman Tom Johnson applies the lumber to the Big M) was honored with his sixth Vezina Trophy in seven years.

Provost Bats In a Career-High 33

In 1961-62, Montreal right winger Claude Provost (shown relaxing in an easy chair along with teammate Jean Guy Talbot) enjoyed a career-high 33 goals, tying him for second in the league. He combined with Henri Richard and Dickie Moore on the Habs' dangerous second line. Provost played 15 NHL seasons and contributed to nine Stanley Cups, all with Montreal.

Jean Guy Talbot, Claude Provost

- On March 14, 1962, Gordie Howe scores his 500th goal, joining Maurice Richard in the two-man club.

- Gordie Howe's 77 points aren't enough to keep Detroit from finishing out of the playoffs for only the second time in the last 24 years.

- The playoffs feature Montreal vs. Chicago and Toronto vs. New York.

- The Black Hawks and Canadiens face off in the semis, and Montreal wins the first two games.

- Chicago defeats Montreal in each of the next four games, outscoring the

Canadiens 15-7 to pull off a mild upset and advance to the Finals.

- Toronto and the Rangers are tied after four games, but Red Kelly scores in double O.T. of Game 5.

- The Leafs crush New York 7-1 in the decisive sixth semifinal game.

Mikita Scores When He's Not in the Box

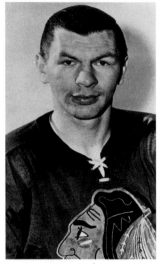

Stan Mikita

Stan Mikita, emerging as a two-way threat in the NHL, finished the 1961-62 season with 25 goals and 97 penalty minutes, combining skill with an extremely nasty disposition to achieve his goals. Playing with Ab McDonald and Kenny Wharram, Mikita tied Billy Hay for the team lead in assists (52) and established himself as a big-league playmaker, finishing fourth in the league in scoring (77).

Player/Coach Harvey Wins Seventh Norris

Doug Harvey

After 14 brilliant seasons in Montreal, during which he won six Norris Trophies, Doug Harvey left the Habs for New York to become player/coach of the Rangers, actually commuting home to his family in Montreal whenever possible. Harvey's Rangers finished fourth in 1961-62, just four points ahead of Detroit, but the veteran backliner notched 30 points and won his seventh Norris Trophy.

Hull Beats the Gump for Goal No. 50

On March 25, 1962, Bobby Hull became the third NHL player ever to score 50 goals in a season. During a 4-1 loss at Madison Square Garden, Hull fired a 10-footer past Rangers goalie Gump Worsley as Reggie Fleming (#6) awaited a rebound that never came and Rangers defenseman Doug Harvey struggled in vain to bring down the Golden Jet. Hull (wearing sweater #7) switched to his famous #9 the following year.

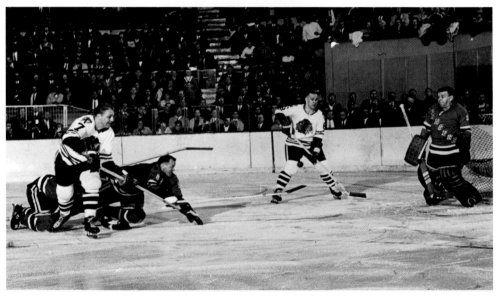

Chicago Black Hawks vs. New York Rangers

1961-62

- Bobby Hull opens the scoring in Game 1 of the Stanley Cup Finals, but Toronto nets four unanswered goals to win 4-1.

- Two goals by Chicago's Stan Mikita in Game 2 are wasted, as the Leafs go on to win 3-2.

- Glenn Hall shuts out the Leafs 3-0 in Game 3 of the Finals. In Game 4, Bobby Hull and Reggie Fleming each score twice to lead the Hawks to a 4-1 win.

- The powerful Leafs attack explodes for eight goals in Game 5—three by Bob Pulford and two more by Frank Mahovlich—as the Leafs win 8-4 and take a 3-2 lead in games.

- Bobby Hull's third-period goal gives the Hawks a 1-0 lead in Game 6. However, Bob Nevin ties it for Toronto and Dick Duff scores at 14:14 of the third period. Toronto wins 2-1 to clinch the Cup.

Red Kelly

Kelly Joins Parliament, Pots 22 Goals

Red Kelly, Toronto's graceful defenseman-turned-center, became a different kind of "two-sport" superstar when, prior to the 1961-62 season, he ran for office in the Canadian Parliament—and won a seat. He then reported for duty with the Maple Leafs and scored 22 goals while centering the top line with Frank Mahovlich and Bob Nevin. A four-time Lady Byng winner and one-time Norris Trophy defenseman, Kelly played five more seasons before retiring.

Stanley Cup Finals

Leafs' D Puts the Screws to Chicago

The Black Hawks entered the 1962 Finals determined to defend their Stanley Cup title, but they ran into a suffocating Toronto defense, led by Allan Stanley and Bobby Baun (shown crushing Chicago tough guy Reggie Fleming into the wall as Hawks center Eric Nesterenko, #6, searches for the puck). The Leafs were backed by the brilliant goaltending of Johnny Bower, whose 2.20 goals-against average led all play-off goalies.

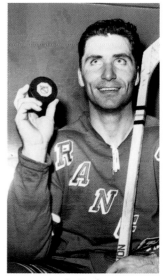

Andy Bathgate

Bathgate Leads in Assists, Nets 200th Goal

The 1961-62 season was a difficult one for the Rangers, who lost more games (32) than they won (26) and were eliminated by Toronto in the playoffs. However, Winnipeg native Andy Bathgate, skating in his 10th NHL season, had a share in his first scoring title, tying Chicago's Bobby Hull for most points (84) while leading the league in assists (54). Bathgate also notched the 200th goal of his career, which he proudly displays.

- Toronto's Tim Horton sets a playoff record with 13 assists by a defenseman. Stan Mikita leads all playoff scorers with 21 points.

- Though they tied with 84 points, Bobby Hull wins the Art Ross Trophy over Andy Bathgate because he had more goals (50 to 28).

- Montreal goalie Jacques Plante wins his sixth Vezina Trophy. He also captures his only Hart Trophy.

- Montreal's Bobby Rousseau, with 21 goals, wins the Calder Trophy.

- Player/coach Doug Harvey wins his seventh (and final) Norris Trophy.

- Toronto's Dave Keon nabs his first Lady Byng Trophy.

- Michigan Tech captures the NCAA hockey championship with a 7-1 win over Clarkson in the finals. Tech's Lou Angotti is named the tournament's MVP.

HOWE DOES HE DO IT? NO. 9 WINS SIXTH HART

It was a measure of Gordie Howe's comprehensive scoring skills that he outlasted his Hall of Fame linemates, Ted Lindsay and Sid Abel, and continued to be a league leader many years later. After Abel retired, Alex Delvecchio became Howe's center, followed by Norm Ullman. In every case, Howe never missed a beat.

At age 34 in 1962-63, No. 9 was outskating and outshooting players a dozen years younger—and outfighting the biggest, toughest brutes as well. Rangers defenseman Lou Fontinato made the discovery a couple of years earlier, when Howe pulverized him in a bout at Madison Square Garden.

"Gordie is likely the greatest hockey player that ever played," said Bobby Hull, the Black Hawks' ace. "And he's likely the best who ever will play."

Howe had scored his 500th career goal in March 1962 and was zeroing in on Maurice Richard's record of 544. Gordie remained at the top of his game because he did everything—skate, stick-handle, and shoot—better than his contemporaries. He was averaging 40-45 minutes per game on the ice—twice the ice time put in by most NHL forwards.

Describing his attacking style, Howe explained: "Many times when I hit the blueline, I have no idea what I'm going to do to put the puck in the net. The more expert a player becomes with every shot in the bag, the less time he wastes worrying about it, and the more worrisome he is to the goalkeeper."

Goalies worried plenty about Howe in 1962-63. He won the scoring title (38-48-86) and his sixth Hart Trophy, setting a new record. While many players were aping Hull's and Andy Bathgate's slapshots, Howe invented and perfected a more controllable drive—the wrist slapshot. He explained: "The blade of the stick should come back waist high or higher on the backswing and should hit the puck clearly off the heel. I snap my wrists as I hit the puck."

Under Howe's orchestration, the Red Wings displayed a wide-open, non-restrictive type of assault that had the forwards sweep down the ice in a series of crisscross designs. Gordie called it the "Play It by Ear" attack, and it changed the basic assault pattern in pro hockey.

Though the Wings finished fourth in 1962-63, Howe did pace the Wings to a semifinal playoff upset over the Black Hawks, pushing Detroit into the Finals against the Maple Leafs. Despite Howe's Promethean efforts, the Red Wings were finished almost as quickly as the Finals began. Dick Duff scored twice in the first 68 seconds of the first contest. Toronto went on to win in five games. "I never had much doubt about our ability to beat Detroit after that," said Maple Leafs G.M./coach Punch Imlach.

Howe, though, would continue to strike fear in his opponents. He made the All-Star team in 1964 and again in 1965. In fact, Gordie would make six more All-Star trips by 1970, giving him 22 such appearances. Howe wouldn't hang up his skates for good until 1980, at the age of 52, 34 years after he first entered the league.

1962-63

- Among the 33 Hall of Fame inductees are Punch Broadbent, Harry Cameron, Reg Noble, Didier Pitre, Sweeney Schriner, and Nels Stewart.

- On June 6, 1962, the site of Bill Barilko's 1951 plane crash is discovered in northern Ontario.

- In New York, Doug Harvey resigns his coaching duties but remains a player.

- When the last-place Bruins win just one of their first 14 games, coach Phil Watson is fired and Milt Schmidt returns to the Boston bench.

- Glenn Hall's consecutive-game streak ends at 502 when a back injury forces him briefly out of the lineup.

- The Maple Leafs win the regular-season title for the first time since 1947-48. They finish 35-23-12, one point ahead of Chicago.

Detroit's Gordie Howe poses with NHL President Clarence Campbell as he receives his unprecedented sixth Art Ross Trophy and holds up his record sixth Hart Trophy. Howe led the league in goals (38) and points (86) and guided the Red Wings back into the playoffs. He had to outplay Chicago's Stan Mikita for the Hart Trophy and Ranger Andy Bathgate for the Art Ross. Though he still had many All-Star years left in him, Howe would never again win either award.

• Johnny Bower and Don Simmons (acquired from Boston for Ed Chadwick) provide solid goaltending for the Leafs, while Frank Mahovlich leads the attack.

• After five straight years atop the standings, Montreal finishes third, three points out of first. The Canadiens do lead the league in goals (225) for the 10th straight year.

• Gordie Howe paces the NHL in goals (38) and wins his sixth (and last) scoring title (86 points).

• Camille Henry, the Rangers' wiry center, enjoys a career year (37 goals), while teammate Andy Bathgate is second in the league in scoring with 81 points.

• Maple Leafs star Frank Mahovlich is third in the league in goals (36). He ties Montreal's Henri Richard for fourth in points (73).

Lou Fontinato

Fontinato's Career Grinds to a Halt

Muscleman Lou Fontinato, who skated for the Rangers and Canadiens during his nine-year career, suffered a career-ending injury during the 1962-63 season when he missed a body-check on Rangers rookie Vic Hadfield and crashed into the boards. Fontinato, a fearless fighter and a friendly, colorful character, sustained a crushed cervical vertebra and some brief paralysis, ending his NHL journey with 26 goals and 1,247 penalty minutes in 535 games.

Pint-Sized Henry Slips In 37 Goals

Considered too small for the NHL at just 5'8" and 150 pounds, Rangers left winger Camille "The Eel" Henry enjoyed a 14-year NHL stint that included a Calder Trophy, a Lady Byng Trophy, and 279 career goals. His finest season came in 1962-63 when, playing on a second line, he ripped 37 goals—second in the league behind Gordie Howe's 38. Unfortunately, the Rangers finished fifth, 14 games under .500 and out of the playoffs.

Camille Henry

Bill Barilko, Gordie Howe

Site of Barilko Crash Finally Found

On June 6, 1962, the site of Bill Barilko's 1951 plane crash was discovered in Northern Ontario. Barilko (shown seated in the penalty box during a clash with Detroit while Gordie Howe prepares to return to the ice) starred for Toronto during a brief five-year career, one that ended when he was just 24 years old. His most famous goal was his last: a sudden-death winner against Montreal to clinch the 1951 Stanley Cup.

1962-63

- Stan Mikita tallies 31 goals and 76 points for the Black Hawks and trails only Gordie Howe and Andy Bathgate in the scoring race.

- Playing beside Gordie Howe and Alex Delvecchio, left winger Parker MacDonald scores a career-high 33 goals for Detroit.

- Terry Sawchuk has an outstanding season in Detroit, leading the NHL in goal-against average (2.48).

- Montreal's Jacques Plante is second in goals-against average (2.49) and ties Chicago's Glenn Hall for first in shutouts (five).

- Detroit's Howie Young sets a new standard for rough play when he spends 273 minutes in the box.

- Lou Fontinato's career ends when he misses a hit on Rangers rookie Vic Hadfield and crashes into the boards, crushing a cervical vertebra and suffering brief paralysis.

Tough, Clean Keon Claims the Lady Byng

Toronto's offense in 1962-63 was sparked by crafty second-line pivot Dave Keon, whose 28 goals were second on the team behind Frank Mahovlich's 36. Centering a line with Veterans Dick Duff (16 goals) and George Armstrong (19), Keon was the league's best symbol of tough, clean sportsmanship. In 68 games, the diminutive center (generously listed at 5'9" and 165 pounds) was called for just two minutes in penalties en route to his second Lady Byng Trophy.

Dave Keon

Young Spends 273 Minutes in the Cooler

Despite his charming smile and good looks, Detroit defenseman Howie Young was a fearsome figure on the ice. In 1962-63, Young established a new standard of miscreant behavior when he was whistled for an astonishing 273 penalty minutes (4.26 per game). Prior to Young's not-so-sterling achievement, the NHL record for single-season penalty minutes had belonged to Lou Fontinato of the 1955-56 Rangers (202 minutes in 70 games).

Howie Young

Detroit Red Wings vs. Toronto Maple Leafs

Sawchuk's Play Lifts the Wings

Detroit climbed back into the playoff picture in 1962-63 as a result of goalie Terry Sawchuk (shown following the puck as defenseman Bill Gadsby, #4, and winger Norm Ullman, #7, cover up in the defensive zone). While the Red Wings finished fourth in the standings, Sawchuk's 2.48 goals-against average led all NHL goalies and he was able to carry the team to the Stanley Cup Finals.

- Boom Boom Geoffrion misses five games when he's banned for throwing his gear at referee Vern Buffy.

- The playoffs feature Toronto vs. Montreal and Detroit vs. Chicago.

- The defending-champion Leafs win the first three games of the semifinals.

- Montreal staves off elimination with a 3-1 victory in Game 4, but the Leafs shut out the Habs 5-0 in Game 5 to advance to the Finals.

- The Red Wings are heavy underdogs in their semifinal series with Chicago—especially after dropping the first two games, 5-4 and 5-2.

- Shockingly, the Red Wings rattle off four straight wins against Chicago, as Terry Sawchuk shines in goal.

- The Stanley Cup Finals pit rivals Detroit and Toronto—with the Wings having won six of the last seven playoff meetings.

Stanley Cup Semifinals

Leafs Beat Habs Badly in Semis

The Canadiens have faced Toronto 13 times in the playoffs, but never were they beaten as badly as in the 1963 semifinals. The Leafs defeated the Habs in five games, outscoring Montreal 14-6. Goalie Johnny Bower and defenseman Tim Horton (both pictured) shut down a Canadiens offense that was the best in the league during the season. Jean Beliveau (background) managed two goals in the series, but Bower pitched a 5-0 shutout in Game 5.

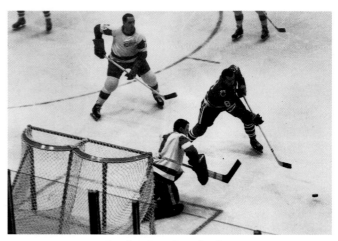

Stanley Cup Semifinals

Detroit Ousts Chicago in Semis

Chicago right winger Murray Balfour chases the puck in front of Detroit netminder Terry Sawchuk during Game 5 of the 1963 Stanley Cup semifinals. After dropping the first two games of the series, Detroit ripped off four straight wins to advance to the Finals. Balfour, who had scored a triple-overtime winner in the 1961 semifinals against Montreal, couldn't muster any magic against Sawchuk, who was playing his best hockey in years.

Chicago Black Hawks vs. Montreal Canadiens

Pilote, Hall Protect the Hawks' Net

The Black Hawks had the league's most proficient defensive scheme in 1962-63, thanks largely to the work of captain Pierre Pilote (shown lugging the puck out of harm's way as Montreal's Henri Richard gives chase) and goalie Glenn Hall, who led the league in wins (30), was third in goals-against average (2.55), and won the Vezina Trophy. Pilote celebrated the 1962-63 season with his first of three straight Norris Trophies.

1962-63

• The Leafs erupt for three quick goals in Game 1 to win 4-2.

• Ed Litzenberger scores for Toronto in the first six minutes of Game 2, and the Leafs go on to win 4-2.

• Detroit rookie Alex Faulkner—the first native of Newfoundland to play in the NHL—scores two goals for the Red Wings in Game 3 of the Finals, as Detroit wins 3-2.

• Dave Keon breaks a 2-2 tie in the third period of Game 4, and Red Kelly adds late insurance, as the Leafs win 4-2. They're one win away from repeating as Cup champs.

• Free-spirited winger Eddie Shack, an unlikely scoring hero, nets the Cup-clinching goal with 6:32 left in Game 5. Toronto wins 3-1.

• Dave Keon leads the Leafs in scoring (12 points), but Detroit's Gordie Howe and Norm Ullman tie for the playoff scoring lead (16).

Eddie Shack

Stanley Cup Finals

Leafs Beat Wings in Ho-Hum Finals

The Maple Leafs were back in the Stanley Cup Finals in 1963, defending their title against the Red Wings, who had failed to qualify for the postseason the year before. The powerful Toronto offense was bolstered by Dave Keon and Bob Pulford (pictured, left and right, around Detroit goalie Terry Sawchuk). This wasn't the most nail-biting series ever played; the Leafs won in five games, and all four of their victories were by exactly two goals.

Shack Smacks In the Cup Winner

Eddie "The Entertainer" Shack scored just six playoff goals in 74 postseason games during his 17-year NHL career. The biggest came on April 18, 1963, during Game 5 of the Stanley Cup Finals between Shack's Maple Leafs and the Red Wings. With the Leafs up three games to one and the score tied 1-1 late in the third period, Shack knocked the puck past Terry Sawchuk on a feed from Kent Douglas to put the Leafs ahead and clinch their 11th Stanley Cup title.

• Detroit legend Gordie Howe wins his sixth Hart Trophy, beating out Chicago's Stan Mikita.

• Dave Keon wins his second straight Lady Byng Trophy, while teammate Kent Douglas captures the Calder Trophy.

• Glenn Hall captures his first Vezina Trophy, topping Toronto's Johnny Bower and Don Simmons.

• Chicago's hard-hitting Pierre Pilote wins the first of his three straight Norris Trophies. Toronto's Carl Brewer is runner-up.

• North Dakota nips Denver 6-5 in the finals to win the NCAA hockey championship. North Dakota forward Al McLean is named tourney MVP.

• The Soviet Union begins its dominance in international hockey, as it wins its first of nine straight world championships.

HULL, BIG M, MIKITA GIVE THE NHL SOME PIZZAZZ

While its competitors in professional basketball, football, and baseball expanded across the continent, big-league hockey remained a six-team cocoon in 1963-64. The upside of this was that only the highest quality performers could play in the NHL, which meant hockey's superstars were really something special. Two of the most interesting glamour boys—Frank Mahovlich and Bobby Hull—were totally contrasting personalities, although they had much in common on the ice.

Hull, who skated for the Black Hawks, was aptly nicknamed the Golden Jet. His blond hair, broad smile, and natural good looks gave him a magnetism attained by few players in big-league sports. This attractiveness was further embellished by his style. Hull had turned a slapshot into a lethal weapon, intimidating goalies whenever he wound up.

Hull's shot was only one feature in his armament. Bobby's mighty legs and equally powerful arms enabled him to withstand body-checks that would have demoralized lesser players. With such raw power at his disposal, Hull could have been a menacing player, but he chose to play clean hockey.

By contrast, Toronto's Mahovlich was a brooding introvert who could not enjoy the center stage on which Hull reveled. But once on the ice, the Big M was a riveting figure. His long, smooth strides gave him superior driving power, not unlike Hull's, and his shot created similar thunder. What Mahovlich lacked in superficial glamour, he more than made up for with his intrinsic grace. He was a Robert Redford among hockey players and the centerpiece of a Toronto club that had won Stanley Cups in 1962 and 1963.

Blocking the Leafs' route in 1963-64 was a Black Hawks club oozing with talent. Alongside Hull was an incendiary and creative stick-handler who had emigrated from Czechoslovakia to Canada as a youth and now ranked among the NHL's best centers. Unlike Mahovlich and Hull, Stan Mikita wore his truculence on his sleeve. He fought everyone in sight while moving right to the top of the scoring list. In 1963-64, he led all NHL players in points (39-50-89).

The Canadiens debuted a glamour player of their own in Yvan Cournoyer. Yvan played just a fraction of the 1963-64 season for the Habs, but the speedy "Roadrunner" would soon become the most popular Montreal player since Rocket Richard.

Montreal, which went a league-best 36-21-13, and Chicago were both upset in the playoffs, however, as Mahovlich's Leafs and Gordie Howe's Red Wings reached the Finals. The series went a full seven games before another of the 1960s glamour skaters, Toronto's Andy Bathgate, scored the Cup-winning goal.

The presence of these superstars spurred interest in hockey across the continent. Other major-league cities, attracted by Hull, Mahovlich, Mikita, etc., clamored for teams of their own. Reacting to the pressure, some NHL leaders—led by New York's Bill Jennings—began laying plans for expansion.

1963-64

• The Hall of Fame nominates seven new members—including Ebbie Goodfellow, Joe Primeau, and Earl Seibert.

• On June 5, 1963, at the Queen Elizabeth Hotel in Toronto, a total of 21 players are selected by NHL teams in the first-ever Amateur Draft.

• The Central Professional Hockey League is formed, with clubs operated by NHL franchises. These farm teams are formed in the Midwestern cities of Minneapolis, St. Paul, Indianapolis, and Omaha.

• The Rangers swap goalie Gump Worsley to Montreal for Jacques Plante, Phil Goyette, and Don Marshall.

• On November 10, 1963, Terry Sawchuk shuts out Montreal for his 94th career whitewash, tying him with Hall of Famer George Hainsworth.

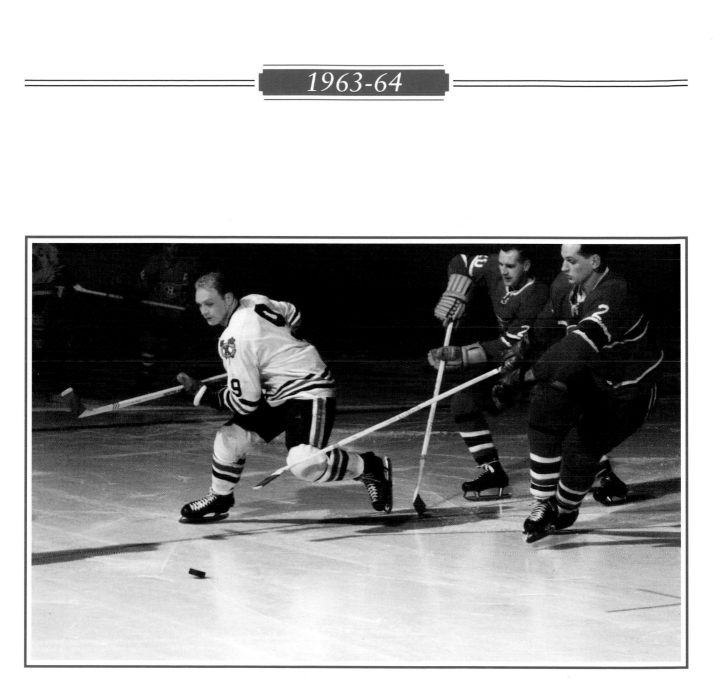

In 1963-64, two years after registering his first 50-goal season, Bobby Hull led the NHL in goals for the third time in five years when he scored 43 times. Hull (shown being pursued by Montreal defenseman Jacques Laperriere, #2, and winger Dave Balon) led his Black Hawks to a second-place finish. He combined with Stan Mikita and Ken Wharram (each of whom scored 39 goals) to make the Hawks the highest-scoring team in the NHL (3.11 goals per game).

• During the Red Wings' November 10 shutout of Montreal, Gordie Howe scores his 545th career goal, surpassing Maurice Richard for the all-time lead.

• A late-season blockbuster trade sees Andy Bathgate—the Rangers' perennial scoring champ—swapped with Don McKenney to Toronto for Arnie Brown, Dick Duff, Bob Nevin, Rod Seiling, and Bill Collins.

• Montreal (36-21-13) finishes first, one point ahead of Chicago.

• Chicago's Bobby Hull leads the league in goals with 43.

• Chicago's Stan Mikita is second in both goals (39) and assists (50), and he leads the league in points (89).

• Andy Bathgate, who splits the season between New York and Toronto, leads the NHL in assists (58) and is fourth in points (77).

Johnston, Bruins Take a Beating

The Bruins, in the midst of a terrible stretch of hockey seasons, finished the 1963-64 season dead last, winning just 18 times. Eddie Johnston was in nets for every second of the action, leading the league in minutes (4,200) as well as losses (40). The 28-year-old NHL sophomore would one day share in the Bruins' return to Stanley Cup glory, but for the time being he was saddled with backstopping an over-the-hill mob that couldn't win.

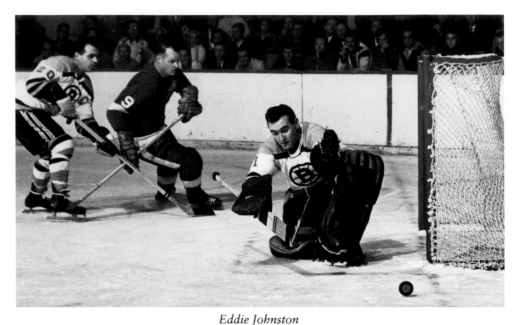

Eddie Johnston

Charlie Hodge

Howe Scores NHL-Record 545th Goal

On October 27, 1963, in his 18th NHL season, the Red Wings' Gordie Howe tied Rocket Richard on the all-time goals list when he scored against Richard's former team, the Canadiens, for his 544th career tally (pictured is the stick he used). Two weeks later, Howe scored No. 545, also against the Habs, and Richard said, "How about that—scoring both goals against my old team."

Gordie Howe's Stick

Hodge Finally Gets to Play

The Canadiens had kept goalie Charlie Hodge around for nearly a decade, using him sparingly as a fill-in for Jacques Plante. When Plante was traded to New York in 1963, Hodge finally got his chance. Hodge, now age 30, responded by posting a 2.26 GAA and winning the Vezina Trophy. Either Hodge had wasted many of his years on the bench, or it was the great Montreal defense that helped him win the Vezina. Acutally, both statements are probably true.

1963-64

- Chicago's Ken Wharram (39), New York's Camille Henry (29), and Montreal star Jean Beliveau (28) round out the top five goal-scorers.

- Trailing Stan Mikita in the overall scoring race are Bobby Hull (87 points), Jean Beliveau (78), Andy Bathgate (77), and Gordie Howe (73).

- Chicago defenseman Pierre Pilote cracks the top five assist-makers (46) and is the NHL's top scoring defender (53 points).

- Johnny Bower, the Maple Leafs' 39-year-old goalie, wins the goals-against average title (2.11).

- Montreal installs Charlie Hodge in goal. He wins 33 games and compiles a league-leading eight shutouts.

- On February 1, 1964, left winger Bobby Rousseau of the Canadiens burns Detroit goalie Roger Crozier for five goals.

Precious Few Love Mikita

For many hockey fans, it was difficult to conjure up the image of Chicago's Stan Mikita as a loving family man. The fiery Czech-born center, pictured with wife Jill and daughter Margaret Ann, doled out heavy punishment on the ice. In 1963-64, Mikita moved to the forefront of NHL superstars when he led the league in scoring (89 points). The fact that he also tied Montreal's Terry Harper for second in penalty minutes (149) left some fans nonplussed.

Stan, Margaret Ann, and Jill Mikita

Toronto Maple Leafs vs. Montreal Canadiens

Leafs Sign Bathgate for Stretch Run

After more than a decade on Broadway, right winger Andy Bathgate left the Rangers late in the 1963-64 season in a seven-player deal and joined the Maple Leafs in time for their playoff run. Bathgate (shown battling Montreal defensemen Jean Guy Talbot, #17, and Ted Harris, #10, for position in front of Jacques Plante's goal) scored five playoff goals for the Leafs, including the Cup clincher against Detroit early in Game 7.

• The playoffs feature Montreal vs. Toronto and Detroit vs. Chicago.

• The two-time defending-champion Maple Leafs engage Montreal in a seesaw battle, as the Habs win Games 1, 3, and 5 while the Leafs take Games 2, 4, and 6.

• The Leafs hold Montreal's powerful offense to just one goal in Game 7 of the semis. They score three goals of their own to advance to the Finals.

• In the other semis matchup, Detroit and Chicago battle back and forth and are tied 3-3 after six games. Detroit wins Game 7 4-2.

• The Finals are tightly fought, with five of the first six games decided by one goal.

• Toronto wins Game 1 3-2 when Bob Pulford beats Terry Sawchuk with just two seconds left in the third period.

Soviets Win Olympic Gold

The 1964 Olympics at Innsbruck, Austria, featured a gold-medal hockey matchup between the Soviet Union, in search of its second hockey title, and Canada, winner of six of the last nine gold medals in hockey. The Soviets, featuring Viktor Kuskin (#5) and Anatoly Firsov (#13), notched a 3-2 win over the Canadians, beating goalie Ken Broderick (pictured) for the winner. The Soviet team went 8-0 in the Olympics.

Olympic Games

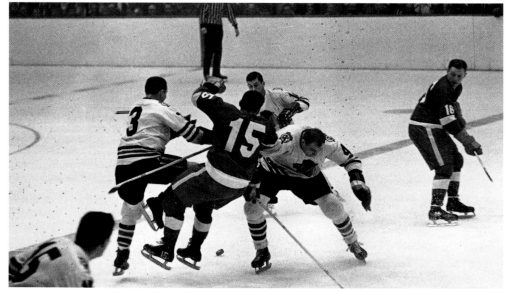

Stanley Cup Semifinals

Wings Bust Up the Hawks in Cup Semifinals

Chicago defenders Pierre Pilote (#3) and Moose Vasko (#4) make an Andre Pronovost sandwich during Game 4 of the 1964 semifinals. The Black Hawks beat Detroit 3-2 in sudden-death on a Murray Balfour goal, then prevailed again in Game 5. The Wings, though, responded with wins in Games 6 and 7. This contest was the NHL's first sudden-death playoff game in two years, ending the league's longest playoff overtime drought since 1927.

1963-64

• Detroit musters a 4-3 win in Game 2, as Larry Jeffrey scores at 7:52 of overtime.

• In yet another thriller, Detroit's Alex Delvecchio wins Game 3 4-3, as he scores with 17 seconds left in the game.

• The Leafs take Game 4 of the Finals 4-2 thanks to a pair of goals from Dave Keon—plus Andy Bathgate's winner midway through the third period.

• In Game 5, Gordie Howe and Eddie Joyal score to give Detroit a 2-1 win and a 3-2 series lead.

• Toronto's Bobby Baun, a rugged defenseman, scores 2:43 into sudden-death to win Game 6 and tie the Finals at three games each.

• Andy Bathgate scores the Cup-clinching goal for Toronto in Game 7, as Johnny Bower throws a 4-0 shutout against Detroit.

Stanley Cup Finals

Hobbled Baun Nets O.T. Goal in Cup Finals

The Maple Leafs returned to the Finals in 1964 and faced the Red Wings, whom they'd beaten in the 1963 Finals in five games. Among the many heroes for the Leafs, who captured their third straight title in 1964, was defense-man Bobby Baun, who scored in sudden-death of Game 6 to tie the series 3-3. Baun's heroics came while the rugged backliner was skating on a broken leg.

Bobby Baun

Leafs Edge Detroit, Howe in Finals

The Red Wings were able to gain a berth in the 1964 Stanley Cup Finals on the strength of their unparalleled scoring genius, Gordie Howe (pictured shooting the puck against Toronto's Johnny Bower while Allan Stanley tries, in vain, to hold him off). But the Leafs, en route to their third straight Cup, held off the Wings and won a grueling seven-game series. Bower, the league's GAA leader (2.11), shut out Detroit 4-0 in Game 7.

Leafs Relish Third Cup in a Row

The 1963-64 Stanley Cup champion Maple Leafs crowd around the ultimate sports trophy. Frank Mahovlich (upper left) led the team in playoff scoring with 15 points, while George Armstrong (#10) earned his third straight Cup as team captain. The Leafs, who featured 10 future Hall of Famers on their team, had now won a dozen Stanley Cups. They would win just one more mug over the next 30 years.

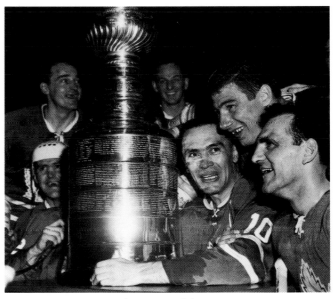

Stanley Cup Celebration

- Detroit's Gordie Howe is the playoffs' leading scorer (19 points) for the sixth time in his career.

- Montreal's Jean Beliveau wins the Hart Trophy, edging out Bobby Hull.

- Chicago winger Ken Wharram wins the Lady Byng Trophy.

- Montreal's Charlie Hodge captures the Vezina Trophy.

- Montreal defenseman Jacques Laperriere beats out teammate John Ferguson for the Calder Trophy.

- Chicago's Pierre Pilote takes his second straight Norris Trophy.

- In the Olympics, the Soviet Union captures its first of four straight hockey gold medals.

- Michigan wins its record seventh NCAA title, beating Denver 6-3 in the finals. Wolverines goalie Bob Gray is the tourney MVP.

FERGIE GIVES THE HABS THE PUNCH THEY NEED

Ever since his Canadiens were bludgeoned out of the 1961 Stanley Cup playoffs by Chicago, Montreal's managing director, Frank Selke Sr., realized that a major roster change was necessary. Skilled players such as Jean Beliveau, Yvan Cournoyer, and J.C. Tremblay required protection from enemy tough guys, yet the Habs were egregiously weak in the muscle department. Selke finally got the word out to his scouts: Find a muscleman who can play.

In 1963, Montreal bird dogs found their man in Cleveland, where John Bowie Ferguson was terrorizing foes for the American League's Cleveland Barons. Built like a bull, Ferguson made the Canadiens' varsity and was placed on a line with captain/center Beliveau, who had been so terribly abused by enemy marauders.

Starting with the Bruins' mean defenseman, Ted Green, Ferguson mopped up every significant enemy goon until the Canadiens began to obtain considerably more room and respect. For more physical support, Selke again reached to the American League and signed Ted Harris out of Springfield. In no time at all, Harris and Ferguson became the NHL's top enforcer tandem. In 1964-65, the Canadiens fused the tough and smooth elements together for a solid second-place finish (36-23-11).

Montreal finished just four points behind the first-place Red Wings. The Black Hawks finished third, even though Bobby Hull won the Hart and Lady Byng Trophies, Stan Mikita took the Art Ross (28-59-87), and Pierre Pilote nabbed the Norris. The Maple Leafs, who were growing tired of Punch Imlach's iron-fisted coaching techniques, dropped to fourth and faced Montreal in the first round of the playoffs.

The Maple Leafs, trying to win their fourth straight Stanley Cup, couldn't handle the muscular Habs. Montreal won the first two games at home, lost two in Toronto, and then rebounded (3-1 and 4-3 in overtime) to oust the champs. Meanwhile, Chicago edged past Detroit in seven games, setting up a classic Final that would also go the seven-game limit.

Unlike the 1961 Chicago-Montreal series in which the Hawks vehemently outhit the Habs, the 1965 Finals featured Ferguson and Harris intimidating the Hawks. In Game 7, Beliveau beat Glenn Hall just 14 seconds into the game. Before the 17-minute mark, Chicago was down 3-0. The "coup de grace" was applied by Ferguson—and his fists. He challenged the Hawks' Eric Nesterenko, knocking him and his club out of Cup contention.

"I warned Nesterenko that he was going to get it, and he got it," said Ferguson. "It has been said that the sight of Nesterenko unconscious on the ice demoralized the Black Hawks, and maybe it did. We shut down Hull, Mikita, and Ken Wharram completely and watched the clock click off our 4-0 win."

The Stanley Cup win reinforced the logic of Selke's enforcer plan. Other teams in the league immediately realized the importance of a guy like Ferguson, and soon each team was searching for its own tough cop.

1964-65

- The NHL passes a new rule prohibiting body contact on faceoffs. It also mandates that, during playoffs, backup goalies must be on the bench and in uniform.

- The Hall of Fame adds seven men, including Doug Bentley, Bill Durnan, Babe Siebert, and Jack Stewart.

- A new trophy is cast in the name of Conn Smythe. It will be given to the MVP of the Stanley Cup playoffs.

- Canadiens manager Frank Selke retires and is replaced by Sam Pollock, who'll build another dynasty in Montreal.

- The Habs lose 33-year-old Bernie Geoffrion, who retires after 14 years to coach the Quebec Aces (AHL).

- The Rangers debut the NHL's first Swedish player—Ulf Sterner.

- Detroit signs 39-year-old Ted Lindsay. But after four years of

A product of the rugged Western Hockey League minor program,
John Bowie Ferguson—though not overly imposing at 5'11" and 190 pounds—
was nonetheless one of hockey's most feared players, thanks to his aggressive,
pugnacious style and willingness to fight anyone who looked at him sideways. In
1964-65, he scored 17 goals on a line with Ralph Backstrom and Claude
Larose and was fifth in the league in penalty minutes (156).

retirement, Lindsay's production is modest (14 goals in 69 games).

• Terry Sawchuk is drafted by Toronto, where he pairs with 40-year-old Johnny Bower.

• In New York, Jacques Plante loses the No. 1 job to Marcel Paille.

• Dickie Moore, 33, attempts a comeback in Toronto after a one-year retirement, but the former scoring ace nets just two goals in 38 games.

• Detroit finishes with the best record in the league, 40-23-7, four points ahead of second-place Montreal.

• Chicago center Stan Mikita captures his second straight scoring title (87 points).

• The NHL crowns a new goal-scoring king, as Norm Ullman lights the lamp 42 times for the first-place Red Wings.

Terrible Ted Is Back; Wings Finish First

The Red Wings captured their first regular-season title in eight years in 1964-65, as they went 40-23-7 to beat out Montreal by four points. Ted Lindsay (pictured with Gordie Howe, far left, and defenseman Bill Gadsby, center) was purchased from Chicago after four years of retirement and returned to his old stomping grounds. Lindsay, however, scored only 14 goals. He retired for good at the end of the season at age 39.

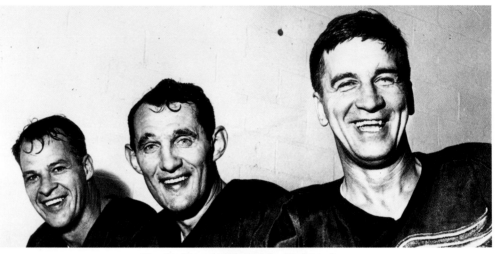

Gordie Howe, Bill Gadsby, Ted Lindsay

Johnny Bower

40-Year-Old Bower Leads NHL in GAA

The defending-champion Leafs acquired goalie Terry Sawchuk from Detroit prior to the 1964-65 regular season as insurance against Johnny Bower's age (40) catching up with him. Bower played less than half of Toronto's games and chalked up a 13-13-8 record, but he also boasted the league's finest goals-against average (2.38) for the second consecutive year. He shared the Vezina Trophy with Sawchuk as Toronto iced the best defense in hockey.

Frank Selke Sr.

Selke Retires After Years of Cup Glory

Frank Selke Sr., one of the most hallowed figures in NHL history, made his first impact on the league as assistant G.M. of the Maple Leafs. After a falling out with Leafs owner Conn Smythe, Selke joined Montreal and became the architect of six Stanley Cup winners. In 1964, he retired with a total of nine Cups under his belt. In 1978, Selke was immortalized with a trophy bearing his name and presented to the league's best defensive forward.

1964-65

- Norm Ullman is second in points, followed by teammate Gordie Howe (76) and Chicago's Bobby Hull (71).

- Bobby Hull (39 goals), Gordie Howe (29), Stan Mikita (28), and Montreal's Claude Provost (27) round out the top five goal-scorers.

- Toronto's Carl Brewer (177 PIM) leads the league in penalty time, but Detroit's Ted Lindsay (173) is as feisty as ever.

- With Terry Sawchuk gone to the Leafs, the Red Wings rely on Roger Crozier full-time, and he leads the NHL in wins (40) and shutouts (six).

- In Toronto, the goaltending of Terry Sawchuk and Johnny Bower—who leads the NHL with a 2.38 GAA—helps the Leafs finish in fourth place.

- Boston finishes in last place for the fifth straight year, despite the scoring of John Bucyk (55 points) and Murray Oliver (43).

Sterner's the First Swede to Join NHL

The 1964-65 Rangers didn't have much to brag about, finishing out of the playoffs and 18 games under .500. However, their future was full of hope as youngsters Rod Gilbert, who led the team in scoring (25-36-61), and Vic Hadfield began to assert themselves. The Rangers also debuted the NHL's first Swedish import, a 6'2" left winger named Ulf Sterner, who played just four games in a Rangers sweater and was held without a goal or assist.

Ulf Sterner

Bobby Hull

Hull Skates with Brother, Wins Byng

The Black Hawks dropped to third place in the 1964-65 standings, though it was not the fault of Bobby Hull, who was second in the league in goals (39), or crafty centerman Stan Mikita, who led the NHL in assists (59) and points (87). It was an eventful season for Hull: His younger brother, Dennis, made his NHL debut with the Hawks (10 goals in 55 games) and the Golden Jet (71 points and just 32 PIM) earned his one and only Lady Byng Trophy.

Conn Smythe Trophy

New Smythe Trophy Honors Playoff MVP

In 1964-65, the NHL announced a new trophy, named for Maple Leafs legend Conn Smythe, to be presented to the most valuable player of the Stanley Cup playoffs. The trophy's first recipient was Montreal center Jean Beliveau, who led his Canadiens to their 12th playoff championship with eight goals and 16 points. Smythe, who was inducted into the Hall of Fame in 1958, was a coach, manager, president, and owner of the Leafs during his career.

• In his first full season, Phil Esposito scores 23 goals for Chicago. The Hawks also debut Dennis Hull, a hard-shooting left winger who's the brother of Bobby Hull.

• The playoffs feature Montreal vs. Toronto and Chicago vs. Detroit.

• Detroit sniper Norm Ullman sets a playoff record with two goals in five seconds vs. the Hawks.

• After dropping the first two games, the Hawks force the series to seven games. Chicago then wins in Detroit, 4-2, to advance to the Finals.

• Montreal wins two games at home to open its semifinal series with Toronto, then drops two in Maple Leaf Gardens.

• Montreal wins Game 5 at home, then wins the decisive game in Toronto when Claude Provost scores 16:33 into sudden-death.

Norm Ullman, Sid Abel

Ullman's 42 Red Lights Lead League

Red Wings center Norm Ullman, pictured at left with coach Sid Abel, wears a hat symbolizing one of his 17 career hat-tricks. The classy veteran celebrated his 10th season in the NHL by leading the league in goals (42) and finishing second only to Stan Mikita for the scoring title (83 points). His six goals in seven postseason games were not enough, however, to launch the Red Wings past Chicago in the opening round of playoffs.

Mikita Leads League in Points, PIM

Stan Mikita (white jersey) fights off rival center Jean Beliveau. When Mikita became an NHL regular in 1959-60, he was known as much for his dirty stickwork and eagerness to fight any and all comers as for his clever playmaking talent. In 1963-64, he won his first scoring title while sitting out 146 penalty minutes. In 1964-65, he won his second consecutive scoring title (28-59-87) and again challenged for the penalty crown (154 PIM).

Stan Mikita, Jean Beliveau

Habs Put an End to Leaf Dynasty

The 1965 Stanley Cup semifinals pitted bitter rivals Montreal and Toronto, who met the previous year with Toronto advancing after a hard-fought, seven-game series. In this rare overhead photo, Toronto's Brit Selby (#8), Tim Horton (#7), and Johnny Bower (goalie) seal off Montreal's Bobby Rousseau. Montreal won this series when Claude Provost scored in overtime of Game 6. It also ended Toronto's dream of four straight Stanley Cups.

Stanley Cup Semifinals

1964-65

- Montreal wins Game 1 of the Finals 3-2 on Yvan Cournoyer's late goal.

- The Canadiens beat the Hawks 2-0 in Game 2, as Gump Worsley records the shutout.

- The Hawks draw even in the series with a pair of home-ice wins, 3-1 and 5-1, but the Canadiens take Game 5 with a 6-0 shelling of Glenn Hall at the Montreal Forum.

- Game 6 sees Ralph Backstrom give Montreal a second-period lead, but Moose Vasko and Doug Mohns score to give Chicago a 2-1 win and tie the series at 3-3.

- Jean Beliveau scores 14 seconds into Game 7 at Montreal, and Gump Worsley stops everything the Hawks throw at him, as the Habs win 4-0 for their 12th Stanley Cup.

- Jean Beliveau's 16 points pace the Habs, and he wins the first Conn Smythe Trophy as the playoff MVP.

Stanley Cup Finals

Beliveau Wins Three Finals Games

Montreal legend Jean Beliveau was a juggernaut in the 1965 Stanley Cup playoffs, scoring eight goals including five in the Finals against Chicago. Of his five championship round goals, he counted three game-winners: his second-period tally during the Habs' 2-0 win in Game 2, his first-period goal in the Habs' 6-0 win in Game 5, and his Cup-clinching goal just 14 seconds into Game 7, which held up as the winner when Montreal took the game 4-0.

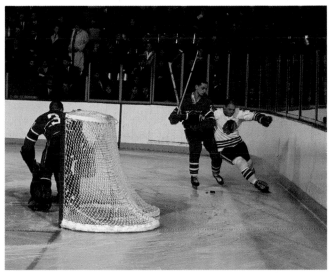

Stanley Cup Finals

Habs Gang Up on Hull in Finals

Not even a 10-goal playoff performance by Bobby Hull (right) could spark the Black Hawks past Montreal in the 1965 Finals. The Habs employed strong-arm tactics (including sending tough guy John Ferguson out to hound Hull) and superlative defense, led by Jacques Laperriere (pictured forcing Hull into the boards), to hold the high-scoring Hawks at bay. Canadiens goalie Gump Worsley (1.75 playoff GAA) was the difference in the Finals.

• Bobby Hull wins his first Hart Trophy, edging out goal-scoring champ Norm Ullman.

• Bobby Hull wins his first and only Lady Byng Trophy.

• For the first time, the Vezina Trophy is awarded to two goalies, as Toronto netminders Terry Sawchuk (36 games) and Johnny Bower (34 games) share the honor.

• Roger Crozier, runner-up for the Vezina, wins the Calder Trophy. He finished ahead of 23-goal scorer Ron Ellis of Toronto.

• Pierre Pilote, Chicago's blueline specialist, captures his third straight Norris Trophy.

• Michigan Tech claims the NCAA hockey championship, crushing Boston College 8-2 in the finals. Tech forward Gary Milroy is named tourney MVP.

While the NHL's conservative bloc, led by President Clarence Campbell, preached in favor of the status quo, Young Turks pushed even harder for expansion. Much of the rumbling came from California, where Los Angeles and San Francisco had to settle for spots in the Western Hockey League. The NHL wouldn't let them in.

In the spring of 1962, columnist Jim Murray of the *Los Angeles Times* wrote: "The National Hockey League makes a mockery of its title by restricting its franchises to six teams, waging a kind of private little tournament of 70 games just to eliminate two teams."

"Other big-money sports are expanding," he continued, "but hockey likes it there in the back of the cave. Any businessman will tell you that in a dynamic economy you either grow or perish. Baseball had to be dragged kicking and screaming out of its rut. Football groped its way on the end of a short rope. Hockey just can't sit there in the dark forever, braiding buggy whips."

At the same time, Harold Ballard, one of the owners of the Maple Leafs, said: "If the right kind of people come to us with $5 million and the right kind of

L.A. TO NHL: 'WE WANT A PIECE OF THE ACTION'

plans, we'll listen. We'd be crazy not to."

By the mid-1960s, rumblings from the West Coast were edging toward the seismic. Colley Hall, owner of the San Francisco Seals, said: "The time has come for the NHL to realize that Los Angeles and San Francisco can't wait. Our hockey fans are just as major-league conscious as fans of baseball and football and feel they should be up there. An angry feeling is developing."

NHL power brokers anticipated the threat but were distracted by their cash cow and the glittering performances of so many stars. In addition to Bobby Hull—who won the 1965-66 scoring crown and the Hart Trophy—Jacques Laperriere emerged as a defensive jewel, winning the Norris Trophy. New York's Jean Ratelle, Rod

Gilbert, and Harry Howell and Detroit's Roger Crozier were among the headline-grabbers who filled NHL arenas to 95-percent capacity.

But finally, on March 11, 1965, at a special meeting of club owners in New York's Plaza Hotel, the NHL lords decided to make the big step. They announced the formation of a second six-team division, saying they would begin evaluating applications from responsible groups.

In February 1966, the NHL officially accepted Los Angeles, San Francisco/Oakland, St. Louis, Pittsburgh, Philadelphia, and Minneapolis-St. Paul as the members of the new division. St. Louis was a surprise since representatives had not filed a formal application. Buffalo and Baltimore had been rejected. So had Vancouver, and this rankled many Canadians. After all, here were six additions to the NHL and not one city was located in the country that was the cradle of hockey.

Expansion talk was so incessant that it deflected attention from the Stanley Cup championship, which again was won by the Canadiens, this time in a six-game Final with Detroit.

1965-66

- The NHL rules that teams must dress two goaltenders for every contest.

- The NHL announces plans for a six-team expansion in 1967-68.

- The Hall of Fame nominates 12 inductees, including Marty Barry,

Clint Benedict, Syd Howe, Bill Mosienko, and Red Horner.

- The last preseason All-Star Game is played and a midseason format is adopted for 1966-67.

- The NHL casts a new trophy—in honor of Lester Patrick—to be

awarded to a player, coach, official, executive, or referee who gives "outstanding service to hockey in the United States."

- Mario Lemieux is born on October 5, 1965, in Montreal. On the same day, Patrick Roy is born in Quebec City, Quebec.

It was not surprising that Los Angeles, San Francisco, and other big cities were clamoring for NHL franchises in the mid-1960s, considering all the rich talent to go around. Budding star Phil Esposito (pictured) was hardly noticed on a Chicago team that boasted future Hall of Famers Bobby Hull, Stan Mikita, Glenn Hall, and Pierre Pilote. In 1965-66, each NHL team featured at least three future Famers, led by Toronto with eight.

• On November 27, 1965, Detroit's Gordie Howe beats Montreal's Gump Worsley for his 600th career goal.

• The Rangers drop goalies Jacques Plante and Marcel Paille in favor of Eddie Giacomin, Cesare Maniago, and Don Simmons.

• The Bruins debut a pair of talented rookie goalies—Bernie Parent and Gerry Cheevers.

• Toronto's Carl Brewer, 27, retires when his contract negotiations with G.M. Punch Imlach stall. He'll remain out of action for four years.

• The Maple Leafs swap fading star Andy Bathgate to Detroit for old-timer Marcel Pronovost, a 15-year Red Wing veteran.

• Montreal goes 41-21-8 to finish in first place, eight points ahead of second-place Chicago.

Bruins Debut a Pair of Aces in Goal

The Bruins suffered through a miserable campaign in 1965-66, losing 43 of 70 games. Nevertheless, Boston debuted two rookie goalies who would both wind up in the Hall of Fame: Gerry "Cheesy" Cheevers and Bernie Parent. Cheevers posted an embarrassing 6.00 goals-against average in six games, while Parent registered a 3.69 GAA in 35 games. Both goalies would make their marks in 1967-68, Cheevers with Boston and Parent with Philadelphia.

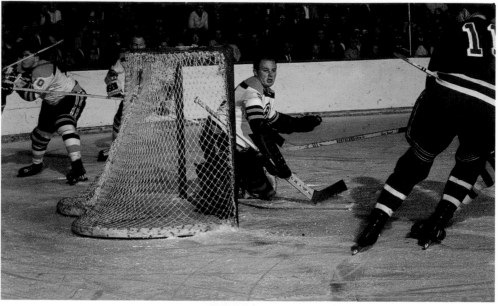

Gerry Cheevers

Gordie Howe

Howe Hits New Milestone: Goal No. 600

On March 14, 1962, Gordie Howe scored the 500th goal of his career against Rangers goalie Gump Worsley. Three years later, Howe notched No. 600, during a 3-2 loss at Montreal. This goal, which came late in the third period and was assisted by Gary Bergman and Don McKenney, was also scored against Worsley, who had since been traded to the Canadiens.

Lester Patrick Trophy

NHL Debuts the Lester Patrick Trophy

In 1965-66, the NHL premiered a new achievement award, the Lester Patrick Trophy. Patrick, whose New York Rangers teams finished out of the playoffs just once in his first 16 years as manager, went into nets at age 44 during the 1928 Stanley Cup Finals. The award, for "outstanding service to hockey in the United States," first went to Detroit legend Jack Adams.

1965-66

- In Chicago, Bobby Hull sets a pair of NHL records: most goals (54) and points (97) in a single season.

- Toronto's Frank Mahovlich (32 goals) is a distant second to Bobby Hull in the goal-scoring race. Detroit's Norm Ullman and Alex Delvecchio tie for third (31).

- Stan Mikita and Montreal's Bobby Rousseau tie for second in points (78). Montreal's Jean Beliveau finishes with 77 and Gordie Howe tallies 75.

- Stan Mikita, Bobby Rousseau, and Jean Beliveau tie for the league lead in assists (48). Gordie Howe (46) and Bobby Hull (43) make the top five.

- New York's Reg Fleming, acquired from Boston, leads the league in penalty minutes (166).

- The Canadiens boast the finest defense in the league (173 goals against) behind the goaltending of Gump Worsley and Charlie Hodge.

Laperriere Wins the Norris

The Montreal defense, steeped in a tradition that included seven-time Norris Trophy winner Doug Harvey, was led in 1965-66 by rangy Jacques Laperriere (pictured checking Chicago's Doug Jarrett). Laperriere, who was the league's top rookie in 1963-64, was a tough, clean player who used his size (6'2", 190 pounds) and tremendous reach to tie up attacking forwards rather than trying to physically punish them. He won the Norris Trophy in 1965-66.

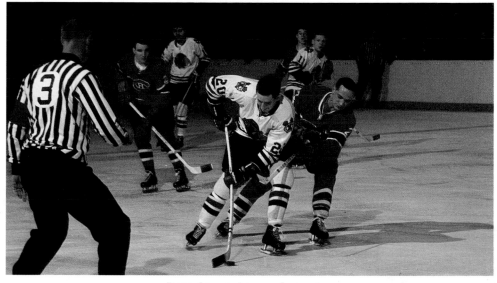

Doug Jarrett, Jacques Laperriere

Bobby Hull

Hull Shatters Scoring Marks

On March 2, 1966, Bobby Hull notched his 50th goal of the season, against Detroit's Hank Bassen, becoming the first player ever to reach the 50-goal plateau twice. Maurice Richard (1944-45), Bernie Geoffrion (1960-61), and Hull (1961-62) had previously reached the mark once each. The Golden Jet then set two more records. He became the first player to score *more than* 50 goals in a season (54), and he finished with an NHL-record 97 points.

Bobby Rousseau

Montreal's Own Rousseau Leads in Assists

The Canadiens were famous for cultivating home-grown talent. In 1965-66, Montreal native Bobby Rousseau—a slightly built forward—established himself as a bona fide scoring threat. In 70 games, Rousseau, playing with Jean Beliveau and John Ferguson, notched 30 goals and tied Beliveau and Chicago's Stan Mikita for the league lead in assists (48). Rousseau and Mikita tied for second in total points (78).

• Chicago is the most potent scoring team (240 goals).

• Toronto's Johnny Bower wins his third straight GAA title (2.25) as the Leafs finish third in the standings.

• Detroit takes the fourth playoff spot by 26 points over fifth-place Boston,

as goalie Roger Crozier ironically leads the league both in shutouts (seven) and losses (24).

• The playoffs feature Montreal vs. Toronto and Detroit vs. Chicago. The Hawks and Red Wings meet in the semis for the fourth straight year.

• After the Hawks take a 2-1 series lead, the Red Wings reel off three straight victories, outscoring the Hawks 13-6 to advance to the Finals.

• The Canadiens, defending Cup champs, have no trouble with Toronto, sweeping the Leafs in four games and outscoring them 15-6.

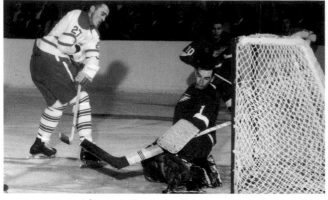

Frank Mahovlich, Roger Crozier

Beliveau, Habs Blast Past Toronto

In his 13th NHL season, Montreal captain Jean Beliveau, at age 34, still dominated the game with his superior playmaking, tying linemate Bobby Rousseau for the league lead in assists (48) and finishing fourth overall in points (77). Beliveau (shown checking Maple Leaf Bob Pulford, #20) led the Habs to a four-game sweep over Toronto in the NHL semifinals. Goalie Gump Worsley and the Montreal defense yielded just six goals in the series.

Stanley Cup Semifinals

Losing Goalie Crozier Wins Smythe

The Red Wings entered the 1966 playoffs as the fourth-seeded team in a four-team race, finishing the season just four games over .500. Goalie Roger Crozier (pictured applying a left pad to stop Toronto scoring star Frank Mahovlich) had a mercurial year, leading the NHL both in losses (24) and shutouts (seven). His playoff performance—a 2.21 GAA while losing in the Finals to Montreal—earned him the Conn Smythe Trophy.

Stanley Cup Semifinals

Wings Shut Down Hull in Semifinals

Chicago boasted the NHL's most potent scoring attack in 1965-66, thanks to Bobby Hull (shown firing on Detroit netminder Roger Crozier while Billy Harris, #14, tries to tie up his stick). During the Stanley Cup semifinals, the Hawks ran into a stone wall in Crozier, who allowed the Hawks just 10 goals in six games as Detroit won it in six. The Wings scored 22 goals in the series; Hull netted just two.

1965-66

- In the Finals, Detroit takes Game 1 3-2 on Paul Henderson's third-period winner. The Wings follow up with a 5-2 trashing of the Habs in Game 2.

- The Canadiens fight back in Game 3, as Gilles Tremblay scores a pair and the Habs win 4-2.

- Game 4 is tied 1-1 until Ralph Backstrom wins it for Montreal with 6:23 to play in the third period.

- Five different Habs score in Game 5, as Montreal rolls to a 5-1 win.

- Game 6 of the Finals goes to overtime tied 2-2. Montreal's Henri

Richard, mirroring the O.T. heroics of his big brother Maurice, scores the Cup-clinching goal at 2:20 of the first extra period.

- The Canadiens win their 13th Stanley Cup, taking the all-time lead over Toronto (12).

Henri Richard

Richard Pots Cup Winner vs. Wings

Game 6 of the 1966 Stanley Cup Finals between Montreal and Detroit was tied 2-2 after regulation. The Habs held a three-games-to-two advantage over the Wings, who had opened the series with a pair of shocking victories on Montreal ice. The Canadiens fought back in the series and even took a 2-0 lead in Game 6. Detroit tied the score, but feisty Henri Richard scored at 2:20 of sudden-death to give Montreal its 13th Stanley Cup.

Stanley Cup Finals

Ullman's 15 Playoff Points Wasted

The Red Wings made the Stanley Cup Finals in 1966—their fourth trip to the championship round in the last six years—and faced a powerful Montreal team looking to defend its 1965 crown. Despite a playoff-leading 15-point performance from Norm Ullman (pictured, #7, preparing for a faceoff), the Red Wings lost in six games when Henri Richard (pictured facing off against Ullman) scored in sudden-death to win Game 6 3-2 and give the Habs the title.

• Detroit goalie Roger Crozier wins the Conn Smythe Trophy, while teammate Norm Ullman wins the playoff scoring race (15 points).

• Chicago's Bobby Hull captures his second straight Hart Trophy, beating out runner-up Jean Beliveau.

• Alex Delvecchio, Detroit's veteran center, wins the Lady Byng Trophy.

• Gump Worsley and Charlie Hodge, Montreal's ace goalies, share the Vezina Trophy.

• Toronto's Brit Selby wins the Calder Trophy over Detroit's Bert Marshall.

• Montreal's Jacques Laperriere cops the Norris Trophy.

• Jack Adams wins the first Lester Patrick Trophy.

• Michigan State beats Clarkson 6-1 in the NCAA finals, as MSU goalie Gaye Cooley is named MVP.

BRUINS DEBUT A GEM IN DEFENSEMAN BOBBY ORR

Throughout most of the 1960s, Boston's beloved Bruins broke the hearts of loyal Beantown fans with some of the most dreadful hockey known to man. From 1959-60 through 1966-67, the Bruins finished fifth twice and sixth six times. The salvation, Boston management insisted, would be a wunderkind defenseman from Parry Sound, Ontario, named Bobby Orr.

Orr had a quality that only a few have brought to the game—charisma. He could skate upwards of 27 mph and created the illusion of a mercury on skates. Big-league scouts noticed Orr before he reached his teens, but it was Boston that made the decisive move. After watching Orr play as a 12-year-old, the Bruins put his name on their protected list, meaning Orr was their property. That done, the Bruins waited for Bobby to mature.

Orr's ripening as a hockey star was faster than anyone could imagine. By the time he was 16, he had become the talk of Canada. Meanwhile, the Bruins began to tout Orr as the eventual messiah who would save the franchise.

But then Orr shook the NHL establishment, because he did what neither Gordie Howe nor

Rocket Richard had done when they were invited to the bigs: Bobby brought an agent with him. His representative, Toronto attorney Alan Eagleson, stunned Bruins manager Hap Emms by declaring that Orr would not come to Boston unless he was rewarded with a contract commensurate with his ability. Emms eventually gave in. The result was a two-year, $150,000 contract that caused reverberations throughout the league.

Orr's eventual impact on the Bruins would be immense, as he would help transform them into a dynastic juggernaut. By 1970, Orr would become the biggest drawing card in the game. "Bobby," said Eagleson, "is the only player capable of filling every rink in the NHL."

The "Orr Effect," as his style came to be known by analysts, had a profound impact on the manner in which hockey was played. Before Bobby donned a Bruins uniform, defensemen concentrated on defense. While there were rushing backliners of note in the past—Eddie Shore and Red Kelly being the most prominent—none of them influenced a major change in the mode of play. But Orr did.

Bobby's idea of playing defense was to poke the puck away from the foe and then carry it the length of the rink for either a shot on goal or a pass to a teammate. In no time at all, every Canadian kid wanted to be Bobby Orr.

Orr didn't carry Boston into a playoff berth in his rookie season of 1966-67—the Bruins finished last while Chicago was on top and Toronto won the Stanley Cup—but his impact was irrevocable. Bobby won the Calder Trophy, although New York's Harry Howell took the Norris Trophy as best defenseman.

At the awards luncheon in 1967, Howell accepted his prize and said, "I am glad I won the Norris Trophy this year, because in 10 years it will be the Bobby Orr Trophy."

1966-67

- The NHL rules that substitutions will now be allowed on coincidental major penalties.

- The NHL's sponsorship of junior teams ends, and all players not on NHL lists are eligible for the amateur draft.

- Los Angeles, Minnesota, Philadelphia, Pittsburgh, St. Louis, and Oakland are awarded NHL franchises for 1967-68.

- The Hall of Fame names 10 inductees, including Max Bentley, Toe Blake, Butch Bouchard, Frank Brimsek, Ted Kennedy, Elmer Lach,

Ted Lindsay, Babe Pratt, Ken Reardon, and Clarence Campbell.

- Boston installs a new coach, as G.M. Milt Schmidt steps down in favor of Harry Sinden.

- The Bruins debut an 18-year-old defenseman who will revolutionize

The Bruins got a good—but depressing—look at their future when 18-year-old
Bobby Orr emerged from junior hockey and, in 1966-67, made his NHL debut.
While Orr was destined to become a trailblazing skater who would lead the Bruins
to greatness, he also proved brittle. In his rookie year, in a sign of things to
come, Orr was hospitalized with a knee injury. It was a series of debilitating
knee injuries that ultimately cut short his brilliant career.

the game and bring greatness to
Boston. His name is Bobby Orr.

• Chicago leads the league with a
41-17-12 record, finishing 17 points
in front of second-place Montreal.
The Black Hawks set an NHL record
for total goals (264).

• Chicago's Bobby Hull leads the
NHL in goals with 52. He becomes
the first player to record back-to-back
50-goal seasons.

• The top three NHL goal-scorers are
Black Hawks, as Bobby Hull's 52
goals are followed by Stan Mikita's
35 and Ken Wharram's 31.

• Stan Mikita wins his third scoring
title, tying Bobby Hull's NHL record
(97 points). Hull is second this year
with 80 points.

• Stan Mikita leads the NHL in
assists (62), while New York's Phil
Goyette is second (49).

Bernie Geoffrion

Boom Boom Comes Out of Retirement

After 14 outstanding seasons in Montreal, Bernie "Boom Boom" Geoffrion ended two years of retirement to try his skills on Broadway, skating for the Rangers. His first year in the Big Apple, during which he scored 17 goals in 58 games, was not without its moments of high drama. At one point the fiery 35-year-old winger was suspended for three games by NHL President Clarence Campbell for deliberately throwing an elbow at linesman Walt Atanas.

Harry Howell

New Yorkers Throw Party for Howell

Hall of Fame defenseman Harry Howell won the 1967 Norris Trophy and was feted at Madison Square Garden on the night of his 1,002nd NHL game (he is pictured with his mother and wife Marilyn). Howell's career spanned three decades and included stops in New York, Oakland, and L.A. of the NHL and New Jersey, San Diego, and Calgary of the World Hockey Association. He retired in 1976 with more than 1,580 professional games to his credit.

Dave Keon

Keon Leads His Leafs to the Promised Land

The oddsmakers who failed to recognize the Maple Leafs as legitimate playoff contenders forgot to submit their memos to Dave Keon, who centered Toronto's top line with Frank Mahovlich and George Armstrong. Although the Leafs finished third with a 32-27-11 record, they hit their stride in the playoffs, beating the favored Black Hawks in the semis and dethroning the Canadiens in the Finals. Keon, with eight playoff points, won the Conn Smythe Trophy.

1966-67

- Detroit's Norm Ullman finishes third in the league in points (70) and ties for third in assists (44).

- Chicago's Denis DeJordy, who pushes ahead of Glenn Hall as the team's No. 1 goalie, leads the NHL in GAA (2.46).

- Terry Sawchuk records 15 of Toronto's 32 victories, as the Leafs—coached briefly by King Clancy—maintain their hold on third place.

- The surprising Rangers finish fourth on the goaltending of Eddie Giacomin, who leads the NHL in wins (30) and shutouts (nine).

- Ex-Habs star Bernie Geoffrion comes out of retirement and scores 17 goals in 58 games for the Rangers.

- Bernie Geoffrion is suspended for three games for throwing an elbow at a linesman. Montreal's John Ferguson is banned for three games for hitting another linesman.

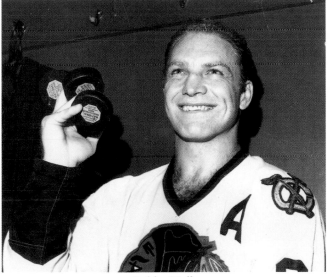

Bobby Hull

Hull Crashes 50 Barrier Once More

In 1966-67, Chicago's premier left winger, Bobby Hull, continued his domination of the NHL by leading the league in goals for the fifth time in eight seasons. The Golden Jet, teaming with playmaker extraordinaire Stan Mikita, notched 52 goals—his second consecutive season with more than 50—and became the first NHLer ever to record three 50-goal campaigns. Hull was second overall in scoring (behind Mikita) with 80 points.

Mikita Wins the Trophy Trifecta

The Black Hawks reigned supreme over the NHL in 1966-67 largely due to the play of Stan Mikita. After building a reputation as a "stick" man with a dirty streak, Mikita underwent a 180-degree transformation. While winning his third scoring title in 1966-67—tying Bobby Hull's NHL points record of 97—the former brawler sat out only 12 minutes and won the Art Ross, Hart, and Lady Byng Trophies.

Stan Mikita

Harry Sinden

Sinden Ready to Resurrect Bruins

The arrival of two new faces in Boston marked the beginning of a new era in 1966-67. One, of course, was Bobby Orr, but the other was coach Harry Sinden (pictured in jacket and tie), who took over for Milt Schmidt. Sinden's Bruins struggled badly in 1966-67, going 17-43-10 and icing the worst offense and defense in the league. In the next season, though, Sinden and Orr would soar to 37 victories.

- Bobby Rousseau and Jean Guy Talbot of Montreal are fined and suspended after physically abusing referees Art Skov and John Ashley, respectively.

- The playoffs feature Chicago vs. Toronto and Montreal vs. New York.

- The Rangers, who have missed the playoffs seven of the last eight years, are no match for the Habs. Montreal wins the first three games.

- The Canadiens advance to the Finals when tough guy John Ferguson, the 1966-67 penalty leader, scores at 6:28 of sudden-death in Game 4.

- Chicago is favored in its semifinal series against Toronto, but the Hawks go down two games to one before eking out a 4-3 win in Game 4.

- The Leafs beat Chicago in Games 5 and 6 to advance to the Stanley Cup Finals.

Fergie Scores to Eliminate Rangers

Despite finishing second to Chicago in the regular season, the Canadiens roared to the 1967 Finals after pounding the Rangers in a four-game sweep in the opening round. The Habs were tested in Game 4 of that series as Rangers goalie Ed Giacomin held Montreal to one goal through regulation. The Habs needed just 6:28 of overtime to eliminate New York as John Ferguson (pictured with teammates J.C. Tremblay and Rogie Vachon) notched the winner.

J.C. Tremblay, John Ferguson, Rogie Vachon

Denis DeJordy

DeJordy Does the Job in Hawks' Net

Chicago goalie Denis DeJordy, playing in only his second full NHL season, was a huge factor in the Black Hawks' rise to first place in the standings in 1966-67. While Bobby Hull and Stan Mikita were combining to give the Hawks the league's best offense (264 goals), DeJordy usurped the No. 1 goaltending job from Glenn Hall and posted the NHL's best GAA among first-stringers (2.46). DeJordy and Hall shared the Vezina Trophy.

Stanley Cup Semifinals

Leafs Fight Off Chicago in Semifinals

Toronto and Chicago, both victims of first-round defeats the previous year, met in the semifinals in 1967. It was a seesaw series that saw the teams split the first four games before Toronto took the edge in Game 5 with a 4-2 win at Chicago Stadium. Flying high from their road win, the Leafs pumped three goals past Glenn Hall at Toronto in Game 6 and prevailed 3-1. Dave Keon (pictured battling Pierre Pilote) set the pace with his usual hard work and tenacity.

1966-67

• The Canadiens win Game 1 of the Finals 6-2, as Henri Richard tallies three goals.

• Toronto's Johnny Bower, taking over for Terry Sawchuk in the Maple Leafs' goal, deflects every shot in Game 2 and wins 3-0.

• Game 3 goes to sudden-death tied 2-2. Toronto's Bob Pulford scores the winner at 8:26 of double overtime.

• In Game 4, Ralph Backstrom and Jean Beliveau each score twice as Montreal wins 6-2. The Leafs then shock the Habs in Montreal, winning Game 5 4-1.

• In Game 6, Toronto's Jim Pappin scores at 19:58 of the second period, and the Leafs skate off with a 3-1 victory. Toronto claims its 13th Stanley Cup, tying Montreal.

• Toronto's Dave Keon is awarded the Conn Smythe Trophy.

Leafs One Goal Better Than Habs

The Canadiens returned to the Stanley Cup Finals in 1967 in hopes of defending their championship, but they ran into a streaking Toronto club that had just survived a six-game war with the Black Hawks. The Maple Leafs exploited novice goalie Rogatien Vachon (pictured kicking the puck out as defenseman Jacques Laperriere, #2, looks on) and barely outscored Montreal (17-16 in six games) en route to their 13th NHL title.

Stanley Cup Finals

Leafs' Glory Years Come to a Close

As members of the Maple Leafs gathered around their fourth Stanley Cup in six years, it was a final moment of celebration for a franchise that would not even make it to the semifinals for more than a quarter-century (they lost to Los Angeles in the 1993 conference finals). The Leafs would hover around .500 for the next dozen years before bottoming out entirely in the 1980s. Sixteen-year veteran George Armstrong (shown holding the Cup as teammate Marcel Pronovost, #3, and others look on) captained the Leafs to their last four Cups.

Stanley Cup Celebration

- Jim Pappin leads all playoff scorers in goals (seven) and points (15), and Johnny Bower notches a 1.67 GAA.

- Stan Mikita wins the Art Ross, Hart, and Lady Byng Trophies, becoming the first to pull off the sweep.

- Chicago's Glenn Hall and Denis DeJordy share the Vezina Trophy.

- Bobby Orr, with 13 goals and 41 points, captures the Calder Trophy.

- Harry Howell, the longtime Rangers stalwart on the blueline, wins his only Norris Trophy.

- Cornell beats Boston University 4-1 in the NCAA hockey finals. Cornell defenseman Wally Stanowski is named tourney MVP.

- The Toronto Marlboros win their fourth Memorial Cup as Canada's top junior team.

NHL Doubles in Size; Six Teams Join the Party

The NHL's decision to balloon from six to twelve teams in 1967-68 made a few ice moguls nervous. Some doubted that cities such as St. Louis and Oakland could sustain franchises over the long haul, while others questioned the method chosen by the established teams for stocking the new clubs.

The approved plan called for each existing team to protect one goalie and 11 other players for the draft. When a team lost a player, it could fill its protected list with another player. This meant that if a team lost its 13th best player, it could put its 14th best on the protected list. If it lost its 15th best, then the 16th best could be protected.

The system didn't seem to favor the league's new clubs. However, NHL President Clarence Campbell felt that an extended backup plan—which called for all teams to be able to protect two goalies and only 14 others for the 1968 and 1969 drafts—would help in the equalization. "The new teams won't have trouble picking out which 14 to protect," he said, "but the older teams... they're going to have problems."

"I visualize definite improvement in the new teams by 1968-69 because of the backup plan," Campbell added. "By 1970, they should have a glorious field day, and I hope they do."

On June 6, 1967, the expansion draft was held in Montreal, and the new teams finally saw what they were getting for their $2 million initiation fees. When the cigar smoke had cleared, many observers felt the new clubs had been taken. After all, they had just paid $100,000 each for bodies that ordinarily, under the regular draft price, cost only $30,000. Of course, for $2 million one not only received 20 players but also got the chance to rake in attendance, radio, and TV revenues.

Even the players had differing opinions. Forward Billy Hicke, drafted by the California Seals (soon to be renamed the Oakland Seals), said of the new owners: "They didn't get a fair shake. Of the 20 players each team drafted, only six or seven are of NHL caliber."

Later, toward the end of the season, Philadelphia Flyers defenseman Ed Van Impe reacted positively to the new division. "Expansion was a good thing for hockey. It's hard to imagine that, until this year, there were only 120 spots open for major-league hockey players. Now it's 240. Expansion hasn't hurt. These guys are proving they belonged."

By the conclusion of the season, expansion did indeed seem like a success. The new teams, with the exception of Oakland, were all contenders for the four playoff spots. While Philadelphia finished first with 73 points, Pittsburgh was fifth with 67 points. The six new teams went a somewhat-respectable 40-86-18 against the established clubs.

The West Division playoffs were so closely played that all three series went to seven games. When the St. Louis Blues bowed to mighty Montreal in four one-goal Finals games—two of them in overtime—the creators of expansion could sit back and admire their artistic triumph.

1967-68

- The NHL doubles in size from six teams to 12. Los Angeles, St. Louis, Philadelphia, Pittsburgh, California, and Minnesota join the party.

- The expansion teams make up the West Division, while the "Original Six" comprise the East. Teams will play a 74-game schedule.

- Prior to the expansion draft, L.A. owner Jack Kent Cooke purchases the entire Springfield (AHL) club from Eddie Shore, giving the Kings a fully stocked farm team.

- The L.A. Kings select legendary goalie Terry Sawchuk with the first pick in the expansion draft.

- The New York Rangers move into the newly constructed Madison Square Garden, built directly above Manhattan's famous Penn Station.

- The Hall of Fame inducts four members: Turk Broda, Neil Colville, Harry Oliver, and Red Storey.

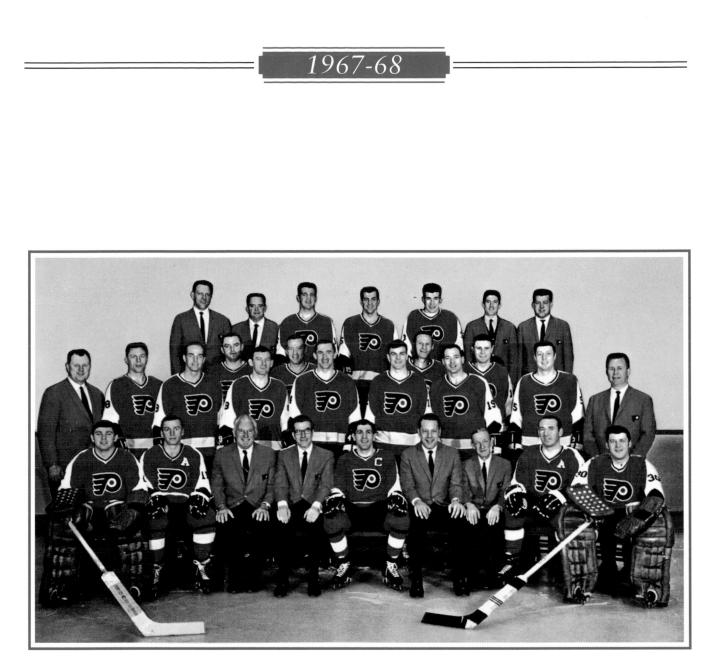

The Philadelphia Flyers emerged as the first regular-season champions of the West Division, in which all six expansion teams were placed. Lou Angotti (front row with the captain's "C" on his sweater), a former Michigan Tech college star who had skated briefly in the Rangers and Black Hawks organizations, led the team in scoring (49 points), while former Montreal farmhand Leon Rochefort (second row, third from left) led the Flyers in goals (21).

• Boston steals Phil Esposito, Ken Hodge, and Fred Stanfield from Chicago for Pit Martin, Gilles Marotte, and Jack Norris.

• Toronto ships Frank Mahovlich, Garry Unger, and Pete Stemkowski to Detroit for Norm Ullman, Paul Henderson, and Floyd Smith.

• Scotty Bowman, who will become one of the great coaches in NHL history, assumes the bench duties in St. Louis after Lynn Patrick gets the Blues off to a 4-10-2 start.

• On October 11, 1967, Montreal's Jean Beliveau scores his 400th NHL goal.

• On December 8, 1967, the California Seals change their name to the Oakland Seals.

• On December 30, 1967, CBS airs its first "Game of the Week." If features L.A. and Philadelphia in the first-ever game at the Los Angeles Forum.

Beliveau Gets 400th Goal, 1,000th Point

Montreal legend Jean Beliveau (#4) recorded the 400th goal of his career on October 11, 1967, against the Pittsburgh Penguins. After a disappointing 12-goal performance the year before, Beliveau was back in top form in 1967-68, scoring 31 times as he led the first-place Canadiens in goals and points (68). On March 3, 1968, he became the NHL's second-ever 1,000-point scorer, joining Gordie Howe.

Jean Beliveau

Expansion Seals Play Like Dogs

The Oakland Seals were a study in futility during their entire NHL existence, starting in their inaugural season, 1967-68, when they won only 15 games and saddled goalie Charlie Hodge (front row, far left) with a league-leading 29 losses. Right winger Bill Hicke (second row, far left) led the team in goals (21) while Gerry Ehman (back row, third from left) led in points (44). Coach Bert Olmstead was fired when the team started out 11-37-16.

Oakland Seals

1967-68

• On January 13, 1968, Minnesota North Star Bill Masterton is checked by Seals defensemen Larry Cahan and Ron Harris. Masterton flips backward and falls hard on his head. He dies 30 hours later of a brain injury.

• The death of Bill Masterton accelerates the movement toward helmets.

• The Canadiens, with Gump Worsley and Rogie Vachon in goal, win the East Division (42-22-10).

• The Rangers take second in the East largely because of goalie Eddie Giacomin, who leads the NHL in wins (36) and shutouts (eight).

• Rangers winger Rod Gilbert ties Detroit's Alex Delvecchio for second in the league in assists (48) and is fifth in total points (77).

• The revamped Bruins, with Bobby Orr on defense, Phil Esposito at center, and Gerry Cheevers in goal, climb from sixth place to third as

Terry Sawchuk

Kings Pluck Sawchuk in '67 Draft

By 1967-68, Terry Sawchuk had celebrated four Vezina Trophies, a Calder Trophy, and four Stanley Cups. When expansion arrived in 1967, Sawchuk—fresh from a Stanley Cup with the Maple Leafs—was left available in the draft and grabbed by the Los Angeles Kings; he was the first player chosen in the draft. Sawchuk played 36 games for the freshman Kings before returning to Detroit (his third tour of duty with the Wings) in 1968-69.

Bobby Hull

Hull Fires 364 Shots, Scores 44

The Black Hawks' preeminence in the league faltered in the first year of the NHL's major expansion. Chicago fell from first to fourth in the East Division (the original six teams) despite a league-leading 44-goal performance from future Hall of Famer Bobby Hull. The Golden Jet blasted an unparalleled 364 shots on goal, many of them set up by his centerman, Stan Mikita, who captured the scoring title.

Bobby Orr

Young Orr Cops His First Norris Trophy

The Bruins had begun the 1967-68 season with a blockbuster deal that pried Phil Esposito loose from Chicago, along with Ken Hodge who would become Espo's most successful linemate ever. The presence of Espo at center and Bobby Orr on the blueline gave the Bruins a one-two offensive punch that few NHL teams would be able to match. In 1967-68, Orr—just a second-year pro—captured his first Norris Trophy after notching 11 goals and 31 points in 46 games.

Esposito leads the league in assists (49) and is second in points (84).

• Chicago falls from first place to fourth even though Stan Mikita leads the league with 87 points. Mikita is second in the NHL in goals (40) and fourth in assists (47).

• Bobby Hull, Stan Mikita's linemate, leads the NHL in goals (44) for the sixth time.

• Gordie Howe's 39 goals are third best in the league, as are his 82 points, but the Wings are among the worst teams in the NHL.

• The Philadelphia Flyers go 31-32-11. They win the Clarence Campbell Trophy, symbolizing supremacy in the West Division.

• The Kings take second in the West—one point behind Philly—as Eddie Joyal leads in points (57).

Jack Kent Cooke

Cooke Buys Kings, Farm Team

Jack Kent Cooke, owner of the Washington Redskins football team, stepped into the hockey world when he was granted the Los Angeles Kings franchise in 1967. Cooke built the $16 million Forum in Inglewood, California, where the Kings—as well as his L.A. Lakers basketball team—would be based. Cooke went even further in his preparations for competing in the NHL, purchasing the entire Springfield (AHL) team from Eddie Shore to use as his farm team.

Masterton Dies After On-Ice Injury

Pictured is the funeral of NHL player Bill Masterton. On January 13, 1968, against the visiting Seals, the 29-year-old Minnesota center was sandwiched by Larry Cahan and Ron Harris as he broke into Oakland's zone. Masterton flipped, hitting his head on the ice. He died two days later. The Masterton Trophy, for perseverance and dedication, was soon established and presented to Montreal's Claude Provost in 1968.

Worsley Wins Vezina, Stars in Playoffs

Lorne "Gump" Worsley knew the best and worst as an NHL goalie, toiling for years in the Rangers' system before finding glory with the Canadiens. In the 1968 Stanley Cup playoffs, he was brilliant, winning 11 games—including a 1-0 shutout of the Blues in Game 2 of the Finals. He finished with a 1.88 playoff goals-against average, a marvelous end to a campaign that earned him a Vezina Trophy.

Gump Worsley

Bill Masterton Funeral

- St. Louis gets 51 points from Red Berenson and 50 points from rookie Gerry Melnyk and marches to a third-place finish.

- Minnesota takes the last playoff spot with an excellent power play and Cesare Maniago's strong goaltending.

- The Pittsburgh Penguins fail to make the playoffs, although 35-year-old Andy Bathgate leads all West Division scorers with 59 points.

- The Oakland Seals replace their first coach, Bert Olmstead, after 64 games and just 11 victories.

- St. Louis' Barclay Plager, one of three Plager brothers in the NHL, leads the league with 153 PIM.

- Montreal's Gump Worsley leads the NHL with a 1.98 GAA. Toronto's Johnny Bower, age 43, is second (2.24).

Madison Square Garden

Fans Give Thumbs Down to New MSG

Built in the middle of Manhattan, the new Madison Square Garden—replacing the old version that stood for years in the middle of Hell's Kitchen—opened for business prior to the 1967-68 season, making a new home for the Rangers. To the dismay of fans and designers, the sight lines were terrible, the game was "out of reach" of the audience, and the entire atmosphere was initially viewed as antiseptic. Alterations have since improved the site.

Stan Mikita

Stosh Repeats His Triple Trophy Feat

Stan Mikita earned his fourth scoring title in five years when he finished the 1967-68 season with 40 goals and 87 points. Moreover, Mikita earned his second straight Lady Byng, Hart, and Art Ross Trophies, giving him his second straight "triple crown." He remains the only player in NHL history to capture the triple crown once, let alone twice. Wayne Gretzky won the Hart and Lady Byng in 1979-80 but finished a point shy of the Art Ross.

'Professional' Soviets Win Gold

The 1968 Winter Games at Grenoble, France, featured a high-flying Soviet team that trounced the Americans 10-2 before winning the gold medal with a 5-0 thrashing of Canada. It was an omen of things to come as the Soviet hockey program—padded with soldiers who trained for hockey year-round—emerged as a dominant power. USA skater Len Lilyholm is shown taking out his aggressions on Viktor Zinger.

Olympic Games

• On March 3, 1968, Jean Beliveau notches his 1,000th point.

• In the West playoffs, third-place St. Louis overcomes first-place Philadelphia in seven games—winning Game 3 in double O.T. on Larry Keenan's goal.

• The fourth-place North Stars drop the first two games of their quarter-final series against the Kings, but they survive in seven.

• In the East playoffs, first-place Montreal sweeps third-place Boston (4-0), while fourth-place Chicago upsets second-place New York (4-2).

• In the semifinals, the Canadiens make short work of Chicago, winning in five games. They take the series on Jacques Lemaire's overtime goal.

• The semifinal series between Minnesota and St. Louis goes seven games, including four sudden-death games beginning in Game 2.

Goldsworthy Shines in Playoffs

Bill Goldsworthy, a former Bruins farm hand, quickly became a crowd favorite in Minnesota with his agile skating, hard shooting, and rugged play. As quick to trade punches as to fire the puck on goal, Goldy's hard-nosed approach earned him a lot of room in which to function. He put this tactic to excellent use during the 1968 playoffs when he led the league in scoring (15 points), even though his team lost to St. Louis in the semifinals.

Phil Esposito

Esposito Comes Alive with Bruins

The Bruins took a quantum leap forward in their pursuit of a championship team when they began the 1967-68 season by swinging a deal with Chicago that brought Phil Esposito to Boston. In his first year in Beantown, the hulking center led the league in assists (49) and was second in overall points (84), trailing only Chicago's Stan Mikita. Maybe it had something to do with his stick, made by ex-Bruin scoring ace Woody Dumart's company.

Bill Goldsworthy

1967-68

- Minnesota wins Game 2 3-2 when Parker MacDonald scores in O.T.

- The Blues take a pair of thrillers in overtime, winning 4-3 on Gary Sabourin's goal in Game 4 and 3-2 on Bill McCreary's O.T. goal. St. Louis' Ron Schock scores the series winner in double overtime of Game 7.

- A courageous St. Louis squad plays the Habs tough, losing Game 1 of the Finals 3-2 in O.T. on Jacques Lemaire's goal.

- The Canadiens manage a 1-0 win in Game 2, as Glenn Hall and Gump Worsley star in goal. Serge Savard scores in the third period.

- In Game 3, Bobby Rousseau breaks a 3-3 score at 1:13 of overtime to put the Habs up 3-0 in the series.

- In Game 4, the Blues take a 2-1 lead into the third period, but Henri Richard ties it and J.C. Tremblay scores the Cup winner with 8:20 on the clock.

Jacques Lemaire

Lemaire Goal Sends Habs to Finals

Montreal finished atop the East Division in 1967-68 with a 42-22-10 record and six players with 20 or more goals, including rookie center Jacques Lemaire. In the opening round of playoffs, the Habs swept the Bruins, outscoring them 15-8, then squashed Chicago in five games. Lemaire, who had 13 playoff points, netted the clinching goal in O.T. against the Hawks to send Montreal to the Finals.

Habs' Tremblay Nets Cup Winner

Jean-Claude Tremblay played 13 years in the NHL and sipped Stanley Cup champagne five times. In the 1968 Finals, when Montreal took on a game but outclassed St. Louis Blues team, Tremblay enjoyed a serene moment of personal glory in Game 4. He untied a 2-2 tie with a goal against Glenn Hall late in the game to give Montreal a 3-2 victory and a four-game sweep of the Blues.

Jean-Claude Tremblay

Red's Heroics Not Enough in Cup Finals

Gordon "Red" Berenson (shown flipping a backhander over the stick of Montreal goalie Gump Worsley), made the most of his first real chance to play in the NHL, leading the fledgling Blues in scoring (22 goals and 51 points) in 1967-68. His two goals in Game 3 of the Stanley Cup Finals were wasted when Montreal's Bobby Rousseau scored early in sudden-death to give the Habs a 4-3 win en route to their four-game sweep.

Stanley Cup Finals

- Glenn Hall is awarded the Conn Smythe Trophy.

- Chicago's Stan Mikita wins a "trophy triple crown"—the Art Ross, the Hart, and the Lady Byng.

- Montreal's Gump Worsley and Rogie Vachon share the Vezina.

- The Calder Trophy goes to flashy Bruin Derek Sanderson. Teammate Bobby Orr wins his first of eight straight Norris Trophies.

- Montreal's Claude Provost wins the first Bill Masterton Trophy for perseverance, sportsmanship, and dedication to hockey.

- The Soviet Union takes the Olympic gold medal, as it rolls to a 5-0 win over Canada in the decisive game.

- Denver wins the NCAA title with a 4-0 victory over North Dakota in the finals. Denver goalie Gerry Powers is the tourney MVP.

BLUES SING A HAPPY TUNE UNTIL HABS SHUT 'EM UP

When St. Louis was granted an NHL expansion franchise in 1967, it was suggested that the Mound City might not be able to support big-league hockey. But the astute managing of Lynn Patrick and Scotty Bowman's clever coaching delivered a playoff berth and a trip to the Finals.

In 1968-69, the Blues established themselves as the premier expansion club both financially and artistically. Owner Sid Salomon Jr. ran a first-class organization, and his club was bolstered by solid trades. Patrick laid the cornerstone for success at two positions when he obtained center Red Berenson and defenseman Barclay Plager from the Rangers. He got each player for practically nothing.

The goaltending of Glenn Hall was world-class. However, the 37-year-old Hall needed help in the nets and Bowman went scouting for another netminder. Scotty learned that Jacques Plante, who had retired in 1965 when his wife fell ill, wanted to make a comeback, so he drafted Jacques from the Rangers. "We both knew he could still play goal," Bowman said. "After all, he hadn't quit because he couldn't do the job."

But Bowman didn't stop there. Aware that left wing needed shoring up, he obtained Camille "The Eel" Henry and Ab McDonald. Finally, he added Billy Plager, kid brother of the Blues' Bob and Barclay, to the defense. Immediately, St. Louis staked its claim as the premier team in the West Division.

"They propose," wrote Mark Mulvoy of *Sports Illustrated*, "that on any given rink they can damn well skate those cocky East teams right up into the stands." That's precisely what they did during one week in November. First, the Blues played the Bruins to a 1-1 tie on Boston Garden ice; they next defeated New York 3-1 at Madison Square Garden; and then they tied Detroit 1-1 at Olympia Stadium.

The Blues' success turned St. Louis into a raving hockey city. St. Louis Arena, built in 1929 but still a handsome edifice, often bulged with huge crowds. The Blues finished the season at 37-25-14, winning the division by 19 points. Plante and Hall were both spectacular, posting GAAs close to 2.00 and winning the Vezina Trophy. Berenson led the West Division in scoring with 82 points.

Playing a physical, intimidating brand of hockey, the Blues obliterated Philadelphia in a four-game, opening-round sweep, then swept the Los Angeles Kings in another four-game affair. Once again, the Blues went head-to-head in the Stanley Cup round with the Montreal Canadiens.

"I know it is going to be tough," said Bowman, "but we're proud of ourselves. You've really got to have something to win eight straight games." However, the Canadiens had infinitely more scoring and a more mobile defense, and they routed St. Louis in four straight games.

The Blues had now dropped eight Finals games to Montreal, but St. Louis fans shrugged off the losses. Even though St. Louis hadn't conquered the NHL, the NHL had conquered St. Louis.

1968-69

- One year after limiting draft eligibility to 20-year-olds (or older), the NHL adopts rules making players all over the world eligible for the NHL draft.

- The Hockey Hall of Fame inducts three members: Bill Cowley, James Dunn, and Jim Hendy.

- The defending-champion Canadiens replace Toe Blake behind the bench with 30-year-old Claude Ruel.

- The Rangers hire former scoring ace Bernie Geoffrion as coach, but Boom Boom lasts just 43 games (22-18-3) before ulcers cause his resignation.

- On October 16, Toronto rookie defenseman Jim Dorey sets an NHL record with nine penalties—four minors, two majors, two 10-minute misconducts, and one game miscon-duct—totaling 48 penalty minutes.

- On November 7, 1968, St. Louis center Red Berenson scores six goals

Despite having legends Doug Harvey (#2) and Glenn Hall (goalie) in the lineup, the Blues were unable to stop Montreal's momentum in the 1969 playoffs—even though the Blues had advanced to the Finals with four-game sweeps of Philadelphia and Los Angeles. The Blues had physical players, such as defenseman Bob Plager (#5), and plenty of scoring talent in Red Berenson (wearing helmet), but the Habs dominated them in the Finals.

at Philadelphia as the Blues win 8-0. He's the only NHL player ever to score six in a game on the road.

• On February 16, 1969, Alex Delvecchio notches his 1,000th point.

• The Canadiens (46-19-11) win the East Division by three points over Boston, as Yvan Cournoyer leads them in goals (43) and points (87).

• The Bruins' Phil Esposito totals 126 points—shattering the NHL record of 97.

• Boston sets records for most goals (303) and penalty minutes (1,297), as they form their reputation as the Big, Bad Bruins.

• The Rangers, fueled by the Goal-a-Game Line of Jean Ratelle (78 points), Rod Gilbert (77), and Vic Hadfield (66), take third place in the East Division.

Red Berenson

Berenson Nets a Half-Dozen in One Game

St. Louis continued to dominate the West Division in 1968-69, finishing 19 points ahead of second-place Oakland. Red Berenson led the team in goals (35), assists (47), and points (82) and set a modern-day record when he scored six goals against Philadelphia's combative goalie Doug Favell during an 8-0 win on November 7, 1968. Berenson remains the only NHL player ever to score six goals in a road game.

Dorey: Nine Penalties in One Game

Toronto rookie defenseman Jim Dorey made a crashing debut in the NHL when, on October 16, 1968, he set a league record with nine penalties in one game, including four minors, two majors, two 10-minute misconducts, and a game misconduct, totalling a record 48 minutes. Dorey's total-penalty mark would later be eclipsed by Boston's Chris Nilan in 1991 (10 penalties), while three others would surpass Dorey's penalty minutes-per-game record. More than just a fighter, Dorey finished the season with 30 points.

Jim Dorey

Ed Giacomin

Giacomin's No. 1 Again in Wins

In 1968-69, the Rangers' goaltending hopes were in the able hands of future Hall of Famer Ed Giacomin, whose workhorse durability made him a favorite among Madison Square Garden fans. Fast Eddie appeared in 70 of the team's 76 regular-season games and won a league-high 37 contests (the third straight time he led the NHL in victories). He was third overall in GAA (2.55) and was one behind Glenn Hall in shutouts with seven.

1968-69

- Eddie Giacomin, the Rangers' slick goalie, leads the league in wins (37) for the second straight year.

- Toronto takes fourth place as Norm Ullman tallies 77 points.

- The Red Wings finish fifth despite 103 points from 40-year-old Gordie Howe and the 49-goal performance of Frank Mahovlich.

- Bobby Hull scores an NHL-record 58 goals, but Chicago finishes last in the East with a 34-33-9 record.

- In the West Division, the St. Louis Blues capture first place (37-25-14), as Red Berenson leads the division with 82 points.

- The second-place Seals are led by veteran Ted Hampson (75 points).

- The Philadelphia Flyers finish third in the West. Graceful center Andre Lacroix leads with 56 points.

Yvan Cournoyer

Super-Swift Cournoyer Sparks Habs

The Canadiens finished with the best record in hockey in 1968-69 (46-19-11), although they did not have the league's best offense. They did get some explosive scoring from right winger Yvan "The Roadrunner" Cournoyer, a fifth-year vet who compensated for a lack of size (5'7") with blazing speed and tremendous shooting. Cournoyer, skating on the Habs' top line with center Jacques Lemaire and Dick Duff, led the team in goals (43) and points (87).

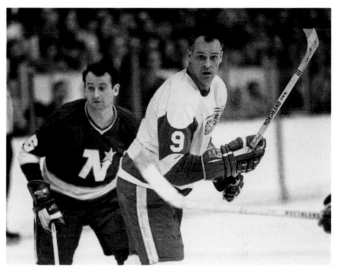

Gordie Howe

40-Year-Old Howe Breaks 100 Mark

At age 40, Detroit legend Gordie Howe (#9), winner of six league scoring titles, enjoyed the most productive season of his entire career. He finished with 103 points, including 59 assists. Ironically, he was a distant third in the Art Ross Trophy race, which was won by Boston's Phil Esposito who finished 23 points ahead of Howe. The Red Wings star was fifth overall in goals (44) and fourth in assists, though his team finished fifth in the East.

- Los Angeles falls to fourth place. Eddie Joyal has a career year (33 goals), but goalie Gerry Desjardins leads the NHL in losses (34).

- The Penguins fail to make the postseason, as the offense of Keith McCreary (25 goals) and Ken Schinkel (52 points) isn't enough.

- Minnesota goes 3-7-1 with Wren Blair behind the bench, switches to John Muckler (6-22-7), and then goes back to Blair (9-14-7).

- Minnesota's Danny Grant and Oakland's Norm Ferguson (34 goals each) are second only to Red Berenson (35) in goals in the West.

- Frank Mahovlich and Phil Esposito tie for second in goals (49 apiece) behind Bobby Hull. Ken Hodge (45) and Gordie Howe (44) follow.

- With 77 assists, Phil Esposito far surpasses Stan Mikita (67), Gordie Howe (59), and Alex Delvecchio (58).

Danny Grant

Stars' Grant Debuts with a Bang

In 1968-69, speedy left winger Danny Grant made a huge first impression on the NHL when he scored 34 freshman goals for a struggling Minnesota team that finished dead last in the West Division. Grant led the North Stars in goals and points (65) and edged Oakland's Norm Ferguson for the Calder Trophy. A former Montreal farm hand, Grant later attained superstar status by scoring 50 goals for the 1974-75 Red Wings.

Espo's 126 Points Smash NHL Mark

The 1968-69 Bruins were known both for their bruising physical style as well as for their devastating offensive attacks. The Big, Bad Bruins featured Phil Esposito at center and Bobby Orr on defense. Between them, they scored 70 goals and 190 points. Espo won his first of five scoring titles with 49 goals, a record 77 assists, and 126 points—29 points better than the previous league record (97) shared by Bobby Hull and Stan Mikita.

Journeyman Hampson Stars with Oakland

Ted Hampson made up for a lack of size (he was just 5'8", 170 pounds) with unrelenting desire. Originally property of the Maple Leafs, he bounced from Toronto to New York to Detroit to Oakland and on to Minnesota before jumping to the rival WHA in 1972. In 1968-69, he led the Oakland Seals in assists (49) and points (74) and was second to 34-goal scorer Norm Ferguson in goals (26). He won the Bill Masterton Trophy for perseverance in 1969.

Ted Hampson

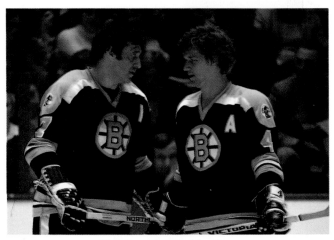

Phil Esposito, Bobby Orr

1968-69

• Phil Esposito's 126 points outdistance second-place Bobby Hull (107) and third-place Gordie Howe (103). They're the first three NHL players to record 100-point seasons.

• St. Louis' Jacques Plante leads the league with a 1.96 GAA, while teammate Glenn Hall is runner-up

(2.16). Hall leads the league in shutouts with eight.

• Flyer/Leaf Forbes Kennedy leads the NHL with 219 PIM.

• Boston's Bobby Orr leads the NHL in plus/minus with a +65 rating. (When he was on the ice—and teams

were at full strength—his team scored 65 more goals than it gave up.)

• In the East Division semifinals, the Canadiens sweep the Rangers and the Bruins broom the Maple Leafs.

• In the West semis, St. Louis sweeps Philadelphia while Los Angeles goes

Detroit Red Wings vs. Pittsburgh Penguins

Big M's 49 Goals Can't Save Wings

Frank Mahovlich (right), whose March 1968 trade from Toronto to Detroit in exchange for Norm Ullman rocked the NHL, scored 49 goals in 1968-69 but couldn't help the Red Wings gain a playoff berth. Nevertheless, his presence on the team along with fellow legends Gordie Howe, Alex Delvecchio, and Terry Sawchuk stirred up many golden memories within Detroit's Olympia. The Big M would move on to Montreal in 1970-71.

Hull's 58 Goals Just Not Enough

The 1968-69 season was a source of frustration for the Black Hawks. They finished last in the East Division (out of the playoffs) despite a 34-33-9 record—while Oakland (29 wins), L.A. (24), and Philadelphia (20) qualified for the playoffs in the West Division. The lone bright spot was Bobby Hull, who notched his fourth season with at least 50 goals. The Golden Jet blasted 58 goals (a new record) and was second overall in points (107).

Bobby Hull

the limit against Oakland. The Kings win Game 7 on the road 5-3 to advance.

• The Habs win the first two East finals games against Boston, as Ralph Backstrom and Mickey Redmond each score overtime goals.

• Montreal advances to the Finals with a 2-1 victory over the Bruins in Game 6, as Jean Beliveau scores at 11:28 of double overtime.

• The Blues, on the goaltending of Glenn Hall and Jacques Plante, sweep Los Angeles in four games and go to the Finals against Montreal.

• The Canadiens take just four games to successfully defend the Stanley Cup, as they outscore the Blues 12-3.

• Dick Duff and Bobby Rousseau score in the first five minutes of Game 1 to stake the Habs to a 2-0 lead. They cruise to a 3-1 win.

Fully Healed Ratelle Paces the Rangers

Jean Ratelle's NHL career was nearly over before it began. A graceful skater with outstanding play-making skill, Ratelle was plagued by back injuries early in his professional career and needed spinal fusion surgery to save his livelihood. By 1968-69, he was at full strength and, playing between Rod Gilbert and Vic Hadfield, led the Rangers in goals (32) and points (78). Gilbert was first in assists (49) and second in points (77).

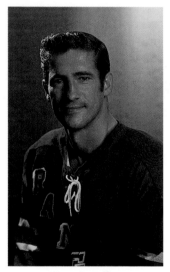

Jean Ratelle

Delvecchio's the Third to Hit 1,000

On February 16, 1969, Detroit's Alex Delvecchio became only the third player in NHL history to reach the 1,000-point plateau. He earned the point with an assist—one of 825 in his career—as the Wings trounced Los Angeles before a packed Olympia Stadium in Detroit. Delvecchio, a longtime linemate of Gordie Howe, finished his 24-year career with 1,281 points and entered the Hall of Fame in 1977.

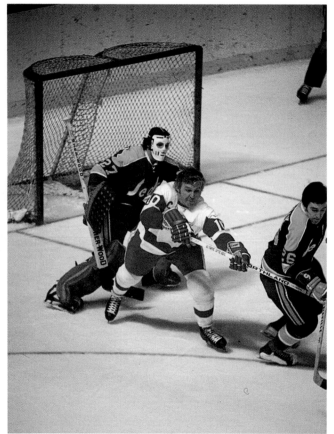

Alex Delvecchio

Savard Stars on D, Cops Conn Smythe Trophy

The Canadiens went a league-best 46-19-11 in 1968-69 thanks to, once again, an excellent team defense. Montreal yielded fewer goals than the league average for the 26th straight year. (Incredibly, they would run the streak to 61 years in a row in 1993-94.) Serge Savard was one of the stars on the blueline. Besides his stellar work in his own end, Savard tallied 10 playoff points and became the first backliner to win the Conn Smythe Trophy.

Serge Savard

1968-69

- In Game 2, Montreal wins 3-1 thanks to goals by Ralph Backstrom, Dick Duff, and Yvan Cournoyer.

- A pair of goals by Dick Duff, as well as the perfect goaltending of Rogie Vachon, helps Montreal win Game 3 4-0.

- Habs tough guys Ted Harris and John Ferguson lead a third-period comeback in Game 4, as Harris ties the game and Fergie scores the winner to give Montreal a 2-1 victory and the Stanley Cup.

- Montreal defenseman Serge Savard wins the Conn Smythe Trophy.

- The Bruins waste a brilliant eight-goal, 18-point performance by playoff scoring leader Phil Esposito.

- In postseason awards, Phil Esposito cops the Hart Trophy.

- The Lady Byng Trophy goes to Alex Delvecchio—his third.

Stanley Cup Finals

Habs' O.T. Goals Do In the Bruins

In the 1969 semifinals, the Bruins, despite Phil Esposito, Bobby Orr, and Ted Green (pictured on his knees while Montreal's Yvan Cournoyer stands by), were snake-bitten against the Habs, losing the first two games of their series in sudden-death on goals from Ralph Backstrom and Mickey Redmond. Then, after fighting back to tie the series, the Bruins lost a deciding Game 6 thriller on a double-O.T. goal by Jean Beliveau.

Stanley Cup Semifinals

Ferguson, Vachon Cool off the Blues

Tempers ran hot in the 1969 Stanley Cup Finals as the St. Louis Blues sought to avenge their four-game sweep by Montreal in the 1968 championship round. Habs enforcer John Ferguson (#22) was often at the center of the trouble (he is shown sparring with Craig Cameron, #16, as Montreal goalie Rogie Vachon looks on). The Blues played valiantly but were outscored 12-3 and were swept again.

- The Vezina Trophy is shared by future Hall of Fame goalies Jacques Plante and Glenn Hall of St. Louis.

- Danny Grant of the North Stars and Norm Ferguson of Oakland (both 34-goal scorers) finish 1-2, respectively, in the Calder Trophy race.

- Bobby Orr takes his second of eight straight Norris Trophies.

- Oakland's Ted Hampson wins the Bill Masterton Trophy, while the Lester Patrick Trophy is awarded to Bobby Hull and Edward Jeremiah, a fabled collegiate coach.

- Denver repeats as NCAA champion, beating Cornell 4-3 in the finals. Denver defenseman Keith Magnuson is named tourney MVP.

- The Montreal Jr. Canadiens capture the Memorial Cup as champions of Canadian major junior hockey.

GREEN NEARLY DIES AFTER FIGHT WITH MAKI

If ever there was a case of a hockey player living by the sword—and almost dying by the sword—it occurred during the 1969 preseason. The victim was Ted Green, a Boston Bruins defenseman who, during the 1960s, was among the most fearsome players in the NHL.

Green was on the Beantown defense when the Bruins played an exhibition game at Ottawa on September 21, 1969. Normally, such contests were relatively mild, but late in the first period St. Louis Blues forward Wayne Maki charged Green behind the Boston net.

"I then reached out with my glove hand and shoved Maki in the face," Green remembered. Maki fell to the ice but managed to spear Green in the abdomen. Green counter-attacked with a stick swipe that caught Maki below the shoulder. "My last thought was, 'I guess that'll straighten him out,'" said Green, "and I turned to skate away."

But Maki struck back, clipping Green in the head with his stick. This time, the Bruin hit the ice. He was lying on his side, his head turning violently. "I didn't know what had happened, where I had been hit, what I had been hit

with, how badly I was hurt," he said.

In fact, Green's life was in danger. He had suffered a compound skull fracture, and a 2½-hour operation was necessary. "There was even a rumor that he died," said teammate Ed Westfall.

At one point, Westfall entered the recovery room at the hospital, where Green was on a stretcher-type bed, moaning. He was the only patient in a big room, and the two nurses kept yelling at Green and jostling him. "I took his hand," Westfall remembered, and said, 'Greenie, it's 18.' Instead of calling me Ed, the guys called me by my uniform number. Teddy didn't move, and I said, 'It's 18. Can you hear me? If you can, squeeze my hand.' He squeezed my hand, and I felt like a new father who just got the

news that the mother and infant are doing fine."

Green didn't die, but he did emerge with temporary paralysis. Meanwhile, the Crown charged both players with assault with attempt to injure. Eventually, in separate trials, each was acquitted. NHL President Clarence Campbell suspended both without pay—Green for 13 games and Maki for 30 days. In Green's case, the suspension was technical because he didn't play at all that year, although he did return to the Bruins in 1970-71.

Without their defensive leader, the Bruins managed an outstanding season, going 40-17-19 and topping the league in goals. Led by the irrepressible Bobby Orr—he won the Art Ross, Hart, and Norris Trophies—the Bruins swept Chicago in four straight East finals games and then did the same to St. Louis in the Finals.

Appropriately, Orr scored the overtime winner in Game 4, giving his Bruins their first Stanley Cup since 1941. As much as the Bostonians missed Green, they demonstrated that their core of Orr, Phil Esposito, and goalies Gerry Cheevers and Ed Johnston had the makings of a dynasty.

1969-70

• In June 1969, Montreal uses the first two picks in the Amateur Draft to acquire both Rejean Houle and Marc Tardif of the Montreal Jr. Canadiens.

• The Hall of Fame inducts six members, including Sid Abel, Bryan Hextall, Red Kelly, and Roy Worters.

• Carl Brewer ends four years of premature retirement to join the Detroit Red Wings.

• Terry Sawchuk joins the Rangers for the final season of his career. He'll retire with NHL goalie records for games (971), wins (453), and shutouts (103).

• The NHL receives unwanted notoriety as the result of a preseason stick fight between the St. Louis Blues' Wayne Maki and Boston's Ted Green that leaves Green hospitalized with a fractured skull.

• Toronto replaces longtime coach Punch Imlach with John McLellan,

The 1969-70 Bruins finished second to the Black Hawks, who won the East Division after finishing last the previous year. Boston was big and bad without its biggest and baddest defenseman, Terrible Ted Green (shown looking for a rebound as Ranger Don Marshall, #22, lingers around the net). Green suffered a life-threatening skull fracture during a preseason stick fight with St. Louis winger Wayne Maki. He missed the entire season.

who steers the Leafs to a last-place finish in the East Division.

• Using a strong team approach, the Black Hawks win the regular-season title with a 45-22-9 record.

• Chicago's Bobby Hull misses 15 games due to injury but reaches a milestone on February 21, 1970, as he scores his 500th career goal, becoming the third to do so.

• Chicago rookie Tony Esposito—kid brother of Phil Esposito—leads the NHL in wins (38) and shutouts (15) while posting a 2.11 GAA.

• The Bruins finish with 99 points, tying Chicago, but finish second with five fewer wins.

• Boston's Phil Esposito leads the NHL in goals (43) for the first time.

• Bobby Orr leads all NHLers in points with a whopping 120.

Future NHL Stars Power Junior Habs

The Montreal Junior Canadiens, who captured their second straight Memorial Cup in 1970, boasted two-thirds of what would become one of the most dominant lines in the NHL. Gilbert Perreault (front row, wearing captain's "C") and Rick Martin (second row, fourth from right) later reunited in Buffalo and formed the French Connection Line with Rene Robert. Ian Turnbull (back row, second from left) went on to a sterling career in Toronto.

Montreal Junior Canadiens

Michel Briere

Briere Injured in Car Crash

The young Pittsburgh franchise got a major boost when rookie center Michel Briere, the 25th player picked in the 1969 draft, immediately established himself, finishing first on the team in assists (32) and third in points (44). Tragically, the promising youngster suffered fatal injuries in an auto crash in the spring of 1970 that took his life the following spring (April 13, 1971). His jersey, No. 21, was subsequently retired.

Gary Smith

Smith Packs His Suitcase

Over a 14-year NHL career, goalie Gary Smith earned the nickname "Suitcase." The huge netminder, who stood 6'4", played for Toronto, the Seals, Chicago, Vancouver, Minnesota, Washington, and Winnipeg in the NHL, as well as Indianapolis and Winnipeg of the World Hockey Association. He led the NHL in losses three times. In 1969-70, he helped the Seals to their last-ever playoff appearance.

1969-70

• The Red Wings finish in third place thanks to a 42-goal year from Garry Unger and 38 goals from Frank Mahovlich.

• The fourth-place Rangers feature the GAG Line of Jean Ratelle centering Rod Gilbert and Vic Hadfield, as well as the Bulldog Line of Walt Tkaczuk between Dave Balon and Billy Fairbairn.

• The Canadiens, two-time defending champs, match the Rangers' record (38-22-16) but fail to make the playoffs by virtue of two fewer goals (246 to 244).

• Yvan Cournoyer, a speedy right winger, is the Habs' leading scorer (63 points).

• The Blues win the West on the scoring of Phil Goyette (division-leading 78 points) as well as the goaltending of Ernie Wakely (league-leading 2.11 GAA) and Jacques Plante.

Orr Garners 120 Points, Four Trophies

A defenseman by trade, Bobby Orr made his mark on the NHL as one of the greatest offensive geniuses the game ever saw. In 1969-70, he became the first defenseman ever to eclipse the 100-point mark and the first to win a scoring title. He finished with 120 points, including a record 87 assists. Orr scored the Cup-winning goal and earned four trophies: the Art Ross, Hart, Norris, and Conn Smythe.

Bobby Orr

Wakely and Plante Star in Blues' Net

Goaltender Ernie Wakely, who started his career in the Montreal farm system, got his chance to play in the NHL following a 1969 trade to St. Louis, where he was the second-stringer behind Jacques Plante. Wakely got into 30 games in 1969-70, posting a 12-9-4 record, four shutouts, and a tremendous 2.11 GAA. The West Division champions yielded just 179 goals.

Ernie Wakely

Tony Esposito

Younger Espo Wields His Magic in Goal

Just as Phil Esposito was establishing himself as the NHL's premier power forward, along came his kid brother, Tony, who wowed Chicago as a rookie in 1969-70. Tony O appeared in 63 games, led the league in wins (38), and led all first-string goalies in GAA (2.17). He won both the Calder Trophy and Vezina Trophy, a feat that would not be duplicated for 14 years (until Buffalo's Tom Barrasso turned the trick).

• Coach Red Kelly guides the Penguins to a second-place finish in the West. Dean Prentice tops the team in scoring (51 points) and rookie sensation Michel Briere leads with 32 assists.

• After 32 games, Minnesota G.M. Wren Blair appoints veteran center Charlie Burns to be player/coach, but Burns' North Stars finish third at just 19-35-22 in the weak West Division.

• Bill Goldsworthy's 36 goals lead the North Stars and all West scorers. Minnesota's J.P. Parise bags 72 points to tie Red Berenson for second in the West.

• The Oakland Seals get 24 goals from defenseman Carol Vadnais and capture the final playoff spot.

• Philadelphia, under rookie coach Vic Stasiuk, falls to fifth place while debuting rookie Bobby Clarke. The Flyers (17-35-24) set an all-time NHL record for ties.

Rejean Houle

Pollock Plucks Two Stars in Draft

Sam Pollock, G.M. of the Canadiens from 1964-78, was one of the shrewdest wheeler-dealers of all time, pulling off deals that qualified as highway robbery. In 1969, the defending champions owned the right to the top pick in the summer draft, thanks to a deal Pollock made with Minnesota. With it, they selected Rejean Houle, the 1968-69 OHA scoring champ. They also owned the second overall pick, which they used to select future star Marc Tardif.

Goldy Pots 36, Breaks into Dance

The North Stars climbed from sixth place in the West Division in 1968-69 to third place in 1969-70, as Bill Goldsworthy elevated himself from a 14-goal scorer to a 36-goal performer. The hard-nosed winger, whose post-goal dance earned the name "The Goldy Shuffle," fused with American-born center Tommy Williams and left winger J.P. Parise to give the North Stars a legitimate scoring attack.

Bill Goldsworthy

1969-70

- The Flyers boast a burly right wing, Gary Dornhoefer, whose strategy of camping in the slot enables him to score a team-high 26 goals.

- In Los Angeles, Hal Laycoe is replaced by Johnny Wilson after a 5-18-1 start, but the team finishes in the basement with a 14-52-10 record.

- Goal-scoring leader Phil Esposito finishes ahead of Garry Unger (42), Stan Mikita (39), Frank Mahovlich (38), and Bobby Hull (38).

- Bobby Orr's 87 assists set a new league record. He is followed by Phil Esposito (56), Minnesota's Tommy Williams (52), and Walt Tkaczuk (50).

- With his 120 points, Bobby Orr outshines teammate Phil Esposito (99), Stan Mikita (86), Phil Goyette (78), and Walt Tkaczuk (77).

- Chicago rookie defenseman Keith Magnuson brawls his way to a league-high 213 penalty minutes.

Brad Park

Year After Year, Park Is Second Best

Brad Park was a superb defenseman whose only shortcoming was his bad luck to play in the NHL during the era dominated by Bruins backliner Bobby Orr. Park (shown slamming a Black Hawk to the ice in front of goalie Ed Giacomin) was runner-up for the Norris Trophy six times in his career, never winning. In 1969-70, the sophomore defenseman notched 37 points and 98 penalty minutes and finished second to Orr in Norris Trophy voting.

Hull Kicked Off Top Line, Nets 500th

In 1969-70, Bobby Hull actually lost his spot on Chicago's top line (with Stan Mikita and Cliff Koroll) to his kid brother Dennis. But the Golden Jet, teaming up with Jim Pappin and Pit Martin, wasn't through terrorizing the NHL. Despite missing 15 games due to a broken jaw, he recorded his 500th career goal against the Rangers on February 21, 1970. Hull became the third 500-goal player, joining Maurice Richard and Gordie Howe.

Esposito Knocks In the Rebounds

The banners at the Boston Garden read: "Jesus Saves But Espo Scores on the Rebound." Boston center Phil Esposito made an art form of standing in the slot and using his sheer strength to hold his position, waiting for loose pucks to slam past sprawling goalies. In 1969-70, Espo led the league in goals (43) and power-play goals (18). He was second in assists (56) and points (120), trailing only his teammate, Bobby Orr, in each category.

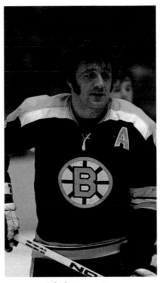

Phil Esposito

Bobby Hull

- In opening-round playoff action, Chicago sweeps Detroit and Boston beats New York 4-2.

- Pittsburgh knocks off Oakland in four quarterfinal games, while St. Louis survives a challenge from Minnesota, winning in six games.

- The Bruins sweep Chicago in the Stanley Cup semifinals, outscoring the Black Hawks 20-10.

- The Blues and Pens swap home-ice wins through five games until the Blues break through in Pittsburgh. They win 4-3 to earn their third straight berth in the Finals.

- In Game 1 of the Stanley Cup Finals, the Bruins score four third-period goals and Johnny Bucyk records a hat-trick as Boston rolls to a 6-1 win.

- Eddie Westfall, a respected checking forward, scores a pair of first-period goals in Game 2. Boston wins 6-2.

Stanley Cup Semifinals

Sanderson Quiets Hull in Cup Semis

When Boston took on Chicago in the 1970 Stanley Cup semifinals, it was obvious that, to win, the Bruins would have to neutralize Bobby Hull (center). To do the job, Boston assigned Derek Sanderson (left), one of the game's supreme defensive forwards, to shadow the Golden Jet. As a result, the Bruins shut down Hull—who had just three goals in eight playoff games—and swept the Hawks 4-0 to gain a berth in the Finals against St. Louis.

Cashman Does Bruins' Dirty Work

The 1969-70 Bruins squad wasn't only talented, it was tough and nasty. Wayne Cashman (pictured fighting St. Louis defenseman Noel Picard, #4) was one of Boston's most feared wingers. It was Cashman who crashed the corners to dig out pucks for Phil Esposito, and it was Cashman who dropped the gloves to pound anyone foolish enough to start trouble with a Bruins player. Cashman could also find the net, proving it with a pair of goals in Game 3 of the Finals.

Broken-Down Sawchuk Dies from Injuries

The brilliant 21-year career of goaltender Terry Sawchuk was winding down when the New York Rangers acquired him for the 1969-70 season. Sawchuk, the NHL's all-time winningest goalie (435 victories) and shutout leader (103), played just eight games for the Rangers. Troubled and bitter in his later years, Sawchuk died in 1970 after a bad scuffle with teammate Ron Stewart on the lawn of Sawchuk's home. Pictured are the remains of his stick.

Terry Sawchuk's Stick

Stanley Cup Finals

• Frank St. Marseille opens the scoring for St. Louis in Game 3, but Boston answers with a pair. Wayne Cashman then scores twice in the third period for a 4-1 final and a 3-0 series lead.

• The desperate Blues take Boston to O.T. of Game 4, tied 3-3.

• The Bruins win their first Stanley Cup in 29 years when Bobby Orr scores at 00:40 of sudden-death in Game 4 to beat St. Louis 4-3.

• Phil Esposito's 27 playoff points set an NHL record, but Bobby Orr (20 points) is honored with the Conn Smythe Trophy.

• Besides the Conn Smythe, Bobby Orr wins his first of three Hart Trophies as well as his third Norris Trophy.

• The Lady Byng Trophy is presented to Blues center Phil Goyette, as Boston's Johnny Bucyk is runner-up.

Stanley Cup Finals

Orr Scores Cup Winner in Overtime

In the 1970 Stanley Cup Finals, it was clear that the Blues would have to stop Bobby Orr (#4) if they had a hope of beating the Bruins. In that pursuit, St. Louis coach Scotty Bowman assigned Jimmy Roberts (#6) to shadow Orr. Roberts, an outstanding defensive forward, held Orr to four assists through the first three games. But in Game 4, Orr netted his ninth playoff goal, in sudden-death, to foil St. Louis and win the Cup for Boston.

Bruins Enjoy First Cup in 29 Years

In the spring of 1970, the Bruins (shown lifting coach Harry Sinden on their shoulders) celebrated their first Stanley Cup title since 1940-41. Boston permanently ended a 28-year stretch in which three teams hoarded the Stanley Cup: Montreal 12, Toronto 10, and Detroit five (plus Chicago with one). Phil Esposito scored 13 goals in the postseason and set a new playoff record with 27 points.

Stanley Cup Celebration

• Tony Esposito, runner-up for the Hart Trophy, wins both the Vezina and Calder Trophies.

• Chicago's Pit Martin, a 5'9" center, is awarded the Masterton Trophy.

• Eddie Shore is one of two recipients of the Lester Patrick Trophy. James

Hendy, longtime owner of the AHL Cleveland Barons, is also honored.

• Cornell defeats Clarkson 6-4 for the NCAA championship. Daniel Lodboa, Cornell's outstanding defenseman, is the MVP of the tournament.

• The Montreal Jr. Canadiens retain the Memorial Cup as champions of major junior Canadian hockey.

• During the spring of 1970, Pittsburgh rookie standout Michel Briere is injured in an automobile crash that will ultimately claim his life on April 13, 1971.

DRYDEN PUTS THE SCREWS TO THE BIG, BAD BRUINS

Never in NHL history has a team been as utterly terrifying as the 1970-71 Boston Bruins. The Big, Bad Bruins left opposing goalies in tears, as they scored 399 goals—108 more than any other team. Center Phil Esposito lit the lamp 76 times, breaking the NHL record by 18, and his 152 points smashed his own NHL record by 26. Yet it was defenseman Bobby Orr who skated off with the Hart Trophy. Orr's 37 goals set an NHL record for a backliner, while his 102 assists were the most by anybody ever.

Boston's depth left other hockey executives gasping. The Bruins boasted the league's top four scorers (Johnny Bucyk had 116 points and Ken Hodge 105) and featured seven of the league's 10 top scorers. Boston finished at 57-14-7 and were the odds-on favorites for a second straight Stanley Cup—and maybe even three more beyond that.

Boston was set to meet Montreal in the first round of the playoffs, and nobody gave Montreal a chance. The Habs had missed the playoffs in 1969-70; and in December 1970, coach Claude Ruel resigned and was replaced by Al MacNeil. The offense, which sputtered the year before, got a boost when G.M.

Sam Pollock obtained Frank Mahovlich from Detroit for Mickey Redmond and two others. Still, the club was short in goal.

When Pollock elevated netminder Ken Dryden from the American League late in the season, few were impressed. The tall, studious Dryden seemed too inexperienced to be a factor for Montreal. Nevertheless, MacNeil made Dryden his goaltender of choice for the homestretch and the opening playoff round.

The defending Cup champions weren't too concerned after beating Dryden 3-1 in Game 1 at Boston Garden. In fact, when the Bruins piled up a 5-1 lead in Game 2, they were feeling pretty darn confident. Perhaps too confident.

"Few of us were really up for the playoffs," said Bruins defenseman Ted Green. "Our club suffered a letdown after clinching the Prince of Wales Trophy. Possibly we were fat cats, and certainly the Canadiens were hungry."

So hungry that they rebounded in Game 2 for a 7-5 win. That done, the Canadiens pushed forward behind Dryden's marvelous goaltending and forced the Bruins to a seventh game at Boston Garden. By now, the Bruin snipers were thoroughly befuddled by Dryden. "He seemed all arms and legs," said Green. "He turned the Canadiens into an inspired team." The inspiration carried through Game 7, which the Habs captured 4-2.

There have been few upsets in sports history to match the Canadiens' defeat of Boston. "No question," said Green, "Dryden was the star. He made fantastic stops."

Dryden pursued the miracle through the Stanley Cup Finals, in which Montreal maintained its poise and beat Chicago in seven games. Ironically, coach MacNeil—who didn't get along with his players—soon resigned under pressure. Dryden, though, would stick around in goal another seven seasons—and lead the Canadiens to five more Stanley Cups.

1970-71

- The NHL expands from 12 teams to 14, as the Buffalo Sabres and Vancouver Canucks are admitted. Buffalo and Vancouver are placed in the East, while Chicago gets to move to the easy West Division.

- In a freak accident, goalie great Terry Sawchuk is fatally injured in a fight at his home with Ranger teammate Ron Stewart. Sawchuk dies at age 40.

- With the first pick in the 1970 Amateur Draft, Buffalo selects Gil Perreault, MVP of the Ontario Hockey Association the previous season.

- The Hall of Fame inducts four new members: Babe Dye, Bill Gadsby, Tom Johnson, and Bob LeBel.

- The defending-champion Boston Bruins install a new coach, Tom Johnson, as Harry Sinden gives up the bench duties.

The Canadiens had gone most of the 1970-71 season with Rogie Vachon and Phil Myre in goal, but come playoff time, they installed former Cornell University standout Ken Dryden (pictured) in goal. Dryden pulled off the upset of the century when he defused the powder-keg offense of the Bruins, beating them in seven opening-round games. The lanky netminder played all 20 playoff games, won the magic number of 12, and skated away with the Conn Smythe Trophy.

• The Bruins roar to 57-14-7, as they demolish the NHL scoring record with 399 goals. Boston boasts the NHL's top four scorers and seven of the top 10.

• Boston's Phil Esposito shatters NHL marks for goals (76) and points (152), as well as shots on goal (550).

• Boston defenseman Bobby Orr charts new territory in playmaking when he records 102 assists.

• Johnny Bucyk (51 goals, 116 points) and Ken Hodge (43-62-105) finish third and fourth on the Bruins—and in the NHL—in scoring.

• Goaltenders Ed Giacomin and Gilles Villemure lead the Rangers to a second-place finish in the East.

• The Canadiens acquire Frank Mahovlich from Detroit for Mickey Redmond, Bill Collins, and Guy Charron.

Gordie Howe Statue

Mr. Hockey Immortalized in Bronze

In 1970-71, the once-proud Detroit franchise deteriorated into a dismal seventh-place team, embarrassingly finishing behind the expansion Vancouver Canucks. Among the few cheerful notes in a season of frustration and humiliation was the casting of a statue of Gordie Howe, commemorating the brilliant career of Mr. Hockey. In 1970-71, the 42-year-old Howe scored 23 goals in his 25th and final season with the Red Wings.

Magnuson Punches Way to PIM Title

Keith Magnuson arrived on the NHL scene as a snarling rookie in the fall of 1969. He was among the league's most impressive newcomers —and most fearsome. The former star at the University of Denver took his post on the Chicago blueline and proceeded to lead the NHL in penalty minutes his first two years—213 PIM in 1969-70 and 291 PIM in 1970-71. Magnuson scored only three goals in his first two years, however.

Keith Magnuson

Vancouver Canucks

NHL Adds Third Canadian Team

The NHL expanded from 12 teams to 14 as the 1970-71 season commenced, adding the Vancouver Canucks and Buffalo Sabres. (For "balance," the league switched Chicago to the West Division and put both new teams in the East Division.) The Canucks, who became just the third Canadian team in the NHL, finished ahead of Detroit and California in the overall standings. They played their home games in the Pacific Coliseum, pictured here.

1970-71

- New coach Al MacNeil leads Montreal to a third-place finish. Jean Beliveau leads the team in scoring (76 points) and scores his 500th goal.

- After acquiring Jacques Plante from St. Louis, the Maple Leafs clinch the last playoff spot. Norm Ullman notches a team-high 85 points.

- Under coach Punch Imlach, the first-year Sabres win 24 games but finish fifth in the East. Gil Perreault leads in goals (38) and points (72).

- The Canucks, with ex-Kings coach Hal Laycoe at the controls, finish sixth in the East. Tough guy Rosie Paiement scores 34 goals.

- Detroit finishes seventh in the East, behind both expansion clubs.

- Chicago grabs the West title by 20 points, as Tony Esposito leads the league in victories (35) and Bobby Hull paces the Hawks with 44 goals. Brother Dennis Hull nets 40.

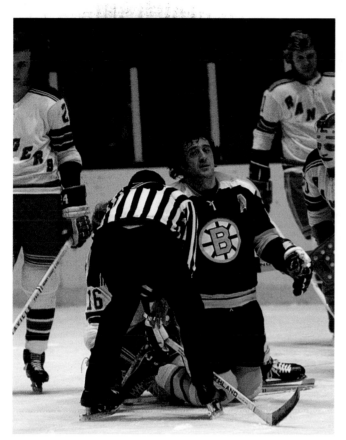

Phil Esposito

Espo Spanks In a Record 76 Goals

The NHL had never witnessed anything like the show put on by Boston's Phil Esposito in 1970-71, when the hulking center banged home an unprecedented 76 goals—shattering Bobby Hull's single-season mark of 58. It was suggested of Esposito that if you tallied the cumulative length of his successful shots on goal (76), they'd measure out to about 80 feet total. To which he was said to have responded, "They don't ask how; they ask how many."

Bobby Orr

Orr Records 102 Helpers, Wins the Hart

No player dominated the game of hockey—taking control of games and turning them in favor of his team with singular splendor—as did Bobby Orr in his brief but shining era (1966-1976). During the Bruins' 121-point 1970-71 season, Orr set a new NHL record with 102 assists and finished second to teammate Phil Esposito in total points (139). He was rewarded with his fourth straight Norris Trophy and second straight Hart Trophy.

Dennis Hull

Younger Hull Scores 40 Goals Too

Dennis Hull was an up-and-down-the-wing sniper who lacked his famous older brother's natural flair and skating speed. However, Dennis' slapshot was nearly as deadly. In 1970-71, the younger Hull ripped 40 goals as the Black Hawks' second-line left winger. Meanwhile, older brother Bobby Hull was filling the net with 44 goals of his own, giving the NHL a first: brothers with 40-plus-goal seasons in the same year.

- After a 21-15-14 start, Al Arbour is replaced as Blues coach by Scotty Bowman. St. Louis goes on to finish second in the West Division.

- Bobby Clarke emerges as a star, as he notches 63 points and leads Philadelphia to a third-place finish.

- Minnesota boasts a pair of 34-goal scorers—Danny Grant and Bill Goldsworthy—and claims the final playoff spot.

- The Kings have five 20-goal scorers but fail to make the playoffs, as they finish sixth in the West.

- Andy Bathgate comes out of retirement but scores just 15 goals for the Penguins, who drop to sixth place in the West.

- The last-place Seals (now known as the California Seals) give up the NHL's most goals (320).

Gil Perreault

Sabres Draft a Great One in Perreault

Most expansion teams in NHL history have begun with one distinct disadvantage: the lack of a franchise player. The Buffalo Sabres, who debuted in October 1970, did not suffer this indignity thanks to the astute scouting of their management staff, which picked Gil Perreault first overall in the 1970 Amateur Draft. A splendid skater with endless offensive talent, Perreault won the Calder Trophy after leading the Sabres in goals (38) and points (72).

Gilles Villemure, Emile Francis, Ed Giacomin

Giacomin, Villemure Share Vezina

The Rangers were the second-best team in hockey during the 1970-71 season, winning 49 games and boasting the game's top goaltending tandem—Eddie Giacomin and Gilles Villemure. The two netminders helped give G.M./coach Emile Francis one of his most successful seasons as an NHL executive. Giacomin and Villemure won the Vezina Trophy with goals-against averages of 2.16 and 2.30, respectively.

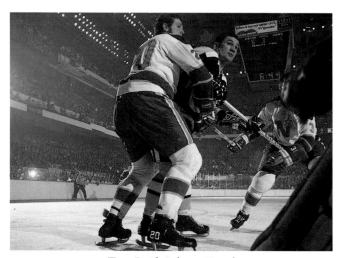

Tom Reid, Johnny Bucyk

Bucyk's 51 Get Lost in the Shuffle

The 1970-71 Bruins set an NHL record when they filled enemy nets 399 times. Overshadowed by the brilliant work of Phil Esposito and Bobby Orr was the 51-goal performance of future Hall of Fame left winger Johnny Bucyk (shown battling Minnesota's Tom Reid for position in front of the North Stars' goal). The Chief played on Boston's second line and was the NHL's third-leading scorer (116 points). He earned the Lady Byng Trophy.

1970-71

- Three Bruins are among the top four goal-scorers: Phil Esposito (76), Johnny Bucyk (51), and Ken Hodge (43). Bobby Hull finishes third (44).

- The top five assist men are Bruins: Bobby Orr (102), Phil Esposito (76), Johnny Bucyk (65), Ken Hodge (62), and Wayne Cashman (58).

- Chicago's Keith Magnuson leads in PIM (a record 291).

- Jacques Plante leads the league in GAA (1.88), while Eddie Giacomin tops the NHL with eight shutouts.

- In the playoffs, the Bruins suffer a seven-game upset at the hands of the

Habs. Rookie goalie Ken Dryden sparks the upset.

- In the other East opener, the Rangers beat the Leafs in six games.

- In the West, Chicago sweeps the Flyers and Minnesota upsets the Blues in six.

Plante's Now a Leaf; Leads NHL in GAA

At the age of 41, Jacques Plante proved he wasn't through shining in the NHL. St. Louis sold Plante, owner of six Stanley Cup rings (but none in the two years the Blues went to the Finals), to Toronto prior to the 1970-71 season. He proceeded to win 24 times in 40 games, and his 1.88 goals-against average was the best in the league. Plante pushed the Leafs back into the playoffs, but they fell to the Rangers in the first round.

Jacques Plante

Players Honor Espo with New Pearson Award

While the voting for the league's Hart Trophy (NHL MVP) remained with the members of the Professional Hockey Writers' Association, a new award was established in the name of former Canadian Prime Minister Lester B. Pearson. The new trophy would go to the NHLer who the players voted the best in the league. The Lester B. Pearson Award would become a prestigious honor. The first one went to Phil Esposito in 1971.

Lester B. Pearson Award

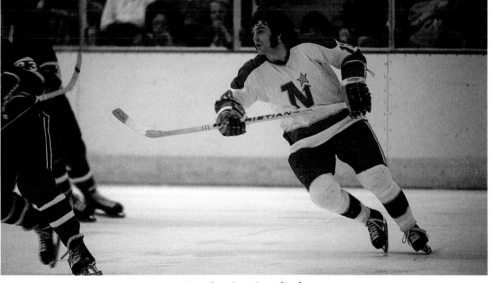

Stanley Cup Semifinals

Habs Shoot Down Stars in Cup Semifinals

After dispatching the heavily favored Bruins in seven games during the opening round of the 1971 playoffs, the Canadiens took on Minnesota in a semifinals shootout. Montreal won by scores of 7-2, 6-3, and 6-1, while the Stars won with scores of 6-3 and 5-2. Finally, the Habs knuckled down and won the series with a 3-2 win in Game 6. Jude Drouin (pictured) was a leader for Minnesota with 12 points in 12 games.

• In a new playoff format, the Habs face Minnesota in the semifinals (instead of their division-rival Rangers), and oust the Stars in six.

• The Rangers and Chicago battle tooth and nail in the semifinals. The Hawks take Game 5 in O.T. before New York evens it with a triple-O.T.

win in Game 6, thanks to a Pete Stemkowski goal. The Hawks take Game 7 4-2.

• Game 1 of the Finals is tied 1-1 through one period of O.T. Chicago's Jim Pappin converts Stan Mikita's pass to win the game 2-1.

• Lou Angotti's pair of third-period goals in Game 2 give the Hawks their 5-3 margin of victory.

• Back in Montreal for Game 3, the Habs overcome a 2-0 deficit with four unanswered goals—three from the Mahovlich brothers plus Yvan Cournoyer's winner—for a 4-2 victory.

Rangers Can't Overcome Chicago's D

After winning a hard-fought, six-game series with Toronto, the Rangers ran into the Black Hawks in the 1971 semifinals. In a battle between the offense of the Rangers (symbolized by Jean Ratelle, #19) and the gritty defense of the Black Hawks (led by Keith Magnuson, #3, and goalie Tony Esposito, #35), the Hawks won in seven games, handing the Rangers a crushing series defeat.

Stanley Cup Semifinals

Jean Beliveau

Classy Vets Lead Montreal to Stanley Cup

By the time the Canadiens won the 1971 Stanley Cup, it was clear that the new regime—most prominently Ken Dryden in goal and Guy Lafleur, who was about to make his NHL debut—was well-prepared to carry the club into the future. Still, members of the old guard, such as Jean Beliveau and Frank Mahovlich, were still making noise. Beliveau had 22 playoff points in 1971, his last NHL season.

1970-71

• Yvan Cournoyer's two goals in Game 4 put the match out of reach, as the Habs even the series with a convincing 5-2 pasting of the Hawks at the Forum.

• Dennis Hull's first-period goal in Game 5 proves the winner, as Tony Esposito blanks the Habs 2-0.

• Down 3-2 entering the third period of Game 6, the Habs rally as Frank Mahovlich ties the game at 5:10 and Pete Mahovlich wins it (on a pass from Frank) less than four minutes later.

• In Game 7, Montreal overcomes a two-goal deficit on a goal by Jacques

Lemaire and two by Henri Richard to win 3-2. The Canadiens thus grab their fifth Stanley Cup in seven years.

• Habs goalie Ken Dryden wins the Conn Smythe Trophy.

• Phil Esposito wins the first Lester B. Pearson Award. It's given to the

Stanley Cup Finals

Habs Put the Wraps on Golden Jet

No team ever truly believed it could stop Bobby Hull, but one of the keys to the Canadiens' seven-game victory against Chicago in the 1971 Finals was their successful containment of the Golden Jet. Here, J.C. Tremblay (#3) and Rejean Houle (right) wrap up the Hawks' superstar. While Hull finished the playoffs with 11 goals and 25 points (second to Frank Mahovlich's 14 goals and 27 points), he scored only three goals in the Finals.

Henri Richard

NHL Cracks Down on Curvy Sticks

The NHL, in an effort to reduce injuries to goalies, established a limit on the amount of curve a player could put to the blade of his stick. Because of pioneers Bobby Hull (whose stick is pictured) and Stan Mikita, who invented the "banana" blade stick that caused slapshots to become all-the-more deadly for their erratic flight, the NHL put a half-inch limit on the amount of bend allowed on the blade (from heel to toe).

Bobby Hull's Stick

Richard Nets the Cup Clincher

The 1971 Stanley Cup Finals between Chicago and Montreal were a nail-biting, thrill-a-minute roller-coaster ride featuring brilliant goaltending—Tony Esposito for the Hawks and rookie Ken Dryden for the Habs—and the heroics of veteran center Henri Richard. In Game 7 at Chicago Stadium, after the Habs fell behind 2-0 early, Richard tied the game late in the second period and scored the Cup-clinching goal in the third period.

NHL's outstanding player as selected by the players themselves.

• Bobby Orr wins both the Hart Trophy and Norris Trophy.

• John Bucyk wins the Lady Byng Trophy, while Buffalo's Gil Perreault takes the Calder Trophy.

• Rangers Eddie Giacomin and Gilles Villemure share the Vezina Trophy while teammate Jean Ratelle claims the Masterton.

• Quebec wins the Memorial Cup as its star, Guy Lafleur, leads the Quebec junior league in scoring.

• Boston University claims the NCAA championship, defeating Minnesota 4-2 in the finals. B.U. goalie Dan Brady wins the tournament's MVP award.

• The Soviet Union wins its record ninth straight world championship.

PARK'S GOOD BUT HE'S NO ORR; BOSTON WINS THE CUP

Determined to regain the Stanley Cup, the Bruins regrouped in 1971-72 behind Bobby Orr and Phil Esposito, who again rampaged through enemy defenses. For the second straight year, Esposito and Orr finished 1-2 in the league in scoring. Once again, Boston sped to the top of the heap (54-13-11), and only overtures from a proposed new major league—dubbed the World Hockey Association—distracted observers from the bewildering Bostonians.

Although the WHA had not actually organized a schedule, it laid out a heavily franchised circuit for 1972-73 and warned the NHL that it would freely raid its rosters. Of course, the well-stocked Bruins would be a WHA target, and already there was talk of fabulous offers being made to Esposito and Ted Green.

Interestingly, Orr's name was omitted from such talk, as it was just assumed that Bobby would never leave Boston. The loss of Orr would have sparked a revolt in Beantown worse than the Boston Tea Party. "Bobby had become the best player in the world," said Hall of Fame referee Bill Chadwick.

As powerful as Orr's Bruins had become, they nevertheless had a worthy challenger in New York. In addition to the GAG (Goal-A-Game) Line of Rod Gilbert, Vic Hadfield, and Jean Ratelle, the Rangers had a competitive goalie in Ed Giacomin and a clever defense. But most of all, the Blueshirts had Brad Park, the league's second-best defenseman.

Though less flamboyant than Orr, Park was more competent in other ways. Brad was a better body-checker, a more accomplished stick-handler in close to his body, and more creative in some ways on the attack. Park's only problems were that he lacked Orr's starry supporting cast and that he played for a less physical team, one that could be intimidated. "We get pushed around too much," confirmed Gilbert.

Despite these shortcomings, the Rangers finished at 48-17-13 and were given a shot at making the Finals. And that they did. They ousted Montreal in the quarterfinals four games to two, then swept Chicago in four semifinal games. Boston easily reached the Stanley Cup Finals by beating Toronto in five games and the Blues in four.

In many ways, the Boston-New York Final was a battle between stars Orr and Park. Orr sparked the Bruins to 6-5 and 2-1 wins, and then Park took over and orchestrated a 5-2 Rangers victory in Game 3. Orr scored twice in Game 4, leading his club to a 3-2 victory. Park then turned Game 5—also a 3-2 result—in the Rangers' favor. Orr wrapped up the series in Game 6. He scored the opening goal and assisted on the second, as Boston blanked the Rangers 3-0 for its second Stanley Cup in three years.

When the postseason awards were announced, Park learned that he had finished runner-up for the Norris Trophy for the third straight year. Meanwhile, Orr proudly accepted his fifth straight Norris Trophy, third straight Hart Trophy, and second career Conn Smythe award. As good as Park was, he was no Bobby Orr.

1971-72

- In measures to reduce full-scale brawls, the NHL installs a rule to eject any player who joins a fight in progress.

- The Hall of Fame inducts five new members: Busher Jackson, Gordon Roberts, Terry Sawchuk, Cooney Weiland, and Arthur Wirtz.

- In the Amateur Draft, the Canadiens take QMJHL scoring champ Guy Lafleur with the first overall pick, while Detroit grabs OHA ace Marcel Dionne second.

- The Bruins go 54-13-11 and again lead the league in goals (330). Goalie Gerry Cheevers posts an undefeated streak of 32 games (24-0-8)—an all-time NHL record.

- Boston's Phil Esposito again leads the league in both goals (66) and scoring (113 points), while Bruin Bobby Orr tops the NHL in assists (80) and is second in scoring (117).

Bobby Orr, shown hauling the puck around Gerry Cheevers' cage while Ranger center Walt Tkaczuk gives chase, carried the Bruins to the Stanley Cup in 1972, notching 19 assists and tying Phil Esposito for most points (24). Orr, the playoff MVP, scored just five postseason goals, but four of them came in the Finals against the Rangers. His first-period goal in Game 6 proved to be the Cup winner, as Boston won the game 3-0 to clinch the crown.

• The Rangers finish second in the East, as Eddie Giacomin and Gilles Villemure win 24 games each.

• New York's GAG Line boasts the third, fourth, and fifth top scorers in the NHL. Jean Ratelle tallies 109 points, Vic Hadfield 106 (including 50 goals), and Rod Gilbert 97.

• The Canadiens bid adieu to retired superstar Jean Beliveau, but they say hello to new coach Scotty Bowman, who leads them to a third-place finish. Frank Mahovlich leads the team with 96 points.

• Yvan Cournoyer has a career year for the Canadiens, scoring 47 goals.

"Rookie" goalie Ken Dryden wins a league-best 39 games.

• Toronto gets 38 goals from Paul Henderson and finishes fourth in the East Division. The Leafs' Norm Ullman tallies his 1,000th point on October 16, 1971.

Yvan Cournoyer

Bobby Orr

Cournoyer Sparks the Powerful Habs

Speedy Yvan Cournoyer was the NHL's fourth-best goal-scorer during the 1971-72 season, ripping 47 goals to trail only Phil Esposito (66), Bobby Hull (50), and Vic Hadfield (50). Cournoyer played alongside center Jacques Lemaire (81 points) and left winger Frank Mahovlich (96), as Montreal posted the best third-place record ever (46-16-16). Seven of the eight recent expansion teams, with the exception being Minnesota, finished well below .500.

Mickey Redmond

Orr Wins Norris, Hart, and Smythe

In 1971-72, Boston defenseman Bobby Orr was still at the top of his game, leading the NHL in assists (80) and finishing second only to teammate Phil Esposito for most points (117). Orr captured his fifth straight Norris Trophy and his third straight Hart Trophy, becoming the first player ever to achieve the latter feat. In the spring, he won his second Conn Smythe Trophy thanks to 24 playoff points.

Wings' Redmond Deal Pays Off Big

The Canadiens gave up a budding superstar in Mickey Redmond when they acquired aging star Frank Mahovlich from Detroit in the midst of the 1970-71 season. By the end of his first full year in Motown, Redmond—a hard-shooting right winger with speed and moves—had proven that Detroit's gamble was worth it. In 1971-72, Redmond tallied 42 goals and 70 points, trailing only Marcel Dionne (77) in total points for the fifth-place Red Wings.

1971-72

- Detroit, without Gordie Howe (who has retired after 25 years), wastes 42 goals from Mickey Redmond. The Wings finish fifth.

- The Sabres break in Richard Martin, who scores 44 goals playing alongside Gil Perreault. However, the team wins just 16 games.

- Vancouver wins 20 games (four more than Buffalo), but notches just 48 points and brings up the rear of the East Division.

- Chicago goes 46-17-15 and dominates the still-soft West Division. The Black Hawks yield just 166 goals, fewest in the league.

- Bobby Hull, in his last year with the Black Hawks, scores 50 goals. On December 12, 1971, he notches his 1,000th career point.

- The Minnesota North Stars, led by Bill Goldsworthy (31-31-62), rise to second place in the West.

Ken Dryden

Playoff Vet Dryden Wins Calder

Ken Dryden had only a half-dozen NHL games under his belt when he entered the 1971 playoffs and carried the Habs to the Stanley Cup. Anyone who believed the young goalie was flash-in-the-pan material was sadly misinformed. Dryden quickly established himself in 1971-72 by leading the NHL in wins (39) and finishing second in GAA (2.24) and shutouts (eight). Still considered a rookie, Dryden was eligible for and won the Calder Trophy.

Phil Esposito

Clarke's the Lone Bright Spot in Philly

Bobby Clarke

The 1971-72 Flyers won just 26 games and failed to make the playoffs after a tie-breaker gave the final post-season berth to Pittsburgh. But there was a significant reason for optimism: center Bobby Clarke, a third-year pro whose determination won him the Masterton Trophy in 1972. Clarke's 35 goals led the team, and his 81 points were 32 better than second-place Gary Dornhoefer.

Esposito Sticks In 66 More

The Bruins were the pride of the NHL during the 1971-72 regular season, chalking up 54 wins and finishing with 119 points. At the helm of their unconquerable battleship was the ultimate "immovable force," Phil Esposito. Espo, from his post in the high slot, banged home 66 goals—a more than respectable follow-up to his record-shattering 76-goal showing the year before. Esposito's 133 total points were enough for a second scoring title.

• The Blues employ three coaches— Sid Abel, Bill McCreary, and Al Arbour—as they hold on to third place behind Garry Unger's 36 goals.

• Pittsburgh, bolstered by the 30-goal performances of Jean Pronovost and Greg Polis, ties Philadelphia at 26-38-14. The Penguins make the playoffs because they had a 3-2 win-loss record against the Flyers during the season.

• Despite new coach Fred "The Fog" Shero and rising superstar Bobby Clarke (35 goals, 81 points), the Flyers can't quite make the playoffs.

• The two California teams, the Seals and Kings, finish sixth and seventh in the West, respectively.

• The NHL's top goal-scorers are Phil Esposito (66), Bobby Hull (50), Vic Hadfield (50), Yvan Cournoyer (47), and Jean Ratelle (46).

New Rule Tries to Prevent Major Brawls

The NHL was about to head into a period of unprecedented on-ice violence, as the Broad Street Bullies of Philadelphia prepared to establish their dominance with intimidation. In 1971-72, the league imposed an automatic game misconduct to any player joining a fight in progress, called the "third man" rule. It was hoped that melees—such as this one between New York and Montreal—would less often escalate into full-scale brawls.

Montreal Canadiens vs. New York Rangers

New York Rangers

Rangers Trio Nets a 'Goal a Game'

In 1971-72, the Rangers went 48-17-13 thanks the GAG (Goal-a-Game) Line. The trio included left winger Vic Hadfield (seated, wearing captain's "C"), right winger Rod Gilbert (to Hadfield's left), and center Jean Ratelle (to Gilbert's left). Ratelle (109 points), Hadfield (106), and Gilbert (97) were third, fourth, and fifth in NHL scoring, respectively. Hadfield became New York's first-ever 50-goal scorer, netting 50 exactly.

1971-72

- The top five assist-makers are Bobby Orr (80), Phil Esposito (67), Jean Ratelle (63), Vic Hadfield (56), and Boston's Fred Stanfield (56).

- With a mark of 1.77, Chicago's Tony Esposito boasts the league's best GAA in 21 years. He also tops the league with nine shutouts.

- Montreal's Ken Dryden is second in GAA (2.24) and shutouts (eight).

- In the East semifinals, Boston beats Toronto 4-1 and the Rangers oust the Habs 4-2.

- Over in the West, Chicago dispatches Pittsburgh 4-0 and St. Louis

ekes past Minnesota 4-3, winning the seventh game 2-1 on Kevin O'Shea's sudden-death goal.

- In the Stanley Cup semifinals, the Rangers sweep Chicago in four.

- The Bruins have no trouble with St. Louis in the semis. They sweep the

Richard Martin

Sabres Find Second Piece of Puzzle

In 1971-72, the second-year Buffalo Sabres won only 16 games—eight fewer than in their inaugural year. The good news was they added the second piece of what would become the French Connection Line when rookie Richard Martin, a Quebec junior scoring whiz, joined Gil Perreault on the team's top line and ripped 44 freshman goals. Martin was runner-up to Montreal's Ken Dryden for the Calder Trophy.

Watson's the Best Shadow in the League

Bryan "Bugsy" Watson's NHL career spanned 16 seasons and saw him wear the sweater of six teams (Montreal, Detroit, California, Pittsburgh, St. Louis, and Washington). In 1971-72, the man who was known as the league's most effective shadow led the NHL in penalty minutes (212). In 1975-76, while skating for the Red Wings, he tallied 322 penalty minutes while failing to score even a single goal. Watson finished his career with 17 goals and 2,214 PIM.

Bryan Watson

Tony O Posts Minuscule 1.77 GAA

Chicago goaltender Tony Esposito was getting a little tired of facing brother Phil's devastating wrist shot. "It's been the story of my life," he said. "Ever since we were kids." In 1971-72, Tony O (pictured guarding the post as brother Phil waits for the puck in his customary perch) posted a 1.77 GAA, the league's best mark from 1940-94. He also led in shutouts (nine) as the Hawks cruised to a West Division title with 46 wins.

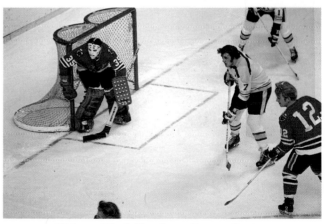

Chicago Black Hawks vs. Boston Bruins

series in four games and outscore the hapless Blues 28-8.

• The Finals pit New York and Boston. The Bruins win 6-5 in Game 1 as Ken Hodge scores a hat-trick.

• Game 2 of the Finals is a goalies' duel between New York's Gilles Villemure and Boston's Ed Johnston. The Bruins win 2-1.

• In Game 3 at New York, Brad Park and Rod Gilbert each score twice to lift the Blueshirts to a 5-2 win.

• In Game 4, Bobby Orr scores twice and assists on Don Marcotte's game-winner, as the Bruins steal a 3-2 decision at Madison Square Garden.

• Facing elimination in Game 5 at Boston, the Rangers overcome a 2-1 deficit on Bobby Rousseau's pair of third-period goals, sending the series back to New York.

Czechs, Not Soviets, Win World Title

The Czechoslovakian National Team captured the 1972 world championship title, briefly interrupting the reign of the Soviet Union, which otherwise held the title of world champ continuously from 1963-75. The Czechs later fell short in the 1972 Olympics at Sapporo when they lost to the Soviets 5-2 in the gold-medal round. Because of an early-round 5-1 loss to Team USA, the Czechs dropped all the way to third and a bronze medal.

Czechoslovakian National Team

Scotty Bowman

Bowman Takes Over Behind Habs' Bench

After winning the 1971 Stanley Cup, Montreal coach Al MacNeil resigned, unwilling to deal with the pressures of being an NHL head coach. The Habs turned to the man who had taken the Blues to the Finals in their first two years of existence, 38-year-old Scotty Bowman. Bowman's first year in Montreal was less than a stunning success, as the team lost in the opening round of playoffs.

Bobby Hull

Hull Pots 50 in His Last NHL Season

Without the fanfare and media attention that would have ordinarily attended such an event, Bobby Hull's 50-goal rampage against NHL goalies in 1971-72 effectively served as his unofficial "farewell" tour. Unbeknownst to hockey fans, the 15-year veteran—whose Black Hawks dominated the West Division—was on the verge of leaving the NHL to join the upstart World Hockey Association.

1971-72

- In Game 6, Bobby Orr scores in the first period and Gerry Cheevers slams the door on New York with a 3-0 shutout, giving the Bruins their second Stanley Cup in three years.

- Bobby Orr wins the Conn Smythe Trophy. He and Phil Esposito each tally 24 playoff points.

- Bobby Orr accepts his third straight Hart Trophy and fifth consecutive Norris Trophy. He's the first player ever to win three straight Harts.

- Jean Ratelle is honored with both the Lady Byng Trophy and Lester B. Pearson Award.

- The Vezina Trophy is awarded to Chicago goalie Tony Esposito and his partner, Gary Smith.

- Ken Dryden, the 1971 Conn Smythe Trophy winner, captures the Calder Trophy. He also finishes runner-up for the Hart Trophy.

New York's Cup Dream Ruined Again

The Rangers' playoff curse was never more evident than in 1972, when they were cruising toward a legitimate run at the Stanley Cup only to see their leader, Jean Ratelle, knocked out of the lineup with a broken ankle. New York, led by defenseman Brad Park (left) eliminated Yvan Cournoyer (right) and the Habs in six opening-round games. They then swept Chicago in the semifinals but, without Ratelle, couldn't compete with Boston in the Finals.

Boston Bruins

Espo, Bruins Polish Off the Rangers

Phil Esposito (#7) was all smiles when his Bruins beat the Rangers in Game 6 of the 1972 Finals to clinch the Stanley Cup—at Madison Square Garden, no less, adding insult to injury. Surrounded by his teammates (Ace Bailey, Bobby Orr, Ed Westfall, and Don Awrey, left to right), Esposito basked in glory after sharing the scoring lead (24 points) with Orr as well as the goal-scoring lead (nine) with teammates Johnny Bucyk and Ken Hodge.

Stanley Cup Quarterfinals

- The Bill Masterton Trophy goes to the Flyers' Bobby Clarke, a diabetic, who has established himself as the team's heart and soul.

- The QMJHL's Cornwall Royals, with future pro star Richard Brodeur in goal, capture the Memorial Cup.

- Boston University successfully defends its NCAA title, beating Cornell 4-0 in the finals. Boston goalie Tim Regan is tourney MVP.

- The Soviet Union wins the Olympic gold medal at Sapporo, Japan, beating Czechoslovakia 5-2 in the decisive game.

- Team USA, with future NHLers Mark Howe and Robbie Ftorek, wins the Olympic silver by virtue of its 5-1 win over the Czechs.

- The Canadians do not participate in the Olympics as they protest the presence of "professional amateurs" from Eastern Bloc countries.

The summer of 1972 left traditional hockey fans and professionals with a collective state of lockjaw, because of two exceptionally traumatic events. The first was the emergence of a baby major league, the World Hockey Association. The second was the truly fabulous eight-game series between the Soviet National Team and the NHL-sponsored Team Canada.

Days after the 1972 Stanley Cup series, agents from the WHA began combing NHL rosters in their efforts to sign players for the new 12-team league. By far the most decisive development occurred in June, when Black Hawks great Bobby Hull signed a 10-year, $2.75 million contract to play for and coach the Winnipeg Jets. Hull's move made front pages across the continent and promptly forced the hitherto smug NHL owners to sit up and take notice.

Hull's switch inspired other NHL stars to consider a change. A month later, Montreal defenseman J.C. Tremblay signed with the Quebec Nordiques, while Bruins goalie Gerry Cheevers left Beantown for the Cleveland Crusaders.

By now, panic gripped the NHL front offices. Fearful of being

SOVIETS, WHA PUT THE HEAT ON THE NHL

raided, the New York Rangers signed their better players to outlandishly high salaries. The more frugal Bruins lost Johnny McKenzie and Derek Sanderson to the Philadelphia Blazers and Teddy Green to the New England Whalers. The New York Islanders, who had yet to play a single NHL game, also lost several players—two to the aptly named New York Raiders.

Meanwhile, Team Canada prepared for the eight-game series—four in Canada and four in Russia—that supposedly would be a breeze for the NHL aces. "If we don't win this series in eight straight," said Montreal goalie Ken Dryden, "it will be a dark day for Canada, judging by the way people are talking."

There was little sunshine early on. On September 2, 1972, in the series' first game, the Soviets triumphed 7-3 at the Montreal Forum. "This," said one NHL official, "is the catastrophe of the century."

The NHL skaters rebounded in the second game for a 4-1 win, but the third game ended in a 4-4 tie. In the final game of the Canadian tour, the Soviets humiliated Team Canada 5-3, as the Vancouver fans booed the NHLers off the ice.

When the series resumed in Moscow, Team Canada rolled up a 3-0 lead in the first game, but the astonishing Soviets rallied for a 5-4 victory. "The Russians," said Dryden, "are not 20 guys dependent on a star to bail them out. They have an organized plan of attack that pays off."

Now it was Team Canada's time to rally. Trailing 3-1-1, the NHL skaters suddenly came alive and took the next three games and the series. Maple Leafs forward Paul Henderson emerged as the hero, scoring the winning goal in the last minutes of the seventh and eighth games. His game-winner with 34 seconds left in Game 8 filled Canadians with national pride. However, it couldn't erase the uneasy feeling that Canada was no longer the world's dominant hockey power.

1972-73

• The World Hockey Association is founded by Dennis Murphy and former American Basketball Association founder Gary Davidson.

• After scoring 604 goals in his 15 seasons in Chicago, Bobby Hull signs a $2.75 million contract with the WHA's Winnipeg Jets in June 1972.

• Among the NHLers who jump to the WHA are Boston's Gerry Cheevers, John McKenzie, and Derek Sanderson; Chicago's Andre Lacroix; and Montreal's J.C. Tremblay.

• The NHL adds the Atlanta Flames to the West Division and the New York Islanders to the East.

• The expansion Islanders use the first pick in the Amateur Draft to pluck OHA ace Billy Harris.

• The Hall of Fame inducts five new members, including Jean Beliveau, Bernie Geoffrion, Hap Holmes, Gordie Howe, and Hooley Smith.

As the 1972-73 season began, the Bruins lost several players to the WHA. Among the "names" to jump ship were Gerry Cheevers (pictured), Derek Sanderson, and Johnny McKenzie. Sanderson quickly returned to the fold after his contract with the Philadelphia Blazers went up in the same cloud of smoke that ultimately enveloped the franchise. Cheevers, who signed with Cleveland, stayed in the WHA for three-plus years before returning to Boston in the spring of 1976.

• Before the regular season, a team of NHL All-Stars plays an eight-game exhibition against the Soviet Union.

• Expected to ravage the Soviet club, the NHLers are stupefied when, on September 2, 1972, the Soviets prevail 7-2 at the Montreal Forum.

• With the series tied 3-3-1 and just 34 clicks left on the clock in Game 8, Paul Henderson crashes the net and bangs his own rebound past Soviet goalie Vladislav Tretiak to give Canada the series win.

• Johnny Bucyk notches his 1,000th career point on November 9, 1972.

• On November 22, 1972, Pittsburgh scores five goals within two minutes and seven seconds vs. St. Louis.

• On January 28, 1973, Detroit's Henry Boucha scores six seconds into the game at Montreal—a new NHL record.

WHA Drops Its First Puck in Ottawa

On the night of October 11, 1972, hockey history was made when the World Hockey Association made its debut in Ottawa, the capital city of Canada. The Ottawa Nationals, who would last only one season in the fledgling league, hosted the Alberta Oilers, who later changed their name to the Edmonton Oilers. The rival league, which many NHL patrons thought would crumble in a year or two, would actually last seven seasons.

Team Canada vs. Soviet Union

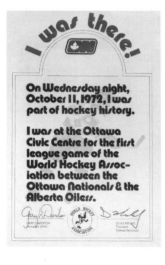

First WHA Game

NHL Stars, Soviets Go to Battle

An historic summit series between NHL stars and their Soviet counterparts was staged in September 1972. The Soviets stunned fans with wins in Montreal and Vancouver, while the NHLers (a.k.a. Team Canada) managed a tie in Winnipeg and a win in Toronto. After the Soviets won Game 5 in Moscow, the NHLers rallied for three one-goal wins (3-2, 4-3, and 6-5, all in Moscow) to capture the series, 4-3-1. Phil Esposito led all scorers (13 points).

Espo's Tops Again in Goals, Points

Despite falling to second place, 13 points behind division-champion Montreal, the Big, Bad Bruins continued to dominate the scoring charts in 1972-73. Phil Esposito knocked home 55 goals to lead the NHL. He added a league-high 75 assists as linemates Ken Hodge (37 goals) and Wayne Cashman (29) were his direct beneficiaries. Espo's scoring title was his fourth in five years, and he was runner-up for the Hart Trophy to Bobby Clarke.

Phil Esposito

• Frank Mahovlich records his 1,000th point on February 13, 1973, and his 500th goal on March 21.

• Montreal goes 52-10-16 to win the East by 13 points. The Canadiens feature a spectacular offense and the brilliant goaltending of Ken Dryden (league-best 2.26 GAA).

• The Bruins score one more goal than the Canadiens and finish second in the East. Phil Esposito wins the triple crown.

• The third-place Rangers boast seven 20-goal scorers. Center Jean Ratelle (41-53-94) leads the attack.

• The Sabres climb into fourth place, as Rene Robert joins Gil Perreault and Rick Martin on the French Connection Line. They score 105 goals.

• Mickey Redmond becomes the first Red Wing ever to score 50 goals when he nets 52, but the team finishes two points out of the playoffs.

Henry Boucha

Ken Dryden

Dryden Paces Goalies in Wins, GAA

Ken Dryden, whose lanky 6'4" physique and introspective demeanor often belied his intensity as an NHL competitor, began his stranglehold on the Vezina Trophy in 1972-73. Besides leading the NHL in wins for the second straight year (33) and winning the GAA title (2.26), Dryden led the Habs to a division title and was voted the game's top goalie. His Vezina Trophy was one of five he would enjoy over his brief eight-year career.

Boucha Scores at Six-Second Mark

Known as much for his tough, physical approach as for his abilities with the puck, Detroit's Henry Boucha (pictured with his trademark headband) nevertheless set an NHL scoring record on January 28, 1973. Boucha scored just six seconds into the game at the Montreal Forum, thus setting the record for the quickest goal in league history. Winnipeg's Doug Smail would shave a second off the record in 1981.

• Despite 37 goals from Dave Keon, the Maple Leafs fall to sixth place ahead of only the Canucks (who get 38 goals from Bobby Schmautz) and the expansion Islanders.

• The Islanders, who begin to steal fans from the Rangers, have a miserable first year (12-60-6).

• In the West, Chicago takes the division by a diminishing margin, edging out the Flyers by eight points.

• Chicago features the MPH Line of Jim Pappin (41-51-92), Dennis Hull (39 goals), and Pit Martin (90 points).

• Still ever-skillful, Stan Mikita notches 83 points for the Hawks in just 57 games, including his 1,000th point on October 15, 1972.

• The Flyers, led by Bobby Clarke (104 points) and Rick MacLeish (50-50-100), are on the rise.

Rick MacLeish

Billy Harris

Andre Lacroix

MacLeish Booms In 50 for Philly

Once a Boston prospect, Rick MacLeish never got a chance to show his wares in Beantown, but after his trade to Philadelphia (for Mike Walton) in 1971, he never looked back. A crafty skater with a booming shot and a relentless desire to score, MacLeish erupted for 50 goals in 1972-73, his first full NHL campaign. He thus became the first player from an expansion team to reach the magical half-century mark.

Harris Scores 50 But Isles Lose 60

The NHL expanded from 14 teams to 16 in the fall of 1972 with the addition of the New York Islanders and Atlanta Flames. The Isles, by virtue of a coin toss, won the right to pick first in the 1972 draft and opted for Toronto native Billy Harris, a brilliant junior scoring ace with the OHA Toronto Marlies. Harris' 28 rookie goals and 50 points in 1972-73 led all Islanders scorers, but his team set an NHL record with 60 losses.

Lacroix Wins the First WHA Scoring Title

The WHA burst upon the scene just as Andre Lacroix was reaching his prime. After five years in the NHL, he jumped to the Philadelphia Blazers, where he won the 1972-73 WHA scoring title. Lacroix, a shifty little centerman with plenty of moxie, notched 124 points and was second in assists (74) and fifth in goals (50). He won the assists title the next year, playing for New York in the ever-shifting franchise circus that was the WHA.

1972-73

- The North Stars are led by rugged Dennis Hextall (30 goals and 82 points) and finish third.

- The Blues finish fourth with Jean Guy Talbot behind the bench.

- The Penguins finish out of the playoffs for the fourth time in six years. L.A. can do no better than sixth, despite 37 goals from Mike Corrigan and 36 from Bob Berry.

- The expansion Atlanta Flames, with yeoman goaltending from Phil Myre and Daniel Bouchard, finish ahead of California.

- The league's top goal-scorers include Phil Esposito (55), Mickey Redmond (52), Rick MacLeish (50), and Montreal's Jacques Lemaire (44).

- Phil Esposito also leads in assists (75), followed by Bobby Orr (72), Bobby Clarke (67), Pit Martin (61), and Gil Perreault (60).

Bobby Hull, Reggie Fleming

WHA Lands a Big Fish—Bobby Hull

The NHL community was shocked and dismayed when superstar Bobby Hull jumped ship in Chicago and signed up with the WHA's Winnipeg Jets franchise for $2.75 million. Hull, shown tangling with former Black Hawks teammate Reggie Fleming, who was now a member of the Chicago Cougars, scored 51 goals and 103 points for Winnipeg, the West Division champs and runners-up for the league championship.

Frank Mahovlich

Mahovlich Reaches Major Milestones

As the 1972-73 season unfolded, Montreal left winger Frank Mahovlich continued to make the Red Wings look foolish for giving up on him in January 1971. The Big M scored 38 goals, notched a team-high 55 assists, and finished with 93 points—the second-best point total of his career—as Montreal won the East Division title. On February 13, 1973, he notched his 1,000th career point; on March 21, 1973, he scored his 500th goal.

Leiter Fires Up Atlanta's New Flames

The expansion Atlanta Flames fared much better in their first year in the NHL than did the New York Islanders, who entered the league with them in 1972-73. The Flames, who hired Boom Boom Geoffrion to coach the club, got a career year from 5'9" center Bobby Leiter, a former prisoner of the Boston farm system who came to Atlanta via Pittsburgh in the Expansion Draft. Leiter, who eventually jumped to the WHA, led the Flames in goals (26) and assists (34).

Bobby Leiter

- Phil Esposito grabs his fourth scoring title (130 points), ahead of Bobby Clarke (104), Bobby Orr (101), and Rick MacLeish (100).

- Philadelphia has four players in the top five for penalty minutes: Dave "The Hammer" Schultz (tops with 259), Bob "Hound Dog" Kelly, Andre "Moose" Dupont, and Don "Big Bird" Saleski.

- Twelve WHA teams begin play. New England, Cleveland, Philadelphia, Ottawa, Quebec, and New York comprise the East, and Winnipeg, Houston, L.A., Alberta, Minnesota, and Chicago make up the West.

- The New England Whalers march to a first-place finish in the East, as Tom Webster notches 53 goals.

- The Cleveland Crusaders take second place behind goalie Gerry Cheevers, while third-place Philadelphia boasts 33 wins from Bernie Parent.

Clarke Makes Headlines in Philly

Chicago's domination of the NHL's West Division dwindled in direct proportion to the rise of Bobby Clarke and his Philadelphia Flyers. In 1972-73, the 23-year-old center from Flin Flon, Manitoba, emerged as an NHL superstar when he notched 37 goals and 104 points. His wingers, rookie Bill Barber and Bill Flett, scored 30 and 43 goals, respectively, and helped Clarke earn his first Hart Trophy—as well as the Lester B. Pearson Award.

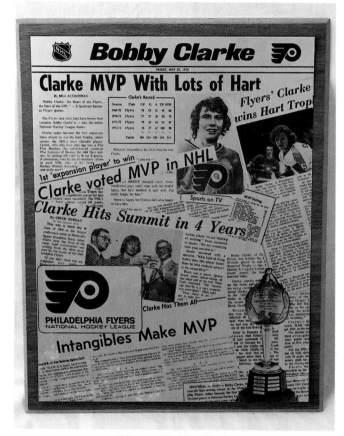

Clips on Bobby Clarke

Recreation of Super Series

Henderson's Goal Wins Super Series

Team Canada entered the final game of its Super Series with the Soviet team needing a win to preserve its status as the world's hockey power. Having fallen behind 1-3-1 in the series, the NHLers fought back to 3-3-1. In Game 8, the teams were tied 5-5 when Paul Henderson—whose late goal won Game 7—scored with 34 seconds to play to win the game and the series. This recreation, with Henderson raising his stick (far right), depicts the winning goal.

1972-73

- The Philadelphia offense is powered by Danny Lawson (61 goals) and Andre Lacroix (124 points).

- Ottawa finishes fourth, as Wayne Carleton leads the team in scoring (42-49-91). Maurice Richard coaches Quebec for two games before Maurice Filion takes over.

- Bobby Hull's 51 goals pace Winnipeg to a first-place finish in the West, while Gord Labossiere propels Houston to second place with 96 points. L.A. and Alberta finish third and fourth, respectively.

- The top four teams in each WHA division make the playoffs, and New England, Cleveland, Winnipeg, and Houston reach the semifinals.

- In the WHA semis, New England harpoons Cleveland 4-1 and Winnipeg jettisons Houston in four straight. The Whalers then beat the Jets 4-1 to take the championship.

Toronto Marlboros

Marlies Win Record Fifth Memorial Cup

Few Canadian Major Junior hockey programs enjoyed the reputation of the Toronto Marlboros, who in 1972-73 won the Memorial Cup for a record fifth time. The Marlies, once known as the training ground for the Maple Leafs, won the OHA title as Mike Palmateer (front row, far right) was the top netminder in the league. Several Marlies went to the NHL: Bob Dailey, Bruce Boudreau, Mark Howe, John Hughes, and Wayne Dillon.

Robert Teams with Martin, Perreault

Buffalo climbed past Detroit, Toronto, Vancouver, and the expansion Islanders in the East Division standings in 1972-73, as the third member of the French Connection Line—right winger Rene Robert—was installed. Robert combined with Gil Perreault and Rick Martin for 105 goals and 244 points. Acquired from Pittsburgh, Martin led the Sabres in goals (40). Perreault, the team leader in scoring, notched 88 points.

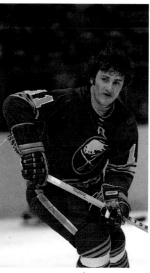

Rene Robert

Redmond: First Wing to Score 50

The continued excellence of Frank Mahovlich in Montreal—after Detroit had unloaded the aging superstar—had to hurt Red Wings fans, but the agony was assuaged by the emergence of Mickey Redmond, who, on March 27, 1973, became the first player in team history to reach the 50-goal plateau, a feat never reached by Gordie Howe in his 25 years in the Motor City. Redmond developed his "heavy" wrist shot by practicing with a metal puck in juniors.

Mickey Redmond

- Andre Lacroix wins the WHA scoring title (124 points). He's followed by New York Raider Ron Ward (118) and Philly Blazer Danny Lawson (106).

- The NHL playoffs see Montreal defeat Buffalo 4-2 and the Rangers blast Boston 4-1 in the East. In the West Division, Chicago disposes of St. Louis 4-1 and Philadelphia beats Minnesota 4-2.

- Montreal takes just five semifinal games to eliminate the Flyers, while Chicago upsets the heavily favored Rangers in five games.

- In Game 1 of the Stanley Cup Finals, Montreal strafes Tony Esposito and Gary Smith for eight goals and wins 8-3.

- Ken Dryden holds off the Hawks in Game 2, as Yvan Cournoyer scores a pair and the Habs win 4-1.

Flyers' Tough Approach Takes Them to Semis

Stanley Cup Semifinals

Fred Shero, coach of the Flyers, had a philosophy he insisted his players adopt: "Take the shortest, quickest route to the puck and arrive in an ill-humor." The tough-boy tactics worked in Round 1 of the 1973 playoffs, as Philly and Dave "The Hammer" Schultz (#8) pounded Minnesota into submission in six games. The Flyers even won Game 1 of the semifinals against Montreal, though the Habs' talent soon won out and Montreal prevailed in five games.

Stanley Cup Semifinals

Rangers Beat Bruins, Fall in Semis

The Rangers won 47 games in 1972-73 but finished only third in the heavily stacked East Division. After exacting a pound of revenge by eliminating the rival Bruins in five opening-round playoff games, New York—led by center Walt Tkaczuk (#18)—took on the Black Hawks, a tough defensive team led by rowdy Keith Magnuson (#3). The favored Rangers won the first game of the series but then dropped four straight.

Yvan Cournoyer

Cournoyer Goes On Scoring Binge

Yvan Cournoyer was a one-man wrecking crew in the 1973 Stanley Cup playoffs, scoring 15 goals and 25 points in 17 games. He scored six goals against the Black Hawks in the Finals, including the game-winner in Game 2 and the Cup-clinching goal in Game 6, breaking a 4-4 tie at 8:13 of the third period to send the Habs to victory and their 17th Stanley Cup. Cournoyer was voted the Conn Smythe Trophy.

1972-73

- Chicago assaults goalie Ken Dryden in Game 3, winning 7-4.

- Montreal silences the Chicago Stadium crowd with a 4-0 win in Game 4 of the Finals.

- Chicago exacts a measure of revenge with an 8-7 shootout win at Montreal in Game 5, as Stan Mikita and Jim Pappin each score twice.

- In Game 6 in Chicago, Yvan Cournoyer breaks a 4-4 tie in the third period and Montreal goes on to win 6-4. The Habs hoist their 17th Stanley Cup.

- Yvan Cournoyer, the playoffs' top scorer (15-10-25), is presented with the Conn Smythe Trophy.

- Philadelphia center Bobby Clarke edges Phil Esposito for the Hart Trophy. Clark also claims the Lester B. Pearson Award.

Stanley Cup Finals

Robinson's D Gives Habs an Edge in Finals

Although several of the games in the 1973 Stanley Cup Finals were shootouts (Game 1: 11 goals; Game 3: 11 goals; Game 5: 15 goals; and Game 6: 10 goals), the Habs actually used defense to gain a margin of victory over the heavily weaponed Black Hawks. Larry Robinson (#19, checking a Black Hawk by the side of the net) was a menacing physical presence on the Montreal backline, neutralizing the Hawks' attack in tight.

Hull's Heroics Fall Short in Cup Finals

Dennis Hull was the Black Hawks' most dangerous weapon in the 1973 play-offs, following a season in which he scored 39 goals and 90 points in his big brother's absence. Dennis (pictured battling behind the Habs' goal with Serge Savard as goalie Ken Dryden eyeballs the puck and Larry Robinson keeps the crease clear) scored nine playoff goals, but he couldn't lift the Hawks past Montreal.

Stanley Cup Finals

- Gil Perreault (88 points, 10 PIM) accepts the Lady Byng Trophy.

- Ken Dryden wins the Vezina Trophy over New York's tandem of Eddie Giacomin and Gilles Villemure.

- The Rangers' Steve Vickers, a 30-goal left winger, cops the Calder.

- Bobby Orr again accepts the Norris Trophy, giving him a half-dozen.

- Pittsburgh's Lowell MacDonald wins the Masterton Trophy, while Walter L. Bush Jr.—who brought NHL hockey to Minnesota—is honored with the Lester Patrick Trophy.

- The Toronto Marlboros win the Memorial Cup for a record fifth time.

- In NCAA action, coach Bob Johnson guides Wisconsin to a 4-2 title-game win over Denver. Badger forward Dean Talafous is named tourney MVP.

FIGHTIN' FLYERS BULLY THEIR WAY TO STANLEY CUP

In a matter of two years, the Philadelphia Flyers underwent one of sportsdom's rare metamorphoses. Though a patsy in 1971-72 (26-38-14), the Flyers emerged in 1973-74 as the most controversial, the most hated, the most respected, and the most colorful team since the Big, Bad Bruins of 1970.

This new group of Flyers went 50-16-12 in 1973-74 and stormed to a six-game thumping of Boston in the Stanley Cup Finals, thus becoming the first recent expansion club to win the silver mug. The Flyers were amazing, from their owner, Ed Snider, to their iconoclastic coach, Fred Shero, to their diabetic superstar, captain Bobby Clarke.

More than anything, though, the Flyers' reputation was built on sock. "If you keep the opposition on their behinds," said Shero, "they don't score goals." In 1973-74, the "Broad Street Bullies" spent 1,750 minutes in the penalty box—an alarming figure considering that no other team had ever topped 1,400 minutes. The Flyers were able to play shorthanded because they had the NHL's best goalie, Bernie Parent, co-winner of the Vezina Trophy and recipient of the Conn Smythe award.

High on the Flyers' superstar pole was young center Rick MacLeish, who scored 32 goals during the season and then tallied the only goal of the Cup-clinching game. Clarke provided the most offensive pop (35-52-87), while Dave "The Hammer" Schultz offered some "pop" of his own. Schultz spent a record 348 minutes in the box. "I get so worked up, I don't know what's going on," Schultz admitted.

What went on when the Flyers played was legalized mayhem. "In pro sports," said Shero, "the strong survive and the weak fall by the wayside." Purists denounced the Flyers as a collection of brawling no-goods. Enemies needled them as overrated phonies. And the NHL office warned them that they were treading on thin, punitive ice.

Though despised by many, the Flyers' gashouse style filled rinks from L.A. to Montreal. "After five years of arriving at rival arenas to the accompaniment of yawns," wrote Bill Fleischman in the *Philadelphia Daily News,* "the Flyers are now a genuine attraction. At nearly every NHL stop, people go out and boo the mad squad."

Detroit fans were fighting mad on February 28, 1973, when the Red Wings and visiting Flyers engaged in four major battles and 134 record-breaking penalty minutes. Detroit coach Johnny Wilson blew his cool after the game.

"Something should be done about this!" demanded the irate Wilson. "They're letting brutality get in the game. No team will back down man-to-man, but all that holding, hooking, and spearing doesn't make sense. You don't win games playing like animals."

They might not have been animals, but the Flyers did win games—and Stanley Cups (they would repeat in 1974-75). Years earlier, Conn Smythe had said, "If you can't beat 'em in the alley, you can't beat 'em on the ice." The Flyers had become living proof of that.

1973-74

- The Hall of Fame inducts five members, including players Doug Harvey, Chuck Rayner, and Tommy Smith.

- With the first pick in the Amateur Draft, the Islanders select Denis Potvin from Ottawa of the OHA.

- Gordie Howe ends his retirement at age 46 to play with his teenage sons, Mark and Marty, on the WHA's Houston Aeros.

- Habs goalie Ken Dryden "retires" for one year to act as a law clerk in order to earn his law degree.

- Vancouver's Wayne Maki dies of brain cancer at age 29. Buffalo's Tim Horton, a 24-year NHL veteran, dies in a car crash.

- A team of WHA All-Stars faces the Soviet Union in an eight-game series. The Soviets prevail 4-1-3. Bobby Hull leads all scorers with seven goals.

The Philadelphia franchise took a major step forward—as well as a philosophical step backward—during the 1973-74 season. On the plus side was the brilliant play of center Bobby Clarke and goalie Bernie Parent, who contributed to the Flyers' first league championship. On the down side, the Flyers' concept of team intimidation through thuggery gave the league a "black eye." Dave "The Hammer" Schultz (pictured) set a new record with 348 penalty minutes.

• Montreal's Henri Richard scores his 1,000th point on December 20, 1973, while Boston's Phil Esposito does the same on February 15, 1974.

• The powerful Bruins capture the East Division title (52-17-9). They crank out a league-leading 349 goals.

• Phil Esposito leads the NHL in both goals (68) and points (145) for the fourth straight year.

• The top four NHL scorers are Bruins: Phil Esposito, Bobby Orr (122), Ken Hodge (105), and Wayne Cashman (89).

• The Canadiens rely on the line of Frank Mahovlich, Pete Mahovlich, and Yvan Cournoyer (107 goals, 226 points) to take second place.

• Without Ken Dryden in goal, the Habs turn to Wayne Tomas (23 wins), Bunny Larocque (15), and Michel Plasse (seven).

Richard Pockets His 1,000th Point

On December 20, 1973, Canadiens winger Henri Richard collected his 1,000th career point, becoming the ninth NHLer ever to reach four digits. The 19-year veteran won the Masterton Trophy (for dedication) at the age of 38 and played just one more season before calling it quits. Richard retired with 11 Stanley Cup rings, more than any other player in history. (Jean Beliveau and Yvan Cournoyer had 10 apiece; Maurice Richard won eight.)

Mike Walton

Henri Richard

Knee Surgery Doesn't Slow Down Esposito

Recovering from major knee surgery in the off-season, Boston's Phil Esposito (pictured whistling for the puck) was right back in the fast lane in 1973-74. He lit the lamp 68 times, giving him three 60-plus-goal campaigns while no one else even had one. The Bruins were back atop the East Division as Esposito won his fifth (and last) scoring title with 145 points. He also captured the Hart Trophy and the Lester B. Pearson Award.

Walton Finds Solace in the WHA

Mike "Shaky" Walton never received the respect he deserved in the NHL, despite scoring 30 goals for the 1967-68 Maple Leafs and 28 more for the 1971-72 Stanley Cup champion Bruins. In 1973-74, Walton jumped to the WHA's Minnesota Fighting Saints and won a league scoring title with 57 goals and 117 points. A dazzling playmaker loved by fans wherever he played, Walton skated for five NHL teams and notched 201 NHL goals.

Phil Esposito

1973-74

- The high-powered, high-salaried Rangers feature eight 20-goal scorers, but the team finishes a distant third in the East.

- Coach Red Kelly's Maple Leafs earn a playoff spot. Darryl Sittler emerges as the team's scoring leader (38 goals, 84 points).

- The Sabres drop to fifth place despite Rick Martin's 52 goals.

- Alex Delvecchio becomes coach of the Red Wings, who finish sixth.

- Gary Smith leads the NHL in losses (33) for the seventh-place Canucks.

- The New York Islanders hire Al Arbour as their new coach and finish last (19-41-18) in the East.

- In the West Division, the Flyers finish first (50-16-12) with a mix of skill and toughness. They are tabbed the "Broad Street Bullies."

Houston Aeros

Howe Leads Houston to WHA Title

At age 46, Gordie Howe (left) was coaxed out of retirement, four years after retiring from the NHL, to play with teenaged sons Mark (wearing helmet) and Marty on the Houston Aeros of the WHA. The Aeros won the West Division in 1973-74, as the Howe trio combined for 73 goals and 203 points. With Gordie and Mark on the forward line and Marty on defense, the Aeros captured the Avco Trophy. Gordie was named league MVP.

Parent Wins a Record 47 Games

Flyers goalie Bernie Parent (pictured holding fort against Rangers Jean Ratelle, #19, and Steve Vickers, #8) emerged as an NHL superstar in 1973-74, when he led the league in wins (an all-time record 47), GAA (1.89), and shutouts (12). Despite these extraordinary numbers, he shared the Vezina Trophy with Black Hawk Tony Esposito (34 wins and a 2.04 GAA), marking the only time that goalies from different teams shared the Vezina.

Avco Trophy Not Quite the Stanley Cup

The WHA's playoff trophy, donated in 1973-74, was antiseptically named the Avco World Trophy after a deal was cut with the Avco Financial Services Company. Reportedly, the company paid just $500 for the honor of having its name on the piece of hardware. The Avco Trophy bore a conspicuous resemblance to the NHL's fabled Stanley Cup, but it would always remain a poor second cousin to the grand master of all awards.

Avco Trophy

Philadelphia Flyers vs. New York Rangers

• Bernie Parent returns to the NHL with the Flyers and leads the league in wins (47, an NHL record), GAA (1.89), and shutouts (12).

• Philly features four 30-goal scorers: Bobby Clarke (35), Bill Barber (34), Ross Lonsberry (34), and Rick MacLeish (32).

• The Chicago Black Hawks fall to second in the West despite 34 victories from goalie Tony Esposito and 80 points from Stan Mikita.

• The L.A. Kings climb to .500 on the shoulders of 5'9" center Butch Goring (28 goals, 61 points) and netminder Rogie Vachon.

• Rookie Tom Lysiak leads the Atlanta Flames in scoring (64 points), as the second-year team qualifies for the playoffs with 74 points.

• The Penguins waste a pair of 40-goal seasons (43 goals from Lowell MacDonald and 40 from Jean Pronovost) and drop to fifth place.

Mickey Redmond

Redmond Bangs In 51 Goals

Detroit's fortunes continued to wane during the 1973-74 season as the once-proud franchise fell to sixth place and used a league-high six goaltenders. Among the few bright spots was the goal-scoring of Mickey Redmond, who moved to the team's top line with center Marcel Dionne. Redmond knocked home 51 goals and led the NHL in power-play tallies with 21.

Marc Tardif

Sharks Yank Tardif Away from Habs

The WHA, brash in its approach to raiding the NHL, continued to typify the anything-goes attitude of the early 1970s when the entire spectrum of established values experienced societal challenges. The Canadiens, hockey's monument to stability and honor, lost a major star when Marc Tardif virtually thumbed his nose at NHL tradition to sign a megabuck deal with the WHA's Los Angeles Sharks.

Orr Skates to Seventh Norris Trophy

Bobby Orr was head and shoulders above the rest of the league's defensemen because he could cover so much ice with his skating and change the course of a game with a single rush of the puck. His passing was never less than brilliant—as evidenced in 1973-74 when he led the league with 90 assists. In 1973-74, Orr won his seventh Norris Trophy.

Bobby Orr

1973-74

• St. Louis misses the playoffs for the first time despite Garry Unger's 33 goals, while the North Stars waste Bill Goldsworthy's 48 goals and Dennis Hextall's 82 points.

• Gilles Meloche, the basement-dwelling Seals' beleaguered goalie, ties for the NHL lead in losses (33).

• The league's top goal-scorers are Phil Esposito (68), Rick Martin (52), Mickey Redmond (51), Ken Hodge (50), and Bill Goldsworthy (48).

• Philadelphia's Dave "The Hammer" Schultz sets a new NHL record with 348 penalty minutes.

• In the WHA, New England takes its second straight East Division title, as Tom Webster (43 goals) and John French (72 points) spark an offense with nine 20-goal scorers.

• The Toronto (formerly Ottawa) Toros join the WHA while Philadelphia drops out. Toronto finishes

Denis Potvin

No. 1 Pick Potvin Cops the Calder

It didn't take rookie Denis Potvin long to establish himself in the NHL. Chosen No. 1 overall by the New York Islanders in the 1973 draft, Potvin scored 17 goals in 1973-74 and led the Isles in points with 54. A former star of the Ottawa 67s of the OHA, the husky defenseman combined rugged physical play with brilliant puck-handling and a cannon for a shot. In the spring of 1974, he was honored with the Calder Trophy.

24-Year Vet Horton Dies in Car Crash

The hockey world was deeply saddened by the death of one of its most popular members when Tim Horton, age 44, died in a car crash on February 21, 1974. A 24-year vet whose NHL career spanned four decades (1949-74), Horton's clean, tough style earned kudos around the league. "Tim was an All-Star on the ice," said longtime teammate George Armstrong, "and a superstar off it." Horton, who won four Stanley Cups with Toronto, entered the Hall of Fame in 1977.

Tim Horton

second in the East thanks to a high-powered offense led by Wayne Carleton.

• Cleveland cruises to a third-place finish in the East. Former NHL star Ralph Backstrom (33 goals) guides the Chicago Cougars to fourth place.

• Quebec, with Jacques Plante behind the bench, wastes 37 goals from Serge Bernier. The New Jersey (formerly New York) franchise teeters near extinction, even with Andre Lacroix.

• Houston finishes first in the WHA West, as the Howe Line of Gordie, Mark, and Marty registers 99 goals.

• Minnesota's league-best offense is led by Mike Walton (57 goals), as the Saints finish second in the West.

• Edmonton edges out Winnipeg for third place, as Bobby Hull notches 53 goals for the fourth-place Jets. Vancouver wastes Danny Lawson's 55 goals with a fifth-place finish.

Rick Martin

Martin's the Youngest to Score 50

The 1973-74 season marked the first of two straight 50-goal campaigns for Buffalo left winger Rick Martin. One-third of the famed French Connection Line, Martin made up for linemates Gil Perreault (who missed 23 games due to injury) and Rene Robert (who slumped badly, scoring only 21 goals). On April 7, 1974, the 22-year-old Martin became the youngest player in NHL history to reach the 50-goal mark (he finished with 52).

Hodge Nets 50 in His Biggest Year

Ken Hodge played 13 seasons in the NHL—most of them as Phil Esposito's right winger—and none were more productive than the 1973-74 campaign. He scored 50 goals and equaled his personal high for points in a season with 105. Hodge later became the focus in one of hockey's most lopsided trades ever. In 1976, the over-the-hill Hodge was traded to the Rangers for up-and-coming superstar Rick Middleton.

Ken Hodge

1973-74

• Mike Walton (117 points) wins the WHA scoring title, finishing ahead of Andre Lacroix (111) and Gordie Howe (100).

• In the WHA playoffs, Houston beats Winnipeg 4-0 and Minnesota 4-2, while Chicago ousts New England 4-3 and Toronto 4-3.

• The WHA finals are never in doubt, as the Houston Aeros outscore Chicago 22-9 in a four-game sweep.

• In the NHL playoffs, the Bruins sweep Toronto while the Rangers eliminate Montreal in the East. Chicago skates past L.A. and the Flyers brawl past Atlanta in the West.

• Down 2-1 in games in the Stanley Cup semifinals, the Bruins rip off three straight wins against Chicago to advance to the Finals.

• The series between the finessing Rangers and bullying Flyers goes to seven games. The hungry Flyers eke out a 4-3 win in Game 7.

Woeful Pens At Least Have One Good Line

The Penguins suffered mightily in the early years, finishing below .500 in their first seven campaigns. In 1973-74, they cost Ken Schinkel his coaching job after opening 14-31-5. Still, they enjoyed some explosive scoring from the Century Line of Lowell MacDonald, Syl Apps Jr., and Jean Pronovost. MacDonald posted a team-record 43 goals, Apps notched a club-record 61 assists, and Pronovost scored 40 goals.

Lowell MacDonald

New Adams Award Honors Top Coach

At the start of the 1973-74 season, the NHL announced the establishment of a trophy, the Jack Adams Award, to honor the year's best coach. The award was named for the legendary bench boss of the Red Wings (1927-47), the architect of their finest teams. He left the Wings in 1963 to become president of the Central League until his death in 1968. The first Jack Adams Award was presented to Philadelphia's Fred Shero.

Jack Adams Award

Minnesota, Michigan Tech Battle It Out

Since 1948, the University of Minnesota had been to the NCAA title game three times (1953, 1954, and 1971), and three times had come up empty in the clutch. In 1974, under coach Herb Brooks (pictured) and standout goalie Brad Shelstad, the Gophers took on powerful Michigan Tech and beat them 4-2. It was the first of three straight title games between the teams (Michigan Tech won in 1975, the Gophers in 1976).

Minnesota Golden Gophers

- In Game 1 of the Stanley Cup Finals, Wayne Cashman and Gregg Sheppard score first-period goals and the Bruins hold on for a 3-2 win.

- The Flyers and Bruins are tied 2-2 after regulation of Game 2. Bobby Clarke scores at 12:01 of sudden-death to tie the series.

- The Flyers win Game 3 at home 4-1, as Bernie Parent holds the awesome Bruins to one goal.

- Game 4 is tied 2-2 with only five minutes to play, but Philly's Bill Barber scores against Gilles Gilbert and Andre Dupont adds insurance as the Flyers win 4-2.

- The proud Bruins avoid elimination in Game 5 at Boston Garden, as Bobby Orr scores twice in a 5-1 cakewalk.

- Bernie Parent throws a 1-0 shutout in Game 6 at the Spectrum, as the Flyers become the first recent expansion team to win the Cup.

Bruins Kayo Esposito in Cup Semis

Chicago's hopes were riding high in the 1974 NHL playoffs, particularly after goalie Tony Esposito tossed a couple of shutouts against Los Angeles in the opening round. Against Boston in the semifinals, the Hawks took a 2-1 series lead when Jim Pappin won Game 3 in sudden-death. But the Bruins climbed off the canvas and won the next three games, outscoring Chicago 15-6, as Greg Sheppard and Phil Esposito provided the offensive thrust.

Fat Cat Rangers Fall to Philly

The Rangers were favored to win the 1974 Stanley Cup, but then they ran into the Flyers in the Cup semis. (Here, Bobby Clarke shakes off New York's Pete Stemkowksi as Joe Watson, #14, looks for the puck.) The Rangers, accused by their boss, Emile Francis, of being "fat cats," lost this bitter series in seven games. A turning point was Dave Schultz's attack on Dale Rolfe as the Rangers stood by and failed to rescue their overmatched teammate.

Tony Esposito

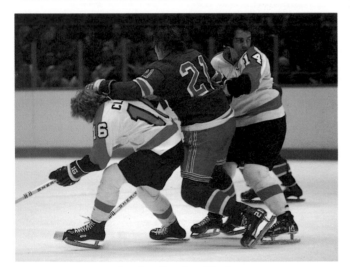

Stanley Cup Semifinals

1973-74

- Rick MacLeish, whose Game 6 goal is the Cup clincher, is the playoff scoring leader with 13 goals and 22 points.

- The Conn Smythe Trophy goes to Bernie Parent, with 12 wins, a 2.02 GAA, and two shutouts.

- On the strength of his outstanding goal-scoring—and his remarkable comeback from an injury in the 1973 playoffs—Phil Esposito wins his second Hart Trophy.

- Boston's Johnny Bucyk earns his second Lady Byng, out-balloting Pittsburgh's Lowell MacDonald.

- Philly's Bernie Parent and Chicago's Tony Esposito tie for the Vezina Trophy. It's the only time there has ever been a tie for the Vezina—or any major award.

- Islanders defenseman Denis Potvin beats out Tom Lysiak of the Flames for the Calder Trophy.

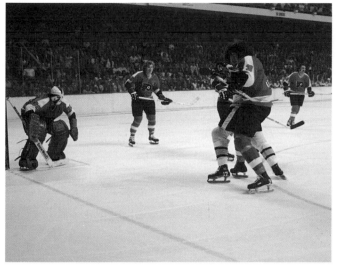

Stanley Cup Finals

Flyers' D Overwhelms the Bruins

The Flyers used physical intimidation and explosive offense to win their first Stanley Cup in 1974. Among the keys to beating Boston in the Finals was the Flyers' ability to clear opponents from the slot. Tom Bladon (#3, tying up Fred Stanfield, #17) displays his strength in the defensive zone. The Flyers matched their opponents man for man in every zone; forwards Rick MacLeish, far right, and Bobby Clarke are shown back-checking.

Orr's Magic Not Enough in Finals

Boston's Bobby Orr, winner of two playoff MVP awards, chalked up 18 points in the 1974 Stanley Cup playoffs, including a league-leading 14 assists. Orr (shown being held off by bruising Flyers defenseman Moose Dupont) had three goals—including the winner in Game 1—and seven points in the Finals. However, he couldn't carry his Bruins past the more balanced Flyers, who won the series in six games.

Smith Sings Her Heart Out for Flyers

Kate Smith's pre-game rendition of "God Bless America" became a symbol of victory for the Flyers. Her recorded version of the song was first played at the Spectrum on December 11, 1969. Philly won the game and Smith became the team's good-luck charm. She performed the song live at the Spectrum three times, and the Flyers won all three. The most famous occurrence came before Game 6 of the 1974 Finals. Philly won the game 1-0 to claim the Cup.

Kate Smith

Stanley Cup Finals

- Bobby Orr wins the Norris Trophy for the seventh straight time. Brad Park is runner-up again.

- The Lester B. Pearson Award goes to Phil Esposito.

- Montreal's Henri Richard wins the Masterton Trophy.

- Alex Delvecchio is among four winners of the Lester Patrick Trophy.

- Philadelphia coach Fred Shero wins the new Jack Adams Award, which is given to the NHL's top coach.

- The powerful Regina Pats of the Western (junior) Hockey League

boast MVP Dennis Sobchuk, who takes them all the way to the Memorial Cup title.

- Minnesota, coached by Herb Brooks, wins the NCAA title game 4-2 over Michigan Tech. Golden Gopher goalie Brad Shelstad is named tourney MVP.

ISLES FALL ONE MIRACLE SHORT ON WAY TO CUP

When the New York Islanders entered the NHL in 1972-73, an automatic rivalry with the cross-county New York Rangers began immediately. In addition to paying a handsome entrance fee, the new franchise was milked by the Rangers for further millions to cover territorial and television indemnity. Islanders owner Roy Boe resented the costs, but he had little choice but to pay through the nose.

The animosity was further aggravated by the Rangers' artistic dominance. The Broadway Blueshirts were one of the most powerful clubs in the NHL through the early 1970s and regularly trashed the Islanders at Madison Square Garden, as well as at the Islanders' Nassau Coliseum.

When the Islanders made the playoffs in 1974-75, for the first time ever, they faced the Rangers in a best-of-three opening round. Most observers expected the series to be a two-game sweep for the Rangers, but it wasn't to be.

Game 1 at the Garden began as expected, and after two periods the home club had built a 2-0 lead. But the Islanders struck back with goals by Billy Harris and Jean Potvin and it was a fresh

hockey game. Then, with six-plus minutes remaining, the Isles' Clark Gillies wristed one off the goalpost and into the net. The Islanders held strong and came away with the biggest win of their existence.

Game 2 at Nassau Coliseum was a penalty-filled affair that the Rangers won big, 8-3, to regain the momentum going back to the Garden. In the first two periods of Game 3, the visitors from Uniondale piled up a 3-0 lead, and 17,500 Rangers fans seemed prepared to throw in the towel. But Emile Francis' skaters still had the blood lust. They probed for Islander soft spots and found one when Bill Fairbairn beat Isles goalie Billy Smith.

Still, the Islanders led 3-1 as time ticked away. But at 13:27 of the third period, Fairbairn again

beat Smith. And then, with just 14 seconds to go, Steve Vickers pumped the puck past Smith and the game was tied 3-3. Rangers fans went nuts as the game entered sudden-death.

Sudden-death, though, was more sudden than anyone expected. Off the opening faceoff, the puck was sent behind the Rangers' net and retrieved by Islander Jude Drouin. Drouin passed it to an open J.P. Parise, who deflected the rubber past goaltender Ed Giacomin for the winning goal.

The Islanders had won the game 4-3 and the series 2-1. More than that, the three-year-old club was quickly thrust to the top of the heap. The Isles had earned the title "Hockey Kings of New York."

The Islanders proceeded to lose the first three games of their next series to Pittsburgh, but they rallied to win the next four and move on to the semifinals against Cup champion Philadelphia. Once again, the Isles lost the first three and won the next three, but this time they couldn't pull off the miracle comeback. The Flyers took Game 7 4-1, advanced to the Finals, and defeated Buffalo in six games for their second straight Stanley Cup.

1974-75

- The NHL expands to 18 teams, as it welcomes the Kansas City Scouts and Washington (D.C.) Capitals.

- The NHL realigns into four divisions: the Patrick and Smythe Divisions (Campbell Conference) and the Norris and Adams Divisions (Wales). Teams will play 80 games.

- The Hall of Fame inducts six new members, including players Billy Burch, Art Coulter, Tom Dunderdale, and Dickie Moore.

- The NHL imposes an additional minor penalty to any player who does not proceed "immediately and directly" to the penalty box.

- Using the first pick in the 1974 Amateur Draft, Washington selects WHL (junior) star Greg Joly, a future flop.

- In the Patrick Division, the Flyers dominate (113 points) while the Rangers (88), Islanders (88), and Flames (83) battle for playoff spots.

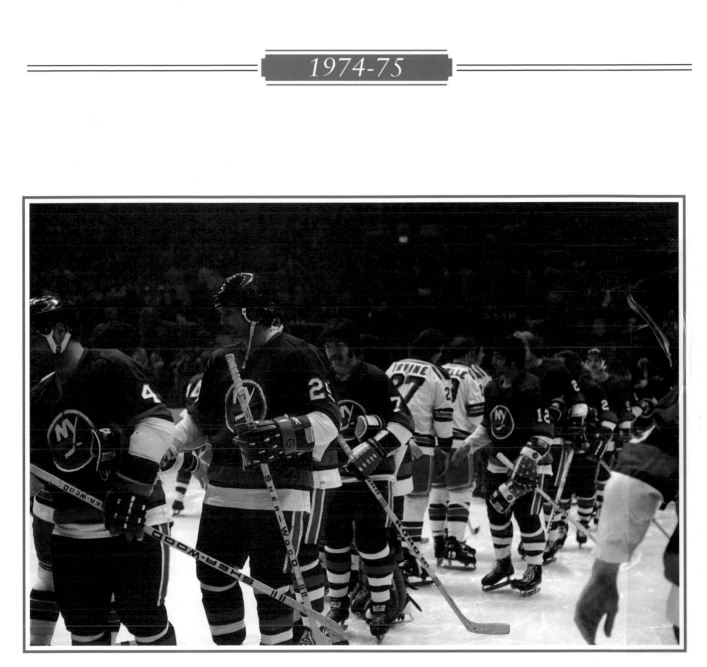

The new and growing rivalry between the Rangers and Islanders reached a new level when, in the preliminary round of playoffs in 1975, the upstart Isles upset the established favorites, winning the series-clinching game at Madison Square Garden, no less. As a capacity crowd hurled epithets down on both teams (hostility for the Isles, disgust for the Rangers), the teams called a temporary truce for the traditional post-series handshake.

- The Smythe Division is won by Vancouver (86 points), as St. Louis (84), Chicago (82), Minnesota (53), and Kansas City (41) follow.

- The Norris Division is won by Montreal (113 points), followed by L.A. (105), Pittsburgh (89), Detroit (58), and Washington (21).

- Buffalo wins the Adams title (113 points), as Boston (94), Toronto (78), and California (51) give chase.

- In Philadelphia, Bobby Clarke ties for the NHL lead in assists (89) as the Flyers win 51 games (tops in the league). Bernie Parent leads in wins (44) and GAA (2.03).

- The second-place Rangers trade Vic Hadfield to Pittsburgh, sign Derek Sanderson, and turn to Gilles Villemure for the bulk of the goaltending.

- Denis Potvin sparks the up-and-coming Islanders with 76 points.

First-Year Scouts Win 15 Games

The NHL expanded to 18 teams in 1974-75 by adding the Kansas City Scouts and Washington Capitals. The Scouts won only 15 games despite 26 goals each from Simon Nolet (front row, wearing captain's "C") and rugged 19-year-old Wilf Paiement (top row, fourth from left). The Scouts boasted one of the best names in hockey in defenseman Bart Crashley (top row, far left), but their woeful offense and defense gave fans little to cheer about.

Kansas City Scouts

Don Cherry

Cherry's Old-School Tactics Work in Boston

Don Cherry, known for his sartorial splendor as well as his pugnacious attitude and "old-style hockey" mentality, took over as coach of the Bruins in 1974-75 and guided them to a 94-point second-place finish in the Adams Division, one of four divisions in the newly restructured NHL. Cherry's Bruins continued the bang-and-crash style that earned them two Stanley Cups in the early 1970s, as Cherry stocked his lineup with tough guys.

Don Lever

Lever Shoots Canucks to Smythe Title

One of the most underrated players of his generation, Don Lever (the third player picked in the 1972 Entry Draft after a brilliant career at Niagara Falls) became a bona fide NHL sniper in 1974-75, when he led the Vancouver Canucks in goals (38) and was second to linemate Andre Boudrias in total points (68). Lever led the Canucks to first place in the Smythe Division. It was their only division title in their first 21 years of existence.

- Bernie Geoffrion steps down as coach in Atlanta, while rookie Eric Vail blasts 39 goals.

- The Canucks win their first division title thanks to Don Lever's 38 goals.

- Garry Unger leads the second-place Blues in goals (36) and points (80),

while Pierre Plante chips in an unexpected 34 goals.

- Stan Mikita, at age 34, leads the Black Hawks in points (86) while Tony Esposito wins 34 games.

- The North Stars win just 23 games despite Bill Goldsworthy's 37 goals.

- The Scouts get 26 goals from rookie Wilf Paiement and former Flyer Simon Nolet, but they win just 15 games.

- The Norris champion Canadiens, with Ken Dryden back in goal, win 47 games for coach Scotty Bowman.

Phil Esposito

Esposito: Lone Member of 60-Goal Club

In 1974-75, Phil Esposito celebrated his 12th NHL season by leading the league in goals for the sixth straight year. His 61 red lights were tops in a league that featured three other 50-goal scorers. To date, no other NHLer had reached the 60-goal mark to join Esposito, who had four years with at least 60 tallies. The lumbering center finished fifth overall in assists (66) and was second to Bobby Orr in points (127).

Bernie Parent

Parent's Tops in GAA, Shutouts

After sharing the 1974 Vezina Trophy with Chicago's Tony Esposito, Flyer goalie Bernie Parent won the award outright in 1975 after leading the NHL in GAA (2.03), wins (44), and shutouts (12). Parent was so magnificent, backups Wayne Stephenson and Bobby Taylor saw action in only 15 games between them. Flyers captain Bobby Clarke said of Parent, the MVP of the 1974 playoffs, "Bernie is the most valuable player in all of hockey."

Rick Martin

Sabres' Top Line Piles Up 131 Goals

The French Connection Line—comprised of left winger Rick Martin, center Gil Perreault, and Rene Robert—didn't just click in 1974-75, it exploded upon the league, accumulating 131 goals and 291 points. Martin scored 52 goals for the second straight year, while Robert scored 40 times and set up 60 goals. Perreault accounted for 39 goals and 96 points. The Sabres won a team-record 49 games and finished atop the Adams Division.

- Guy Lafleur emerges as Montreal's new scoring ace (53-66-119). His center, Pete Mahovlich, tallies 82 assists and 117 points.

- Former Ranger Bob Nevin (31-41-72) leads L.A. to its surprising second-place finish.

- The Penguins make the playoffs thanks to Jean Pronovost (43 goals), Rick Kehoe (32), Pierre Larouche (31), and Vic Hadfield (31).

- The Red Wings waste a 50-goal performance from Danny Grant and 47 goals and 121 points from Marcel Dionne.

- The Washington Caps go a horrendous 8-67-5, setting NHL records for losses, longest losing streak (17 games), longest road losing streak (37 games), and goals against (446).

- Caps goalies Ron Low (8-36-2, 5.45 GAA) and Michel Belhumeur (0-24-3, 5.36) hang their heads.

Hull's Numbers Zoom Out of Sight

As rivals in the NHL, Bobby Hull and Gordie Howe enjoyed many pitched battles for supremacy. In the WHA, Hull was the greater force. In 1974-75, the Golden Jet—now a Winnipeg Jet—scored 77 goals, a mark that would forever remain a WHA record. During his seven-year WHA tenure, Hull ripped 303 goals in 411 games, while the forty-something Howe managed 174 goals in 419 games.

Howes' Aeros Storm to WHA Crown

Houston dominated the WHA in the 1974-75, outscoring opponents 369-247 in the regular season and then sweeping Quebec in the championship series. Houston featured six players with at least 30 goals, including Gordie Howe (34 goals) and Mark Howe (36), and one 40-goal scorer—Frank Hughes (48). Marty Howe (pictured exiting the rink ahead of his father) solidified a strong defense.

Bobby Hull, Gordie Howe

Houston Aeros

Clarke Wins Second Hart, Second Cup

Bobby Clarke never won a scoring title (although he finished second twice), but he won the Hart Trophy three times, his second coming in 1974-75 when he led Philadelphia to a regular-season title. Clarke tied Bobby Orr for the assists lead (89) and topped the Philly scoring chart with 116 points. He then guided the Flyers through the mine field of playoff booby traps and led them to their second straight Stanley Cup title.

Bobby Clarke

1974-75

• In Buffalo, the French Connection Line (Rick Martin-Gil Perreault-Rene Robert) erupts for 131 goals. The Sabres set an NHL record by boasting six 30-goal scorers.

• Don "Grapes" Cherry coaches the second-place Bruins, as Phil Esposito leads the league in goals (61). Bobby

Orr is tops in points (135) and tied for tops in assists (89).

• Darryl Sittler's team-high 80 points help the mediocre Leafs finish third.

• The struggling Seals edge closer to extinction as their production falters. They win just 19 games.

• On December 22, 1974, Phil Esposito scores his 500th goal.

• On February 15, 1975, Yvan Cournoyer scores five goals as Montreal crushes Chicago 12-3.

• The NHL's top goal-scorers are Phil Esposito (61), Guy Lafleur (53), Rick

Gerry Cheevers

Ed Staniowski

Soviets Beat a Team of WHA Stars

In a WHA version of the famous 1972 summit series between the NHL and the Soviet national team (won by Team Canada), the Soviet nationals in 1974 took on an All-Star team from the WHA, led by goalie Gerry Cheevers, who was in goal for seven of eight games and notched a 3.43 goals-against. The Canadian team managed three ties and a single victory (at Toronto in Game 2), but it dropped the remaining four contests as Soviet goalie Vladislav Tretiak redeemed himself.

Orr Enjoys One Last Year of Glory

Nobody knew it at the time, but the 1974-75 season—during which he tied for the NHL assists lead (89) and won his second scoring championship (135 points)—would be the swan song of Bobby Orr's record-setting career. Orr took home an Art Ross Trophy, his first Lester B. Pearson Award, and his unprecedented eighth straight Norris Trophy. In 1975-76, Orr played just 10 games as his knees began to go.

Staniowski Wins Major Junior Award

The Regina Pats of the Western Hockey League (one of the three circuits making up the Canadian Hockey League, along with the Ontario and Quebec leagues) were the WHL reigning champs entering 1974-75. With goalie Ed Staniowski in nets, they were a favorite to repeat—until the Victoria Cougars unseated them. Nevertheless, Staniowski was honored with a prestigious award—the first-ever Canadian Major Junior Player of the Year Award.

Bobby Orr

Martin (52), Danny Grant (50), and Marcel Dionne (47).

• The top five point-producers include Bobby Orr (135), Phil Esposito (127), Marcel Dionne (121), Guy Lafleur (119), and Peter Mahovlich (117).

• Philadelphia's Dave Schultz sets an NHL record for PIM (472).

• The WHA realigns into three divisions: Canadian, Western, and Eastern.

• Houston, with Gordie Howe and sons, wins the Western Division.

• The Quebec Nordiques win the Canadian Division, as Serge Bernier (54 goals) and Rejean Houle (40) spark the offense.

• The New England Whalers repeat as Eastern Division champs, as Al Smith wins 33 games.

Expansion Caps Stink Up the Joint

The expansion Capitals of 1974-75 rivaled Watergate for the worst fiasco in Washington, D.C. The Caps went a shameful 8-67-5 and won just once on the road. Their goaltenders were Ron Low (pictured pulling an olé routine as Boston's Bobby Orr pumps one into his goal) and Michel Belhumeur, who posted records of 8-36-2 and 0-24-3, respectively. The Caps allowed an all-time record 446 goals and scored just 181 themselves.

Washington Capitals

Guy Lafleur

Lafleur Blooms in Montreal

In 1974-75, Guy Lafleur began to fulfill his tremendous potential, leading the Habs in goals (53) and points (119). The Flower, whose graceful skating was balanced by a lightning-quick shot, trailed only Phil Esposito for the league lead in goals. In 1970-71, this super-prospect scored 130 goals in 62 games for Quebec of the QJHL.

Marcel Dionne

Dionne Nets 47, Demands Trade

Detroit's Marcel Dionne spent 1974-75 proving to the NHL community that he was superstar material. The brilliant centerman lit the lamp 47 times and finished third in the league in points (121). After winning the Lady Byng Trophy for sportsmanship, Dionne ironically demanded that the Red Wings trade him— which they did, to L.A.

1974-75

• Bobby Hull, playing alongside future NHL stars Anders Hedberg and Ulf Nilsson, scores 77 goals for the third-place Winnipeg Jets.

• The WHA's top five scorers are Andre Lacroix (147 points), Bobby Hull (142), Serge Bernier (122), Ulf Nilsson (120), and Larry Lund (108).

• In the playoffs, Houston reaches the championship series again after series wins over Cleveland (4-1) and San Diego (4-0).

• The Quebec Nordiques reach the finals with series wins over Phoenix (4-1) and Minnesota (4-2).

• Houston outscores Quebec 20-7 in a four-game sweep to capture its second straight Avco Trophy—both by sweeps.

• In the NHL playoffs, a best-of-three opening round is added, during which Toronto beats L.A. (2-1), Chicago eliminates the Bruins (2-1),

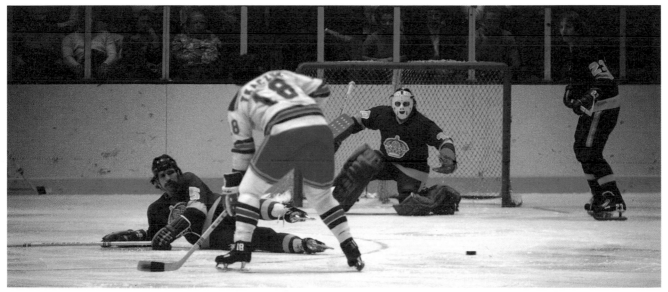

Los Angeles Kings vs. New York Rangers

Goalie Vachon Carries Kings on His Back

Once a star in Montreal, goalie Rogatien Vachon (pictured facing Ranger Walt Tkaczuk) found his way to Los Angeles via a trade. In 1974-75, he was the NHL's second-most stingy netminder, finishing with a GAA of 2.24. Though the Kings lacked a scoring star, Vachon carried the team to a best-ever 42-17-21 record. In the playoffs, Los Angeles fell in the first round to Toronto.

Dave Schultz

Schultz Sets PIM Record: 472 Minutes

In 1974-75, the Flyers were the NHL's best team, and its dirtiest. The Broad Street Bullies terrorized the NHL, and no player more typified their nasty approach than designated pugilist Dave "The Hammer" Schultz (right). While the Flyers soared, Schultz sank to new lows. He spent an all-time record 472 minutes (6.21 PIM per game) in the sin bin while scoring just nine goals.

the Penguins oust St. Louis (2-0), and the Islanders—in a significant series—oust the crosstown Rangers (2-1).

• In the quarterfinals, Philadelphia sweeps Toronto (4-0), Buffalo beats Chicago (4-1), and the Habs erase Vancouver (4-1).

• In an historic series, the Islanders overcome a three-games-to-none deficit to beat Pittsburgh.

• In the Stanley Cup semifinals, the Sabres shock Montreal in six games, winning the clinching game 4-3 at the Montreal Forum.

• The Flyers take the first three games of their series with New York, but the Isles again win the next three—as they did against Pittsburgh.

• The powerful Flyers win their Game 7 semifinal showdown against the Isles 4-1. They go on to face the Sabres in the Stanley Cup Finals.

Stanley Cup Semifinals

Isles, Flyers Duke It Out in Semis

The Flyers were well on their way to a second straight Stanley Cup when they ran into the Cinderella Islanders, who had shocked the Rangers in the opening round of the 1975 playoffs. Dave Schultz (#8), the chief goon of the Broad Street Bullies, lost this battle against the Isles' Clark Gillies, but the Flyers wound up winning the war. After winning the first three games and dropping the next three, Philly won Game 7 4-1 to advance to the Finals.

Ed Giacomin, Garry Howatt

Sabres Slide Past Montreal in Semis

Montreal's Serge Savard (left) may have gotten the better of this exchange with Buffalo's Gil Perreault (right), but Buffalo got the last laugh, deflating the Habs' hopes for another Stanley Cup by ousting the Canadiens in the 1975 NHL semifinals. Rene Robert scored in sudden-death of Game 5 to give Buffalo a 3-2 series edge. The Sabres then skated into Montreal and stole Game 6 4-3 to advance to the Finals against Philadelphia.

Stanley Cup Semifinals

Giacomin Pows Howatt in the Kisser

In a moment of historic transition, Rangers goalie Ed Giacomin, normally an even-tempered performer known for cool under fire, attacks Islanders superpest Garry Howatt during the preliminary round of the 1975 Stanley Cup playoffs. It was Howatt's first trip to the postseason and Giacomin's last. The Rangers, who were eliminated by the Isles in a Game 3 overtime thriller, were soon dismantled, with Giacomin waived to Detroit.

1974-75

- The Flyers win the first two games of the Finals, 4-1 and 2-1. The Sabres win Game 3 5-4 on Rene Robert's overtime goal.

- Buffalo ties the series with a 4-2 win in Game 4, but the Flyers respond with a 5-1 win in which goon Dave Schultz scores two goals.

- Game 6 at Buffalo is scoreless until Philly's Bob "Hound Dog" Kelly scores 11 seconds into the third period. Bernie Parent pitches a 2-0 shutout as the Flyers repeat as Stanley Cup champions.

- Bernie Parent receives his second straight Conn Smythe Trophy.

- Philadelphia's Bobby Clarke edges L.A. Kings goalie Rogie Vachon for the Hart Trophy.

- Bernie Parent claims his second straight Vezina Trophy, beating out L.A.'s Rogie Vachon and Gary Edwards.

Stanley Cup Finals

Flyers' D Carries Them to Title

During the 1975 Finals, the Flyers' defense was characterized by the toughness of Ed Van Impe (far left), the two-way mobility of Jimmy Watson (foreground), and the unparalleled goaltending of Bernie Parent, a two-time Conn Smythe Trophy winner. The Sabres, whose offense ranked second overall (354 goals) during the regular season, scored only one goal apiece in Games 1, 2, and 5 of the Finals and were shut out in the decisive Game 6.

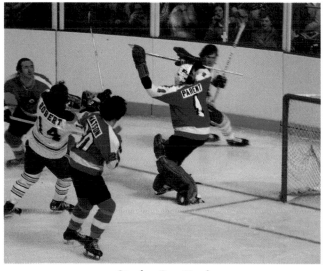

Stanley Cup Finals

Parent Foils the Sabres in Finals

Philadelphia's Bernie Parent was brilliant in the 1975 playoffs, sporting a 1.89 GAA. On the down side, he did allow Rene Robert (#14 in white) to beat him at 18:29 of O.T. in Game 3 of the Finals, and he also surrendered four goals in Game 4 as the Sabres tied the series. But Parent allowed only one goal in Game 5 (a 5-1 win) and shut out the Sabres 2-0 in Game 6 to win the Stanley Cup—and his second straight playoff MVP award.

- Atlanta's Eric Vail wins the Calder Trophy, edging out Pierre Larouche of Pittsburgh. Detroit's Marcel Dionne wins the Lady Byng.

- Bobby Orr sets an NHL record for consecutive trophies when he accepts his eighth Norris Trophy. Orr also wins the Lester B. Pearson Award.

- Buffalo's Don Luce is honored with the Masterton Trophy. The Jack Adams Award goes to Kings coach Bob Pulford.

- Led by OHA scoring leader Bruce Boudreau, the Toronto Marlies capture the Memorial Cup.

- Regina goalie Ed Staniowski is the first-ever recipient of the Canadian Major Junior Player of the Year Award.

- Michigan Tech trounces Minnesota 6-1 in the NCAA finals. Tech goalie Jim Warden is named tourney MVP.

CANADIENS TEACH BAD BOY FLYERS A LESSON

Hockey purists cringed at the prospect of Philadelphia's Flyers winning a third straight Stanley Cup in 1975-76. The Broad Street Bullies had blemished hockey's image, and NHL officials privately hoped that some club would beat the "bad guys" at their own game. But nobody believed that the Canadiens would be that team. Too often, the stylish Habs were bashed into submission by Dave "The Hammer" Schultz and his rough-and-ready mates.

"Even when we would play them in an exhibition game, they would try to beat us up, intimidate us," said Montreal's Jacques Lemaire. "That year, we played an exhibition and we brought up some fighters from the minors—Glenn Goldup, Rick Chartraw, and Sean Shanahan.... They didn't beat up on us that night."

Indeed, the 1975-76 Canadiens refused to be intimidated by anybody. Montreal favored artistry over mayhem, but when trouble erupted, big, skilled players like defenseman Larry Robinson would flex their muscles and tame the unruly opposition.

During the season, the Norris-champion Canadiens went 58-11-11 and excelled in every phase of the game. Guy Lafleur led the league in points (125), while goalie Ken Dryden won the Vezina Trophy. The Canadiens had no trouble in the playoffs, outclassing Chicago in four straight and then whipping the up-and-coming Islanders in five semifinal games.

Over in the Patrick Division, the Flyers took first place with a 51-13-16 mark. Captain Bobby Clarke led the league in assists (89) and won the Hart Trophy, while his teammates took care of the dirty work. Surprisingly, though, Philly was almost upset in the playoffs' first round. Toronto took the Flyers to seven games before succumbing 7-3 in the final match. The weary Flyers lost Game 1 of the semifinals to Boston, but they responded with a Game 2 win in overtime and then three straight easy victories.

And so the Stanley Cup Finals pitted the Canadiens and Flyers, the two teams with dramatically contrasting images. If ever there was a Good vs. Evil confrontation, this was it.

The "fight" began at the Montreal Forum in Game 1. The Habs fell behind 3-2, but Lemaire tied the score in the middle of the third period. With less than two minutes remaining, the Habs' Guy Lapointe scored the winner for a 4-3 decision. The Canadiens took the second game 2-1, and the teams flew to the City of Brotherly Love for Game 3.

The Canadiens took no abuse from the Flyers at the Spectrum, as they whizzed by such intimidators as Schultz, Andre Dupont, and Bob "Hound Dog" Kelly. Montreal won the two games in Philly, 3-2 and 5-3, and grabbed the Stanley Cup.

Most hockey fans, especially those in the NHL's public relations department, were delighted that the "good guys" prevailed and taught the bullying Flyers a lesson. Little did anyone realize, though, that they were witnessing the formation of yet another Canadiens dynasty.

1975-76

- The Hall of Fame inducts seven members, including players George Armstrong, Ace Bailey, Gordie Drillon, Glenn Hall, and Pierre Pilote.

- The Stanley Cup champion Flyers, who traded up for the first pick in the Entry Draft, use it to take center Mel Bridgman of Victoria (WHL).

- At his request, the Red Wings trade Marcel Dionne. He goes to Los Angeles for Dan Maloney, Terry Harper, and a draft pick.

- The Rangers retool with a series of astounding roster moves—including selling Eddie Giacomin to the Red Wings.

- On October 30, 1975, Boston's John Bucyk scores his 500th goal.

- On November 7, 1975, in one of the most shocking deals ever, New York ships Jean Ratelle and Brad Park to the hated Bruins for Phil Esposito.

Montreal was three years past its last Stanley Cup title when the 1976 playoffs began and it was clear that Philadelphia would be its chief competition for the silver trophy. The awaited showdown came in the Finals and, with the help of splendid checking from players like Jimmy Roberts (shown tying up the stick of Bill Barber, #7), the Canadiens stunned their rivals with a four-game sweep, winning by the slimmest of margins (4-3, 2-1, 3-2, and a whopping 5-3).

• On February 7, 1976, Toronto's Darryl Sittler racks up six goals and an NHL-record 10 points in an 11-4 beating of the Bruins.

• The Flyers (51-13-16) win the Patrick on the scoring of Reg Leach (61 goals), Bill Barber (50 goals), and Bobby Clarke (119 points). Philly sets a record for home wins with 36, including 20 in a row.

• After Bernie Parent suffers retina damage, Wayne Stephenson takes over in Philly and wins 40 games.

• The Islanders roar to a second-place finish in the Patrick.

Defenseman Denis Potvin leads the team with 98 points, while rookie Bryan Trottier tallies 95.

• The third-place Flames get 34 goals from overachiever Curt Bennett and an 82-point performace from Tom Lysiak.

Bill Barber

Boston Gets Best of Espo-Park Deal

The most dramatic trade in the history of the Rangers and Bruins took place on November 7, 1975, as All-Star defenseman Brad Park, award-winning center Jean Ratelle, and Joe Zanussi went to the Bruins for Phil Esposito and Carol Vadnais. The Rangers struggled even after Espo's arrival, but Park successfully replaced oft-injured Bobby Orr. Brad finished runner-up for the Norris Trophy in 1975-76 (for the fifth time).

Bobby Clarke

Barber Stars on Goal-Happy Clarke Line

On April 3, 1976, the Flyers' Bill Barber scored his 50th goal of the year against Buffalo's Al Smith, joining linemate Reggie Leach (who scored his 50th goal in March) as the team's top goal-getters. Barber, the left winger on Bobby Clarke's line, finished fourth in the league in points (112) and was the second-best plus/minus player in the NHL (+74). He finished his career with 420 goals in 12 seasons.

Brad Park

Tough-as-Nails Clarke Powers Philadelphia

Flyer captain Bobby Clarke, one of the toughest men ever to skate in the NHL, played despite a diabetic condition that required daily insulin injections. In 1975-76, he led the Flyers to a first-place Patrick finish with 119 points and an NHL-best 89 assists. Clarke was largely responsible for Reggie Leach, his right winger, leading the NHL in goals (61) and Bill Barber, his left winger, scoring 50. For his efforts, Clarke received the Hart Trophy.

1975-76

- Rod Gilbert's 36 goals lead the Rangers, as Phil Esposito finishes with just 35 goals and 83 points.

- The Black Hawks (32-30-18) win the Smythe Division by one point over Vancouver, as Pit Martin leads in scoring (32-39-71).

- Phil Maloney's Canucks enjoy a 37-goal season from third-year pro Dennis Ververgaert and win 33 games (best in the Smythe).

- The Blues go through three coaches and finish third in the Smythe. Chuck Lefley (43 goals) and Garry Unger (39) lead the attack.

- Minnesota and Kansas City bring up the rear in the Smythe with woeful offense and worse defense. K.C. goes 12-56-12 and uses three coaches.

- Les Canadiens (58-11-11) win the Norris by 42 points, as Guy Lafleur (56 goals), Steve Shutt (45), and Pete Mahovlich (34) lead the way.

Darryl Sittler

Sittler Scores 10 Points in One Game

Toronto center Darryl Sittler entered the record books on February 7, 1976, when he posted six goals and four assists, becoming the first player ever to score 10 points in a game. His six goals all came against Boston goalie Dave Reece (who would play only 14 NHL games) as the Leafs trounced the Bruins 11-4. No other NHLer has ever notched more than eight points in a regular-season game. Only six others have scored six goals in a game.

Lefley Stars on Turbulent Blues Squad

The 1975-76 season was a test of fortitude and survival for the St. Louis Blues. Despite the brilliant goal-scoring of former Montreal prospect Chuck Lefley, the team played just well enough to gain a playoff berth with a third-place finish in the Smythe, but poorly enough to get two coaches (Garry Young and Lynn Patrick) replaced. Lefley, a left winger with a cannon shot, blasted a team-high 43 goals and led the Blues in points as well (85).

Chuck Lefley

Marc Tardif

Tardif Wins a Tarnished Triple Crown

Marc Tardif, in his first full season with the Quebec Nordiques, recorded the WHA's first triple crown, leading the league in goals (71), assists (77), and points (148) in 1975-76. The 26-year-old left winger was so devastating, his performance even overshadowed the 60-goal output of teammate Real "Buddy" Cloutier. An asterisk sits beside Tardif's triple crown because 37-year-old Nordiques defenseman J.C. Tremblay also notched 77 assists.

• Montreal's Ken Dryden leads the NHL in wins (42) and GAA (2.03).

• Marcel Dionne, in his first year as an L.A. King, notches 40 goals and 94 points to lead the team to a second-place finish in the Norris Division.

• Pittsburgh climbs into third place in the Norris, as both Pierre Larouche (53) and Jean Pronovost (52) crack the 50-goal mark.

• Detroit fails to qualify for the playoffs for the sixth straight year. Walt McKechnie's 82 points are tops on the club.

• Milt Schmidt goes 3-28-5 coaching the woeful Washington Caps. Tommy McVie replaces him and goes 8-31-5.

• Led by Jean Ratelle (105 points), Boston (48-15-17) captures the Adams Division. Netminder Gilles Gilbert wins 17 straight games—an NHL record.

Bryan Trottier

Larouche Is the Youngest to Score 50

On April 3, 1976, the Penguins' Pierre Larouche notched his 50th goal of the year. At age 20, Larouche became the youngest player to reach the prestigious mark. He finished with 53. Teammate Jean Pronovost closed the campaign with 52 goals to give the club two 50-goal scorers, a feat that only Boston had accomplished prior to 1975-76.

Pierre Larouche

Trottier Gets a Quick Trick

Islander rookie Bryan Trottier, in a rare photograph without his moustache, holds up the prizes from the first of his 16 career NHL hat-tricks. Trottier, in his first NHL campaign in 1975-76, was the team's driving force as the Isles finished second in the Patrick Division. The former WHL junior star tallied 95 points and won the Calder Trophy.

Gare Scores 50 the Hard Way

On April 4, 1976, hard-shooting Danny Gare became the second player in Buffalo history to score 50 goals in a season when he beat Toronto's Gord McRae. A tough player with a quick temper and a quicker shot, Gare played much of the year on the checking line with super penalty-killers Don Luce and Craig Ramsay, but he still found the net with great frequency.

Danny Gare

1975-76

• The Sabres' French Connection Line (Rick Martin, Rene Robert, and Gil Perreault) notches 128 goals and Danny Gare reaches 50, as Buffalo finishes eight points behind Boston.

• The Leafs, on Darryl Sittler's 100-point season, finish third in the Adams Division.

• The California Seals bring up the rear in the Adams Division in this their final season.

• The NHL's top goal-scorers are Reg Leach (61), Guy Lafleur (56), Pierre Larouche (53), Jean Pronovost (52), Bill Barber (50), and Danny Gare (50).

• The NHL's top assist-makers are Bobby Clarke (89), Pete Mahovlich (71), Guy Lafleur (69), and Jean Ratelle (69).

• The top scorers include Guy Lafleur (125 points), Bobby Clarke (119), Gil Perreault (113), Bill Barber (112), and Pierre Larouche (111).

Denis Potvin

Potvin Usurps Orr as Game's Top Blueliner

A dominating force in the NHL, Islanders backliner Denis Potvin captured the Norris Trophy in 1975-76, ending the eight-year reign of Boston's Bobby Orr. Potvin, an intense competitor who was feared for his punishing physical play, also displayed excellent offensive skills. In 1975-76, he finished among the league leaders in assists with 67.

Jean Ratelle

Ratelle Tallies Up 105, Wins the Byng

Jean Ratelle was a pivotal player in the huge trade between the Rangers and Boston. He gracefully stepped into a Bruins uniform and finished the year with 36 goals and 105 points, the second-best point total of his 21-year career. Boston finished atop the Adams Division as Ratelle's production helped the Bruins to 48 regular-season wins. Ratelle captured the Lady Byng Trophy for the second time in his career.

Marcel Dionne

Dionne Becomes the King of Kings

Disgruntled with the performance of the lowly Red Wings, All-Star center Marcel Dionne demanded a trade. He got his wish prior to the 1975-76 season, as Detroit swapped him and Bart Crashley to Los Angeles for Dan Maloney, Terry Harper, and a draft pick. Dionne gave the Kings their first potent scorer ever, as he established L.A. records for goals (40) and points (94).

• Steve Durbano, who skates for the Penguins and Kansas City Scouts, takes the penalty crown (370 PIM).

• In the WHA, the Minnesota and Denver clubs fold while Vancouver shifts to Calgary. Cincinnati enters the league and Chicago exits.

• Winnipeg wins the WHA's Canadian Division as Bobby Hull, Ulf Nilsson, and Anders Hedberg combine for 141 goals and 342 points.

• Indianapolis, under future NHL coach Jacques Demers, moves from last to first in the East Division despite a 35-39-6 record.

• Houston leads the WHA with 53 wins. Gordie Howe, at age 47, leads the team with 102 points.

• The WHA's top goal-scorers include Marc Tardif (71) and Real Cloutier (60) of Quebec, Toronto's Vaclav Nedomansky (56), Bobby Hull (53), and Quebec's Rejean Houle (50).

Johnny Bucyk

Bucyk Quietly Scores 500 Goals

Boston left winger Johnny Bucyk celebrated his 21st season in 1975-76 by becoming the seventh player to score 500 NHL goals. On October 30, 1975, in a 3-2 win over St. Louis, the 40-year-old vet slipped the puck past Yves Belanger. Bucyk played seemingly his whole career in relative obscurity, as he suffered for a decade on miserable Bruins teams and then, when the team rose to the top, played in the shadows of Phil Esposito and Bobby Orr.

Shutt Scores 45 from the Port Side

In 1975-76, Steve Shutt knocked home 45 goals while skating the left wing on Montreal's top line with right winger Guy Lafleur and center Pete Mahovlich. While Lafleur won the league scoring title with 125 points and Mahovlich notched 71 assists and 105 points, Shutt—in his fourth NHL season—was the league's third-best plus/minus player, tying Philadelphia's Reg Leach with a +73 rating.

Steve Shutt

1975-76

- The WHA's top point-getters are Marc Tardif (148), Bobby Hull (123), Real Cloutier (114), and Ulf Nilsson (114).

- After ousting Edmonton (4-0) and Calgary (4-1), Winnipeg sweeps Houston in four games for the Avco Trophy.

- In the opening round of the NHL playoffs, Buffalo beats St. Louis (2-1), Toronto ousts Pittsburgh (2-1), the Isles sweep Vancouver (2-0), and L.A. douses the Flames (2-0).

- In the Stanley Cup quarterfinals, the Bruins oust the Kings (4-3), while Philly ekes past the Leafs (4-3).

Toronto's Darryl Sittler scores five goals in one game.

- Montreal sweeps Chicago in the quarterfinals, while the Isles need six games to do away with Buffalo.

- In the semifinals, Montreal crushes the Isles in five games.

Pittsburgh's Pronovost Knocks In 52

Jean Pronovost's 14-year NHL career reached its pinnacle in 1975-76. In his eighth campaign with Pittsburgh, the 31-year-old right winger ripped 52 goals, netting No. 50 on March 24, 1976, against Boston goalie Gilles Gilbert. Skating with Lowell MacDonald and Syl Apps Jr., Pronovost made excellent use of Apps' superb playmaking. Jean finished runner-up to Boston's Jean Ratelle for the Lady Byng Trophy.

Guy Lafleur

Chico Resch

Only Dryden Is Better Than Resch

As an NHL sophomore in 1975-76, Islanders goalie Glenn "Chico" Resch assumed a major portion of the team's goaltending chores and went 23-11-10. His brilliant 2.07 goals-against average was second best in the NHL behind Ken Dryden's 2.03. Resch tossed seven shutouts (second best behind Dryden's eight) and was a runner-up with partner Billy Smith for the Vezina Trophy, which was won by Dryden.

Jean Pronovost

La Creme de la Creme Rises to the Top

In the spirit of the Flying Frenchmen, Guy Lafleur excited Montreal crowds with his speed, grace, and scoring ability. In 1975-76, he won his first of three straight Art Ross Trophies (56 goals and 125 points), led the Habs to the league's best record, and scored the Cup-winning goal in Game 4 of the Finals against the Flyers. Lafleur was also the players' choice as player of the year, winning the Lester B. Pearson Award.

• Philadelphia returns to the Finals after thrashing Boston in five semifinal games (in which the Flyers' Reg Leach scores five goals in one game).

• The Cup Finals pit the Flying Frenchmen of Montreal against the Broad Street Bullies of Philly. It's a test of "good versus evil," NHL style.

• The Canadiens win Game 1 4-3 when Guy Lapointe converts a pass from Steve Shutt with 1:22 to go.

• Game 2 is a goaltenders' war, ending 2-1 in favor of the Canadiens on goals from Jacques Lemaire and Guy Lafleur.

• After the Flyers take a 2-1 lead in the first period of Game 3 in Philadelphia, the Habs come back on Steve Shutt's tying goal and Pierre Bouchard's winner.

• In Game 4, Reg Leach scores his 19th playoff goal, setting an NHL record.

Hull, Swedes Power the Jets to WHA Title

In 1975-76, Bobby Hull scored 53 goals in his fourth WHA season as his line (shared by Swedish stars Ulf Nilsson and Anders Hedberg) combined for 141 goals and 342 points. At age 37, Hull still had the legs and the shot that made him one of the NHL's most feared competitors. His Winnipeg Jets won the Canadian Division in the regular season and then advanced to the finals, where they swept Houston to win the Avco Trophy.

Bobby Hull

Olympic Games

Soviets Capture Olympic Gold

The Soviets prevailed again in the 1976 Winter Games at Innsbruck, Austria. CCCP claimed its fifth gold medal in six Olympics by defeating Czechoslovakia in the championship game. Here, Soviet Juriy Liapkin stands triumphant as Czech goalie Jiri Holecek looks up in awe. The Czechs had to forfeit an earlier game to Poland when one of their players failed a post-game drug test.

Reggie Leach

Leach Breaks Record with 80 Combined Goals

In 1975-76, Reggie Leach notched 61 regular-season goals (first overall) and added 19 more in the play-offs for a total of 80 tallies in 96 games. In the process, he set NHL records for most playoff goals as well as most goals in the regular season and playoffs combined. Leach captured the Conn Smythe Trophy despite playing on a losing team.

1975-76

- In Game 4, Montreal breaks a 3-3 tie with goals from Guy Lafleur and Peter Mahovlich. The Habs skate off with a 5-3 win, a 4-0 sweep, and their 18th Stanley Cup.

- With his 19 playoff goals, Reg Leach earns the Conn Smythe Trophy.

- Bobby Clarke takes his third and final Hart Trophy, while the Islanders' Denis Potvin is runner-up.

- Boston's Jean Ratelle, nicknamed "Gentleman Jean," wins his second Lady Byng Trophy. Jean Pronovost is runner-up.

- Ken Dryden cops the Vezina Trophy, beating out Billy Smith and rookie Chico Resch of the Islanders.

- Islander rookie Bryan Trottier edges teammate Chico Resch for the Calder.

- Denis Potvin wins the Norris Trophy, ending Bobby Orr's reign.

Flyers Figure Out Gilbert in Cup Semis

With a pair of Stanley Cups under their belts, the Flyers took on a tough Boston team in the 1976 semifinals. Bruins goalie Gilles Gilbert (pictured) was a crafty and agile force in nets, using his stick to stop the puck as well as to make life difficult for the opposition. Gilbert became Boston's No. 1 playoff goalie after Gerry Cheevers lost a pair of O.T. games to L.A. in the quarter-finals. Still, the Flyers skated past Gilbert's Bruins in five.

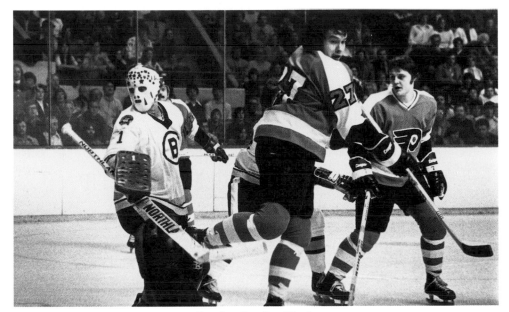

Stanley Cup Semifinals

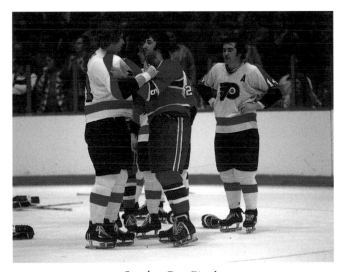

Stanley Cup Finals

Flyers Can't Bust Habs' Tough D

Montreal's Guy Lapointe (center) and Philadelphia's Don "Big Bird" Saleski (left) discuss ongoing violence in the NHL, as the Stanley Cup Finals pitted the grace and artistry of the Flying Frenchmen against the ill-tempered style of the Broad Street Bullies. The Flyers dropped the first two games (4-3 and 2-1), as they were unable to break through Montreal's win-at-all-costs defense to severely test goalie Ken Dryden.

- Rod Gilbert wins the Masterton Trophy, while Stan Mikita is one of three to receive the Lester Patrick.

- Guy Lafleur's peers honor him with the Lester B. Pearson Award, while Boston coach Don Cherry receives the Jack Adams Award.

- The Soviets win their fifth Olympic gold medal, beating Czechoslovakia 4-3 in the title game.

- For the second straight Olympics, Canada opts to boycott ice hockey in protest against the "professional amateurs" skating for the Soviets and other communist countries.

- Ottawa's Peter Lee is voted the Canadian Major Junior Player of the Year, while Hamilton wins the Memorial Cup.

- Minnesota wins the NCAA title, defeating Michigan Tech 6-4 in the finals. Gopher forward Tom Vanelli is the tourney's MVP.

When looking back on the 1976-77 Canadiens—a record-breaking powerhouse featuring such stars as Guy Lafleur, Steve Shutt, and Ken Dryden—one mustn't forget the grand master behind the bench. Though often disliked and misunderstood, the wily Scotty Bowman had no peer.

"Scotty played favorites, no doubt about it, and he loved playing one guy against another," said forward Peter Mahovlich. "The important thing is, Scotty's way worked. His teams might have hated him, but he got them to play to their capabilities and not too many coaches can say that. Agree or disagree, love him or hate him, he won and that's all people remember now." Or as hockey writer Al Strachan remembered: "The players hated Scotty 364 days a year. On the other day, they cashed their Stanley Cup cheques."

On the ice, Lafleur was the marquee attraction, leading the league in scoring for the second straight year (56-80-136) and winning his first of two straight Hart Trophies. He teamed with the high-scoring Shutt (who set an NHL record for a left wing with 60 goals) and center Jacques Lemaire, yet the club's checkers were no less important. Doug

LAFLEUR LEADS HABS TO 60 WINS, ANOTHER CUP

Jarvis, Bob Gainey, and Jim Roberts had no peers, while another Kid Line—Doug Risebrough, Mario Tremblay, and Yvon Lambert—could hold its own with anybody.

"And then if you could take care of that group of forwards," said former Bruins coach Don Cherry, "you came up against the Big Three at the blueline and Ken Dryden in net."

Serge Savard, Guy Lapointe, and Larry Robinson blended all aspects of solid defense without any Bobby Orr-type histrionics. They were backed by a pair of young aces, Bill Nyrop and Brian Engblom. With that armada in front of him, goalie Ken Dryden had little trouble maintaining his mastery in goal. His second straight Vezina Trophy was a given.

With literally every piece in place, the 1976-77 Canadiens thoroughly dominated opponents, outscoring them 387-171. The Habs went 60-8-12 and set records that still stand for victories, points (132), and road wins (27). From November 1 through April 26 (38 games including playoffs), the Canadiens went undefeated at the Forum.

"We were a family," said Lafleur. "We used to stick more together with the players than with our wives. Our wives used to criticize us. They'd say, 'You're always with the players. You go on the road with the guys. Why don't you stay home with your wife instead of going out with the players again?' It was that kind of chemistry between all the players. We had fun."

The Canadiens had no trouble defending their 1975-76 Stanley Cup. In the playoffs, they trashed St. Louis in four straight and disposed of the Islanders in six. In the Finals, Montreal vanquished Boston in four games, outscoring the Bruins 16-6.

This Canadien club was more than just a hockey team. This was a precision-crafted, finely tuned machine. "The '75-'76 and '76-'77 Canadiens teams," said Cherry, "may have been the best ever in the NHL."

1976-77

- The NHL adopts a new rule calling for an extra five-minute penalty and a game misconduct to any player clearly instigating a fight.

- The California Seals transfer to Cleveland and change their name to the Barons. The Kansas City Scouts become the Colorado Rockies.

- The Hall of Fame inducts five new members, including players Johnny Bower and Bill Quackenbush.

- Using the first pick in the 1976 Entry Draft, Washington selects defenseman Rick Green from London (OHL).

- The Canada Cup is staged prior to the season, as Canada, the U.S., Czechoslovakia, the Soviet Union, Sweden, and Finland face each other.

- Canada tops the Canada Cup standings (4-1-0) and then beats Czechoslovakia in a best-of-three championship round, 6-0 and 5-4 in

Tremendous skating ability—agility as well as speed and explosiveness characterized the game of Guy Lafleur. In 1976-77, he captured his second straight Art Ross Trophy with a league-leading 136 points. The Flower also led the league with 80 assists and enjoyed his third consecutive 50-goal season (finishing with 56). At the end of the season, he received his first Hart Trophy and second Lester B. Pearson Award.

overtime. Darryl Sittler scores the O.T. goal.

• Rather than returning to the Bruins, legendary defenseman Bobby Orr signs a free-agent deal with Chicago.

• On October 12, 1976, the Rangers' Don Murdoch ties Howie Meeker's rookie record when he scores five goals against Minnesota.

• On February 2, 1977, Toronto's Ian Turnbull becomes the first NHL defenseman to score five goals in a game, as he victimizes the Red Wings in a 9-1 rout.

• On February 14, 1977, Philly rookie Al Hill sets a record with five points in his first NHL game, as the Flyers beat St. Louis 6-4.

• On February 19, 1977, Rangers right winger Rod Gilbert becomes the 11th NHLer to record 1,000 points.

Six Countries Square Off in Canada Cup

The Canada Cup tournament preceding the 1976-77 season included six teams (Canada, Czechoslovakia, Finland, Sweden, the United States, and the Soviet Union). Team Canada advanced to the finals and faced a strong Czech team anchored by Olympic goaltending hero Vladimir Dzurilla (#1). The Canadian squad was bolstered by the NHL's most dangerous scorer, Montreal's Guy Lafleur (#10).

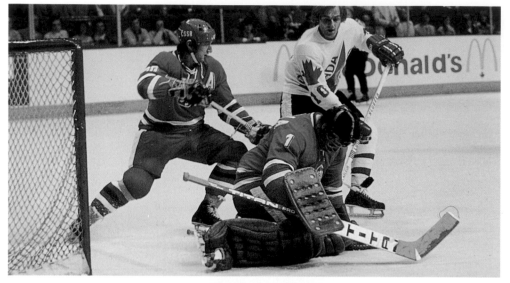

Canada Cup Series

Hull, Canada Prevail in Canada Cup

The high drama of international competition in the Canada Cup series was always balanced by mutual respect among the players. After Team Canada defeated Czechoslovakia 5-4 in overtime in the finals, Bobby Hull (left) took part in the traditional exchange of jerseys with one of his opposite numbers from Czechoslovakia. Hull's teammate, Bobby Orr, was voted the tournament MVP.

Canada Cup Series

1976-77

• On February 27, 1977, Chicago legend Stan Mikita becomes the eighth NHLer to score 500 goals.

• On April 3, 1977, Boston's Jean Ratelle records his 1,000th point.

• Montreal goes 60-8-12, setting NHL records for victories, road victories (27), points (132), and longest home undefeated streak (34 games).

• Montreal's Steve Shutt scores 60 goals—most ever by an NHL left winger. Teammate Guy Lafleur's 80 assists and 136 points are tops around the NHL.

• Ken Dryden's 2.14 GAA is topped only by part-time teammate Bunny Larocque's 2.09.

• L.A. adds an aging Dave Schultz for muscle and gets 53 goals from Marcel Dionne, as the Kings finish second in the Norris, 49 points behind the Canadiens.

Barons No Better Than Hapless Seals

At the start of the 1976-77 campaign, following 10 years of losing seasons and near financial ruin, the California Seals franchise moved to Richfield, Ohio, where they were renamed the Cleveland Barons. The city of Cleveland had enjoyed a history of popular minor-league clubs in the AHL, but the NHL Barons were a flop on the ice (25-42-13) and at the gate.

Cleveland Barons Mask

Gil Perreault

Perreault Keys Sabres' High-Powered Attack

With a team-high 95 points, Gilbert Perreault helped Buffalo finish second in the Adams Division in 1976-77. As the leader of the French Connection Line—with Richard Martin (36 goals, 65 points) on the left wing and Rene Robert (33 goals, 73 points) on the right—Perreault used his great speed and puck control to create scoring chances. The Sabres scored 301 goals, fourth best in the league.

Orr Signs with Chicago, Plays Just 20 Games

After 10 years in Boston, defenseman Bobby Orr, at age 28, signed a free-agent contract with Chicago prior to the start of the 1976-77 season. To the disappointment of fans around the NHL, the legendary Orr was unable to play more than 20 games as knee injuries continued to plague him. In typical fashion, Orr counted four goals and 23 points in those 20 games. Bobby would play through the 1977-78 season before calling it quits.

Bobby Orr

Swedes, Hull Fuel Jets

The WHA crowned a new goal-scoring champion in 1976-77 when Winnipeg's Anders Hedberg, a Swedish right winger playing on a line with Bobby Hull and fellow countryman Ulf Nilsson, ripped 70 goals. (Nilsson accumulated a league-high 85 assists.) Hedberg finished second in the league behind Quebec's Buddy Cloutier (66-75-141) in total scoring with 131 points, while Nilsson had 124 points. The Jets lost to Quebec in the WHA finals.

Anders Hedberg

• Pittsburgh finishes third in the Norris, as former 50-goal scorers Pierre Larouche and Jean Pronovost finish with 29 and 33, respectively.

• With 36 goals from free agent Guy Charron, the Washington Caps climb past Detroit for fourth in the Norris.

• Philadelphia is back atop the Patrick Division (48-16-16). Bernie Parent returns from an eye injury and wins 35 games.

• The Flyers ride the scoring of Rick MacLeish (49 goals) and Bobby Clarke (90 points).

• The ever-improving Islanders boast the stellar goaltending of Glenn Resch (26 wins, 2.28 GAA) and Billy Smith (21 wins, 2.50 GAA). They finish second in the Patrick with 106 points.

• Atlanta boasts three 30-goal scorers (Willi Plett, 33; Eric Vail, 32; and Tom Lysiak, 30) and finishes third.

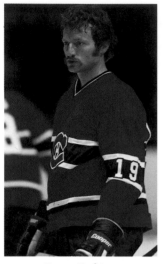

Larry Robinson

Rick MacLeish

Ian Turnbull

Norris-Winning Robinson Is a Big, Big Plus

Montreal defenseman Larry Robinson gave the Habs an offensive catalyst off the blueline as well as a hard-nosed back-checker in the defensive zone. In 1976-77, Robinson proved his skill with the puck when he tied for third overall in assists (66). At season's end, Robby had an unheard-of +120 plus/minus rating and was an overwhelming first choice for the Norris Trophy. Toronto's Borje Salming finished second.

MacLeish's 49 Help Philly Finish First

A 50-goal scorer in 1972-73, Rick MacLeish narrowly missed the magic mark in 1976-77, finishing with 49 tallies as the Flyers captured their fourth straight Patrick Division title. MacLeish was the top scorer (97 points, fourth overall in the NHL) on a team that boasted eight players with at least 20 goals. MacLeish centered the Flyers' second line with Ross Lonsberry and crease-crasher Gary Dornhoefer.

Turnbull Nets Five in a Game

On February 2, 1977, Toronto's Ian Turnbull (center) did what no defenseman in the history of the game had ever done: score five goals in a game. The offense-minded backliner achieved the mark in a 9-1 rout of Detroit, scoring twice on Eddie Giacomin and three times against reliever Jim Rutherford. A guitarist and composer, Turnbull was a longtime favorite of Leafs owner Harold Ballard, who appreciated Turnbull's flair for the dramatic.

1976-77

- The Rangers continue to struggle under coach John Ferguson, as Phil Esposito (80 points) and Rod Gilbert (75) just aren't enough.

- St. Louis installs Emile Francis as coach and wins the Smythe Division (32-39-9), as rookies Bernie Federko and Brian Sutter debut.

- Led by Tim Young's 95 points, the North Stars edge Chicago by one point for second place in the Smythe Division.

- Tony Esposito leads the NHL in losses (36) as Chicago suffers through a 26-43-11 season, its worst in years.

- Vancouver fails to make the playoffs, as do the Colorado Rockies (despite Wilf Paiement's 41 goals).

- Boston's Gerry Cheevers wins 30 for the Adams champs (49-23-8).

- Peter McNab, a free agent from Buffalo, leads Boston in goals (38)

McDonald Keys a Tough Leafs Line

The Maple Leafs struggled to keep pace with the Bruins and Sabres in the 1976-77 Adams race, but the scoring of Lanny McDonald kept them in the hunt. McDonald formed a dangerous line with playmaking whiz Darryl Sittler (90 points) and the pugnacious Dave "Tiger" Williams, who led the NHL in penalty minutes (338). Toronto won only 33 games in 1976-77 but McDonald knocked home a career-high 46 goals, fifth best in the NHL.

Lanny McDonald

Paiement Nets 41 in Mile High Country

Wilf Paiement, younger brother of former NHL and WHA tough guy Rosaire Paiement, set a franchise record when he scored 41 goals for the 1976-77 Colorado Rockies. The hard-nosed right winger bounced around the league from Kansas City and Colorado (one franchise, two cities) to Toronto, Quebec, the Rangers, Buffalo, and Pittsburgh during his 14 years in the NHL. He retired in 1988 with 356 goals, 814 points, and 1,757 penalty minutes.

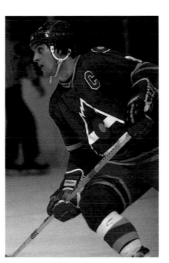

Wilf Paiement

Dionne Scores 53 Goals, Wins the Lady Byng

Before Marcel Dionne went to Los Angeles, the Kings had never had a 50-goal scorer—or a player with 50-goal potential. In 1976-77, Dionne ripped 53 goals (third best in the league) and finished with 122 points (second to Guy Lafleur). Dionne was a one-man juggernaut for Bob Pulford's Kings, who finished second in the Norris Division. Marcel led the NHL in shots (378) and won his second Lady Byng Trophy.

Marcel Dionne

while Jean Ratelle continues his outstanding production (94 points).

• The Sabres finish second in the Adams on the scoring of Gil Perreault (95 points) and Rene Robert (73).

• Toronto's line of Darryl Sittler (90 points), Lanny McDonald (46 goals), and Dave Williams (league-high 338 PIM) makes big noise, as the Leafs finish third in the Adams.

• Dennis Maruk's 78 points are wasted as Cleveland takes up where the Seals left off, finishing last in the Adams.

• The NHL's top goal-scorers include Steve Shutt (60), Guy Lafleur (56), Marcel Dionne (53), Rick MacLeish (49), and Lanny McDonald (46).

• The top point men are Guy Lafleur (136 points), Marcel Dionne (122), Steve Shutt (105), Rick MacLeish (97), and Gil Perreault (95).

Cloutier Pots 66 on Powerful Quebec Line

The WHA continued to shift teams and realign divisions in 1976-77, but the Quebec Nordiques attacked the regular-season schedule without missing a beat. Hard-shooting right winger Real "Buddy" Cloutier skated on a devastating line with Marc Tardif and Serge Bernier. Cloutier, a lefty shot playing the off-wing, won the league scoring race with 66 goals and 141 points, while his line combined for 158 goals and 346 points.

Real Cloutier

Jean Ratelle

Steve Shutt

Ratelle Still Has What It Takes

Many had questioned the caliber of Jean Ratelle's play when the Rangers traded him to Boston in 1975-76, but the veteran playmaker proved he was far from over the hill. On April 3, 1977, Ratelle capped off a 94-point season (best on the Adams Division-leading Bruins) by recording the 1,000th point of his career during a 7-4 win over Toronto.

Shutt's 60 Goals Set Left Wing Record

Steve Shutt's steady improvement as a goal-scorer continued in 1976-77, as he set a new NHL record for goals by a left winger with 60. In his first five NHL campaigns, Shutt's output grew from eight goals as a rookie to subsequent years of 15, 30, 45, and 60. Shutt was a brilliant capitalist, using a quick release and deadly accuracy to turn many of Guy Lafleur's league-leading 80 assists into goals.

1976-77

- The WHA plays its first "exhibition" games against NHL teams, going 13-6-2 in the series.

- The WHA's Toronto Toros move to Birmingham, Alabama, while the Howes (Gordie and sons Mark and Marty) threaten to depart Houston.

- The WHA shifts back to two divisions (East and West). Quebec wins the East on the scoring of Real Cloutier (66 goals and 141 points).

- Houston wins the West thanks to top scorers Rich Preston (38 goals) and Cam Connor (35).

- The WHA's top scorers are Real Cloutier (141 points), Anders Hedberg (131), Ulf Nilsson (124), league MVP Robbie Ftorek (117), and Andre Lacroix (114).

- Quebec makes it to the Avco finals with playoff series wins over New England (4-1) and Indianapolis (4-1).

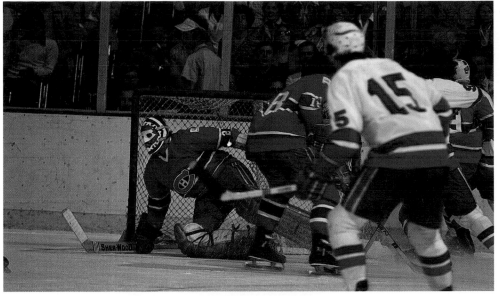

Ken Dryden

Any Way You Look at It, Dryden's No. 1

The Montreal dynasty was in full swing in 1976-77, as Ken Dryden led the league in victories (41) for the fourth time in five seasons. The lanky ex-Cornell star posted a 2.14 GAA and led all NHL goalies in shutouts (10). Stingy defense was the cornerstone of the Habs' successful foundation and Dryden—who captured his second straight Vezina Trophy in 1976-77—was the chairman of the board.

Young's 95 Points Set Stars Record

The North Stars finished second in the Smythe Division in 1976-77, as team captain Tim Young turned in a sparkling performance. He registered a career-high 95 points, a club record that would stand for five years. A shifty skater with tremendous passing skills, Young tied Montreal's Larry Robinson and Toronto's Borje Salming for third in the NHL in assists (66) and tied Buffalo's Gil Perreault for fifth overall in total points.

Tim Young

Mikita's 500th Brightens a Bleak Season

Late in the 1976-77 season, his 19th NHL campaign, Black Hawks legend Stan Mikita became the eighth player in league history to score 500 career goals. Mikita's big moment came on February 27, 1977, when he beat Canucks goalie Cesare Maniago before an ecstatic Chicago Stadium crowd. The Hawks finished the season at 26-43-11, as Mikita's 49 points were just 13 off the team lead.

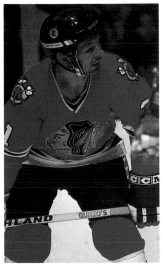

Stan Mikita

- The high-powered Jets, led by Anders Hedberg's 70 goals, reach the finals with playoff series wins over San Diego (4-3) and Houston (4-2).

- Quebec dethrones Winnipeg in seven finals games. The Nordiques overcome a 12-3 thrashing in Game 6 to win the deciding game 8-2.

- In the opening round of the NHL playoffs, the Isles sweep Chicago (2-0), Buffalo sweeps Minnesota (2-0), Toronto beats Pittsburgh (2-1), and the Kings oust Atlanta (2-1).

- In the Stanley Cup quarterfinals, the Flyers need six games to dispose of Toronto, while the Bruins take six to erase the Kings. Montreal sweeps St. Louis and the Islanders sweep Buffalo.

- In the semifinals, the Bruins avenge previous defeats with a sweep of the Flyers, while Montreal needs six games to dump the Islanders.

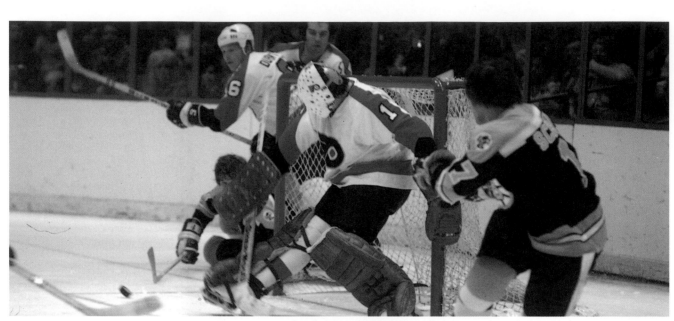

Stanley Cup Semifinals

Bruins Send the Flyers Home Early

In the 1976-77 Stanley Cup semifinals, Boston emphatically ended Philadelphia's string of three straight Finals appearances. Against Philly, the Bruins won the first two games in overtime, squeaked by in Game 3 2-1, and skated off with a 3-0 shutout in Game 4. Boston winger Bobby Schmautz (pictured) wound up as the playoffs' leading goal-scorer with 11.

Stanley Cup Semifinals

Habs Shut Down Isles in Semis

The Islanders won six straight playoff games to open the 1977 Stanley Cup season, ousting Chicago 2-0 in the prelims and sweeping Buffalo 4-0 in the quarters. They met their match in the semifinals, however, when Montreal shut them out twice in the first four games. Islander Andre St. Laurent (#21) celebrates his one goal of the playoffs, but goalie Ken Dryden ultimately prevailed, winning Game 6 2-1.

1976-77

• In Game 1 of the Finals, Montreal crushes Boston 7-3.

• The Bruins play better defense in Game 2 but muster no offense, as Ken Dryden frustrates Boston 3-0.

• Despite the home ice in Game 3, the Bruins go down 3-0 in the first period as Guy Lafleur, Steve Shutt, and Jacques Lemaire pace the Habs to an eventual 4-2 win.

• With 4:32 gone in overtime of Game 4, playoff wizard Jacques Lemaire beats Boston goalie Gerry Cheevers, giving Montreal a 2-1 win and its 19th Stanley Cup.

• Guy Lafleur, with 26 points, wins the Conn Smythe Trophy.

• Having already won the Art Ross award, Guy Lafleur is awarded the Hart Trophy. Bobby Clarke is second.

• Marcel Dionne wins his second Lady Byng, edging Jean Ratelle.

Stanley Cup Finals

Jacques Lemaire

Lemaire Comes Up Big at Crunch Time

Jacques Lemaire scored the winning goal in Game 3 of the 1977 Stanley Cup Finals—the third goal in a first-period barrage that led to a 4-2 Habs victory. In more dramatic fashion, the fleet-footed Lemaire clinched the Canadiens' 19th Stanley Cup when he beat Gerry Cheevers at 4:32 of sudden-death to win Game 4 2-1. It was his second goal of the game and 19th point of the playoffs.

Bruins and Habs Square Off in Finals

With Gerry Cheevers back in nets after a brief hiatus in the WHA, the Bruins roared back into Cup contention in 1976-77 and earned a berth in the Finals with series victories over Los Angeles (4-2) and Philadelphia (4-0), while Montreal skated past St. Louis (4-0) and the Islanders (4-2) en route to the Finals. Guy Lafleur (pictured attacking the Bruins' net) was the playoff's leading scorer (26 points) and was the Conn Smythe Trophy winner.

Habs Hammer Bruins in Cup Finals

One year after destroying the defending Stanley Cup champion Flyers in four games in the championship round, the Canadiens won eight of 10 playoff games to reach the Finals in 1977, where they met their old rival, Boston. The Bruins proved to be no match for the brilliant goaltending of Ken Dryden (shown turning away Boston's sleek centerman, Jean Ratelle). Montreal won four straight games, outscoring the Bruins 16-6, to win the Cup.

Stanley Cup Finals

• Ken Dryden nabs his third Vezina Trophy, sharing the honor with Montreal teammate Bunny Larocque.

• Atlanta rookie Willi Plett (33 goals) wins the Calder Trophy.

• Guy Lafleur claims one more honor—the Lester B. Pearson Award.

His coach, Scotty Bowman, wins the Jack Adams Award.

• Montreal's Larry Robinson wins the Norris Trophy.

• Islander winger Ed Westfall, a checking specialist in his 16th NHL season, cops the Masterton Trophy.

• Dale McCourt of St. Catherines cops the Canadian Major Junior Player of the Year Award. New Westminster wins the Memorial Cup.

• Wisconsin scores a 6-5 O.T. win over Michigan in the NCAA title game. Badger goalie Julian Baretta is tourney MVP.

WHA WON'T GO AWAY; NHL GETS ANXIOUS

A full six years after NHL President Clarence Campbell opined that the World Hockey Association "wouldn't take off the ground," the WHA was still alive, doing moderately well, and refusing to fold its tent. Not only that, but the maverick league managed to retain some of hockey's biggest names.

Bobby Hull starred for Winnipeg, Gordie Howe pumped in 34 goals for New England, and Frank Mahovlich patrolled left wing on the Birmingham Bulls. Moreover, two Swedes—Ulf Nilsson and Anders Hedberg—added an international flavor that dazzled spectators more than any European counterparts in the NHL.

"Much as the NHL had hoped we'd disappear," said WHA President Howard Baldwin, "we kept hangin' in and hangin' in." Of course, the league was not without its problems, as the once 12-team circuit was now down to eight teams. "Still," said Baldwin, "we had enough resources to keep going for some time, and that drove the NHL to distraction."

It also drove players' salaries to all-time highs, as WHA teams offered exceptionally high fees that NHL teams often had to match or even top. Additionally, the new league developed a fan-appealing cast of swash-buckling tough guys. Birmingham Bulls Steve Durbano (284 penalty minutes), Frank Beaton (279), Gilles Bilodeau (258), and Dave Hanson (241) were goons with a flair, and they helped draw more fans than the purists would care to believe.

Once the NHL's top power brokers—Chicago owner Bill Wirtz and Detroit's Bruce Norris—believed that the WHA could last into the 1980s, they decided to take affirmative action. They united behind Detroit lawyer John Ziegler as a successor to Campbell, and on September 4, 1977, Ziegler became the NHL's fourth president.

Ziegler's orders were unequivocal: Make peace with the WHA and then eliminate it as a competitor. To that end, secret meetings between Ziegler and Baldwin were held in the hopes of hammering out a peace pact. They came close in 1978, but a final agreement wouldn't come for another year.

In the meantime, hockey fans got to witness two spectacular teams—the NHL's Montreal Canadiens and the WHA's Winnipeg Jets. Nearly as strong as the year before, the Habs went 59-10-11. Guy Lafleur led the league in goals (60) and points (132) and accepted another Hart Trophy. Goalie Ken Dryden won another Vezina Trophy (2.05 GAA), while Larry Robinson headed a fearsome defense. Not surprisingly, the Canadiens rolled to their third straight Stanley Cup, beating Boston in six Finals games.

Montreal's WHA counterpart was the Jets, whose Hull-Nilsson-Hedberg line matched anything the NHL had to offer. In the playoffs, Winnipeg knocked off Birmingham four games to one and then swept New England in four straight to capture the Avco Trophy.

Many fans wondered how the top WHA teams would fare against NHL opponents. They would find out by decade's end, as a WHA-NHL merger was just around the corner.

1977-78

- The NHL elects a new president in September 1977. John A. Ziegler steps in after Clarence Campbell retires after 31 years.

- The Hall of Fame inducts five members, including players Alex Delvecchio and Tim Horton.

- The NHL debuts the Frank Selke Trophy, named for the former Montreal boss. It's awarded to the game's best defensive forward.

- With the first pick in the Entry Draft, Detroit selects Dale McCourt from St. Catherines.

- On December 11, 1977, Philadelphia defenseman Tom Bladon notches four goals and four assists in an 11-1 rout of Cleveland.

- The New York Islanders (48-17-15) finish atop the Patrick Division for the first time, as Bryan Trottier leads the league in assists (77).

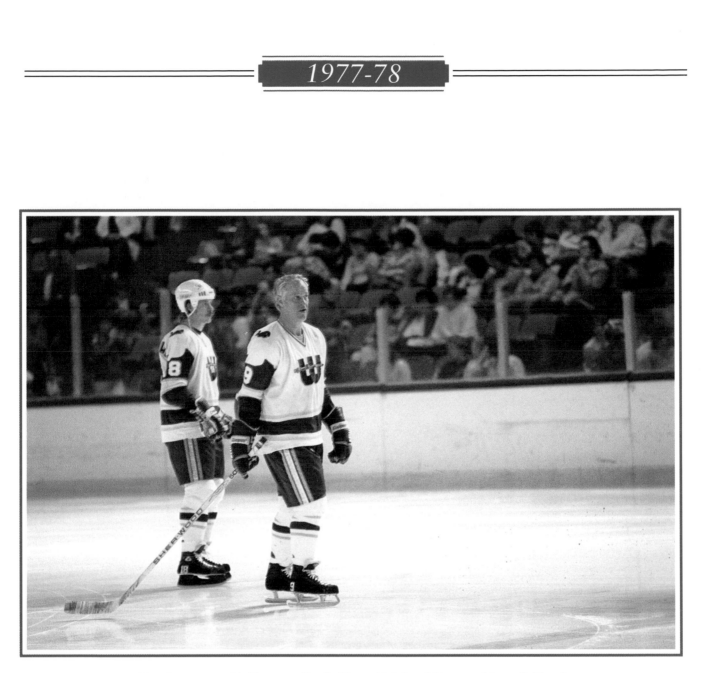

After four years with Houston, Gordie Howe (right) and his sons, Marty (left) and Mark, had a "falling out" with Aeros ownership and joined New England in 1977-78. Gordie Howe, at age 49, led the Whalers in scoring (34-62-96) and carried them to the WHA championship series, where they were swept by Bobby Hull's Winnipeg Jets. Howe and Hull, two of the biggest drawing cards in hockey history, helped keep the WHA afloat throughout the 1970s.

• Islanders rookie Mike Bossy sets an NHL record with 53 first-year goals. Five other Isles score 30-plus goals.

• The Flyers drop to second in the Patrick. Bill Barber leads the team in goals (41), while Bobby Clarke is tops in points (89 in 71 games).

• With seven 20-goal scorers, Atlanta grabs third place in the Patrick Division.

• Controversy swirls around the Rangers as G.M. John Ferguson "retires" Rod Gilbert, an old nemesis when Fergie skated for the Habs.

• Pat Hickey (40 goals) and Phil Esposito (81 points) pace the Rangers, as the team finishes fourth in the Patrick.

• The Black Hawks install Bob Pulford behind the bench and win the Smythe (32-29-19). Ivan Boldirev leads Chicago in scoring (35-45-80).

Junior Bruins Cop Another Memorial Cup

The 1977-78 New Westminster Bruins were the pride of the Western juniors, winning the WHL playoff championship and going on to capture their second consecutive Memorial Cup in the round-robin tournament that followed their league playoffs. The Bruins got lots of help from future Red Wings star John Ogrodnick (back row, fourth from left), who scored 59 regular-season goals and added 14 in the playoffs.

New Westminster Bruins

Darryl Sittler

Sittler Sets Career Highs, Sets Up Mates

The Maple Leafs went 41-29-10 in 1977-78, third in the Adams Division, on the scoring of team captain Darryl Sittler, who enjoyed career highs in goals (45), assists (72), and points (117). The hard-skating center finished third in the league in points and second to the Islanders' Bryan Trottier in assists. Sittler's right winger, Lanny McDonald, finished fourth overall in goals (47).

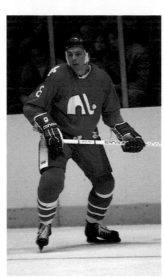

Marc Tardif

Tardif Nets 65 on His Way to 500

The WHA, reduced to eight teams in 1977-78, saw Quebec's Mark Tardif—a former NHLer with Montreal—win the league scoring title. Tardif led the WHA in goals (65) and points (154) and tied Winnipeg's Swedish sensation, Ulf Nilsson, in assists (89). Tardif returned to the his former league when Quebec merged into the NHL in 1979-80. In his 14-year career in the two leagues, he tallied 510 goals.

1977-78

- The Colorado Rockies take second in the Smythe as Wilf Paiement (31 goals), Paul Gardner (30), and rookie defenseman Barry Beck (22) star.

- The Canucks, coached by former NHL enforcer Orland Kurtenbach, drop to third place in the Smythe Division with a 20-43-17 record.

- Garry Unger is the Blues' leading scorer with just 52 points, as St. Louis fails to make the playoffs.

- Minnesota goes through three coaches—Ted Harris, Andre Beaulieu, and Lou Nanne—en route to an 18-53-9 season, its worst ever.

- The Canadiens go 59-10-11 and win the Norris again, this time by 51 points. Guy Lafleur leads the league in goals (60) and captures his third straight scoring title (132 points).

- Ken Dryden is second in the NHL in wins (37) and first in GAA (2.05).

Stay-at-Home Bladon Scores Eight in Game

Tom Bladon carved out a place in hockey history on December 11, 1977, when he became the first NHL defenseman ever to notch eight points in a game. The Flyers destroyed Cleveland 11-1 before a screaming Spectrum crowd as Bladon ripped four goals and added four assists. Known as a smart, stay-at-home defenseman who employed brains over brawn, Bladon scored just 73 career goals in 610 NHL games.

Tom Bladon

Dale McCourt

McCourt Revs It Up in Motor City

The Red Wings struggled mightily through the 1970s, but one of their bright spots was center Dale McCourt, the first player chosen in the 1977 Entry Draft. After a brilliant junior season at St. Catherines, McCourt was voted the 1977 Canadian Major Junior Player of the Year. Then, in 1977-78, he led Detroit to a second-place finish behind Montreal in the Adams Division. McCourt led the Red Wings in scoring at 33-39-72.

Trottier Nets 46, Feeds Baby Bossy

The up-and-coming Islanders posted the best record in the Campbell Conference in 1977-78 (48-17-15) and Bryan Trottier led the charge. Trottier, in just his third NHL season, registered 46 goals and a league-leading 77 assists. A physically aggressive playmaking ace, Trottier finished with 123 points (second only to Montreal's Guy Lafleur) and was instrumental in the Isles' Mike Bossy setting an NHL rookie record for goals.

Bryan Trottier

• The Red Wings climb from last to second in the Norris, as rookie Dale McCourt leads the team in goals (33) and points (72).

• The Kings drop to third in the Norris as Marcel Dionne falls to 36 goals. Butch Goring, a future playoff hero, leads the Kings in goals (37).

• The Penguins get 25 goals from Pete Mahovlich, acquired from Montreal for Pierre Larouche, but finish fourth in the Norris. Jean Pronovost leads the team with 40 goals.

• The Capitals continue to struggle, finishing last in the Norris despite 38 goals from veteran Guy Charron.

• The Bruins boast an all-time record 11 players with at least 20 goals (led by Peter McNab with 41), as they capture the Adams Division title (51-18-11).

• Ex-WHA goalie Ron Grahame joins the Bruins and goes 26-6-7.

Selke Trophy Goes to Hard-Nosed Forwards

Frank Selke Trophy

The NHL forged a new award in 1977-78 in the name of Frank J. Selke. A legend in the formation and administration of the league from 1918 through the 1960s, Selke was an executive with Toronto (winning three Stanley Cups) and a six-time champion as manager of the Canadiens. The inaugural Selke Trophy—given to the league's best defensive forward—was presented to Montreal's Bob Gainey, a hard-checking defensive specialist.

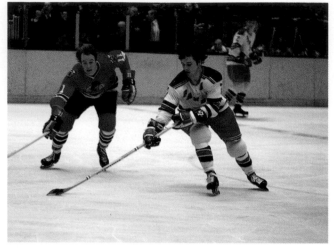

Rod Gilbert

G.M. Fergie Gives Rocky the Boot

Rod "Rocky" Gilbert (right) gave the Rangers 16 full seasons of brilliant play on the right wing, notching 406 goals and 1,065 points. But in 1977-78, he was "fired" by G.M. John Ferguson after 19 games. Fergie and Gilbert had been bitter rivals when the former was a hard-nosed left winger for Montreal and Gilbert was a high-scoring right winger for New York. Gilbert never played again in the NHL.

Ken Dryden

Dryden Stops All But Two a Game

The Habs were well on their way to a fourth consecutive Stanley Cup in 1977-78, as goalie Ken Dryden erected a wall in front of the Montreal net and rarely allowed the opposition to dent the twine. While leading the NHL in goals scored (359), the Habs—thanks to the miserly goaltending of Dryden—also led the league in goals against, giving up just 183 tallies. Dryden's league-best 2.05 GAA won him his third straight Vezina Trophy.

1977-78

- Despite 105 points, Buffalo settles for second in the Adams. Goalie Don Edwards leads the league with 38 wins, while Danny Gare (39 goals) replaces Rene Robert on the French Connection Line.

- Toronto boasts a pair of 40-goal scorers—Lanny McDonald (47) and Darryl Sittler (45)—but finishes 21 points behind Boston.

- Cleveland speedster Dennis Maruk notches 36 goals, but the Barons win only 22 games.

- The NHL's leading goal-scorers are Guy Lafleur (60), Mike Bossy (53), the Canadiens' Steve Shutt (49), Lanny McDonald (47), and Bryan Trottier (46).

- Guy Lafleur wins another scoring title (132 points), as Bryan Trottier (123), Darryl Sittler (117), Montreal's Jacques Lemaire (97), and Denis Potvin (94) give chase.

Mike Bossy

John Ziegler

Ziegler Takes Over as the NHL's Prez

After 31 years of service to the NHL, Clarence Campbell retired as league president and was replaced by John A. Ziegler in 1977. A Detroit native and graduate of the University of Michigan Law School, Ziegler began providing legal services for the Red Wings in 1959 and later became an alternate governor for the team on the NHL Board of Governors. In 1976, he succeeded Chicago's Bill Wirtz as Chairman of the NHL Board of Governors.

Bossy's the First Frosh to Net 50

One of the most dangerous snipers in the history of the game, Michael Bossy made his NHL debut with the Islanders in 1977-78 and rewrote the record books. Playing alongside Bryan Trottier, Bossy shattered the rookie goal-scoring record when he lit the lamp 53 times (breaking Richard Martin's record of 44 set in 1971-72). Though drafted just 15th in the 1977 draft, Bossy won the Calder Trophy by a considerable margin.

• Dave Schultz, now with L.A., wins another penalty crown (405 PIM).

• In the WHA, the San Diego, Phoenix, and Calgary franchises all cease operations.

• Only eight WHA teams compete in a single division. Winnipeg is the regular-season champion with 102 points, nine ahead of New England.

• Winnipeg superstars Ulf Nilsson and Anders Hedberg are offered $2.4 million each over two years to jump to the New York Rangers. It's a reversal of previous raiding trends.

• Unhappy with their owner in Houston, the Howe trio—Gordie and sons Mark and Marty—joins New England. The senior Howe notches 96 points to lead the team.

• The Birmingham Bulls boast four of the top five WHA penalty leaders, led by Steve Durbano (284 PIM).

NHL Honors Goring with Two Trophies

Injuries limited Marcel Dionne to 70 games in 1977-78, but L.A.'s scoring slack was picked up by small-but-speedy veteran Butch Goring. In his ninth NHL season, Goring reached a personal high in goal-scoring when he led the Kings with 37 tallies. After suffering with a losing team for so many years yet always maintaining high standards, Goring was honored with the year's Lady Byng Trophy as well as the Masterton Trophy.

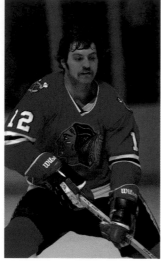

Ivan Boldirev

Boldirev Helps Hawks Win the Smythe

After several years lost in the depths of Boston's farm system and wasting away on the hapless California Seals, Ivan Boldirev finally got a chance to play with a contender when he was traded to Chicago in 1974. By the end of the 1977-78 season, he had elevated his status to that of team scoring leader. With 35 goals and 80 points (the best season of his 15-year career), the Yugoslavian center helped the Hawks capture the Smythe Division title.

Butch Goring

Park Pushes Boston to Adams Title

At age 29, Brad Park proved he still had lots of hockey left in him in 1977-78 when he scored 22 goals for the Bruins, who finished first in the Adams Division. A 10-year veteran, Park was the fourth-leading scorer on the club with 79 regular-season points—and he was the third overall scorer in the playoffs (20 points in 15 games). To his chagrin, he was the runner-up for the Norris Trophy for the sixth time in nine years.

Brad Park

1977-78

- Frank "Rarely" Beaton (279 PIM), Gilles Bilodeau (258), and Dave Hanson (241) are the other ornery Bulls.

- Quebec's Marc Tardif (65-89-154) sets a WHA record for points. He's followed by Real Cloutier (129), Ulf Nilsson (126), Anders Hedberg (122), and Bobby Hull (117).

- With a playoff bye and a five-game triumph over Birmingham, Winnipeg earns its fourth trip to the WHA finals. New England beats Edmonton (4-1) and Quebec (4-1) to reach the final round.

- The Jets outscore New England 24-8 (including a 10-2 pasting in

Game 3) en route to a four-game sweep and their second Avco Trophy.

- In the NHL playoffs, Philadelphia sweeps Colorado (2-0), Detroit brooms Atlanta (2-0), the Leafs sweep L.A. (2-0), and Buffalo erases the Rangers (2-1) in the opening round.

Don Edwards

Edwards' 38 Wins Lead the League

It took Don Edwards a little time to get to the NHL—he was 22 starting his sophomore season in 1977-78—but he didn't take much time to make an impression. The Sabres sent Edwards into 72 games and he rewarded them with a league-leading 38 wins and a brilliant 2.64 goals-against average (fifth best in the NHL). Edwards registered five shutouts and was a main reason why Buffalo posted a splendid 44-19-17 record.

Lafleur, Habs Remain a Cut Above

As the Canadiens charged toward another league title in 1977-78 (59-10-11), Guy Lafleur—their unstoppable scoring machine—led the league in points for the third straight year (132). He also paced the NHL in goals (60) and captured his second straight Hart Trophy. Lafleur's 60 goals gave him four straight seasons with more than 50, a feat never before achieved by a Habs skater.

Guy Lafleur

• Boston needs just four games to eliminate Chicago in the quarterfinals, while Philadelphia beats Buffalo in five. Montreal ousts Detroit (4-1) and Toronto shocks the Isles with an O.T. win in Game 7.

• In the Stanley Cup semifinals, Montreal outscores the Leafs 16-6 in a four-game sweep, while Boston thrashes the Flyers in five games.

• In Game 1 of the Finals, Guy Lafleur scores once and assists two other goals as the Habs win 4-1.

• Game 2 goes to sudden-death before Guy Lafleur beats Boston goaltender Gerry Cheevers at 13:09 of overtime to give the Canadiens a 3-2 victory.

• Boston's Gary Doak scores 59 seconds into Game 3 at Boston. The Bruins cruise to a 4-0 win on Gerry Cheevers' shutout.

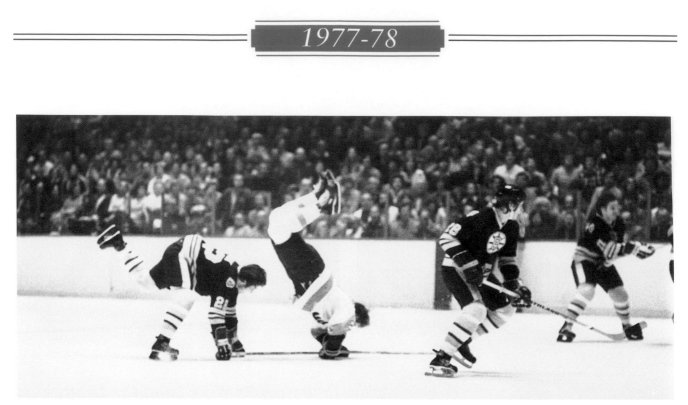

Stanley Cup Semifinals

Bruins Trip Up Flyers in Cup Semis

During the 1978 Stanley Cup semifinals between Philadelphia and Boston, Bobby Clarke, the Flyers' captain and inspirational leader, took a major-league header after being tripped up by defenseman Brad Park (far left). It was an ominous moment that symbolized the overall outcome of the series, as the one-time Big, Bad Bruins flipped the one-time Broad Street Bullies right out of the playoffs with a five-game triumph.

Pint-Sized Palmateer Comes Up Big

A big player in the Toronto success story of 1977-78 was diminutive Mike Palmateer, the southpaw goalie who stood just 5'9" but made up for a lack of bulk with great quickness and agility. Palmateer tied for second in regular-season shutouts (five) and pitched two more in the playoffs, beating Los Angeles 4-0 in the opening round and then blanking the Islanders 2-0 in Game 3 of the quarterfinals.

Mike Palmateer

1977-78

• Game 4 goes to sudden-death tied 3-3. Bruins winger Bobby Schmautz scores to tie the series at two games apiece.

• In Montreal for Game 5, the Habs build a 2-0 lead after one period, make it 4-0 after two periods, and win the game 4-1.

• Boston scores first in Game 6 but the Habs go on to win 4-1. Montreal, which has now beaten the Bruins in 13 consecutive playoff series, claims its third straight Stanley Cup.

• Montreal defenseman Larry Robinson, with 17 playoff assists, is voted the Conn Smythe Trophy.

• Guy Lafleur accepts his second consecutive Hart Trophy, finishing ahead of Bryan Trottier. Lafleur also wins his third straight Lester B. Pearson Award.

• Montreal's Bob Gainey, a hard-working winger, wins the first Frank Selke Trophy.

Stanley Cup Finals

Habs Bash Boston Again in Finals

The Boston Bruins charged through the 1978 playoffs, sweeping Chicago (4-0) and shellacking Philadelphia (4-1) to earn the right to challenge the Canadiens. But Habs goalie Ken Dryden (pictured) was waiting for them. He finished the playoffs with a minuscule goals-against average (1.89) as Montreal tore through the postseason with a 12-3 record, ousting Boston in six.

Habs Get Help from Underdogs

It wasn't only the superstars who contributed to the Canadiens' playoff success. So-called "blue-collar plumbers" such as Rick Chartraw (pictured celebrating with the Stanley Cup) also had significant roles to play. In the case of Montreal's strapping defenseman/winger (and the only NHLer ever born in Caracas, Venezuela), the role was of protector, defender, and enforcer.

Schmautz's O.T. Goal Wins Game 4 of Cup Finals

After being humiliated by Montreal in the 1977 Stanley Cup Finals, the Bruins charged into the 1978 Finals bent on exacting revenge. Right wing sniper Bobby Schmautz evened the series at two games apiece when he won Game 4 in sudden-death, beating Ken Dryden at 6:22 of the first overtime. Schmautz, who led all playoff goal-scorers the previous year (11), fell to seven goals in the 1978 playoffs.

Bobby Schmautz

Stanley Cup Celebration

- Ken Dryden takes his third straight Vezina Trophy, sharing it with goaltending partner Bunny Larocque.

- Right winger Mike Bossy beats out Barry Beck for the Calder Trophy.

- Denis Potvin edges the Rangers' Brad Park for the Norris Trophy.

- Detroit coach Bobby Kromm is voted the Jack Adams Award. L.A.'s Butch Goring wins both the Lady Byng Trophy and Masterton Trophy.

- Bobby Smith of the OHL's Ottawa 67s is voted the Canadian Major Junior Player of the Year.

- Led by John Ogrodnick, New Westminster captures its second straight Memorial Cup.

- Boston University beats Boston College in the NCAA title game. B.U. defenseman Jack O'Callahan, a future Olympian, is voted tourney MVP.

When the Houston Aeros dropped out of the World Hockey Assocation before the 1978-79 season began, the maverick league was down to seven teams and struggling to stay afloat. But those who believed it would go under misjudged the young league's creativity and the NHL's obtuseness.

While the senior league twiddled its thumbs over what to do about 17-year-old phenom Wayne Gretzky (league rules didn't permit teams to sign kids under age 18), the WHA quickly grabbed the future Great One. He started out with Indianapolis, was soon dealt to Edmonton, and in no time at all established himself as pure gold on skates. Gretzky was so good that he deflected attention from the WHA's fiscal problems, and his presence in the rival league inspired the NHL to step up peace talks.

With that in mind, high-level meetings between officials of both leagues were held throughout the 1978-79 season, a year that was captivating on both sides. In the NHL, Montreal drove hard for a fourth consecutive Stanley Cup while a new threat emerged in New York. The Islanders had developed an imposing squad featuring Bryan Trottier, Denis

WHA Finally Dissolves; NHL Absorbs Four Teams

Potvin, Billy Smith, Mike Bossy, and Clark Gillies.

The Gretzky-led Oilers topped the WHA, although Quebec—paced by Real Cloutier—was a strong second. The Nordiques were followed by Winnipeg and New England, which boasted the father-and-sons team of Gordie, Mark, and Marty Howe.

The Islanders finished first overall, a point ahead of Montreal in the NHL's regular-season race. But the Isles suffered a stunning defeat when the Rangers defeated them in a six-game playoff matchup, an upset that put the Rangers in the Stanley Cup Finals against Montreal. The Finals were a lot closer than they appeared on paper, but the Canadiens prevailed in five games and skated off with their fourth consecutive Stanley Cup.

In the WHA playoffs, Gretzky led all scorers with 10 goals and 20 points, but it was Winnipeg that won the Avco Trophy. The Jets ousted the favored Oilers four games to two in the championship round. While all this was happening, merger talks had progressed so far that league consolidation seemed inevitable.

In fact, the NHL and WHA set June 15, 1979, as a deadline for signing a merger/expansion agreement. What the NHL hoped to gain was a huge influx of cash, the return of defected players, and peace in the new decade. All that remained was approval by the players, and on June 9, 1979, the NHL Players' Association ratified the merger which, for legal and egotistical reasons, the NHL called an "expansion."

Quebec, Winnipeg, Edmonton, and New England (which would now be known as Hartford) were accepted for the 1979-80 season. Cincinnati, Birmingham, and Indianapolis were left to find minor-league affiliations for themselves. Meanwhile, with an infusion of $24 million from the four expansion clubs, the NHL embarked on a new era, which, it hoped, would accent peace and prosperity.

1978-79

- The failing Cleveland franchise merges with the Minnesota North Stars (also in financial woes). The new team remains in Minnesota and plays in the Adams Division.

- The Hall of Fame inducts six men, including players Andy Bathgate, Jacques Plante, and Marcel Pronovost.

- Using the first pick in the Entry Draft, Minnesota selects Bobby Smith from the Ottawa 67s of the OHA.

- Don Murdoch of the Rangers is suspended for the season (later commuted to 40 games) when border guards find cocaine in his clothing.

- Buffalo's Tony McKegney becomes the NHL's first "full-time" black skater, as he begins a 13-year career.

- On December 23, 1978, Islander Bryan Trottier scores eight points against the Rangers (five goals and three assists) and sets an NHL record with six points in a single period.

In 1978-79, the Edmonton Oilers won the last WHA regular-season title before merging with the NHL. They were led by 17-year-old phenom Wayne Gretzky (43-61-104), who was purchased from financially strapped Indianapolis eight games into the season. Gretzky's career began in 1976-77, when he played just three games for Peterborough of the OHA. In 1977-78, he tallied 70 goals and 182 points for Sault Ste. Marie of the OHA.

• On January 15, 1979, Minnesota's Tim Young scores five goals against the Rangers.

• On March 11, 1979, Kings defenseman Randy Holt receives one minor, three majors, two 10-minute misconducts, and three game misconducts for a record 67 PIM.

• The Islanders go 51-15-14 and top the NHL in goals (358). Islander right winger Mike Bossy is the league's top goal-scorer (69), while center Bryan Trottier wins the scoring title (134 points).

• Philadelphia G.M. Pat Quinn replaces coach Bob McCammon after a 22-17-11 start, and he guides the Flyers to second place in the Patrick.

• The Flyers use five goalies and get a pair of 34-goal seasons from Bill Barber and Reg Leach.

• Coach Fred Shero leads the Rangers to a third-place finish.

Godfather, Two Dons Make Up Mafia Line

With Fred Shero behind the bench, the Rangers climbed back into playoff contention in 1978-79, going 40-29-11. The Mafia Line, consisting of "Godfather" Phil Esposito (left) and his two Dons—Don Murdoch (center) and Don Maloney (right)—was united following Murdoch's 40-game suspension for cocaine possession. Maloney would go on to score 20 points in the 1979 playoffs, setting an NHL record for a rookie.

Phil Esposito, Don Murdoch, Don Maloney

Trottier Sets a Record, Wins Hart Trophy

On December 23, 1978, Islanders center Bryan Trottier (pictured with Atlanta's Willi Plett) became just the fifth player in league history to post eight points in a game. Included were a record six points in one period, as the Isles clobbered the Rangers 9-4. Trottier wound up pacing the NHL in assists (87) and points (134) and led New York to a league-best 51-15-14 record. He was honored with the Hart Trophy.

Bryan Trottier

Real Cloutier

Cloutier Lives It Up in His Native Quebec

Real "Buddy" Cloutier celebrated his final year in the WHA in 1978-79 by scoring 75 goals (narrowly missing Bobby Hull's league record of 77 goals). The Nords finished second in the regular season as Cloutier won his second scoring title (129 points) in three years. Cloutier was born and raised in Quebec, played junior hockey in the province, and played all but the last two years of his pro career in Quebec.

1978-79

- The Rangers are led by the "Mafia Line" of Phil Esposito and his two Dons (Don Murdoch and rookie Don Maloney).

- The Flames boast their first 50-goal scorer, Guy Chouinard (50). Bob MacMillan (37 goals) and Eric Vail (35) pitch in mightily.

- Chicago (29-36-15) recaptures the Smythe despite an anemic offense. Stan Mikita, at age 38, is second on the club with 55 points.

- Vancouver places second in the Smythe (with a 25-43-13 record) as Ron Sedlbauer knocks home 40 goals.

- St. Louis gets heroic work from Brian Sutter (41 goals), Bernie Federko (31), and Garry Unger (30), but wins just 18 of 80 games. Colorado finishes six points behind the Blues.

- The Canadiens (52-17-11) take the Norris by 30 points, as Guy Lafleur

Bill Wirtz, Bobby Orr

Damaged Knees Force Orr to Retire

Bobby Orr saddened the hockey world on November 9, 1978, when he announced his retirement from NHL action. Unable to compete due to bad knees, Orr (pictured with Black Hawks owner Bill Wirtz) called it quits after just six games. Just 30 years old, Orr's brilliant career ended with 270 goals and 915 points (most ever by a defenseman at the time) in just 657 games, plus a pair of Stanley Cup rings and eight straight Norris Trophies.

NHL Is No Challenge for Soviets

The 1979 Challenge Cup series, a three-game midseason playoff between the USSR and NHL in New York, was captured by the Soviet National Team two games to one. The NHLers took Game 1 4-2, while the Soviets evened the series on Viktor Golikov's winner in Game 2. The "rubber match" was more like a "no contest" exhibition, as the Soviets strafed goalie Gerry Cheevers for a half-dozen goals in a 6-0 rout.

Soviet National Team

Anders Hedberg, Ulf Nilsson

Blueshirts Ink Hedberg and Nilsson

The Rangers emptied their wallets prior to 1978-79 and landed a pair of talented Swedes, Anders Hedberg and Ulf Nilsson, who were plucked from the Winnipeg Jets of the WHA. While right winger Hedberg (33 goals) and left winger Pat Hickey (34) enjoyed outstanding seasons, pivot Nilsson lasted only 59 games. Nilsson broke his ankle when his skate got caught in a rut in the ice of Madison Square Garden.

---

tics Phil Esposito with his fifth straight 50-goal season (52).

• Montreal goalie Ken Dryden's 2.30 GAA is tops in the league.

• Greg Malone (35 goals) and Peter Lee (32) help the Penguins finish second in the Norris.

• Marcel Dionne erupts for 59 goals and 130 points, but the Kings do no better than a .500 record.

• Former collegiate star Dave Taylor notches 43 goals and first-year King Charlie Simmer nets 21, as the Kings see the birth of the Triple Crown Line (with Marcel Dionne).

• Washington climbs out of the cellar as Dennis Maruk (31 goals), Tom Rowe (31), Guy Charron (28), and Ryan Walter (28) add offensive spark.

• The Red Wings revert to old form and drop out of contention, wasting a 38-goal year from Czech star Vaclav Nedomansky.

Ron Sedlbauer

Sedlbauer Scores 40 in Ugly Uni

It was said of the 1978-79 Vancouver Canucks uniform (a multicolored chevron intended to depict strength, but more often inspiring mockery), "It isn't very good-looking, but it sure is ugly!" Left winger Ron Sedlbauer, a hard-shooting second-round pick, enjoyed a career year in 1978-79 when he ripped 40 goals. A one-way skater who never amounted to much as a playmaker, Sedlbauer's career spanned seven seasons (143 goals, 86 assists in 430 games).

Ken Dryden

Dryden Retires at Peak of Career

Ken Dryden won his fourth consecutive Vezina Trophy in 1978-79 as he helped the Habs to a 52-17-11 record and first place in the Norris Division—30 points ahead of second-place Pittsburgh. Dryden led all NHL goalies in GAA (2.30) and shutouts (five) and finished with a 30-10-7 record. Dryden retired after beating the Rangers in the 1979 Finals for his sixth Stanley Cup. The 31-year-old moved to England and wrote a book about his hockey experiences.

Tiger Williams

Williams Lets His Fists Do the Talking

In grade school, on a questionnaire asking children to describe "what they wanted to be when they grow up," Dave "Tiger" Williams wrote "NHL" across the page and left it at that. His approach to the game was much the same once he got there—straightforward, no-nonsense. In 1978-79, skating on a line with Darryl Sittler and Lanny McDonald, the cranky left winger scored 19 goals and hammered his way to a league-leading 298 penalty minutes.

• Eight Bruins surpass the 20-goal mark, including Rick Middleton (38) and Peter McNab (35). Boston takes another Adams title (43-23-14).

• The once-powerful Sabres falter, as the French Connection Line (Gil Perreault, Rick Martin, and Danny Gare) loses some punch.

• Darryl Sittler (87 points) and Lanny McDonald (43 goals) are the best of a .500 Maple Leafs team.

• Minnesota plays "musical coaches" with Harry Howell and Glen Sonmor trading places twice each, but the Stars finish last in the Adams with just 28 wins.

• North Star rookie Bobby Smith lives up to his billing when he nets 30 goals and leads the team in scoring (74 points).

• The leading goal-scorers include Mike Bossy (69), Marcel Dionne (59), Guy Lafleur (52), Guy Chouinard (50), and Bryan Trottier (47).

Tony McKegney

Dionne's the Main Jewel in Triple Crown

After an "off" year in which he scored just 79 points, Marcel Dionne rebounded in 1978-79 when he was teamed with Charlie Simmer and Dave Taylor, forming the famed Triple Crown Line in Los Angeles. (Each wore a crown on his jersey; hence, "triple crown.") Dionne finished second in the league in both goals (59) and points (130) and fired a league-high 362 shots on goal. He won the Lester B. Pearson Award.

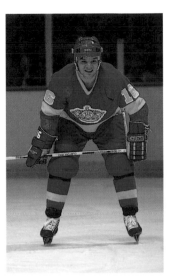

Marcel Dionne

McKegney Finds a Home in NHL

Born in Montreal, Tony McKegney starred at Kingston of the OHA before the Sabres chose him in the second round of the 1978 Amateur Draft. He made his NHL debut in 1978-79, playing 52 games (eight goals, 22 points), and became the NHL's first full-time black player. Others—Willie O'Ree (45 games in 1957-58 and 1960-61) and Mike Marson (196 games in the late 1970s)—had made inroads, but McKegney carved out a 13-year career.

MacMillan Tallies 108, Wins Lady Byng

If the 1978-79 Flames had played in the Smythe, they would have won the division crown by 17 points. As it were, they finished last in the Patrick with 90 points. Speedy right winger Bob MacMillan led the team with 71 assists and 108 points, while veteran goalie Dan Bouchard led the NHL in victories (32). With only 14 penalty minutes, MacMillan won the Lady Byng Trophy.

Bob MacMillan

• The top five scorers include Bryan Trottier (134 points), Marcel Dionne (130), Guy Lafleur (129), Mike Bossy (126), and Bob MacMillan (108).

• In February, a team of NHL All-Stars faces the Soviet National Team in the Challenge Cup in New York. The Soviets win two games to one.

• In the WHA, the Houston franchise folds, leaving only seven teams and bringing on heated negotiations for a partial merger with the NHL.

• In Edmonton, manager Glen Sather acquires 17-year-old Wayne Gretzky from Indianapolis. The Oilers win the regular-season title over Quebec.

• Wayne Gretzky notches 46 goals and 110 points as a first-year pro, while goalie Dave Dryden (brother of Canadiens netminder Ken) gives the Oilers a league-best 2.89 GAA.

• Real Cloutier gives Jacques Demers' Nordiques a 75-goal year and another scoring title (129 points).

Potvin Cops the Norris, His Third

In 1978-79, Denis Potvin scored a career-high 31 goals and was third on the Isles in scoring with 101 points (his most ever). A perennial All-Star who shined on both ends of the ice, Potvin earned his third Norris Trophy, outballoting Larry Robinson. In winning his third Norris, Potvin became the fourth player to win more than two, joining Bobby Orr (eight), Doug Harvey (seven), and Pierre Pilote (three).

Denis Potvin

The Flower Wilts, But Just a Little

While Guy Lafleur's string of league scoring titles ended at three (the Islanders' Bryan Trottier dethroned the Flower in 1978-79), the brilliant Montreal winger notched his fifth straight season with at least 50 goals, tying the mark of former Bruins great Phil Esposito. Lafleur finished the campaign with 52 goals and 129 points (third best in the league in both categories). His 77 assists were second only to Trottier's 87.

Guy Lafleur

Chouinard Pots 50 for Cellar-Bound Flames

The Flames were trapped in the highly competitive Patrick Division in 1978-79 and ended up last with a 41-31-8 record. The superb scoring of fifth-year pro Guy Chouinard ignited them. The slick-skating center from Quebec City erupted in just his third full NHL season, leading all Atlanta snipers with 50 goals. His linemates—Eric Vail (35 goals) and Bob MacMillan (37)—benefitted from his savvy playmaking (57 assists).

Guy Chouinard

1978-79

• The WHA's top five scorers are Real Cloutier (129 points), Robbie Ftorek (116), Wayne Gretzky (110), Mark Howe (107), and Kent Nilsson (107).

• In the final WHA championship, Winnipeg thrashes the Oilers in six games—despite being outscored 32-21.

• Soon after the season, four WHA teams (New England, Edmonton, Winnipeg, and Quebec) join the NHL, while Birmingham, Cincinnati, and Indianapolis cease operations.

• In the first round of the NHL playoffs, Philadelphia beats Vancouver (2-1), Toronto sweeps Atlanta (2-0), Pittsburgh survives Buffalo (2-1), and the Rangers blank the Kings (2-0).

• In the Stanley Cup quarterfinals, Montreal sweeps Toronto (4-0), Boston squelches Pittsburgh (4-0), the Isles sweep Chicago (4-0), and the Rangers handle Philly (4-1).

Winnipeg Jets

Mike Bossy

Jets Win the Last Avco Trophy

Winnipeg captain Lars-Erik Sjoberg hugs the Avco Trophy after the Jets defeated Edmonton in six games for the last-ever WHA championship. The series featured a marquee matchup of the Jets' Bobby Hull and the Oilers' Wayne Gretzky. Ironically, Winnipeg's Rich Preston, a nondescript right winger, skated off with the playoff MVP award.

Bossy Scores 69 Before You Know It

Mike Bossy of the Islanders won the 1978-79 goal-scoring title when he lit the lamp 69 times. His coach, Al Arbour, said of Bossy and his lightning-quick release, "One second the puck is on the way to him, and the next thing you know the red light is on." Known for his gentlemanly play and smooth skating, Bossy tallied 126 points and had a +63 plus/minus rating, evidence of his ability to backcheck.

- In the semifinals, the Habs beat Boston in Game 7 as Yvon Lambert scores at 9:33 of O.T.

- The Rangers and Islanders meet in the semis. The Isles win Games 2 and 4 in O.T., but the Rangers pull off a huge upset by erasing the Stanley Cup favorites in six games.

- In Game 1 of the Stanley Cup Finals, the Rangers beat Ken Dryden with a pair of first-period goals en route to a 4-1 win.

- Montreal rebounds on home ice in Game 2 with a 6-2 thrashing of New York, as six Habs score to overcome an early 2-0 Ranger lead.

- Playing on two bad knees, courageous Rangers goalie John Davidson cannot hold off the powerful Habs in Game 3, as Montreal wins at Madison Square Garden 4-1.

- Game 4 goes to sudden-death tied at 3-3. Montreal's Serge Savard scores at 7:25 of O.T.

John Davidson

The Rangers' Davidson Saves the Day

The brilliant performance of Rangers goaltender John Davidson carried the Blueshirts past the Islanders in the 1979 Stanley Cup semifinals. His 2.28 playoff GAA and countless acrobatic saves—despite damage to both knees that would ultimately require surgery—made J.D. a hero on the streets of Manhattan. Davidson was not nearly as effective in the Finals, however, as Montreal burned him for 19 goals in five games.

Rangers Oust Rival Isles in NHL Semis

The Rangers successfully contained Islanders sniper Mike Bossy (#22) in their 1979 Stanley Cup semifinal series and pulled off a dramatic six-game upset of their crosstown rivals. The scoring of veteran Phil Esposito and rookie Don Maloney (whose brother, defenseman Dave Maloney, #26, is shown covering up in the defensive zone) helped launch the Rangers into their first Stanley Cup Finals appearance in seven years.

Stanley Cup Semifinals

Habs Take Advantage of Boston Blunder

Boston and Montreal couldn't seem to avoid each other in the playoffs, though in 1978-79 they met prior to the Finals. In the semis, the teams battled fiercely for seven games. Game 7 was tied on a late goal by Guy Lafleur after Boston was called for too many men on the ice (Bruins coach Don Cherry refused to name the culprit). At 9:33 of sudden-death, Yvon Lambert (pictured) beat Gilles Gilbert to send the Habs to the Cup Finals.

Stanley Cup Semifinals

• Game 5 at Montreal is tied 1-1 after one period, but the Habs pour three second-period goals past John Davidson and win 4-1, taking their fourth straight Stanley Cup.

• The Canadiens capture their 15th Cup in the last 24 years, capping off the greatest dynastic run in history.

• Canadiens defensive specialist Bob Gainey captures the Conn Smythe Trophy.

• Scoring champ Bryan Trottier edges Guy Lafleur for his first Hart Trophy.

• Atlanta's Bob MacMillan outballots Marcel Dionne for the Lady Byng Trophy, but Dionne wins the Lester B. Pearson Award.

• Montreal goalies Ken Dryden and Bunny Larocque share the Vezina Trophy. It's Dryden's fourth straight.

• Bob Gainey wins the Frank Selke Trophy—his second of four straight.

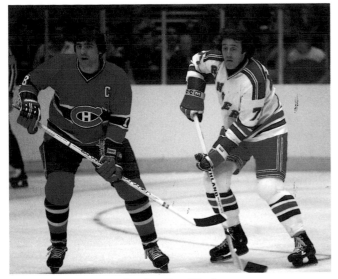

Stanley Cup Finals

Stanley Cup Celebration

Habs Drop Opener, Then Get Serious

The Rangers took Game 1 of the 1979 Finals against the Canadiens—in Montreal—but never won another game. The Habs' defense, led by Masterton Trophy winner Serge Savard (left), successfully shut down Phil Esposito (right) and the rest of the Rangers' offense. The Canadiens outscored New York 18-7 over the next four games and won their fourth straight Cup, becoming only the second NHL team ever to accomplish the feat.

Gainey Helps Habs to 21st Stanley Cup

Montreal survived a playoff mine field, narrowly escaping a semifinal disaster with Boston before advancing to the Finals against the surprising Rangers. Defensive forward Bob Gainey (hoisting the Stanley Cup) was a major force as the Habs became Cup champions for the 21st time. Gainey garnered 16 playoff points, and his goal halfway through Game 5 put the series out of reach. Gainey won the Conn Smythe Trophy.

- Minnesota's Bobby Smith wins the Calder Trophy.

- Denis Potvin wins his second straight Norris Trophy, as Montreal's Larry Robinson is runner-up.

- The Jack Adams Award is given to the Islanders' Al Arbour, while the Masterton Trophy goes to Serge Savard, who has overcome serious injuries.

- Bobby Orr, whose career ends at age 31 due to knee injuries, is the lone recipient of the Lester Patrick Award.

- Pierre Lacroix of Trois Rivieres (QMJHL) wins the Canadian Major Junior Player of the Year Award. The Peterborough Petes (OHL) win the Memorial Cup for the first time.

- Minnesota nips North Dakota 4-3 in the NCAA title game, as Gopher goalie Steve Janaszak is tourney MVP.

U.S. Skaters Shock the Soviets, Win the Gold

Uncle Sam's chances of winning an Olympic gold medal in February 1980 ranged between slim and non-existent. Mother Russia iced an overwhelmingly powerful squad, while Sweden, Czechoslovakia, and Finland all had formidable squads. Team USA was seeded seventh in a 12-team field and, even though the Games were held in Lake Placid, New York, the U.S. was considered a long shot even for a bronze.

USA opened against Sweden and trailed 2-1 with 41 seconds left in the game. It looked hopeless, but with a faceoff in the Swedish end, U.S. coach Herb Brooks pulled goalie Jim Craig in favor of an extra skater. Center Mark Pavelich won the faceoff, and at 19:33 defenseman Bill Baker fired a 45-foot blast past Swedish goalie Pelle Lindbergh, clinching an improbable 2-2 tie.

A loose U.S. squad next faced Czechoslovakia, and fans took notice when USA went up 4-2 after two periods. Goals by Phil Verchota and Buzz Schneider early in the third period sealed a stunning 7-3 victory.

Team USA then routed Norway 5-1, Romania 7-2, and West Germany 4-2, ending the "season" at 4-0-1 and easily earning a spot in the four-team "medal round." However, the first game of the medal playoffs was against the feared Soviet Union, the same team that had defeated the Americans 10-3 two weeks earlier and had outscored Olympic foes 51-11. The U.S. was a huge underdog.

Ten thousand Lake Placid fans, hoping against hope, watched the Soviets take a 1-0 lead at 9:12 of the first period. But at the 14-minute mark, the Americans pulled even when Schneider fired a routine slapshot that somehow eluded Soviet goalie Vladislav Tretiak. The Soviets went up 2-1, but USA's Mark Johnson scored a fluke goal just before the first period ended. "(Dave) Christian fired the puck at me from center ice," Tretiak recalled. "I made a sloppy save and the rebound went out in front of me, but there were no opponents near me anyway. But out of nowhere came Mark Johnson."

The Soviets went ahead 3-2 and held the lead until 8:39 of the third period, when the U.S. tied the score on a power-play goal by Johnson. Then with 10 minutes left, Pavelich found captain Mike Eruzione at the top of the circle. Eruzione fired, using a Russian defenseman as a screen, and beat new goalie Vladimir Myshkin. The Americans held on 4-3, and with the seconds ticking off and the crowd chanting "USA! USA!," announcer Al Michaels screamed, "Do you believe in miracles? Yes!"

The gold, however, was not theirs yet. Two days later, Team USA faced an ever-dangerous Finnish squad and trailed 2-1 after two periods. In need of a jump-start, USA got it early in the third period, as Verchota converted a Christian pass for the tying goal. Three minutes later, speedy Rob McClanahan put the Americans ahead, and then Johnson sealed the game with a shorthanded goal. As the final seconds ticked away, USA rejoiced with a 4-2 gold-medal victory, concluding the final chapter of the Miracle at Lake Placid.

1979-80

- The NHL expands from 17 teams to 21 as four WHA clubs—Edmonton Oilers, Hartford (formerly New England) Whalers, Winnipeg Jets, and Quebec Nordiques—join the NHL.

- The Hall of Fame inducts four members, including Harry Howell, Bobby Orr, and Henri Richard.

- Colorado uses the first pick in the 1979 Entry Draft to select defenseman Rob Ramage of London (OHA).

- Philadelphia loses goalie Bernie Parent, who retires because of vision problems resulting from an eye injury suffered several years back.

- Scotty Bowman—with four straight Stanley Cups—walks away from the Canadiens to join Buffalo.

- The Flyers weave together a 35-game undefeated streak (an NHL record) and finish a league-best 48-12-20. Goalie Pete Peeters goes 29-5-5 and Reg Leach nets 50 goals.

The 1980 Olympic Games delivered a "Miracle on Ice" as the American hockey contingent, led by captain Mike Eruzione (front row, center), upset the Soviets in the semifinal game and Finland in the finals. Eruzione never played a game in the National Hockey League, but many of his Team USA mates did, including Neal Broten, Mark Johnson, Ken Morrow, Rob McClanahan, Mark Pavelich, Dave Christian, Mike Ramsey, and Jim Craig.

• The Islanders drop to second in the Patrick behind Philly. Bryan Trottier and Mike Bossy combine for 93 goals and 196 points, while Swedish rookie Anders Kallur nets 22 goals.

• Phil Esposito leads the Rangers with 78 points, including his 1,500th, as New York places third in the Patrick.

• Ex-WHA star Kent Nilsson joins Atlanta and scores 40 goals and 93 points. Atlanta finishes fourth in the Patrick despite a winning record.

• The Capitals finish last in their new division, the Patrick, despite rookie Mike Gartner's 36 goals.

• The Black Hawks (34-27-19) rule the Smythe Division with the addition of ex-WHA stars Terry Ruskowski and Rich Preston. Stan Mikita plays the last of his 22 seasons in Chicago.

• Red Berenson takes over as coach of the Blues and leads them to second place in the Smythe.

Lafleur Nets 50 for Sixth Straight Year

Guy Lafleur, the indefatigable symbol of Montreal's Flying Frenchmen, set an NHL record in 1979-80 when he registered his sixth straight year of 50-or-more goals (netting 50 exactly). Lafleur finished third overall in a variety of categories including points (125), assists (75), and shots on goal (323). Teammate Steve Shutt once opined, "His intensity about the team's success is unbelievable."

Baby-Faced Gare Paces NHL in Goals

In 1979-80, the Sabres edged past Boston for the Adams Division title as right winger Danny Gare—the baby-faced sniper with the short fuse and nose for the net—tied for the NHL lead in goals with 56 (including 17 power-play goals). Gare, whose tenacious approach and tireless work ethic earned him the honor of wearing the captain's "C" on his jersey, set a Buffalo season record for goals that would stand until 1992-93.

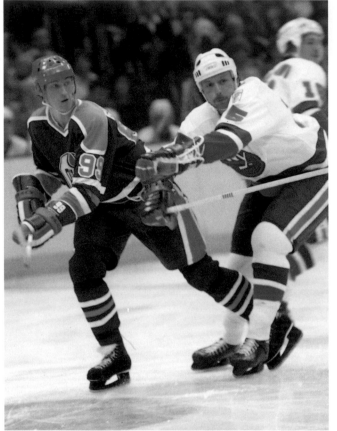

Wayne Gretzky, Denis Potvin

Teenager Gretzky Wins Hart Trophy

Islander Denis Potvin (right) can't contain Wayne Gretzky, as the Oilers' sensational 18-year-old shows the grace and agility that made him the WHA's greatest attraction. In his first NHL campaign, Gretzky tied L.A.'s Marcel Dionne in points (137) but lost the scoring race (and Art Ross Trophy) because Dionne had two more goals (53 to 51). Gretzky did win the Hart Trophy although not the Calder, as WHA imports weren't eligible.

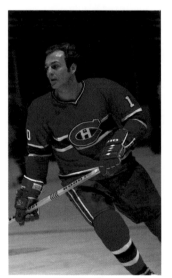

Guy Lafleur

Danny Gare

- In St. Louis, rookie goalie Mike Liut leads the NHL in wins (32).

- Rugged Stan Smyl (31 goals) and Swede Thomas Gradin (30) help Vancouver finish third in the Smythe.

- Edmonton, loaded with future stars—Wayne Gretzky, Mark Messier, Kevin Lowe—makes the playoffs with a 28-39-13 record.

- Edmonton rookie Wayne Gretzky, at age 19, leads the league in assists (86) and ties for tops in points (137).

- Despite the goal-scoring of Rene Robert (28), Lanny McDonald (25), Jack Valiquette (25), and Lucien DeBlois (24), the Rockies crumble (19-48-13).

- The Winnipeg Jets, winners of the final WHA championship, tie Colorado for fewest points in the league (51), wasting Morris Lukowich's 35 goals.

Bowman Bolts Habs for Buffalo

One of the chief traits of coach Scotty Bowman has always been his inability to refuse a challenge. After four straight Stanley Cups in Montreal, the man who would one day become the NHL's winningest coach left Les Habs and took over management of the Sabres, guiding them to a 47-17-16 record and first place in the Adams Division in 1979-80. The success story featured the Bowman touch—great defense. The Sabres allowed the fewest goals in the NHL (201).

Scotty Bowman

Boston Bruins/New York Rangers Brawl

Bruins Jump into Stands, Beat Up Fans

The bitter rivalry between the Rangers and Bruins reached a new level during the 1979-80 season when, following a match at Madison Square Garden, fans hurled beer on the Boston bench and hot-tempered Terry O'Reilly scaled the glass to take on his abusers up-close and personal. Moments later, he was joined by several team-mates, including Mike Milbury, who pried a shoe off one fan and started beating the guy with it.

• Bernie Geoffrion is replaced by Claude Ruel after 30 games, but the Canadiens (47-20-13) win the Norris by 33 points over Los Angeles.

• After eight brilliant seasons, Montreal goalie Ken Dryden retires, leaving Bunny Larocque and Denis Herron to tend the Habs' goal.

• Pierre Larouche becomes the first player to score 50 goals for two different teams when he and Guy Lafleur each score 50 for Montreal.

• L.A.'s Charlie Simmer, Marcel Dionne, and Dave Taylor—the Triple Crown Line—amass a whopping 146 goals and 328 points.

• Injuries to Greg Malone and Orest Kindrachuk hamper the Penguins, who tie Hartford for third in the Norris.

• Hartford is led by NHL newcomers Blaine Stoughton (56 goals) and Mike Rogers (105 points). Gordie Howe skates for the Whalers at age 52.

Gordie Howe

Mr. Hockey Enjoys One Last Hurrah

Nine years after retiring from the NHL and subsequently re-emerging as a star in the WHA, Gordie Howe made a triumphant return to the NHL in 1979-80 at the age of 51. The season was Howe's final year of action. In 80 games, Mr. Hockey tallied 15 goals and 41 points, finishing his NHL career with 801 goals and 1,850 points in 1,767 games. He also amassed 174 goals and 508 points in 419 WHA games.

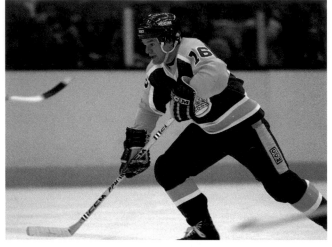

Marcel Dionne

Dionne Ties for Tops in Points

Although few in sunny California cared to notice, Marcel Dionne enjoyed some brilliant seasons with the L.A. Kings. In 1979-80, he won his only scoring championship, edging rookie Wayne Gretzky (whom he tied with 137 points) by virtue of his two extra goals (53 to 51). Dionne won the Art Ross Trophy and his second straight Lester B. Pearson Award. Moreover, he finished runner-up to Gretzky for the Hart and Lady Byng Trophies.

Charlie Simmer

Slow Simmer Boils Over, Scores 56

After the California Seals drafted him in 1974, the slow-skating Charlie Simmer toiled in the minors for nearly five years before a move to Los Angeles afforded him the chance to break into the NHL. Playing with Marcel Dionne on the Kings' dreaded Triple Crown Line, Simmer exploded in 1979-80 for 56 goals (tied for the league lead) in just 64 games. Included were a league-best 21 power-play goals.

1979-80

• The Red Wings sign Rogie Vachon from L.A. (and nearly lose star Dale McCourt as compensation), but Vachon leads the NHL in losses (30) and Detroit finishes last. Ted Lindsay takes over as coach late in the year.

• Scotty Bowman's Sabres go 47-17-16 to capture the Adams. Ric Seiling joins Rick Martin and Gil Perreault on the Sabres' top line. Bob Sauve leads the NHL in GAA (2.36) and Danny Gare scores 56 goals.

• Boston finishes five points behind Buffalo, as Rick Middleton and Peter McNab each score 92 points.

• Sophomore winger Steve Payne and veteran Al MacAdam each score 42 goals, as the North Stars gain a playoff berth in the Adams Division.

• Toronto slides to fourth in the Adams. Wilf Paiement replaces Lanny McDonald on the Darryl Sittler line and scores 20 goals in 41 games.

Cloutier Turns the Trick in First NHL Game

Fresh from his scoring title during the final year of the WHA, Quebec winger Real Cloutier entered the NHL record books when he notched a hat-trick in his first NHL game, tying a 37-year-old record set by Montreal's Alex Smart. Unfortunately for the Nordiques, who finished last in the Adams with just 25 wins, no other Nord scored and they lost to Atlanta 5-3. Cloutier finished the year with 42 goals.

Real Cloutier

Garry Unger

Michel Larocque

Unger Plays in 914 Straight Games

Garry Unger broke into the NHL in 1967 with Toronto and became a regular following his trade to Detroit during his rookie year. Over the next decade, Unger never missed a game. On December 21, 1980, his consecutive-game streak finally came to an end at 914 games. He retired in 1983 with 413 goals and 804 points in 1,105 NHL games.

Larocque, Herron Replace Dryden

The retirement of Ken Dryden after just eight NHL seasons left a huge hole in the Montreal lineup. The burden of filling that void fell partly on the shoulders of career backup Michel "Bunny" Larocque. In 38 decisions in 1979-80, Larocque won 17 times and finished with a 3.32 GAA. Meanwhile, partner Denis Herron went 25-3-3 with a 2.51 GAA, as the Habs took the Norris Division title.

- Despite 42 goals from Real Cloutier, and 33 from Marc Tardif, Quebec fails to make the playoffs.

- Atlanta's Garry Unger sees his consecutive-game streak end at 914.

- Islanders goalie Billy Smith is credited with a goal against Colorado when, after a Smith save, a Rockies player shoots the puck into his own open net.

- The NHL's leading goal-scorers are Charlie Simmer, Blaine Stoughton, and Danny Gare (56 apiece). Marcel Dionne and Mike Bossy are next with 53 each.

- Marcel Dionne and Wayne Gretzky tie for the scoring title (137 points). Guy Lafleur (125), Gil Perreault (106), and Mike Rogers (105) follow.

- The 16 teams with the best overall records make the playoffs. The team with the best record plays the 16th best, second plays 15th, etc.

Larouche Bounces Back, Pumps In 50

A wunderkind in his early years with Pittsburgh, where he became the NHL's youngest 50-goal scorer (53 in 1975-76), Pierre Larouche was traded to Montreal for Pete Mahovlich during the 1977-78 campaign. After a disastrous 1978-79 season (nine goals in 36 games), he erupted for 50 goals in 1979-80, becoming the first player ever to score 50 for two different teams. A gifted golfer, Larouche's career was cut short by back trouble.

Philadelphia's Peeters Goes 29-5-5

The Flyers lost star goalie Bernie Parent to an eye injury that cut short his career after the 1978-79 season, but they wasted no time in finding a more-than-adequate replacement, former Medicine Hat junior Pete Peeters, who was a rookie in 1979-80 and posted a sterling 29-5-5 record in 40 appearances. Peeters was known as something of a flake—many goalies shared such a reputation—but there was nothing wrong with his puck-stopping.

Stoughton's Big Year Goes for Naught

Originally property of Pittsburgh, right winger Blaine Stoughton played three NHL seasons before jumping to the WHA in 1976. It wasn't until the 1979-80 season that he had any measurable NHL success. In his first year back, Stoughton lit up NHL goalies for 56 goals—his best total ever. However, the Whalers won just 27 of 80 games and Stoughton's 100 points (and Mike Rogers' 105 points) were wasted.

Pierre Larouche

Pete Peeters

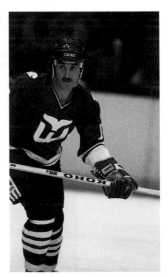

Blaine Stoughton

• In the best-of-five preliminaries, Philly sweeps Edmonton, Minnesota sweeps Toronto, Montreal brooms Hartford, and Boston beats Pittsburgh (3-2).

• Chicago ends a 16-game playoff losing streak (an NHL record) by sweeping St. Louis.

• In other prelims, the Isles best L.A. (3-1), the Rangers erase Atlanta (3-1), and Buffalo beats Vancouver (3-1).

• In the quarterfinals, Buffalo sweeps Chicago (4-0), the Isles trounce Boston (4-1), the Flyers oust the Rangers (4-1), and Montreal is shocked by Minnesota in seven.

• Philadelphia handles the upstart North Stars (4-1) in the semifinals, while the Islanders eliminate Buffalo in six to advance to the Finals.

• Game 1 of the Finals between Philly and the Isles goes to sudden-death before Denis Potvin beats Pete Peeters to give the Isles a 4-3 win.

Billy Smith

Don Edwards

Edwards and Sauve Save the Sabres

The goaltending tandem of Don Edwards and Bob Sauve provided Buffalo with 47 victories in 1979-80, enough to win the Adams Division. Sauve led the league with a 2.36 goals-against average while Edwards was second in GAA (2.57) and posted 27 victories. At season's end, the Buffalo netminding tandem was awarded the Vezina Trophy, ending the four-year reign of Montreal's Ken Dryden.

Goalie Smith Scores a Goal

Rarely has there been a more ill-tempered goalie than Billy Smith, who, in 1979-80, earned the distinction of also being one of the greatest "money" goalies ever to play. His 15 playoff wins capped off a brilliant season in which he was credited with a goal against Colorado. Smith was awarded the goal after a Rockie skater accidentally shot the puck into his own open net following a save by Smith (the last Isle to touch the puck).

• Game 2, still at the Spectrum, features a Paul Holmgren hat-trick, as the Flyers chase goalie Billy Smith in an 8-3 rout.

• The Isles rebound in Game 3 by thumping the Flyers 6-2, as Denis Potvin scores twice.

• Game 4 is never in doubt, as the Isles score twice in the first 13 minutes and breeze to a 5-2 win.

• With their backs to the wall in Game 5 at Philly, the Flyers get two goals from Rick MacLeish (including the winner) in a 6-3 triumph.

• Down 4-2 in the third period of Game 6, the Flyers score twice to force O.T., but Bobby Nystrom scores to win the game 5-4. The Isles hoist their first Stanley Cup.

• Bryan Trottier, who set a playoff record for points with 29, captures the Conn Smythe Trophy.

Stanley Cup Semifinals

Flyers Trip Up Stars in Cup Semis

Although the days of the Broad Street Bullies were all but over, the always-physical Flyers continued to mix intimidation in with their potent firepower. After dispatching Edmonton and the Rangers in the first two playoff rounds in 1980, the Flyers thrashed Minnesota, winning four straight games after losing the first game of the semis 6-5.

Finally, Isles Reach the Finals

After being upset in the 1978 and 1979 playoffs, the Islanders thrashed Buffalo 5-2 in Game 6 of their 1980 semifinal series and earned the right to face the Flyers. The chalkboard in the Islanders' dressing room spoke volumes about the team's exultant state after beating Buffalo and getting a horde of monkeys off their backs.

Stanley Cup Semifinals

1979-80

• Although he ties Wayne Gretzky for the most overall points (137), Marcel Dionne wins the Art Ross Trophy by virtue of more goals (53 to 51).

• Wayne Gretzky wins his first of eight straight Hart Trophies—and he nabs the Lady Byng. At age 19, he's the youngest ever to win either award.

• Marcel Dionne captures his second straight Lester B. Pearson Award.

• The Calder Trophy goes to Boston defenseman Ray Bourque, who edges Detroit's Mike Foligno.

• Buffalo goalies Bob Sauve and Don Edwards share the Vezina Trophy.

• Montreal's Larry Robinson wins his second Norris Trophy, beating out Toronto's Borje Salming.

• Flyers coach Pat Quinn cops the Jack Adams Award, and Montreal's Bob Gainey wins his third Frank Selke Trophy.

Isles Win Game 6 on Nystrom's O.T. Tally

Islanders Lorne Henning (#10) and Bob Lorimer (#4) prepare to celebrate the Cup-winning goal, which was set up by John Tonelli and scored in overtime by Bob Nystrom (against the boards). Nystrom scored four playoff O.T. winners in his career, but none bigger than the one in Game 6 of the 1980 Finals. Nystrom deflected a shot past Pete Peeters at the 7:11 mark to give New York a 5-4 win.

Stanley Cup Finals

Stanley Cup Celebration

Isles Win the First of Four Stanley Cups

The Islanders celebrate their first of four consecutive Stanley Cups as Dave Langevin (far left), Butch Goring (in helmet), Duane Sutter (hand raised), Bob Bourne (#14), and others prepare to take the Cup for a victory lap around Nassau Coliseum. The Islanders joined the Flyers as the first expansion teams to win the mug. (Ironically, during the 1980s, the Canadiens were the only non-expansion team to win the Cup.)

- Minnesota winger Al MacAdam (a 42-goal scorer after years of struggle in California and Cleveland) claims the Masterton Trophy for his perseverance.

- The U.S. Olympic team, coached by Herb Brooks and captained by Mike Eruzione, surprisingly makes it to the medal rounds at the Winter Games in Lake Placid, New York.

- In a stunning upset, the U.S. Olympic team defeats the Soviet Union 4-3. USA then knocks off Finland 4-2 to capture the gold medal.

- Regina's Doug Wickenheiser is the Canadian Major Junior Player of the Year. Dale Hawerchuk powers Cornwall to the Memorial Cup.

- North Dakota tops Northern Michigan 5-2 in the NCAA title game. North Dakota's Doug Smail is tourney MVP.

BOSSY SCORES 50 IN 50... WITH 1:29 TO SPARE

Like Maurice "Rocket" Richard of an earlier decade, Mike Bossy of the Islanders was, at first, considered too brittle for long-term high scoring in the NHL. But Bossy, like Richard, proved his critics wrong. The little right wing who hailed from Richard's hometown, Montreal, scored 50-plus goals in nine consecutive years, 1977-78 through 1985-86, and helped the Isles to four straight Stanley Cups beginning in 1980.

Mike carried an exceptionally hot stick early in 1980-81, and it became apparent that he could conceivably score 50 goals in 50 games—a feat achieved only by Richard. Bossy fueled interest by saying that 50 in 50 would be his deepest personal achievement. Occasionally, Bossy broke stride and fell behind the goal-a-game pace, but in mid-January he came on strong, scoring seven goals in two games. After his 47th game, Bossy had 48 goals.

"It's a challenge," said Bossy before game 48. "I think that I owe it to everybody to get the record now because I sort of announced it and I owe it to myself too."

Game 48 was against Calgary, and the Flames put the screws on Bossy. They double- and sometimes triple-teamed the Islanders' gifted right wing. New York was able to score, winning 5-0, but Bossy was manacled at every turn, especially when tenacious Eric Vail shadowed him.

Two nights later, Bossy took the ice at Joe Louis Arena against the Red Wings. Once again, Bossy was stymied. The final score of game 49 was 3-0 New York, but Mike had zip. "If I didn't get the record," Bossy allowed, "it would have been embarrassing because I had made it such a big thing."

Game 50 was at Nassau Coliseum. He needed not one but two goals to tie the mark, and through two periods of play Bossy seemed almost invisible. He had the look of an anxious young man. "I had never been so frustrated in all my hockey career," he admitted later. "I couldn't do anything right. I felt as if my hands were bound with tape and my stomach was tied in knots."

More than anything, Bossy needed a break. And then, almost miraculously, it happened. With a little more than five minutes left in the game, Quebec was hit with a minor penalty and Bossy was dispatched to the scene for the Islanders' power play. The clock ticked away: "4:15...4:14...4:13...." Suddenly, the puck was cradled on Bossy's stick. He released a backhander in the direction of crouched goalie Ron Grahame and lit the lamp at 4:10.

Goal No. 50 was now a slapshot away, but there were only four minutes left, then three, then two. As the clocked ticked below 1:40, Bossy received a pass near the left faceoff circle. Goalie Grahame prepared for the shot as Mike cracked his wrist and fired the puck goalward. Grahame never touched the rubber. It hit the twine with 1:29 remaining in the game, and the Coliseum reverberated with a noise rarely heard in an arena. Mike Bossy, meanwhile, breathed a sigh of relief.

1980-81

• Prior to the season, the Atlanta franchise—unable to make it in the deep South—moves to Calgary, Alberta. They're still called the Flames.

• Four men join the Hall of Fame, including players Harry Lumley, Lynn Patrick, and Gump Worsley.

• Using the first pick in the 1980 Entry Draft, Montreal selects center Doug Wickenheiser of Regina (WHL).

• Gordie Howe hangs up his skates after 32 pro seasons. He leaves with NHL records for seasons (26), games (1,767), goals (801), assists (1,049), and points (1,850).

• Quebec becomes involved in international intrigue when it signs Czech defectors Peter and Anton Stastny.

• After 41 games, the Rangers' Phil Esposito abruptly retires.

• On January 6, 1981, the Isles' John Tonelli scores five times vs. Toronto.

On January 24, 1981, Islanders sniper Mike Bossy became only the second player in NHL history to score 50 goals in 50 games when—late in the 50th game—he beat goalie Ron Grahame en route to a 7-3 Islanders win over Quebec. Bossy went on to lead the NHL in goals with 68, his fourth straight season with at least 50 goals. Included were a league-best 28 power-play goals. His 119 points placed him fourth in the league in scoring.

• On January 7, 1981, the Kings' Marcel Dionne garners his 1,000th career point.

• On January 24, 1981, Isles sniper Mike Bossy becomes only the second NHLer to notch 50 goals in 50 games.

• On February 22, 1981, the Stastny brothers—Peter (four goals, four assists) and Anton (three goals, five assists)—combine for 16 points as Quebec routs Washington 11-7.

• On February 26, 1981, the North Stars and Bruins brawl their way to 406 penalty minutes—an NHL record.

• On March 4, 1981, Montreal's Guy Lafleur scores his 1,000th point. Fifteen days later, Philly's Bobby Clarke accomplishes the feat.

• On March 19, 1981, Buffalo scores an NHL-record nine goals in one period in a 14-4 rout over Toronto.

Tiger Williams

Tiger: Don't Expect Mr. Nice Guy

One of the most intense players ever to lace on skates, Dave "Tiger" Williams (#22) led the NHL in penalty time in 1980-81, sitting out 343 minutes. Williams rejected the off-ice fraternization common among his peers, saying: "I can't pretend to be friendly to those guys after spending so much time trying to beat 'em up. It's phony." Williams scored 241 goals and sat out a record 3,966 minutes in 962 NHL games.

Four of Six Sutter Bros. Hit the Ice

Never in the history of the NHL had a brother act taken on the dimension of the Sutter boys from Viking, Alberta. In 1980-81, no less than four Sutters suited up for action, including Brian (St. Louis), Darryl (Chicago), Duane (Islanders), and Brent (briefly with the Isles). In 1982-83, two more Sutters—twins Rich and Ron—entered the NHL, giving the league another first: six brothers playing in the league simultaneously.

Sutter Brothers' Jerseys

1980-81

- The Islanders recapture the top spot in the NHL with a mark of 48-18-14, as Mike Bossy rings up 68 goals.

- The Flyers remain a Patrick Division threat as Bill Barber (43 goals), Rick MacLeish (38), and Reg Leach (34) spark the attack.

- Calgary gets 49 goals from Kent Nilsson and unexpected scoring from tough guy Willi Plett (38). The Flames finish third in the Patrick.

- The Rangers slip to fourth in the Patrick as Fred Shero resigns. He's replaced by Craig Patrick.

- The Caps can't climb out of the Patrick cellar despite Dennis Maruk's 50 goals and Mike Gartner's 48.

- St. Louis (45-18-17) wins the Smythe thanks to 10 20-goal scorers. Wayne Babych scores 54 times, while Bernie Federko tops the club in points (104).

Marcel Dionne

Habs Rarely Lose with Sevigny in Net

Despite the decline of Guy Lafleur as well as the loss of Ken Dryden and the infusion of new players, the Habs managed to keep winning. In 1980-81, a new hero emerged in goal as Richard Sevigny took on the bulk of the netminding duties. In 33 games, the former Quebec junior standout went 20-4-3. His 2.40 GAA contributed to a Vezina Trophy, which he shared with Michel Larocque and Denis Herron.

Danny Gare

Richard Sevigny

Dionne Hits 1,000 in Record Time

Marcel Dionne once said: "I don't believe practice makes perfect. It can only hurt a player if he skates his very best in practice." On January 7, 1981, playing in his 740th NHL game, Dionne became the 13th NHLer to notch 1,000 career points when he scored during a 5-3 Kings win over Hartford. It was the quickest 1,000 points ever. No word on whether coach Bob Berry gave him the next morning's practice off.

Gare, Tough Defense Power the Sabres

Buffalo won its second straight division title in 1980-81 with great team defense, the best penalty killing in the league, and some explosive scoring from the line of Derek Smith, Tony McKegney, and Danny Gare. A former 56-goal scorer, Gare "slumped" somewhat during 1980-81 but still led the Sabres in goals (46) and points (85). His line accounted for more than 40 percent of the team's total goal-scoring.

- Darryl Sutter, one of six Sutter brothers who will play in the NHL, leads Chicago in goals (40) in his rookie year. The Hawks finish second in the Smythe.

- Vancouver gets unexpected offense from goon Tiger Williams (35 goals) and finishes third in the Smythe.

- The Oilers add Finnish sensation Jari Kurri to Wayne Gretzky's line and one of the most deadly combos in NHL history is born.

- Wayne Gretzky finishes the year with an NHL-record 164 points—including five goals in a game—but Edmonton posts a losing record.

- Not even the arrival of Chico Resch can help the Rockies from losing 45 games. Lanny McDonald tops the team with 35 goals.

- Winnipeg goes winless during a 30-game span (an all-time NHL record) and finishes 9-57-14. Danny Geoffrion, son of Bernie, nets 20.

Stastny Defects to Quebec

The Nordiques became embroiled in international political intrigue in 1980 when they helped the defection efforts of Peter Stastny, a star in Czechoslovakia. Stastny joined his brother Anton and immediately became a star in the NHL, winning the Calder Trophy with record rookie numbers (70 assists and 109 points). On February 22, 1981, the two Stastnys accounted for seven goals and 16 points in an 11-7 win at Washington.

Mark Howe

Howe Speared by Goal Net Spike

Former WHA superstar Mark Howe entered the NHL in 1979-80 with the Hartford Whalers (who were absorbed into the NHL when the two leagues merged). During the course of a game in 1980-81, the brilliant defenseman nearly lost his life when he was checked into the net and the spike holding the goal cage in place speared his buttock, just missing his spine. Howe missed 17 games that year but went on to play more than another decade in the NHL.

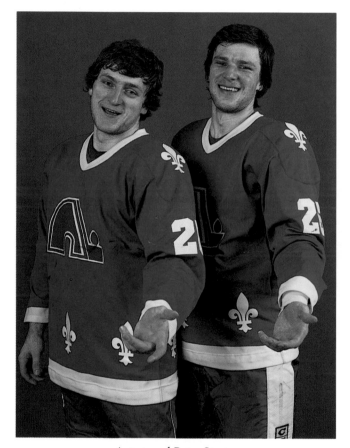

Anton and Peter Stastny

1980-81

- The Canadiens (45-22-13) win the Norris by just four points over L.A., as Guy Lafleur's streak of six 50-goal seasons ends (27 in 51 games).

- Montreal goalie Richard Sevigny notches a 20-4-3 record and also leads the league with a 2.40 GAA.

- The Kings finish second thanks to the Triple Crown Line. Larry Murphy's 76 points set a record for a rookie blueliner.

- Charlie Simmer scores on a miraculous 32.7 percent of his 171 shots, and Kings goalie Mario Lessard leads the NHL in wins (35).

- Pittsburgh finishes third in the Norris, as Rick Kehoe erupts for 55 goals while defenseman Randy Carlyle scores 83 points.

- Blaine Stoughton (43 goals) and Mike Rogers (40) are among the very few bright spots during another season of trials in Hartford.

Dennis Maruk

Randy Carlyle

Carlyle Lugs the Rubber, Cops the Norris

Puck-handling was the trademark of Randy Carlyle's game through the 1980s, as he established himself as one of the premier players in the NHL. Carlyle won the Norris Trophy in 1980-81 after posting a career-high 83 points (16 goals) for the Penguins. Originally property of the Maple Leafs, Carlyle spent six years in Pittsburgh and nine in Winnipeg before retiring in 1993.

Maruk Finally Emerges, Nets 50

His road to NHL stardom was mined with potential disasters—including stays in California and Cleveland—but Dennis Maruk successfully navigated his way along the rocky road and emerged in 1980-81 as one of the game's most prolific scorers. He joined the 50-goal club when he beat Detroit's Larry Lozinski on the final day of the season.

Ex-Baseballer Babych Bats In 54

Wayne Babych was a good—not great—goal-scorer in his first two NHL seasons, with 53 goals in two campaigns. But in his third pro season, 1980-81, he teamed with playmaker extraordinaire Bernie Federko and exploded for 54 goals. Picked third overall in the 1978 draft, Babych also received a contract offer from the Montreal Expos. He chose the NHL and played for four teams in nine years, scoring 192 goals.

Wayne Babych

• Whalers defenseman Mark Howe narrowly averts a career-ending injury when checked into the net, as the spike holding the cage in place misses his spine by a half-inch.

• Red Wings sophomore John Ogrodnick rips 35 goals as Detroit finishes last in the Norris again.

• Danny Gare (46 goals), Tony McKegney (37), and Andre Savard (31) power the Sabres to an Adams Division title (39-20-21).

• The Bruins finish 12 points behind Buffalo, as Rick Middleton tallies 44 goals and 103 points. Rogie Vachon wins 25 games.

• The North Stars tie Boston for second in the Adams Division. Don Beaupre, Minnesota's 19-year-old goalie, goes 18-14-11.

• Quebec makes the playoffs as Peter Stastny (109 points) and brother Anton each score 39 goals. Former Flame Jacques Richard rips 52.

Ducky Powers Cornwall to Memorial Cup

The Cornwall Royals of the Quebec Major Junior Hockey League successfully defended their Memorial Cup title in 1981 thanks largely to the play of center Dale "Ducky" Hawerchuk, who earned honors as the QMJHL and Canadian Major Junior Player of the Year in 1980-81 after scoring 81 goals and 183 points. In June of 1981, Hawerchuk became the first player chosen overall (by the Winnipeg Jets) in the 1981 Entry Draft.

Dale Hawerchuk

Gretzky Sets Marks for Points, Feeds

It didn't take Wayne Gretzky long to live up to his nickname, the "Great One." On February 18, 1981, en route to a 55-goal season, Gretzky filled the St. Louis net with four goals in one period, becoming only the fifth player ever to achieve such a feat. Edmonton won the game 9-2 and Gretzky went on to set NHL records for assists (109) and points (164). The 20-year-old also accepted his second Hart Trophy.

Wayne Gretzky

Minnesota's Broten Wins Baker Award

Neal Broten, a native of Roseau, Minnesota, enjoyed an entire career in his own backyard, playing high school hockey at Roseau, college hockey at the University of Minnesota—where in 1981 he won the first Hobey Baker Award as the college game's premier player—and pro hockey for 12 years with the North Stars. His home streak came to an end in 1993-94 when the Minnesota franchise relocated to Dallas, but he continued with the same team nonetheless.

Neal Broten

1980-81

- Toronto just makes the playoffs despite the scoring of Darryl Sittler (43 goals), Wilf Paiement (40), Bill Derlago (35), and Rick Vaive (33).

- The NHL's top goal-scorers include Mike Bossy (68), Marcel Dionne (58), Charlie Simmer (56), Wayne Gretzky (55), and Rick Kehoe (55).

- Scoring leaders are Wayne Gretzky (164), Marcel Dionne (135), Kent Nilsson (131), and Mike Bossy (119).

- Tiger Williams is the NHL's most penalized player (343 PIM).

- The best-of-five first round of the playoffs features five sweeps: Buffalo over Vancouver, Minnesota over Boston, Calgary over Chicago, the Oilers over Montreal, and the Isles over Toronto.

- In other preliminary-round action, St. Louis survives Pittsburgh (3-2), Philadelphia outlasts Quebec (3-2), and the Rangers oust L.A. (3-1).

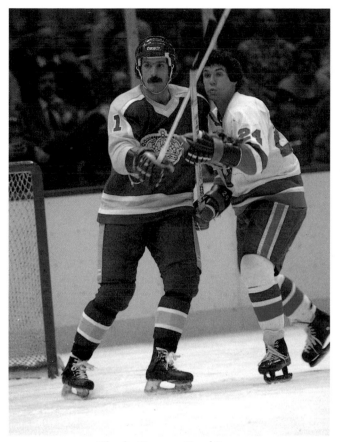

Charlie Simmer, Gord Lane

Nilsson Packs His Bags, Puts Puck in Net

Originally drafted by Atlanta in 1976, Swedish-born Kent Nilsson spent two years in the WHA with the Winnipeg Jets before joining his NHL team after the 1979 merger. Following a brilliant 40-goal rookie year (1979-80), Nilsson moved to Calgary with the relocating Flames and exploded for 82 assists and 131 points in 1980-81. He trailed only Wayne Gretzky and Marcel Dionne in the final scoring race.

Liut's Puck-Stopping Wows His Peers

Due largely to the brilliant performance of ex-Bowling Green goalie Mike Liut, St. Louis finished first in the Smythe in 1980-81 for the first time in four years. Liut won 33 of 60 decisions and posted a 3.34 GAA. NHL players knew that Liut's somewhat modest numbers didn't tell the whole story, as they honored him with the Lester B. Pearson Award as the league's best player. Liut also finished runner-up to Wayne Gretzky for the Hart Trophy.

L.A.'s Simmer Cleans Up the Trash

Kings left winger Charlie Simmer (shown fighting for position with Islanders defenseman Gord Lane) was known for his very slow feet and very quick hands, particularly in front of the net. A big skater (6'3", 210 pounds), Simmer would park himself in the slot and score the majority of his goals on deflections and rebounds. In 1980-81, Simmer scored 56 goals (for the second year in a row) despite missing 15 games due to injury.

Kent Nilsson

Mike Liut

- In the quarterfinals, Minnesota shocks Buffalo (4-1), the Isles beat Edmonton (4-2), the Rangers skate past St. Louis (4-2), and Calgary squeaks past Philadelphia (4-3).

- The semifinals in the Campbell Conference see Minnesota stun Calgary 4-2.

- In the Wales Conference final, the Isles sweep the Rangers, outscoring their Broadway enemies 22-8.

- In Game 1 of the Stanley Cup Finals, the heavily favored Islanders build a 3-0 lead and go on to beat Minnesota 6-3.

- After Dino Ciccarelli's early goal for the Stars in Game 2, Mike Bossy and Denis Potvin each score twice as the Isles skate to another 6-3 win.

- New York wins a Game 3 shootout in Minnesota. Mike Bossy (two goals) and Butch Goring (three) lead the Isles to a 7-5 victory.

Isles Crush Rival Rangers in Semifinals

The cross-county playoff rivalry between the Isles and Rangers resumed in 1981 after the Isles eliminated Toronto and Edmonton in the early rounds and the Rangers knocked off Los Angeles and St. Louis. In the semis, the Rangers' offense died while their defense collapsed under the Isles' avalanche (22 goals in four games). Wayne Merrick (pictured on the ice) was one of many Islanders to heap misery on the Rangers.

Butch Goring

Stanley Cup Semifinals

Goring Leads the Isles' Playoff Charge

In the first defense of their Stanley Cup championship, the Islanders overcame Toronto, Edmonton, and the Rangers thanks to the goaltending of Billy Smith and the clutch scoring of Butch Goring (20 points in 18 games). Goring arrived in New York prior to the 1979-80 playoff season as a complement to Bryan Trottier. But Goring was the top dog in the 1981 playoffs, winning the Conn Smythe Trophy.

Stanley Cup Semifinals

Stars Shoot Down Flames in Cup Semis

In 1980-81, the North Stars finished third in the Adams Division and going into the playoffs their prospects looked chancy at best. But they shocked Boston in three straight to start their miracle journey, then eliminated powerful Buffalo in five games. In the semifinals, Minnesota faced Calgary. Led by 93-point center Bobby Smith (pictured beating Reggie Lemelin of the Flames), the North Stars eliminated Calgary in six.

1980-81

- The North Stars avoid elimination in Game 4 with a dramatic 4-2 win.

- The Islanders begin Game 5 with a three-goal outburst. They win 5-1 and claim their second straight Cup.

- Butch Goring, who scored twice in Game 5, is voted the Conn Smythe Trophy. Mike Bossy, though, tallied 17 goals and a playoff-record 35 points.

- Islanders goalie Billy Smith confirms his role as the team's "money" goalie with 14 postseason victories and a 2.54 playoff GAA.

- For the second year in a row, Edmonton's No. 99, Wayne Gretzky, wins the Hart Trophy. Blues goalie Mike Liut (33 wins) is runner-up.

- Rick Kehoe, the Penguins' 55-goal scorer, wins the Lady Byng Trophy, topping Wayne Gretzky in the voting.

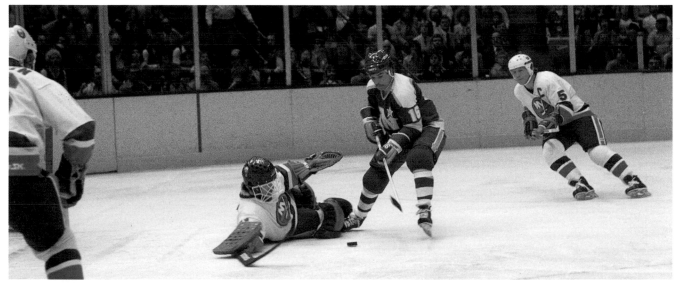

Stanley Cup Finals

John Ziegler, Denis Potvin

Smith Shines at Crunch Time

Islanders goalie Billy Smith earned his second Stanley Cup ring with 14 wins and a 2.54 GAA in the 1981 postseason. He cemented his reputation as a clutch goalie by winning close games and shutting the door when his team was blowing out opponents. Smith's best performance came against the Rangers in the semis, as he allowed just eight goals in the Islanders' four-game sweep.

Isles Breeze Past Stars, Grab the Cup

NHL President John Ziegler congratulates Denis Potvin after the Islanders won the 1981 Stanley Cup, their second straight. Potvin posted 17 postseason assists, tying for second overall. Goring, the playoff MVP, scored three goals in Game 3 of the Finals and added two more in the decisive Game 5. New York's series triumph over Minnesota was never in doubt, as they outscored the Stars 26-16 and won the finale 5-1.

- Quebec's Peter Stastny, who set a league record for assists (70) and points (109) by a rookie, wins the Calder Trophy. Pittsburgh's Randy Carlyle wins the Norris Trophy.

- Mike Liut is voted the Lester B. Pearson Award. His coach, Red Berenson, wins the Jack Adams.

- Montreal's Bob Gainey wins his fourth (and last) Frank Selke Trophy, while Blues forward Blake Dunlop wins the Masterton Trophy.

- Dale Hawerchuk, the Canadian Major Junior Player of the Year, helps the Cornwall Royals to their second consecutive Memorial Cup.

- Wisconsin, with tourney MVP Marc Behrend in nets, beats Minnesota 6-3 in the NCAA championship game.

- Minnesota center Neal Broten wins the first Hobey Baker Award, which is presented to the top college player in the U.S.

GRETZKY TIPS, WOBBLES, AND WISHES IN 92 GOALS

Throughout NHL history, the idea of a hockey player scoring more than 90 goals in a season seemed preposterous. Ridiculous. No way. That is, until Wayne Gretzky matured as a scoring machine in 1981-82. A year earlier, he had tallied a league-leading 164 points on 55 goals and 109 assists. Some figured Gretzky might someday reach 65 goals in a year, or even 70. But in 1981-82, the dice rolled perfectly for the Great One.

Teamed with Finnish star Jari Kurri, Gretzky catapulted to the top of the scoring pack early and sprinted far ahead of even Mike Bossy, who would finish with 64 goals. Gretzky's touch was unfathomable. He scored his 50th goal in his 39th game, making a mockery of the mythical 50-in-50 feat achieved by Rocket Richard and by Mike Bossy one year earlier.

"After 35 games," said Gretzky, "I had 38 goals. But the pucks get bigger and the net smaller as the season wears on. But right then, just before the All-Star break, all heaven broke loose. Pucks started going into the net on their own. I'd tip 'em in, bounce 'em in, wobble 'em in, elbow 'em in, wish 'em in. No matter what I tried,

they kept finding their way past goaltenders.

"In one stretch of four games, I got 10 goals—three against Minnesota, two against Calgary, one against Vancouver, and four against L.A. I had 45 goals in 38 games." Philadelphia was the next opponent, on December 30 at Northlands Coliseum. "That night," said Gretzky, "turned out to be one of the greatest of my life."

By the six-minute mark of the third period, Gretzky had beaten Philly goalie Pete Peeters four times and was up to 49 goals. With time running out, the Flyers were down only one, 6-5, and pulled the goaltender for an extra skater. But before the horn blew, Glenn Anderson fed Gretzky, who flipped it into the empty net. Five goals in one game. Fifty goals in

39 games. "I knew then," said Gretzky, "that I'd beat Phil Esposito's record of 76 goals in a season."

Wayne broke the record at the Aud in Buffalo, beating goalie Don Edwards in his 66th game. (Esposito needed 70 games for his mark.) Gretzky eventually became the first player to break the 200-point barrier (212), although he fell eight goals short of the 100-goal level to which he aspired. "I don't know if anyone can get 100," said Gretzky.

What Wayne and his Oilers did get was a lesson in maturity. Despite finishing the season at 48-17-15 and scoring an NHL-record 417 goals, the too-cocky Oilers lost in the first round of the playoffs to Los Angeles. The Kings, 21-41-15 on the year, defeated Edmonton three games to two in the opening round.

With Gretzky's Oilers out of the picture, the Islanders were able to storm through the playoffs, sweeping Vancouver in four Finals games. However, when fans generations from now look back on 1981-82, they'll likely gloss over the Isles' third straight Stanley Cup. "Gretzky's 92 goals," they'll say. "Now *that* was something."

1981-82

- The NHL re-aligns its divisions as several teams shift: Minnesota from the Adams to the Norris; Winnipeg, Chicago, and St. Louis from the Smythe to the Norris; and Toronto from the Adams to the Norris.

- Other franchise shifts include Calgary moving from the Patrick to

the Smythe; L.A. from the Norris to the Smythe; Pittsburgh from the Norris to the Patrick; and Montreal and Hartford from the Norris to the Adams.

- Four men join the Hall of Fame, including players Johnny Bucyk, Allan Stanley, and Frank Mahovlich.

- With the first overall pick in the 1981 Entry Draft, Winnipeg selects Cornwall star Dale Hawerchuk.

- Washington, with the third pick overall, chooses high schooler Bobby Carpenter from Massachusetts, making him the highest-drafted U.S.-born player ever.

No hockey player has ever dominated a season like Wayne Gretzky of the Edmonton Oilers did in 1981-82, when he shattered Phil Esposito's single-season record of 76 goals. Gretzky, pictured scoring his 77th goal of the year against Buffalo goaltender Don Edwards, set season records for goals (92), assists (120), and hat-tricks (10) and became the first player ever to notch 200 points in a season (212). He also led the Oilers to an NHL-record 417 goals.

• USSR wins the six-country Canada Cup tournament with an 8-1 thrashing of Canada in the finals.

• On December 20, 1981, Winnipeg's Doug Smail scores five seconds into a 5-4 win over St. Louis for the fastest opening goal ever.

• In a one-month span, three players score five goals in a game: Chicago's Grant Mulvey (February 3), Islander Bryan Trottier (February 13), and the Jets' Willy Lindstrom (March 2).

• On April 3, 1982, Buffalo's Gil Perreault tallies his 1,000th point.

• Edmonton explodes for an NHL-record 417 goals, as the Oilers go 48-17-15 and win the Smythe.

• On December 30, 1981, Wayne Gretzky scores five goals to give him 50 in 39 games. He goes on to set NHL records for goals (92), assists (120), and points (212).

Dennis Maruk

Maruk Scores 60 for Lowly Caps

Washington got off to one of its patented slow starts in 1981-82, losing 12 of its first 13 games and costing coach Gary Green his job. Not even the magnificent goal-scoring of Dennis Maruk could keep the Caps from a fifth-place finish in the Patrick Division. Maruk, a flashy winger whose lack of size never hindered his ability to produce, set a team record with 60 goals, third best in the NHL. He also finished fourth overall in points (136).

Billy Smith

Smith Wins Vezina, Stanley Cup

Battlin' Billy Smith made almost as much hay with his aggressiveness as with his brilliant goaltending. In 1981-82, as the Isles captured another Patrick Division title, Smith posted a 2.97 GAA and enjoyed a 32-9-4 record, good enough to win him the Vezina Trophy. In the playoffs, he was nearly unbeatable, with 15 victories in 18 games and a 2.52 GAA as the Islanders sewed up their third straight Stanley Cup.

Super Frosh Stastny Gets Even Better

Trapped in the highly competitive Adams Division, Quebec fell to fourth place in 1981-82 despite a better-than-.500 record and the fourth-best offense in the NHL. Much of the Nordiques' firepower came from brilliant sophomore Peter Stastny, who improved on his record-setting 109-point rookie season by notching 46 goals and 139 points and finishing third overall in scoring. His 93 assists were second only to Wayne Gretzky's 120.

Peter Stastny

- Overshadowed by Wayne Gretzky is teammate Mark Messier (50 goals).

- The Canucks grab second place in the Smythe as Thomas Gradin leads in goals (37).

- Lanny McDonald's career gets a charge when Calgary acquires him from Colorado. He leads the Flames in goals (34), as the team finishes third in the Smythe.

- The Kings' Triple Crown Line is dethroned when Charlie Simmer scores only 15 goals in 50 games, though Marcel Dionne nets 50 and Dave Taylor 39. L.A. finishes fourth.

- Chico Resch leads the league in losses (31) for Colorado, the worst team in the league.

- The Islanders win an NHL-record 15 games in a row and capture another regular-season championship (54-16-10). Mike Bossy pots 64 goals while Bryan Trottier scores 50.

Vaive's the First Leaf to Reach 50

Rick Vaive suffered a dismal rookie season with Vancouver in 1979-80 that resulted in his being traded to Toronto before the year was out. But in 1981-82 with the Leafs, Vaive did what no Toronto skater had ever done before: reach the 50-goal plateau. On March 24, 1982, the hard-shooting right winger beat St. Louis goalie Mike Liut for his 50th red light of the year. He finished the season with 54 goals, a Toronto record.

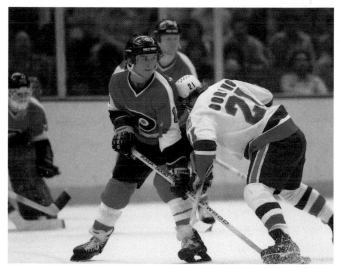

Ken Linseman

Flyers Find a New Star in Linseman

With Bobby Clarke entering his 13th NHL season in 1981-82, the torch of leadership in Philadelphia was being passed to a fiery kid from Kingston, Ontario. Ken Linseman was a speedy center with a huge chip on his smallish shoulders. In 1981-82, Linseman led the Flyers in assists (68) and points (92), many of which came against the Rangers, who had forfeited his junior rights to sign coach Fred Shero in 1978.

Rick Vaive

• The Rangers hire U.S. Olympic coach Herb Brooks, trade for Mike Rogers (38-65-103), and see the emergence of matinee idol Ron Duguay (40 goals).

• Philadelphia falls to third in the Patrick behind both New York teams. Bill Barber (45 goals), Brian Propp (44), and Ken Linseman (92 points) lead the way.

• In his first full NHL season, Mike Bullard nets 36 for the Penguins, who finish fourth in the Patrick.

• Washington loses 12 of its first 13 games, fires Gary Green, and installs Bryan Murray as coach. Dennis Maruk scores 60 goals but the Caps finish last in the Patrick.

• The Canadiens capture the Adams Division title with a 46-17-17 record. Rookie goalie Rick Wamsley posts a 23-7-7 record while Keith Acton (88 points) leads a well-balanced attack.

Stoughton's 52 Goals Go to Waste

Hartford finished out of playoff contention for the second straight season in 1981-82 despite a brilliant one-man performance by right winger Blaine Stoughton. The injury-plagued Whalers won only 21 games, but Stoughton enjoyed his second 50-goal season. On March 28, 1982, the ex-WHA star beat North Stars goalie Gilles Meloche for his 50th. "Stosh" finished the year with 52 tallies, sixth best in the NHL.

Blaine Stoughton

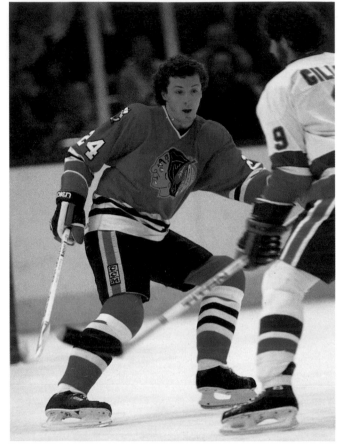

Doug Wilson

Wilson Blasts In 39, Wins Norris

Prior to the 1981-82 season, only one Black Hawk player (three-time Norris Trophy winner Pierre Pilote) had ever been honored as the league's outstanding defenseman. In 1981-82, Doug Wilson (pictured backchecking against Islander left winger Clark Gillies) became the second. Wilson scored 39 goals on the strength of his tremendous slapshot en route to his first and only Norris Trophy.

1981-82

- The Bruins take second place in the Adams, as Rick Middleton reaches a career-high 51 goals and rookie Barry Pederson connects for 44.

- After the Sabres sputter under coach Jimmy Roberts, G.M. Scotty Bowman takes over as coach. The Sabres finish a disappointing third in the Adams.

- Quebec finishes fourth in the Adams on the scoring of Peter Stastny (46 goals), Michel Goulet (42), Marc Tardif (39), and Real Cloutier (37).

- The Nordiques boast an all-brother line—Peter Stastny centering for Anton and Marian—and they collect 107 goals and 300 points.

- Blaine Stoughton's 52 goals are the only bright spot in Hartford as the Whalers finish out of the playoffs.

- The North Stars (37-23-20) win the Norris for their first-ever division title. Dino Ciccarelli (55 goals), Bobby Smith (43), Neal Broten (38), and Steve Payne (33) lead the way.

Ron Duguay, Herb Brooks, Barry Beck, Mark Pavelich   Dino Ciccarelli

Brooks Finds Few Friends in New York

When Herb Brooks joined the Rangers as head coach in 1981, he was known for his demanding style and taciturn manner. A coaching style that worked to perfection with collegians and amateurs was a difficult pill to swallow for Brooks' squad of highly paid professionals. Brooks enjoyed the loyalty of his former Minnesota winger Mark Pavelich (#40), but clashed with matinee idol Ron Duguay (#10) and oft-injured captain Barry Beck.

Denis Savard

Fully Healed Ciccarelli Rings Up 55

A broken leg suffered during his final year of junior hockey nearly cost Dino Ciccarelli his shot at an NHL career. But in 1981-82, he established himself as one of the game's premier snipers, scoring a club-record 55 goals as the North Stars captured the Norris Division title. Ciccarelli made the most of Neal Broten's clever playmaking and finished with 106 points, second on the team behind Bobby Smith's 114.

Savard Carries Hawks on His Back

There were few bright spots in Chicago during the 1981-82 regular season, as the Black Hawks won just 30 games. However, offensive catalyst Denis Savard exploded for his first 100-point season (119). His 87 assists were third best in the league, and he led Chicago through a brilliant playoff run. He scored 18 playoff points and took the Hawks to the Stanley Cup semifinals, where they lost to Vancouver in five games.

• The Jets hire a new coach, Tom Watt, and finish second in the Norris. Rookie Dale Hawerchuk (45 goals, 103 points) makes an immediate impact, while veteran Morris Lukowich nets 43.

• The Blues waste strong production from Brian Sutter (39 goals), Jorgen Pettersson (38), Perry Turnbull (33), and Bernie Federko (92 points). They finish third in the Norris.

• Chicago finishes fourth in the Norris despite center Denis Savard (119 points), defenseman Doug Wilson (39 goals), and tough guy Al Secord (44 goals).

• Rick Vaive's 54 goals go for naught in Toronto, as the Leafs stumble to a 20-44-16 record under coach Mike Nykoluk and place fifth in the Norris.

• Detroit's stay in the Norris basement continues, as John Ogrodnick (28 goals) and Mark Osborne (67 points) are the only bright spots.

Dale Hawerchuk

Hawerchuk Gives Jets a Needed Jolt

Despite their success as a WHA franchise, Winnipeg struggled mightily during their early years in the NHL—until they made Dale Hawerchuk the first pick in the 1981 Entry Draft. A former Canadian Major Junior Player of the Year at Cornwall (QMJHL), Hawerchuk made a splendid NHL debut in 1981-82, leading the Jets in goals with 45 and points with 103— third most ever by a fresh- man. He was an over- whelming choice for rookie of the year.

Bobby Carpenter

Caps Draft an American in Round 1

The Capitals made history on June 9, 1981, when they made Bobby Carpenter their first pick (third overall) in the Entry Draft. / ar prospect from St. John's High School in Massachusetts, Carpenter thus became the first American- born player ever picked in the first round. Despite his family's efforts to dissuade the Caps from drafting Bobby (who preferred Boston or Hartford), the talented center scored 32 goals for Washington in 1981-82.

Mark Messier

Gretzky's Not the Only Star in Edmonton

The predominance of Wayne Gretzky overshadowed many great players in Edmonton, but one player who overcame it was Mark Messier, whose 50-goal performance in 1981-82 catapulted him out of his good buddy's shadow. A lightning-quick center with a mean streak (119 PIM) and an indomitable spirit, Mess quickly became the Oilers' heart and soul even as Gretzky remained the team's symbol of grace and execu- tion.

1981-82

- Leading NHL scorers are Wayne Gretzky (212), Mike Bossy (147), Peter Stastny (139), Dennis Maruk (136), and Bryan Trottier (129).

- Leading goal-scorers include Wayne Gretzky (92), Mike Bossy (64), Dennis Maruk (60), Dino Ciccarelli (55), and Rick Vaive (54).

- Although he plays just 27 games, Montreal's Denis Herron wins the GAA title (2.64).

- In a new playoff format, each division's top four teams play down to a division champion. The Norris champ then faces the Smythe winner for the Campbell Conference champi-

onship, while Adams meets Patrick for the Wales Conference title.

- In the Adams Division semifinals, Boston erases Buffalo (3-1) and Quebec upsets Montreal (3-2).

- In the Patrick semis, the Rangers top Philly (3-1) and the Isles beat

Barry Pederson

Bryan Trottier

Trottier Bangs In 50; Isles Rule Again

The Islanders went a league-best 54-16-10 in 1981-82, as Bryan Trottier reigned as the circuit's most dangerous all-around player. A tenacious hitter, he showed his explosive scoring punch when he scored four goals in one period against Philadelphia on February 13. Trottier concluded the year with exactly 50 goals and finished runner-up to Wayne Gretzky for the Hart Trophy.

Pederson Scores 44 Frosh Goals

The Bruins tapped a gold mine when they brought Barry Pederson—their top pick in the 1980 draft—to the NHL in 1981-82. Fresh from a brilliant three-year career at Victoria, Pederson teamed on a line with right wing sniper Rick Middleton. While Middleton tallied 51 goals and 94 points, Pederson was right behind at 44 and 92. Pederson finished runner-up to the brilliant Dale Hawerchuk for the Calder Trophy.

Pittsburgh (3-2)—in which Islander Bryan Trottier establishes a record by scoring in 27 straight playoff games.

• In the Norris semis, Chicago defeats Minnesota (3-1) and St. Louis beats Winnipeg (3-1). In the Smythe semis, L.A. shocks Edmonton (3-2) and Vancouver blanks Calgary (3-0).

• Quebec edges Boston (4-3) in the Adams finals, while Chicago tops St. Louis (4-2) in the Norris. Vancouver beats L.A. (4-1) in the Smythe, and the Isles eliminate the Rangers (4-2) in the Patrick.

• The Islanders sweep Quebec (4-0) in the Wales Conference finals, while

Vancouver continues its Cinderella act with a five-game win over Chicago in the Campbell Conference.

• In Game 1 of the Stanley Cup Finals, Mike Bossy scores with two seconds to play in the first O.T. to give New York a 6-5 win over Vancouver.

Campbell Conference Finals

Canucks Upset Chicago in Semis

Vancouver and Chicago engaged in a tough semifinal battle in 1982, as each team pressed for the opportunity to unseat the Cup holders from Long Island. Left winger Lars Molin (pictured, left, attacking the goal of Murray Bannerman as Black Hawks center Denis Savard looks on) played just three seasons in the NHL but made it to the Finals in 1982 when his Canucks fashioned a five-game upset of the favored Hawks. He had 11 points in 17 playoff games.

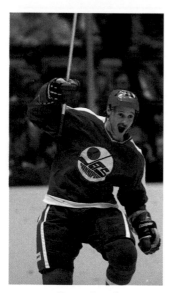

Doug Smail

Smail Scores Quickest Goal in History

On December 20, 1981, Doug Smail gave Winnipeg an early Christmas present when he sparked the Jets to a 5-4 win over St. Louis with a goal just five seconds after the opening faceoff. Smail thus entered the NHL record books with the fastest goal ever scored at the start of a game. A smallish skater with excellent speed and great defensive prowess, Smail averaged one goal every four games through his 13-year NHL career.

Wales Conference Finals

Isles Dump Quebec—and the Ref

Longtime NHL general manager Emile Francis once said, "Hockey is a slippery game. It is played on ice." It is also a rough game, even for the officials. During the 1982 semifinals between Quebec and the Islanders, linesman Ray Scapinello was dumped into the New York bench as Buddy Cloutier (#9) and Billy Carroll (#25) fought for the puck. The two-time defending-champion Isles handled Quebec easily, outscoring them 18-9 in a four-game sweep.

1981-82

- The Canucks take a 3-2 lead into the third period of Game 2, but the Isles score four goals and win 6-4.

- Billy Smith blanks Vancouver in Game 3, as New York prevails 3-0.

- Mike Bossy's goal in the second period of Game 4 breaks a 1-1 tie, as the Isles win 3-1 and take their third straight Stanley Cup.

- Mike Bossy leads all playoff scorers with 17 goals, while teammate Bryan Trottier is the points leader (29). Bossy skates off with the Conn Smythe Trophy.

- Wayne Gretzky nabs his third straight Hart Trophy, while Bryan Trottier is runner-up. Gretzky also takes the Lester B. Pearson Award.

- Boston winger Rick Middleton annexes the Lady Byng Trophy, while teammate Steve Kasper earns the Frank Selke.

Vancouver's Dream Goes Up in Smoke

The Canucks floated through the first three rounds of the 1982 playoffs as if on some magic carpet ride, but reality hit hard quickly in the Stanley Cup Finals. Here, Vancouver's Thomas Gradin gets mugged by a mob of New Yorkers. The Canucks lost the first two games in New York (including Game 1 in overtime) and then dropped the next two in Vancouver, losing by the scores of 3-0 and 3-1.

Stanley Cup Finals

Stanley Cup Finals

Bossy's 81st Goal Wins the Stanley Cup

Mike Bossy's tremendous shooting ability earned him his fifth straight season with at least 50 goals, as he drilled in 64 in 1981-82. Bossy's 17th goal of the Stanley Cup playoffs (pictured) broke a 1-1 tie in Game 4 of the Finals and enabled the Islanders to complete their four-game sweep of Vancouver for their third consecutive championship. Bossy led all playoff goal-scorers and won the Conn Smythe Trophy.

• Islander Billy Smith wins his first and only Vezina Trophy, beating out Edmonton rookie Grant Fuhr. Winnipeg freshman Dale Hawerchuk beats out Boston rookie Barry Pederson for the Calder Trophy.

• Chicago's hard-shooting Doug Wilson wins the Norris Trophy.

• Colorado goalie Chico Resch receives the Masterton Trophy.

• Tom Watt, Winnipeg's first-year bench boss, wins the Jack Adams Award.

• Dave Simpson of the London Knights (OHL) is named the

Canadian Major Junior Player of the Year, while the Kitchener Rangers capture their first Memorial Cup.

• Phil Sykes leads North Dakota to a 5-2 win over Wisconsin for the NCAA title, while Bowling Green's George McPhee wins the Hobey Baker Award.

ISLES OUST THE OILERS FOR FOURTH STRAIGHT CUP

Starting its fourth season since its merger with the WHA, the NHL began boasting about parity, whereby the gap between rich and poor was narrowed to a competitively healthy point. By 1982-83, three of the former WHA teams—Edmonton, Winnipeg, and Quebec—had demonstrated the ability to keep up with the others. The question was: Could anyone keep up with the Islanders?

Winners of three consecutive Stanley Cups, the Isles were as well-balanced as they had been when they won their first title. "A problem," said top forward Bob Bourne, "was wear and tear. We already had been through a lot of playoff action (78 games from 1980 through 1983), and it was taking its toll on us, physically and mentally."

Nevertheless, the championship core was still intact and young enough to keep winning. Billy Smith's feisty goaltending was enhanced by a tight defense led by Denis Potvin, Ken Morrow, Stefan Persson, and Dave Langevin. Meanwhile, forwards Bourne, Butch Goring, Bryan Trottier, Mike Bossy, Clark Gillies, and Anders Kallur were splendid two-way attackers. "We had size, speed, and enough sharpshooters

to keep the opposition off-balance," said Gillies.

Not that the Islanders were without imposing challengers. The Flyers and Capitals were tough in the Patrick Division, while the Wayne Gretzky-led Oilers were scoring goals at a record-breaking rate. "We felt we were closing in on the Islanders," said Oilers defenseman Kevin Lowe. "Our club was getting stronger by the year now that Mark Messier and Glenn Anderson were coming into their own."

Edmonton finished the season with 106 points and in first place in the Smythe Division. They steamrolled over Winnipeg, Calgary, and Chicago to reach the Finals for the first time. In defense of their title, the Islanders wound up in second place with 96 points, 10 points behind the Flyers. The

Islanders then disposed of Washington, the New York Rangers, and Boston, clinching their fourth straight trip to the Stanley Cup Finals.

Despite Gretzky, Edmonton was totally outmatched by the Islanders in the final round. New York prevailed in four games with an exhibition of defense stymieing offense. In Game 1, Smith deflected every Edmonton shot—and there were plenty of them—as New York won 2-0. In Game 2, the Islanders beat the Oilers at their own game, scoring three goals in the first period and eventually winning 6-3.

In Game 3, the Isles again shut down the Edmonton machine, taking the game 5-1. Game 4 saw the New Yorkers score three goals in the first period—all within a minute and 37 seconds. Smith held the score to 4-2, executing some saves that left the crowd breathless.

The New York Islanders became the first U.S.-based team to win four consecutive Stanley Cups—and only the third team ever to win four in a row. Smith emerged as the Conn Smythe Trophy winner, as he held the Oilers to six goals in the final series.

1982-83

- Prior to the season, John McMullen buys the Rockies and moves them to New Jersey. He pays upwards of $30 million in "territorial" indemnity fees to the Rangers, Islanders, and Flyers.

- The New Jersey Devils move into the Patrick Division. The Winnipeg Jets leave the Norris Division and fill

the vacancy left by Colorado's departure from the Smythe.

- The Hall of Fame inducts four men, including players Yvan Cournoyer, Rod Gilbert, and Norm Ullman.

- Using the first pick in the 1982 Entry Draft—acquired from

Colorado—Boston selects WHL defenseman Gord Kluzak.

- On October 23, 1982, between periods of a Canucks-Bruins game, young Boston defenseman Norm Leveille suffers a brain hemorrhage, which will lead to partial paralysis.

Leading 3-2 in Game 4 of the Finals, the Islanders scored with 1:09 left to complete the series sweep over Edmonton and clinch the Stanley Cup. Here, John Tonelli (left), Ken Morrow (right), and Bobby Nystrom (obscured) celebrate the final goal, which was scored by Morrow. Morrow, the ultimate defensive defenseman, was getting used to big victories. From February 1980 through May 1983, he won one Olympic gold medal and four Stanley Cups.

- On December 14, 1982, L.A.'s Marcel Dionne becomes the ninth player ever to reach 500 career goals.

- On January 20, 1983, Flyer Darryl Sittler notches his 1,000th point.

- On February 23, 1983, Ranger center Mark Pavelich becomes the first American ever to score five goals in a game when he strafes Hartford's Greg Millen in an 11-3 win.

- In Edmonton, the Wayne Gretzky Show continues, as the Great One leads the NHL in goals (71), assists (a record 125), and points (196).

- The Oilers go 47-21-12 to take the Smythe. Mark Messier (48 goals), Glenn Anderson (48), and Jari Kurri (45) add to the high-octane offense.

- The mediocre Flames finish second in the Smythe, as Lanny McDonald reaches a career high in goals (66) and Kent Nilsson amasses 104 points.

Peter Stastny

Stastny Trio Rolls Up 295 Points

Quebec's offensive attack in 1982-83 boasted three brothers among the team's top four scoring leaders. Peter Stastny, with brothers Anton and Marian, formed a line that accounted for 115 goals and 295 points. Peter led with 47 goals and 124 points, while Anton (32-60-92) and Marian (36-43-79) followed. The Czech brothers played together in Quebec for four years until Marian went to Toronto in 1985.

Pete Peeters

Peeters Leads in GAA, Victories

The Bruins were hockey's predominant regular-season team in 1982-83, amassing 110 points. Much of the credit went to ex-Flyers goalie Pete Peeters. The flaky netminder, who had come over from Philadelphia in a trade for Brad McCrimmon, won the Vezina Trophy after leading the league with a 2.36 GAA, eight shutouts, and 40 wins.

Michel Goulet

Goulet Pots 57 from the Port Side

Michel Goulet, who played one season in the WHA (at Birmingham) before joining the Nordiques, emerged as the NHL's premier left winger during the 1982-83 season. His 57 goals were fourth best in the league and tops on the Nords. He reached the 100-point plateau for the first of four times when he finished the year with 105 points. Goulet combined gritty determination with accurate shooting and graceful puck-handling.

1982-83

- The Canucks fall to third in the Smythe—despite Darcy Rota (42 goals) and Stan Smyl (38).

- Dale Hawerchuk (40 goals) helps the Jets make the playoffs.

- L.A. finishes in the Smythe basement, as Marcel Dionne (56 goals) is the only one who shines on the Triple Crown Line.

- Boston's nifty 50-20-10 record is the league's best. Pete Peeters leads the NHL in wins (40) and GAA (2.36), while Rick Middleton (49 goals) and Barry Pederson (46) lead the attack.

- Montreal finishes second in the Adams as Mark Napier (40 goals), Steve Shutt (35), and Mario Tremblay (30) make headlines.

- The Sabres fall to third in the Adams, as Tony McKegney (36 goals) proves to be a bona fide threat.

Langway Scores Three Goals, Wins Norris

The Canadiens, long known for their brilliant player transactions, erred badly when they traded Rod Langway to Washington prior to the 1982-83 season for Ryan Walter. A large (6'3", 218 pounds) and mobile defenseman, Langway blossomed into an immediate superstar behind the blueline. Though he garnered a measly three goals and 29 assists in 1982-83, Langway won the Norris Trophy thanks to his great defensive skills.

Secord: First Hawk Since Hull to Net 50

The Black Hawks unveiled an unlikely scoring hero in 1982-83 when Al Secord was put on the left side of Denis Savard's line (with Steve Larmer on the right wing). Secord (pictured helmetless with Larmer left and Savard right) was a feared tough guy with knockout power who suddenly became an offensive weapon. In 80 games, Secord scored 54 goals to become only the second Hawk ever, along with Bobby Hull, to score 50.

Rod Langway

Steve Larmer, Al Secord, Denis Savard

- The Nordiques capture the final playoff spot in the Adams Division as Michel Goulet (57 goals) emerges as the league's premier left winger.

- Peter Stastny notches 47 goals and 124 points for Quebec, while brothers Anton (92 points) and Marian (79) make more modest contributions.

- Hartford goes through three coaches en route to a 19-54-7 season, squandering the production of Blaine Stoughton (45 goals), Mark Johnson (31), and Ron Francis (31).

- Bob McCammon guides the Flyers to a 49-23-8 record and a Patrick Division title. Swedish goaltending ace Pelle Lindbergh, a rookie, wins 23 games.

- Philly's Darryl Sittler notches 43 goals, but Bobby Clarke (85 points) remains the team's offensive leader.

- The Cup champion Islanders drop to second in the Patrick.

LaFontaine Scores 104 for Verdun

Born in St. Louis, speedy center Pat LaFontaine earned Canadian Major Junior Player of the Year honors in 1983 after leading the Quebec Major Junior Hockey League in goals (104), assists (130), and points (234) while playing at Verdun. In the 1983 Entry Draft, the New York Islanders made LaFontaine (pictured with 1980 Olympic hero Ken Morrow) the third player chosen overall, but they wouldn't sign him to a pro contract until after the 1984 Olympics.

Fuzzy-Lipped McDonald Nets 66

Lanny McDonald (left) had two distinctive features that made him easily recognizable: his cannon shot off the right wing and his Yosemite Sam whiskers. In 1982-83, the former Leafs hero set a Calgary record when he ripped 66 goals— second best in the league behind Wayne Gretzky's 71.

Pat LaFontaine, Ken Morrow

Bobby Clarke

Clarke Enjoys Last Hurrah

Bobby Clarke was 33 years old and one year away from retiring when he won his final award in 1982-83. Clarke earned the Frank Selke Trophy as the game's top defensive forward. It seemed like old times for Bobby, as he led the Flyers in scoring (85 points) and finished fifth in the league in assists (62). Clarke captained Philly to a Patrick title, although they were swept in the first round of the playoffs by the Rangers.

Lanny McDonald

1982-83

• The still-potent Isles are led by Mike Bossy, who has his sixth straight 50-goal season (60).

• Under Bryan Murray, the much-improved Capitals move into third place in the Patrick. Mike Gartner (38 goals), Bob Carpenter (32), and Dennis Maruk (31) provide offense.

• Mark Pavelich, a former Olympic hero, scores 37 goals for former U.S. Olympic coach Herb Brooks, bench boss of the Rangers. New York goes .500 and places fourth in the Patrick.

• The Devils, in their first year in the Patrick, post a 17-49-14 record.

• Pittsburgh (18-53-9) has an even worse time than the Devils, despite five 20-goal scorers.

• The Norris is won by Chicago (47-23-10). Al Secord, a rugged left winger, scores 54 goals while Denis Savard tallies 121 points.

Bossy Again Smashes the 50 Mark

The Islanders dropped out of first place in the Patrick Division in 1982-83 but Mike Bossy, the game's most fearsome right winger, never missed a beat. In his sixth NHL season, he recorded his sixth straight year with at least 50 goals. On March 12, 1983, he beat Washington's Al Jensen for his 50th of the year. With 60 goals (third overall) and 118 points (fourth)—combined with just 20 penalty minutes—Bossy won his first Lady Byng Trophy.

Wayne Gretzky

Gretzky Nets 71 of Oilers' 424 Goals

Wayne Gretzky powers past Philadelphia's Brian Propp en route to another sensational scoring season. In 1982-83, the Great One knocked home 71 goals (best in the NHL) and won his third straight scoring title (196 points). He captured the Hart Trophy as well as the Lester B. Pearson Award as the players' choice for MVP. His Oilers went a Smythe best 47-21-12 and again set an NHL record for goals (424).

Mike Bossy

- Murray Bannerman and Tony Esposito—nearing the end of his long career—split the goal duties for the Hawks.

- Minnesota finishes second in the Norris, as Dino Ciccarelli (37 goals) and rookie Brian Bellows (35) provide offensive spark.

- Rick Vaive's second straight 50-goal season (51) helps propel Toronto to third in the Norris Division.

- The Blues struggle to a fourth-place finish in the Norris despite the work of Brian Sutter (46 goals) and Bernie Federko (84 points).

- Detroit wastes a 41-goal season from John Ogrodnick, as it lands in the Norris cellar again.

- Wayne Gretzky wins the scoring title by 72 points over Peter Stastny (124). Denis Savard (121) and Mike Bossy (118) follow.

New Jersey Devils

Devils Lay Dormant in New Jersey

John McMullen, owner of the Houston Astros baseball team, bought the crumbling Colorado Rockies in 1982 and moved them to the Meadowlands in East Rutherford, New Jersey. The New Jersey Devils got off to a difficult start in their first year in the Patrick Division, going 17-49-14. Their offense was so anemic that Aaron Broten led the team in scoring with just 55 points. Glenn "Chico" Resch did a respectable job in goal.

Marcel Dionne

Dionne is L.A.'s Only Shining Jewel

In 1982-83, the Kings' Triple Crown Line continued to struggle amid injury and frustration. A year after Charlie Simmer missed 30 games due to injury, Dave Taylor was knocked out of 34 games. Only Marcel Dionne was able to stay healthy and productive, finishing with 56 goals. On December 14, 1982, he scored on Washington's Al Jensen, making him the NHL's ninth 500-goal scorer.

Pavelich Sets an American Record

The Rangers' Mark Pavelich made history on February 23, 1983, when he scored five goals in a game in an 11-3 trouncing of Hartford. Since Joe Malone first did it in 1917, the NHL had experienced 37 five-goal performances, but all were tallied by Canadians. Pavelich, a native son of Eveleth, Minnesota, became the first American to turn the trick. Pavelich left the NHL in 1987 to pursue fishing interests.

Mark Pavelich

1982-83

- Top goal-scorers are Wayne Gretzky (71), Lanny McDonald (66), Mike Bossy (60), and Michel Goulet (57).

- In the Patrick Division semifinals, the Rangers sweep Philly and the Isles erase Washington (3-1). In the Adams semis, Boston trounces Quebec (3-1) and Buffalo shocks Montreal (3-0).

- In the Norris semifinals, Chicago skates past St. Louis (3-1) and Minnesota eliminates Toronto (3-1). In the Smythe semis, Calgary beats Vancouver (3-1) and the Oilers blank Winnipeg (3-0).

- In the Patrick finals, the Isles beat the rival Rangers in six games. The

Black Hawks need just five games to knock off Minnesota in the Norris finals.

- In the Adams finals, Boston beats Buffalo in overtime of the seventh game. Boston's Rick Middleton tallies an NHL-record 19 points in the series.

Behrend Wins Second MVP Award

Two years after being named the Most Outstanding Player of the 1981 NCAA tournament, Wisconsin goalie Marc Behrend won the award again in 1983, thus becoming the second player to do so (after Lou Angotti). Behrend won the second honor after defeating Harvard in the championship game 6-2. He wasn't the only star on the Wisconsin team, however. Future NHLers Chris Chelios, Patrick Flatley, and Bruce Driver also skated for the Badgers.

Norm Leveille, Larry Robinson

Teenage Leveille Nearly Dies

Tragedy struck the Boston franchise on October 23, 1982, when Norm Leveille, a promising 19-year-old left winger playing in just his second NHL season, was stricken with a cerebral hemorrhage. Leveille (pictured at a charity golf function with Larry Robinson) lingered near death for several days before his condition—caused by a congenital defect—stabilized. He suffered minor paralysis and underwent extensive rehabilitation.

Marc Behrend

• The Smythe finals are never in doubt as Edmonton outscores the Flames 35-13 over five games, including 10-2 in Game 3.

• In the Wales Conference finals, the Isles beat Boston (4-2) as Mike Bossy scores all four game-winning goals for New York.

• Edmonton makes a shambles of Chicago's defense in the Campbell Conference finals, outscoring the Hawks 25-11 in a four-game sweep.

• In a quest for their fourth straight Stanley Cup, the Islanders win Game 1 of the Finals 2-0, as Billy Smith shuts out the heralded Oiler offense.

• A pair of goals from sophomore Brent Sutter helps the Isles pull away in Game 2, as New York wins 6-3 and builds a two-game lead.

• In Game 3 at Northlands Coliseum, New York blows open a 1-1 game with four straight goals to win 5-1.

Adams Division Finals

Bruins Escape Buffalo But Fall in Semis

Isles defenseman Stefan Persson fires on Boston rookie Gord Kluzak (the top pick in the 1982 draft) during New York's series triumph in the Wales Conference finals. The Bruins reached the Wales finals thanks to a Game 7 overtime goal by Brad Park against Buffalo. However, they fell in six games to the Islanders, as Mike Bossy scored four game-winning goals. It was the 15th straight playoff series that New York had won.

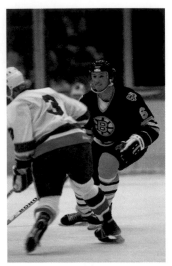

Wales Conference Finals

Boston Prevails in Adams Thriller

The 1983 Adams Division finals, between Buffalo and Boston, extended to seven games, with each team swapping victories like heavyweights trading body punches. Game 7, played at Boston Garden, was tied at 2-2 when regulation time expired. This tight-checking game (as illustrated by Mike Foligno, left, and Dave Barr, right) ended at 1:52 of sudden-death when Boston's Brad Park beat Bob Sauve to end the series.

Gretzky, Mates Blow Out Chicago

Edmonton steadily rose to power in the NHL with Wayne Gretzky (pictured at right) at the helm. In 1982-83, the Oilers finished with 106 points and averaged more than five goals per game. In the Stanley Cup playoffs, after sweeping Winnipeg and thrashing Calgary, the Oilers took on Chicago and totally strafed Hawks goalie Murray Bannerman (#30), scoring 25 goals in a four-game romp. Gretzky finished the playoffs with an NHL-record 38 points.

Campbell Conference Finals

1982-83

- Unable to focus their tremendous offense, the Oilers sputter under the constant pressure of the Islanders and lose Game 4 4-2. The Isles hoist their fourth straight Stanley Cup.

- On the strength of 13 playoff wins and a 2.68 GAA, Islander Billy Smith wins the Conn Smythe Trophy.

- Despite no goals in the Finals, Wayne Gretzky sets a playoff record with 38 points. The Isles' Mike Bossy is tops with 17 postseason goals.

- Wayne Gretzky becomes the first player to win four straight Hart Trophies. He also claims his second straight Lester B. Pearson Award.

- Boston goalie Pete Peeters, in his first year with the team, wins the Vezina Trophy and finishes runner-up for the Hart.

- Mike Bossy (60 goals, 20 penalty minutes) wins his first Lady Byng Trophy, while Washington's Rod Langway claims the Norris.

Smith Puts the Clamp on the Oiler Offense

In a scene typifying their struggles in the Finals, Wayne Gretzky camps behind the net—in his "office"—while Jari Kurri (#17) struggles to convert one of the Great One's magical passes. Backchecking forward Butch Goring (left) lends goalie Billy Smith defensive support. The Oilers could muster only six goals in four games against Smith. In the conference finals, Edmonton had averaged six goals a game.

Stanley Cup Finals

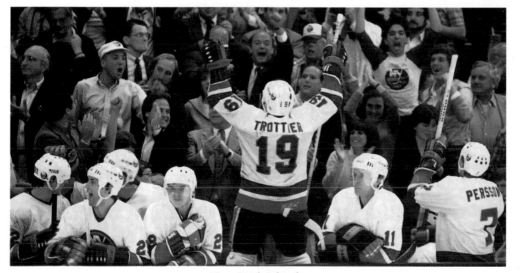

New York Islanders

Trottier, New Yorkers Begin the Celebration

Bryan Trottier, the heart of the Islanders, leads the Nassau Coliseum crowd in a cheer as the team puts the final touches on its fourth straight Stanley Cup championship. In its playoff march to the four titles, New York won 60 games against just 18 defeats and won all 16 series in six games or less. Goalie Billy Smith, the Conn Smythe Trophy winner in 1983, went 57-13 during the four-year playoff binge.

• Chicago's Steve Larmer (43 goals) captures the Calder Trophy, while Chicago coach Orval Tessier wins the Jack Adams Award.

• Lanny McDonald wins the Masterton Trophy, while Bobby Clarke cops the Frank Selke Trophy.

• With 104 goals and 130 assists, Verdun's Pat LaFontaine—a Michigan native—is named the Canadian Major Junior Player of the Year.

• The Portland Winter Hawks, led by Cam Neely, Ray Ferraro, and Richie Kromm, win the Memorial Cup.

• Wisconsin beats Harvard 6-2 for the NCAA title, as Wisconsin Badgers goalie Marc Behrend becomes the second player to twice earn the tourney MVP honors.

• Harvard defenseman Mark Fusco wins the Hobey Baker Award.

HIGH-OCTANE OILERS WHIP THE WEARY ISLES

During the early 1980s, hockey purists fell in love with the style of the New York Islanders. Their well-balanced approach, fortified by strong defensive checking, enabled them to win four consecutive Stanley Cups. However, their No. 1 challenger, Glen Sather's Edmonton Oilers, had its own theory of how to play the game. And defense had little to do with it.

The Oilers' style of play was purely run-and-gun, and they were talented enough to get away with it. Wayne Gretzky was in his prime in 1983-84, ringing up 87 goals and 205 points. He was backed by such able weaponry as Mark Messier (37-64-101), Jari Kurri (52-61-113), Glenn Anderson (54-45-99), and high-scoring defenseman Paul Coffey (40-86-126).

"We were winning a lot of hockey games with this system," said Oilers defenseman Kevin Lowe, "but we hadn't won a Stanley Cup yet. The thinking was that we had to win it in 1983-84 or the club would be dismantled and a new approach would be tried."

By contrast, Islanders G.M. Bill Torrey was satisfied that he had an ideal formula. Sure, he iced a potent offense, led by Mike Bossy, Brian Trottier, and Clark Gillies, but his team essentially depended on a stout defense led by Denis Potvin, Stefan Persson, and Ken Morrow. As always, Bill Smith was the ace between the goalposts.

"A lot of teams had been gunning for us for three years after we had won the first Cup," said Islanders forward Bob Bourne. "We had suffered plenty of wear and tear, but there was still plenty of talent and grit on the team."

The Islanders remained a respectable defending champion through the 1983-84 season, going 50-26-4, but they were pushed to the limit in the first round of the playoffs against the Rangers. Only a goal by Morrow in overtime of Game 5 allowed them to advance. The Isles then managed to squeeze past both Washington and Montreal, but in each case the toll was heavy.

The Oilers, who had blown through the season at 57-18-5 and amassed an NHL-record 446 goals, routed Winnipeg in the first round of the playoffs. They then edged Calgary in a seven-game series and blew out the North Stars in four games. That set the stage for a showdown between the kings of offense and hockey's most balanced club.

In Game 1 of the Finals, it was Grant Fuhr who made the difference in goal. After Edmonton utility forward Kevin McClelland banked an angle shot past Smith, Fuhr shut down the Islanders the rest of the way and gave Edmonton a critical 1-0 win. The Isles rallied to win Game 2, but they were beginning to show the physical and mental effects of having won 19 consecutive playoff series. The Oilers, smelling blood, took over the series when they returned home and reeled off three straight victories in convincing fashion.

Wayne Gretzky hoisted the Stanley Cup for the first time in his career. "I've held women and babies and jewels and money," said the Great One, "but nothing will ever feel as good as holding that Cup."

1983-84

- The NHL adds one five-minute sudden-death period to regular-season games ending in ties.

- In the Entry Draft, five Americans go in the first round, including Brian Lawton (first) by Minnesota, Pat LaFontaine (third) by the Isles, and Tom Barrasso (fifth) by Buffalo.

- The Hall of Fame inducts four new men, including players Ken Dryden, Bobby Hull, and Stan Mikita.

- Early in the season, L.A.'s Marcel Dionne scores career goal No. 545, passing Maurice Richard for second overall.

- On November 19, 1983, Oiler Jari Kurri scores five goals in a 13-4 win over New Jersey, prompting Wayne Gretzky to call the Devils a "Mickey Mouse" organization.

- On December 20, 1983, Montreal's Guy Lafleur becomes the 10th NHLer to score 500 goals.

New Jersey Devils Fans

Gretzky Calls Devils a Mickey Mouse Team

On November 19, 1983, Edmonton thrashed the hapless Devils 13-4 as Jari Kurri scored five goals. Oiler captain Wayne Gretzky, who notched three goals and eight points of his own during the game, referred to the Devils as a "Mickey Mouse" organization, prompting a vehement outcry from Devils fans during the Oilers' next visit to the Meadowlands. New Jersey finished at 17-56-7.

Coffey Pours It On, Piles Up 126 Points

Defenseman Paul Coffey, the Oilers' offensive catalyst, entered the record books when he finished 1983-84 with 126 points, second best in the league and the third-highest total ever amassed by a backliner. Bruins legend Bobby Orr, with whom many compared the brilliant-skating Coffey, had seasons of 135 and 139 points. In 1985-86, Coffey would break Orr's single-season record for goals by a defenseman (48 compared to Orr's 46).

Paul Coffey

Pederson's 116 Help Boston Win the Adams

The Bruins captured their second straight Adams Division title in 1983-84, as Rick Middleton and Barry Pederson combined for 86 goals and 221 points. Pederson was Boston's top scorer, notching 39 goals and 116 points. Barry would later suffer a cancer scare and then be traded to Vancouver for Cam Neely and the rights to junior Glen Wesley. He finished his 12-year NHL career with 238 goals and 654 points in 701 games.

Barry Pederson

while Tom McCarthy (39 goals) and Dino Ciccarelli (38) chip in big.

• The sub-.500 Blues finish second in the Norris, as Bernie Federko (107 points) leads the charge.

• Detroit staggers into third place in the Norris, just a point ahead of Chicago. Rookie Steve Yzerman leads the Wings in points (87).

• The Black Hawks—whose owner, Arthur Wirtz, died in July—waste the scoring of Denis Savard (94 points).

• Toronto's Rick Vaive records his third straight 50-goal season (netting 52 this year), but the Leafs win just 26 games.

• The Islanders, four-time defending Stanley Cup champions, go 50-26-4 and win the Patrick Division. Mike Bossy (51 goals, 118 points) tops the team in scoring once again.

Goulet Belts Out Another 50-Goal Season

Called "the best left winger in hockey," Quebec's Michel Goulet continued his awesome goal-scoring during the 1983-84 season when he notched his second of four straight years with at least 50 goals. The three-time first-team All-Star racked up 56 goals and a career-high 121 points, finishing two points ahead of teammate Peter Stastny. Goulet was the league's third-highest scorer and helped Quebec to a 42-28-10 record.

Vaive Can't Revive the Maple Laughs

Toronto captain Rick Vaive uses his strength and balance to stave off Rangers backliner Barry Beck. A formidable shooter at any range, Vaive tortured enemy goalies with his third straight 50-goal season in 1983-84, finishing the year with 52 goals and 93 points. However, his team—derided in the local media as the Maple Laughs—went 26-45-9 and finished out of the playoffs for the third time in four years.

Pain-Racked Kerr Scores 54 Goals

Injuries played havoc with Tim Kerr's career—from leg injuries that kept him from being drafted out of juniors to endless shoulder damage that continually interrupted and ultimately shortened his career. Entering the 1983-84 campaign, Kerr had 54 career goals in three years. By season's end, Kerr (pictured battling Islander Paul Boutilier in the low slot) had doubled his career output with a titanic 54-goal season.

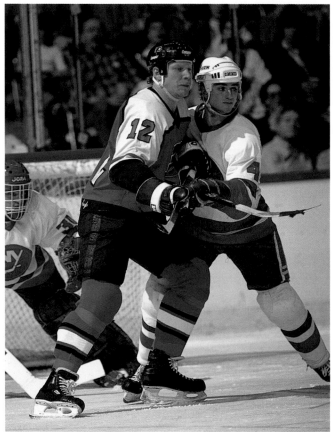

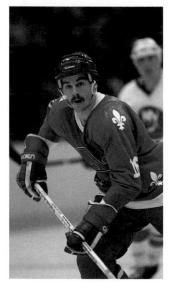

Michel Goulet

Rick Vaive

Tim Kerr, Paul Boutilier

1983-84

- The ever-improving Capitals finish just three points behind the Isles. Mike Gartner leads the club with 40 goals.

- Philadelphia rides the goal-scoring of free agent Tim Kerr (54) and playmaking of Brian Propp (53 assists) to finish third in the Patrick.

- The Rangers, in the midst of a revolt against coach Herb Brooks, place fourth in the Patrick. Mark Pavelich (82 points) and Pierre Larouche (48 goals) lead the way.

- The Devils (17 wins, 41 points) are not much better than the pitiful Penguins (16 wins, 38 points). New Jersey President Bob Butera accuses the Pens of losing games to ensure gaining the top pick (Mario Lemieux) in the 1984 draft.

- With Barry Pederson (116 points) and Rick Middleton (105), Boston goes 49-25-6 and wins the Adams.

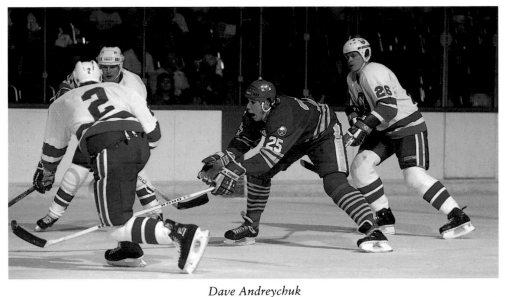

Dave Andreychuk

Andreychuk Picks Up Where Gil Left Off

While Sabres rookie goalie Tom Barrasso was yielding just 2.84 goals a game en route to the Calder and Vezina Trophies, Buffalo fans were also treated to a new, young scoring star—left winger Dave Andreychuk. The second-year pro potted 38 goals in helping Buffalo to a 48-25-7 record. The Sabres needed someone to take over the scoring leadership from the aging Gil Perreault, and Andreychuk became the guy.

Soviets Flatten Olympic Foes

The Soviet Union returned to Olympic dominance in the 1984 Winter Games at Sarajevo, Yugoslavia. In their match against Poland, for example, they pummeled goalie Wlodzimierz Olszewski (pictured face down in the crease after another goal), beating the Poles 12-1. The Soviets skated to a gold medal while Czechoslovakia took silver. The 1984 Games were a huge disappointment for Canada and USA, who finished out of medal contention.

Olympic Games

- Buffalo, which wins an all-time record 10 road games in a row, finishes a point behind Boston. Rookie Tom Barrasso stars in nets and Dave Andreychuk nets 38.

- The Nordiques, under coach Michel Bergeron, enjoy their best season yet (42-28-10). Michel Goulet (56 goals, 121 points) and Peter Stastny (46-73-119) burn the nets.

- The Canadiens (35-40-5) suffer their first losing record since 1950-51. Guy Lafleur leads in goals with just 30.

- The Whalers are the most improved team in the league but they still wind up last in the Adams. Rookie Sylvain Turgeon scores 40 goals and Mark Johnson leads with 87 points.

- The top NHL scorers are Wayne Gretzky (205 points), Paul Coffey (126), Michel Goulet (121), Peter Stastny (119), and Mike Bossy (118).

Lafleur Nets 500th Before Hanging 'Em Up

Clearly past his prime, Montreal's Guy Lafleur nonetheless remained a potential weapon through his years of diminishing returns. In 1983-84, the 13-year veteran notched his 500th career goal en route to a 30-goal campaign. Less than 20 games into the 1984-85 season, Lafleur suddenly retired at age 33. He was not heard from again until he made a dramatic comeback with the New York Rangers in the fall of 1988.

Sylvain Turgeon

Turgeon Nets 40 Goals in Rookie Year

The future of the Hartford Whalers began to look considerably brighter following the 1983 Entry Draft when they secured the rights to former Quebec junior scoring ace Sylvain Turgeon with the second overall pick. Turgeon wasted no time proving his talent was legitimate when he scored 40 rookie goals, the sixth most ever by an NHL frosh. Sly later was plagued by a series of injuries that diminished his career.

Tony Tanti

Tanti Comes Alive, Scores 45

The Blackhawks had high hopes for Tony Tanti when they selected him in the first round of the 1981 Entry Draft, particularly since he had scored 177 goals in just 154 junior games at Oshawa over two-plus seasons. But Tanti became trade bait when the Hawks went after Vancouver's rugged Curt Fraser in a one-for-one swap. Tanti, of Maltese extraction, quickly made Chicago regret the move, setting a Canuck record for goals in a season (45) in 1983-84.

Guy Lafleur

1983-84

- The leading NHL goal-scorers include Wayne Gretzky (87), Michel Goulet (56), Glenn Anderson (54), Tim Kerr (54), Rick Vaive (52), and Jari Kurri (52).

- In the Norris Division playoffs, Minnesota beats Chicago (3-2) while St. Louis tops Detroit (3-1). In the Smythe semifinals, Edmonton sweeps Winnipeg (3-0) and Calgary beats Vancouver (3-1).

- The Patrick semis see the Caps stun Philly (3-0) and the Isles survive the Rangers (3-2). In the Adams, Montreal shocks Boston (3-0) and Quebec eliminates Buffalo in three.

- Minnesota beats St. Louis (4-3) in the Norris finals, while Edmonton outlasts Calgary in seven.

- Montreal beats Quebec (4-2) to take the Adams playoff title in a festival of bad blood and brawling. In the Patrick finals, the Isles take out Washington in five games.

Dale Hawerchuk

Langway Gets Things Done in Washington

The Capitals made a concerted effort to put space between themselves and the Patrick Division basement in 1983-84. The steady play of Rod Langway on defense gave them the confidence to perform at a higher level and the foundation on which to build a winner. Langway tallied just nine goals and 33 points but won his second straight Norris Trophy. He also finished runner-up for the Hart Trophy.

Rod Langway

Lowly Jets At Least Have Hawerchuk

Winnipeg continued to struggle in 1983-84, going 31-38-11, despite the outstanding play of Dale Hawerchuk (left). In just his third season, the baby-faced center nicknamed "Ducky" posted his second 100-point season. His 102 points (including 65 assists) established him as one of the game's most dangerous forces. He notched an all-time record five assists in one period during a game against Los Angeles.

Gretzky: 87 Goals, 205 Points

In 1983-84, Wayne Gretzky amassed 87 goals and 205 points, put together an NHL-record 51-game points-scoring streak, won his fourth Art Ross Trophy, and copped his fifth Hart Trophy. Gretzky's brilliance could be attributed to his grace and skill—not his muscle. In fact, physical-strength tests in training camp showed that Gretzky had the weakest upper body of any player on the team and that he wasn't much stronger than the average teenager.

Wayne Gretzky

- The Oilers and North Stars are a study in mismatches, as Edmonton ousts the inferior Stars in four games in the Campbell Conference finals.

- After dropping the first two games of the Wales Conference finals, the Islanders win four straight to reach the Finals for the fifth straight year.

- In Game 1 of the Finals, Oilers goalie Grant Fuhr outduels New York's Billy Smith as Edmonton wins a surprising 1-0 game.

- In Game 2, the Islanders show the firepower that made them four-time Cup winners, as they prevail 6-1.

- In Game 3 at Northlands Coliseum in Edmonton, the Oilers thrash New York 7-2 to take a two-games-to-one lead.

- The Oilers are relentless in Game 4, as they again stick it to the Isles by the score of 7-2.

Tom McCarthy

McCarthy's Goals Lifts Stars

The North Stars had the privilege of two first-round draft picks in 1979. The first one was spent on defenseman Craig Hartsburg (sixth overall). Four picks later, the Stars chose again, selecting strapping left winger Tom McCarthy from the Oshawa (OHA) Generals. He played modestly in his early NHL career, but in 1983-84 McCarthy blasted home 39 goals. He helped the North Stars finish first in the Norris Division.

Steve Yzerman

Yzerman Nets 39 in Rookie Season

Chosen fourth overall in the 1983 draft by Detroit, former Peterborough junior star Steve Yzerman made a big rookie impression during the 1983-84 NHL season, scoring 39 goals and 87 points, tops on the team. A franchise-type player, Yzerman made the transition from junior hockey to the pros without so much as one game on the farm. "Stevie Wonder" became the captain of the Motown club at the tender age of 21.

Gillies Lifts Isles Past Habs in Cup Semis

Known as a hard-hitting left winger who could beat you as effectively with goals as with punishing body-checks, Clark Gillies (#9, celebrating a semifinal goal against Montreal) had a brilliant 1984 Stanley Cup season, ripping 12 goals in 21 games. The Islanders dropped the first two games of their series with the Canadiens, but roared back with four consecutive wins to gain a berth in the Finals for the fifth straight year.

Wales Conference Finals

1983-84

- The Islander dynasty comes to an end in Game 5, as the Oilers whip the four-time champs 5-2 and hoist the Cup.

- Wayne Gretzky tops all playoff scorers with 35 points, but hard-nosed teammate Mark Messier (26 points) wins the Conn Smythe.

- Wayne Gretzky wins his fifth straight Hart Trophy, outballoting Rod Langway. Gretzky also accepts the Lester B. Pearson Award.

- For the second straight year, Mike Bossy nabs the Lady Byng Trophy and Boston's Rick Middleton finishes second.

- Buffalo rookie Tom Barrasso wins the Vezina Trophy thanks to a 2.84 GAA. He also wins the Calder Trophy over Steve Yzerman.

- Rod Langway claims his second straight Norris Trophy, edging out Paul Coffey.

Stanley Cup Finals

Oilers, Isles Face Off Again in Cup Finals

The 1984 Stanley Cup Finals were a rematch of the previous year's combatants, as the four-time defending-champion Islanders girded for another assault from Wayne Gretzky's powerful Oilers. Here, Brent Sutter (#21), Denis Potvin (#5), and goalie Billy Smith fall victim to a goal by Edmonton center Mark Messier (right). The teams split the first two games in New York.

Oilers Blast Isles in Games 3, 4, and 5

The Islanders, decimated by injuries, just couldn't contain the Oilers' attack in the 1984 Finals, nor could they muster much offense of their own. Here, New York rookie Pat LaFontaine is thwarted by Oilers goalie Andy Moog. In Games 3, 4, and 5—all in Edmonton—the Oilers won by scores of 7-2, 7-2, and 5-2, putting an abrupt end to the Islander dynasty. The Oilers' 94 playoff goals gave them 540 for the season (in 99 games).

Stanley Cup Finals

• Washington's Doug Jarvis receives the Frank Selke Trophy, while Brad Park—now with Detroit—is honored with the Masterton Trophy.

• Bryan Murray, coach of the improved Capitals, is the recipient of the Jack Adams Award.

• At the Olympic Games in Sarajevo, Yugoslavia, the Soviet Union goes undefeated in seven games to regain the gold medal. Canada finishes fourth and the U.S. seventh.

• Mario Lemieux of Laval is named Canadian Major Junior Player of the Year on the strength of 133 goals and

282 points. Ottawa, however, wins the Memorial Cup.

• Bowling Green beats Minnesota-Duluth 5-4 in overtime to win the NCAA championship. BGU goalie Gary Kruzich is the tourney MVP and Minnesota-Duluth's Tom Kurvers claims the Hobey Baker Award.

HE LOOKS MARVELOUS! MARIO STARS IN PITTSBURGH

Before 1984, few junior players had ever been so highly touted as Mario Lemieux. Nevertheless, the 18-year-old Montreal native deserved the platitudes, as he displayed a rare assortment of skills at the highest level. So special was this teenage wonder that they called him Le Magnifique.

Despite his tremendous 6'4", 200-pound frame, Mario was a deceptively fast, graceful skater who packed a traumatizing shot. Lemieux was by far the most prolific scorer in Quebec Major Junior Hockey League history, amassing three-year totals of 247 goals and 562 points in 200 games. In his final year with Laval, 1983-84, Lemieux notched 133 goals and 149 assists for 282 points in 70 games—and then he tallied 52 points in 14 playoff games.

Hailed as the greatest player to come out of the Quebec junior system since Guy Lafleur, Mario would go to the NHL team that finished dead last in 1983-84. The Pittsburgh Penguins "won" the race for last with a mere 38 points, three fewer than the New Jersey Devils. New Jersey brass accused Pittsburgh of tanking games to ensure finishing with the worst record. Nothing came of

the charge and the Devils were forced to pick second in the Entry Draft, taking Kirk Muller (who would become a steady 30-goal scorer).

As a Pittsburgh rookie in 1984-85, Lemieux fulfilled all the artistic expectations, dazzling the Pittsburgh crowd with his graceful yet lethal offensive prowess. His innate shyness and initial difficulties in speaking English may have been public relations debits, but the once somnolent Penguins fans enthusiastically embraced their budding superstar.

Lemieux scored his first NHL goal in his first game on his first shift off his first shot. He earned a spot in the midseason All-Star Game and emerged as the contest's Most Valuable Player with two goals and an assist. By season's end, he had garnered 43

goals and 100 points and skated off with the Calder Trophy.

The sudden ascent of Lemieux immediately led to comparisons with Wayne Gretzky, although their respective sizes, styles, and personalities were vastly different. Whereas Gretzky was just as at home in front of the camera as in front of the goalcrease, Mario lacked his innate charisma. In a symbol of just how different they were, Lemieux wore the jersey number "66," the inverted version of Gretzky's "99."

Moreover, Lemieux's Penguins and Gretzky's Oilers were polar opposites on the ice. While the Penguins languished in the Patrick cellar again in 1984-85, Gretzky led his troops to a second straight Stanley Cup, whipping Philadelphia in five Finals games.

But as the years went by, Lemieux gradually climbed the ladder to reach the lofty heights of Gretzky. In 1987-88, he outscored Gretzky for the first time (168 to 149) and ended Wayne's streak of eight consecutive Hart Trophies. And while the Great One would again hoist back-to-back Stanley Cups in the springs of 1987 and '88, Le Magnifique would do the double himself, pulling off the feat in 1991 and 1992.

1984-85

- The Hall of Fame inducts six men, including players Phil Esposito, Jacques Lemaire, and Bernie Parent.

- Amid controversy following charges that they had "tanked" the end of the season to ensure finishing last, the Penguins draft first overall and take junior superstar Mario Lemieux.

- In Canada Cup play, Canada beats the USSR in the semifinals as Mike Bossy scores in overtime. Canada then knocks off Sweden in the finals.

- On December 19, 1984, 23-year-old Wayne Gretzky records his 1,000th career point in only his 424th game.

- On January 29, 1985, Islander Bryan Trottier tallies his 1,000th point.

- The Flyers have the league's top record (53-20-7), relying heavily on Tim Kerr (54 goals), Brian Propp (96 points), and goalie Pelle Lindbergh (league-leading 40 wins).

The most celebrated rookie in many years, Mario Lemieux made a sudden and dramatic impact on the NHL during his freshman season, scoring 43 goals and 100 points en route to the Calder Trophy. Largely overshadowed by Lemieux was rookie teammate Warren Young, who knocked in 40 goals of his own. However, Young would score only 32 more goals in his career, while Lemieux would one day become the greatest player on the globe.

• The Caps finish second to the Flyers in the Patrick Division with a second straight 101-point season, thanks to a team GAA of 2.97.

• The Caps get 50-goal performances from Mike Gartner (50) and Bobby Carpenter (53)—the first American ever to reach the 50-goal mark.

• The Isles drop to third in the Patrick Division despite Mike Bossy (58 goals), Brent Sutter (42), and John Tonelli (42).

• The Rangers stumble to fourth in the Patrick, as defenseman Reijo Routsalainen leads in scoring (73 points).

• Midway through the season, Rangers G.M. Craig Patrick replaces Herb Brooks behind the bench after Brooks loses control of the team.

• New Jersey finishes one point ahead of Pittsburgh in the Patrick, as ex-Flyer Mel Bridgman tops all scorers with 61 points.

Bernie Federko

Jari Kurri

Federko Helps the Blues Cop the Norris

St. Louis won the Norris Division title in 1984-85 thanks largely to the play-making of ace center Bernie Federko. The slick veteran finished with 103 points and cracked the NHL's top-10 scoring chart for the third time in five years. Federko's assist-making (73) was instrumental in helping Joe Mullen emerge as a 40-goal scorer. Federko also fed Brian Sutter, who netted 37.

Dale Hawerchuk

Hawerchuk: First Jet to Score 50

The arrival of Dale Hawerchuk in 1981 marked a new beginning for the Jets franchise. In 1984-85, the fourth-year veteran became the first player in club history to reach the 50-goal plateau when he beat Chicago's Warren Skorodenski during a 5-5 tie. At just 21 years of age, Hawerchuk tallied 53 goals and 130 points, third most in the league.

Kurri Scores 71 Before You Can Blink

Jari Kurri revolutionized hockey while playing the right side on Wayne Gretzky's top line in Edmonton. In 1984-85, the Finnish sensation perfected the "one-timer." Perched in shooting position, Kurri would accept passes from Gretzky, then fire on net without stopping the puck. This technique helped him set a league record for goals by a right winger (71) and win the Lady Byng Trophy.

1984-85

- The Penguins introduce Mario Lemieux, but "The Savior" cannot raise the team out of the cellar—despite 43 goals and 100 points.

- Career minor-leaguer Warren Young scores 40 goals as Mario Lemieux's winger/protector. He'll later earn a huge contract, though his performance is clearly flash-in-the-pan material.

- Montreal rebounds from a bad year by winning the Adams Division (41-27-12). Mats Naslund leads the Habs in scoring (42-37-79) and rookie defenseman Chris Chelios makes a splash with 55 assists.

- Quebec finishes three points behind the Canadiens, as Peter Stastny enjoys his fifth straight 100-point season (32 goals, 68 assists) and Michel Goulet rips 55 goals.

- Buffalo falls to third in the Adams, as G.M. Scotty Bowman briefly demotes 1984 Vezina and Calder

Raymond Bourque

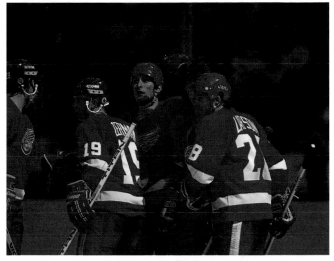

Detroit Red Wings

Motor City's Johnny O Drives In 55

John Ogrodnick, flanked by Steve Yzerman (left) and defenseman Reed Larson, celebrates one of the 55 he scored in 1984-85 en route to First All-Star Team honors. A hard-shooting Ontario native who apprenticed in the rugged Western Canadian juniors, Johnny O was a two-time 40-goal scorer (41 in 1982-83 and 42 in 1983-84) before reaching the elite 50-goal club, achieved for the first time on March 13, 1985, against Edmonton's Grant Fuhr.

Bourque Stars on So-So Boston Team

The Bruins struggled through an uncharacteristically mediocre season in 1984-85, finishing in fourth place. Defenseman Ray Bourque had an outstanding offensive season (86 points) as did former Kings winger Charlie Simmer (33 goals), but the team couldn't overcome serious defensive lapses and fell from 104 points in 1983-84 to just 82 in 1984-85. Coach Gerry Cheevers was fired before the season ended.

Trophy winner Tom Barrasso to the minors, causing a minor controversy. Gil Perreault leads the Sabres in scoring (83 points).

• Boston goes 36-34-10, its worst record in 18 years. The Bruins boast excellent offense—Ray Bourque (86 points), Charlie Simmer (33 goals

with Boston), and Keith Crowder (32 goals)—but mediocre defense.

• The Whalers win 30 games—their most since joining the NHL—but remain in the Adams basement.

• Edmonton breezes to a Smythe Division title (49-20-11), as Wayne

Gretzky tops 200 points for the third time in four years (73-135-208) and Jari Kurri nets 71.

• Winnipeg, second in the Smythe, is led by Dale Hawerchuk, who becomes the first Jet to score 50 goals (53). Five other Jets score 30-plus goals, led by Paul MacLean (41).

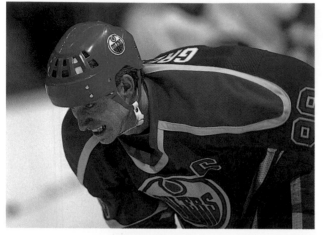

Wayne Gretzky

Gretzky Cops His Sixth Hart

The grace and fluidity of Wayne Gretzky's game often overshadowed the intensity he brought to the rink. In 1984-85, he won his fifth straight scoring title (73 goals and 208 points) and was the overwhelming choice for the league MVP award (his sixth in a row). With his unequaled leadership and creativity, the Oilers topped the 400-goal mark for the fourth straight season.

Bossy Scores 58 for Fading Isles

Mike Bossy scored 58 goals in 1984-85 (his eighth straight 50-goal season) but the Islanders dropped to third place in the Patrick Division and lost in the second round of the playoffs to Philadelphia. With stars like Bryan Trottier, Denis Potvin, Billy Smith, and (soon) Bossy on the decline, the Islanders were tumbling toward mediocrity.

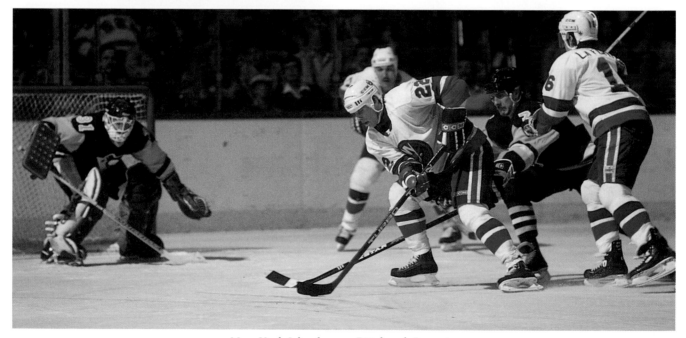

New York Islanders vs. Pittsburgh Penguins

1984-85

• Calgary finishes third in the Smythe, as Swedes Kent Nilsson and Hakan Loob tie for the team lead in goals (37). The Flames set an all-time NHL record by going 264 games without being shut out.

• Los Angeles powers out of the Smythe basement on the strength of

Marcel Dionne (46 goals, 126 points) and Bernie Nicholls (46 goals).

• The Canucks waste eight 20-goal scorers, including Tony Tanti (39), as they miss out on the playoffs.

• St. Louis (37-31-12) wins the Norris Division, getting big numbers from

Bernie Federko (103 points), Joe Mullen (40 goals), and Brian Sutter (37 goals).

• Chicago jumps to a second-place finish in the Norris, as Denis Savard (105 points) and Steve Larmer (46 goals) continue to set the pace.

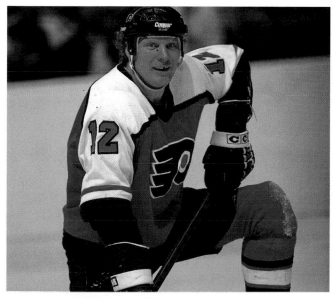

Tim Kerr

Kerr Just Gets 'Em and Bangs 'Em In

There wasn't anything fancy about the way Tim Kerr approached his job as a goal-scoring machine (54 goals in 1984-85). He didn't have much skating speed, his shot was average, and he didn't use intimidation to buy space on the ice. At 6'3" and 235 pounds, the Flyers' Gentle Giant relied strictly on strength and determination, camping in the high slot and banging home rebounds and centering passes from his wingers.

Lindbergh Pilots Flyers to Best Record

The Flyers ascended to the top of the league in 1984-85, outpointing the Oilers 113-109, thanks in large part to the brillant goaltending of Swedish sensation Pelle Lindbergh. While center Tim Kerr led the team in goals (54) and Brian Propp racked up 96 points, Lindbergh—a lightning-quick goalie with acrobatic balance and mobility—led the NHL with 40 wins and had a 3.02 goals-against average.

Michel Goulet

Goulet's 55 Goals Nothing to Brag About

Nordiques left winger Michel Goulet skates away from Islanders defenseman Stefan Persson in pursuit of the puck. In the third year of a streak that would see him notch at least 53 goals in four straight seasons, Goulet knocked in 55 goals in 1984-85. He did not, however, earn first- or second-team All-Star status, as 50-goal scorers were becoming a dime a dozen by the mid-1980s.

Pelle Lindbergh

• Detroit fades to a distant third in the Norris, as sophomore Steve Yzerman suffers through a rugged year (30 goals). John Ogrodnick (55 goals) picks up the slack.

• The North Stars fall from first to fourth in the Norris, as injuries and slumps plague the team.

• Toronto's porous defense leads to 52 losses, as young goalies Allan Bester and Ken Wregget struggle.

• The NHL's top five scorers are Wayne Gretzky (208 points), Jari Kurri (135), Dale Hawerchuk (130), Marcel Dionne (126), and Edmonton defenseman Paul Coffey (121).

• The league's leading goal-scorers include Wayne Gretzky (73), Jari Kurri (71, an NHL record for a right wing), Mike Bossy (58), John Ogrodnick (55), and Michel Goulet (55).

• Buffalo's Tom Barrasso leads in GAA (2.66), while Montreal's Chris Nilan leads in PIM (358).

Carpenter: First American to Net 50

After years of struggle and humiliation, the Capitals emerged as a power to be reckoned with in 1984-85, finishing second in the Patrick Division for the second straight time and boasting the first American-born player ever to notch a 50-goal season. Massachusetts-born Bobby Carpenter, the club's up-and-coming superstar, fired home 53 goals and joined sniper Mike Gartner (who scored 50) to give the Caps their first 50-goal duo.

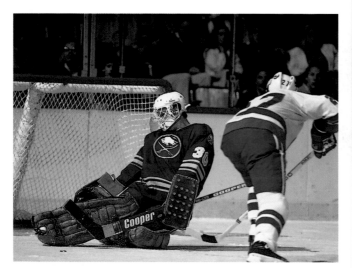

Tom Barrasso

Banished Barrasso Bounces Back

Tom Barrasso's sophomore season got off to a horrific start when the previous year's Calder and Vezina Trophy winner was dispatched to the minor leagues by Buffalo boss Scotty Bowman early in the campaign. Barrasso, a highly confident performer, went down to Rochester where he allowed just six goals in five games. Bowman then brought Barrasso back up again and he ended up leading the NHL with a 2.66 GAA and five shutouts.

Bobby Carpenter

1984-85

• In the Smythe semifinals, Edmonton sweeps L.A. (3-0) and the Jets skate past Calgary (3-1) for their first-ever series win. In the Norris semis, Chicago sweeps Detroit (3-0) while Minnesota brooms the Blues (3-0).

• In the Patrick semifinals, the Isles edge the Caps (3-2) while the Flyers sweep the Rangers (3-0). In the Adams, Quebec beats Buffalo (3-2) and the Habs outlast Boston (3-2) for their 16th straight playoff win over the Bruins.

• Edmonton sweeps Winnipeg (4-0) to capture the Smythe playoff title. The Oilers outscore the Jets 22-11.

• Chicago wins a high-scoring, six-game battle with the North Stars, as the teams average 10 goals per game before the Hawks win the Norris title.

• The once-dynastic Islanders fail to escape their division finals, as Philadelphia trounces them (4-1) to win the Patrick.

Paul Coffey

Hodgson Wins Cup, Named Top Player

Dan Hodgson is one of the few lucky players in Canadian juniors history to reap all of the postseason glory. Not only did he lead Prince Albert (WHL) to the Memorial Cup, but he was also voted the Canadian Major Junior Player of the Year Award. Hodgson registered 70 goals and 182 points during the 64-game season. He would play just 114 games in the NHL.

Dan Hodgson

Coffey Pots 37, Wins the Norris

On October 26, 1984, Edmonton's Paul Coffey became just the seventh NHL defenseman to notch four goals in a game. The fleet-footed offensive genius finished the season with 37 goals and 121 points and won the first of his two Norris Trophies, even though many criticized him for his soft defensive-zone play.

Chelios Helps Habs Win the Adams

Montreal's Chris Chelios (#24) heads up ice as defensive partner Larry Robinson covers his back. A rugged skater with equal measures of offensive genius and bad temper, Chelios emerged as an up-and-coming star in the NHL when he notched 55 rookie assists in 1984-85. Chelios, a Chicago native, finished runner-up for the Calder Trophy after helping the defensive-minded Canadiens finish first in the Adams Division.

Chris Chelios

- Quebec wins Game 7 of its Adams final against Montreal 3-2, as the teams each score 24 goals in the tightly contested series.

- The Oilers set records for consecutive playoff wins (12) and goals in a series (44) during their six-game triumph over Chicago in the conference finals. Jari Kurri scores 12 goals in the series—an NHL record.

- The Flyers oust Quebec (4-2) to earn their first Finals berth in five years.

- In Game 1 of the Stanley Cup Finals, host Philadelphia pumps four goals past Grant Fuhr as the Flyers shock the Oilers 4-1.

- The Oilers rebound in Game 2, winning 3-1.

- Wayne Gretzky's first-period hat-trick in Game 3 paces the Oilers to a 4-3 win.

Oilers Blast Hawks in Wild Semis

Kevin Lowe puts the screws to Chicago's Ken Yaremchuk during the 1985 Cup semifinals, but it was one of the few defensive highlights of the series. In fact, this was the highest-scoring NHL series of all time, as the two teams combined for 69 goals. Edmonton's 44 goals smashed the individual record by nine. The Oilers won the first two games 11-2 and 7-3, dropped the next two 5-2 and 8-6, and won the last two 10-5 and 8-2 to advance to the Finals.

Campbell Conference Finals

Howe Helps Flyers Knock Off Isles

The last time the Flyers met the Islanders in the playoffs, they fell to the New Yorkers in the 1980 Finals. Philly got revenge in the 1985 playoffs, however, beating the Isles in five division-final games. Defenseman Mark Howe, shown laying the lumber across the back of the Islanders' Pat LaFontaine, was a major offensive spark for the Flyers, exhibiting his usual brand of brilliant skating and passing.

Patrick Division Finals

Wales Conference Finals

Lindbergh, Flyers Rout Quebec

The Flyers hadn't been to the Stanley Cup Finals since 1980, when Bob Nystrom's sudden-death goal in Game 6 gave the Isles their first of four championships. In 1985, with goalie Pelle Lindbergh in nets, the Flyers beat Quebec in the semifinals to advance to the Finals against Edmonton. Lindbergh played brilliantly in the semifinals, allowing just 12 goals in six games versus the Nords and shutting them out 3-0 in the deciding game.

1984-85

- Down 3-1 in the first period, the Oilers fight back to win Game 4 with four unanswered goals. They win 5-3 to take a 3-1 series lead.

- Mark Messier and Paul Coffey each score twice as the Oilers roll to an 8-3 win in Game 5. Edmonton hoists its second straight Cup.

- The Conn Smythe Trophy is presented to Wayne Gretzky, who tallies an all-time record 47 playoff points. Paul Coffey sets the scoring record for a defenseman (37).

- Wayne Gretzky accepts his sixth straight Hart Trophy and fourth straight Lester B. Pearson Award.

- Jari Kurri wins the Lady Byng Trophy with 135 points and 30 PIM.

- Philadelphia goalie Pelle Lindbergh outballots Buffalo sophomore Tom Barrasso for the Vezina Trophy.

- Mario Lemieux is a hands-down Calder Trophy winner.

Flyers, Oilers Split Two in Philly

The Flyers had few moments of celebration in the Stanley Cup Finals, although they did split the first two games at the Spectrum. Here, Philly's Dave Poulin (wearing the captain's "C") celebrates a goal with Brian Propp (#26). Oilers goalie Grant Fuhr (masked) is way out of position as teammates Randy Gregg (#21), Glenn Anderson (#9), and Don Jackson (holding down Tim Kerr) cannot help.

Stanley Cup Finals

Fuhr Contains Flyers in Cup Finals

Edmonton goalie Grant Fuhr scrambles back into position as one of his defenders holds off Flyers forward Derrick Smith behind the net. After allowing four goals to the Flyers in a 4-1 loss to open the Finals, Fuhr allowed Philadelphia just one goal in Game 2 and three goals in each of the three games at Northlands Coliseum—while his Oilers teammates scored 21 times over the five-game span. Fuhr finished the playoffs with 15 wins in 18 games.

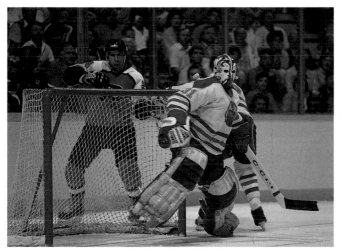

Stanley Cup Finals

Stanley Cup Celebration

Oilers Down Philly in Five, Sip Champagne

Mark Napier sips champagne from the Stanley Cup as teammate Charlie Huddy (right) lends support. The Oilers quaffed the bubbly after downing the Flyers in five games, including an 8-3 blowout in the finale. The 1985 playoffs were the Gretzky and Coffey Show. While Wayne set the all-time record for playoff points with 47, Paul Coffey established the standard for points by a defenseman with 37.

• Paul Coffey wins his first Norris Trophy, while Boston's Ray Bourque finishes second.

• Craig Ramsey, the veteran Sabre known for his checking and penalty-killing, captures the Frank Selke Trophy.

• Anders Hedberg of the Rangers wins the Masterton Trophy, while first-year Philly coach Mike Keenan nabs the Jack Adams Award.

• Dan Hodgson leads Prince Albert to the Memorial Cup and is voted the Canadian Major Junior Player of the Year.

• Rensselaer Polytechnic Institute beats Providence 2-1 in the NCAA title game, but Friars goalie Chris Terreri is named tournament MVP.

• Minnesota-Duluth's Bill Watson, a future Black Hawks winger, accepts the Hobey Baker Award.

'UNBEATABLE' OILERS END UP BEATING THEMSELVES

When the 1985-86 season began, there was every reason to believe that the Edmonton Oilers would become hockey's next dynasty and win a third straight Stanley Cup. Their lineup was never stronger. The incomparable Wayne Gretzky set all-time records for assists (163) and points (215) and again annexed the Hart Trophy. Defenseman Paul Coffey, who captured the Norris Trophy, was looking more like Bobby Orr every day.

With their explosive talent and Glen Sather's astute coaching, the Oilers rolled to a 56-17-7 record and seemed indomitable. But, as it happened, the Oilers were conspicuously weak in one area: luck.

This shortcoming did not manifest itself until the playoffs. The Oilers' postseason opened calmly enough against the Vancouver Canucks, as high-scoring right wing Glenn Anderson scored for Edmonton only 38 seconds into the opening game. Coffey scored less than two minutes later, and Edmonton ran away with a 7-3 triumph. The Oilers continued their dominance and easily sealed the series with a pair of 5-1 victories.

The Oilers next faced a Calgary team that had finished second to the Oilers in the Smythe Division with 89 points and had swept Winnipeg in the opening playoff round. The bitter series opened in Northlands Coliseum, where the Oilers had won 18 straight playoff games. The Flames were unimpressed, as Lanny MacDonald beat goalie Grant Fuhr at 1:26 of the first session. Calgary took a 2-1 lead into the third period and refused to fold, as goals by Joe Mullen and Hakan Loob sealed the victory.

The Oilers won a sloppily played Game 2, 6-5 in overtime, on a goal by Anderson. In Game 3 at Calgary, the Flames outplayed the Oilers in the final 40 minutes and came away with a well-deserved 3-2 victory. War broke out in Game 4, as 196 minutes in penalties were called, but Edmonton won every battle, including the game, 7-4. Gretzky dominated with a hat-trick and Fuhr turned in his best performance of the series.

Edmonton, though, could not keep the momentum going and dropped Game 5, again 4-1. The Oilers went back to Calgary facing what everybody believed was impossible—elimination. With the Saddledome buzzing with excitement, the Flames jumped quickly to a 2-0 lead. The Oilers wouldn't quit, and goals by Esa Tikkanen, Mark Messier, and Glenn Anderson led the champs to a 5-2 win.

The decisive Game 7 at Northlands Coliseum will never be forgotten. The Flames again took a 2-0 lead, but Edmonton rallied to tie the count 2-2 as the third period began. Then it happened. Young Edmonton defenseman Steve Smith—a late replacement for injured Lee Fogolin—fired the puck from behind his net, through the crease. The puck caromed off Fuhr's leg and into the net.

More than half a period remained, but the Oilers were continually thwarted. They lost the game 3-2 and the series 4-3. From that point on, the Oilers became known as the Dynasty That Never Was.

1985-86

- Due to the brilliant five-on-five play of the Oilers, the NHL adopts a rule allowing substitutions (six-on-six play) in the event of coincidental minors.

- The Hall of Fame inducts five men, including players Gerry Cheevers, Bert Olmstead, and Jean Ratelle.

- Toronto picks Wendel Clark with the first pick in the 1985 draft.

- On November 19, 1985, Flyers goalie Pelle Lindbergh, age 26, is killed in a car crash.

- On December 11, 1985, Edmonton beats the Black Hawks 12-9, tying the NHL record for combined goals in a game.

- On January 2, 1986, the Isles' Mike Bossy scores his 500th goal. He gets his 1,000th point 22 days later.

- On March 9, 1986, Buffalo's Gil Perreault scores his 500th goal.

The two-time Stanley Cup champion Oilers were poised—and heavily favored—to successfully complete the "three-peat," but they ran into a buzz saw from Calgary in the second round of the playoffs. The seesaw battle between the bitter Alberta rivals lasted seven games and was decided on a fluke play. Oilers defenseman Steve Smith (pictured), attempting an up-ice pass, shot the puck off goalie Grant Fuhr and into his own net, giving Calgary its margin of victory.

• The two-time champion Oilers win the regular-season title, going 56-17-7, as Wayne Gretzky sets the all-time record for points with 215.

• Wayne Gretzky sets a new league record with 163 assists—including seven on December 11, 1985, and seven more on Valentine's Day.

• Jari Kurri (68 goals) and Glenn Anderson (54) contribute to Edmonton's astonishing 426 goals.

• Calgary finishes a distant second to Edmonton in the Smythe. Joe Mullen, acquired from St. Louis in midseason, scores 44.

• Winnipeg finishes 60 points behind Edmonton, unable to capitalize on Dale Hawerchuk's 105-point season.

• The Canucks match Winnipeg's 59 points but finish fourth with three fewer wins. Tony Tanti scores 39 goals while lightning-fast Finn Petri Skriko rips 38.

Gretzky Racks Up a Record 215 Points

Wayne Gretzky, who has set more NHL scoring records than anyone in history, established a new league standard in 1985-86 with 163 assists. Needless to say, the Great One won another scoring title (his sixth), this time with an NHL-record 215 points. Gretzky's 163 set-ups alone gave him more points than the league's second-leading scorer, Pittsburgh's Mario Lemieux, who had 141 points in his sophomore campaign.

John Vanbiesbrouck

Vanbiesbrouck Wins 31 Games, Vezina Trophy

The Rangers turned to sophomore goalie John "Beezer" Vanbiesbrouck to carry the load in nets in 1985-86, as they barely eked out the final playoff spot in the highly competitive Patrick Division. Vanbiesbrouck suited up for 61 games, posted a 3.32 GAA, and led the NHL in victories with 31. The acrobatic 5'8" puck-stopper won the Vezina Trophy, becoming the first Ranger to do so since Ed Giacomin and Gilles Villemure shared the award in 1971.

Wayne Gretzky

Doug Brown, Scott Fusco

Another Fusco Wins the Baker

Scott Fusco (pictured on the ice stopping future NHLer Doug Brown in white) was a highly touted college player after a brilliant career at Harvard. But even after winning the 1986 Hobey Baker Award as the top U.S. college player in the country, Fusco never played a single game in the NHL. His older brother Mark, who won the Hobey Baker Award in 1983, played parts of two seasons with Hartford.

1985-86

• Los Angeles drops out of the playoffs, as Bernie Nicholls (36-61-97) and Marcel Dionne (36-58-94) cannot compensate for a porous defense.

• Chicago (39-33-8) takes the Norris title, as Denis Savard tallies another 100-point season (116) while defensive specialist Troy Murray explodes for 45 goals and 99 points.

• Minnesota finishes second, one point behind Chicago. Dino Ciccarelli (44 goals) returns to form, Scott Bjugstad (43) has a career year, and Neal Broten tallies 105 points.

• The Blues fall to third in the Norris despite Bernie Federko's 102 points and a stunning 44-goal season from rugged winger Mark Hunter.

• Toronto climbs out of the Norris Division cellar, finishing fourth. Miroslav Frycer (75 points) and Rick Vaive (33 goals) lead the attack.

Sylvain Turgeon

Turgeon's 45 Lead Powerful Whaler Offense

Huge expectations were placed on the broad shoulders of Sylvain Turgeon (shown firing on the Flyers' net) after the Whalers picked him second in the 1983 draft. Following Turgeon's 40-goal rookie season, Hartford appeared to be a team of the future. They tasted the fruits of success in 1985-86, as Turgeon scored 45 goals and led them to their first winning record ever (40-36-4). The Whalers placed fourth in the Adams but led the division in scoring.

Thanks to the Spin-o-Rama, Savard Nets 47

Chicago soared to the top of the Norris Division in 1985-86. Denis Savard, creator of the "Spin-o-Rama" move (in which he would complete a 360-degree turn while carrying the puck in order to elude defensemen), was Chicago's scoring ace, notching his fourth season with at least 100 points (116). In 1985-86, he reached a career high in goals with 47.

Denis Savard

Lindbergh Killed in Car Crash

The Flyers were dealt a tragic blow on November 19, 1985, when their dazzling goalie, Pelle Lindbergh, was fatally injured in a high-speed automobile accident. Lindbergh lost control of his turbo-charged Porsche and careened into a concrete wall. The former Vezina Trophy winner was just 26 years old. Bob Froese replaced Lindbergh in the Philly nets and wound up leading the NHL in goals-against average (2.55).

Pelle Lindbergh

• Detroit falls to last in the division, yielding 415 goals, as Steve Yzerman misses 29 games due to injury.

• In the Adams Division, Quebec goes 43-31-6 and wins its first division title. Peter Stastny (122 points) and Michel Goulet (53 goals) lead the offense.

• The Canadiens, with Guy Lafleur now retired, place second in the Adams. Mats Naslund (110 points) and rookie goalie Patrick Roy star.

• Boston finishes one point behind the Habs in the Adams Division, as Keith Crowder emerges as the team's top scorer (38 goals, 84 points).

• The Whalers make the playoffs for the first time in six years, as Sylvain Turgeon (45 goals) heads a list of seven 20-goal scorers.

• Buffalo, fifth in the Adams, can't make the playoffs despite a .500 record. Hard-nosed Mike Foligno rips 41 goals.

Paul Coffey

Murray Nets 45, Honored for Defense

Known primarily for his tenacious checking, tireless work ethic, and tremendous leadership abilities, the Hawks' Troy Murray captured the 1985-86 Frank Selke Trophy as the NHL's best defensive forward. Ironically, Murray earned the honor during a terrific offensive season—45 goals and 99 points. He proved to be just a one-year wonder offensively, however, as he would never again tally more than 28 goals or 71 points in a season.

Coffey's 48 Tallies Break Orr's Record

On March 14, 1986, during a 12-3 devastation of the Red Wings, magnificent Oilers defenseman Paul Coffey racked up eight points (two goals and six assists), tying the NHL record for points in a game by a defenseman set in 1977 by Philadelphia's Tom Bladon. Coffey finished the year with 48 goals—breaking the record of Bruins legend Bobby Orr (46)—and amassed a staggering 138 points. He skated off with his second Norris Trophy.

Troy Murray

Joe Mullen

Mullen's 44 Goals Fire Up Flames

In 1981-82, Joe Mullen became the first player to score 20 goals in two different leagues in the same year (21 at Salt Lake City and 25 for the Blues). In 1985-86, traded from the Blues to Calgary midway through the season, Mullen notched his third straight season with at least 40 goals (44). Mullen, who grew up on the streets of Hell's Kitchen in New York City, led the Flames' drive to the 1986 Stanley Cup Finals.

1985-86

• Buffalo's Dave Andreychuk notches 36 goals, including five in a game.

• The Flyers overcome the death of Pelle Lindbergh to go 53-23-4 and win the Patrick Division. Tim Kerr scores 58 goals (an NHL-record 38 on the power play) and Brian Propp garners 97 points.

• Fully recovered from a near-catastrophic injury, Philly's Mark Howe notches 82 points and is a remarkable +85. Goalie Bob Froese steps into a tough position and leads the NHL with a 2.55 GAA in 51 games.

• Washington finishes three points behind Philadelphia in the Patrick Division. Dave Christian nets 41 goals while Al Jensen and Pete Peeters star in goal.

• The Islanders register a 90-point season but finish third in the Patrick. Mike Bossy has another monster year (61 goals, 123 points).

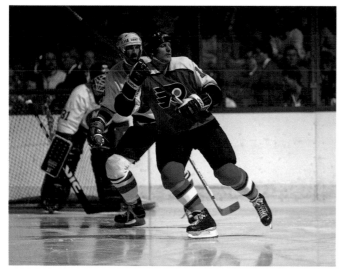

Tim Kerr

Sabre Vet Perreault Pots No. 500

Buffalo fans suffered through a tough 1985-86 season as their Sabres missed the playoffs despite chalking up 80 points in 80 games (while three other teams qualified with less than 60 points apiece). One bright spot came on March 9, 1986, when veteran hero Gil Perreault beat Devils goalie Alain Chevrier for his 500th career goal. Perreault retired after the 1986-87 season following a 17-year, 512-goal career in Buffalo.

Gil Perreault

Kerr Works Out of His Office

Flyers center Tim Kerr avoids the check of Islanders defenseman Ken Morrow as he sets up in his "office"—15 feet in front of the enemy net. In 1985-86, Kerr posted the third of his four straight seasons of 50-plus goals, finishing with 58. The hulking native of Windsor, Ontario, was almost unstoppable when the Flyers had the man advantage, leading the league with 34 power-play goals. He also notched eight game-winners.

Stastny-Led Nords Win the Adams

Relying on a combination of scoring skill and physical toughness, the Nordiques captured their first division title in 1985-86. Peter Stastny spearheaded the attack with 81 assists and 122 points while left winger Michel Goulet fired home a team-high 53 goals. Hard-nosed center Dale Hunter, the team's "squad sergeant," scored 28 goals and crashed his way to 265 penalty minutes as the team nosed out Montreal in the Adams Division race.

Peter Stastny

• The Rangers grab the final Patrick Division playoff spot. Rookie Mike Ridley's 65 points lead a mild attack.

• Mario Lemieux, the Penguins' new heart and soul, notches a team-record 93 assists, as hockey fans begin flocking to the Civic Arena. Still, the Penguins finish below .500.

• The New Jersey Devils improve slightly (28 wins) but still finish in the Patrick Division basement.

• The top five scorers are Wayne Gretzky (215 points), Mario Lemieux (141), Paul Coffey (138), Jari Kurri (131), and Mike Bossy (123).

• Leading goal-scorers include Jari Kurri (68), Mike Bossy (61), Tim Kerr (58), Glenn Anderson (54), and Michel Goulet (53).

• In the playoffs, Toronto shocks Chicago in the Norris Division semis (3-0), while St. Louis outlasts Minnesota (3-2) in their series.

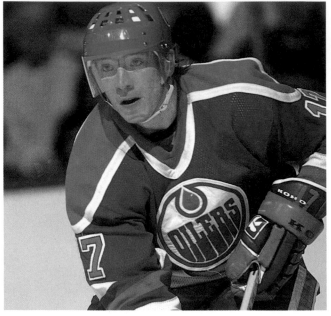

Jari Kurri

Mike Bossy

Kurri's 68 Pace Wicked Oiler Attack

In 1985-86, Edmonton right winger Jari Kurri led the league in goal-scoring for the only time in his career. Playing alongside buddy Wayne Gretzky, Jari found the back of the net 68 times. Kurri, who had one of the hardest shots in the league, helped the Oilers surpass the 400-goal mark for the fifth straight time. The Oilers finished with 426 team goals.

Bossy Scores No. 500 in Record Time

On January 2, 1986, goal-scoring superstar Mike Bossy became only the 11th player in NHL history to reach the 500-goal plateau. With his team up 6-5 against the Bruins at Nassau Coliseum, Bossy fired the puck into Boston's vacated net for the magic number. In just his 647th game, Bossy recorded the fastest 500 goals yet. "It's a milestone," he said, "but it's not the kind of record you have to get in a specific amount of time."

1985-86

- In the Smythe, Edmonton needs the minimum three games to dispatch Vancouver, while Calgary puts the broom to Winnipeg.

- Over in the Adams, Hartford stuns Quebec with a 3-0 sweep while the Canadiens continue their domination of Boston (3-0).

- In the Patrick, the Rangers knock off Philadelphia (3-2) while the Caps hand the Isles their first opening-round loss in eight years (3-0).

- After a seven-game tussle, St. Louis beats Toronto for the Norris title, winning the finale 2-1.

- In the Smythe finals, Calgary shocks the defending-champion Oilers (4-3) after Edmonton defenseman Steve Smith puts the puck in his own net to give the Flames the Game 7 win.

- Montreal sneaks past a surprising Hartford squad with a 2-1 O.T. win in Game 7 of the Adams finals.

Mario Lemieux

Roy Heats Up in Playoffs

Patrick Roy's rookie season was far from spectacular. He played 47 games in goal for Montreal and produced a 23-18-3 record with a 3.35 goals-against average, which belied the Habs' commitment to team defense. In the playoffs, however, Roy displayed his true genius, winning 15 of 20 starts and boasting a microscopic 1.92 GAA. The Habs ultimately won their 22nd Stanley Cup and the rookie goalie nabbed the Conn Smythe Trophy as playoff MVP.

Patrick Roy

Mario Pumps Life into the Penguins

With Mario Lemieux leading the charge, Pittsburgh showed a marked improvement in 1985-86, increasing its regular-season point total to 76 (from 53 the previous year). Mario, who finished second to Wayne Gretzky in overall scoring, set franchise records with 93 assists and 141 points. The silky-smooth Lemieux won the Lester B. Pearson Award.

Christian Gives the Caps Some Pop

Years of ineptitude were behind them when the 1985-86 Capitals roared to the third-best record (50-23-7) in the league and boasted a trio of high-powered snipers. Included was 41-goal scorer Dave Christian, a former U.S. Olympian who played in Winnipeg, Washington, Boston, St. Louis, and Chicago in a 14-year run. Christian's 41 goals set the pace as Mike Gartner (35) and Alan Haworth (34) followed.

Dave Christian

• The Rangers eliminate Washington in six games (4-2) to win the Patrick Division playoff title.

• Calgary outlasts St. Louis (4-3) in the Campbell Conference finals, winning the deciding game 2-1. Montreal makes it to the Finals with a five-game pasting of the Rangers.

• In Game 1 of the Cup Finals, Calgary thrashes visiting Montreal 5-2, as Dan Quinn and Lanny McDonald break open a close game with goals early in the third period.

• Montreal wins Game 2 3-2, as Brian Skrudland scores just nine seconds into sudden-death.

• At the Montreal Forum for Game 3, the Habs score four goals in the first period (two by Mats Naslund) and streak to a 5-3 win.

• Game 4 remains scoreless until 11:10 of the third period, when Habs rookie Claude Lemieux scores to win the game 1-0.

Vernon Pops Blues' Balloon in Cup Semis

As if the life of a goalie wasn't tough enough already, Calgary netminder Mike Vernon had to combat both the point-blank attack of St. Louis winger Doug Wickenheiser (#14) as well as the distraction of a beach ball, which had been hurled on the ice at St. Louis Arena during the 1986 Stanley Cup semifinals. The Flames took the series as Vernon won a Game 7 goalies battle, 2-1, over Blues netminder Rick Wamsley.

Campbell Conference Finals

Wales Conference Finals

Rangers Hit a Brick Wall in Habs' Roy

The 1985-86 Rangers, with a 25-goal performance from chippy Swede Tomas Sandstrom, were favorites to gain a berth in the Stanley Cup Finals...that is, until they ran into a human buzz saw named Patrick Roy (shown stopping Sandstrom at close range). Roy and the Canadiens prevailed in five games as the Rangers mustered only nine goals in the series.

1985-86

- Montreal builds a 4-1 lead through 56:46 of Game 5. Calgary makes it 4-3, but the Habs hold on and win the game and the series.

- The Habs hoist the Stanley Cup for the record 22nd time, and rookie goalie Patrick Roy, age 20, wins the Conn Smythe Trophy.

- Wayne Gretzky, winner of six straight Art Ross Trophies, also accepts his seventh consecutive Hart.

- Mario Lemieux wins the Lester B. Pearson Award.

- Mike Bossy wins his third Lady Byng Trophy, edging Jari Kurri.

- Rangers goalie John Vanbiesbrouck, who took his team to the conference finals, wins the Vezina Trophy, beating out Philly's Bob Froese.

- Calgary's Gary Suter (68 points) wins the Calder Trophy, as Wendel Clark is second.

Stanley Cup Finals

Habs Win Four Straight to Claim Cup

Patrick Roy (left), a first-time Stanley Cup champion, receives congratulations from Flames forward John Tonelli (right), a four-time Cup champ (with the Islanders), after the Habs put the final touches on their five-game Stanley Cup series victory over Calgary. Montreal dropped the opening game of the Finals before storming back with four straight victories, outscoring the run-and-gun Flames 13-8.

Patrick Roy, John Tonelli

Vernon Duels Roy in Cup Showdown

The 1986 Stanley Cup Finals between Montreal and Calgary were characterized by the splendid goaltending of both Patrick Roy (Habs) and Mike Vernon (Flames). The diminutive Vernon—pictured making a kick-save as Montreal's Bobby Smith maneuvers for a rebound—played all 21 playoff games and achieved a sterling 2.93 GAA.

Claude Lemieux

Lemieux's Goals Help Habs Win Cup

Claude Lemieux, pictured hoisting the Stanley Cup, played only 10 games during the 1985-86 regular season, but when the playoffs began he was a force. A "disturber" who irked even his own teammates with his on-ice histrionics (faking injuries, starting trouble and skating away, etc.), Lemieux notched 10 playoff goals including the winner in Montreal's 1-0 victory in Game 4 of the Finals.

- Paul Coffey, whose 48 goals broke Bobby Orr's record for goals by a defenseman, wins the Norris Trophy.

- Boston's Charlie Simmer receives the Masterton Trophy, while Troy Murray gladly accepts the Frank Selke Trophy.

- NHL broadcasters present Edmonton coach Glen Sather with the Jack Adams Award.

- Luc Robitaille of Hull (QMJHL) is the Canadian Major Junior Player of the Year, two years after the Kings selected him 171st in the draft.

- The Guelph Platers win their first-ever Memorial Cup.

- With tourney MVP Mike Donnelly, Michigan State beats Harvard 6-5 in the NCAA championship game, while Harvard's Scott Fusco claims the Hobey Baker Award.

ALL-STARS AND SOVIETS RENDEZVOUS IN QUEBEC

A unique sporting event conceived by a French-Canadian entrepreneur highlighted the 1986-87 regular season. Held in Quebec City, Rendez-Vous '87 featured two hockey titans: the NHL's All-Stars and the Soviet National Team. The result was a unique spectacle that no one would ever forget. The NHLers won the first game 4-3 on February 11, then lost the finale 5-3 on February 13.

The event was created by Marcel Aubut, president of the Quebec Nordiques. When Quebec was designated to host the 1987 NHL All-Star Game, Aubut decided that the annual event should be different. He proposed a two-game series between the NHLers and Soviets.

"It shouldn't be a party just among us, the hockey fans," Aubut told the NHL governors. "It should be an event where sports fans who otherwise have no interest in hockey have no choice but to watch, and where even the people who are not interested in sports have no choice but to watch. That is the way to promote a sport."

NHL owners were both intrigued and skeptical. Would it sell? They allowed Aubut to proceed with his concept, and he turned the event into more than a hockey match. It was a gigantic cultural celebration centered around the game. There were black-tie dinners, fashion shows, rock concerts, and international celebrities. Moreover, almost the entire Hockey Hall of Fame was imported and put on display.

The games themselves featured superb hockey by the best players in the world. The series opened with a ceremonial faceoff between the NHL's Wayne Gretzky and the Soviets' Viacheslav Fetisov and—despite some chauvinistic officiating and questionable post-game awards—it was an exhilarating event, further enhanced by the split-decision.

When the spectacle was over, hockey fans turned their attention back to the NHL, where the Edmonton Oilers were putting on a show of their own. The trio of Gretzky (62-121-183), Jari Kurri (54-54-108), and Mark Messier (37-70-107) powered Edmonton to a 50-24-6 record, best in the NHL.

The Oilers, trying to regain the Cup they had lost a year earlier, stormed through the playoffs. They crowned the L.A. Kings in five opening-round games, highlighted by a 13-3 laugher in Game 2. After sweeping Winnipeg in the Smythe Division finals, Edmonton beat Detroit in five games in the conference finals. The Oilers entered the Finals against the bullying Philadelphia Flyers.

Oilers coach Glen Sather, aware that the Flyers would use force, countered with three heavyweights of his own: Kevin McClelland, Marty McSorley, and rookie Kelly Buchberger. The two clubs slugged it out for seven low-scoring games. The Oilers overwhelmed Philly in Game 7 but were unable to open more than a one-goal gap. They finally moved ahead by two goals in the dying moments of the game, as Glenn Anderson unloaded a tremendous slapshot past goalie Ron Hextall. When the final horn sounded, the Oilers were Stanley Cup champions once again.

1986-87

- To speed the game, the NHL enacts a rule suspending delayed off-sides once the offending player leaves the opponent's defensive zone.

- The Hall of Fame inducts four members, including players Leo Boivin, Dave Keon, and Serge Savard.

- Detroit uses the first pick in the 1986 Entry Draft to select Michigan State center Joe Murphy, while Jimmy Carson goes No. 2 to the Kings.

- Phil Esposito takes over as Rangers G.M., fires coach Ted Sator in favor of Tom Webster, and begins a series of trades that will gut the team.

- Scotty Bowman, the winningest coach in NHL history, is fired by Buffalo.

- On November 20, 1986, the Habs and Bruins stage a brawl that results in $14,000 in fines. Boston Mayor Ray Flynn warns that arrests will result from future such riots.

Wayne Gretzky (left) and Soviet star Viacheslav Fetisov participate in the ceremonial opening faceoff for Rendez-Vous '87, a two-game tournament pitting the NHL's finest against the best of the Soviet Union. Also participating in the ceremony were hockey legends Vladislav Tretiak, Gordie Howe, and Jean Beliveau (left to right). The NHL stars won Game 1 4-3, while the Soviet team—loaded with future NHLers—took Game 2 5-3.

- On November 26, 1986, Toronto's Borje Salming is accidentally cut by a skate, requiring more than 200 stitches in his face.

- Four members of Swift Current (WHL.)—Scott Kruger, Chris Mantyka, Brent Ruff, and Trent Kresse—are killed in a bus crash.

- On January 9, 1987, Kings coach Pat Quinn is expelled by NHL President John Ziegler for signing a deal to become Vancouver's G.M. in 1987-88 and taking money from the Canucks while employed by L.A.

- In mid-February, the NHL stages a two-game extravaganza in Quebec,

"Rendez-Vous '87," pitting NHL stars against a team of Soviet stars. Each team wins once.

- Edmonton wins the regular-season championship, going 50-24-6.

- On November 22, 1986, Wayne Gretzky records his 500th goal.

Gilmour Comes Alive, Cracks the 100 Mark

A former OHL scoring champ, Doug Gilmour spent his first three years in the NHL as an understudy to Bernie Federko in St. Louis, as the coaching staff relegated the speedy center to defensive assignments. In 1986-87, Gilmour exploded offensively with 42 goals and 105 points, pushing the .500 Blues to a first-place finish in the Norris Division. Actually, Gilmour first came alive in the 1986 playoffs, when he scored 21 points in 19 games.

Doug Gilmour

Jacques Demers, Joe Murphy

Fans Boo Murphy, Cheer Demers

Joe Murphy and coach Jacques Demers represented two vastly different sides of the Red Wings' story. Murphy, a collegiate star at Michigan State, was the first player picked in the 1986 draft but was an NHL flop until 1990-91 (by which time he'd gone to Edmonton). Demers, the ultimate player's coach—a rah-rah leader with boundless enthusiasm—sparked the once-dormant Red Wings to the 1987 conference finals.

L.A.'s Robitaille Named Top Rookie

When the Kings picked Luc Robitaille 171st overall in the 1984 Draft, he was at best a long shot to make the NHL. By the end of 1985-86, the Montreal native was elected the top player in Canadian junior hockey. As an NHL rookie in 1986-87, playing alongside fellow novice Jimmy Carson, the smooth left winger scored 45 goals and was selected as the league's outstanding rookie, edging Flyers goalie Ron Hextall, who won the Vezina as a freshman.

Luc Robitaille

1986-87

- Five of Wayne Gretzky's 62 goals come in a game on December 6.

- Calgary takes second place in the Smythe Division as Joe Mullen (47 goals) leads the offense and Al MacInnis and Paul Reinhart (144 points between them) spark the attack from the blueline.

- Winnipeg improves by 29 points but finishes third in the Smythe. Rookies Eldon "Pokie" Reddick and Daniel "The Bandit" Berthiaume shine in goal.

- The Kings make the playoffs thanks to rookies Luc Robitaille (45-39-84) and Jimmy Carson (37-42-79).

- Vancouver manages only 66 points despite Tony Tanti's 41 goals and ex-Bruin Barry Pederson's 76 points.

- The Norris is tightly bunched but no one has a winning record. St. Louis (32-33-15) comes out on top, as scrappy center Doug Gilmour explodes for 105 points.

Joe Mullen

Ron Francis

Francis Helps Resuscitate Whalers

When a team improves from fourth place to first place in one year, there's usually a pretty good reason. The 1986-87 Whalers had a very good reason, and his name was Ron Francis, who had his best year yet by scoring 30 goals and leading the team with 93 points. Francis, a native of Sault Ste. Marie, Ontario, established himself as a brilliant playmaking center who could find the net, play in traffic, and carry a team on his 6'2", 200-pound frame.

Mullen Pots 47, Wins the Byng

Calgary virtually stole Joe Mullen from St. Louis in a six-player trade late in the 1985-86 season, and the rifle-shot right winger made the Flames look extra smart when he scored 47 goals in 1986-87 and led the team in scoring with 87 points. The 5'9" Mullen always played a hard-but-clean game. His lack of penalty time (just 14 minutes on the season) helped him capture his first Lady Byng Trophy.

• With drastically improved defense, Detroit rebounds from dead last to finish just a point behind St. Louis. Steve Yzerman tallies 90 points.

• Chicago players are now officially known as "Blackhawks" (as opposed to "Black Hawks"). Whatever the name, the club drops to third place.

• The Leafs barely eke out the final Norris playoff spot. Wendel Clark's 37 goals lead Toronto.

• Dino Ciccarelli registers 52 goals and 103 points for the North Stars, who lose Neal Broten for 34 games due to injury.

• In the Adams, Hartford (43-30-7) wins its first division title. Ron Francis (93 points) and Kevin Dineen (40 goals) propel the Whalers.

• Montreal finishes one point behind Hartford, as Brian Hayward (league-leading 2.81 GAA) and Patrick Roy (2.93) star in the nets.

Potvin: First NHL Blueliner to Hit 1,000

On April 4, 1987, Islanders legend Denis Potvin achieved what no other NHL defenseman had ever done: notch 1,000 career points. The record-setting 1,000th point came when Islander Mikko Makela's shot glanced off the arm of Potvin and bounced into the Buffalo net during a 6-6 shootout at Nassau Coliseum. Potvin missed five weeks of the season with a sprained left knee, while the Isles finished third in the Patrick Division.

Denis Potvin

Espo Tinkers with the Rangers

In 1986-87, Phil Esposito returned to the league as Rangers G.M. In the next three years, Espo would come to be known as Trader Phil. In his first year, he got Bob Carpenter from the Caps for Mike Ridley, then traded him to L.A. for Marcel Dionne. In a bizarre sequence, he traded Mark Pavelich to Minnesota for a draft pick, which he sent back to Minnesota when he got Tony McKegney, whom he then sent to St. Louis.

Phil Esposito

1986-87

• The Bruins finish third in the Adams. Ray Bourque leads in scoring (95 points) while newcomer Cam Neely rips 36 goals.

• Quebec drops from first to fourth in the Adams despite acquiring sniper John Ogrodnick from Detroit and getting 49 goals from Michel Goulet.

• The Sabres miss the playoffs, although rookie Christian Ruuttu (22-43-65) is a bright spot.

• The Patrick-winning Flyers (46-26-8) introduce rookie goalie Ron Hextall, who leads the league in games (66), wins (37), and save percentage (.902). Tim Kerr nets 58.

• Washington, second in the Patrick, is led by Mike Gartner (41 goals). Defenseman Larry Murphy, "stolen" from the Kings for Ken Houston and Brian Englbom, leads with 81 points.

• The Islanders debut new coach Terry Simpson, after the retirement of Al Arbour, and finish third. Mike

Kerr Cracks 50 Again, Flyers Finish First

With rookie sensation Ron Hextall in goal and veteran center Tim Kerr continuing to knock home goals at a rate of more than 50 per year, the Flyers soared to their fourth division title in five years. With goal-scoring seasons of 54, 54, and 58 to his credit, Kerr piled up 58 more red ones in 1986-87—second best in the league—despite missing five games due to injury. He also led the league in power-play goals (26) for the second time.

Tim Kerr

Stars Waste Ciccarelli's Big Numbers

A 52-goal performance from Dino Ciccarelli (shown charging off the bench) could not keep Minnesota from finishing last in the Norris Division in 1986-87 as the Stars posted a 30-40-10 record. A scrappy right winger who scored 55 goals as a sophomore in 1981-82, Ciccarelli reached the 100-point mark for the second time in his career when he finished the year with 103 points.

Dino Ciccarelli

99's Trophy Case Getting Mighty Crowded

Wayne Gretzky continued to dominate the NHL as no professional athlete had ever dominated any sport, leading the league in goals (62), assists (121), and points (183) in 1986-87. The NHL scoring runner-up, Jari Kurri, had fewer points (108) than Gretzky had assists. Gretzky captured his eighth straight Hart Trophy, his seventh straight scoring title, and his fifth career Lester B. Pearson Award—not to mention his third Stanley Cup.

Wayne Gretzky

Bossy sees his string of 50-goal seasons end at nine. He scores 38.

• On April 4, 1987, Islander Denis Potvin becomes the first NHL defenseman to record 1,000 points.

• The Rangers stumble to fourth place after trading for Walt

Poddubny, Marcel Dionne, Tony McKegney, Ron Duguay, Curt Giles, Jeff Jackson, Pat Price, Stu Kulak, and Bob Froese.

• Mario Lemieux misses 17 games due to injury but still manages 54 goals. The Penguins fail to make the playoffs for the fifth year in a row.

• NHL scoring leaders include Wayne Gretzky (183 points), Jari Kurri (108), Mario Lemieux (107), Mark Messier (107), and Doug Gilmour (105).

• The league's five 50-goal scorers are Wayne Gretzky (62), Tim Kerr (58), Jari Kurri (54), Mario Lemieux (54), and Dino Ciccarelli (52).

Raymond Bourque

Mario Lemieux

Iron Man Jarvis Plays 964 Straight

Doug Jarvis (right) scored 45 goals one year in junior hockey, but in his NHL career he scored just 139 goals in 964 games. Nevertheless, the 5'9" defensive specialist played a dozen years without ever missing a game. In 1985-86, he played 82 games (in an 80-game schedule) when Washington traded him to Hartford. He broke Garry Unger's "iron man" record of 914 games during the 1986-87 season and won the Masterton Trophy for dedication.

Bourque Racks Up 95 Points, Wins Norris

Former rookie of the year Raymond Bourque led the Bruins in scoring in 1986-87 with 95 points and demonstrated his patented tough-but-clean play, accumulating just 36 penalty minutes. The Bruins placed third in the Adams Division while Bourque established himself as the NHL's premier defenseman, winning his first of five Norris Trophies. From 1981 through 1994, Bourque played in all but one NHL All-Star Game.

Lemieux Nets 54 Despite a Bad Back

The Penguins suffered a setback in 1986-87 as they chalked up four fewer points than the previous year and again missed the playoffs. What scared Pittsburgh officials even more was that Mario Lemieux began to suffer from a bad back. Mario notched 54 goals and 107 points (third in the league) but had to sit out 17 games. Back ailments would continue to plague Lemieux —but not defeat him— throughout his career.

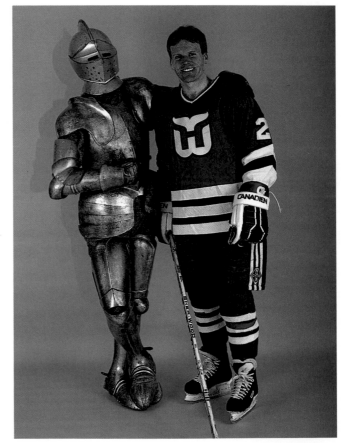

Doug Jarvis

1986-87

- In the divisional semifinals—now best-of-seven series—the Flyers need six games to beat the Rangers.

- The Caps and Islanders engage in a seven-game clash, and Game 7 goes to quadruple O.T. Pat LaFontaine scores to advance the Isles to the Patrick Division finals.

- In the Adams semis, Quebec upsets Hartford (4-2) and Montreal sweeps Boston. The Habs have now beaten the Bruins in the 18 straight playoff series in which they've met.

- In the Norris semis, Toronto upsets St. Louis (4-2) while Detroit sweeps Chicago.

- In the Smythe Division semifinals, the Jets douse the Flames (4-2). The Oilers score a playoff-record 13 goals in Game 2 on their way to a five-game rout of the Kings.

- Philly beats the Isles (4-3) in the Patrick finals. Montreal ousts Quebec (4-3) in the Adams finals.

Salming's Face Sliced by Skate

Maple Leafs defenseman Borje Salming was lost by the team for 24 games in 1986-87 when he was accidentally cut in the face by the skate of Detroit winger Gerard Gallant. The gash, which required more than 200 stitches, snaked its way along Salming's right cheek, to the inside of his right eye, and up over his brow. It was the third injury around Salming's eye in recent months and prompted the veteran to consider attaching a face-shield to his helmet.

Ron Hextall

Nasty Hextall Wins Vezina, Smythe

In 1986-87, the Flyers debuted a big, mean rookie goalie with a name associated with hockey greatness: Ron Hextall, grandson of NHL Hall of Famer Bryan Hextall. At 6'3", Hexy combined quick reflexes with a nasty competitive streak that enabled him to survive a league-high 66 games, plus 26 in the playoffs as the Flyers went to the Stanley Cup Finals. Hextall won both the Vezina Trophy as well as the Conn Smythe Trophy (pictured).

Borje Salming

- Detroit outlasts Toronto (4-3) in the Norris finals to advance against the Oilers, who sweep Winnipeg in the Smythe finals.

- Philadelphia beats Montreal in six games (4-2) to win the Wales title, while the Oilers outclass Detroit (4-1) to win the Campbell crown.

- In Game 1 of the Finals, the Oilers break open a 1-1 tie with goals from Glenn Anderson, Paul Coffey, and Jari Kurri to win 4-2.

- Game 2 is tied 2-2 after regulation, but Jari Kurri beats Ron Hextall at 6:50 of O.T.

- Game 3 at Philly sees the Oilers take a 3-0 lead before the Flyers score five goals to win 5-3.

- Game 4, won by Edmonton 4-1, is marred by Flyer goalie Ron Hextall's slash against Oiler Kent Nilsson, for which Hextall is suspended eight games to start the 1987-88 season.

Flyers Break Down Habs' D, Win the Semis

The 1987 Stanley Cup semifinals between Philadelphia and Montreal were characterized by hard hitting and fast-paced play. Here, Pelle Eklund, the Flyers' ace playmaker, is chased down by defensive forward Brian Skrudland. In a series pitting two brilliant young goalies—Ron Hextall for Philly against Montreal's Patrick Roy—the Flyers were able to overcome Montreal's superb team defense and beat the Habs in six games.

Wales Conference Finals

Isles Beat Caps in Fourth O.T.

On April 18, 1987, the Islanders and Capitals played the fifth-longest game in NHL history. Tied at 2-2 after regulation in Game 7 of their division semifinal series, the teams couldn't score through three overtime periods and nearly half of the fourth. Finally, Pat LaFontaine's turnaround shot from the high slot beat Caps goalie Bob Mason, ending the game after 68:47 of sudden-death—and at 1:56 a.m.

Patrick Semifinals

Stanley Cup Finals

Anderson's Late Goal Seals the Cup

Oilers winger Glenn Anderson (#9) always attracted a crowd in the offensive zone. Anderson scored 14 goals in the 1987 Stanley Cup playoffs, second best behind teammate Jari Kurri (15). With the Oilers leading 2-1 late in Game 7 and the Flyers pressing frantically to tie, Anderson unloaded a blast that beat Ron Hextall and sealed the game 3-1.

1986-87

- Game 5 at Edmonton is tied 3-3 when Flyer winger Rick Tocchet beats Grant Fuhr to give Philly a 4-3 win.

- Back in Philadelphia for Game 6, the Oilers jump out to a 2-0 lead. But Lindsay Carson, Brian Propp, and J.J. Daigneault score to give the Flyers a dramatic 3-2 victory.

- The Flyers take a 1-0 lead in Game 7 at Edmonton, but the Oilers bounce back for a 3-1 win. They hoist their third Cup in four years.

- Losing goalie Ron Hextall—who plays in a record 26 playoff games—wins the Conn Smythe Trophy.

- Wayne Gretzky collects his eighth straight Hart Trophy and fifth career Lester B. Pearson Award. Ray Bourque is runner-up for the Hart.

- Calgary's Joe Mullen, with 47 goals and 14 penalty minutes, wins his first Lady Byng Trophy.

Stanley Cup Finals

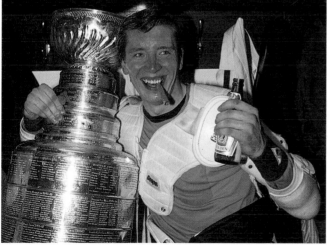

Jari Kurri

Flyers Stay Alive, Force Game 7

After their disastrous 1986 playoff season, the Oilers—led by the tenacious Mark Messier (right)—took on the equally feisty Flyers, whose never-quit attitude was personified by center Ron Sutter (#14). In the Finals, the Oilers took a three-games-to-one lead before Philly staved off elimination with a pair of dramatic one-goal victories to force a seventh game at Edmonton.

Kurri Lights It Up, Sips from Cup

Although Flyers goalie Ron Hextall won the 1987 Conn Smythe Trophy, many argued that Jari Kurri (pictured) was a deserving candidate. The Finnish Finisher deposited 15 playoff goals (best in the league) and was huge in the clutch. He scored the O.T. winner in Game 2 of the Finals, netted the Cup-clinching goal in Game 7, and counted five game-winners among his 15 tallies.

- Rookie Ron Hextall wins the Vezina with a 3.00 GAA and 104 PIM, but Luc Robitaille claims the Calder Trophy.

- Boston's Ray Bourque wins his first Norris Trophy, while Philly's Dave Poulin takes the Frank Selke Trophy.

- Hartford's Doug Jarvis, who sets a record for consecutive games (964), wins the Masterton Trophy.

- Detroit coach Jacques Demers wins the Jack Adams Award.

- Rob Brown of Kamloops (WHL) is named the Canadian Major Junior Player of the Year. Meanwhile, Medicine Hat (WHL) wins its first Memorial Cup.

- North Dakota beats Michigan State 5-3 for the NCAA title. UND's Tony Hrkac, the tourney MVP, wins the Hobey Baker Award.

FEISTY DEVILS STIR UP A LITTLE BIT OF HELL

In many ways, the New Jersey Devils' 1988 homestretch run was as pulsating as the 1951 pennant rush of baseball's New York Giants. Behind two electrifying newcomers—rookie head coach Jim Schoenfeld and freshman goaltender Sean Burke (from the Canadian Olympic team)—the perennial cellar-dwellers closed the season with a sensational 7-0-1 streak, gaining a playoff berth that earlier had seemed hopelessly out of reach.

New Jersey needed a win in its final regular-season game, at Chicago, in order to overtake the New York Rangers for the fourth and final Patrick Division playoff spot. New Jersey and Chicago skated to a 3-3 tie at the end of regulation, but the Devils could not afford a stalemate. To clinch a playoff berth, they needed a win. They got it at 2:21 of sudden-death, when red-hot John MacLean—who had scored the game-tying goal—slammed in a rebound of a Joe Cirella shot for the game-winning goal. New Jersey entered the playoffs for the first time ever.

In Round 1 of the Patrick Division playoffs, the Devils squared off against the division-champion New York Islanders.

Playing an outrageously physical style, Schoenfeld's skaters ousted the Isles four games to two, with both New Jersey losses coming in overtime.

Riding the wave of their upset, New Jersey went on to face Washington in the Patrick finals. The Devils dropped the first game 3-1, but they evened the count in Game 2 with a 5-2 drumming of the Caps. The Devils had clearly taken charge, keyed by the line of left wing Patrik Sundstrom, right wing MacLean, and center Mark Johnson. When the series moved to Byrne Arena, the Jerseyites hammered Washington 10-4, as Sundstrom set an NHL playoff record with eight points. Washington was dumped in the seventh game, as MacLean scored the winning goal once again.

Incredibly, the Devils had advanced to the Wales Conference finals against the Boston Bruins. The series proved to be grueling, extending to seven games, and it included a Devils overtime win in Game 2. In Game 3 at Byrne, the Devils were devastated by the Bruins, 6-1. Seconds after game's end, Schoenfeld verbally assaulted referee Don Koharski, who later charged that the coach had floored him.

With NHL President John Ziegler mysteriously unavailable, Vice-President Brian O'Neill suspended Schoenfeld prior to Game 4. In a bizarre turn of events, a New Jersey court overturned the ruling and Schoenfeld was behind the bench by game time. In protest, the three NHL game officials walked out and were replaced by three amateurs.

The Devils won Game 4, whereupon Ziegler reappeared and re-suspended Schoenfeld for Game 5, which the Bruins dominated 7-1. The Devils evened the series in Game 6, but their miracle year ended in the final match, which the Bruins won 6-2. Despite the loss, the New Jersey Devils—once known as hockey's "Mickey Mouse team"—had won the hearts of a continent, as well as league-wide respect.

1987-88

- Team Canada wins the Canada Cup, defeating the Soviets two games to one in the finals. Mario Lemieux scores the winners in Game 2 (double O.T.) and Game 3 (with 1:26 to go).

- The Hall of Fame inducts five men, including players Bobby Clarke, Ed Giacomin, and Jacques Laperriere.

- The Sabres pick first in the 1987 Entry Draft and select scoring ace Pierre Turgeon of Granby (QMJHL).

- Edmonton's Paul Coffey says he will not return to the Oilers due to contract problems, and G.M. Glen Sather lets him sit on the sidelines until Thanksgiving.

- Goalie Andy Moog joins the Canadian National Team rather than play for Glen Sather in Edmonton. He will later be traded to Boston.

- Brian Spencer, a former NHLer charged with murder in West Palm Beach, Florida, is found not guilty.

After finishing out of the playoffs for nine straight years (four
as the Colorado Rockies and five as the Devils), New Jersey made an unlikely
and thrilling run for the Stanley Cup in the spring of 1988. They charged all the
way to the semifinals, where the Bruins beat them in seven. A major contributor
to the Devils' effort was right winger John MacLean (#15). Johnny Mac had
18 points in the postseason, including seven goals.

• On December 8, 1987, Philadelphia goalie Ron Hextall shoots the puck the length of the ice into Boston's open net, becoming the first NHL goalie to score with a shot on goal.

• On March 1, 1988, Wayne Gretzky records his 1,050th assist, breaking Gordie Howe's all-time record.

• On March 19, 1988, Bernie Federko notches his 1,000th point.

• Calgary emerges as the NHL's best team (48-23-9). Flames rookie Joe Nieuwendyk (51 goals), Hakan Loob (50), and Mike Bullard (48) lead the potent offense.

• The Oilers finish second in the Smythe as Wayne Gretzky misses 16 games. Craig Simpson, acquired from Pittsburgh for Paul Coffey, notches 56 goals. He's the first NHLer to score 50 while being traded in midseason.

• Dale Hawerchuk (121 points) helps the Jets finish third in the Smythe.

Canada Wins a Canada Cup Thriller

The 1987 Canada Cup tournament culminated in a best-of-three championship round between Canada and the Soviet Union. With the finals tied 1-1, the Soviets jumped to a 4-2 first-period lead in Game 3 before goals by Larry Murphy (pictured, #8), Brent Sutter, and Dale Hawerchuk put the Canadians in front 5-4. Future NHLer Alexander Semak tied it up in the third, but Canada's Mario Lemieux scored with 1:26 left to win the game and the title.

Fuhr's 40 Wins Earn Him the Vezina

During the 1987-88 season, Oilers goalie Grant Fuhr didn't crack the top five in two main categories: goals-against average (3.43) or save percentage (.881). However, he proved his superiority by winning the most games (40) and tying for the lead in shutouts (four). Fuhr was in net for 90 percent of the Oilers' victories and won 16 of 19 playoff games. He was honored with his first Vezina Trophy.

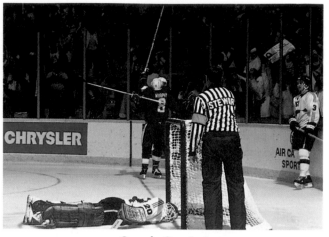

Canada Cup Series

Grant Fuhr

NHL Honors Toronto's King Clancy

In 1987-88, the NHL established a new award in honor of Hall of Famer Francis "King" Clancy. It recognized "the player who best exemplifies leadership qualities on and off the ice and has made a noteworthy humanitarian contribution in his community." Calgary right winger Lanny McDonald was the inaugural winner in 1988. Clancy played in the NHL from 1921-37, for Ottawa and Toronto, and was a Maple Leaf executive for much of five decades.

King Clancy Award

- Los Angeles earns the final playoff berth in the Smythe as Luc Robitaille (53-58-111) and Jimmy Carson (55-52-107) star.

- Vancouver (with Pat Quinn in charge after a legal battle ends in his reinstatement as G.M.) wins just 25 games despite Tony Tanti's 40 goals.

- Steve Yzerman's first 50-goal, 100-point season helps the 41-28-11 Red Wings capture the Norris. It's their first first-place finish in 23 years.

- The Blues acquire Tony McKegney (40 goals) and future star Brett Hull, who combine with Bernie Federko (89 points) and Doug Gilmour (36 goals). St. Louis places second in the Norris Division.

- Thanks to Denis Savard (44 goals), Steve Larmer (41), and recently acquired Rick Vaive (43), Chicago overcomes bad goaltending to finish third in the Norris.

Knee Injury Sidelines Gretzky

After missing just eight games in eight NHL seasons, Wayne Gretzky was forced to sit out 16 contests during the 1987-88 season with a knee injury, costing him a chance at his eighth straight scoring title. He finished with "only" 40 goals and was second overall with 149 points in 64 games (2.33 points per game). Mario Lemieux, who won the scoring title, averaged 2.21 points per contest.

Stephane Richer

Richer Shoots Till He Hits No. 50

After two mediocre scoring seasons in the NHL, third-year pro Stephane Richer—a hard-shooting winger known for shooting when there's nothing to shoot at—scored 50 goals in 1987-88, leading all Canadiens in goals and becoming the first Hab since 1979-80 to reach 50. Richer, who led the NHL in game-winning goals (11), hit the half-century mark on the final day of the season, when he beat Tom Barrasso in a 4-4 tie at Buffalo.

Wayne Gretzky

• Toronto makes the playoffs as Ed Olczyk rips 42 goals.

• Despite Dino Ciccarelli (41 goals) and Brian Bellows (40), the North Stars win just 19 games.

• Montreal (45-22-13) wins the Adams Division thanks to Stephane Richer (50 goals), Bobby Smith (93 points), and Patrick Roy (2.90 GAA).

• Defenseman Ray Bourque leads the Bruins in scoring (81 points) as the Bruins place second in the Adams.

• In the wake of Gil Perreault's retirement after 17 seasons, the Sabres regroup and climb into third place in the Adams.

• The Whalers collapse to fourth in the Adams. Ron Francis leads the team in scoring with just 75 points.

• The Nordiques miss the playoffs for the first time in eight years.

Oilers Dump Coffey, Get Simpson

The Penguins picked Michigan State center Craig Simpson second overall in the 1985 draft, then traded him early in November 1987 to the Oilers for malcontent Paul Coffey (a holdout in Edmonton). Simpson, a highly imaginative and rugged playmaker, erupted for 43 goals in 59 games following his trade to Edmonton and finished the season with 56 red lights, No. 50 coming on March 15, 1988, against Buffalo.

Raymond Bourque

Craig Simpson

Blueliner Bourque Pours It On

Despite finishing 14 games over .500 in 1987-88, Boston trailed the Adams-leading Canadiens by nine points in the final standings. The Boston attack was led by defenseman Ray Bourque, whose 64 assists and 81 points led the team. Bourque unleashed 344 shots on goal, second only to Mario Lemieux's 382, and was third among NHL defensemen in points behind Calgary's Al MacInnis and Gary Suter. Bourque earned his second Norris Trophy.

1987-88

• Peter Stastny (46 goals) and Michel Goulet (48) can't save Quebec.

• Mike Bossy retires but the Isles win the Patrick (39-31-10), as Pat LaFontaine (47 goals) blossoms.

• The Capitals finish second in the Patrick for the fifth straight year, as

Mike Gartner rips 48 goals and Pete Peeters leads the NHL in GAA (2.78).

• The Flyers boast the same record as Washington (38-33-9). Rick Tocchet tallies 31 goals and 301 PIM.

• The Devils barely make the playoffs, as Canadian Olympian Sean

Burke goes 10-1-0 down the stretch. Kirk Muller (94 points) and Pat Verbeek (46 goals) provide offense.

• The Rangers tie New Jersey with 82 points, but New York misses out on the Patrick's final playoff berth because of two fewer victories.

Joe Nieuwendyk

Rookie Nieuwendyk Knocks In 51

Before Joe Nieuwendyk arrived as a rookie in the NHL in 1987-88, the most famous player to come out of Cornell University was Ken Dryden. In Calgary, the former All-American challenged the record for rookie goals (53) set by Islanders icon Mike Bossy in 1977-78. Nieuwendyk found the back of the net 51 times and won the Calder Trophy.

Lemieux Wins the Hart, Art Ross

Mario Lemieux nearly played his first full NHL schedule in 1987-88, missing only four games due to persistent back trouble. The magnificent Mario emerged as the league's newest scoring champion, ending the seven-year reign of Wayne Gretzky. Lemieux won his first Art Ross Trophy (70-98-168) as well as his first Hart Trophy.

Jimmy Carson

Young Carson Nets 55 Goals

Jimmy Carson was a highly touted rookie when he entered the NHL as the second player picked in the 1986 draft, and he responded with a sterling 37-goal rookie performance. The Detroit-area product faced the sophomore jinx in 1987-88 and never even blinked. By season's end, Carson had fired home 55 goals (third best in the league) and tallied 107 points (eighth best).

Mario Lemieux

- Mario Lemieux leads the NHL with 70 goals and 168 points, but his Pens finish a point back of the Devils.

- Following Mario Lemieux, the NHL's top scorers are Wayne Gretzky (149 points), Denis Savard (131), and Dale Hawerchuk (121).

- Top goal-scorers include Mario Lemieux (70), Craig Simpson (56), Jimmy Carson (55), Luc Robitaille (53), and Joe Nieuwendyk (51).

- In the Patrick Division semis, New Jersey upsets the Isles (4-2) while Washington nips Philadelphia in seven.

- In the Adams Division semis, the Habs dispose of Hartford (4-2) while Boston beats Buffalo (4-2).

- Calgary needs just five games to eliminate L.A. (4-1) in the Smythe semis, while Edmonton similarly ousts Winnipeg (4-1).

Keenan Fired After Flyers Fall

Flyers coach Mike Keenan huddles with Rick Tocchet (#22) as Murray Craven (#32), Peter Zezel (head bowed), and Derrick Smith (extreme right) look on. Keenan established himself as an intense, dedicated strategist who demanded nothing but 100-percent effort from his players. The Flyers finished atop the Patrick Division in Keenan's first three years in Philly. After placing third in his fourth year, 1987-88, he was fired.

Mike Keenan

Sather Sends Bitter Coffey to Pittsburgh

Despite tremendous success in Edmonton, All-Star defenseman Paul Coffey refused to play for G.M. Glen Sather in 1987-88, citing contract differences that proved irrevocable. Sather let Coffey sit for almost two months, finally trading the disgruntled blueliner to Pittsburgh. Under strict orders from owner Peter Pocklington, the Oilers' savvy manager began a campaign of playing contractual hardball with all of his stars.

Glen Sather

Steve Yzerman

Yzerman Nets 50th, Then Blows His Knee

Under coach Jacques Demers, the Red Wings won the Norris Division in 1987-88—their first first-place finish since 1964-65. Detroit captain Steve Yzerman, who was born in '65, led the way with 50 goals and 102 points in just 64 games. Yzerman, a gifted skater and playmaker with natural goal-scoring ability, tore the ligaments in his right knee on March 1, 1988, the same game in which he scored his 50th goal.

1987-88

• In the Norris Division semis, Detroit beats Toronto (4-2) while St. Louis eliminates Chicago (4-1).

• The Devils shock the Caps in seven fight-filled games to win the Patrick playoff title. New Jersey's Patrik Sundstrom sets a playoff record with eight points in a Game 3 10-4 win.

• The Bruins end the Habs' playoff domination of them with a five-game Adams final triumph (4-1). Montreal had beaten Boston in 18 straight playoff series.

• Edmonton sweeps Calgary in a surprisingly easy Smythe final series, outscoring the Flames 18-11.

• Detroit advances to the conference finals with a five-game series win over St. Louis in the Norris.

• During the Wales finals between Boston and New Jersey, the referees and linesmen strike for one game following an attack by Devils coach Jim Schoenfeld on Don Koharski.

Kent Nilsson, Ron Hextall

Schoenfeld Punished for Rude Remark

The Devils were a surprise power in the 1988 playoffs, but the team fell into trouble in the Cup semifinals when coach Jim Schoenfeld got into a ruckus with referee Don Koharski. After berating Koharski for his handling of the game, an irate Schoenfeld shouted, "Go eat another doughnut, you fat pig..." and was suspended by the league. A court injunction reversing the suspension led to a brief officials strike.

Jim Schoenfeld

Hextall Gets Nasty, Scores Goal

Following a brilliant rookie season, Flyers goalie Ron Hextall suffered the consequences of his hot temper in 1987-88, drawing 104 penalty minutes. Moreover, he was suspended for the season's first eight games after viciously slashing Oiler Kent Nilsson (pictured) in the 1987 Finals. Hextall also scored a goal in 1987-88 when he fired the puck into Boston's empty net, making him the first goalie in NHL history to actively score a goal.

Gartner Stars on Second-Fiddle Caps

A franchise known for its inability to win the big games, the Capitals finished the 1987-88 season in second place in the Patrick Division (for the fifth straight time). At the head of the parade was 48-goal scorer Mike Gartner, the game's fastest skater and one of the hardest shooters in the league. Gartner, who donated money to charity for every goal he scored, piled up huge dividends for worthy causes.

Mike Gartner

• Boston outlasts the Devils (4-3) in the Wales finals, while Edmonton smashes the Red Wings (4-1) in the Campbell Conference finals.

• In Game 1 of the Stanley Cup Finals, Keith Acton breaks a 1-1 tie early in the third period to give Edmonton a 2-1 victory over Boston—and former Oiler goalie Andy Moog.

• In Game 2, Wayne Gretzky nets the winner at 11:21 of the third period. The Oilers go on to win 4-2.

• In Game 3 at Boston, the Oilers score four straight goals en route to a 6-3 win. Edmonton's Esa Tikkanen notches a hat-trick.

• Just as Oiler Craig Simpson scores at 16:37 of the second period of Game 4 at Boston Garden to tie the game 3-3, a power failure knocks out the lights and the game is ultimately suspended.

Oilers Hold Off Wings in Semis

The Red Wings were the class of the Norris Division in 1987-88, going 41-28-11 and beating the Leafs and Blues to go to the semifinals. Steve Yzerman, trying to break through Craig Simpson (left) and Glenn Anderson (right), played only three games in the post-season after recovering from torn knee ligaments. His diminished presence wasn't enough to inspire Detroit over the Oilers, who won the series in five games.

Campbell Conference Finals

Olympic Games

Soviet Union Wins an Early Gold Medal

The Soviet Union celebrates a 7-1 trouncing of Sweden to clinch the 1988 Olympic gold medal in Calgary, Alberta. Although they would lose to Finland two days later, their gold medal was already assured. Eight of the Soviets' top scorers eventually moved to the NHL: Vladimir Krutov, Slava Fetisov, Igor Larionov, Sergei Makarov, Alexei Kasatonov, Valeri Kamensky, Anatoli Semenov, and Alexander Mogilny.

1987-88

• Game 4 is replayed in Edmonton, as the Oilers break open a 2-2 game. They win 6-3 and claim their fourth Stanley Cup in five years.

• With 43 playoff points—including a record 13 in the Finals—Wayne Gretzky wins his second Conn Smythe Trophy.

• Mario Lemieux, who broke Wayne Gretzky's seven-year reign as scoring champ, ends Gretzky's eight-year domination of the Hart Trophy. Lemieux also wins the Lester B. Pearson Award.

• Montreal's Mats Naslund wins the Lady Byng Trophy, while Oiler Grant Fuhr—who sets an NHL record with 75 games played—captures the Vezina.

• Joe Nieuwendyk wins the Calder Trophy over Buffalo's Ray Sheppard, while Ray Bourque wins his second straight Norris Trophy.

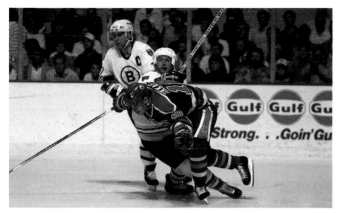

Stanley Cup Finals

Lights Go Out in Game 4 of Finals

The Oilers won the first three games of the 1988 Finals and were tied 3-3 with Boston in Game 4. But with 3:23 left in the second period, the Boston Garden suddenly lost power. Members of the Oilers stood on the darkened ice in sweat clothes as technicians tried to find a quick solution to the electrical malfunction. After a lengthy delay, however, the game was suspended (statistics were retained) and the series returned to Edmonton.

Stanley Cup Finals

Oilers Fight Through Boston Checks

The close checking and spirited play of the Bruins helped veteran goalie Reggie Lemelin lead all playoff puck-stoppers with a 2.63 GAA in 1988. However, it wasn't enough to untrack the Oilers in the Stanley Cup Finals. Edmonton's Esa Tikkanen, shown fighting past the check of Ken "Rat" Linseman as Ray Bourque follows the puck, notched 27 points and typified Edmonton's combination of skill and toughness.

Janet Jones, Wayne Gretzky

Gretzky's 43 Points Lead to Cup

Wayne Gretzky, who rang up a whopping 43 playoff points, won the 1988 Conn Smythe Trophy as Edmonton completed its five-game "sweep" of the Bruins, winning the replayed fourth game 6-3 on Oilers ice. Gretzky is shown sharing the Cup with wife Janet Jones. Just two months later, when Gretzky was traded to Los Angeles, Jones was blamed for breaking up the Oilers much as Yoko Ono was once blamed for breaking up the Beatles.

• Montreal checking specialist Guy Carbonneau wins his first Frank Selke Trophy, while L.A.'s Bob Bourne claims the Masterton Trophy.

• Detroit's Jacques Demers becomes the first coach to win back-to-back Jack Adams Awards.

• A new award, in honor of Toronto legend King Clancy, is presented to Calgary's Lanny McDonald for leadership and humanitarianism.

• Joe Sakic of Swift Current (WHL) is the Canadian Major Junior Player of the Year, while Medicine Hat wins its second straight Memorial Cup.

• Lake Superior State, with tourney MVP Bruce Hoffort in nets, beats St. Lawrence 4-3 to claim the NCAA title. Minnesota goalie Robb Stauber wins the Hobey Baker Award.

• In the 1988 Winter Games at Calgary, the Soviets win their seventh Olympic gold medal.

GRETZKY GOES TO L.A. IN BIGGEST TRADE EVER

When Edmonton Oilers hero Wayne Gretzky was traded to the Los Angeles Kings on August 9, 1988, the media hailed it as the biggest trade in 68 years. Only Boston's sale of Babe Ruth to the Yankees in 1920 carried the weight of this mega-blockbuster deal.

Not only did Gretzky go to L.A., but Edmonton also threw in Marty McSorley and Mike Krushelnyski. In return, the Oilers received scoring whiz Jimmy Carson, Martin Gelinas, first-round draft picks in 1989, 1991, and 1993, and $15 million.

Some speculated that owner Peter Pocklington made the deal for financial reasons. But others thought that Pocklington and G.M. Glen Sather both wanted Gretzky gone because Wayne had protested against recent management decisions (such as its unwillingness to give in to Paul Coffey's contract demands). Gretzky implied that Sather—not just Pocklington—wanted the deal to go through. "Hey," said Gretzky, "Slats has made every trade in Edmonton that there's been for 10 years. You think he didn't have a hand in this one?"

The only deal in NHL history comparable to the Gretzky package was made in November

1947. That's when Chicago shipped scoring ace Max Bentley to Toronto for an entire front line—Bud Poile, Gus Bodnar, and Gaye Stewart—as well as a complete defensive pair, Bob Goldham and Ernie Dickens.

Nevertheless, the Gretzky deal inspired even more attention—and considerable dismay in Canada. Oilers fans by the thousands protested that Pocklington had sold his team down the Saskatchewan River. Some even pointed the finger at Wayne's wife, Janet Jones, a Los Angeles native and aspiring actress. They believed she influenced Wayne to leave frigid Edmonton for the glitter of Hollywood.

Kings fans, though, were thrilled to have the Great One on board. Ticket sales soared, and Gretzky didn't disappoint. In 1988-89, he tallied 54 goals and 114 assists and captured his ninth Hart Trophy in 10 years. He also led his new team to a second-place finish and a first-round playoff meeting against his old team.

Interest in the Oilers-Kings clash was obviously immense. The first two games were played in L.A., where Edmonton captured the opener 4-3. The Kings bounced back in Game 2, beating the Oilers 5-2 thanks to a Chris Kontos hat-trick. The series then moved to Edmonton, where Gretzky received a surprisingly hostile reception. Boos rained upon him. "It didn't bother me," he asserted. "In a way it was nice. People can stop talking about the trade now."

The Kings overcame a three-games-to-one deficit to force a seventh game at the L.A. Forum. A capacity crowd cheered like never before as Gretzky scored two goals to lead L.A. to a 6-3 victory. The Kings went on to lose the next series to the Calgary Flames, the eventual Cup champions. Nevertheless, fans in subsequent years would continue to flock to the Forum, all eager to set their sights on No. 99, a star among Hollywood stars.

1988-89

- On August 9, 1988, Edmonton trades Wayne Gretzky, Mike Krushelnyski, and Marty McSorley to the Kings for Jimmy Carson, Martin Gelinas, three first-round picks, and $15 million.

- The Hall of Fame inducts six members, including players Tony Esposito, Guy Lafleur, Buddy O'Connor, and Brad Park.

- Minnesota uses the first pick in the 1988 draft to select U.S.-born Mike Modano of Prince Albert (WHL).

- Guy Lafleur comes out of retirement to join the Rangers.

- Over the summer, Dino Ciccarelli goes to jail (briefly) after an Ontario court finds him guilty of assault in a game against Toronto's Luke Richardson in 1987-88.

- On December 31, 1988, Mario Lemieux tallies five goals and eight points in an 8-6 win over New Jersey.

The largest trade in hockey history would be a 10-player deal between Toronto and Calgary in 1992. The *biggest* trade in hockey history came on August 9, 1988, when the Edmonton Oilers traded Wayne Gretzky (pictured), the greatest player in the history of the game, to Los Angeles with Mike Krushelnyski and Marty McSorley for Jimmy Carson, Martin Gelinas, L.A.'s No. 1 draft picks in 1989, 1991, and 1993, and a reported $15 million in cash.

• On January 10, 1989, Wayne Gretzky notches his 2,011th career point (regular season and playoffs), surpassing Gordie Howe's combined record of 2,010.

• On March 2, 1989, Detroit's Bob Probert is arrested after crossing the Canadian border with 14.3 grams of cocaine. He will be expelled from the NHL, then allowed to return.

• On March 21 1989, just 14 days after notching his 1,000th NHL point, Calgary winger Lanny McDonald scores his 500th (and last) career goal.

• On March 22, 1989, Sabres goalie Clint Malarchuk has his jugular vein slashed by the skate of St. Louis' Steve Tuttle, requiring surgery.

• Calgary posts a 54-17-9 record, the best in the league, as Joe Mullen sets a record for most points in a season by an American-born player.

Chris Chelios, Brian Propp

Esposito Lets Ridley Get Away

In three years as the G.M. of the Rangers, Phil Esposito made a lot of bad trades. One of his very worst came right at the start of his reign of terror when he shipped Mike Ridley, a quietly effective center, to Washington for Bobby Carpenter, who was sent packing after only 28 games. Ridley immediately established himself as the Caps' most reliable skater. In 1988-89, he led the first-place team with 89 points.

Mike Ridley

Chelios K.O.'s Propp, Wins Norris

Hard-nosed Chris Chelios (left) and finesse winger Brian Propp (right) have waged many a war of words over the years. In the 1989 playoffs, Chelios elbowed Propp into unconsciousness, inciting Flyers goalie Ron Hextall to eventually "lose it" and attack Chelios. Propp on Chelios: "He's just a lousy person." Chelios on Propp: "He's a gutless jerk." While Hextall was later suspended for his attack, Chelios skated away with the Norris Trophy.

Malarchuk's Neck Sliced by Skate

In one of the scariest moments in the history of the game, Buffalo goaltender Clint Malarchuk suffered a slashed neck when the skate of St. Louis winger Steve Tuttle sliced open his exterior jugular vein. Malarchuk was rushed from the ice to the operating room where surgery was performed to repair the damage. Were it not for the quick work of Buffalo trainer Jim Pizzutelli, Malarchuk might not have made it to the hospital.

Clint Malarchuk

1988-89

- The Flames' Joe Nieuwendyk nets 51 goals, including five in a game.

- The Kings, with Wayne Gretzky (168 points), Bernie Nicholls (150), and Luc Robitaille (98), finish in second place behind Calgary in the Smythe Division.

- The defending Cup champion Oilers fall to third place despite 49 goals from an unhappy Jimmy Carson.

- Vancouver rookie Trevor Linden scores 30 goals as the Canucks take the final playoff berth in the Smythe Division.

- Despite Dale Hawerchuk's 41 goals, the Jets finish last in the Smythe, costing coach Rick Bowness his job.

- The Red Wings, without Bob Probert for 55 games, finish atop the Norris (34-34-12). Steve Yzerman amasses 65 goals and 155 points.

Steve Yzerman, Craig Simpson

Yzerman Nets 65; Wings Win Norris

Detroit superstar Steve Yzerman tries to erase the numbers from Craig Simpson's jersey. The 1988-89 season saw Detroit capture its second straight Norris Division title as Yzerman, fully recovered from torn knee ligaments, finished third overall in goals (65), assists (90), and points (155) while leading the NHL in shots (388). He had the NHL's longest point-scoring streak of the year (28 straight games) and won the Lester B. Pearson Award.

Ciccarelli Thrown in the Slammer

Dino Ciccarelli of the North Stars was briefly jailed in an Ontario jail cell during the summer of 1988 for assaulting Toronto defenseman Luke Richardson during a game played January 6, 1988, in Toronto. In the incident, Ciccarelli hit Richardson over the head with his stick and punched him in the mouth. Ciccarelli was sentenced to one day in the hoosegow and fined $1,000.

Dino Ciccarelli

Patrick Roy

Roy Carries the Torch for Powerful Habs

Thanks to the work of their splendid goaltender, Patrick Roy, the Canadiens won 53 games in 1988-89 and were the second-best team in the NHL with 115 points (to Calgary's 117). Roy, a 23-year-old veteran of four NHL seasons, led the league in goals-against average (2.47), posted the best save percentage (.908), and won his first Vezina Trophy. He also finished second overall in wins (33) and tied for second in shutouts (four).

• St. Louis finishes just two points behind Detroit, as Brett Hull erupts for 41 goals and 84 points.

• Minnesota finishes third in the Norris despite a 27-37-16 record. Dave Gagner leads the team in goals (35) and points (78).

• Chicago stumbles to fourth place after Denis Savard misses 22 games. Steve Larmer leads with 43 goals.

• The Maple Leafs enjoy the productivity of linemates Ed Olczyk (38-52-90) and Gary Leeman (32-43-75) but finish out of the playoffs.

• Montreal (53-18-9) wins the Adams Division title by 27 points over Boston. Mats Naslund (33 goals) and Bobby Smith (32) lead the attack.

• Boston struggles to overcome the loss of Ray Bourque for 20 games. Tough guy Cam Neely (37 goals, 190 PIM) helps the team finish second.

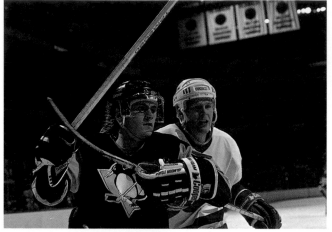

Rob Brown

Laissez-Faire Brown Scores 49

Voted the 1987 Canadian Major Junior Player of the Year, Pittsburgh winger Rob Brown (pictured jousting with an Islander defender) notched 49 goals and 115 points in just 68 games in 1988-89 while playing the right side of Mario Lemieux's line. A gifted player with a hard, accurate shot (he had a league-best 29.0 shooting percentage in 1988-89), Brown has played much of his NHL career under heavy criticism for an unsound work ethic.

Nicholls Pots 70 as L.A.'s No. 2 Guy

Years of struggle in Los Angeles finally paid off for Bernie Nicholls. With opposing teams putting their best checkers on new arrival Wayne Gretzky, the eight-year veteran center recorded 70 goals (second in the NHL), 80 assists (fifth best), and 150 points (fourth best). His 10-game goal-scoring streak was the league's longest, and he was among the NHL's top five in power-play goals (21), shorthanded goals (eight), and shots (385).

Bernie Nicholls

1988-89

• Buffalo sophomore Pierre Turgeon leads the team in goals (34) and assists (54), helping the Sabres to a third-place finish in the Adams.

• Kevin Dineen overcomes the effects of Crohn's Disease and leads the Whalers in scoring (45 goals, 89 points), as Hartford finishes fourth.

• Peter Stastny (35 goals, 85 points) and newcomer Walt Poddubny (38 goals) spark the Nords' offense, but the team finishes out of the playoffs.

• After five straight second-place finishes, the Caps go 41-29-10 and finish atop the Patrick. Mike Ridley (89 points), Geoff Courtnall (42 goals), and late-season pickup Dino Ciccarelli lead the charge.

• Pittsburgh places second in the Patrick. Mario Lemieux (85-114-199), Rob Brown (49-66-115), and Paul Coffey (30-83-113) lead the attack.

Mario Lemieux

Super Mario Erupts for 85 Red Lights

Mario Lemieux not only won his second scoring championship in 1988-89, but this time he took the Penguins with him for the ride. Pittsburgh finished at 40-33-7. Mario scored 85 goals (second most ever at the time), notched 114 assists (tying Wayne Gretzky), and outscored the Great One by 31 total points (199 to 168). No. 66 was a special-teams monster, netting 31 power-play goals and 13 shorthanded goals, both tops in the NHL.

Joe Mullen

Flames' Mullen Sets American Scoring Record

Joe Mullen set a record in 1988-89 for most points by an American-born skater (110), as he helped the Flames to a franchise-best 117 points. Mullen, 32, led the Flames in scoring and reached the 50-goal mark on the second-to-last day of the season, scoring on the Jets' Bob Essensa. "Fifty is nice, but 40 goals year after year is more important because I want to be known for my consistency," said Mullen, a six-time 40-goal man.

Lafleur's Back in the Action

In 1988, former Canadiens superstar Guy Lafleur announced he was ending his three-year retirement and making a comeback with the Rangers. At age 37, Lafleur still had enough magic to find the net for 18 goals in 67 games, as enthusiastic chants of "Guy, Guy, Guy" resounded throughout the league. Lafleur played the 1989-90 and 1990-91 seasons with Quebec.

Guy Lafleur

• The Penguins set an NHL record for power-play goals (120), while Mario Lemieux sets the league standard for shorthanded goals (13).

• The Rangers collapse late and finish third in the Patrick. Brian Leetch sets an NHL record for goals by a rookie defenseman (23).

• Philadelphia finishes fourth in the Patrick as Tim Kerr scores 48 goals in just 69 games and enforcer Rick Tocchet nets 45.

• The Devils win just 27 games, wasting the scoring of John MacLean (42 goals).

• Without Mike Bossy, who has retired because of back pain, the Islanders finish in the Patrick cellar. Pat LaFontaine scores 45 goals.

• The top five NHL scorers are Mario Lemieux (199 points), Wayne Gretzky (168), Steve Yzerman (155), Bernie Nicholls (150), and Rob Brown (115).

Leetch Sets Rookie Scoring Record

The Rangers had to wait two years for Brian Leetch to make it to the NHL after drafting him ninth overall in 1986. Following a brilliant year at Boston College and another with the U.S. Olympic team, the sleek, mature defenseman began his first full NHL season in the fall of 1988. By the close of the 1988-89 campaign, Leetch had established a new NHL record for goals by a rookie defenseman (23) and had captured the Calder Trophy.

Wayne Gretzky

Gretzky Named MVP, Breaks a Howe Record

After all of the hubble-bubble surrounding his trade to L.A., Wayne Gretzky quickly got down to business. The Great One tallied 54 goals, 114 assists, and 168 points, finishing second to Mario Lemieux in the scoring race. Gretzky, however, wound up with the Hart Trophy, his ninth. On January 10, 1989—against Edmonton—Gretzky notched his 2,011th NHL point (regular season and playoffs combined), passing Gordie Howe for the all-time record.

Brian Leetch

Bob Probert

Wings' Bad Boy Probert Caught with Cocaine

Detroit left winger Bob Probert, one of the game's most dreaded brawlers despite possessing remarkably "soft" hands when carrying the puck around the net, got himself into a world of legal trouble on March 2, 1989. Border police arrested him crossing from Canada to the U.S. holding 14.3 grams of cocaine. Probert, a multiple arrestee for driving under the influence, was suspended indefinitely by league boss John Ziegler.

1988-89

- Leading goal-scorers include Mario Lemieux (85), Bernie Nicholls (70), Steve Yzerman (65), and Wayne Gretzky (54).

- Calgary goalie Mike Vernon leads the NHL in wins (37), while Montreal netminder Patrick Roy takes the GAA crown (2.47).

- In the playoffs, Chicago upsets Detroit (4-2) while St. Louis skates past Minnesota (4-1) in the Norris Division semifinals. The Blackhawks derail the Blues (4-1) to win the Norris playoff title.

- In the Smythe semis, Calgary barely escapes an upset by Vancouver (4-3) while the Kings stun the Oilers (4-3). Calgary then sweeps Los Angeles (4-0) to win the division crown.

- In the Adams semifinals, Montreal sweeps Hartford (4-0) while Boston thrashes Buffalo (4-1). Montreal clubs Boston in five games to take the Adams playoff title.

Lane MacDonald

MacDonald Wins Baker, NCAA Title

On its third trip to the NCAA title game, Harvard (loser in 1983 and 1986) pulled off a thrilling sudden-death overtime win over Minnesota in 1989. Sophomore winger (and future Boston star) Ted Donato was the MVP. Lane MacDonald (#19) finished the year with a team championship and a personal thrill when he won the Hobey Baker Award as the top college player in the nation. He rejected an NHL career despite the interest of several pro teams.

Smythe Division Semifinals

Gretzky Beats Ex-Mates in Playoffs

In the opening round of the 1989 playoffs, Wayne Gretzky (right) led his new team against the team with whom he'd won four Stanley Cups. In an emotion-packed series, the Kings and Oilers swapped the series lead through six games. In Game 7, Gretzky opened the scoring with a goal at 52 seconds, assisted Bernie Nicholls' go-ahead goal in the second period, and notched an empty-netter in the third period as the Kings upset the reigning champs.

• In the Patrick, Philly stuns the Caps (4-2) while the Penguins rout the Rangers (4-0). The Flyers then upset the Pens (4-3) in the division finals, as Mario Lemieux tallies five goals and eight points in Game 5.

• On April 11, 1989, Philadelphia goalie Ron Hextall shoots the puck into Washington's vacated net, becoming the first NHL goalie ever to score in the playoffs.

• In the Campbell Conference finals, Chicago falls to Calgary in five games. In the Wales Conference finals, the Habs outlast Philly in six.

• In Game 1 of the Stanley Cup Finals, Calgary's Theo Fleury unlocks a 2-2 tie with a second-period goal that gives the Flames a 3-2 win.

• With the score 2-2 in Game 2 of the Finals, Montreal scores twice in 1:34 during the third period to prevail 4-2 and tie the series.

Super Shot MacInnis Wins Conn Smythe

There are players with big slapshots—like Raymond Bourque and Doug Wilson—and then there are players with scary slapshots, such as the one owned by Allan MacInnis, who won the 1989 Conn Smythe Trophy after leading his Calgary team to its first Stanley Cup. His 31 points led all scorers and he had the most assists (24) as well. "Mr. Clutch," MacInnis notched four game-winners, accounting for one-fourth of the team's 16 victories.

Campbell Conference Finals

Allan MacInnis

Otto, Flames Burn Hawks in Semis

Calgary center Joel Otto was an unsung hero of the 1989 playoffs. He scored a key overtime goal to eliminate Vancouver, then helped the Flames stampede the Blackhawks in five conference final games. In the Stanley Cup Finals, Otto scored a goal 28 seconds into Game 5 to spark the Flames to a 3-2 win. His 19 playoff points (including 13 assists) were fourth best on the team.

Hextall Scores; Flyers Fall in Semis

The Flyers got past the Caps in the first round of the 1989 playoffs as goalie Ron Hextall scored another goal, firing the puck into the Caps' empty net during an 8-5 victory. The Flyers then beat Pittsburgh in seven games but lost to Montreal in six games in the conference finals. Hextall (shown fighting Mats Naslund for position) was outdueled in the Wales finals by Montreal goalie Patrick Roy, who posted two shutouts.

Wales Conference Finals

1988-89

- Down 3-2 late in Game 3, the Habs tie the score on Mats Naslund's goal with 41 seconds left, then win it on Ryan Walter's goal in double O.T.

- Joe Mullen scores twice in Game 4 to help the Flames to a 4-2 victory. Calgary then takes a 3-2 triumph in Game 5 to take a 3-2 series lead.

- Calgary's Lanny McDonald scores in the second period of Game 6, giving the Flames a 2-1 lead, and Doug Gilmour's two goals in the third cement a 4-2 victory. The Flames thus win their first-ever Stanley Cup.

- Flames defenseman Al MacInnis wins the Conn Smythe Trophy.

- Wayne Gretzky receives his ninth Hart Trophy in 10 seasons, while Steve Yzerman captures the Lester B. Pearson Award.

- Montreal goalie Patrick Roy wins his first Vezina Trophy. Rangers defenseman Brian Leetch wins the Calder Trophy.

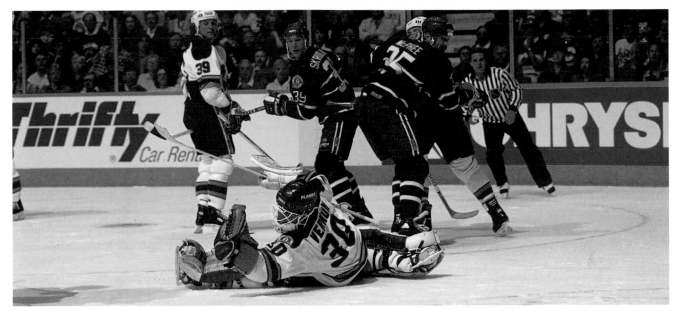

Stanley Cup Finals

Lanny McDonald

Vernon Wins 16 as Flames Cop Cup

Flames goalie Mike Vernon was a major roadblock between the Canadiens and their 23rd Stanley Cup. Here, Vernon makes a split save as teammate Doug Gilmour (#39), Montreal's Brian Skrudland (#39), and Canadien Mike McPhee (#35) admire the effort. Vernon played all 22 of the Flames' postseason games and won the magic number (16). His 2.26 playoff GAA was second to Patrick Roy's 2.09.

McDonald Goes Out with a Bang

The 1988-89 season was a storybook finish to the illustrious career of Lanny McDonald. On March 7, 1989, McDonald notched his 1,000th career point (a goal) during a 9-5 win over Winnipeg. Just 14 days later, he scored the 500th (and final) goal of his 16-year NHL career. Two months later, the man with the big moustache and the warm smile hugged the Stanley Cup. "I've had the time of my life," he said.

• Chris Chelios of the Habs wins his first Norris Trophy, while teammate Guy Carbonneau wins his second straight Frank Selke.

• Flyer Tim Kerr is honored with the Masterton Trophy, while first-year Montreal coach Pat Burns claims the Jack Adams Award.

• Niagara Falls defenseman Bryan Fogarty is the Canadian Major Junior Player of the Year, but Swift Current wins the Memorial Cup.

• Harvard wins the NCAA championship with a 4-3 O.T. win against Minnesota. Harvard's Ted Donato is tourney MVP, and the Crimson's Lane MacDonald captures the Hobey Baker Award.

• In May 1989, Alexander Mogilny, a member of the Central Red Army team, defects while his Soviet team is touring Sweden. Mogilny ends up in Buffalo with the Sabres.

MESSIER, OILERS DO IT WITHOUT GRETZKY

For legitimate reasons, the 1989-90 Calgary Flames didn't strike fear in the hearts of opponents like recent defending champions had (i.e., the Islanders and Oilers). Despite a strong and well-balanced offense, a tough defense (led by Al MacInnis), and a stellar goaltender (Mike Vernon), the Flames did not dominate. Of their 80 games, they won 42.

In fact, a whole crop of teams had a legitimate chance at claiming the first Stanley Cup of the '90s. Chicago, Boston, and the Rangers—all division champions—as well as Buffalo were regarded as potential threats. "This was a year when we felt that the field was wide open," said Rangers G.M. Neil Smith. "A lot would depend on which team got hot at the right time."

It wasn't Calgary. The Flames lost in the first playoff round to the Los Angeles Kings, four games to two.

Meanwhile, few paid attention to the Edmonton Oilers. The loss of Wayne Gretzky to the Kings was considered irreparable, and despite a second-place finish in the Smythe, the Oilers were not taken too seriously. An offense that once scored more than five goals per game was now down below the four mark.

Further diminishing the Oilers' prospects was the absence of their ace goaltender, Grant Fuhr. A shoulder injury sidelined Fuhr, compelling the Oilers to go with second-stringer Bill Ranford. To everyone's amazement, Ranford played as well as—if not better than—Fuhr, giving the Oilers some hope as they entered the playoffs.

With Gretzky gone, Mark Messier accepted the Oiler captaincy and took leadership to the highest plane. Seething for a victory in every game, the hard-driving forward finished second in the scoring race, behind Gretzky, with 129 points. The effort earned him the Hart Trophy, a prize that nobody challenged.

In the first round of the playoffs, the Oilers edged Winnipeg 4-3. They then swept Gretzky's Kings in four games, thus earning a spot in the Campbell Conference finals against Chicago. "By this time," said Messier, "the road to the Cup had widened considerably."

Chicago took a two-games-to-one lead in their series, but the Oilers rallied to win the next three to enter the Finals. The Boston Bruins also roared into the championship round, as they swept Washington in four Wales finals games.

Ranford and the Oilers showed their grit in Game 1 of the Finals, at Boston. For 115 minutes, the two clubs battled to a 2-2 tie. Finally, Edmonton's Petr Klima scored the winner against Bruins goalie Andy Moog—who ironically had been traded for Ranford.

The deflated Bruins then lost their second straight Finals game at home, 7-2. They rallied for a victory in Alberta, 2-1 in Game 3, but could not withstand the Oilers' attack. Edmonton completed the rout with 5-1 and 4-1 wins. Ranford won the Conn Smythe Trophy.

"It was," said Messier, "a year I would never forget." It also was the last year in which Edmonton could stake a claim to hockey leadership.

1989-90

- The Hall of Fame inducts five members, including players Darryl Sittler, Herbie Lewis, and the Soviet Union's Vladislav Tretiak.

- Using the first pick in the 1989 Entry Draft, the Quebec Nordiques select Swedish sensation Mats Sundin.

- The Canucks create a storm of protest and controversy when they select Soviet superstar Pavel Bure with the 113th overall pick after it was understood that Bure's eligibility ran out after the third round.

- At a July 1989 press conference, the New Jersey Devils announce they have signed former Red Army stars Viacheslav Fetisov and Sergei Starikov.

- Among the prominent Soviets to join the NHL are Igor Larionov and Vladimir Krutov (Vancouver), Sergei Makarov (Calgary), and Alexander Mogilny (Buffalo).

Two of the NHL's premier players—Boston's Ray Bourque and Edmonton captain Mark Messier—went head-to-head in the 1990 Stanley Cup Finals. Messier tied linemate Craig Simpson for the overall points lead (31) while Bourque had 17 points in 17 games. Messier's Oilers won their fifth Stanley Cup in seven years thanks largely to goalie Bill Ranford, who went 16-6 with a 2.53 GAA and won the Conn Smythe Trophy.

• After a qualified success in his comeback with the Rangers (18 goals), Guy Lafleur signs with the Nordiques.

• On October 15, 1989, Wayne Gretzky surpasses Gordie Howe's career scoring mark (1,850 points) with a pair of goals against Edmonton to give him 1,852 career points in 780 games.

• On October 17, 1989, Detroit's Bob Probert is sentenced to three months in jail for smuggling cocaine across the U.S.-Canadian border back in March.

• On October 19, 1989, Quebec's Peter Stastny records his 1,000th point.

• On January 2, 1990, Edmonton's Jari Kurri tallies his 1,000th point.

• On February 13, 1990, the Isles' Bryan Trottier nets goal No. 500.

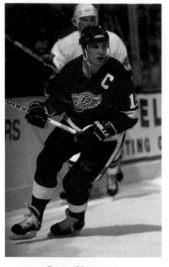

Steve Yzerman

Wings Crumble But Yzerman Flies High

Steve Yzerman's meteoric rise to superstardom was propelled by a second straight 60-goal season. Though the Red Wings played miserably in 1989-90, winning just 28 games and finishing last in the Norris Division, Yzerman finished second in the league in goals (62) and third in points (127). "Stevie Wonder" shared the NHL lead for shorthanded goals (seven).

Cam Neely

Neely Picks Up the Pace, Scores 55

Before knee injuries forestalled his progress, Cam Neely was on his way to superstar status in the NHL. In 1989-90, he made the quantum leap from rugged winger to lethal weapon, finishing third overall in goals (55), second in power-play goals (25), and tied for first in game-winners (12). Boston won the Adams Division as Neely (92 points) was the club's top scorer.

Bellows Nets 55 to Pace the Stars

Brian Bellows came to the NHL in 1982-83 with an endless supply of scoring ability, but it wasn't until the 1989-90 season, his eighth in the league, that he found his way to the 50-goal club. Brian led the North Stars in goals (55), points (99), power-play goals (21), game-winners (nine), and shots on goal (300).

Brian Bellows

1989-90

- On February 14, 1990, Pittsburgh's Mario Lemieux leaves the lineup with severe back pain stemming from a herniated disc, ending a 46-game point-scoring streak.

- On March 11, 1990, Chicago's Denis Savard notches his 1,000th point.

- On March 22, 1990, Detroit's Bob Probert plays his first game after a one-year ban for drug possession.

- On April 16, 1990, Bob Clarke is fired as G.M. of the Flyers.

- Boston posts the NHL's best record (46-25-9) thanks to an outstanding defense led by Ray Bourque. Cam Neely (55 goals) leads the offense.

- The Sabres finish second in the Adams, as Pierre Turgeon and Dave Andreychuk each score 40 goals.

- Montreal falls to third in the Adams despite Stephane Richer's 51 goals

Roy Proves Dominant in Montreal Net

The Canadiens fell to third place in the hotly contested Adams Division in 1989-90 despite winning 41 games. Goalie Patrick Roy was first in the league in goals-against average (2.53), wins (31), and save percentage (.912) and tied for second with three shutouts. Roy won his second consecutive Vezina Trophy to become the eighth goalie in Canadiens history to win it more than once—an achievement no other team has approached.

Patrick Roy

Makarov, 31, Wins Calder

Former Red Army left winger Sergei Makarov joined the Flames for the 1989-90 season. Makarov had 11 years of international experience and was a three-time Soviet Player of the Year. He ended up scoring 24 goals for Calgary and won the Calder Trophy, which upset some people because he was 31 years old. In response, the NHL ruled that, in the future, no one who began the season at age 26 or older would be eligible for future Calder Trophies.

Sergei Makarov

Savard Reaches the 1,000 Mark

The 1989-90 Blackhawks won the Norris Division title despite losing their best player, Denis Savard, for 20 games due to injury. Savard, though, reached an historic milestone on March 11, 1990, when he assisted on an Al Secord goal and became the 26th player in NHL history to total 1,000 points. "I'm very proud of this," said Savvy. "It was one of my goals as a kid: to play in the NHL, win the Stanley Cup, and score 1,000 points."

Denis Savard

and Patrick Roy's league-best 2.53 goals-against average.

• Hartford captures the final playoff berth in the Adams Division (by 54 points over Quebec), as Pat Verbeek notches 44 goals and Ron Francis accumulates 101 points.

• The lowly Nordiques win an embarrassing 12 games, wasting the scoring of Joe Sakic (39-63-102).

• The Rangers (36-31-13) win the Patrick title by two points as new arrivals Bernie Nicholls and Mike Gartner team up with a resurgent John Ogrodnick (43 goals).

• The Devils finish second in the Patrick, as Kirk Muller (86 points) and John MacLean (41 goals) star.

• Washington falls to third despite Dino Ciccarelli (41 goals).

• The Isles make the playoffs thanks to Pat LaFontaine (54 goals).

Gary Leeman

Leeman Turns It Up a Notch, Nets 51

Gary Leeman's career-high goal production entering the 1989-90 season was the 32 goals he scored in 1988-89—and that includes his junior career at Regina as well as in the minors. In 1989-90, however, Leeman became just the second player in Leafs history to reach the 50-goal plateau. Skating the right wing on Ed Olczyk's line, the Toronto native blasted 51 goals, joining three-time 50-goal man Rick Vaive in the Leafs' record book.

LaFontaine Sticks Out Among Isles

Pat LaFontaine (pictured jostling with the Rangers' Mark Hardy) led the Islanders in scoring in 1989-90 for the third straight year. After scoring 45 and 47 goals in the two years previous, LaFontaine potted 54 in 1989-90. He finished with 105 points and was a runner-up to Brett Hull for the Lady Byng Trophy. LaFontaine was actually a one-man band for the Isles, as Brent Sutter, with 68 points, was the team's second-leading scorer.

Pat LaFontaine

1989-90

• The Penguins play 21 of their last 22 games without Mario Lemieux, who still notches 123 points. Paul Coffey's 103 points go for naught as the team just misses the playoffs.

• Philadelphia fails to make the playoffs for the first time in 18 years despite seven 20-goal scorers. Rick Tocchet (37 goals, 96 points, 196 PIM) is the central figure.

• Calgary (42-23-15) repeats as Smythe champion. Joe Nieuwendyk (95 points), Doug Gilmour (91), Al MacInnis (90), and newcomer Sergei Makarov (86) give the Flames an NHL-best 348 goals.

• Edmonton's Mark Messier rebounds with 45 goals and 129 points as the Oilers enjoy a 90-point season.

• Winnipeg finishes third in the Smythe thanks to Dale Hawerchuk (81 points) and rookie goalie Bob Essensa.

Sakic Goes It Alone on the Lowly Nords

Despite the return of coach Michel Bergeron (after his debacle with the Rangers), the lowly Nordiques won only 12 games in 1989-90. The only bright spot was 20-year-old sophomore Joe Sakic, who somehow managed 39 goals and 102 points. It was quite an achievement considering Quebec scored just 240 goals, fewest in the league since 1983-84. The second-leading scorer on the Nords was defenseman Michel Petit with a piddling 36 points.

Joe Sakic

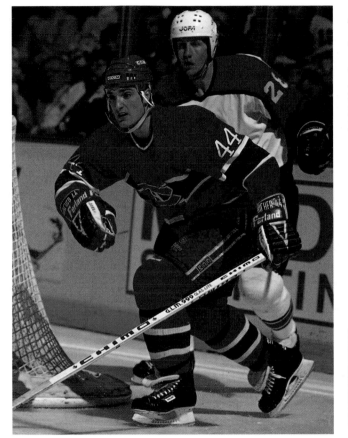
Stephane Richer

Richer Pots 50, Joins Elite Company

The mercurial Stephane Richer, who followed his 50-goal output of 1987-88 with just 25 goals in 1988-89, was back in the fast lane in 1989-90 when he blasted 51 goals. He became Montreal's second-ever two-time 50-goal scorer, joining Guy Lafleur who managed it six seasons running. Maurice Richard, Bernie Geoffrion, Steve Shutt, and Pierre Larouche each reached 50 once, while 500-goal scorer Jean Beliveau never turned the trick.

Bourque Adds a Seven, Wins Norris Trophy

By 1989-90, Boston's Ray Bourque had surrendered his No. 7 jersey (previously worn by Phil Esposito and subsequently retired) in favor of No. 77 and was on track for yet another award-winning year. Bourque finished third among all NHL defensemen in scoring (19-65-84), trailing Paul Coffey (103 points) and Calgary's Al MacInnis (90), but he wound up winning the Norris Trophy, making him the game's fifth three-time winner.

Raymond Bourque

• Los Angeles stumbles into fourth in the Smythe, although Wayne Gretzky (142 points) and Luc Robitaille (101) continue to shine.

• Vancouver drops out of the playoff picture, as Dan Quinn leads a limp offense with just 63 points.

• Chicago goes 41-33-6 to win the Norris race. Rookie Jeremy Roenick scores 26 goals and Denis Savard notches 80 points in 60 games.

• The Blues finish five points back of Chicago, as Brett Hull (72 goals) and Adam Oates (79 assists) make a devastating scoring combo.

• Toronto rises to third in the Norris, as Gary Leeman (51 goals), Vincent Damphousse (94 points), and Ed Olczyk (88 points) fuel the uprising.

• The North Stars overcome off-ice turmoil surrounding their future and place fourth in the Norris. Brian Bellows (55 goals) leads the way.

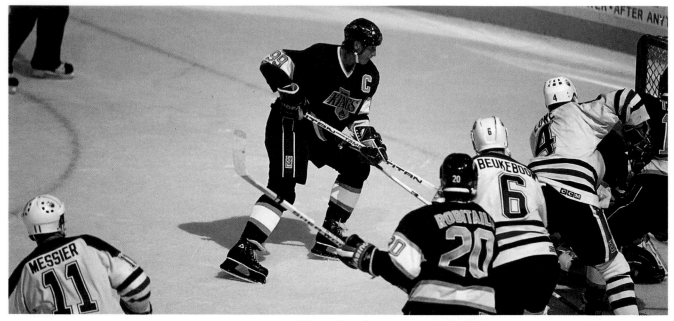

Wayne Gretzky

Gretzky Sets NHL Scoring Record

On October 15, 1989, Wayne Gretzky became the NHL's all-time leading scorer when he notched his 1,851st career point to surpass the legendary Gordie Howe. The Great One did it in grand style too, scoring with 53 seconds left in regulation to tie Edmonton; he later netted the winner in overtime. Howe's 1,850 points came in 1,767 games while Gretzky needed just 780 games to equal that total.

Gretzky, Howe Share Respect

For the few games leading up to Wayne Gretzky's record-breaking 1,851 career points, Gordie Howe was on hand for all of No. 99's games. When Gretzky broke the all-time scoring record on October 15, 1989, in Edmonton, Howe said of the young superstar, "He's a super hockey player and a super young man." Gretzky had worn No. 9 as a youngster in honor of Howe, his favorite all-time player.

Wayne Gretzky, Gordie Howe

• The Red Wings waste Steve Yzerman's 62-goal, 127-point effort, as they fail to make the playoffs.

• The NHL's top scorers are Wayne Gretzky (142 points), Mark Messier (129), Steve Yzerman (127), Mario Lemieux (123), and Brett Hull (113).

• Leading goal-scorers include Brett Hull (72), Steve Yzerman (62), Cam Neely (55), Brian Bellows (55), and Pat LaFontaine (54).

• In the playoffs, Chicago outlasts the North Stars (4-3) while St. Louis blows past Toronto (4-1). The Black-hawks then claim the Norris playoff

title with a seven-game win over the Blues.

• In the Smythe semis, Los Angeles upsets the Flames (4-2) and the Oilers survive a scare from Winnipeg (4-3). Edmonton then sweeps the Kings (4-0) for the Smythe playoff title.

Mario Lemieux

Mario Scores Big Despite Bad Back

Playing in terrible pain was common for Pittsburgh hero Mario Lemieux. In 1989-90, Lemieux was forced to the sidelines after 58 games due to a herniated disc in his back, ending a 46-game point-scoring streak. Still, he finished fourth overall in assists (78) and points (123). Projected over 80 games, his 2.08 PPG average would have given him 166 points and another scoring title.

Like Father, Like Son; Brett Nets 72

On April 2, 1972, Bobby Hull scored his 50th goal of the 1971-72 season while his seven-year-old son, Brett, watched on TV. A mere 18 years later, on February 6, 1990, Brett Hull scored his 50th goal of the year for St. Louis en route to a new record for goals by a right winger (72). Brett's 50th goal marked the first time in NHL history that a father-son tandem had recorded 50-goal seasons.

Trottier Nets 500 Thanks to Isles' System

Bryan Trottier

Islanders icon Bryan Trottier scored his 500th NHL goal on February 13, 1990, against Calgary goalie Rick Wamsley. In his trademark "team first" fashion, Trottier credited the Islanders' attack methodology for his achievement. "We've all got to stick to the system," he said. "That system put 500 goals on the board for me." Trottier concluded his 15th season with the Isles in 1989-90 before signing as a free agent with Pittsburgh.

Brett Hull

• In the Adams, Boston beats Hartford (4-3) while Montreal skates past Buffalo (4-2). Boston avenges itself with a 4-1 series win over the Habs to win the division playoff title.

• In the Patrick, the Rangers erase their nemeses, the Isles (4-1), while Washington caps the Devils (4-2). The Capitals then take out the Rangers in five games in the division finals.

• Edmonton outskates Chicago in the Campbell Conference finals (4-2), while Boston sweeps Washington (4-0) for the Wales Conference championship.

• In Game 1 of the Finals, Boston's Ray Bourque ties the game at 2-2 with two third-period goals, but Edmonton's Petr Klima wins it at 15:13 of triple overtime.

• In Game 2, Jari Kurri notches his seventh career playoff hat-trick as Edmonton wins 7-2.

Ballard, 86, Dies After Long Illness

On April 11, 1990, the NHL lost one of its more colorful characters when Maple Leafs owner Harold Ballard (pictured leaning through the brick window) died at age 86 after a lengthy and difficult illness. His final years were spent in a swirl of controversy, as various members of his immediate and extended family battled in court and in the media to gain control of Ballard's considerable estate—including the Leafs.

Harold Ballard

Boston Bruins

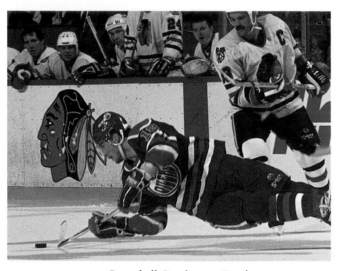
Campbell Conference Finals

Simpson Helps Oilers Soar Past the Hawks

Oilers left winger Craig Simpson (shown sprawling on the ice as Chicago captain Dirk Graham watches) was coming off a disappointing 29-goal season when he suddenly caught fire in the 1990 playoffs. In 22 games, the strapping winger led all players in goals (16, including three game-winners) and tied for first in points (31). The Oilers defeated Chicago in six Campbell Conference final games, winning the finale 8-4.

Boston Routs the Caps in Four Straight

The Bruins pose with the Wales Conference championship trophy after whipping the Capitals in four games. TV analyst John Davidson interviews Ray Bourque (wearing the captain's "C") while Cam Neely (#8) and Brian Propp (far right) look on. Boston outscored the Caps 15-6 over the four games, including a Game 2 shutout by Andy Moog (#35 at left). The Bruins made the playoffs for the 23rd straight year in 1990—an NHL record.

1989-90

- After dropping the first two games at home, Boston wins Game 3 2-1 thanks to goalie Andy Moog.

- Edmonton's Glenn Anderson scores twice in the first period of Game 4 to pace the Oilers to a 5-1 win and a 3-1 series lead.

- Glenn Anderson starts the scoring in Game 5, and Craig Simpson scores the winner at 9:31 of the second period, as the Oilers win 4-1 and take their fifth Stanley Cup in seven years.

- Oilers goalie Bill Ranford (2.53 playoff GAA) wins the Conn Smythe Trophy.

- Mark Messier wins the Hart Trophy as well as the Lester B. Pearson.

- Brett Hull secures the Lady Byng Trophy, while teammate Rick Meagher captures the Frank Selke.

- Patrick Roy wins the Vezina, edging out Buffalo's Daren Puppa.

Stanley Cup Finals

Bruins Manage Just One Win in the Finals

The 1990 Stanley Cup Finals were a rematch of the Edmonton-Boston Finals of 1988, which were thoroughly dominated by the Oilers who won four games to none. Despite the outstanding goaltending of Boston's Andy Moog in the '90 Finals, the Bruins couldn't stop the scoring of Craig Simpson (seen fighting through the check of Dave Christian, #27, and Randy Burridge, #12). The Bruins scored a victory in Game 3 but lost the series 4-1.

Oilers Enjoy the Last of the Good Times

Esa Tikkanen (in white hat) was one of four Oilers among 1990's top five playoff scorers—along with Craig Simpson, Mark Messier, and Jari Kurri. This locker room celebration would be the last of the good times for the Oilers, who would finish around .500 in 1990-91 and 1991-92 and plunge to the depths of the league in 1992-93 and 1993-94.

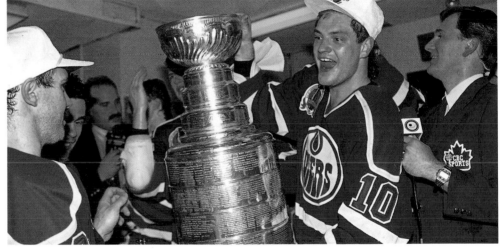

Stanley Cup Celebration

• Ray Bourque, runner-up for the Hart, nabs his third Norris Trophy, outballoting Al MacInnis.

• "Rookie" Sergei Makarov, age 31, wins the Calder Trophy, causing an age restriction to be written into the rule for the future.

• Boston's Gord Kluzak, who has long battled serious knee problems, wins the Masterton Trophy, while Winnipeg bench boss Bob Murdoch takes the Jack Adams Award.

• Mike Ricci of the OHL Peterborough Petes is named the Canadian Major Junior Player of the Year. The Oshawa Generals win the Memorial Cup.

• Wisconsin wins its fourth NCAA title in 14 years with a 7-3 triumph over Colgate in the title game. The Badgers' Chris Tancill is tourney MVP, while Michigan State's Kip Miller wins the Hobey Baker Award.

Prior to 1989, many Soviet and European hockey stars had the talent—and the desire—to skate in the NHL. Unfortunately for them, NHL teams didn't exactly throw out the welcome mat.

For one thing, neither Canadian nor American players favored the idea of losing jobs to foreigners. Also, many NHL coaches and managers believed that Europeans couldn't handle the physical pounding in the NHL. The slur "Chicken Swede" had been bandied about since the Rangers signed Ulf Nilsson and Anders Hedberg in the 1970s, despite the courageousness of both skaters.

However, the prejudice against Europeans gradually evaporated. For one reason, the NHL was beginning another expansion—adding the San Jose Sharks in 1991-92 and the Ottawa Senators and Tampa Bay Lightning in 1992-93. The NHL's talent was now being spread thin, and general managers looked across the ocean for needed players. Also, the crumbling of the Soviet Union eased immigration restrictions for Soviet aces.

Yet even before the Iron Curtain finally collapsed, the New Jersey Devils were seeking ways of breaching the barrier. "I knew that there was a wealth of talent

SOVIETS SKATE INTO AMERICAN TERRITORY

over there," said Devils owner John McMullen. "It was only a matter of finding a way of getting the players over here."

The first breakthrough came in June 1989 when New Jersey signed Viacheslav Fetisov and Sergei Starikov (and Alexei Kasatonov in December). Also in 1989, Vancouver landed Igor Larionov and Vladimir Krutov, and Calgary inked Sergei Makarov. While the assimilation into the NHL was not smooth for everyone, the success of Makarov and Fetisov inspired other clubs to exploit the Russian market.

In 1990, the Red Wings gobbled up fleet forward Sergei Fedorov. It was an unauthorized move that angered the Soviet hockey brokers, but the NHL money proved more powerful than the Soviet hockey bureaucracy. Fedorov went on to lead all

NHL rookies in scoring in 1990-91 with 79 points.

"It was pretty apparent by then," said Rangers G.M. Neil Smith, "that European players were going to have a major impact on the NHL in the years to come."

Other European stars who joined the NHL included Sweden's Mats Sundin, a tall, lanky sharpshooter who scored 23 goals for Quebec in 1990-91. Czechoslovakia, which had sent the great Stastny brothers to the NHL in the early 1980s, now offered Bobby Holik, a rangy winger who scored 21 goals for Hartford in 1990-91. Holik also proved his toughness as he logged 113 minutes in the box.

One European import even helped a team win the Stanley Cup. Czechoslovakia's Jaromir Jagr joined Pittsburgh as an 18-year-old in 1990 and soon captivated Civic Arena crowds with his determination and stick-handling. He reminded many of teammate Mario Lemieux; in fact, the letters of his first name could even spell "Mario Jr." When Pittsburgh won its first-ever Stanley Cup in the spring of 1991, Jagr had a large hand in it, tallying five assists in the Finals against Minnesota.

1990-91

- The Hall of Fame inducts four men, including players Bill Barber, Fern Flaman, and Gil Perreault.

- Winnipeg Jets prospect Tod Hartje, a Harvard grad from Minnesota, becomes the first North American ever to play for a Soviet team when he joins Sokol Kiev.

- Prior to the season, the Jets trade Dale Hawerchuk and a first-round pick to Buffalo for Phil Housley and others. Also, Chicago ships Denis Savard to Montreal for Chris Chelios.

- Longtime star Jari Kurri abandons the Oilers to play in Italy.

- Using the first pick in the Entry Draft for the second straight year, Quebec chooses highly touted Owen Nolan of Cornwall (OHL).

- The Nordiques pay $350,000 to the Djurgarden Hockey Club (Sweden) for Mats Sundin's release, then ink 1989's top draft pick.

Alexander Mogilny's defection from the Soviet Union in 1989 caused a huge uproar in Moscow, where Mogilny was a star on the Red Army powerhouse. Mogilny joined Buffalo as a sky's-the-limit prospect, but his rookie season (1989-90) was a nightmare. He had a hard time adapting to his North American teammates and he also had a fear of flying. By 1990-91, however, many of his problems were behind him and his production began to rise (30-34-64).

• On August 31, 1990, Edmonton goalie Grant Fuhr admits to past "substance abuse." He'll later be suspended for a year by NHL President John Ziegler.

• On October 26, 1990, Wayne Gretzky notches an assist against Winnipeg—his 2,000th career point.

• On January 25, 1991, Blues sniper Brett Hull becomes the third person in NHL history to score 50 goals in less than 50 games when he scores a pair in a 9-4 win over Detroit.

• On March 31, 1991, Boston's Chris Nilan receives six minor penalties, two majors for fighting, a 10-minute misconduct, and a game misconduct, totaling a record 10 penalties.

• Chicago (49-23-8) wins the Norris Division title, as Steve Larmer enjoys his only 100-point season (101), Jeremy Roenick scores 41 goals, and rookie Ed Belfour stars in net.

Brett Hull

Luc Robitaille

Theo Fleury

Hull Pots 50 in 50, Then Adds 36 More

Brett Hull had a lot to smile about in 1990-91. He shattered his own record for goals by a right winger (72) with a league-high 86 red lights—the second-highest single-season goal production in NHL history. Only Wayne Gretzky's 92 goals in 1981-82 surpassed Hull's stunning achievement. Hull scored his 50th goal on January 25, 1991, in his 49th game, making him just the third person ever to score 50 NHL goals in less than 50 games.

Robitaille, Gretzky, & Co. Rev Up L.A.

Hockey interest in Tinseltown reached new heights in 1990-91 as the Kings rose to the top of the Smythe. One of the most popular Kings was left winger Luc Robitaille. A fifth-year pro with a pair of 50-goal, 100-point seasons under his belt, Robitaille blended with center Wayne Gretzky and right wing sniper Tomas Sandstrom to form one of the NHL's deadliest lines. Robitaille and Sandstrom each scored 45 goals while Gretzky chipped in 41.

Tiny Fleury Rises to New Heights

In 1990-91, Calgary's Theo Fleury made a quantum leap from NHL prospect to bona fide scoring threat. A third-year NHLer, the diminutive right winger (generously listed at 5'6" and 160 pounds) led the Flames in both goals (51) and points (104). He joined the elite 50-goal club at age 22 when he beat Vancouver's Bob Mason on March 26, 1991. He was one of only four players to surpass the 50-goal plateau for the year.

1990-91

• The Blues finish with the second-best record in the NHL (47-22-11) thanks to Brett Hull (86 goals) and Adam Oates (25-90-115).

• Detroit finishes a distant third in the Norris despite Steve Yzerman (51-57-108) and rookie Sergei Fedorov (31 goals).

• Primarily on the scoring of Dave Gagner (40-42-82), Minnesota grabs the final playoff berth in the Norris.

• The Maple Leafs are the second-worst team in the league (57 points). Ten new players acquired in trades (including Peter Zezel and Bob Rouse for Al Iafrate) don't help much.

• The L.A. Kings (46-24-10) capture their first-ever division title, as Wayne Gretzky wins another scoring crown (163 points) and Luc Robitaille and Tomas Sandstrom each net 45 goals.

• Second-place Calgary is led by both Theo Fleury (51 goals) and Joe Nieuwendyk (45).

Paul Coffey

Defenseman Coffey Scores 1,000

On December 22, 1990, veteran Paul Coffey notched an assist during Pittsburgh's 4-3 win over the Islanders. The point was his 1,000th and made him only the second defenseman in NHL history, after Denis Potvin, to reach the millennium. Coffey, pictured unloading his big slapshot while Bryan Trottier flanks him on the left wing, finished third among NHL defensemen in scoring in 1990-91 with 93 points.

Eagle, Hawks Fly High in the Norris

In 1990-91, Eddie "The Eagle" Belfour won the unofficial triple crown of goaltending when he led the NHL in GAA (2.47), save percentage (.910), and wins (43). That he accomplished all of this as a rookie (despite playing 23 games during the 1989-90 season) was further testament to his brilliance. Belfour, whose Blackhawks won the Norris Division, earned the Calder Trophy and the Vezina Trophy.

Eddie Belfour

• Third-place Edmonton finishes at exactly .500 and yields as many goals as it scores (272-272). Mark Messier misses 27 games due to injuries.

• Vancouver takes the last Smythe playoff spot by two points over Winnipeg. The Canucks surge after a late-season trade lands Geoff Courtnall, Cliff Ronning, and Sergio Momesso.

• The Jets trade for 30-goal scorer Ed Olczyk but fail to make the playoffs.

• Boston (44-24-12) wins the Adams Division and enters the playoffs for a record 24th straight year. Ray Bourque (94 points), Craig Janney (92), and Cam Neely (51 goals) lead the way.

• Montreal finishes second to Boston, although Russ Courtnall leads the Habs with just 76 points and Stephane Richer slumps to 31 goals.

Phenom Lindros Terrorizes OHL Opponents

Not since Mario Lemieux scored 133 goals in his final season of junior hockey (1983-84) had a teenager received the attention given to Oshawa's Eric Lindros. In 1990-91, Lindros—a player with the skills of Wayne Gretzky and the temperament of a junkyard dog—led the OHL in goals (71) and points (149) and garnered 189 penalty minutes in just 57 games. Named the Canadian Major Junior Player of the Year, he was the top pick in the 1991 draft.

Chris Nilan

Eric Lindros

Wayne Gretzky

Nilan: 10 Penalties in One Game

Boston's designated tough guy, Chris Nilan (shown in a rare moment with the puck), set an inauspicious NHL record against Hartford on March 31, 1991, when he was called for 10 penalties. Nilan received six minor penalties (for holding, roughing, unsportsmanlike conduct, instigating, and two for elbowing), two fighting majors, and a pair of misconducts for a grand total of 42 minutes. Nilan had led the league in PIM in 1983-84 and 1984-85.

Gretzky Surpasses 2,000 Points

Wayne Gretzky captured his ninth league scoring crown in 11 years in 1990-91 when he finished the season with 163 points. He captured his second Lady Byng Trophy and, more importantly, led the Kings to a 46-24-10 record and their first division title of their 24-year existence. Along the way, he reached two more milestones: 2,000 career points (an assist at Winnipeg on October 26) and 700 career goals.

1990-91

- The Sabres finish third in the Adams thanks to Dale Hawerchuk (89 points) and Pierre Turgeon (79). Alexander Mogilny—cured of his fear of flying—smashes 30 goals.

- Pat Verbeek (43 goals) helps Hartford finish fourth in the Adams. In March, the Whalers deal Ron Francis and Ulf Samuelsson to Pittsburgh for John Cullen and Zarley Zalapski.

- The Nordiques remain the NHL's worst team (46 points), although Joe Sakic (48-61-109) stars and rookie Mats Sundin (23 goals) shows his potential.

- In the Patrick Division, the Penguins win their first-ever division title. Mario Lemieux notches 45 points in just 26 games (because of back surgery), while Mark Recchi and Kevin Stevens each score 40 goals.

- Veteran sniper Mike Gartner (49 goals) and Brian Leetch (88 points)

Grant Fuhr

Ziegler Bans Goalie Fuhr for 60

Grant Fuhr, one of the great "money" goalies of his era, was suspended by NHL President John Ziegler for the entire 1990-91 season when he admitted to having suffered from past substance abuse. Speculation was that Fuhr had formerly used cocaine, although a specific "substance" was never named by the All-Star goalie. Ziegler's year-long ban was later commuted to 60 games, but it remained the longest such suspension in NHL history.

Hull and Oates Star in St. Louis

Detroit management erred badly in June 1989 when it traded up-and-coming Adam Oates (right) and Paul MacLean to St. Louis for the over-the-hill pair of Bernie Federko and Tony McKegney. In 1990-91, Oates set a Blues record for assists (90) and finished third in the NHL in scoring (115 points). His chemistry with right wing Brett Hull was key in Hull's record-breaking 86-goal season.

Raymond Bourque

Bourque Powers the Bruins to Adams Title

In 1990-91, Boston finished 11 points ahead of second-place Montreal in the Adams Division, thanks largely to the leadership of Ray Bourque, the team's best player since Bobby Orr. The classy, hard-hitting defenseman was third in the league in shots (323) and had the NHL's sixth-best plus/minus rating (+33). With 94 points, Bourque trailed only Calgary's Al MacInnis for scoring among defensemen. Ray won his fourth Norris Trophy in five years.

Adam Oates

lead the Rangers to a second-place finish in the Patrick.

• Washington finishes third in the Patrick, as defenseman Kevin Hatcher leads the team in points (74).

• John MacLean's 45 goals help pace the Devils to a fourth-place finish in

the Patrick Division. Newcomer Claude Lemieux rips 30 goals.

• Philadelphia fails to make the playoffs for the second year in a row despite Rick Tocchet's 40-goal output.

• The Islanders suffer through a contract holdout and brief walkout

by Pat LaFontaine, their leading scorer (41-44-85), and win just 25 games.

• The NHL's leading scorers are Wayne Gretzky (163 points), Brett Hull (131), Adam Oates (115), Mark Recchi (113), and John Cullen (110).

Tiny Verbeek Claws His Way to 43 Goals

Pat Verbeek made a name for himself in the NHL by overcoming huge obstacles. At only 5'9", he had to battle the "too small" rap until he scored 20 goals and racked up 158 penalty minutes as an NHL rookie (1983-84). He came back from an off-season farm accident that required surgical reattachment of his thumb and still put together several 40-goal seasons. In 1990-91, he led the Whalers in goals (43) and penalty minutes (246).

Pat Verbeek

Discarded by Philly, Clarke Joins Stars

Bob Clarke and the Philadelphia Flyers had been synonymous for more than 20 years, with Clarke serving 15 as a player and six as general manager. When the Flyers "fired" Clarke in 1990 (calling it a parting of ways due to philosophical differences), he was immediately hired by the new owner of the Minnesota North Stars, Norm Green. Clarke hired Bob Gainey as coach and the team went to the 1991 Stanley Cup Finals.

Bobby Clarke

NMU Wins a Wild NCAA Title Game

The 1991 NCAA title game between Northern Michigan and Boston University turned into a heart-stopping free-for-all as the game went to triple overtime tied at 7-7. The NMU Wildcats got a couple of hat-tricks, one from the nation's leading scorer, Scott Beattie, and the other from defensive ace Darryl Plandowski, whose third goal came at 1:57 of the third session as the Wildcats won 8-7 for their first-ever title.

NCAA Championship Game

- Only four NHLers score 50 goals, including Brett Hull (86), Cam Neely (51), Theo Fleury (51), and Steve Yzerman (51).

- Five players—Paul Coffey, Mark Messier, Dave Taylor, Michel Goulet, and Dale Hawerchuk—reach the 1,000-point mark during the season.

- In the playoffs, Pittsburgh survives a scare from New Jersey (4-3) while Washington eliminates the Rangers (4-2). The Pens then oust the Caps (4-1) to take the Patrick crown.

- In the Adams semis, Boston skates past Hartford (4-2) while Montreal dispatches Buffalo (4-2). The Bruins knock off the Habs in seven games in the Adams Division finals.

- In the Norris, Minnesota shocks Chicago (4-2) while St. Louis gets past Detroit (4-3). The North Stars eliminate the favored Blues (4-2) to win the Norris playoff title.

Patrick Division Semifinals

Mario Powers the Pens in Playoffs

In 1990-91, chronic back trouble kept Mario Lemieux out of the lineup for all but 26 regular-season games. Yet he scored 19 goals and 45 points in those 26 contests and was equally devastating in the playoffs. In 23 postseason games, he carried the Penguins on his broad shoulders, scoring 16 goals and finishing with 44 points—second best ever for a single-playoff year. Lemieux won the Conn Smythe Trophy as playoff MVP.

Mario Lemieux

Defenseman Hatcher Scores Big

Washington defenseman Kevin Hatcher clears the crease during the opening round of the 1991 playoffs. Hatcher gave the Caps a player with size (6'4", 225), strength, aggressiveness, and pure talent. He led the 1990-91 team in scoring with 74 points and set a club mark for goals by a defenseman with 24. Hatcher and the Caps erased the Rangers in the opening round of the playoffs before falling to Pittsburgh.

• In the Smythe, L.A. tops Vancouver (4-2) while Edmonton beats Calgary (4-3). The Oilers upset Gretzky's Kings in a six-game division final series that features four overtimes.

• In the Wales Conference finals, Pittsburgh beats the Bruins (4-2) to earn its first-ever berth in the Stanley Cup Finals. In the Campbell finals, the North Stars shock the Oilers in five games.

• In Game 1 of the Stanley Cup Finals, the North Stars win a 5-4 shootout at Pittsburgh, as Neal Broten scores twice for Minnesota.

• The Penguins rebound in Game 2, winning 4-1, as Pittsburgh goalie Tom Barrasso makes 39 saves and Kevin Stevens scores the game-winner.

• On home ice, the North Stars skate to a 3-1 win in Game 3 as Dave Gagner, Bobby Smith, and Gaetan Duchesne all score for Minnesota.

Stars Sock It to the Oilers in Semis

Chris Dahlquist (left) and Adam Graves collide as their respective teams, Minnesota and Edmonton, battle in the Campbell Conference finals. The Cinderella North Stars, who finished fourth in the Norris but shocked Chicago (in six games) and St. Louis (in six), went all the way to the Finals after dispatching Edmonton in five games. The Oilers, in search of their sixth Cup in eight years, eliminated Calgary and L.A. before running into the Stars.

Campbell Conference Finals

Cam Neely

Neely Falls Victim to Cheap Shot

The 1991 playoffs remain a haunting memory in the mind of Boston's Cam Neely. Neely, who scored 51 regular-season goals and was the team's leading playoff goal-scorer (16), was the victim of an Ulf Samuelsson cheap shot during the Wales Conference finals, as the Pittsburgh defenseman took out Cam's left knee. Neely later underwent arthroscopic surgery and missed 71 games of the 1991-92 season while his career hung in jeopardy.

Bellows and Recchi Pile Up the Points

Two of the leading scorers in the 1991 Stanley Cup play-offs were Minnesota right winger Brian Bellows (#23) and Pittsburgh left winger Mark Recchi (#8). The North Stars' surprising advancement to the Finals would never have happened without Bellows, who accounted for 10 goals and 29 points in 23 games. Recchi, the second-leading scorer (after teammate Mario Lemieux), scored 10 goals and added 24 assists for 34 points.

Stanley Cup Finals

1990-91

- Pittsburgh's potent attack comes alive in Game 4 of the Finals, as Kevin Stevens, Ron Francis, and Mario Lemieux score in the first three minutes and the Pens go on to win 5-3.

- In Pittsburgh for Game 5, Mario Lemieux, Kevin Stevens, and Mark Recchi (twice) score in the first period as the Pens build a 4-0 lead and hold on for a 6-4 win.

- Pittsburgh goalie Tom Barrasso stars in Game 6 as the Penguins roar to an 8-0 win and their first Cup.

- For his brilliant offensive work (44 playoff points) and inspirational leadership, Mario Lemieux wins the Conn Smythe Trophy.

- Brett Hull wins both the Hart Trophy and the Lester B. Pearson Award.

- Wayne Gretzky, runner-up for the Hart Trophy, receives the Lady Byng.

Craig Patrick

Patrick Builds Winner in Pittsburgh

Stanley Cup titles and the name "Patrick" are hardly strangers. Penguins G.M. Craig Patrick (shown hoisting the silver mug while being doused in celebratory beer) is the grandson of Rangers legend Lester Patrick, architect of three Stanley Cup titles in New York. Craig Patrick, a former NHL player of modest repute, was a driving force as G.M. of the Rangers (1981-86) before building the Pens into a championship team.

Pens Beat Stars 8-0 in Finals Finale

Mario Lemieux (#66) and Larry Murphy (#55) celebrate one of the 28 goals scored by Pittsburgh during its six-game Stanley Cup-winning series against Minnesota. With the series tied at two games apiece, the Pens exploded for four first-period goals in Game 5 en route to a 6-4 victory. They then humiliated the North Stars at the Met Center with an 8-0 win, the most one-sided Cup-deciding score in the history of the NHL.

Stanley Cup Finals

• Chicago's Ed Belfour, who led the NHL in GAA (2.47), wins (43), and save percentage (.910), wins both the Calder Trophy and Vezina Trophy.

• Ray Bourque becomes the first four-time winner of the Norris Trophy since Bobby Orr. The Blues' Brian Sutter wins the Jack Adams Award.

• Chicago's Dirk Graham wins the Frank Selke Trophy, while Kings veteran Dave Taylor takes the Masterton Trophy.

• Oshawa's Eric Lindros is selected as the Canadian Major Junior Player of the Year, while Spokane wins its first Memorial Cup.

• Northern Michigan, led by tourney MVP Scott Beattie, wins the NCAA championship with an 8-7 O.T. win over Boston University in the title game.

• Boston College center David Emma wins the Hobey Baker Award.

Ordinarily, the Pittsburgh Penguins would have been favored to retain the Stanley Cup they had won in 1991. Besides the brilliant Mario Lemieux, the champs boasted such scorers as Joe Mullen, Ron Francis, Jaromir Jagr, Kevin Stevens, and Rick Tocchet. "It was as good a collection of forwards as you'll see on any team, any time," said New York Islanders coach Al Arbour.

However, the 1991-92 Penguins would have to overcome the tragic loss of their coach. Bob "Badger" Johnson, one of the most beloved coaches in NHL history, underwent surgery for cancer in the summer of 1991. He died three months later.

Johnson's replacement, Scotty Bowman, had a long history of success but hadn't been a bench boss since 1987. Some observers questioned whether the aloof and acerbic Bowman could effectively control the freewheeling champions.

Bowman's strategy was simple. He let artists like Lemieux and Jagr do their own thing and turned much of the off-day coaching over to assistants like Barry Smith. The plan was partially successful during the regular season, but still the

PLAYERS GO ON STRIKE; PENS STRIKE GOLD AGAIN

Penguins fell behind the Mark Messier-led Rangers in the standings.

New York got a stranglehold on first place in the homestretch and appeared capable of winning its first Stanley Cup since 1940. Then, the unthinkable happened. After months of threats and counter-threats, the league owners and the NHL Players' Association reached an impasse over a new collective bargaining agreement. On April 1, 1992, the players went on strike.

For a time, it appeared that neither side would budge and the 1992 playoffs would be canceled. But at the 11th hour—after 10 non-hockey days—an agreement was sealed and players returned to the rinks. "We were happy to be back in action," said Rangers coach Roger Neilson, "but the break disrupted our momentum."

Sure enough, the Rangers faded quickly and were eliminated from the playoffs by a suddenly aroused Pittsburgh club—even though New York's Adam Graves broke Lemieux's hand. Lemieux returned to action in the Wales Conference finals against Boston, where he led his troops to a four-game sweep and a spot in the Finals against Chicago.

The Blackhawks, on the heels of 11 straight playoff wins, busted out of the gates in Game 1 of the Finals, twice opening three-goal leads. Undaunted, the Penguins struck back and came away with a 5-4 triumph. Chicago coach Mike Keenan tried to use heavyweights Mike Peluso and Stu Grimson as intimidators, but the Penguins could not be grounded. They won the next three games by scores of 3-1, 1-0, and 6-5 for their second straight Stanley Cup.

Having scored 16 playoff goals, Lemieux was the unanimous winner of the Conn Smythe Trophy. Moreover, the Penguins loomed as an NHL dynasty. "It looked to us that a third straight Cup was well within our grasp," said Penguins owner Howard Baldwin. "All we needed to do was avoid injuries and keep our heads on straight."

1991-92

• The NHL expands to 22 teams, as the San Jose Sharks—owned by former North Stars owners George and Gordon Gund—begin play.

• The NHL adopts several rule changes in regards to the goalcrease. Also, video replays are employed to assist refs in goal/no-goal situations.

• Using the first pick in the 1991 draft (their third straight No. 1 pick), Quebec drafts Eric Lindros, who immediately announces he will not sign with the Nordiques.

• The Hall of Fame inducts five men, including players Mike Bossy, Denis Potvin, Bob Pulford, and Clint Smith.

• In July 1991, the Blues sign free agent Brendan Shanahan to a $5 million contract. NHL boss John Ziegler then awards standout defenseman Scott Stevens to the Devils as compensation.

• Canada wins its third straight Canada Cup series, defeating the U.S.

NHL President John Ziegler (left) and NHL Players' Association boss John Goodenow (right) ended the 1992 players strike after 10 days. More than a dozen key issues were decided. The players made modest gains in free agency and also won on such issues as trading card revenue (which was turned over to the players) and playoff money (they won a larger share). The owners were able to lengthen the season to 84 games and, if they chose, reduce their rosters to 19 players.

two games to none in the finals. Goalie Bill Ranford is tourney MVP.

• Pavel Bure, the Central Red Army star around whom controversy and lawsuits focused after Vancouver "illegally" drafted him in 1989, leaves Russia for the NHL.

• The Oilers clean house, trading Grant Fuhr and Glenn Anderson to Toronto for Vince Damphousse and Luke Richardson, and shipping Mark Messier to the Rangers for Bernie Nicholls.

• The Oilers also trade away Jari Kurri and Steve Smith.

• Eric Lindros returns to junior hockey, rejecting a reported $50 million contract offer by Quebec.

• On October 14, 1991, Ranger Mike Gartner scores his 500th goal.

• Pat LaFontaine walks out on the Islanders, demanding a trade.

Carbonneau Dishes Out the Checks

Montreal captain Guy Carbonneau, a 72-goal scorer during his final year at Chicoutimi (Quebec juniors), never made an offensive impact at the NHL level. His career high in goals in the NHL was 26 in 1988-89. Carbonneau's unrivaled merit came from his tireless work ethic and dedication to checking. In 1991-92, he won his third career Selke Trophy as the game's top defensive forward, symbolic of the Canadiens' winning strategy.

Patrick Roy

Roy Remains NHL's Best in the Nets

Montreal's Patrick Roy continued to slam the door on NHL shooters in 1991-92. He led all NHL goalies in goals-against average (2.36) and save percentage (.914), was second in games played (67) and minutes (3,935), and finished third in wins (36). Roy, a three-time first-team All-Star, captured his third Vezina Trophy. Montreal yielded just 207 goals, fewest in the league since 1979-80, on its way to an Adams Division title.

Guy Carbonneau

Roberts Scores Big When He's Not in the Box

Intensity and physical conditioning are the trademarks of Calgary left winger Gary Roberts. Known as one of the NHL's most physically fit skaters, the Ontario native emerged as a legitimate scoring threat in 1989-90 when he notched 39 goals. In 1991-92, he joined the elite 50-goal club with 53 tallies. He also racked up 207 penalty minutes—the fifth straight year he spent at least 200 minutes in the box.

Gary Roberts

1991-92

- The Isles trade Pat LaFontaine to Buffalo for Pierre Turgeon.

- After just nine games, Pat LaFontaine is knocked out of the Sabres' lineup when Calgary's Jamie Macoun breaks his jaw in two places with a slash, resulting in major reconstructive facial surgery.

- The hockey world mourns the death of Pittsburgh coach Bob Johnson, 60, who succumbs to cancer on November 26, 1991.

- On November 30, 1991, the North Stars' Bobby Smith scores his 1,000th point.

- On December 8, 1991, the Sabres and Flames engage in a 29-minute brawl as an aftermath of the Jamie Macoun-Pat LaFontaine incident.

- On January 2, 1992, in the biggest trade in history, Calgary ships Doug Gilmour and four others to Toronto for Gary Leeman and four Leafs.

Steve Yzerman

Yzerman Leads Wings to Norris Title

After a two-year slump, the Red Wings climbed back into first place in the Norris Division in 1991-92 behind captain Steve Yzerman, who suffered through what, for him, was an "off" year. He scored just 45 goals and 103 points after seasons of 50, 65, 62, and 51 goals. Still, the slick center led the league in shorthanded goals (eight), tied for second in game-winners (nine), and enjoyed a nine-game goal-scoring streak.

Kirk McLean

McLean Helps Canucks Win Smythe

Largely due to the superb play of goalie Kirk McLean, the Canucks captured the Smythe Division title in 1991-92, their first in 17 years. Originally property of (but virtually ignored by) the Devils, McLean arrived in Vancouver via a trade in September 1987. In 1989-90, he led the league in games played (63). In 1991-92, he tied for the NHL lead in wins (38) and shutouts (five), was third in GAA (2.74), and finished runner-up for the Vezina.

- On January 4, 1992, Mike Gartner registers his 1,000th point.

- On February 16, 1992, Chicago's Michel Goulet scores his 500th goal.

- On February 29, 1992, Boston's Ray Bourque becomes the third NHL defenseman to reach 1,000 points.

- On March 5, 1992, Quebec's Mats Sundin scores five goals in a 10-4 rout of Hartford.

- On March 24, 1992, Pittsburgh's Mario Lemieux tallies his 1,000th career point. He accomplishes the feat in just his 513th game.

- On April 1, 1992, the NHL players go on strike, rejecting the owners' collective bargaining agreement offer.

- On April 12, 1992, the players ratify a new collective bargaining agreement by a vote of 409 to 61 and resume play after a 10-day strike.

Messier Stars on Broadway, Named MVP

Mark Messier was the last of the major stars to leave Edmonton (after Paul Coffey, Wayne Gretzky, Jari Kurri, Glenn Anderson, and Grant Fuhr departed). The Rangers acquired the former league MVP for Bernie Nicholls, assigned him the captaincy, and watched him take the team to its first regular-season title in 50 years. Messier was a smash on Broadway, posting 107 points en route to his second Hart Trophy and his second Lester B. Pearson Award.

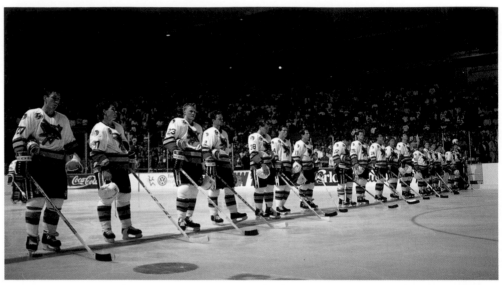

San Jose Sharks

Gunds' Sharks Sell a Lot of Jerseys

In 1990, North Stars owners George and Gordon Gund did the NHL a "favor" by selling the club to someone who would keep the team in Minnesota. The NHL rewarded the brothers with the league's next expansion franchise, the San Jose Sharks, who took the ice for the first time in 1991-92. The Sharks won only 17 games but were a merchandising phenomenon, as brisk sales of team memorabilia compensated for the team's on-ice futility.

Leetch Scores 102, Wins Norris

Former Calder Trophy winner Brian Leetch emerged as the game's most dangerous offensive defenseman in 1991-92. A fourth-year pro, Leetch scored 22 goals and assisted on 80 more as he led all NHL defenders with 102 points. A brilliant skater with smarts and poise far beyond his youth, Leetch brought an exciting explosiveness to the Rangers' attack. He was honored at season's end with the Norris Trophy.

Mark Messier

Brian Leetch

1991-92

- The Rangers (50-25-5) post the NHL's best record for the first time in 50 years. Mark Messier notches 107 points and defenseman Brian Leetch explodes for 102.

- Washington finishes second to the Rangers in the Patrick Division, as Michal Pivonka (80 points) combines with Dino Ciccarelli (38 goals) and Dimitri Khristich (36 goals).

- Pittsburgh places third in the Patrick, as Mario Lemieux (44 goals and 131 points in 64 games) and Kevin Stevens (54-69-123) power the league's best offense.

- Despite losing John MacLean for the year with knee damage, New Jersey makes the playoffs. Claude Lemieux notches 41 goals.

- The Islanders again finish out of the playoffs, although Pierre Turgeon, Ray Ferraro, and Derek King each score exactly 40 goals.

Canada Cup Series

Gretzky Drops to Third in Scoring Race

In his 13th NHL season, Wayne Gretzky led the Kings to a second-place finish in the Smythe Division, pacing the league in assists with 90 and finishing third in points with 121. It was the first year that he did not finish first or runner-up in scoring. Nevertheless, Gretzky scored his 732nd goal on December 21 to surpass Marcel Dionne for second on the NHL list. He also won his second straight Lady Byng Trophy.

Wayne Gretzky

Canada Beats U.S. in Canada Cup

Canada and the United States were the premier teams of the 1991 Canada Cup tournament. The canucks went 3-0-2 in the round-robin, while the yanks went 4-1-0. Both teams prevailed in the semifinals and met in the best-of-three finals. Dale Hawerchuk (pictured) and the Canadians won easily, 4-1 and 4-2, for their third straight triumph in the event. Canadian goalie Bill Ranford was named tourney MVP.

Red Rocket Soars in Vancouver

In 1991-92, the Canucks unveiled a Soviet rookie, Pavel Bure, who had been a building block for the Red Army team that was quickly crumbling due to NHL defections. Bure, an explosive skater with astonishing puck-handling skills, finished the year with 34 goals in 65 games. Dubbed the "Red Rocket," Bure won the Calder Trophy.

Pavel Bure

• Philadelphia misses the playoffs for the third straight year. Mark Recchi finishes with 43 goals.

• Montreal (41-28-11) takes the Adams Division title, as Patrick Roy leads the NHL in GAA (2.36) and Kirk Muller turns in a 36-goal, 77-point season.

• Boston finishes second to Montreal, although Cam Neely misses 71 games from an injury suffered by a "dirty" knee check from Pittsburgh's Ulf Samuelsson during the 1991 playoffs.

• The Sabres, who set an NHL record for penalty minutes (2,713), finish third in the Adams. Pat LaFontaine (46 goals in 57 games) and Dale Hawerchuk (98 points) star on offense.

• Hartford stumbles into the playoffs with a 26-41-13 record, as John Cullen, Pat Verbeek, and Bobby Holik all have disappointing seasons.

Super Skater Roenick Flips In 53 Goals

Born in Boston and a graduate of the often nasty, always high-scoring Quebec junior league, Jeremy Roenick arrived in the NHL with a reputation as one of the best skaters the game had ever known. In 1991-92, the hard-nosed center became just the third player in Blackhawks history to reach the 50-goal plateau (along with Bobby Hull and Al Secord). He finished the season with 53 goals, 103 points, and 98 penalty minutes.

Brett Hull

Hull Takes a Licking, Keeps On Ticking

Brett Hull learned the hard way what NHL checking can really mean. After scoring 86 goals in 1990-91, the Hull Watch was on red alert during the 1991-92 season, and the winger with the lightning-quick release began to wear not only his own jersey but the jerseys of some of the game's best "shadows." Nevertheless, the happy-go-lucky Blues sniper led the NHL in goals for the third straight year, scoring 70 in 73 games.

Jeremy Roenick

First Pick Lindros Sticks It to Quebec

In a somewhat startling and unprecedented gambit, Eric Lindros (right, holding a Nordiques sweater in his left hand) politely greeted the Quebec management team that made him the first pick in the 1991 draft. But then, after refusing to don the jersey for the customary photo session, Lindros announced he would not sign with or play for the Nordiques, choosing instead to forego a year in the NHL while some kind of deal could be arranged.

Eric Lindros

1991-92

- Quebec's woes continue despite the emergence of Joe Sakic (94 points) and Mats Sundin (76).

- Detroit goes 43-25-12 to win the Norris thanks to the scoring of Steve Yzerman (45-58-103), Ray Sheppard (36 goals), Paul Ysebaert (35), Jimmy Carson (34), and Sergei Fedorov (32).

- The Blackhawks finish second as Jeremy Roenick scores 53 goals and Ed Belfour has the NHL's second-best GAA (2.70). Mike Peluso leads the NHL in PIM (408).

- Brett Hull enjoys his third straight season scoring at least 70 goals, as the Blues finish third in the Norris.

- Ten games under .500, the North Stars limp into the playoffs. Mike Modano tops the team with 77 points.

- The midseason acquisition of Doug Gilmour helps the Maple Leafs surge late, but they cannot overcome the North Stars for a playoff berth.

Doug Gilmour

Bob Johnson

Johnson Dies After Winning Cup

"It's a great day to play hockey." Those words were the trademark of Bob Johnson, longtime coach of the University of Wisconsin (15 years and three NCAA titles) and a man of unlimited enthusiasm for the game. Johnson, pictured with his famous notepad, led Calgary to the Stanley Cup Finals in 1986 and took Pittsburgh to its first Stanley Cup in 1991. The hockey world mourned his death, from cancer at age 60, on November 26, 1991.

Leafs Land Gilmour in 10-Man Deal

On January 2, 1992, Doug Gilmour was the central figure in the biggest trade in NHL history when Calgary and the Maple Leafs swapped 10 players. The Flames shipped Gilmour, Jamie Macoun, Ric Nattress, Kent Manderville, and Rick Wamsley to the Leafs for Gary Leeman, Alexander Godynyuk, Jeff Reese, Michel Petit, and Craig Berube. The Leafs didn't make the playoffs in 1991-92 but they improved tremendously in 1992-93—thanks largely to Gilmour.

• The Canucks go 42-26-12 to win the Smythe. Goalie Kirk McLean (2.74 GAA) is the key.

• The Kings finish second in the Smythe. Wayne Gretzky (121 points), Luc Robitaille (107), Tony Granato (39 goals), and late-season pickup Paul Coffey lead the assault.

• Edmonton struggles to a third-place finish in the Smythe, as first-year Oiler Vince Damphousse erupts for 38 goals and Joe Murphy rips 35.

• Bob Essensa (2.88 GAA) propels the Jets to a fourth-place finish, just one point behind Edmonton.

• Calgary fails to qualify for the playoffs despite the work of Gary Roberts (53 goals).

• San Jose wins just 17 games in its inaugural season. Highly touted rookie winger Pat Falloon (25-34-59) leads a limp offense.

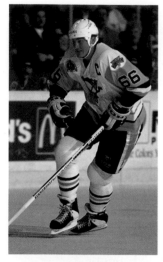

Mario Lemieux

Lemieux, Mates Fight Through Tough Times

Mario Lemieux was a study in courage during a difficult 1991-92 season. While fighting the effects of a degenerative disc problem in his back, Lemieux missed 16 games yet still won his third scoring title (44-87-131). Making the season more demanding was the death of coach Bob Johnson. The Cup-defending Penguins finished 39-32-9.

Madison Square Garden Scoreboard

Gartner Rips No. 500 vs. Ex-Mates

The scoreboard at Madison Square Garden commemorates the 500th career goal of Rangers right winger Mike Gartner, scored on October 14, 1991, against Washington goaltender Mike Liut. Gartner, who staked the Rangers to an early lead with his historic goal, watched Washington roar back and beat New York 5-3. Gartner had played nearly 10 seasons and scored 397 of his goals with the Capitals.

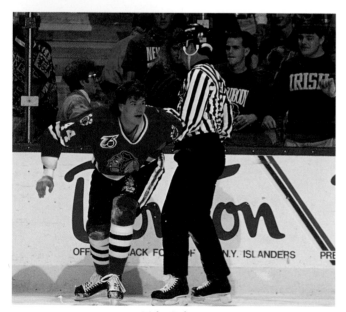

Mike Peluso

Peluso Fights His Way to 408 PIM

Chicago's Mike Peluso (shown scrambling out of the clutch of a peacemaking linesman after one of his many fights) led the NHL in penalty minutes in 1991-92 and was the first player in 10 years to surpass the 400-minute mark, finishing with 408 penalty minutes in just 63 games. Peluso was penalized the equivalent of nearly seven full games. Much of his time was for misconducts, which he spent in the dressing room after getting kicked out of games.

1991-92

- The NHL's top scorers are Mario Lemieux (131 points), Kevin Stevens (123), Wayne Gretzky (121), Brett Hull (109), Luc Robitaille (107), and Mark Messier (107).

- The only 50-goal scorers are Brett Hull (70), Kevin Stevens (54), Gary Roberts (53), and Jeremy Roenick (53).

- In the Patrick Division playoffs, the Rangers edge New Jersey (4-3) while Pittsburgh survives the Caps (4-3). The Pens then erase the Rangers (4-2) in the division finals.

- Adam Graves of the Rangers is suspended for four games after he breaks Mario Lemieux's hand.

- In the Adams semis, Montreal beats Hartford in seven games on Russ Courtnall's double-overtime goal in Game 7. Boston narrowly edges Buffalo (4-3) before sweeping the Habs (4-0) to take the Adams crown.

- In the Norris semifinals, Detroit ousts the North Stars (4-3) and

Criticism Builds Against Ziegler

John Ziegler

John A. Ziegler, NHL president from 1977-92, was often criticized for being a "mouthpiece" for the owners rather than a nonpartisan arbiter. His absence from the scene when the on-ice officials went on strike during the 1988 playoffs spelled the beginning of the end. In 1991-92, when the players struck for 10 days, Ziegler was roundly criticized for his passivity. He resigned after the season.

Campbell Conference Finals

Hawks Broom Edmonton in Semis

Edmonton enjoyed a glimmer of hope in Game 2 of its 1992 Stanley Cup semifinal series against Chicago when Bernie Nicholls (shown firing the puck on Ed Belfour) scored to give the Oilers a 2-0 lead. But Belfour, who was en route to a record 11 straight playoff victories, slammed the door shut on Edmonton and his Blackhawks rebounded with four unanswered goals to win the game. Chicago went on to sweep Edmonton (4-0) to go to the Finals.

Olympic Games

Unified Team Wins Olympic Gold

Future NHLers Clark Donatelli (right) and Vitali Prokhorov shared a friendly greeting after the Unified Team defeated USA 5-2 in the semifinals of the 1992 Winter Games in France. Prokhorov's CIS squad eventually won the gold medal with a rousing 3-1 defeat of Canada, while Donatelli's club lost to Czechoslovakia and finished out of the medals. Donatelli finished the 1991-92 season at Boston while Prokhorov joined St. Louis in 1992-93.

Chicago eliminates St. Louis (4-2). The Blackhawks then sweep the Red Wings (4-0) in the division finals.

• In the Smythe semis, Vancouver survives the Jets (4-3) and Edmonton beats the Kings in six. In the division finals, the Oilers erase the Canucks in six games.

• In the Wales Conference finals, Pittsburgh sweeps Boston (4-0) to secure its second straight Stanley Cup Finals appearance.

• In the Campbell Conference, Chicago brooms Edmonton (4-0) to stretch its playoff winning streak to 11 games.

• In Game 1 of the Stanley Cup Finals, the Penguins forge a 5-4 comeback victory. Mario Lemieux scores twice, including the winner.

• Mario Lemieux scores twice in Game 2, including the winner to break up a 1-1 tie, as Pittsburgh wins 3-1 to take a 2-0 series advantage.

Wales Conference Finals

Tocchet, Pens Club Boston in Wales Finals

Penguins G.M. Craig Patrick made a profoundly significant trade late in the 1991-92 season when he swapped high-scoring winger Mark Recchi to Philadelphia for hard-nosed Rick Tocchet (pictured skating past Boston goalie Andy Moog during the 1992 Wales Conference finals). Tocchet scored 19 points in 14 playoff games and helped the Penguins rip through the Bruins in four straight.

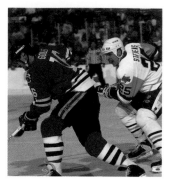

Stanley Cup Finals

Pens Halt the Streaking Hawks

Pittsburgh's Kevin Stevens harasses Michel Goulet during the 1992 Stanley Cup Finals. The Blackhawks, led by goalie Ed Belfour, roared into the Finals with 11 straight wins (three against St. Louis followed by four-game sweeps of Detroit and Edmonton), but they were swept in four straight by the Penguins. Pittsburgh rallied from a 3-0 deficit in Game 1 to win 5-4, then followed with 3-1, 1-0, and 6-5 triumphs. Stevens scored the only goal in Game 3.

Francis Does the Job as No. 2 Center

During several stretches of the season when Mario Lemieux was forced out of the lineup, the Penguins' No. 2 center, Ron Francis, quietly but effectively filled in. Here, Francis crashes the Blackhawks' crease during the 1992 Finals as goalie Ed Belfour and winger Michel Goulet attempt to hold him at bay. Francis topped all playoff scorers with 19 assists. He was the team's most effective faceoff man and an inspirational leader.

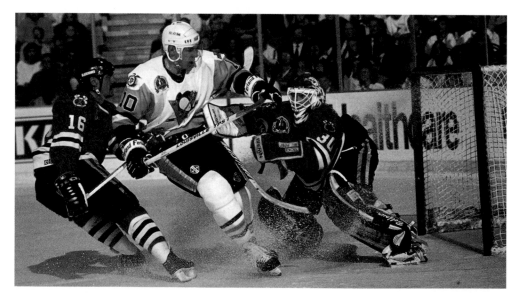

Stanley Cup Finals

- In Chicago for Game 3, Pittsburgh's Kevin Stevens is the only player to score, as the Pens win 1-0.

- The Pens and Hawks each score thrice in the first period of Game 4, but third-period goals by Larry Murphy and Ron Francis give the Pens a 6-5 win and the Stanley Cup.

- Ed Belfour and Tom Barrasso each break an NHL record by posting 11-game winning streaks in the playoffs.

- Mario Lemieux, with 34 points in just 15 playoff games, wins his second straight Conn Smythe Trophy.

- Mark Messier receives both the Hart Trophy and Lester B. Pearson Award.

- Patrick Roy, runner-up for the Hart Trophy, wins his third Vezina Trophy. Canucks rookie Pavel Bure (34-26-60 in 65 games) wins the Calder Trophy.

Pens Hug Cup After 11 Straight Wins

The close-knit Penguins huddle together for this Stanley Cup celebration photo. Bryan Trottier, who just won his sixth Stanley Cup, lies flat on the ice with his head on Mario Lemieux's lap. Not only did the Penguins win their last 11 games of the playoffs, but they opened the 1993 postseason with three more straight wins against New Jersey. That gave them 14 playoff victories in a row, setting an NHL record.

Stanley Cup Finals

Barrasso Has Best Stat of All: 16 Wins

Pittsburgh was able to repeat as Stanley Cup champion largely on the brilliant goaltending of Tom Barrasso (shown keying on the puck as defenseman Ulf Samuelsson ties up Blackhawks left winger Michel Goulet). Often criticized for lacking intensity, Barrasso proved unbeatable in clutch situations. While he finished fifth among playoff goalies in GAA (2.82), he earned all of Pittsburgh's 16 wins including the last 11 in a row.

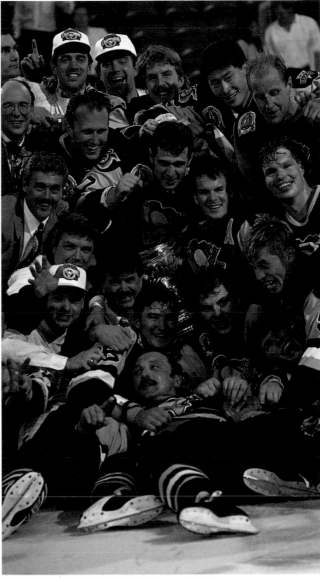

Stanley Cup Celebration

- Brian Leetch captures the Norris Trophy, beating out Ray Bourque.

- Islanders goalie Mark Fitzpatrick, who battles a rare blood disorder (EMS), wins the Masterton Trophy, while Vancouver G.M./coach Pat Quinn accepts the Jack Adams.

- Wayne Gretzky takes his second straight Lady Byng Trophy, while Montreal's Guy Carbonneau accepts his third Frank Selke Trophy.

- Charles Poulin of St. Hyacinthe is the Canadian Major Junior Player of the Year. Kamloops wins the Memorial Cup.

- In the Olympics, the Unified Team defeats Canada 3-1 in the gold-medal game.

- Lake Superior State beats Wisconsin 5-3 in the NCAA title game, as LSSU's Paul Constantin is named tourney MVP. Maine's Scott Pellerin receives the Hobey Baker Award.

HABS COME OUT ON TOP IN THE YEAR OF THE UPSET

More than anything, the 1992-93 season was marked by upheaval—a new commissioner, new teams, uncertainty in Pittsburgh and New York, and a slew of playoff upsets.

The NHL was undergoing massive administrative tremors. Gary Bettman, formerly third in command at the National Basketball Association, was named the league's first commissioner. Almost immediately, Bettman reorganized and beefed up the New York office and then announced that, starting in 1993-94, the league would be divided into Eastern and Western Conferences with division names being changed to Pacific, Central, Northeast, and Atlantic.

Two new teams took the ice in 1992-93, the Tampa Bay Lightning and Ottawa Senators, and two more were announced for 1993-94—one in South Florida (the Florida Panthers) and one in Southern California (the Mighty Ducks of Anaheim, owned by Disney).

Goofy things were happening all over. Before the season, Quebec agreed to trade prodigy Eric Lindros to Philadelphia—and also agreed to trade him to the

Rangers! After considerable study, a league arbiter decided that Lindros belonged to Philadelphia. The problem, Ranger-wise, was that several New York players had learned that they had been part of the aborted deal, and this caused dissension within the club. Once considered a Stanley Cup contender, the Rangers fizzled.

Pittsburgh, of course, was the No. 1 favorite to win the Cup, but the Penguins endured a roller-coaster year. Mario Lemieux got off to a tremendous start, but in January he discovered he was suffering from Hodgkin's disease. Le Grande Mario missed 24 games yet, showing startling resilience, came back to lead the NHL in scoring (69-91-160).

With Lemieux steering the ship, the Penguins again looked invincible; down the stretch, they won an NHL-record 17 straight games. After defeating New Jersey in the opening playoff round, however, the Pens' roller-coaster ride took another dip. In the Patrick finals, the Islanders beat the champs in seven games, with New York bench-warmer David Volek winning it in overtime.

Meanwhile, playoff upsets were popping up all over the place. Division champions Chicago and Boston were *swept* in the opening round. The other two first-place teams, Pittsburgh and Vancouver, were gone by Round 2. Moreover, Quebec and Detroit—the fourth- and fifth-best teams during the regular season—were eliminated in the opening round.

In fact, of the seven teams that had amassed 100 points during the season, only one, Montreal, made it to the conference finals. The Canadiens' journey through the playoffs was pure adventure. Eleven times the Habs entered sudden-death during the postseason, and 10 times they prevailed. Three of the O.T. wins came in the Finals against Los Angeles, with John LeClair scoring the overtime winners in Games 3 and 4. Montreal clinched the Stanley Cup with a 4-1 win in Game 5, putting the cap on a dizzying season.

1992-93

- The NHL expands from 22 to 24 teams by adding the Tampa Bay Lightning and Ottawa Senators. Also, the season is expanded to 84 games.

- Helmet wearing is made optional in the NHL, but the league invokes stricter penalties for fighting and high-sticking.

- Tampa Bay chooses first in the 1992 Entry Draft, taking Czechoslovakian star Roman Hamrlik, while Ottawa takes Russian ace Alexei Yashin.

- The Hall of Fame inducts seven members, including players Marcel Dionne, Woody Dumart, Bob Gainey, and Lanny McDonald.

- After a one-year holdout, Eric Lindros (property of Quebec) is traded to both Philadelphia and the Rangers in separate, simultaneous deals necessitating third-party arbitration.

- On June 30, 1992, arbitrator Larry Bertuzzi rules that Philadelphia and

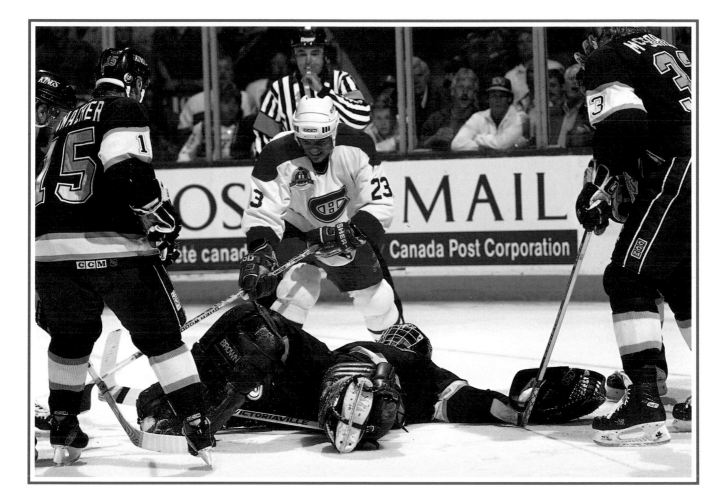

Montreal's tenacious assault on L.A.'s goalmouth made life difficult for
the Kings during the 1993 Stanley Cup Finals. Here, Brian Bellows (#23) digs
for a loose puck under Kings goalie Kelly Hrudey as Pat Conacher (left) and Marty
McSorley (right) hover above. The Kings played disciplined defensive hockey
but were unable to crack the wall of defense erected by Montreal's superb
backliners and outstanding netminder, Patrick Roy.

Quebec have a binding agreement. Eric Lindros goes to the Flyers for Ron Hextall, Mike Ricci, Steve Duchesne, three other players, two No. 1 picks, and $15 million.

• On August 8, 1992, NHL brawler John Kordic dies of heart failure in police custody following a violent arrest in Quebec. A pathologist will claim that alcohol, cocaine, and steroids caused his death.

• On September 22, 1992, the Kings announce Wayne Gretzky will miss at least half of the regular season with a herniated thoracic disc in his back.

• On September 30, 1992, the 15-year tenure of NHL President John A. Ziegler officially ends as the league's former general counsel, Gil Stein, takes over on an interim basis.

• On October 5, 1992, Mario Lemieux signs a seven-year, $42 million contract with the Penguins.

Eric Lindros

Flyers Empty the Bank to Land Lindros

After sitting out an NHL season because he did not want to play in Quebec, former No. 1 draft pick Eric Lindros was traded simultaneously to the Rangers and Flyers in June 1992. An independent arbiter ruled the Philly deal was binding. The Flyers dealt six players, two No. 1 picks, and $15 million to Quebec, yet Lindros proved his value with 41 goals and 75 points, even though knee injuries limited his season to 61 games.

Bure Blasts 60 Past Enemy Goaltenders

In 1992-93, after a dazzling rookie season, the Red Rocket was on a one-man seek-and-destroy mission against NHL goaltenders. Pavel Bure, the Canucks' 21-year-old winger, shattered every team record for goal-scoring when he blasted 60 goals and 110 points. He surpassed Tony Tanti's 45-goal mark (1983-84) and Patrik Sundstrom's 91-point feat (1983-84). On March 1, 1993, Bure became Vancouver's first-ever 50-goal scorer.

Pavel Bure

Eddie Belfour

Belfour Lifts Hawks to Norris Title

The 1992-93 season was highlighted by several superb goaltending performances, not the least of which was the Vezina Trophy-winning show put on by Chicago's hot-tempered Eddie "The Eagle" Belfour. The former Calder Trophy netminder took the Hawks to the top of the Norris Division as he led the NHL in games (71) and shutouts (seven), was second in wins (41) and GAA (2.59), and was third in save percentage (.906).

1992-93

• On December 4, 1992, Eric Lindros is charged with common assault after Marie Lynn Nunney alleges he elbowed her and spat beer on her in a Whitby, Ontario, bar.

• For the first time in four years, since his 1989 drug bust, Detroit's Bob Probert is allowed to travel across the Canadian border without fear of deportation.

• The NHL announces that, on February 1, 1993, former NBA Vice-President Gary Bettman will take over as the NHL's new commissioner (instead of "president").

• On December 13, 1992, goalie Manon Rheaume of the Atlanta Knights (IHL) becomes the first woman to play a professional regular-season game.

• On January 8, 1993, while disabled by back pain, Mario Lemieux is diagnosed with Hodgkin's disease.

Mario Lemieux

Mario Hit with Hodgkin's Disease

In a year of dramatic highs and lows, Mario Lemieux began the season by celebrating his 27th birthday (October 5, 1992) with a seven-year contract worth $42 million. In January, while Lemieux was out of the lineup with recurring back trouble, shocking news arrived that he had been diagnosed with Hodgkin's disease. Yet, after only a month of treatment, Lemieux returned to the lineup in March in time to chase down and pass Pat LaFontaine for the NHL scoring title.

Mogilny Shares in the Spirit of 76

In 1992-93, Buffalo's Alexander Mogilny (shown skating past the hook of another former Soviet, Dmitri Yushkevich) used blazing speed, a lightning-quick release, and the playmaking skills of linemate Pat LaFontaine to forge one of the most stunning goal-scoring performances in NHL history. The splendid winger shared the NHL lead in goals (76, fifth most ever), led in hat-tricks (seven), and tied for the lead in game-winning goals (11).

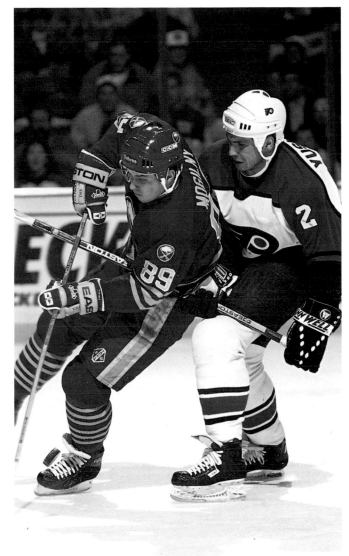

Alexander Mogilny, Dmitri Yushkevich

• On January 21, 1993, after nine shoulder operations, hernia surgery, a broken leg, three knee surgeries, and the tragic death of his wife, four-time 50-goal scorer Tim Kerr retires.

• On February 22, 1993, Toronto's Glenn Anderson records his 1,000th point.

• On February 24, 1993, Detroit's Steve Yzerman nets his 1,000th point.

• On March 2, 1993, after missing nearly two months battling Hodgkin's disease, Mario Lemieux returns.

• On March 10, 1993, two years after promising not to move the team, North Stars owner Norman Green announces the team will move to Dallas for the 1993-94 season.

• On March 19, 1993, five games after returning from a serious neck injury, Rangers defenseman Brian Leetch breaks his right ankle while stepping out of a New York taxi.

Luc Robitaille

Robitaille Flies High at Left Wing

Adding to his growing reputation as the NHL's steadiest, most deadly left winger, Kings portsider Luc Robitaille enjoyed a career year in 1992-93, notching 63 goals (fourth best in the NHL) and 24 power-play goals (tied for fifth). He also set an NHL record for points by a left winger (125). With Wayne Gretzky gone for 39 games due to back trouble, Robitaille filled in and earned his fifth First All-Star Team berth in six years.

Doug Gilmour

The Lightning Flashes a Little Thunder

Under the watchful eye of G.M. Phil Esposito, the Tampa Bay Lightning entered the NHL in 1992-93 and were remarkably competitive, by expansion expectations. While they finished last in the Norris Division, they counted 23 wins and were inspired by some promising young players, such as defenseman Roman Hamrlik, the No. 1 overall pick in 1992, and center Brian Bradley, who erupted for 42 goals and 86 points.

Gilmour and Leafs Shatter Team Records

The blockbuster deal of 1991-92 that brought Doug Gilmour from Calgary to Toronto paid huge dividends in 1992-93, as the Leafs climbed into third place in the Norris Division and set a franchise record for wins (44) and points (99). Gilmour, runner-up to Mario Lemieux for league MVP honors, set club records for assists (95) and points (127) and won the Frank Selke Trophy as the NHL's best defensive forward.

Roman Hamrlik

1992-93

- On April 10, 1993, the Penguins beat the Rangers 4-2 and establish an NHL record with 17 straight wins.

- The Penguins go a league-best 56-21-7, as Mario Lemieux notches 69 goals and 160 points in just 60 games.

- Washington finishes second in the Patrick Division, as Kevin Hatcher becomes the seventh defenseman in NHL history to score 30 goals (34).

- The surprising Islanders take third place in the Patrick. Pierre Turgeon (58-74-132), Derek King (38 goals), and Steve Thomas (37) lead the way.

- New Jersey finishes fourth in the Patrick, as Claude Lemieux (81 points) again leads the team in scoring while Stephane Richer (38 goals) and Alexander Semak (37) contribute.

- A late-season surge thrusts the Flyers into fifth place. Mark Recchi

Selanne Rifles In 76 Rookie Goals

Teemu Selanne started his rookie NHL season in a contract dispute with the Jets, signed an offer sheet with Calgary, then inked a deal in Winnipeg in time for the regular season. He then proceeded to shatter Mike Bossy's rookie goal-scoring record (53) with 76 tallies, tying Alexander Mogilny for the NHL lead. He also crushed Peter Stastny's rookie points-scoring record (109) by posting 132 points. He was a runaway winner for the Calder Trophy.

Mats Sundin

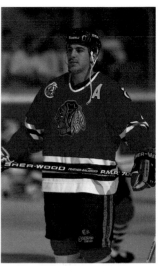

Chris Chelios

Teemu Selanne

Sundin's Scoring Skein Ends at 30

On December 12, 1992, the Nordiques survived an 8-7 shootout in San Jose. Ironically, their top player, Mats Sundin, was held without a point, bringing to an end his 30-game point-scoring streak. During the phenomenal run—the fourth-longest streak in NHL history—Sundin scored 21 goals and 46 points. He finished the season with 47 goals and 114 points (up from 76 points the year before) and was 11th in league scoring.

Chelios Makes Enemies, Wins the Norris

Hated in 23 of 24 NHL cities for his chippy aggressiveness (282 penalty minutes) and strong offensive skills, Blackhawks defenseman Chris Chelios—a native son of Chicago—was the recipient of his second Norris Trophy in 1992-93 (his first coming in 1988-89 when he skated for Montreal). Eight defensemen recorded more points than Chelios, who scored 73, but none combined the physical and skill elements so successfully.

---

notches 53 goals and Eric Lindros scores 41 times in 61 games.

• The Rangers miss the playoffs despite 45 goals from veteran Mike Gartner.

• Boston (51-26-7) takes first place in the Adams Division, as Adam Oates

(45-97-142) and rookie linemate Joe Juneau (102 points) come up big.

• Quebec takes second in the Adams thanks to Mats Sundin (47-67-114) and Joe Sakic (48-57-105).

• Montreal gets newfound scoring from Brian Bellows (40 goals), Vince

Damphousse (39), and Kirk Muller (37) and finishes third with 102 points.

• Buffalo's tandem of Pat LaFontaine (53-95-148) and Alex Mogilny (76 goals, 127 points) guides the Sabres to fourth place in the Adams.

Kariya Wins Baker, NCAA Title

Paul Kariya basked in glory during 1992-93. The smallish left wing scored 93 points for the University of Maine, won the Hobey Baker Award, and led his Black Bears to the national championship. In June, the NHL's Mighty Ducks of Anaheim made Kariya their first-ever draft pick.

Yzerman Fuels Wings' Offense

The 1992-93 Red Wings set new franchise records for victories (47) and points (103) and finished a close second to Chicago in the Norris Division. Their star centerman, Steve Yzerman, had another spectacular season, scoring 58 goals (sixth overall) and 137 points (fourth). In a year of heavy offense, the Wings led the league in goals with 369.

Paul Kariya

Steve Yzerman

LaFontaine Racks Up 148

Pat LaFontaine's first year in Buffalo (1991-92) was cut short when Calgary's Jamie Macoun shattered his jaw with a slash. In 1992-93, LaFontaine (shown with the protective mask that allowed him to return following his injury) scored 53 goals and was second in the NHL in points with 148, most ever by an American. His 95 assists were crucial in linemate Alexander Mogilny's 76-goal outburst.

Pat LaFontaine

1992-93

• Hartford and first-year Ottawa fail to make the Adams Division playoffs. The Senators finish 10-70-4.

• Chicago goes 47-25-12 to finish atop the Norris. Jeremy Roenick (50 goals) and goalie Ed Belfour (second in GAA at 2.59) are the keys.

• Detroit places second in the Norris thanks to the NHL's best offense. Steve Yzerman (58-79-137), Dino Ciccarelli (41 goals), Sergei Fedorov (34), and Paul Ysebaert (34) star.

• The Maple Leafs are third with 99 points—their most ever—as Doug Gilmour records 127 points and Dave

Andreychuk leads the NHL in power-play goals (32 of his 54 goals).

• Brett Hull (54 goals) and Craig Janney (106 points) help St. Louis finish fourth in the Norris.

• The North Stars, amid well-founded rumors of their transfer to Dallas,

Ottawa Senators' Opening Ceremony

Adam Oates

Owner Says Senators Tanked Games

The expansion Ottawa Senators kicked off their 1992-93 season with the extravaganza pictured here. A terrible team on the ice (10-70-4), the Senators were the focus of a postseason investigation after owner Bruce Firestone made comments suggesting the team had tanked some games to ensure finishing last and guaranteeing a better drafting position. The team was cleared but Firestone decided to step aside.

Blues Dump Oates, Live to Regret It

The Blues traded Adam Oates to Boston for Craig Janney late in 1991-92 in a dispute over money. Blues winger Brett Hull, the chief recipient of Oates' superb playmaking skills, blasted St. Louis management for ditching his buddy and benefactor. In Boston, Oates proved that Hull was right, notching a league-high 97 assists and finishing third overall in scoring with a career-best 142 points, combining smartly with rookie forward Joe Juneau.

collapse in the stretch and finish out of the playoffs. So does Tampa Bay, which wins 23 games.

• Vancouver (46-29-9) takes first place in the Smythe Division, as sophomore Pavel Bure totals 60 goals and 110 points.

• The Flames rebound for a second-place finish in the Smythe. Theo Fleury leads the way with 100 points.

• Wayne Gretzky notches 65 points in 45 games while Luc Robitaille (63 goals, 125 points) sets NHL marks for goals and points by a left winger. L.A. finishes third in the Smythe.

• Teemu Selanne sets new NHL rookie records with 76 goals and 132 points, helping the young Jets finish fourth in the Smythe.

• Edmonton undergoes major personnel changes in a rebuilding season, while San Jose (11 wins) plays poorly and accomplishes little.

Manon Rheaume

Gartner Nets 30 for 14th Straight Year

History was made on January 23, 1993, when Mike Gartner scored his 30th goal of the 1992-93 season. In so doing, he became the only player in the history of the league to register 14 straight NHL seasons with at least 30 goals. A brilliant 45-goal season ended with an early summer, as Gartner's Rangers dropped like a rock through the standings and finished out of the playoffs.

Mike Gartner

Atlanta Debuts a Female Goalie

History was made on December 13, 1992, when Manon Rheaume, a goaltender in the Tampa Bay Lightnings' farm system, became the first woman ever to play in a professional hockey game. Suiting up for the Atlanta Knights of the International League, Rheaume—a 22-year-old rookie free agent from Quebec—played in just a pair of games and recorded a fairly husky 6.36 goals-against average.

Bettman's the NHL's First Commish

With the resignation of John A. Ziegler and the self-inflicted shame attached to interim boss Gil Stein (who rigged his own induction into the Hall of Fame in 1993), the NHL went outside its own backyard for a new boss. It chose Gary Bettman, who served as assistant commissioner of the NBA before agreeing to become the NHL's first "commissioner" (after 76 years of NHL presidents).

Gary Bettman

1992-93

- Leading NHL scorers include Mario Lemieux (160 points), Pat LaFontaine (148), Adam Oates (142), Steve Yzerman (137), Teemu Selanne (132), and Pierre Turgeon (132).

- The top goal-scorers are Teemu Selanne (76), Alexander Mogilny (76), and Mario Lemieux (69).

- In the Adams Division semifinals, Buffalo shocks the Bruins (4-0) while Montreal skates past Quebec (4-2). Montreal then sweeps the Sabres, who are without the injured Pat LaFontaine and Alexander Mogilny.

- In the Patrick semifinals, the Isles shock Washington (4-2). In Game 6

of the series, Washington's Dale Hunter cheap-shots Pierre Turgeon, knocking him out of the lineup and incurring a 21-game suspension in 1993-94.

- In the other Patrick semifinal series, Pittsburgh whips New Jersey (4-1). The Isles then stun the Penguins in

Isles Lasso Penguins in Patrick Final

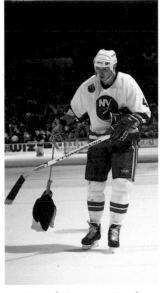

Patrick Division Finals

For the Islanders, the 1993 playoffs were a Cinderella story that rivalled their 1975 upset of the prohibitively favored New York Rangers. They survived Washington in the first round and pulled a stunning upset of the Stanley Cup champion Penguins in the Patrick finals. The image of defenseman Uwe Krupp disposing of a penguin doll hurled on the ice at Nassau Coliseum captured the essence of the Islanders' rude treatment of the reigning champs.

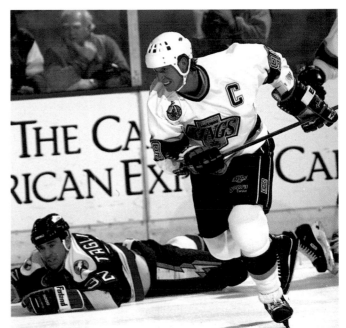

Wayne Gretzky

Gretzky Warms Up in the Springtime

By the 1993 playoffs, Wayne Gretzky was back in top form after a back injury kept him out of 39 games. Gretzky took the Kings where they'd never been before: to the Stanley Cup Finals. The Great One led all playoff scorers in points (40). He notched three game-winning goals and recorded his 100th playoff goal (as did teammate Jari Kurri).

Lemieux Showered with Awards

Mario Lemieux

In a comeback story of epic proportion, Mario Lemieux returned to NHL action following a month of radiation treatment for Hodgkin's disease and still had the wherewithal to win his fourth scoring title with 69 goals and 160 points in just 60 games. Lemieux won his third Lester B. Pearson Award, his second Hart Trophy, and his first Masterton Trophy for perseverance and dedication.

---

the division finals, winning Game 7 in sudden-death.

• In the Norris semis, the Blues sweep Chicago (4-0) while Toronto beats Detroit (4-3) with an O.T. win in Game 7. The Leafs then outlast the Blues (4-3) to win the Norris title.

• In the Smythe, Vancouver takes Winnipeg (4-2) and L.A. surprises Calgary (4-2). The Kings then defeat Vancouver in six games in the division finals.

• The Islanders are no match for Montreal in the Wales Conference finals, losing in five games.

• Los Angeles survives the Leafs (4-3) in the Campbell Conference finals, as L.A.'s Wayne Gretzky and Jari Kurri each score their 100th career playoff goals. In Game 6, Gretzky tallies his record eighth playoff hat-trick.

• The Finals open in Montreal, but L.A. wins Game 1 4-1.

Aftermath of Hunter/Turgeon Incident

Caps' Hunter Cheap-Shots Turgeon

Washington's playoff frustrations boiled over in Game 6 of its opening-round series against the Islanders. After blowing leads in three games, the Caps faced elimination in Game 6. When Pierre Turgeon scored the fifth goal in New York's 5-3 series-clinching win, Dale Hunter slammed the unsuspecting Turgeon into the boards, sparking a full-scale brawl and a shower of debris from Islanders fans. Hunter was later suspended for 21 games.

Isles Run into a Habs Buzz Saw

After their dramatic series triumph against Washington and their Game 7 sudden-death survival vs. the Penguins, the Islanders faced the Adams Division champion Canadiens in the Wales finals. While the Isles avoided the embarrassment of a sweep by Montreal, winning Game 4 4-1, they were clearly outmatched and succumbed in five games, losing the finale 5-2. Here, New York's Brad Dalgarno gets mugged behind the Montreal net.

Wales Conference Finals

Campbell Conference Finals

Leafs Lose to Lost Angelenos

The 1993 Campbell Conference championship matched two up-and-coming powers: the Smythe Division champion Kings, led by Wayne Gretzky, and the Norris champion Maple Leafs, with Doug Gilmour at the helm. Fans in Toronto displayed their partisan sentiments during the Leafs' 3-2 nail-biter victory in Game 5, but the Kings would have the last laugh, edging the Leafs 5-4 in a thrill-a-minute Game 7 showdown featuring a hat-trick from Gretzky.

1992-93

- Montreal takes Game 2 3-2 as Eric Desjardins scores all three goals— including one in O.T.

- Montreal wins the next two Finals games in L.A., 4-3 and 3-2, as John LeClair wins both games with overtime goals. The Habs have now won 10 straight playoff O.T. games.

- Back in Montreal for Game 5, the Canadiens dust off the Kings 4-1 to claim their 23rd Stanley Cup.

- Though Wayne Gretzky garners 40 playoff points, Patrick Roy (2.13 playoff GAA) wins his second Conn Smythe Trophy.

- By a large voting margin, Mario Lemieux is awarded the Hart Trophy over Doug Gilmour. Lemieux also receives the Lester B. Pearson Award and the Masterton Trophy.

- Ed Belfour wins the Vezina Trophy, edging out Pittsburgh's Tom Barrasso.

Montreal Canadiens

Damphousse, LeClair Power Habs

Montreal won its record 23rd Stanley Cup in 1993 by eliminating L.A. in five games. Vince Damphousse, John LeClair, and Kirk Muller each scored three game-winning goals in the playoffs, with LeClair netting sudden-death winners in Games 3 and 4 of the Finals. Damphousse (at center, holding the Cup) led the team with 23 playoff points.

Montreal Goes 10 for 11 in O.T.

Montreal backliner Eric Desjardins (at right, #28) scored three goals in Game 2 of the 1993 Finals, including the winner in sudden-death. The Canadiens played in 11 overtime games in the 1993 playoffs and won the last 10 of them (two vs. Quebec, three against Buffalo, two vs. the Isles, and three vs. L.A.). Patrick Roy, pictured stopping Kings winger Mike Donnelly, won the Conn Smythe Trophy.

Stanley Cup Finals

- Chicago's Chris Chelios wins his second Norris Trophy, beating out runner-up Ray Bourque.

- The Calder Trophy goes to Teemu Selanne, who outballots Joe Juneau.

- Pierre Turgeon is honored with the Lady Byng Trophy, while Boston's Dave Poulin earns the King Clancy Trophy.

- Doug Gilmour wins the Frank Selke Trophy, while Toronto coach Pat Burns cops the Jack Adams Award.

- Pat Peake of the Detroit Jr. Red Wings is named Canadian Major Junior Player of the Year, while Sault Ste. Marie wins the Memorial Cup.

- The University of Maine wins the NCAA title with a 5-4 win over Lake Superior State in the finals. Maine's Jim Montgomery is named tourney MVP, while the school's Paul Kariya wins the Hobey Baker Award.

For decades, the Rangers proved that extravagant spending couldn't purchase the Stanley Cup. But finally, generations after the Blueshirts annexed Lord Stanley's mug in 1940, the best team money could buy ended the championship drought.

To do so, Paramount Communications, which owned the team and Madison Square Garden, pumped an inordinate amount of cash into the purchase of players, such as forward Steve Larmer and goalie Glenn Healy. They also hired coach Mike Keenan, paying him almost $1 million a year.

These players were added to a nucleus that included Philadelphian Mike Richter in goal and Connecticut-reared Brian Leetch on defense. They melded neatly with three gifted Russians—Alexei Kovalev, Sergei Zubov, and Sergei Nemchinov.

Keenan adhered to his previous coaching trends by selecting one goalie as his top banana and sticking with him. "I decided in training camp that Mike Richter would be my primary goaltender," added Keenan, "and that Glenn Healy would be there for motivation and to fill in from time to time. Obviously, it worked out for the best."

RANGERS PUT AN END TO 54-YEAR DROUGHT

By midseason, the Rangers had taken a firm hold on first place overall. Captain Mark Messier was in mint condition and Adam Graves, one of many ex-Oilers on the team, was on his way to a 52-goal season. To the league's surprise, Zubov developed into the club's highest-scoring defenseman, even better than the gifted Leetch.

"We had the best power play and the best penalty-killing," said Richter, "which is a pretty good parlay."

When the Rangers slipped in late winter, management gambled at the trade deadline, unloading popular Mike Gartner to Toronto for Glenn Anderson, obtaining checking forwards Stephane Matteau and Brian Noonan from Chicago, and nabbing yet another Oiler veteran, Craig MacTavish.

The Rangers finished a league-best 52-24-8, then opened the playoffs with an easy sweep of the Islanders. They followed that by eliminating Washington in five games, whereupon they met the Devils in one of the best playoff series of all time.

Trailing three games to two and 2-0 in Game 6, the Rangers rallied behind Messier to tie the series. Game 7, played at Madison Square Garden, went into double overtime after the Devils tied the score with 7.7 seconds remaining in regulation. Finally, a fluke shot by Matteau, from behind the net, somehow bounced off New Jersey goalie Martin Brodeur and into the cage.

That sent the Rangers into the Finals against Vancouver. After losing the opener at home, the Blueshirts reeled off three straight wins. Delirious New Yorkers, some of whom paid $1,500 or more for a ticket, packed the Garden for Game 5, but the Canucks won that game, 6-3, and the next, 4-1.

More nervous than optimistic, the Garden faithful sweated through a nip-and-tuck Game 7. The Rangers took a 3-1 lead, yielded a goal in the third period, and hung on for a 3-2 triumph. The Blueshirts hoisted the Stanley Cup and paraded it around the ice, showing their fans a trophy they hadn't seen in 54 years.

1993-94

• The NHL opens the season with two new teams—the Florida Panthers and the Mighty Ducks of Anaheim. The Minnesota North Stars move to Texas and become the Dallas Stars.

• The NHL's conferences are renamed the Eastern and Western. The Atlantic and Northeast Divisions make up the Eastern Conference, and the Central and Pacific make up the Western Conference.

• The Hall of Fame inducts eight men, including players Steve Shutt, Guy Lapointe, Billy Smith, and Edgar Laprade.

• The Ottawa Senators, who reportedly threw their final game of the 1992-93 season to guarantee the first pick in the 1993 draft (Alexandre Daigle), are fined $100,000 by NHL boss Gary Bettman.

• On October 9, 1993, the Tampa Bay Lightning sets an NHL atten-

The Rangers were clearly the favorites in the 1994 Stanley Cup Finals. After all, they were the No. 1 seed in the playoffs, while Finals opponent Vancouver was seeded 14th. Nevertheless, Vancouver won the series opener and—after the Rangers copped the next three—won two straight to send the series to seven games. Craig MacTavish (#14) and the Rangers sweated out a 3-2 win in Game 7 to end a 54-year Stanley Cup drought.

dance record when 27,227 fans fill the ThunderDome for a match with the Florida Panthers.

• The NHL's on-ice officials strike on November 14, 1993, and are indefinitely replaced by referees and linesmen from other leagues. The strike ends November 30.

• On December 5, 1993, Mike Gartner, playing for the Rangers, becomes the sixth player in NHL history to reach the 600-goal plateau.

• On February 2, 1994, the Red Wings beat Tampa Bay 3-1, giving coach Scotty Bowman his 1,000th NHL win.

• On February 5, 1994, Washington's Peter Bondra scores five goals in a 6-3 win over Tampa Bay.

• In the same February 5 game, Peter Bondra scores four goals in 4:12 against goalie Daren Puppa, setting a record for the fastest four goals ever.

Mighty Ducks Fans

Fans Can't Get Enough of the Ducks

The NHL continued its expansion mode in 1993-94 with the addition of two new teams: the Mighty Ducks of Anaheim and the Florida Panthers. The Mighty Ducks, owned by the Disney Corporation and named after a successful Disney movie, were an instant marketing hit. They were also a remarkably competitive team, winning 33 games and finishing ahead of both Los Angeles and Edmonton in the Pacific Division. The Ducks played their games in The Pond.

Bure Fires In a League-High 60

A brilliant skater and a dynamic offensive player, Pavel Bure suffered through some rough times in 1993-94, missing eight games due to a variety of aches and pains. Nevertheless, he managed to fire home 60 goals to lead the league. It was Bure's second straight 60-goal season and his second 100-plus-point season, as he tied for fifth in the NHL in total points (107). His Canucks finished at 41-40-3 but turned it on come playoff time.

Pavel Bure

1993-94

- On February 13, Pittsburgh's Tom Barrasso ties Frank Brimsek as the winningest American-born goalie in NHL history when he records his 252nd NHL victory.

- On February 17, 1994, Quebec's Mike Ricci scores five goals against the San Jose Sharks in an 8-2 win.

- On March 3, 1994, Alan Eagleson, former director of the NHL Players' Association, is indicted by a U.S. Federal Grand Jury on 32 criminal counts, including fraud, racketeering, and obstruction of justice.

- Kings center Wayne Gretzky ties the NHL record for career goals, held by Gordie Howe (801), with a March 20th goal against San Jose.

- On March 23, 1994, Wayne Gretzky beats Vancouver's Kirk McLean for career goal No. 802, with assists from Marty McSorley and Luc Robitaille, and becomes the NHL's all-time leading goal-scorer.

Sergei Fedorov

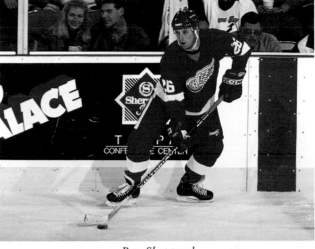

Ray Sheppard

Slow-Footed Sheppard Scores 52

Detroit's Ray Sheppard has always been known for two things: his nose for the net and his caterpillar-like skating speed. In 1993-94, the classy sniper reached new heights when he fired home 52 goals (tying for fifth in the league). With Steve Yzerman out of the lineup for 26 games, Sheppard—who scored 38 goals as a Sabres rookie in 1987-88—filled in as a bona fide offensive threat.

Fedorov Stars on Both Ends of the Ice

Sergei Fedorov was recognized in 1992-93 as one of the NHL's premier defensive forwards, but in 1993-94 the ex-Soviet star blossomed into one of the game's most prodigious scorers, chasing Wayne Gretzky for the NHL scoring title. Ultimately, Sergei finished second with 120 points (56 goals). More impressively, he won both the Hart and the Frank Selke Trophy. Among forwards, Fedorov was the league's best plus/minus player at +48.

• Six members of the Hartford Whalers—Pat Verbeek, Geoff Sanderson, Chris Pronger, Marc Potvin, Todd Harkins, and Mark Janssens—are arrested March 24 in Buffalo following a barroom brawl.

• Pittsburgh's Ron Francis, New Jersey's Bernie Nicholls, Hartford's Brian Propp, and Detroit's Dino Ciccarelli all notch their 1,000th NHL point. Ciccarelli also scores his 500th career goal.

• The Rangers win the Atlantic Division and have the best record in hockey (52-24-8). Adam Graves leads the team in goals (52).

• Goalie Martin Brodeur (2.40 GAA) helps New Jersey compile 106 points and finish second to the Rangers in the Atlantic.

• Led by playmaker Joe Juneau (19-66-85), the Capitals finish third in the Atlantic Division.

Dave Andreychuk

Andreychuk Lights It Up 53 Times

After several above-average scoring seasons in Buffalo, Dave Andreychuk became a legitimate NHL game-breaker after his trade to Toronto in 1992-93, finishing that season with a combined 54 goals. In 1993-94, Andreychuk blasted home 53 goals, including 21 on the power play and five more while shorthanded. The lumbering winger has remarkably soft hands around the net and can absorb tremendous punishment to get the job done.

Adam Graves

Graves Cracks the Half-Century Mark

No Ranger since Vic Hadfield in 1971-72 had ever scored 50 goals in a season, although several had made serious runs. In 1993-94, Adam Graves, heir apparent to Mark Messier as the Rangers' next spiritual and emotional leader, set a franchise record with 52 tallies, tying for fifth in the league. Graves combined toughness and skill, scoring 20 power-play goals and sitting out 127 minutes in penalties.

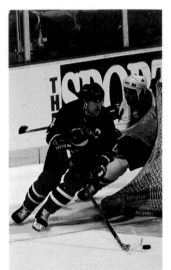

Scott Stevens

Stevens Does It All for New Jersey

In 1993-94, for the first time in Devils history, a defenseman was the team's leading scorer. Scott Stevens, a finalist for the season's Norris Trophy, finished with 18 goals (second best of his career) and a career-high 78 points. His +53 plus/minus rating was the best in the NHL. Thanks to the play of their team captain, the Devils finished with the second-best record in the league (47-25-12) and nearly made it to the Stanley Cup Finals.

1993-94

- Center Pierre Turgeon scores 94 points but the Islanders finish at .500, fourth in the Atlantic.

- The Florida Panthers set an NHL expansion record with 33 wins in their inaugural campaign, thanks largely to goalie John Vanbiesbrouck (2.53 GAA, .924 save percentage).

- Despite the outstanding play of Eric Lindros, Mark Recchi, and rookie sensation Mikael Renberg, the Flyers fail to make the playoffs for the fifth straight year.

- Tampa Bay cannot muster any offense and finishes last in the Atlantic.

- Pittsburgh wins the Northeast Division, going 44-27-13, as Jaromir Jagr emerges as the team's new scoring leader (99 points). Mario Lemieux finishes with 37 points in just 22 games.

- Boston finishes second to the Penguins, as injury-plagued sniper

Richter Helps Rangers Finish First

After a comparatively dismal 1992-93 campaign, Rangers goalie Mike Richter had a brilliant 1993-94 season, setting a team record with a 20-game unbeaten streak. He broke Dave Kerr's mark of 19, which was set in 1939-40, the last time the Rangers won the Stanley Cup. Richter topped the league with 42 wins and had the fifth-best GAA (2.57), helping the Rangers to the best overall record in the NHL (52-24-8).

Felix Potvin

Mike Richter

Leafs Jump Off to a 10-0-0 Start

No team ever got off to a better start than the 1993-94 Maple Leafs, who won their first 10 games thanks to the brilliant goaltending of sophomore Felix Potvin. In his first 10 starts, Potvin was 9-1 with a league-best 2.33 GAA. "La Chat" ended the season with 34 wins, a 2.89 GAA, and a .907 save percentage. The Leafs cooled off and finished with a 43-29-12 record, second in the Central Division.

Cam Neely scores 50 goals while playing a total of just 49 games.

• Montreal is just a point behind Boston, as goalie Patrick Roy and Vince Damphousse (91 points) star.

• Buffalo's 95 points are one fewer than the Canadiens' in the Northeast Division. Goalie Dominik Hasek leads the league in GAA (1.95).

• Joe Sakic's 92 points can't help Quebec from finishing a distant fifth in the Northeast.

• Hartford wins just 27 games and finishes sixth in the Northeast

Division, despite Geoff Sanderson's 41 goals.

• Rookie center Alexei Yashin (79 points) is the only saving grace for Ottawa, which wins 14 games.

• Detroit (46-30-8) wins the Central thanks to the league's best offense.

NHL Officials Go on Strike for Two Weeks

In a move unprecedented in NHL history, the game's on-ice officials went on strike on November 14, 1993, after they failed to hammer out a new contract with the league brass. For the next two weeks, the NHL continued its schedule with replacement officials from the various Canadian major junior leagues as well as professional minor leagues. On November 30, a new deal was struck and the veteran officials returned to action.

Replacement Officials

ThunderDome

Fans Flock to ThunderDome

After playing their initial NHL campaign at Expo Hall, a 10,400-seat facility, the Tampa Bay Lightning played the 1993-94 season in a new building, the ThunderDome, with a 28,000-seat capacity. Though the team was only moderately successful on the ice, it was a huge hit with Florida fans. The club set an NHL attendance record when 27,227 ticket-holders showed up for the home opener against their down-state rivals, the Panthers.

1993-94

- Sergei Fedorov (56-64-120) stars for the Wings.

- The Maple Leafs set an NHL record by starting off the season with 10 consecutive victories. They finish second in the Central thanks to Doug Gilmour (111 points) and Dave Andreychuk (53 goals).

- The Stars shine bright in Dallas, as Mike Modano scores 50 goals and the club finishes with 97 points.

- Brett Hull (57 goals) and Brendan Shanahan (52) lead St. Louis to a fourth-place finish in the Central Division.

- Jeremy Roenick (107 points) and goalie Eddie Belfour help Chicago finish three games over .500.

- Tie Domi (league-high 347 penalty minutes) and a fleet of tough guys can't help Winnipeg escape the Central cellar.

Dominik Hasek

VBK Leads Panthers to Record 33 Wins

Until very late in their inaugural season, the 1993-94 Florida Panthers were vying for a playoff spot in the Eastern Conference. A major reason for their outstanding freshman campaign was goalie John Vanbiesbrouck, who had the league's fourth-best GAA (2.53) and earned 21 of the team's 33 wins (tying Anaheim for most ever by an expansion team). VBK was a finalist for both the Hart Trophy and Vezina Trophy.

John Vanbiesbrouck

Wayne Gretzky

Gretzky Breaks Howe's Goal-Scoring Record

Revered in hockey as the "Great One" for much of his brilliant 15-year career, L.A.'s Wayne Gretzky finally became the game's greatest all-time goal-scorer when, on March 23, 1994, he rifled one past Vancouver goalie Kirk McLean on a set-up from longtime buddy Marty McSorley. The goal, No. 802 of his career, edged him past Gordie Howe, who had held the record since his retirement in 1979-80, the year Gretzky arrived on the NHL scene. Gretzky also led the league in scoring (38-92-130) and won the Lady Byng Trophy.

Hasek Comes to the Rescue

Early in the 1993-94 campaign, the Sabres lost Pat LaFontaine and goalie Grant Fuhr to bad knees, and many thought the season would be lost. Then Czech goalie Dominik Hasek stepped into the void left by Fuhr and was nothing short of spectacular. In 58 games, he chalked up a 30-20-6 record with a league-best 1.95 goals-against average. It was the first time in 20 years that an NHL goalie had a GAA under 2.00. Hasek was honored with the Vezina Trophy.

• Defenseman Al MacInnis (82 points) and three 40-goal scorers help Calgary go 42-29-13 and win the Pacific Division.

• Led by goal-scoring champ Pavel Bure (60-47-107), Vancouver finishes second in the Pacific Division, a game over .500.

• San Jose winds up three points behind Vancouver, as 5'7" Arturs Irbe sparkles in net.

• Terry Yake leads Anaheim in scoring with just 52 points, yet the expansion Ducks win 33 games and place fourth in the Pacific.

• Despite the heroics of Wayne Gretzky (38-92-130), the Kings fail to qualify for the playoffs one year after making it to the Finals. It is Gretzky's first-ever playoff shutout.

• The Oilers sink to the Pacific floor, as rookie Jason Arnott (33 goals) is one of few bright spots.

Modano's the Biggest Star in Dallas

Mike Modano spent four years in Minnesota trying—but failing—to live up to the expectations he brought as the first player picked in the 1988 Entry Draft. In 1993-94, the Detroit native finally fulfilled his promise, scoring 50 goals to lead the newly relocated Dallas Stars. Modano, a great skater with a tremendous shot, also notched 93 points for the second straight season.

Mike Modano

Scotty Bowman

Bowman Records His 1,000th Win

William "Scotty" Bowman coached some of the game's greatest players: Guy Lafleur in Montreal; Gilbert Perreault in Buffalo; Mario Lemieux in Pittsburgh; and, in 1993-94, a cast of Detroit stars including Steve Yzerman and Sergei Fedorov. Thus, it's no wonder Bowman became the game's winningest coach. In 1993-94, he reached the 1,000-win mark (including regular season and playoffs) with a 3-1 victory over Tampa Bay in early February.

Olympic Games

Sweden Wins Olympic Shootout

The 1994 Winter Games in Lillehammer, Norway, featured a hotly contested gold-medal game between Canada and Sweden. Tied 2-2 after regulation, the teams staged the first-ever Olympic shootout, during which Swedish goalie Tommie Salo (shown stopping Canada's Dwayne Norris) outdueled Canadian puck-stopper Corey Hirsch. Peter Forsberg scored during the shootout to give Sweden the final margin of victory.

1993-94

- Leading scorers include Wayne Gretzky (130), Sergei Fedorov (120), Adam Oates (112), and Doug Gilmour (111).

- Top goal-scorers are Pavel Bure (60), Brett Hull (57), Sergei Fedorov (56), and Dave Andreychuk (53).

- Divisional playoffs are abandoned. The top eight teams from each conference make the playoffs, with the No. 1 team facing No. 8, No. 2 meeting No. 7, etc.

- In the Eastern Conference quarterfinals, the Rangers embarrass the Isles (4-0), Washington survives Pittsburgh

(4-2), New Jersey squeaks by Buffalo (4-3), and Boston outlasts the Canadiens (4-3).

- In the Western Conference quarterfinals, San Jose shocks top-seeded Detroit (4-3), Toronto beats Chicago (4-2), and Dallas sweeps St. Louis (4-0). Vancouver wins its last three

Lake Superior State Lakers

Alan Eagleson

Jury Convicts Eagleson

Alan "The Eagle" Eagleson, chief architect of the NHL Players' Association, was the subject of a protracted investigation that culminated on March 3, 1994, when a United States Federal Grand Jury indicted him on 32 separate criminal charges, including fraud, racketeering, and obstructing justice. The Toronto-based lawyer was still fighting extradition procedures as the 1993-94 season came to an end.

Lakers Claim Another NCAA Title

The Lake Superior State Lakers won their third NCAA title in seven years when they crushed the Boston University Terriers 9-1 in the 1994 championship game. Laker sophomore Sean Tallaire was voted the tournament MVP. LSSU, which won the crown in 1988 and 1992, was the pride and joy of Sault Ste. Marie, Michigan—a sleepy town located in the state's Upper Peninsula.

Goalie Irbe, Sharks Play Cinderella

Thanks to the heroic performance of goalie Arturs "The Wall" Irbe, San Jose was the surprise of the 1994 playoffs, first by beating Central Division champion Detroit in the first round (in seven games), and then by stretching the Maple Leafs to seven games in the next series. Irbe made huge saves and refused to be intimidated by the bigger, more aggressive Detroit and Toronto clubs.

Western Conference Semifinals

games—in overtime—to upset Calgary (4-3).

• In the Eastern semis, the Rangers beat Washington in five while New Jersey—after dropping Games 1 and 2—roars back to beat the Bruins in six.

• In the Western semis, Toronto beats San Jose in Game 7, while the surprising Canucks roar past Dallas in five.

• New York defeats New Jersey in a seven-game Eastern Conference final, as Stephane Matteau scores the clincher in double overtime.

• In the Western finals, the favored Maple Leafs are stymied by the bigger, faster, more aggressive Canucks, who prevail in five games.

• Vancouver steals a win in New York in Game 1 of the Cup Finals, as Greg Adams scores in overtime.

Gilmour Piles Up the Playoff Points

Until his Maple Leafs were eliminated in the third round by Vancouver, Doug Gilmour (#93) was the leading scorer in the 1994 playoffs, notching 28 points in 18 games (including 22 assists). Playing on an injured ankle, the gritty centerman could muster just four points in the five-game semifinals, as Toronto lost four straight to the Canucks after winning Game 1 in overtime.

Doug Gilmour

Rangers Roar Back to Beat Devils

The Rangers trailed New Jersey in the 1994 Eastern finals. However, New York's Mark Messier and his former Edmonton teammates (including Esa Tikkanen, #10) proceeded to take over. New York won Game 6 on Messier's hat-trick and Game 7 on Stephane Matteau's goal in double O.T.

Eastern Conference Finals

Richter, Leetch Make Rangers Go

The Rangers gained their first berth in the Stanley Cup Finals since 1979 thanks largely to the play of goalie Mike Richter (pictured) and defenseman Brian Leetch (#2). Richter notched four shutouts (including two against the Isles in the opening round) and Leetch led all scorers (34 points) en route to the Conn Smythe Trophy. Leetch spoke on the phone to U.S. President Bill Clinton immediately after the Rangers won the Stanley Cup.

Eastern Conference Quarterfinals

1993-94

- New York wins Games 2 and 3 of the Finals, 3-1 and 5-1, as Glenn Anderson scores both game-winners. Down 2-0 in Game 4, the Rangers rally to win again, 4-2.

- With the Cup in sight, the Rangers lose Game 5 at home 6-3, as eight goals are scored in the third period.

- Vancouver wins Game 6 at home 4-1, as Geoff Courtnall and Jeff Brown each score twice.

- Back in New York, the Rangers take a 3-1 lead in Game 7 and hang on to win 3-2. They hoist the Stanley Cup for the first time in 54 years.

- Rangers defenseman Brian Leetch (34 playoff points) becomes the first American-born player to earn the Conn Smythe Trophy.

- Sergei Fedorov becomes the first Red Wing since Gordie Howe to win the Hart Trophy. He also wins the Frank Selke.

Western Conference Finals

Canucks Burn Leafs in Cup Semis

Leafs center Peter Zezel (#25, on knees) scored a pair of goals in the first game of the 1994 Western Conference finals against Vancouver, including the winner in sudden-death. However, Canucks goalie Kirk McLean (pictured) proceeded to slam the door, pitching shutouts in Games 3 and 4. Vancouver won the series four games to one, as McLean posted a 1.59 goals-against average in five games.

McLean Keeps Canucks in the Hunt

The general opinion during the 1994 playoffs was that the Canucks, seeded seventh in the Western Conference, would never have gotten past Calgary in the opening round, let alone all the way to the Finals, were it not for the brilliant goaltending of Kirk McLean. McLean pitched four shutouts in the early rounds and went toe to toe with New York netminder Mike Richter in the Finals.

Stanley Cup Finals

Stanley Cup Finals

Messier Knocks In the Big Goals

The Rangers rode the shoulders of captain Mark Messier (right) through a relatively easy first-round sweep of the Islanders, a slightly more challenging second-round set with the Capitals, and an extremely difficult seven-game war with the Devils, during which Mess predicted a Game 6 win and then delivered it with a hat trick. Messier also scored the Cup-clinching goal in Game 7 of the Finals, which New York won 3-2.

• Boston's Ray Bourque wins his fifth Norris Trophy, while Dominik Hasek takes the Vezina.

• Other trophy winners include Wayne Gretzky (Lady Byng), Cam Neely (Masterton), and New Jersey coach Jacques Lemaire (Jack Adams).

• During the gold-medal hockey match between Canada and Sweden in the 1994 Winter Games, a 2-2 deadlock ends in a shootout. Sweden's Peter Forsberg nets the winning goal.

• The Kamloops Blazers win the Memorial Cup, while London's Jason

Allison captures the Canadian Major Junior Player of the Year Award.

• Lake Superior State wins the NCAA title with a 9-1 win over Boston University in the finals, as Laker Sean Tallaire is tourney MVP. Minnesota-Duluth's Chris Marinucci wins the Hobey Baker.

In 1994-95, the NHL faced the real possibility that labor unrest could force the cancellation of the season. Despite weeks of negotiation, representatives of the NHL Players' Association and the league were unable to reach a settlement on a new collective bargaining agreement. Consequently, after the completion of the exhibition schedule on October 1, NHL owners locked out the players and waited for an agreement.

Both sides remained at a standstill despite numerous threats of "final offer" after "final offer." The most pressing issues separating the two sides were free agency, salary arbitration, entry-level salaries, the Entry Draft, and revenue sharing. With no real end in sight, players began to go back to juniors or flee to Europe to stay sharp during the interim, causing some bitterness among those not invited to Europe.

"I don't think it's right," Edmonton's Jason Arnott, who had narrowly missed winning the 1994 Calder Trophy, outspokenly said. "We're getting locked out. We're part of a union; we should get locked out together."

Finally, on January 11, after three months and 468 missed games, both sides hammered out a new deal allowing the players to

SHORTENED BY LOCKOUT; DEVILS COP STANLEY CUP

return to the ice. Since half of the season had been wasted, the 1995 schedule consisted of just 48 games. Perhaps Calgary captain Joe Nieuwendyk summed up the abridged schedule best: "Nobody wins in this situation. We lost. They lost. The fans lost."

While much of the attention on the ice during the shortened season focused on the triumphs in Detroit and the troubles with the New York Rangers, a quiet revolution was taking place in New Jersey under the direction of defensive genius Jacques Lemaire. The Devils had come within a double-overtime goal of reaching the Finals in 1994, and Lemaire had a surprise in store for his opponents in 1995. Lemaire employed the "neutral zone trap," which proved to be the most debated defensive maneuver in decades. Instead of focusing on his lack of offense, Lemaire concentrated on his hard-

working forwards, veteran mobile defensemen, and one of the top young goalies in the league, Martin Brodeur.

During the regular season, the Devils had only moderate success with the trap. New Jersey finished only four games over .500 and captured the fifth seed in the Eastern Conference playoffs. Lemaire remained confident that the tables would turn in the playoffs, when defensive hockey is the norm, not the exception. He was right.

Conn Smythe winner Claude Lemieux had the task of shadowing the NHL's top power forwards throughout the playoffs: Cam Neely, Jaromir Jagr, Eric Lindros, and Keith Primeau. Lemieux did more than just shut them all down; he outscored them 13-7 in 20 games.

The Devils smothered opponents in the playoffs. Even Scotty Bowman, whose Detroit Red Wings finally made it to the championship round, couldn't find a way to beat the heat of the New Jersey express. Lemaire's Devils, using purposeful forechecking, opportunistic scoring, and bone-rattling body-checking, buried the Motowners in four straight contests, outscoring the Wings 16-7. The Devils thus won the first Cup in the 21-year history of the franchise.

1994-95

- Citing fatigue and the inability to play up to his usual level, Mario Lemieux, 28, announces he will sit out the 1994-95 season.

- The NHL Hall of Fame inducts three men: Lionel "Big Train" Conacher, Harry Watson, and executive Brian O'Neill.

- Already a staple of two cable-TV networks (ESPN and espn-2), the NHL signs an exclusive over-the-air TV deal with Fox Sports.

- After a dozen years in Calgary, All-Star defenseman Al MacInnis is traded to St. Louis for Phil Housley.

- Barely a month after coaching the Rangers to a Stanley Cup, Mike Keenan leaves for St. Louis. NHL Commissioner Gary Bettman suspends Keenan for 60 days and fines him $100,000 for jumping to the Blues.

- Without a collective bargaining agreement in place between themselves

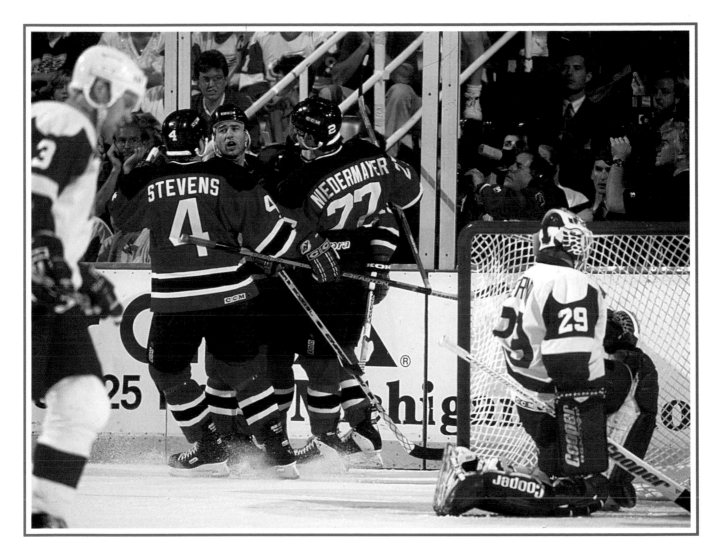

John MacLean (obscured by his jubilant teammates) scored just once during the 1995 Stanley Cup Finals. But his timely tally midway through the second period of Game 2 against Red Wings goalie Mike Vernon erased Detroit's 1-0 lead. New Jersey won the game 4-2 en route to a sweep of the Wings and the first Stanley Cup in franchise history.

and the Players' Association, NHL owners vote to lock the players out of camp, delaying the start of the season.

• Negotiations between the owners and the NHLPA last until late January 1995, when a new collective bargaining agreement is finally hammered out.

• On February 7, 1995, Pittsburgh's Joe Mullen becomes the first U.S.-born player to reach 1,000 points.

• On February 9, 1995, Philadelphia trades Mark Recchi to Montreal and acquires John LeClair, who joins Eric Lindros and Mikael Renberg to form the Legion of Doom Line.

• On March 8, 1995, Rangers winger Steve Larmer notches an assist in a 6-4 win over New Jersey for his 1,000th career point.

• In Minnesota, former North Stars scoring star Bill Goldsworthy announces he is suffering from AIDS.

Gary Bettman, Bob Goodenow

Lockout Ends in Time to Save the Season

NHL Commissioner Gary Bettman (left) and NHLPA boss Bob Goodenow (right) spent three months in heated negotiations before finalizing a new collective bargaining agreement and ending the lockout. The owners never did get the salary cap or luxury tax that they had wanted, but the players—desperate to return to the ice—yielded ground. Players now had to wait longer to become free agents.

Fox Sports

Six Captains Stripped of "C," Shipped Away

The truncated 1995 season was a dangerous time to wear the captain's "C," as no fewer than six squad leaders, including Pat Verbeek (pictured), were traded. Kevin Hatcher was traded by Washington to Dallas for Stars captain Mark Tinordi. Later in the year, Dallas traded Tinordi's successor, Neal Broten, to the Devils. Montreal shipped Kirk Muller to the Isles, and San Jose sent Bob Errey to Detroit.

Pat Verbeek

Fox Brings NHL Back to Network TV

At a September 1994 press conference, the NHL announced its agreement with Fox Sports to expand television coverage in the United States with an exclusive five-year, over-the-air broadcast deal. The NHL also revised its deal with ESPN, the cable television provider. The contract with FOX marked the return of NHL hockey to network TV for the first time in 20 years, with the 1995 All-Star Game as its debut.

1994-95

- On March 25, 1995, Red Wings coach Scotty Bowman records his 900th regular-season win as Detroit beats Vancouver 2-1.

- On April 17, 1995, L.A.'s Wayne Gretzky notches the 2,500th point of his career with an assist in a 5-2 loss to Calgary.

- Led by Paul Coffey's 58 points and Ray Sheppard's 30 goals, the Red Wings finish first overall in the NHL for the first time since 1964-65.

- Brett Hull notches 29 goals and 50 points in 48 games as St. Louis posts a 28-15-5 record, good for second place in the Central Division.

- Bernie Nicholls (23 goals) and Joe Murphy (22) pace the Blackhawks to a third-place finish in the Central.

- In his first year as a Maple Leaf, center Mats Sundin leads the fourth-place team in both goals (23) and points (47).

High-Scoring Olympic Line Powers Jets

The international Olympic Line of left wing Keith Tkachuk (left) from Massachusetts, right wing Teemu Selanne (right) from Finland, and Alexei Zhamnov from Moscow led the Jets in scoring in 1995. Zhamnov, the line's center, was the only NHLer with a five-goal game (April 1, 1995, against the Kings) and tied for third overall in goals (30). The trio combined for 74 goals and 164 points in 48 games.

Keith Tkachuk, Teemu Selanne

An American First: Mullen Reaches 1,000

On February 7, 1995, playing in the 935th game of his NHL career, Pittsburgh right winger Joey Mullen notched an assist during a 7-3 home loss to Florida. The point gave him 1,000 and made him the first U.S.-born player in league history to reach that estimable plateau. Mullen was a Stanley Cup champion with Calgary in 1989 before adding two more Cups with Pittsburgh ('91 and '92).

Joey Mullen

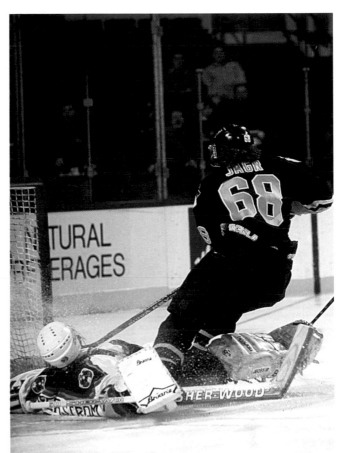

Jaromir Jagr

Globetrotting Jagr Leads in Scoring

During the three-month lockout, Jaromir Jagr found his way to the rosters of three other teams, in his native Czech Republic, Italy, and Germany. But it was his return to NHL action that launched one of his greatest performances. In 48 games, he notched 32 goals and 70 points. He tied Eric Lindros for most points and won the Art Ross Trophy on the basis of more red lights, 32 to 29.

• Dave Gagner leads Dallas in scoring (42 points). Despite just 17 wins, the club makes the playoffs.

• Winnipeg wastes a brilliant performance by their Olympic Line of Alexei Zhamnov (65 points), Keith Tkachuk (51), and Teemu Selanne (48) to finish out of the playoff picture.

• Theo Fleury is the league's seventh-leading goal-getter (29) and sixth overall scorer (58 points). His Flames win the Pacific Division at 24-17-7.

• Vancouver, led by Pavel Bure's 20 goals and 43 points, finishes second in the Pacific Division at 18-18-12.

• The Sharks finish third in the Pacific Division, thanks to veterans Ulf Dahlen and Craig Janney.

• The Nordiques are the Eastern Conference's top team thanks to Joe Sakic (62 points), rookie Peter Forsberg (50 points), and Owen Nolan (30 goals).

Long-Shot Larmer Scores 1,000th Point

Madison Square Garden

Before joining the Rangers in 1993, Steve Larmer was known first as a long-shot draft pick (120th overall in 1980) who blossomed into a regular 40-goal threat and second as an NHL iron man, playing in 884 consecutive games. On March 8, 1995, Larmer again carved his name in the record books when he notched the 1,000th point of his career, an assist in a Rangers 6-4 home win over New Jersey.

Oh, Brother! NHL Is Filled with 'Em

The NHL was a family game in 1995 with more than a dozen brother acts: Rob and Scott Niedermayer (pictured); Neal and Paul Broten; Pavel and Valeri Bure; Geoff and Russ Courtnall; Gord and Kevin Dineen; Derian and Kevin Hatcher; Brett and Eric Lindros; Kelly, Kevin, and Kip Miller; Boris and Dmitri Mironov; Keith and Wayne Primeau; David and Joe Sacco; Kevin and Ryan Smyth; Darrin and Darryl Shannon; and Brent, Rich, and Ron Sutter.

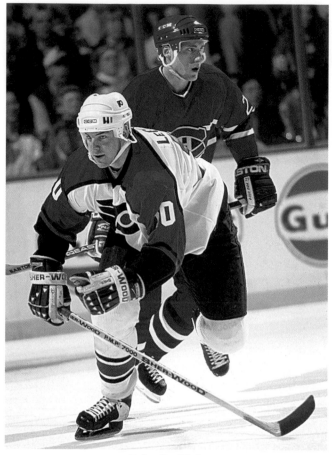

John LeClair

LeClair Spells Doom for Philly's Foes

In search of a complementary finisher for Eric Lindros, the Flyers pulled off a blockbuster deal with Montreal, sending Mark Recchi north for power-play quarterback Eric Desjardins and budding power forward John LeClair (pictured). In no time, LeClair, Lindros, and sophomore Mikael Renberg formed the Legion of Doom Line, with LeClair notching 25 goals in 37 games and the line chalking up 176 points.

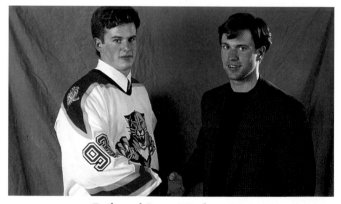

Rob and Scott Niedermayer

1994-95

- The Penguins take second in the Northeast Division, as Jaromir Jagr wins the scoring title with 70 points (32 goals).

- Boston rides the playmaking of Adam Oates (53 points) and goaltending of rookie Blaine Lacher to secure third place in the Northeast Division.

- Buffalo goalie Dominik Hasek dominates again while snipers Alexander Mogilny (47 points) and Donald Audette (24 goals) lead the attack for the fourth-place Sabres.

- Eric Lindros powers the Flyers to first place in the Atlantic Division with 70 points, but he loses the scoring title

to Jaromir Jagr on a goals-scored tiebreaker.

- The Devils get 23 goals from Stephane Richer and brilliant goaltending from Martin Brodeur to finish second in the Atlantic Division at 22-18-8.

Rookie Kariya Lights It Up for Ducks

A former Hobey Baker Award winner as the top U.S. college player, Anaheim's Paul Kariya made the NHL All-Rookie team in 1995 with a 39-point season (in 47 games). He led all freshmen in goals (18) and was the only rookie in the league to lead his team in scoring. Only Peter Forsberg of Quebec (the Calder Trophy winner) notched more points (50) than the Ducks' lightning-quick left winger.

Wayne Gretzky

Gretzky Now Up to 2,500 Career Points

On April 17, 1995, during a 5-2 loss to Calgary, Kings defenseman Rob Blake ripped a power-play goal. The set-up man, Wayne Gretzky, who in the course of his career had taken offensive genius to unprecedented levels, earned an assist on the goal and thus became the first man in NHL history to rack up 2,500 career points. Many believe this is a mark that will never be approached, let alone surpassed.

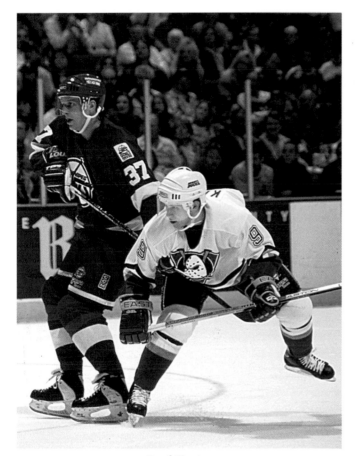

Paul Kariya

• Rookie goalie Jim Carey has the NHL's third-best GAA (2.13), and Peter Bondra leads the league in goals (34), as Washington takes third in the Atlantic Division.

• A year after winning the Stanley Cup, the Rangers finish one game under .500 (22-23-3) and narrowly gain the final playoff berth in the Eastern Conference.

• In the Eastern Conference quarter-finals, the Rangers upset Quebec (4-2), Philadelphia beats Buffalo (4-1), Pittsburgh ousts Washington (4-3), and New Jersey shells Boston (4-1).

• In the Western Conference quarter-finals, Detroit beats Dallas (4-1), San Jose upsets Calgary (4-3), Vancouver shocks St. Louis (4-3), and Chicago tips Toronto (4-3).

• In the Eastern semifinals, the Flyers sweep the Rangers in four while New Jersey plucks the Penguins in five.

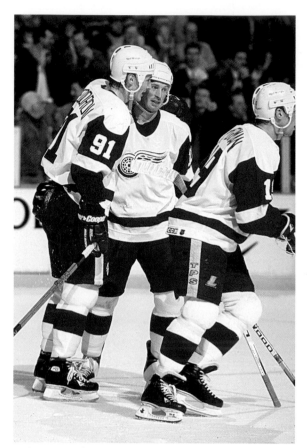

Sergei Fedorov, Doug Brown, Steve Yzerman

Wings Top the League Standings

The Detroit Red Wings, led by Sergei Fedorov (left), Doug Brown (center), and Steve Yzerman (right), finished atop the NHL standings in 1995 for the first time in 30 years, with 33 wins in 48 games. The last time the Hockeytown sextet topped the league charts was in 1964-65, when Norm Ullman led the league with 42 goals and the club won 40 of its 70 regular-season games.

Lindros Cops Hart and Pearson as Game's MVP

Many fans felt that, with 70 points in just 46 games, Eric Lindros (pictured) should have won the Art Ross Trophy over Pittsburgh's Jaromir Jagr (70 points in 48 games), though Lindros lost on the basis of goals scored (32 to 29). Still, Lindros won the respect of writers and colleagues when he captured both the Hart Trophy and the Lester Pearson Award as the game's most valuable player.

Eric Lindros

Eastern Conference Quarterfinals

Underdog Rangers Slay the Nordiques

One year after winning their first Stanley Cup in 54 years, the New York Rangers barely qualified for the 1995 playoffs. However, as the eighth seed in the Eastern Conference, they played David to Quebec's Goliath in the first round and pulled a dramatic upset with a six-game elimination of the regular-season conference champs. The Nordiques subsequently packed their bags and moved to Denver.

1994-95

- In the Western semifinals, the Red Wings hook the Sharks in four straight while Chicago sweeps Vancouver.

- The Eastern Conference finals see the Devils and Flyers take turns winning on the road before New Jersey finally reverses the trend, winning Game 6 and the series (4-2).

- The Red Wings need five games to dispatch the surprising Blackhawks in the Western Conference finals, which features three overtime finishes.

- In the Finals, the Devils employ their defensive "trap" style of defense to neutralize Detroit's powerful attack, winning in Motown 2-1 and 4-2.

- The Devils return to New Jersey with a two-game series lead, then put the final touches on the Red Wings with a pair of 5-2 victories. For the first time in their 21-year existence (dating back to their origins as the Kansas City Scouts and Colorado Rockies), the Devils win the Stanley Cup.

Eastern Conference Finals

Clutch-Shooting Lemieux Cops the Conn Smythe

Due to the lockout and the delayed start to the season, the Stanley Cup was not decided until June 24, the latest an NHL game had ever been played. However, the summer season wasn't nearly as hot as Devils right winger Claude Lemieux, who ripped 13 goals—three of them game-winners. Lemieux led the Devils with 65 shots, and his clutch scoring eventually earned him the Conn Smythe Trophy as playoff MVP.

Claude Lemieux

Devils Roast Flyers in Eastern Finals

In the Eastern Conference finals, the Devils and Flyers took turns winning away from home. In Game 5, Flyers goalie Ron Hextall (shown stopping Stephane Richer) faced 32 shots and was often brilliant. He kept his Flyers in a 2-2 tie until the final minute of regulation, when playoff hero Claude Lemieux scored at 19:15 of the third period to give New Jersey the win. The Devils took Game 6 to win the series.

Brodeur Posts 1.67 GAA in Playoffs

Devils goalie Martin Brodeur became a candidate for playoff MVP honors when he allowed the powerful Red Wings just seven goals in the four-game Finals. Indeed, Brodeur ultimately concluded the playoff season with a microscopic 1.67 goals-against average, giving up 34 goals in 20 games. On his goaltending, New Jersey swept the Finals and lost only four games throughout the playoffs.

Martin Brodeur

- Devils winger Claude Lemieux wins the Conn Smythe Trophy as playoff MVP with 13 goals, three of them game-winners.

- Dominik Hasek wins the Vezina Trophy for the second consecutive season.

- Classy Pittsburgh center Ron Francis earns the Frank Selke Trophy for his outstanding defensive play as well as the Lady Byng Trophy for his sportsmanship.

- Detroit's Paul Coffey takes his third Norris Trophy as the league's top defenseman.

- Quebec center Peter Forsberg wins the Calder Trophy, narrowly edging Washington goalie Jim Carey.

- Eric Lindros grabs the Hart Trophy and the Lester B. Pearson Award.

- Boston University wins the NCAA title with a 6-2 win over Maine.

ROY, SAKIC, AVALANCHE FREEZE OUT FLORIDA

Changes abounded for the 1995-96 season, as more than 150 NHL players changed sweaters. The most noteworthy trade occurred when the L.A. Kings traded Wayne Gretzky in February to St. Louis, where he joined Brett Hull. Gretzky, discouraged by the Kings' poor play, had demanded to be traded, and after much speculation Gretzky was dealt to Mike Keenan's Blues for a handful of prospects.

Midway through the year, the Jets flew Teemu Selanne, the NHL's top rookie in 1993, to the Anaheim Mighty Ducks. The "Finnish Flash" teamed with Paul Kariya, a player with Hart Trophy potential.

Back in Canada, the Canadiens had been facing internal turmoil since missing the playoffs in 1994-95. In Montreal, losing is simply unacceptable. After starting the 1995-96 season with five straight losses, the Habs fired GM Serge Savard and coach Jacques Demers, replacing them with Rejean Houle and Mario Tremblay. Both were former players, but neither had front-office experience. The most vocal opponent of the changes was Patrick Roy, the league's top goalie and an idol among fans in Montreal.

Finally, on December 2, the ill feelings and bitter sentiments came to a head. In a game against Detroit, Tremblay kept Roy in net despite the Red Wings slamming nine goals behind him. When Roy did get yanked, he marched to the bench, turned to Canadiens President Ron Corey, and told him he was quitting the team, claiming Tremblay had humiliated him. Two days later, Roy and team captain Mike Keane were dispatched to Colorado.

Roy and the Avalanche surprised hockey purists who thought the Red Wings, who set an NHL record with 62 victories during the regular season, would find their way back to the Stanley Cup Finals. But the Motowners collided with an Avalanche of talent from Colorado in the Western Conference finals and limped back to Detroit after learning a six-game lesson.

There was, however, more to the Avalanche than Roy. Joe Sakic was the team's offensive sparkplug while Peter Forsberg was a stylish playmaker with speed, tenacity, and a killer instinct. And the Avalanche had also acquired feisty Claude Lemieux, the playoff MVP in 1995.

The Avalanche's road to the Finals was rocky, with each series lasting six games, including four sudden-death affairs against Chicago. But once they reached the Finals, Colorado dispatched the Florida Panthers in four straight games, including an 8-1 thrashing in Game 2 in which Forsberg recorded a hat-trick in the first period.

In Game 4, it was goalies Roy and John Vanbiesbrouck who emerged as stars. In a 104-minute scoreless marathon—the longest scoreless game in Stanley Cup Finals history—it took a blast from the blueline by rearguard Uwe Krupp to give Colorado a 1-0 victory and the Cup.

Sakic, the heart and soul of the Avalanche, led all playoff scorers with 18 goals and set a new playoff record with six game-winners. Colorado became the fifth team in the last five years to hoist the Cup, which gave the fans in Denver a whole new Rocky Mountain high.

1995-96

- After finishing the 1994-95 season atop the Eastern Conference, the Quebec Nordiques move to Denver and become the Colorado Avalanche.

- On August 2, 1995, longtime TV broadcaster Brian Smith, a former NHL player, is shot and killed outside the CJOH-TV studio in Ottawa.

- After a year of rest, Mario Lemieux records the 500th goal of his career on October 26, 1995.

- On November 6, 1995, Hartford assistant coach Paul Maurice, 28, replaces fired coach Paul Holmgren, thus becoming the youngest head coach in professional sports.

- New York's Mark Messier scores his 500th goal vs. the Flames on November 6, 1995.

- On December 6, 1995, only days after vowing never to play for Montreal again, superstar goalie Patrick Roy is traded to Colorado.

Overcoming a valiant effort from the Florida Panthers (the Cinderella team of the 1996 playoffs), the Colorado Avalanche swept to the NHL championship by riding the shoulders of their peerless captain, Joe Sakic. Sakic led all postseason scorers with 18 goals and 34 points in 22 games. Six of Joe's goals were game-winners, which contributed to his choice as playoff MVP.

• On December 13, 1995, Detroit's Paul Coffey becomes the first NHL defenseman to record 1,000 helpers.

• Toronto's Doug Gilmour reaches 1,000 points on December 23, 1995.

• On January 17, 1996, Detroit superstar Steve Yzerman scores his 500th goal, beating Colorado's Patrick Roy in a 3-2 win.

• On January 18, 1996, the NHL approves the sale of the Winnipeg Jets. The team will move to Arizona.

• On January 31, 1996, the Blues' Dale Hawerchuk scores the 500th goal of his career, against the Maple Leafs.

• In a year of huge deals, the Jets and Ducks join the melee. Teemu Selanne joins Paul Kariya in Anaheim while Oleg Tverdovsky and Chad Kilger, touted youngsters, go to Winnipeg.

Mario Turns a Trick, Nets 500th Goal

In a triumphant return to action after a year of rest and recuperation following cancer treatment, Pittsburgh superstar Mario Lemieux resumed his assault on NHL goalies with a brilliant 69-goal output. On October 26, 1995, "Super Mario" became the 20th player in league history to score 500 goals, reaching his magical milestone with a characteristic three-goal performance during a 7-5 win over the Islanders.

Mario Lemieux

Pavel Bure, Alexander Mogilny

For Messier, 500 Goals Is as Easy as 1, 2, 3

Rangers squad leader Mark Messier, the only player in NHL history to captain two different franchises to Stanley Cup championships, earned another major honor on November 6, 1995. Mess ripped a dramatic hat-trick against visiting Calgary goaltender Rick Tabaracci to reach 500 career goals. In so doing, Messier (shown with all three pucks) became the 21st player to reach the hallowed mark.

Mark Messier

Bure Blows a Knee; Mogilny Nets 55

Vancouver and Buffalo cut a major deal in July 1995. Michael Peca and Mike Wilson, two top prospects, were shipped to the Sabres for goal-scoring ace Alexander Mogilny, whom the Canucks planned to team with Pavel Bure. Unfortunately, Bure suffered a severe knee injury just 15 games into the year. Undaunted, Mogilny went on to score 55 goals.

1995-96

- On February 14, 1996, Kings winger Tony Granato undergoes brain surgery to remove an intracranial hematoma resulting from a headlong crash into the boards during a recent game.

- Winnipeg's Deron Quint ties an NHL record with two goals in four seconds on December 15, 1995.

- Wayne Gretzky is traded from the Kings to St. Louis to help the Blues in their playoff hunt.

- The Montreal Forum closes its doors on March 11 following a 4-1 Canadiens win over Dallas. The Habs move into the Molson Centre.

- St. Louis goalie Grant Fuhr appears in 76 straight games.

- Toronto's Larry Murphy becomes the fourth rear guard to notch 1,000 points on March 27, 1996.

- On March 29, 1996, former NHL scoring ace Bill Goldsworthy, 51,

Fuhr Plays in 76 Straight, Wins No. 300

On November 30, 1996, future Hall of Fame goalie Grant Fuhr, winner of five Stanley Cups and a Vezina Trophy, won the 300th game of his career with a 4-1 victory in Winnipeg. Fuhr finished the 1995-96 season with a league-high 79 games played—including 76 straight from the start of the season. Only a knee injury in the final week of the campaign prevented him from perhaps playing all 82 games.

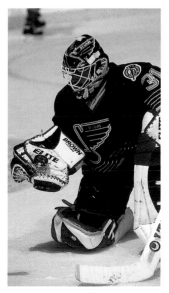

Grant Fuhr

Paul Coffey

Coffey Notches His 1,000th Assist

On December 11, 1996, during a 3-1 win over Chicago, defenseman Paul Coffey, already the highest-scoring rear guard in NHL history, became the first backliner ever to record 1,000 assists. His milestone helper came on a set-up of Igor Larionov's first-period goal. Shortly after, Coffey received a congratulatory phone call from former teammate Wayne Gretzky, who was 730 helpers ahead of Coffey at the time.

Patrick Roy

Roy Heads for the Mountains, Wins 300th Game

The year was full of ups and downs for goalie Patrick Roy. After an embarrassing 11-1 shelling by Detroit, the Montreal goalie feuded with management and demanded a trade. Shipped to Colorado, Roy, 30, later notched his 300th career triumph with a 7-5 win over Edmonton. He was the 12th goalie in NHL history to notch 300 victories and the second youngest ever—just months older than all-time wins leader Terry Sawchuk.

---

succumbs to complications resulting from his long bout with AIDS.

• The Red Wings set an NHL record with 62 victories en route to a second straight Presidents' Trophy.

• Chris Chelios leads the Blackhawks in assists (58) and points (72) and takes the team to second place in the Central Division with 40 wins.

• Swedish sensation Mats Sundin powers the Leafs to a third-place finish in the Central Division.

• Despite the presence of scoring legends Wayne Gretzky (102 points) and Brett Hull (43 goals), the Blues do no better than fourth in the Central.

• Led by Keith Tkachuk (50 goals, 98 points), the Jets make the playoffs.

• The Dallas Stars bring up the rear of the West, though Mike Modano leads the way in goals (36) and points (81).

Granato Needs Surgery After Horrific Crash

Feisty Kings winger Tony Granato began to experience headaches in late January 1996 after crashing into the boards. After he checked himself into a Los Angeles-area hospital, tests revealed an intracranial hematoma. Surgery was performed at UCLA Medical Center, and in a four-hour procedure the hematoma was removed. Of course, Granato sat out the remainder of the season.

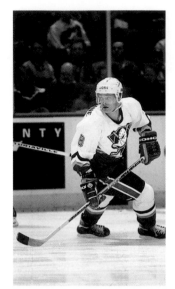

Teemu Selanne

Newest Duck Selanne Racks Up 108 Points

In perhaps the biggest trade of the year, Winnipeg shipped their "Finnish Flash," Teemu Selanne, to Anaheim with Marc Chouinard for Oleg Tverdovsky and Chad Kilger. Selanne, a right winger, quickly teamed up with Paul Kariya to give the Mighty Ducks one of the most lethal one-two combinations in the league. The dynamic duo finished in a tie for seventh overall with 108 points each.

Tony Granato

Steve Yzerman

Yzerman Joins Howe in 500 Club

Detroit's Steve Yzerman, the longest-serving team captain of his era, cemented his entry into the Hall of Fame on January 17, 1996, when he scored his 500th goal, beating Colorado's Patrick Roy in a 3-2 home win. Yzerman and Gordie Howe are the only players in NHL history to score 500 goals for the Red Wings, although much-traveled Dino Ciccarelli scored his 500th NHL goal as a Wing in 1993-94.

1995-96

- The first-year Avalanche take the Pacific Division title with 47 wins, as Joe Sakic is third in the NHL in points (120) and Peter Forsberg is fifth (116).

- Despite an overall losing record, Calgary rides the shoulders of Theo Fleury (46 goals, 96 points) to second place in the Pacific Division.

- Vancouver gets 55 goals from Alexander Mogilny (third best in the league) but barely squeaks into the playoffs with a 32-35-15 record.

- Anaheim boasts two high scorers in Paul Kariya (50 goals) and Teemu Selanne (108 points), but the Ducks miss the playoffs.

- The Oilers miss the playoffs for the fourth straight year despite a 104-point performance from Doug Weight.

- Without Wayne Gretzky, the L.A. Kings finish 16 games under .500.

- San Jose occupies the last spot in the conference, winning just 20 games.

Young Kariya Emerges with 50 Goals

The 1995-96 Mighty Ducks scored 234 goals, and 50 of them came from speedy Paul Kariya, playing in just his second NHL season. Indeed, Kariya finished with 108 points, meaning he had a hand in nearly half of the Ducks' tallies. At 21, he was the youngest 50-goal scorer since Craig Simpson notched 56 goals for the 1987-88 Oilers. For his excellence and sportsmanship, Kariya won the Lady Byng Trophy.

Dale Hawerchuk

Paul Kariya

Ducky Does It for Grandma: No. 500

Center Dale Hawerchuk joined elite company on January 31, 1996, when, playing for St. Louis before a hometown Toronto crowd that included his beloved grandmother, he notched the 500th goal of his illustrious career. "Ducky" beat Maple Leafs goalie Felix Potvin during a 4-0 win.

- In the East, the Flyers get 115 points from Eric Lindros (sixth overall) and 51 goals from John LeClair (fifth) and lead the conference with 103 points.

- The Rangers win 41 games and take second place in the Atlantic Division, as 35-year-old Mark Messier finishes with 47 goals and 99 points.

- The surprising Florida Panthers, led by Ray Sheppard (37 goals) and Scott Mellanby (70 points), finish third in the Atlantic Division.

- Washington's Peter Bondra leads the Caps with 52 tallies (fourth overall), helping Washington to the playoffs.

- Tampa Bay finishes fifth in the Atlantic and earns a playoff berth.

- One year after winning the Stanley Cup, the Devils fail to make the playoffs despite a 37-33-12 record.

- The Islanders (22 wins) waste Ziggy Palffy's 43-goal, 87-point effort.

Ozzie Shines in Net, Scores a Goal

Brilliant at "both" ends of the rink, Detroit goalie Chris Osgood enjoyed a 21-game unbeaten streak en route to 62 wins in 1995-96, most in NHL history. On March 6, 1996, in a 4-2 win at Hartford, "Ozzie" shot the puck into the Whalers' empty net in the closing moments, becoming the third goalie in league history to score a goal.

Brett Hull, Wayne Gretzky

Hull, Gretzky Not Enough for Blues

Two of the greatest goal-scorers of their era, Brett Hull and Wayne Gretzky, were united on the Blues late in the 1995-96 season after the "Great One" was traded by the Kings for Craig Johnson, Patrice Tardif, and Roman Vopat. To the Blues' disappointment, even Gretzky (who led the team in playoff points) could not get St. Louis past the second round of the postseason, where they lost to Detroit in seven games.

Chris Osgood

- In the Northeast, Pittsburgh wins 49 games and the division title. Scoring champ Mario Lemieux (161 points), Jaromir Jagr (149), and Ron Francis (119) finish in the top four overall.

- Ray Bourque (82 points) leads Boston to second in the Northeast at 40-31-11.

- The superstar trio of Pierre Turgeon (96 points), Vincent Damphousse (94), and Mark Recchi (78) leads Montreal to third in the Northeast.

- Hartford misses the playoffs, making high-scoring captain Brendan Shanahan (44 goals) miserable.

- Though their goalie, Dominik Hasek, leads the league in save percentage (.920), the Sabres drop out of playoff contention with 73 points.

- The Senators finish last in the NHL with 18 wins. Rookie Daniel Alfredsson is a bright spot with 26 goals.

Andreychuk Joins Devils, Hits a Grand

On March 13, 1996, veteran left winger Dave Andreychuk, with 990 points to his career resume, was traded by Toronto to New Jersey for a draft pick. Three weeks later, on April 7, Dave scored against the Rangers to notch his 10th point in a Devils uniform. It was also the 1,000th point of his career, making him the third player of the year to reach the millennium mark, and the 46th ever.

Larry Murphy

Murphy Joins Three Backliners with 1,000 Points

One of the most underrated players in NHL history, defenseman Larry Murphy, while skating with Toronto (his fifth team), became only the fourth rear guard ever to notch 1,000 points (along with Paul Coffey, Ray Bourque, and Denis Potvin). His historic moment came on March 27, 1996, with a goal in the Leafs' 6-2 whipping of the Canucks.

Dave Andreychuk

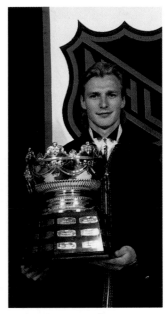

Sergei Fedorov

High-Scoring Fedorov Wins Another Selke

Combining relentless speed and agility, Detroit center Sergei Fedorov finished the 1995-96 season as the Red Wings' top scorer in all three offensive categories (39 goals, 68 assists, 107 points). Moreover, he won praise around the league for his checking. When hardware was distributed, Fedorov took home his second Frank Selke Trophy in three years.

• In the Eastern Conference quarterfinals, Florida stuns Boston (4-1), the Rangers oust Montreal (4-2), Pittsburgh stops Washington (4-2), and Philadelphia outlasts Tampa Bay (4-2).

• In the Western Conference quarterfinals, Chicago sweeps Calgary (4-0), Colorado whips Vancouver (4-2), Detroit beats Winnipeg (4-2), and St. Louis survives Toronto (4-2).

• In the Eastern semifinals, the Penguins overcome the Rangers in five games while the Panthers stun the Flyers in six games, winning two of the last three in sudden-death.

• In the Western semifinals, Colorado eliminates Chicago in six games (four of which go to OT). Detroit wins Game 7 against St. Louis on a dramatic Steve Yzerman overtime clincher.

• In the Eastern Conference finals, Florida upsets the Penguins, winning Game 7 3-1 in Steeltown.

Chris Chelios

Upstart Cats Blow Past Boston in Five

In just their third NHL season, the Panthers earned a playoff berth with the fourth-best record in the Eastern Conference, which pitted them against Boston, the fifth seed. In a shocking turn of events, the heavily favored Bruins managed just one win (a 6-2 face-saver in Game 4) before being eliminated by the Cats in Game 5. Florida winger Scott Mellanby (#27) used his size to dominate the slot.

Eastern Conference Quarterfinals

Chelios Takes Home His Third Norris Trophy

In the 43-year history of the Norris Trophy, only three men have been named the NHL's best defensemen for two different clubs. Doug Harvey won it six times in Montreal and once with the Rangers. Paul Coffey won it twice with Edmonton and once in Detroit. In 1996, Chris Chelios (winner of the 1989 Norris with the Habs) won the award for the third time, his second with his hometown Blackhawks.

Eastern Conference Semifinals

Flyers Not Tough Enough for Panthers

The Eastern Conference semifinals between Florida and Philadelphia were full of surprises. The Panthers, led by such veterans as Dave Lowry (right), stood up to the big, tough Flyers. In Game 5, the Cats battled to a 1-1 tie in regulation, then scratched and clawed until Stu Barnes scored at 8:05 of double-overtime to give the Panthers a 2-1 win. The Flyers were eliminated in Game 6, losing 4-1 in Miami.

1995-96

• Colorado beats Detroit in six heated affairs in the Western finals.

• In the Stanley Cup Finals, Colorado pours it on in Denver, beating Florida 3-1 and 8-1.

• On home ice, Florida builds a 2-1 lead in the first period of Game 3 but cannot hold back the Avs, who get second-period goals from Mike Keane and Joe Sakic and win 3-2.

• Fighting for their hockey lives in Game 4, Florida forces Colorado to a scoreless tie through regulation and two periods of overtime. Colorado's Uwe Krupp scores at 4:31 of triple-OT to win the Cup. Avs goalie Patrick Roy stops 63 shots.

• Joe Sakic sets an NHL playoff record with six game-winning goals and leads all postseason scorers with 34 points in 22 games. He wins the Conn Smythe Trophy.

Florida Shocks the Penguins in East Finals

The rejuvenated Mario Lemieux and emerging superstar Jaromir Jagr were expected to end Florida's storybook playoff run in the Eastern Conference finals. But the Panthers, playing solid defense and exploiting every offensive opportunity, shut down Lemieux and Jagr and stunned the Penguins. The series went seven games before Florida took the deciding contest, 3-1 in Pittsburgh.

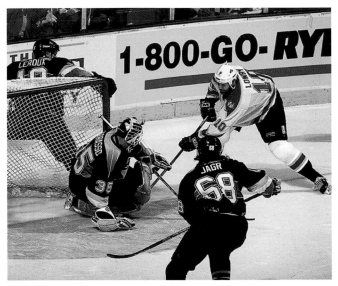

Eastern Conference Finals

Krupp Wins Cup with Goal in Triple-OT

Colorado simply had too much talent for Florida in the Finals, even though the Panthers, on the goaltending of John Vanbiesbrouck, played every game (with the exception of an 8-1 Game 2 shellacking) close. After three straight losses, the Cats played bravely in Game 4. The game was deadlocked at 0-0 until triple-overtime, when this shot from Uwe Krupp eluded Vanbiesbrouck and gave the Avs the Stanley Cup.

Avs Punch Out the Wings in West Finals

In a vicious series that boiled with bad blood, the Avalanche and Red Wings traded punches, high sticks, elbows, and goals for six grueling games before Colorado earned its first trip to the Stanley Cup Finals. Claude Lemieux was ejected from Game 6 for checking Kris Draper face-first into the boards. Draper later underwent facial surgery while the Red Wings, as a team, licked their playoff wounds.

Western Conference Finals

Stanley Cup Finals

- In a storybook finish to a miraculous comeback, Mario Lemieux wins his third Hart Trophy and fourth Lester B. Pearson Award.

- Washington goalie Jim Carey wins the Vezina Trophy with 35 wins, a 2.26 GAA, and nine shutouts.

- Chicago's Chris Chelios wins his third Norris Trophy. Gary Roberts, who returns to action after a serious neck injury, wins the Masterton.

- Ottawa's Daniel Alfredsson takes the Calder Trophy, while Paul Kariya, with 108 points and 20 penalty minutes, wins the Lady Byng.

- Detroit coach Scotty Bowman wins the Jack Adams Award for the second time, while his ace center, Sergei Fedorov, wins his second Frank Selke.

- The University of Michigan wins its eighth NCAA titile with a 3-2 overtime win over Colorado College.

Once the New York Rangers ended their 54-year curse in 1994, the Detroit Red Wings became the team with the longest Stanley Cup drought. But in 1997, for the first time in 42 years, the Wings finally presented the Cup to the fans of Hockeytown.

Losing in the 1996 conference finals following a record-setting 62-win season left a bitter taste in the mouths of the Wings. In 1996-97, coach Scotty Bowman decided to alternate his goaltenders and try MVP forward Sergei Fedorov on defense during the 1996-97 season. Bowman's carefully constructed plan, which centered on a defense-first concept, worked to perfection.

"Scotty could pull those guys out of a tailspin anytime he wants to," coach Ken Hitchcock, whose improved Dallas Stars wound up beating Detroit for the regular-season Central Division title, said in March. "He doesn't want to—yet."

To help bolster the team's chemistry for the 1996-97 season, the Wings acquired two key players. Brendan Shanahan arrived in a trade from Hartford for holdout Keith Primeau and Paul Coffey. And rear guard Larry Murphy, booed out of Toronto, proved he still had life in his 36-

AFTER 42 YEARS, CUP IS BACK IN HOCKEYTOWN

year-old legs by providing veteran leadership from his post on the blueline. Shanahan and Murphy aided 14-year Wings captain Steve Yzerman, providing the leadership needed to win Lord Stanley's mug.

Before the playoff field had been narrowed to two teams, the NHL lost one of its greatest players and box-office attractions when Philadelphia knocked Pittsburgh out of the playoffs in the first round. After overcoming Hodgkin's disease and a chronically bad back during his career, scoring sensation Mario Lemieux announced he was retiring following the season. Lemieux said he had enough of the clutching and interference that had now become an everyday activity in the NHL.

In his swansong season, Lemieux exited like a champion, winning his sixth scoring title and second in a row with a league-leading 122 points. Shortly after

he hung up his skates, the Hockey Hall of Fame announced that Lemieux would be inducted into the Hall without serving the three-year waiting period.

Meanwhile, a heated rivalry between the Colorado Avalanche and the Wings had evolved over the past two years, including "Fight Night at The Joe" on March 26, 1997. Four battles took place that evening, including one involving Detroit goalie Mike Vernon bloodying Colorado goalie Patrick Roy. The two teams met again in the Western Conference finals. After the Wings dominated the opener but lost 2-1, they rolled off three straight, capped off by a 6-0 romp in a 236-minute penalty-fest.

The Wings' next opponent was Philadelphia, which had advanced after eliminating the New York Rangers in five games, only to be ousted in four games by the Wings. The Flyers could blame Conn Smythe winner Vernon for their demise. Bowman decided to start the veteran netminder after Chris Osgood stood between the pipes for a majority of the regular season. Vernon proved to be the right choice after he stopped 102 of 108 shots in the Finals and allowed the Motor City a chance to quench its 42-year thirst from the Cup.

1996-97

- The Winnipeg Jets move to Phoenix, where they become the Coyotes.

- In September, Team USA wins the first-ever World Cup of Hockey title. They claim a 5-2 win over Canada in Game 3 of the best-of-three final. Rangers goalie Mike Richter is tournament MVP.

- Following a brief stint in St. Louis, Wayne Gretzky signs with the Rangers, reuniting with Mark Messier.

- In August 1996, Chicago trades its holdout superstar, Jeremy Roenick, to Phoenix for playmaking ace Alexei Zhamnov.

- Just 13 games into the season, Buffalo's Pat LaFontaine is knocked out for the year with post-concussion syndrome—a growing problem in the NHL.

- In a December 1996 tilt, Wayne Gretzky passes the unprecedented 3,000-point mark (including play-

The last time the Detroit Red Wings won the Stanley Cup (1955), they were led by such luminaries as Terry Sawchuk, Gordie Howe, Red Kelly, Ted Lindsay, Marcel Pronovost, and Alex Delvecchio. During a "dry spell" from 1967 to 1983, they made it to the playoffs twice in 17 years. In the spring of 1997, Motor City once again became known as "Hockeytown" thanks to Steve Yzerman and Co.

offs)—2,639 points in the regular season, 362 points in the postseason.

• On December 22, 1996, Brett Hull scores his 500th career goal, joining father Bobby in the 500 club.

• With injuries to both Tom Barrasso and Ken Wregget, the Penguins turn to rookie goalie Patrick Lalime, who begins his NHL career with a 14-0-2 record.

• Mario Lemieux, who will retire after the season, notches the 600th goal of his career with a tally against Vancouver on February 4, 1997.

• Detroit coach Scotty Bowman wins his unprecedented 1,000th regular-season game on February 9, 1997.

• In mid-March 1997, Pittsburgh's Joe Mullen (the first-ever American) and Devil Dave Andreychuk become the 25th and 26th players, respectively, to join the 500-goal club.

USA, Richter Rev It Up in World Cup

With controversy swirling around Canada Cup founder Alan Eagleson, a new summer tournament—the World Cup of Hockey—was introduced in 1996. Led by New York Rangers goalie Mike Richter (shown with his MVP gift, a Harley-Davidson motorcycle), Team USA pulled off a huge upset. It defeated Canada in the championship round, two games to one, with a stunning 5-2 victory in Game 3.

Mike Richter

Ziggy Cheers Up the Isles with 48 Goals

Although the Islanders struggled all year and finished near the bottom of the league standings, one bright star was sharp-shooter Ziggy Palffy, whose 48 goals led the team and placed him fifth in the NHL. A terrific skater with great puck skills, Ziggy also notched 90 points, tying him (with Penguin Ron Francis) for eighth overall. Six of Ziggy's goals were game-winners.

Wayne Gretzky

Gretzky Takes Scoring Magic to Broadway

After a short—and far from sweet—stint in St. Louis, free-agent superstar Wayne Gretzky signed a contract in 1996 with the New York Rangers. He reunited with old pals Mark Messier, Esa Tikkanen, and Jeff Beukeboom from his Oilers days and with Luc Robitaille from his years in L.A. The "Great One" was a huge hit on Broadway, leading the Blueshirts in assists (72) and points (97).

Ziggy Palffy

1996-97

- Colorado, led by goalie Patrick Roy's NHL-best 38 wins, takes the Presidents' Trophy as the league's regular-season champ (107 points).

- Teemu Selanne (109 points) and Paul Kariya (99)—second and third overall in the NHL—help Anaheim finish second in the Pacific Division.

- For the first time in five years, the Oilers are back in the playoffs, as Doug Weight (82 points) and Ryan Smyth (39 goals) lead the way.

- The Canucks miss the playoffs for the first time in seven years, as Alex Mogilny (31 goals) and Pavel Bure (23) fail to deliver.

- Despite respectable defense (2.87 goals against), the Flames miss the playoffs with a fifth-place division finish.

- The up-and-coming L.A. Kings show promise, but they struggle to a sixth-place Pacific Division finish.

Hot News: Hockey Moves to Desert

After dodging the relocation bullet once, the Winnipeg Jets finally picked up and left Manitoba in 1996. New owner Richard Burke installed his team, renamed the Coyotes, into the America West Arena in downtown Phoenix, bringing NHL hockey to another previously unheard-of region of North America—namely, the desert. Sporting a new look, the Yotes treated their fans to a third-place finish.

Brendan Shanahan

Shanahan: New Wings Scoring Ace

Known and respected around the NHL for his grit and dedication to winning, Brendan Shanahan (center) began the 1996-97 season in Hartford. His public wish for a trade made him a goat in the eyes of Whalers fans even though he had selflessly led the club in scoring the previous year. Shanny got his wish on October 9, 1996, when he was swapped to Detroit for Red Wings holdout Keith Primeau. He led Detroit in goals (47) and points (88).

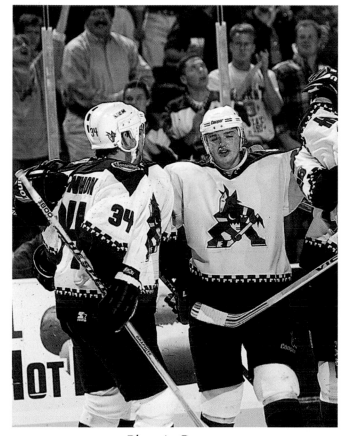

Phoenix Coyotes

- San Jose misses the playoffs despite a 31-goal showing from Owen Nolan and the late-season acquisition of goalie Eddie Belfour.

- The Central Division title goes to Dallas, which wins a franchise-record 48 games. Mike Modano (35 goals) leads the way.

- Brendan Shanahan (47 goals) and goalie Mike Vernon, who notches his 300th career win, help the Red Wings take second in the Central at 38-26-18.

- In a successful first-run in Arizona, the Coyotes get 52 goals from Keith Tkachuk and finish third in the division.

- The Blues survive coach Mike Keenan (who is fired) to finish fourth in the Central. They get a 42-goal performance from Brett Hull and 73 games from goalie Grant Fuhr.

- Chicago rides Tony Amonte's 41 goals to fifth place in the Central Division—and a playoff berth.

Patrick Lalime

Brett Joins His Old Man in 500 Club

One of the most prolific goal-scorers of his era, Brett Hull made his permanent mark in the record books on December 22, 1996, during a 7-4 win over the visiting L.A. Kings, when he scored his 500th NHL goal. The 24th man in league history to score 500, Brett did it 26 years after his father, Bobby Hull, netted his own 500th. This made them the only father-son combo in this hallowed scoring category.

Rookie Lalime Starts Out Career 14-0-2

When injuries knocked both of their starting goalies (Tom Barrasso and Ken Wregget) out of the lineup, the Pittsburgh Penguins reached down to the farm and brought in rookie Patrick Lalime, who had never played in the NHL before. In his first 16 games, he was unbeatable, going 14-0-2. He finished the year with a 21-12-2 record and a 2.94 GAA in 39 games, earning a spot on the NHL All-Rookie Team.

Brett Hull

Pat LaFontaine

LaFontaine Knocked Out for Season

A troubling epidemic of serious concussion injuries around the NHL claimed one of the game's most prominent stars when Buffalo center Pat LaFontaine was knocked out of the lineup just 13 games into the season. Thanks to a vicious elbow from 6'6" Penguins defenseman Francois Leroux, LaFontaine, who is 5'10", sat out virtually the entire season, with his future very much in doubt.

1996-97

- Toronto misses the playoffs with a 30-44-8 season, as Mats Sundin (41 goals) is not enough.

- On the strength of goalie Martin Brodeur's league-leading 1.88 goals-against average, the Devils take the Atlantic Division title with 104 points.

- The Flyers enjoy a 50-goal outburst from John LeClair and 79 points in just 52 games from Eric Lindros and miss the Atlantic title by one point.

- The Panthers continue to rely on team defense, winning 35 games without a 30-goal scorer.

- Wayne Gretzky and Mark Messier take the Rangers to a 38-34-10 record, as Gretzky ties for fourth in league scoring with 97 points.

- For the first time since 1982, Washington misses the playoffs, blowing a 46-goal display from Peter Bondra.

Scotty Bowman

Vernon Wins 300th Before Playoff Joyride

Veteran goalie Mike Vernon, who won a Stanley Cup in Calgary (1989), was a "backup" to Chris Osgood for most of the 1996-97 season. He played in only 33 games and chalked up just 13 wins, although his 12th victory of the year put him in the elite company of 300-game winners. In the play-offs, Vernie was Detroit's go-to man, playing in all 20 games, winning the magic 16, and taking MVP honors.

Mike Vernon

Another Mark for Bowman: Win No. 1,000

Already the most successful coach in NHL history, Scotty Bowman carved another notch in his legendary record with his 1,000th regular-season victory. It came on February 8, 1997, when the Red Wings defeated Pittsburgh 6-5 in overtime, with help from a Brendan Shanahan hat-trick. Bowman finished the campaign with 1,013 wins and an impressive .659 career winning percentage in 1,736 games.

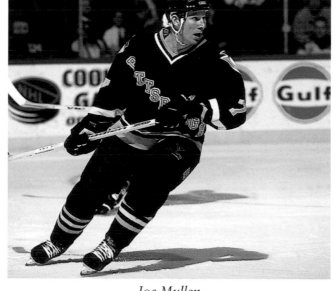

Joe Mullen

Mullen: First American to Net 500 Goals

From the mean streets of New York's Hell's Kitchen district all the way to NHL stardom, the journey of speedy winger Joe Mullen took on legendary propor-tion on March 14, 1997, when he beat Colorado goalie Patrick Roy for his 500th career goal. In so doing, Mullen (a three-time Stanley Cup champ) became the first American-born NHLer to join this fraternity and guaranteed him a spot in the Hall of Fame

---

- Tampa Bay is back on the sidelines despite 35 goals from veteran Dino Ciccarelli.

- The Islanders miss the postseason, but the good news is that Ziggy Palffy (48 goals) and rookie defenseman Bryan Berard are for real.

- Behind brilliant goalie Dominik Hasek, the Sabres win the Northeast Division at 40-30-12.

- The Penguins boast three of the NHL's top-10 scorers—Mario Lemieux (122 points), Jaromir Jagr (95), and Ron Francis (90)—and finish second in the Northeast.

- For the first time in five years, the Senators earn a playoff spot, going 31-36-15. Alexei Yashin (35 goals, 75 points) leads in scoring.

- Montreal drops to fourth in the division, as Vince Damphousse (81 points) and Mark Recchi (34 goals) provide leadership.

Raymond Bourque

Lemieux Bids Adieux after Goal No. 600

Mario Lemieux

The brilliant career of Mario Lemieux, interrupted so often by injury and illness, appeared to end in 1997. Before retiring, the courageous Penguins captain notched his 600th career goal (on February 4, 1997) and won his sixth Art Ross Trophy, finishing his 12th NHL season with 122 points. The "Magnificent One" left with 613 goals and 1,494 points in just 745 games—a ratio of 2.01 points per game. He also won a pair of Stanley Cup titles. Lemieux would make a stunning return in 2000.

Bourque Joins Coffey with 1,000 Assists

Some of the greatest names in hockey have come through Boston, including Bobby Orr, Phil Esposito, Eddie Shore, and Milt Schmidt. Defenseman Raymond Bourque joined that elite company. On March 27, 1997, he became the fifth player in NHL history (and the second defenseman after Paul Coffey) to notch 1,000 career assists. He also became the all-time leading scorer on the Bruins.

Brian Leetch

Leetch Takes Home Second Norris Trophy

Known more for his grace than his brawn, Rangers defenseman Brian Leetch (shown administering a classic hip check) led all NHL rear guards in scoring in 1996-97 with 78 points. He was also a plus-31. For his tremendous two-way play, Leetch was rewarded with the second Norris Trophy of his career. He first won the top-defenseman award in 1991-92, when he notched a career-high 102 points.

1996-97

- In a sad finale, the Whalers finish their last year in Hartford as a bust. Their top three scorers (Geoff Sanderson, Andrew Cassels, and Derek King) are destined to be dealt.

- For the first time in 30 years, the Bruins (26-47-9) fail to make the playoffs, as Jozef Stumpel's team-high 76 points are nothing more than a farewell performance.

- Mario Lemieux wins his sixth scoring title (122 points) while Keith Tkachuk leads the league in goals (52). The Rangers' Brian Leetch tops all defensemen with 78 points.

- In the Eastern Conference quarterfinals, the Devils crush Montreal (4-1), the Flyers eliminate Pittsburgh (4-1), the Rangers tame the Panthers (4-1), and Buffalo survives Ottawa in overtime (4-3).

- In the Western Conference quarterfinals, Colorado beats Chicago (4-2)

Selanne Pots 51, One Off the League Lead

Only four players managed to reach the 50-goal plateau in 1996-97, including Mario Lemieux and John LeClair (50 each). Coyote winger Keith Tkachuk led the way with 52 red lights, and Mighty Ducks sniper Teemu Selanne was sandwiched in this group with 51. Selanne finished second in the NHL with 109 points, 10 ahead of teammate Paul Kariya.

Teemu Selanne

Edmonton Oilers

Sabres Stars Take Home the Hardware

The Buffalo Sabres enjoyed a terrific season, topping the Northeast Division and advancing to the Eastern Conference semifinals before the Flyers ousted them. Much of their success was due to these three stars: goaltender Dominik Hasek, who won his third Vezina Trophy in four years; Michael Peca, winner of the Selke Trophy as the NHL's top defensive forward; and Ted Nolan, the NHL's coach of the year.

Dominik Hasek, Michael Peca, Ted Nolan

Oilers Stun the Stars in First Round

A once mighty playoff power, the Oilers fell on hard times in the 1990s, missing the postseason four years in a row (1993-96). In the spring of 1997, as the seventh seed in the Western Conference, the Oilers—led by Doug Weight and Ryan Smyth—took on the second-seeded Dallas Stars. What many felt would end quickly took seven games to decide, with the Oilers grabbing the thrilling finale 4-3 in sudden-death.

and Detroit ousts St. Louis (4-2), while Edmonton shocks Dallas (4-3) and Anaheim edges Phoenix (4-3).

• In the Eastern semis, the Rangers upset the Devils in five after losing Game 1. The Flyers make quick work of Buffalo, dulling the Sabres in five.

• In the Western semis, the Red Wings take three games in overtime en route to a four-game sweep of Anaheim. Colorado drills the Oilers in six.

• In the Eastern Conference finals, the Flyers dispatch their ancient rivals, the Rangers, in five hard-fought games.

• In the Western finals, the Wings and Avalanche renew their heated rivalry and trade body blows—including back-to-back 6-0 whippings of each other—before Detroit wins in six.

• In Game 1 of the Stanley Cup Finals, the Red Wings defeat the Flyers on the road 4-2.

Lindros Sends Mario Home Empty-Handed

Flyers captain Eric Lindros, feeling the heat to deliver in his third trip to the playoffs, faced a major challenge in the Eastern Conference quarterfinals against veteran Penguins superstar Mario Lemieux. Lindros matched Lemieux in goals (three each) and outpointed the future Hall of Famer nine to six. The Flyers advanced with a five-game victory over their cross-state rivals.

Eric Lindros, Mario Lemieux

Eastern Conference Finals

Flyers Are Too Tough for Mess, Gretzky

The Rangers, armed with Mark Messier (#11) and Wayne Gretzky, figured to give Eric Lindros (left) and his Flyers a run for their money in the Eastern Conference Finals. However, Lindros notched nine points (including five goals) in the five-game series, and the latest round in this bitter rivalry went to the Flyers.

1996-97

- The Red Wings take Game 2—also in Philly—when Kirk Maltby breaks a 2-2 tie in the second period and Brendan Shanahan makes it 4-2 in the third.

- Back in Hockeytown for Game 3, the Red Wings are unstoppable, ripping six goals against Ron Hextall

in a humiliating 6-1 victory and a 3-0 series lead.

- In Game 4, defenseman Nick Lidstrom gives Detroit a 1-0 lead with 33 seconds left in the first period. Darren McCarty scores the eventual winner as the Wings prevail 2-1 to complete the sweep.

- For the first time since 1955, the Red Wings are Stanley Cup champions. Their goalie, Mike Vernon, wins the Conn Smythe Trophy.

- Buffalo goalie Dominik Hasek earns the Hart Trophy, the Vezina Trophy, and the Lester B. Pearson Award.

Shanahan's Shot Sends the Wings on Their Way

Anxious to avenge their embarrassing sweep by New Jersey in the 1995 Finals, the Red Wings stormed the championship round. After beating the Flyers 4-2 in Game 1, Detroit jumped to a quick lead when Brendan Shanahan (left) scored just 1:37 into Game 2, which the Red Wings took 4-2. On home ice, the Red Wings took the next two games, 6-1 and 2-1, to sweep the stunned Flyers and win the Cup.

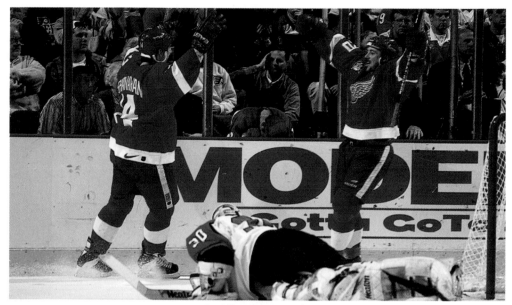

Stanley Cup Finals

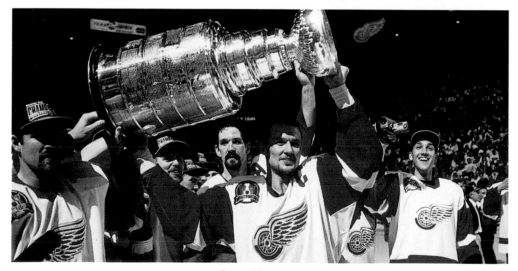

Steve Yzerman

Wings' Drought Finally Ends After 42 Years

Not since Ted Lindsay enjoyed the honor in 1955 had a Red Wings team captain hoisted the Stanley Cup. On June 7, 1997, squad leader Steve Yzerman, captain since 1986, broke the 42-year drought with a victory lap around Joe Louis Arena following the team's four-game sweep of the Flyers.

- Tony Granato of the San Jose Sharks, who returns to action from life-threatening brain surgery a year ago, earns the Masterton Trophy for perseverance and sportsmanship.

- Rangers superstar Brian Leetch accepts his second Norris Trophy, while Anaheim's Paul Kariya takes home his second straight Lady Byng Trophy.

- Buffalo center Michael Peca cops the Frank Selke Trophy, while his boss, Ted Nolan, wins the Jack Adams.

- Bryan Berard, who had refused to play for Ottawa when drafted first overall in 1995, wins the Calder Trophy for the Islanders.

- The NHL announces expansion plans, with Nashville, Atlanta, Columbus, and Minneapolis-St. Paul to join the league in stages from 1998-99 through 2000-01.

Ever since Swedish superstar Ulf Sterner crossed the Atlantic and had a brief sojourn with the New York Rangers in the mid-1960s, the NHL has had a taste of distinct international flavor. However, some may argue that it wasn't until the 1997-98 season that the NHL truly became a global league, especially when the league shut down for two weeks in February to allow its players to compete in the Winter Olympic Games.

The international dominance of the NHL reached record heights in 1997-98. Seven of the league's top 11 scorers—including the first three—were European trained. Jaromir Jagr won his second scoring crown with 102 points, while Teemu Selanne, Pavel Bure, and Peter Bondra all climbed the 50-goal plateau. In a year when the league suffered a power shortage unlike any since the days of Eddie Shore, the league's most exciting players came from across the pond in Europe.

Still, the story of the 1997-98 season was dominated by defense, defense, and goaltender Dominik Hasek. The dwindling goal totals were a topic of concern for the entire season, with an average of only 5.3 goals scored per game, the lowest total in 42 years.

HASEK COPS GOLD MEDAL AND SECOND HART TROPHY

Only Jagr was able to break the century mark in points, while the leading scorer for 17 of the league's 26 teams failed to average a point per game. In reality, the NHL has always feasted on its strengths. In the 1980s, the NHL was stocked with slick-skating forwards with a knack for fancy footwork and picture-perfect plays. In the 1990s, the NHL's strength is goaltending, and a visible reduction in offensive output is the result.

And as goaltending goes, no one can match the heroics of Hasek, known as "The Dominator." The on-ice antics of the Sabres' elastic acrobat from the Czech Republic are well documented, but he put together back-to-back seasons that are statistically breathtaking. In 1997-98, Hasek recorded 13 shutouts, the most by any goaltender since Tony Esposito

blanked the opposition 15 times in 1969-70.

At the end of his glorified season, Hasek was awarded his second consecutive Hart Trophy as league MVP, making him the only goaltender in NHL history to accomplish the feat. But perhaps Hasek's greatest triumph was his outstanding display during the 1998 Olympics. Hasek stonewalled the opposition and led the underdog Czech Republic team to an upset gold-medal victory over Russia.

Hasek hoped to cap off his incredible season with the Stanley Cup. However, one obstacle standing in the way of Hasek's Sabres and the Cup were the surprising Washington Capitals, who were more than Buffalo could handle during the Eastern Conference playoffs.

Three of the Capitals' four wins over Buffalo needed overtime, including the finale. Speedster Joe Juneau knocked home a loose puck past Hasek six minutes into extra time, sending the Capitals to the Finals against the reigning-champion Detroit Red Wings. The Wings won the first three games by one goal each, then copped the Game 4 finale 4-1 for their second straight Stanley Cup.

1997-98

- Just days after winning the 1997 Stanley Cup, Detroit defensemen Vladimir Konstantinov is critically injured in a limo crash.

- Mark Messier leaves the Rangers to sign a free-agent contract with the Canucks.

- On October 3, 1997, the NHL season begins in unique fashion. Anaheim and Vancouver play a two-game set in Nagano, Japan, as a lead-in to the upcoming Winter Olympics.

- On October 26, 1997, Rangers center Wayne Gretzky records his 1,851st career assist, giving him more

helpers than any other NHLer in history has total points.

- On November 8, 1997, Washington's Phil Housley becomes the fifth defenseman to reach 1,000 points.

- On December 14, 1997, Phoenix right winger Mike Gartner becomes

The best goalie in the NHL, Dominik Hasek (center) proved he was also the best goalie in the world when he took his Czech Republic team to an Olympic gold medal in Nagano, Japan, during the 1998 Winter Games. Hasek starred in a thrilling 2-1 shootout victory over Canada in the semifinals before capping off the two weeks of high drama with a classic 1-0 victory over Russia in the gold-medal game.

the fifth player in NHL history to score 700 career goals, beating Detroit's Chris Osgood in a 3-3 tie.

• Jari Kurri (Colorado) and Dino Ciccarelli (Florida) become the eighth and ninth players in NHL history, respectively, to score 600 goals.

• On December 27, 1997, Florida goalie John Vanbiesbrouck becomes only the second U.S.-born goalie in league history to record 300 career wins (joining Tom Barrasso).

• After a lengthy holdout, Anaheim's Paul Kariya returns and is January's Player of the Month—only to be knocked out for the year with a concussion on February 1.

• The NHL suspends play for over two weeks in February to allow many of its stars to play in the Olympics.

• In upsets at the Olympics, Canada and USA are shut out of medal play.

Hurricanes Blow Into Carolina

One of the four World Hockey Association teams to merge into the NHL in 1979, the Hartford Whalers struggled with dwindling fan support through the late 1980s and into the 1990s, eventually forcing ownership to consider relocation. That move came after the 1996-97 campaign—their fifth straight out of the playoffs. In the fall of '97, the club reemerged in Greensboro, North Carolina, as the Carolina Hurricanes.

Carolina Hurricanes

Tom Barrasso

U.S.-Born Barrasso Wins 300th

In 1983-84, goalie Tom Barrasso won both the Calder and Vezina Trophies. Fourteen years and two Stanley Cups later, Barrasso, born in Boston, became the first American-born netminder in NHL history to record 300 regular-season wins when he stopped Florida 4-1 on October 19, 1997. A week later, he passed Maple Leafs legend Turk Broda (302) on the all-time wins list.

1997-98

- NHL star Dominik Hasek leads his Czech Republic team to a gold-medal win over Russia.

- The U.S. women's Olympic team defeats the Canadians to win the gold.

- The Carolina Hurricanes tender a multimillion-dollar offer sheet to free-agent holdout Sergei Fedorov, sparking the Red Wings to ink their Russian superstar to a new deal.

- With a goals-against average of 1.89, Devils netminder Martin Brodeur wins his second William Jennings Trophy (for the goalie whose team surrenders the fewest goals).

- Six NHLers notch their 1,000th point: Adam Oates, Phil Housley, and Dale Hunter of the Caps, Pat LaFontaine (Rangers), Luc Robitaille (Kings), and Al MacInnis (Blues).

- Mark Messier (Vancouver) and Ron Francis (Pittsburgh) reach 1,000 career assists.

Madison Square Garden Scoreboard

Three Caps Rack Up 1,000 Points

The Washington Capitals enjoyed a unique circumstance in 1997-98 when three of their veteran stars—Adam Oates, Phil Housley, and Dale Hunter—reached the 1,000-point plateau. Oates reached 1,000 with a goal in early October. Housley, the second U.S.-born player and the fifth defenseman to join the club, did it in November. Hunter delivered his memorable point in January.

Adam Oates, Phil Housley

Great One Out-Assists Howe's Points

The most brilliant player ever to strap on skates, Wayne Gretzky achieved yet another milestone on October 26, 1997. He notched his 1,851st regular-season assist, giving him more helpers than any other player in league history had points, eclipsing the NHL's second all-time points leader, Gordie Howe (1,850). The "Great One" had only one mark left: Howe's record for most goals, 975 (WHA and NHL).

Mess Leaves Broadway for Canucks

Though he later would admit he left a piece of his heart and soul in Manhattan, fiery captain Mark Messier, who had led the Rangers to a Stanley Cup in 1994, departed Broadway for Vancouver after a simmering contract dispute with GM Neil Smith. The only NHLer ever to captain two different teams to playoff championships, Messier was immediately named Canucks captain, replacing longtime leader Trevor Linden.

Mark Messier

- Penguin Jaromir Jagr grabs his second scoring title and is the league's only 100-point player (35 goals, 102 points).

- With Joe Nieuwendyk leading all Canadian-born players in goals (39), the Stars rise to the top of the NHL standings with a 49-22-11 record.

- Detroit demonstrates superior team play and finishes second in the Central at 44-23-15.

- St. Louis comes together under coach Joel Quenneville—and the goaltending of Grant Fuhr (2.53 GAA) and Jamie McLennan (2.17) —to grab third place in the Central.

- The Coyotes get 40 goals from injury-plagued Keith Tkachuk to narrowly gain a playoff berth.

- Following an 0-7 start, Chicago gets 31 goals each from Tony Amonte and Eric Daze but misses the playoffs for the first time in 29 years.

Vanbiesbrouck Joins Barrasso in 300 Club

On December 27, 1997, goalie John Vanbiesbrouck of the Panthers recorded his 300th career win, joining fellow American Tom Barrasso as the only U.S.-born netminders in NHL history to reach this prestigious mark. A New York Ranger for nine seasons, "Beezer" returned to New York for the momentous win, victimizing his old nemeses, the Islanders, with a 6-2 beating.

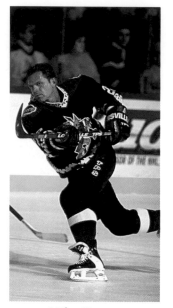

Mike Gartner

John Vanbiesbrouck

Gartner Pots 700th Goal, Then Retires

One of the classiest players of his era, sniper Mike Gartner played 19 years and 1,432 games and never won a Stanley Cup. Still, he placed his name in Hall of Fame contention with brilliant goal-scoring, which culminated on December 14, 1997, when he ripped the 700th tally of his career, a feat matched by only four other men in NHL history. He retired in 1998 with 708 goals and 1,335 points.

Pat LaFontaine

Still Tickin', LaFontaine Cracks 1,000

After several concussions (the most recent of which cost him all but 13 games in 1996-97), Pat LaFontaine was told his services were no longer required in Buffalo. He signed with the Rangers (his third team in New York State) and, on January 22, 1998, scored against Flyers goalie Garth Snow for his 1,000th career point. Only two American-born skaters (Joe Mullen and Phil Housley) had reached the mark before him.

1997-98

- Toronto continues its backward slide, wasting Mats Sundin's 33 goals.

- Colorado's Peter Forsberg finishes second overall in scoring (91 points), and Patrick Roy notches 31 of the club's wins, as the Avalanche win the Pacific Division at 39-26-17.

- The Kings return to the playoffs after a four-year layoff. Jozef Stumpel finishes with 79 points, 10th overall.

- The speedy Oilers acquire Billy Guerin from New Jersey and take third in the Pacific Division on Doug Weight's 70 points and goalie Curtis Joseph's eight shutouts.

- The Sharks take the final playoff berth in the Western Conference thanks largely to goalie Mike Vernon (2.46), who notches 30 wins.

- A late-season surge cannot catapult the low-scoring Flames out of fifth place in the Pacific Division.

LeClair Nets 50 for Third Straight Year

If Eric Lindros didn't play in Philadelphia, many feel left winger John LeClair would be a candidate for league MVP honors. In 1997-98, the hard-shooting power forward from St. Albans, Vermont, banged out 51 goals, making him the first American-born player to record three straight 50-goal seasons (he had 51 in 1995-96 and 50 in 1996-97). In 1997-98, LeClair also led the Flyers in points (87).

John LeClair

Jagr: Only NHLer with 100 Points

With the retirement of Mario Lemieux after the 1997 playoffs, a new period began in Pittsburgh in 1997-98—the Jaromir Jagr era. Feared around the NHL for his power and puck-handling skill, Jagr was called the most dangerous one-on-one player in the game. He finished the year with his second scoring title and was the only NHLer with more than 100 points (102).

Luc Robitaille

"Slow-Footed" Robitaille Hits a Grand

Once considered too slow for the NHL, Luc Robitaille proved that hard work can support natural talent. In 1997-98, during his second tour of duty with the Kings, "Lucky" became the 51st player in league history to notch 1,000 points, thanks to his two assists in a 5-3 win over Calgary on January 29, 1998. One of the highest-scoring left wingers ever, Robitaille continued his march toward the Hall of Fame.

Jaromir Jagr

• Teemu Selanne has a brilliant year, sharing the league lead for goals (52). But without Paul Kariya, the Mighty Ducks finish at 26-43-13.

• Even a tremendous season from Pavel Bure (51 goals, 90 points) cannot keep the trade-torn Canucks from finishing at 25-43-14.

• The Devils ascend to the top of the Eastern Conference with 107 points, as Martin Brodeur wins 43 games with 10 shutouts.

• John LeClair becomes the first U.S.-born player to notch three straight 50-goal seasons, helping Philly take second in the Eastern Division.

• The Capitals ride the massive shoulders of Olie "The Goalie" Kolzig (33 wins), and get 52 goals from Peter Bondra, to grab third in the Eastern Division.

• Islander Ziggy Palffy pots 45 goals, but the team misses the playoffs.

Belfour: 1.88 GAA for NHL's Top Club

The Dallas Stars finished atop the NHL regular-season standings in 1997-98 for the first time in franchise history (including 26 years in Minnesota), thanks to the brilliant goaltending of free-agent acquisition Eddie Belfour. "Eddie the Eagle" set a club record with 37 wins (second in the NHL) and led the league with a 1.88 goals-against average, his best career mark.

Sergei Fedorov

Fedorov Signs Huge Deal to Stay Put

After winning a Stanley Cup, Sergei Fedorov, the league MVP in 1993-94, sat out the start of the 1997-98 season when contract negotiations with Detroit management broke down. A restricted free agent, Fedorov eventually signed a $28 million offer sheet with Carolina, which was quickly matched by Detroit. Fedorov played just 21 games, but he then led all playoff goal-scorers (10) as he helped the Red Wings repeat.

Eddie Belfour

1997-98

- Wasting a brilliant 90-point show from Wayne Gretzky (third overall), the Rangers stumble to fifth in the Eastern Division.

- The Panthers grab Ray Whitney (33 goals, 65 points) on waivers, but they finish at 24-43-15.

- A season in disarray sees Tampa Bay finish last overall in the NHL at 17-55-10, their worst year ever.

- Playing a new system of team defense, the Penguins rally behind scoring ace Jaromir Jagr and take the top spot in the Northeast Division with 40 wins.

- The Bruins finish second in the Northeast as youngster Jason Allison (83 points) complements legendary defenseman Ray Bourque (48 points).

- Buffalo unites behind all-world goalie Dominik Hasek and takes third place in the Northeast Division.

Samsonov: The Best of Boston's Rooks

The Boston Bruins boasted two first-round picks in the 1997 Entry Draft—Joe Thornton (first overall) and Sergei Samsonov (pictured; eighth). While both players joined the Bruins, it was the 19-year-old Samsonov, already a veteran of 73 pro games in Detroit (IHL), who made the bigger impact. In 81 NHL games, the speedy left winger scored 22 goals, colleted 47 points, and took home the Calder Trophy.

Dominik Hasek

The Dominator Shuts Down Flyers in First-Round Series

The Flyers had home-ice advantage in their opening-round playoff series against Buffalo, but the Sabres had four-time Vezina Trophy winner Dominik Hasek in goal. Hasek not only foiled the Flyers' lesser scoring threats, like Colin Forbes (#12), but he also shut down the big guns—Eric Lindros (one goal), John LeClair (one), Rod Brind'Amour (two)—as the Sabres pulled off a shocking five-game upset.

Sergei Samsonov

• Mark Recchi leads Montreal in goals (32) and points (74) and netminder Andy Moog stars in his final NHL season.

• The Senators gain a playoff berth as Alexei Yashin notches 33 goals and the team shines defensively.

• The Carolina Hurricanes are the only team in the Northeast Division not to make the playoffs, ending their first season in the South at 33-41-8.

• In the Eastern Conference quarter-finals, major upsets see Ottawa stun New Jersey (4-2) and Buffalo rip Philadelphia (4-1), while Montreal takes Pittsburgh (4-2) and Washington stops Boston (4-2).

• In the Western Conference quarters, Edmonton shocks Colorado (4-3), Dallas takes San Jose (4-2), Detroit ousts Phoenix (4-2), and St. Louis sweeps Los Angeles.

Eastern Conference Quarterfinals

Eighth Seed Ottawa Shocks the Devils

Doug Gilmour took first-place New Jersey into the Eastern Conference playoffs against the eighth-seeded Senators and led the club in scoring with five goals and seven points. Unfortunately for "Killer" and the Devils, they could not solve goaltender Damian Rhodes—who got help from the crossbar in this Game 5 encounter. In the biggest upset of the playoffs, Ottawa took the series four games to two.

Olie Kolzig

Wings Fight Off Dallas in West Finals

In their quest to defend the Stanley Cup, the Red Wings had to take a route through Dallas, where the Stars—winners of the Presidents' Trophy—waited to knock them off in the Western Conference finals. With a heroic performance from Darren McCarty (#25), who chipped in with some timely goal-scoring in addition to his usual hard hitting, the Red Wings edged Dallas in a hard-fought, six-game conference finals.

Western Conference Finals

"The Goalie" Leads Caps to the Finals

Washington's Olie "The Goalie" Kolzig was a brick wall during the 1998 Stanley Cup playoffs, giving up just 13 goals in a six-game victory over Boston, seven more (including two shutouts) during a five-game spanking of Ottawa, and 11 more as the Caps took six games to eliminate Buffalo. Kolzig outdueled Buffalo's Dominik Hasek in a classic battle of netminders and led Washington to the Finals for the first time ever.

1997-98

• In the Eastern Conference semis, the Capitals knock off the Senators (4-1) and the Sabres sweep Montreal.

• The Western Conference semis see Detroit slam the Blues (4-2) and Dallas avenge its 1997 playoff loss to Edmonton (4-1).

• In the Stanley Cup semifinals, Washington knocks off the Sabres (4-2) and the Red Wings shut down Dallas (4-2).

• Detroit takes the first two games over Washington in the Cup Finals, 2-1 and 5-4, winning the second affair on Kris Draper's overtime goal.

• Sergei Fedorov scores his playoff-leading 10th goal with 4:51 to play in Game 3, breaking a 1-1 deadlock.

• Detroit gets two goals from Doug Brown and the Cup clincher from Martin Lapointe, taking Game 4 4-1 for their second straight Finals sweep.

Capitals' Juneau Nets Four Winners

For the first time since they came into the NHL in 1974-75, the Washington Capitals advanced all the way to the Stanley Cup Finals in the spring of 1998, thanks largely to the brilliant work of star centerman Joe Juneau (90), who shared with Adam Oates the team lead in playoff points (17). Among Juneau's seven postseason tallies were four game-winners, two of them in sudden-death.

Vladimir Konstantinov

Konstantinov Shares in Wings' Win

Detroit successfully defended its playoff title with a four-game sweep of the Capitals in the Finals, although three games were decided by one goal (Game 2 went to overtime). In the aftermath, Steve Yzerman (#19), voted playoff MVP, shared the glory with fallen comrade Vladimir Konstantinov (#16), who was still recovering from injuries suffered in a car accident following Detroit's 1997 Stanley Cup win.

Stanley Cup Finals

• Red Wings captain Steve Yzerman leads all playoff scorers with 24 points. He wins the Conn Smythe Trophy.

• Buffalo's Dominik Hasek is the first goalie to win the Vezina Trophy, the Pearson Award, and the Hart Trophy two years in a row.

• Rob Blake of the Kings takes the Norris Trophy, while Ron Francis wins his second Lady Byng.

• Boston rookie Sergei Samsonov wins the Calder Trophy, while Dallas Star Jere Lehtinen grabs the Frank Selke award.

• Two years after a life-threatening illness, Blues goalie Jamie McLennan wins the Bill Masterton Trophy.

• Boston bench boss Pat Burns takes the third Jack Adams Award of his career. His first two were with Montreal and Toronto.

The 20th century of professional hockey ended with a bang when the Dallas Stars won their first ever Stanley Cup after a triple-overtime win over the Buffalo Sabres. But even more significant was that the century closed concurrently with the conclusion of the single greatest career in the history of the game of hockey.

After 20 years in the NHL, Wayne Gretzky decided to hang up his skates. On Sunday, April 18, 1999, the man simply known as the "Great One" played his last game, a 2-1 overtime loss to the Pittsburgh Penguins, in which he assisted on the Rangers' lone goal. Gretzky then bid fond farewell to a packed house at New York's Madison Square Garden and to millions more watching on television.

"I wish I could have been [Michael] Jordan hitting that last shot to win the championship," he said after the game, "but that wasn't going to happen."

Sadly for Gretzky—and the New York fans who marveled at his play for the final three seasons of his brilliant career—the Rangers failed to qualify for the playoffs his last two years. At 38 years old, he was past his prime—and he knew it.

GRETZKY HANGS 'EM UP AFTER 20 GREAT YEARS

"Not only am I ready to retire," he said, "I'm physically ready to retire. It's hard. This is a great game, but it's a hard game. I'm ready."

Gretzky walked away from the game holding 61 NHL scoring records. Some of his achievements are so mind-boggling, they must be illustrated to be properly comprehended.

He was the greatest set-up man the game has ever seen, finishing his NHL career with 1,963 assists. To put this number in perspective: Gordie Howe amassed 1,850 total points in his career, second all-time on the NHL points list—and 113 points fewer than Gretzky had assists!

When the final buzzer sounded and the books closed on Gretzky's scoring magic, his NHL totals included 894 regular-season goals and 2,857 points (93 goals and 1,007 points ahead of second-place

Howe). Among his 61 records, he had the most career goals, assists, and points; assists per game (1.32); three-goal games (50); 40-goal seasons (12); 50-goal seasons (nine); 60-goal seasons (five); 100-point seasons (15); and consecutive 100-point seasons (13).

His single-season records include high marks for goals (92); assists (163); points (215); three-goal games (10); points per game (2.77); fastest 50 goals (39 games); and points-scoring streak (51 consecutive games).

A winner of four Stanley Cups in five years with the Edmonton Oilers in the early 1980s, Gretzky was not only a true champion but a man who changed the face of hockey. When he found a new home with the Los Angeles Kings in 1988, he revitalized the popularity of a dying sport in Hollywood—and made it possible for another pro team, the Mighty Ducks of Anaheim, to call California home.

Upon his retirement, Wayne's famous No. 99 was immediately retired—by the Rangers as well as the NHL—and the Hockey Hall of Fame quickly voted unanimously to waive the customary three-year waiting period and promptly add Gretzky's name to its legendary rolls.

1998-99

• The NHL grows to 27 teams as the Nashville Predators debut.

• The NHL introduces the Maurice Richard Trophy, given to the player who leads the league in tallies.

• On January 7, 1999, in a 4-2 home win over Buffalo, Luc Robitaille scores

his 500th goal, making him the 27th player (and sixth left wing) to reach the mark.

• In January, Flyers goalie John Vanbiesbrouck shuts out the Islanders, Hurricanes (partial game), Predators, and Capitals in successive appearances.

• On January 12, 1999, former first-overall draft pick Doug Wickenheiser, 37, who played 10 years in the NHL, loses a five-year battle to cancer.

• On February 5, 1999, in Detroit, Patrick Roy, 33, becomes the youngest goalie in NHL history to reach 400 wins.

A sellout crowd of 18,200 fans packed Madison Square Garden on April 18, 1999, and millions more watched on TV, as Wayne Gretzky (joined by longtime friend and two-time teammate Mark Messier) skated in his final NHL game, an overtime loss to the Pittsburgh Penguins. Gretzky capped a brilliant 20-year career with more than 60 NHL scoring records and four Stanley Cup rings. His final regular-season numbers: 894 goals, 1,963 assists, and 2,857 points in 1,487 games. Playoffs: 122 goals, 260 assists, and 382 points in 208 games.

• On February 13, 1999, more than 67 years after opening, Toronto's Maple Leaf Gardens hosts its final NHL game, a 6-2 win by Chicago.

• On March 29, 1999, Wayne Gretzky scores the 1,072nd goal of his pro career, surpassing Gordie Howe for the all-time NHL/World Hockey Association record.

• Sparked by Mike Modano (81 points) and Brett Hull's league-high 11 game-winning goals, the Stars win the Presidents' Trophy at 51-19-12.

• The Coyotes finish second in the Pacific Division. Jeremy Roenick (72 points), Keith Tkachuk (36 goals), and Nikolai Khabibulin (2.13 GAA) lead the way.

• The Mighty Ducks post a 35-34-13 record, as Teemu Selanne (the NHL's top goal-scorer at 47) and Paul Kariya finish second and third overall in points with 107 and 101, respectively.

• The Sharks return to the postseason, as Jeff Friesen tops the team with 57 points.

Jaromir Jagr

Jagr Captures Another Scoring Title

During the 1998-99 campaign, while the Penguins were mired in bankruptcy and worried about their uncertain future in the NHL, Jaromir Jagr overcame the many distractions in Steeltown and won his second straight scoring title, the third of his career. He finished with 127 points and was one of only three NHLers to surpass the 100-point plateau, joining Anaheim's Teemu Selanne (107) and Paul Kariya (101).

Collapsed Lung Sidelines Lindros, Philly's Chances

In a troubling pattern, Philadelphia's Eric Lindros once again saw a productive and superior season interrupted by a serious injury, causing him to spend more time in civilian clothes than the Flyers would like. With 93 points in 71 games, he was on course for a 100-point season when he suffered a collapsed lung in Nashville. He missed the end of the regular season and all of the playoffs, dashing Philly's Cup hopes.

Eric Lindros

Wayne Gretzky

Gretzky Breaks Howe's Record for Most Goals

As the 1998-98 season began, Wayne Gretzky had but one scoring mark yet to achieve: catching Gordie Howe for the most professional goals, WHA and NHL combined, in a career. On March 29, 1999, against the New York Islanders before a thrilled Madison Square Garden crowd, the Great One banged home his own rebound for the game-winning goal and his 1,072nd goal, one more than his idol, Howe.

1998-99

- The fifth-place Kings finish 32-45-5 and waste a one-man show by Luc Robitaille (74 points).

- Colorado finishes atop the Northwest Division at 44-28-10, boasting the fourth and fifth overall scorers: Peter Forsberg (97 points) and Joe Sakic (96).

- Despite playing most of the year without their ace, Doug Weight, the Oilers earn the last playoff spot in their conference, finishing second in the division at 33-37-12.

- In Calgary, Phil Housley becomes the all-time leading scorer among Americans, but the trade of Theo

Fleury to Colorado casts a gloom over the Flames' season.

- Mark Messier's 600th career goal is lost in the morass of a losing season in Vancouver (23-47-12).

- The Red Wings finish atop the Central Division at 43-32-7, as Steve

Chicago Sends One of Their Own Packing

The "sports as a business" debate raged on as usual in 1998-99, with huge contracts, holdouts, and management tussles making as much news as goal-scoring. Still, no one was as shocked as the man himself when Chicago native and hometown favorite Chris Chelios was shipped to the arch-rival Detroit Red Wings at the March 1999 trading deadline. The veteran backliner was quickly inked to a new contract by Detroit.

Patrick Roy

Roy Sets NHL Record for Combined Wins

In a watershed season that began disastrously, Colorado goalie Patrick Roy etched his name in the record books yet again. He carved a place for himself in the annals of hockey history when he passed Terry Sawchuk and Jacques Plante as the winningest goalie in NHL history—regular season and playoffs combined. After the Avalanche lost to the Stars in the Western Conference finals, Roy ended the 1998-99 season with 522 career wins.

Chris Chelios

Selanne Earns First-Ever Richard Trophy

Anaheim's slick right winger, Teemu Selanne, won the NHL goal-scoring title in 1998-99 with 47 tallies. Ironically, it was the first year an award was presented to the NHL's top lamp-lighter (the Maurice Richard Trophy) and also the first nonstrike season since 1969-70 that the NHL did not have at least one 50-goal scorer. It was Selanne's third goal-scoring title.

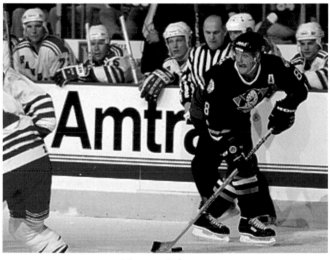

Teemu Selanne

Yzerman is 17th overall in points (74) and Brendan Shanahan leads the team with 31 goals.

• Pavol Demitra is the NHL's 10th overall scorer at 37-52-89. His 10 game-winning goals help St. Louis to a 37-32-13 record, second best in their division.

• The Blackhawks finish out of the playoffs, wasting Tony Amonte's 44 goals.

• The first-year Nashville Predators are surprisingly competitive, finishing at 28-47-7 thanks to Cliff Ronning's 60 points and Sergei Krivokrasov's 25 goals.

• The Devils capture the top spot in the Eastern Conference behind Petr Sykora's 72 points and great goaltending from Martin Brodeur.

• Eric Lindros (93 points in 71 games) suffers a collapsed lung late in the season, but the up-and-down Flyers manage to take second in the Atlantic Division at 37-26-19.

Maple Leaf Gardens

Leafs Leave Garden for Air Canada

One by one, the great old barns of the NHL have been forsaken in the name of corporate sponsorship: Chicago Stadium razed to make a parking lot for the United Center; Boston Garden abandoned in favor of the Fleet Center; the Montreal Forum vacated for the Molson Center. In 1998-99, Maple Leaf Gardens, though saved from the wrecking ball by a historical landmark provision, saw its last NHL game as the Leafs moved to the new Air Canada Centre. Leafs legends were on hand to say goodbye.

Pint-Sized Ronning Comes Up Big

As a junior in the Western league, Cliff Ronning won the WHL scoring title with the New Westminster Bruins in 1984-85. Still, at 5'8" he was considered too small for the NHL. Undaunted, he made his debut with the St. Louis Blues in the 1986 playoffs, and (with the exception of one season in Italy) he has been an NHL fixture ever since. The first-year Predators acquired him in 1998-99, and he led the club with 60 points.

Stars Shining Bright Atop NHL Standings

For the second straight season, the Dallas Stars topped the NHL regular-season standings with a combination of dominant defense and lightning-strike offense. Their leader, Mike Modano, continued his recent evolution as one of the game's most talented and dedicated two-way players, finishing with 81 points (13th overall) in 77 games and a plus-minus ranking of +29, among the top marks in the league.

Mike Modano

Cliff Ronning

• Pittsburgh follows NHL scoring champ Jaromir Jagr (44-83-127) to a 38-30-14 record, but injuries decimate the lineup and bankruptcy threatens the team's future.

• The Rangers fail to make the playoffs for the second straight year despite 38 goals from Adam Graves.

Their leading scorer, Wayne Gretzky (62 points), plays his final game.

• Management turmoil complicates a shaky situation in Nassau County, as the Islanders go 24-48-10.

• The Senators prove they're for real, taking the Northeast Division at

44-23-15 on Alexei Yashin's 94 points and goalie Ron Tugnutt's league-best 1.79 goals-against average.

• With a revamped attack, the Maple Leafs finish at 45-30-7, as Mats Sundin ties for 11th in the league in points (83) and Sergei Berezin rips 37 goals.

Demitra Rips 37 Goals for Blues

In the mid-1970s, the Rangers traded up-and-coming star Rick Middleton to Boston for aging grinder Ken Hodge in what is widely viewed as among the most lopsided trades in NHL history. In November 1996, the Ottawa Senators shipped Pavol Demitra to St. Louis for Christer Olsson. In 1998-99, Demitra exploded for 37 goals and 89 points (10th overall) to lead the Blues. Who says history doesn't repeat itself?

Byron Dafoe

Dafoe Shuts the Door for the Bruins

Throughout NHL history, the common consensus has always been that, in order to contend for a championship, a team must have great goal-tending. Entering the new century, the Bruins are well equipped in that department with Byron Dafoe stationed between the pipes. In 1998-99, Dafoe led the NHL with 10 shutouts, was second in save percentage (.926), and was third in goals-against average (1.99).

Pavol Demitra

Tugnutt Finds a Home with the Senators

In his first five NHL seasons (with Quebec), goalie Ron Tugnutt posted a record of 35-83-19 with a goals-against average in the 4.00 neighborhood. Then, after brief stints in Edmonton, Anaheim, and Montreal, he signed on with Ottawa in 1996. By the end of the 1998-99 season, "Tugger" was among the toasts of the NHL, with a league-leading 1.79 goals-against average and the game's third-best save percentage (.925).

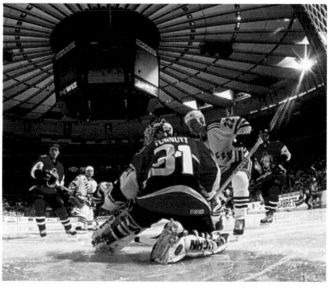

Ron Tugnutt

- Boston goalie Byron Dafoe posts the second-best save pct. in the league (.926) and the third-best GAA (1.99), helping the Bruins to a 39-30-13 finish.

- Dominik Hasek posts a league-best .937 save percentage and sniper Miroslav Satan erupts for 40 goals as Buffalo skates to a 37-28-17 record.

- The Canadiens, facing financial hardship, unload stars Mark Recchi and Vincent Damphousse and end up out of the playoff race at 32-39-11.

- After missing the playoffs six years straight as the Hartford Whalers, the relocated Carolina Hurricanes take the weak Southeast Division at 34-30-18.

- A midseason trade for Pavel Bure cannot help the Panthers, who fail to make the playoffs.

- A year after going to the Stanley Cup Finals, Washington fails to make the playoffs. Late in the year, the Caps unload warriors Dale Hunter, Joe Juneau, and Craig Berube.

Paul Kariya

L.A.'s Robitaille Powers In His 500th Goal

On June 9, 1984, Luc Robitaille, labeled too slow for the NHL, was drafted 171st overall by the Kings. In short order, the Montreal native took 1986 CHL (junior) Player of the Year honors before winning the 1987 Calder Trophy. On January 7, 1999, in his 928th game, Lucky recorded his 500th career NHL goal, becoming the 12th fastest player in history to reach 500 red lights.

Luc Robitaille

Two Ducks Quack the Century Mark

Only three players cracked the 100-point plateau during the 1998-99 season, including the scoring champion (Pittsburgh's Jaromir Jagr) and a pair of high-flying Ducks. Teemu Selanne, who led the circuit in goal-scoring (47), and Paul Kariya paced Anaheim with 107 and 101 points, respectively. Great finishers and playmakers, the duo also ranked among the NHL's top five in assists.

Avalanche Add Another Star in Drury

In a clear case of the rich getting richer, the Avalanche introduced Chris Drury to their fans in 1998-99. Coming off a brilliant collegiate career that included the 1998 Hobey Baker Award and a place on Boston University's '95 national championship team, Drury scored 20 rookie goals. His performance earned him the Calder Trophy, as he beat out Ottawa's Marian Hossa and fellow Av Milan Hejduk.

Chris Drury

• More trouble brews in Tampa Bay, where the Lightning win only 19 games. Darcy Tucker leads the team in scoring with just 43 points.

• In addition to the third Art Ross Trophy of his career, Pittsburgh's Jaromir Jagr takes home his first Hart Trophy.

• Wayne Gretzky wins his fifth Lady Byng Trophy, giving him 32 major NHL awards for his career.

• Buffalo's Dominik Hasek wins his fifth Vezina Trophy in six years.

• Blues defenseman Al MacInnis takes home the Norris Trophy after leading all NHL blue-liners with 62 points.

• Center Chris Drury wins the Calder Trophy after pounding in 20 goals for the Avalanche.

• Dallas Stars winger Jere Lehtinen becomes the first NHL player since

Sakic Shines When Avs Down a Man

Known for his wicked wrist shot and soft-spoken style, Mighty Joe Sakic showed another side of his game in 1998-99, that of premier penalty-killer. He scored short-handed goals in three straight games (one game short of the NHL record) and tied for the league lead in shorties (five). A special player with special-teams excellence, he also ripped 12 power-play goals.

Alexei Yashin

Yashin Smashes Senators Records

A dynamic and powerful skater with grace and skill in equal measure, Alexei Yashin spent the 1998-99 season carving his name in the Ottawa record book. He set franchise marks for goals (44), assists (50), and points (94) and finished sixth overall in the league's scoring race. He also took the Sens to their first division title and first 100-point season (44 wins, 103 points).

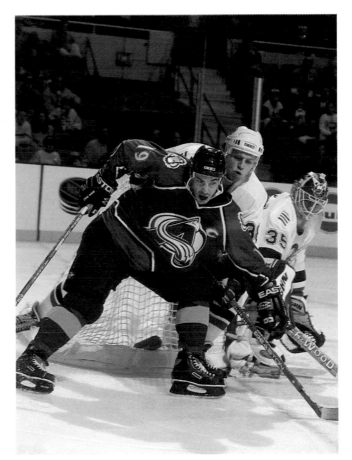

Joe Sakic

Guy Carbonneau (1988 and 1989) to capture back-to-back Frank Selke Trophies.

• Tampa Bay's John Cullen accepts the Bill Masterton Trophy after returning to NHL action following a bout with cancer.

• Stars netminders Ed Belfour and Roman Turek take the William Jennings Trophy as Dallas allows the NHL's fewest goals (168)—a miniscule 2.05 per game.

• On March 23, 1999, Washington trades longtime captain Dale Hunter to Colorado to give Hunter a chance to win the Stanley Cup ring he has pursued for nearly two decades.

• On March 23, 1999, Vincent Damphousse goes to San Jose, becoming the sixth straight captain of the Montreal Canadiens to be traded while wearing the C.

Brodeur Wins 39, Lacks Mates' Help

The model of consistency, New Jersey Devils goalie Martin Brodeur finished the 1998-99 season with a league-high 39 wins. Brodeur became just the sixth netminder in NHL history to post four consecutive 30-win seasons. Unfortunately, with the Devils' new offensive style, Martin's personal stats suffered. Uncharacteristically, he was out of the NHL's top 10 in goals-against average and save percentage.

Martin Brodeur

Sabres Dart Past Leafs into Finals

The seventh-seeded Buffalo Sabres earned a berth in the Stanley Cup Finals for the first time in 24 years after beating Toronto in five games. The Maple Leafs proved no match for the underdog Sabres despite Toronto's fierceness, shown by Alexander Karpovtsev (right) battling Buffalo's Brian Holzinger. In the next round, Buffalo's inexperience emerged, in part to Dallas's roster containing eight players with rings compared to Buffalo's zero.

Roy, Avs End Wings' Bid for Three-Peat

Colorado squashed any hope Detroit had for becoming the next hockey dynasty when the Red Wings were eliminated in the Western Conference semis. Behind goalie Patrick Roy's strong performance, the Avalanche advanced to the next round. Although the Avalanche lost in the conference finals to Dallas, Roy picked up his record 110th career NHL playoff win.

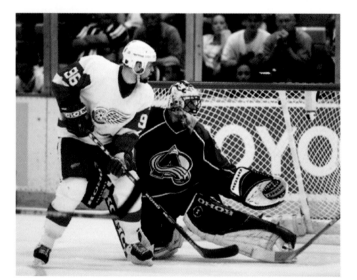

Western Conference Semifinals

Eastern Semis

• At the trade deadline, the Red Wings acquire seasoned netminder Bill Ranford from Tampa Bay.

• In the Eastern Conference quarterfinals, Pittsburgh dethrones top-seeded New Jersey (4-3) while Buffalo pounds Ottawa (4-0).

• In the Western Conference quarterfinals, the Stars skate past the Oilers (4-0), the Avalanche spear the Sharks (4-2), Detroit sweeps Anaheim (4-0), and St. Louis wins the last three games to beat Phoenix (4-3).

• In the Eastern semis, Toronto beats Pittsburgh in six, while Buffalo does likewise to Boston.

• In the Western semis, Dallas rolls over St. Louis in six and Colorado edges Detroit in six.

• Continuing their tremendous postseason run, the Sabres knock off the Maple Leafs in five games to go to the Stanley Cup Finals for the first time since 1975.

Cup Finds New Home in Texas

The Dallas Stars won their first Stanley Cup by defeating Buffalo in six games. After playing in the second-longest overtime game in Finals history and the longest game to decide a winner, the Stars brought the Cup to Dallas, the furthest south the Cup has traveled. Brett Hull (far right) scored the series winner at 14:51 of the third overtime, just 22 seconds shorter than the longest Finals game, back in 1990 between Edmonton and Boston.

Stanley Cup Finals

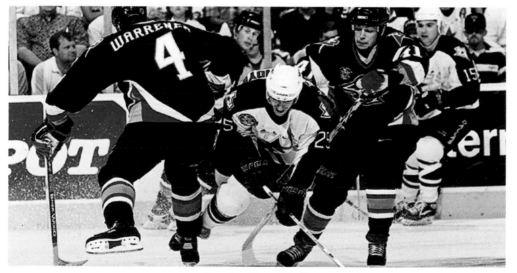

Stanley Cup Finals

Nieuwendyk Earns Conn Smythe Trophy

Conn Smythe winner Joe Nieuwendyk (center) endured the pressure from Buffalo throughout the series. The gritty center bounced back from two knee surgeries over the summer to earn the playoff MVP award. His on-ice performance saw him tally a playoff-high 11 goals, which included six game-winners. His six winners tied a playoff record set by Colorado's Joe Sakic in 1996.

- The Stars endure a grueling seven-game series with the Avalanche to earn a trip to the Finals.

- Buffalo stuns the Dallas crowd by beating the Stars 3-2 in overtime of Game 1. Jason Woolley scores the game-winner.

- The Stars wins Games 2 (4-2) and 3 (2-1), with Joe Nieuwendyk notching both goals in the latter victory.

- After dropping Game 4 2-1, Dallas wins Game 5 2-0.

- With the Cup in its reach, Dallas outlasts Buffalo 2-1 in the third

overtime of Game 6 to capture its first Stanley Cup. Brett Hull's winning goal triggers controversy, as he appears to be in the crease.

- Dallas center Joe Nieuwendyk, who ties a playoff record with six game-winning goals, wins the Conn Smythe Trophy.

While coming to grips with the retirement of Wayne Gretzky, the NHL forged ahead in 1999-00 with a keen eye on the future—which included expansion. The success of the Dallas Stars, who had packed the house and won the 1999 Stanley Cup, proved once and for all that hockey could indeed thrive in the South. In Tennessee, the Nashville Predators had played to huge and adoring crowds, as had the Coyotes in the desert of Arizona.

With this in mind, the NHL returned to Atlanta in 1999, introducing the Thrashers as the league's 28th club. It was the first taste of big-league hockey for Georgians since the 1970s, when the Flames burned up the ice before moving to Calgary.

Prior to the season, the most prominent item on the agendas of the club owners was to tweak the NHL's rules. For example, they addressed Brett Hull's Stanley Cup-winning goal for Dallas in triple overtime of Game 6 that spring. He had scored with a toe in the goalcrease, a clear violation of the league's zero-tolerance policy. In response, the NHL brass decided to create a no-harm, no-foul, no-video replay standard.

This new attitude of tolerance allowed attacking players to take

NEW JERSEY MASTERS THE NHL'S NEW RULES

up incidental residence in the enemy goalcrease so long as they did not physically interfere with the goalie's ability to do his job (that is, see and stop pucks). Among the main reasons for this reform was to eliminate lengthy play stoppages caused by countless video reviews. The new mandate rendered Hull's goal more acceptable, if only retroactively, although it did little to assuage the bitterness of Buffalo fans still fuming over the "illegal" goal.

Moreover, the two-referee system, which had been tried on a part-time basis the previous year, was adopted for most games. The main reason for adding a ref was to put more eyes on the game and facilitate a greater crackdown on obstruction penalties. This, of course, would boost goal-scoring, which had dropped to the lowest levels since the days of the Original Six.

The New Jersey Devils made excellent use of the NHL's new world order, leading the Eastern Conference in goals (251) and finishing second only to Detroit (278) overall. Patrik Elias led the way with 35 tallies, while Petr Sykora (25), Bobby Holik (23), and Jason Arnott (22) also pitched in regularly. Goalie Martin Brodeur topped the league in wins for the third straight year (43), and the team finished with 103 points.

Led by the stalwart play of defenseman Scott Stevens, the Devils roared through the playoffs with series wins over Florida (in four), Toronto (six), and Philadelphia (seven) before taking on the defending-champion Stars in the Finals. The Devils' A Line—comprised of Arnott, Sykora, and Elias—delivered in the crucial moments.

Sykora's second-period goal in Game 3 proved to be the winner, while the Devils' three-goal, third-period barrage in Game 4 led to a 3-1 New Jersey victory. Dallas won a classic Game 5—1-0 in triple overtime—on Mike Modano's winner. But in Game 6, Arnott scored a double-overtime goal to give New Jersey its second Stanley Cup. Fans in Buffalo shed no tears for the Stars.

1999-00

• The NHL expands to 28 teams with the addition of the Atlanta Thrashers.

• The NHL implements a new system in which each team plays 25 home and 25 road games using two referees.

• In the aftermath of Brett Hull's Stanley Cup-winning goal (while he was partially in the goalcrease), the league institutes a no-harm, no-foul, no-video review standard.

• The NHL rules that for regular-season tie games, each team will receive a point in the standings. In the event of an overtime goal, the winning team will earn an additional point.

• Blues center Pierre Turgeon becomes the 55th player to score 1,000 career points with a goal against Edmonton on October 9, 1999.

• On December 27, 1999, in just his 810th career game, Colorado's Joe Sakic collects an assist to mark his 1,000th NHL point.

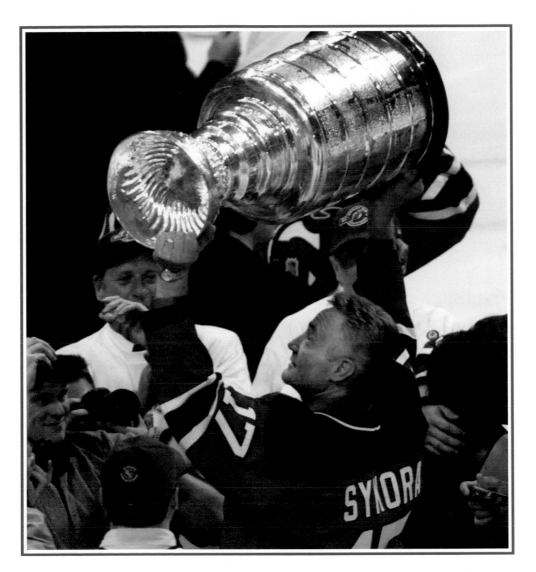

Wearing the sweater of fallen Devils scoring ace Petr Sykora (who was sent to the hospital during the final game of the Finals), New Jersey coach Larry Robinson hoists the Stanley Cup in celebration. Robinson, who had won six Cups as a legendary Canadiens defenseman, took over as New Jersey's bench boss with just eight games remaining in the regular season, replacing the fired Robbie Ftorek.

• Dallas goalie Ed Belfour becomes the 16th man in NHL history to reach the 300-win plateau, beating Washington 2-1 on February 13, 2000.

• On February 27, 2000, Detroit's Pat Verbeek becomes the 57th player to reach 1,000 points. On March 22nd, he scores his 500th NHL goal.

• Pittsburgh's Jaromir Jagr wins his fourth scoring title with 96 points. He's followed by Pavel Bure (94) and Mark Recchi (91).

• Florida's Pavel Bure wins the Rocket Richard Trophy as the league's top goal-scorer with 58 (14 tallies ahead of second-place finisher Owen Nolan).

• Red Wings blue-line ace Nicklas Lidstrom leads all NHL defensemen in points (73).

• Sharks winger Owen Nolan leads the NHL in power-play goals (18).

• Denny Lambert of the Thrashers tops the NHL in PIMs (219).

After 20 Years, Hockey Returns to Hotlanta

The NHL first introduced big-league hockey to Atlanta with the debut of the Flames in 1972. After eight seasons of moderate success (five winning seasons), the club moved to Calgary. Twenty years later, the NHL unveiled the Thrashers, with Don Waddell as general manager and former NHL winger Curt Fraser running the bench. Former IHL MVP Norm Maracle (pictured) played 32 games in goal. Atlanta finished last in scoring and goals allowed and won just 14 games.

Norm Maracle

Chris Pronger

Pronger Mimics Orr as Double Trophy Winner

Not since Hall of Famer Bobby Orr did it in 1972 had an NHL defenseman won both the Norris Trophy and Hart Trophy in the same year. But that's what Blues "Secretary of Defense" Chris Pronger (#44) managed in 1999-00. He logged 62 points, the game's best plus-minus rating (+52), and a staggering 30 minutes per game. Pronger possessed everything a coach could hope for in a defenseman: size, strength, skill, and intelligence.

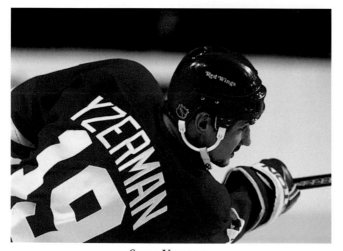

Steve Yzerman

Yzerman Scores No. 600, Joins NHL's Elite

Steve Yzerman celebrated yet another milestone on November 26, 1999: He became the 11th player in league history to score 600 career goals. The historic tally came against the Oilers and sparked a 4-2 home victory. In the new century, Stevie Wonder would climb up the NHL's top-10 ladder for career goals and points.

- Brian Boucher, Philadelphia's first-year netminder, plays 35 games and posts the league's best goals-against average (1.91).

- On the strength of Roman Turek's 1.95 goals-against average, the Blues win the Presidents' Trophy with a league-leading 114 points.

- The playmaking of Steve Yzerman (44 assists) and goal-scoring of Brendan Shanahan (41) earn Detroit a second place finish in the Central Division.

- Tony Amonte's third 40-goal season in four years sparks the Blackhawks to third place in the Central Division,

but the club misses the playoffs for the third straight year.

- Veteran Cliff Ronning paces the second-year Nashville Predators in points (62), but the young team fails to make the playoffs with just 28 victories.

Pavel Bure

Owen Nolan

Lamp-Lighter Nolan Leads the Way in San Jose

Long recognized as one of the game's premier power forwards, Sharks captain Owen Nolan (right) helped San Jose to its best season ever (35 wins) in 1999-00 while enjoying his own finest performance. His 44 goals and 84 points set franchise marks, and he was the NHL's second-leading red-lamp lighter, trailing only Pavel Bure (58). His 18 power-play goals topped the NHL.

Russian Rocket Wins Rocket Richard Trophy

In Year Two of the Maurice "Rocket" Richard Trophy for goal-scoring, Florida's Pavel Bure, a.k.a. the Russian Rocket (left), celebrated a league-high 58 goals and took the namesake trophy. He finished the year as the NHL's only 50-goal scorer, as defenses gained the upper hand throughout the season. For Bure, this was his fourth career 50-goal campaign.

Rookie Boucher Posts Sub-2.00 Goals Against

To say that Flyers goalie Brian Boucher exploded onto the NHL scene in 1999-00 would not be overstating facts. En route to leading the NHL in goals-against average, he became the first rookie goalie since the 1950-51 season to play at least 25 games and post a GAA under 2.00 (1.91 in 35 contests). The last to do it? Toronto's Al Rollins and Detroit's Terry Sawchuk.

Brian Boucher

• Dallas, the defending Stanley Cup champion, rides the shoulders of Mike Modano (38 goals, 81 points) to first place in the Pacific Division.

• The Kings are back in the playoffs after Luc Robitaille (36 goals, 74 points) helps L.A. win 39 games and take second in the Pacific Division.

• With 34 goals and 78 points, Jeremy Roenick is the top desert dog in Phoenix, helping the Coyotes to third place in the Pacific.

• Rough and rugged Owen Nolan registers a career-high 84 points as San Jose takes fourth in the Pacific Division.

• The Mighty Ducks fail to qualify for playoff action despite a combined 75 goals and 171 points from their dynamic duo of Paul Kariya and Teemu Selanne.

• Finishing third in the league in assists (53), Joe Sakic takes Colorado to the top spot in the Northwest.

Quenneville, Blues Hoist the Prez Trophy

A rugged and determined defenseman during his 15-year NHL career, Joel Quenneville made a smooth transition to coaching. After taking over in 1997, it took him only three years to take the Blues to their first-ever Presidents' Trophy as the league's regular-season champion. For his work, he received the 2000 Jack Adams Award as Coach of the Year.

Joel Quenneville

Sundin Captains Leafs to First Title in 37 Years

The first European to serve as Toronto's captain, Mats Sundin provided leadership in a variety of important ways in 1999-00. Not only did he lead the team in scoring (again), but he also set an NHL single-season record when he scored four regular-season overtime goals, proving himself one of the game's greatest clutch players. Sundin helped Toronto win its division for the first time since 1963.

Mats Sundin

Verbeek Reaches 500, 1,000 Marks

Colorfully (and aptly) nicknamed "The Little Ball of Hate," Pat Verbeek (right) reaped the harvest of his own perseverance during the 1999-00 season. He notched his 1,000th point on February 27 and added his 500th career goal on March 22. Verbeek's career had been seriously, albeit temporarily, threatened when he nearly lost his left thumb in an off-season farm accident in 1985. Showing astonishing perseverence, he returned to the Devils in 1985-86 and scored 25 goals.

Pat Verbeek

- Playmaker Doug Weight (51 assists) and scoring ace Ryan Smyth (28 goals) pace the Oilers to a second-place finish.

- Despite 27 goals from Markus Naslund and 25 from Todd Bertuzzi, the Canucks don't make the playoffs, finishing third in the Northwest.

- Calgary's playoff absence reaches its fourth straight year as the Flames waste a career-best 35-goal effort from Valeri Bure (kid brother of Pavel).

- The Flyers are the toast of the Eastern Conference, as Mark Recchi's 91 points help Philadelphia win 45 games and top the Atlantic Division with 105 points.

- Martin Brodeur leads the NHL in wins (43) for the third straight year as the Devils take second in the Atlantic.

- Scoring ace Jaromir Jagr and rookie goalie J.S. Aubin (23 wins) help the

Jagr Wins Scoring Title with Just 96 Total Points

Not counting the 48-game 1995 campaign, the last time a scoring title was won with fewer than 100 points was 1967-68, when Chicago's Stan Mikita took the Art Ross Trophy with 87 points. In 1999-00, Penguins captain Jaromir Jagr regularly raided the crease and paced the NHL with 96 points in just 63 games (1.52 points per game). He was handed his fourth Ross Trophy—and third straight.

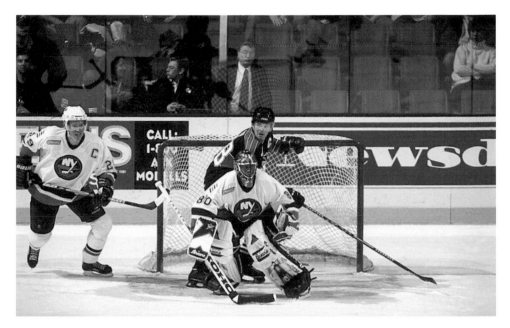

Jaromir Jagr

Scott Gomez

Gomez Makes History, Wins the Calder Trophy

Born in Alaska, and the son of a Mexican immigrant, New Jersey's Scott Gomez arrived on the NHL scene in 1999-00 as a feel-good story based on his status as the league's first Hispanic player. In short order, he earned his way to Calder Trophy honors (and a Stanley Cup) by leading all rookies with 70 points, including 51 assists.

Penguins post a .500 record and finish third in the Atlantic.

• The Rangers fail to make the play-offs for the third year in a row, but rookie Mike York gives fans hope for the future by leading the team in goals with 26.

• The Islanders waste a 35-goal performance from Mariusz Czerkawski and finish 13th in the conference.

• Goalie Olaf Kolzig tops the 40-win mark for the first time in his career (41), and tough guy Chris Simon rips 29 goals, as Washington takes the Southeast Division.

• With 98 points, the Panthers are back in the playoffs after a two-year absence. Pavel Bure's 94 points set a franchise record.

• Despite four 20-goal scorers, the Hurricanes run out of wind and fail to make the playoffs. They finish third in the division.

Olaf Kolzig

"Zilla" Puts Up Monster-Sized Stats in Goal

Two years after backstopping the Capitals to the 1998 Stanley Cup Finals against Detroit, Washington's 6'3", 225-pound Olaf Kolzig enjoyed a personal career year. "Olie the Goalie," or "Zilla" (as in Godzilla), won 41 games, recorded five shutouts, and posted a .917 save percentage while leading NHL netminders in minutes played. He was honored with the Vezina Trophy.

Berard Speared in Eye, Fights to Save Career

Near-tragedy struck star Maple Leafs defenseman Bryan Berard on March 11, 2000, when he was accidently speared by Marian Hossa of Ottawa. Hossa was following through on a shot on goal when the blade of his stick caught Berard in the right eye. Several surgical procedures were required to save the eye, and Berard often thought his young career was over. In 2001-02, however, he returned to the NHL with the Rangers.

Bryan Berard

Eastern Conference Quarterfinals

Straka Powers Pens to First-Round Upset

Martin Straka (#82) was one of the NHL's most creative playmakers in 1999-00. He led Pittsburgh in postseason assists (nine in 11 games) and was instrumental in leading the seventh-seeded Penguins past the Southeast Division champion Capitals in a huge first-round upset. Pittsburgh won the opener in a rout, 7-0, then took three of the next four—all by one goal.

1999-00

• For the seventh time in their eight-year history, the Lightning, with just 19 wins, fail to make the playoffs, wasting a 25-goal effort from Vincent Lecavalier.

• With 61 thrashings, Atlanta takes residence in the Eastern Conference basement.

• For the first time since 1962-63, the Maple Leafs win a division title (Northeast). Captain Mats Sundin (73 points) paces the team to 45 wins and its first-ever 100-point season.

• Five Senators score 20 or more goals (Marian Hossa leads with 29) as Ottawa take second in the Northeast.

• Rookie goalie Martin Biron (41 games) spells oft-injured netminder Dominik Hasek and leads the Sabres to third place in the Northeast Division.

• The goal-scoring exploits of Sergei Zholtok (26) and Martin Rucinsky (25) can't keep the injury-plagued

Eighth-Seeded Sharks Stun Top-Seeded Blues

The image of Sharks defenseman Mike Rathje (left) dumping Blues forward Michal Handzus (#26) was symbolic of San Jose's first-round upset of St. Louis in 2000. Seeded eighth in the Stanley Cup tourney, the Sharks unceremoniously dumped No. 1 seed St. Louis in a hard-fought seven-game series. San Jose won the clincher, 3-1, in the Show-Me State.

Western Conference Quarterfinals

Devils Survive Flyers in Eastern Finals Thriller

The 2000 Eastern Conference Finals saw Philadelphia take a three-games-to-one lead over New Jersey in what would eventually extend to an epic seven-game battle royale. The outcome remained in doubt until late in Game 7. That's when Devils scoring ace Patrik Elias (#26) slipped the decisive goal past Flyers rookie netminder Brian Boucher for a 2-1 win, completing the Devils' dramatic comeback.

Eastern Conference Finals

Canadiens from a second consecutive nonplayoff finish.

• A season of frustration sees the Bruins trade Ray Bourque to Colorado and then fail to make the playoffs despite 60 points from budding star Joe Thornton.

• In the Eastern Conference playoffs, seventh-seeded Pittsburgh pulls off a huge first-round upset by ousting the second-seeded Capitals in five games.

• The Western Conference is turned upside down when eighth-seeded San Jose ousts the top-seeded Blues in a seven-game first-round classic.

• Philadelphia, Dallas, and Colorado take five games to win their first-round series.

• New Jersey and Detroit both sweep their opponents to advance to the second round of the playoffs. Toronto moves on in six.

Lindros Suffers Yet Another Concussion

Slammed by New Jersey's Scott Sevens in the 2000 playoffs, Philly's Eric Lindros suffered a concussion—his fourth in five months and sixth in two years. Eric, who had criticized the team's medical staff for failing to diagnose the severity of his injuries, was stripped of his captaincy for grousing.

Eric Lindros

Western Conference Finals

Dallas Upends Avalanche in Western Finals

Stars forward Guy Carbonneau, a legendary defensive ace, returns an Avalanche player to his bench in the 2000 Western Conference finals. Colorado won Games 1 and 3 of the series on the strength of Patrick Roy shutouts. The Stars, however, prevailed in seven, winning the finale 3-2.

Devils Captain Earns Smythe Trophy

An ageless warrior playing in his 17th playoff tournament in 18 NHL seasons, Devils captain Scott Stevens turned 36 just before the 2000 Stanley Cup playoffs commenced. On June 10, 2000, as a two-time Stanley Cup champion, he won the Conn Smythe Trophy as the postseason's MVP on the strength of his stalwart physical play on the New Jersey blue line. Stevens tied for the playoff lead in plus-minus (+9), and he assisted Jason Arnott's Stanley Cup-winning overtime goal in Game 6.

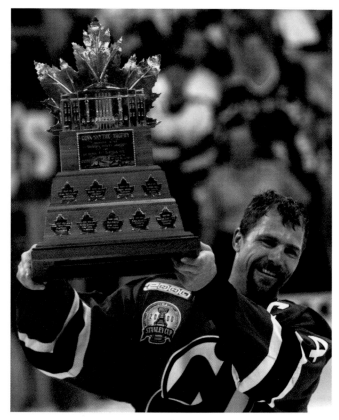

Scott Stevens

1999-00

- In the Eastern Conference semifinals, the Flyers win Game 4 in quintuple overtime en route to a dramatic six-game elimination of the surprisingly difficult Penguins.

- The Devils pull a mild upset by beating Toronto in the second round, while Dallas (over San Jose) and

Colorado (over Detroit) move on with five-game series wins.

- In a nail-biting marathon, the Devils edge the Flyers in the Eastern Conference finals by winning Game 7 2-1.

- The Western Conference finals, matching high-flying Colorado and

Dallas, go the distance before the Stars narrowly eke out a 3-2 win in Game 7.

- Down three games to one in the Stanley Cup Finals, Dallas netminder Ed Belfour records a 1-0 triple-overtime shutout in Game 5 to keep the Stars' hopes alive.

Stanley Cup Finals

Arnott Plays the Hero with Cup-Winning Goal

Bruising center Jason Arnott (#25) was fourth in playoff goals (eight) in 2000, with only one game-winner. That clutch tally, however, was the biggest of his NHL life as it ended Game 6 of the Stanley Cup Finals at 8:20 of double overtime. Arnott's dramatic shot, off assists from Scott Stevens and Patrik Elias, gave the Devils a 2-1 win over Dallas and their second Stanley Cup championship in six years.

Stanley Cup Finals

Modano Ends Scoreless Duel in Game 5 of Cup Finals

Down three games to one and playing in New Jersey, the Stars were on the brink of elimination in the 2000 Stanley Cup Finals. For a full five periods of Game 5, Devils goalie Martin Brodeur and Dallas netminder Eddie Belfour turned back all shots in a heart-pounding duel. Finally, at 6:41 of triple overtime, Dallas center Mike Modano (facing front) netted the winner, keeping the Stars' hopes alive. For Modano, the 1999-00 campaign was one of highs and lows. During the regular season, he was slammed into the boards by Anaheim's Ruslan Salei and had to be carried off on a stretcher. Nevertheless, he led Dallas in scoring (81 points) before taking them to Game 6 of the Cup Finals.

- Jason Arnott's goal at 8:20 of double OT in Game 6 gives the Devils their second Stanley Cup title and dethrones the defending champions.

- Scott Stevens, whose ferocious bodychecks neutralized all comers, wins the Conn Smythe Trophy.

- St. Louis defenseman Chris Pronger, who leads the league in plus-minus, earns the Hart and Norris trophies.

- Blues winger Pavol Demitra accepts the Lady Byng Trophy.

- Washington netminder Olaf Kolzig (2.24 GAA) takes the Vezina Trophy.

- New Jersey's Scott Gomez, the NHL's first Hispanic player, tops the rookie charts in points (70) and grabs the Calder Trophy.

- Detroit's Steve Yzerman takes the Frank Selke Trophy, ending the two-year reign of the Stars' Jere Lehtinen.

Divergent themes characterized the 2000-01 NHL season: Out with the old, in with the new. After 22 brilliant seasons, Raymond Bourque, a five-time Norris Trophy winner and one of the most beloved performers in league history, finally hoisted a Stanley Cup, then retired at age 40.

Just as Bourque was set to embark on his farewell tour, the league once again expanded its already bulging roster, adding the Columbus Blue Jackets and Minnesota Wild to make the NHL a 30-team circuit with two balanced conferences. Both squads showed great heart, winning 28 and 25 games, respectively.

In Steeltown, Penguins owner Mario Lemieux ended 3½ years of retirement with an astonishing return to action. On December 27, 2000, "The Savior" thrilled 17,148 Penguins fans by posting a goal and two assists in a 5-0 shelling of Toronto. His first point came just 33 seconds into the game, when he set up Jaromir Jagr's eventual game-winner. Mario finished the season with 76 points in just 43 games.

Bourque was hardly the only hero wearing a Colorado sweater. On October 17, 2000, during a nine-game winning streak by the Avs, netminder Patrick Roy beat

RAY AND ROY LEAD THE AVS TO THE MOUNTAINTOP

the Capitals for his 448th regular-season victory. The win erased the NHL record held for 30 years by the legendary Terry Sawchuk.

"The record has a special place," Roy said. "This is something that doesn't take one year, but a career."

Bourque, meanwhile, had spent 21 years striving to fulfill one ambition—to win the Stanley Cup—and now he had one year to make it happen. Inspired by his dedication, his determination, his refusal to accept anything less than the ultimate prize, the Avalanche became a juggernaut. They won a franchise-record 52 games and earned the Presidents' Trophy as the NHL regular-season champions. Bourque finished third among league blue-liners in points with 59.

In the playoffs, Colorado's challenges came from unexpected sources. The Avs swept Vancouver

in the opening round, but three of the games were decided by just one goal. Colorado also struggled against goalie Felix Potvin and the Kings, who forced a Game 7 showdown before snapping under the pressure of the Avalanche offense. Colorado beat the Blues in five games in the Western Conference finals, but the series was hard-fought as three games went to overtime.

In the Eastern Conference, defending champion New Jersey defeated Carolina, Toronto, and Pittsburgh en route to the Stanley Cup Finals. As a group, the Devils showed their respect for Bourque by making him fight and scratch for every inch of Stanley Cup success. The Finals were a tense, emotional roller-coaster, with each team taking and then losing the advantage.

The Devils were on the verge of repeating after a 4-1 win in Game 5 (at Colorado). But Roy, capping his monumental season, recorded a shutout in Game 6 and allowed just one goal in Game 7, a 3-1 win, to secure the series. When Commissioner Gary Bettman presented the Stanley Cup to Joe Sakic, the Avs captain immediately handed it off to a teary-eyed Bourque, for whom a life's ambition was fulfilled.

2000-01

- For the third straight season, the NHL expands, adding the Columbus Blue Jackets and Minnesota Wild.

- On June 24, 2000, Mike DiPietro, a star at Boston University, becomes the first goalie ever chosen first overall in the NHL Entry Draft, going to the Islanders.

- After a season of partial use, the NHL turns to the full-time employment of the two-referee system, putting four officials on the ice for all games.

- On November 15, 2000, the Bruins add a homegrown scoring ace when they send contract holdout Anson

Carter to Edmonton for Massachusetts native Bill Guerin.

- A year after adding Ray Bourque to their blue-line corps, Colorado adds Rob Blake from Los Angeles in a blockbuster that exports Adam Deadmarsh and Aaron Miller.

No sooner had NHL Commissioner Gary Bettman presented the Stanley Cup to
Colorado captain Joe Sakic than the unselfish playmaker passed it to Ray Bourque.
The 22-year veteran's single ambition throughout his farewell tour had been to
win the playoff title. With the trophy in hand, Bourque, at 40, jumped up and
down like a teenager.

- Anaheim trades superstar right winger Teemu Selanne to San Jose for Jeff Friesen.

- Pittsburgh's Jaromir Jagr captures his fifth scoring title (121 points), while Joe Sakic (118), Patrik Elias (96), Alexei Kovalev, Jason Allison, and Martin Straka (95 each) follow.

- Florida's Pavel Bure (59) leads the league in goals, with Joe Sakic (54) and Jaromir Jagr (52) joining him as the NHL's only other 50-goal men.

- Washington's Adam Oates ties Jaromir Jagr for the NHL lead in assists (69), with Martin Straka (68) trailing close behind.

- Rookie Stars goalie Marty Turco turns in the game's best GAA (1.90).

- For the fourth straight year, New Jersey netminder Martin Brodeur leads the league in wins (42). Patrick Roy of the Avs wins 40 for the first time.

Goalie DiPietro Picked No. 1

Mike DiPietro

Pictured with GM Mike Milbury (right) and co-owner Sanjay Kumar (left), Mike DiPietro made history on June 24, 2000, when he became the first goalie ever selected first overall in the NHL Entry Draft. He joined the Isles organization after one season at Boston University, where he drew raves for his quickness, athleticism, and competitive fire.

Columbus Blue Jackets

Blue Jackets Skate in Heart of Ohio

The state of Ohio long has been a legitimate hockey hotbed. Cleveland even had an NHL team of its own with the brief tenure of the Barons in the late 1970s. In 2000-01, the NHL grew to 30 teams, adding the Columbus Blue Jackets and Minnesota Wild. The Jackets won 28 games. Among their youngsters were (from left) Greg Gardner, Mathieu Darche, and Jonathan Schill.

Minnesotans Go Wild for New Team

Minnesota hockey fans, still hurting after losing the North Stars to Dallas, rejoiced when the NHL announced that hockey was returning to the frigid state. On October 6, 2000, in Anaheim, Wild rookie Marian Gaborik (center) scored the first goal in Wild history. He celebrated with veteran Jim Dowd (left) and fellow rookie Filip Kuba (right). Minnesota finished the season with a respectable 25 victories.

Minnesota Wild

• Three NHLers post their 1,000th point: Sharks center Vincent Damphousse (October 14), Jaromir Jagr (December 30), and Flyers pivot Mark Recchi (March 13).

• On October 17, 2000, Patrick Roy logs his 448th regular-season win, breaking Terry Sawchuk's NHL mark.

• Powered by scoring ace Joe Sakic, the Avalanche take the Presidents' Trophy with 118 points.

• On the strength of Doug Weight's 90 points, Edmonton enjoys its best record in more than a decade, taking second place in the Northwest Division with 93 points.

• After failing to make the playoffs for four years running, the Canucks ride the 41-goal performance of Markus Naslund to third place in the Northwest and a playoff berth.

• The Flames' playoff hopes are doused by a 27-36-15-4 record despite another strong scoring show

Patrick Roy

Roy One-Ups Sawchuk With Win No. 448

Long respected for his skill as well as his penchant for dramatics, Patrick Roy enjoyed another—perhaps the ultimate—huge moment on October 17, 2000, when he backstopped Colorado to a 4-3 overtime triumph in Washington. The victory gave Patrick 448 regular-season career wins, one more than legendary netminder Terry, who had held the NHL record. Still at the top of his game, Roy finished the season with a career-high 40 wins.

He's Still Got It! Mario Returns, Stars Again

In a comeback of epic proportions, Steeltown hockey savior Mario Lemieux shed his owner's cloak and returned to action on December 27, 2000, with three points against the Maple Leafs. In 43 games, the NHL's only active Hall of Famer posted 76 points, making him the most potent scorer in the league. Mario and his partners had purchased the Penguins in 1999, saving the franchise from potential bankruptcy.

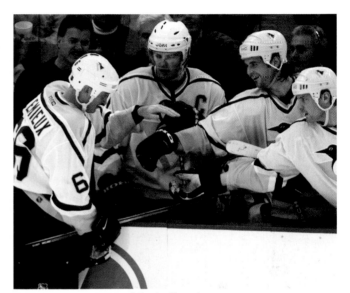

Mario Lemiuex

Nicklas Lidstrom

Lidstrom Sticks Around, Earns Norris Trophy

Nicklas Lidstrom (right), three straight years a runner-up as the league's top defenseman, finally took the Norris Trophy in 2000-01. Lidstrom, a lunch-bucket defender who also scored 71 points, garnered 600 Norris votes to Ray Bourque's 251 and Scott Stevens's 203. A year earlier, Lidstrom had made some noises about leaving the NHL in order to raise his children in his native Sweden.

by budding superstar Jarome Iginla (31 goals, 71 points).

• Minnesota wins 25 games behind goalie Manny Fernandez.

• With 111 points, Detroit takes the Central Division. Brendan Shanahan (76 points) leads in scoring.

• After winning the 2000 Presidents' Trophy, the Blues fall to second in the Central as goalies Roman Turek and rookie Brent Johnson shine.

• Even with a 25-goal outburst from rugged Scott Walker, the improving Predators miss the playoffs.

• Chicago fails to make the playoffs for the fourth straight year despite three 30-goal men (Tony Amonte, Steve Sullivan, and Eric Daze).

• First-year Columbus brings up the rear in the Central Division, posting a competitive 28 wins and boasting a 30-goal scorer in Geoff Sanderson.

Hasek Dominates Again, Captures Sixth Vezina

As goalie Dominik Hasek began the 2000-01 campaign, his ninth in a Sabres sweater, doomsayers insisted that the reign of The Dominator was over. But Hasek proved he still had plenty of gas in the tank, recording a league-high 11 shutouts, winning 37 games, and posting a 2.11 GAA. The upshot was that 30 voting experts (the league GMs) deemed Dom worthy of his sixth Vezina Trophy.

Dominik Hasek

Bure Fires In 59 for Another Goal-Scoring Crown

Few players have the ability to break open games like Pavel Bure, the Russian Rocket. For the second straight season, the Moscow Muzzle-Loader led the NHL in goals (59) in 2000-01 to earn the Maurice Richard Trophy. In his first 10 seasons, Pavel led the circuit in tallies no fewer than four times—twice each for Florida and Vancouver.

Francis Joins League's High-Rent District

Prior to January 29, 2001, only four players in NHL history had registered as many as 1,600 career points—Wayne Gretzky (2,857), Gordie Howe (1,850), Mark Messier (1,781), and Marcel Dionne (1,771). Then, with a three-assist night, Ron Francis joined the elite crowd. Francis finished his 20th season with 1,624 points.

Ron Francis

Pavel Bure

• Mike Modano and Brett Hull combine for 72 goals and 163 points as Dallas grabs the top spot in the Pacific for its fifth straight division title.

• Rookie goalie Evgeni Nabokov wins 32 games and youngster Patrick Marleau notches 25 goals as San Jose jumps to second in the Pacific, its best finish ever.

• Ziggy Palffy (38 goals) and Luc Robitaille (37) share the scoring load as the Kings make the playoffs.

• Phoenix feels the frustration of a tightly contested Western Conference, as 35 wins, 90 points, and a 2.27 GAA from goalie Sean Burke aren't enough for a playoff spot.

• Disappointment turns to bitterness as Anaheim drops to last place in the Western Conference, behind both the Wild and Blue Jackets.

Bondra Powers In the Power-Play Goals

Teams foolish enough to take penalties against the Capitals in 2000-01 were made to pay a premium thanks to the power-play preeminence of Peter Bondra. After a subpar performance in 1999-00, the super sniper finished with a league-leading 22 power-play goals and a healthy total of 45 red lights.

Peter Bondra

Jacques Martin, Alexei Yashin

Martin Leads Sens to 48 Wins

Before he became one of the top coaches in the NHL, Jacques Martin guided Guelph (OHL) to the 1986 Memorial Cup. He was named the NHL's coach of the year in 1998-99 before taking the 2000-01 Senators to their best finish ever: 48 wins and 109 points. Martin got plenty of help from Alexei Yashin (40-48-88).

Patrik Elias

Elias Smashes New Jersey's Scoring Record

A star rising out of the swamps of northern New Jersey, Devils winger Patrik Elias (#26) exploded onto the scoring scene in 2000-01. Elias tallied a franchise-record 96 points, eclipsing the 94 set by Kirk Muller in 1987-88. Patrik finished his fourth full season trailing only Jaromir Jagr and Joe Sakic in the league's scoring race. Moreover, his +45 rating tied Sakic for the NHL lead.

• The Devils finish first in the Eastern Conference, dominating with solid defense and Patrik Elias's explosive scoring (96 points, a franchise record).

• First-year goalie Roman Cechmanek makes a stunning debut with 35 wins and a 2.01 GAA for the second-place Flyers.

• Pittsburgh welcomes owner Mario Lemieux back to the lineup and rides the scoring of Jaromir Jagr (121 points) and Alexei Kovalev (44 goals) to third place.

• The return of Mark Messier after three years in Vancouver is not enough to propel the Rangers to success. They miss the playoffs for the fourth straight year.

• The Islanders miss the playoffs for the seventh year in a row despite the continued fine play of Polish puckmeister Mariusz Czerkawski, who leads the club with 30 tallies.

Scott Stevens

Cechmanek Wins 35 in NHL Debut

At age 29, Czech goalie Roman Cechmanek of the Flyers didn't qualify for rookie honors as he began his NHL career in 2000-01. However, after recording 10 shutouts, posting 35 wins, and chalking up the second-best goals-against average in the league (2.01), he more than qualified for Vezina Trophy consideration. He wound up losing a fairly close vote to fellow country-man Dominik Hasek.

Roman Cechmanek

Sakic Cops Hart, Byng, Pearson

One of the most respected superstars in the world, Joe Sakic finished the 2000-01 season with a roomful of hardware—including his second Stanley Cup. He also took the Hart Trophy, the Lester B. Pearson Award, and the Lady Byng Trophy. Here, the Avs captain poses with the Presidents' Trophy, won by the team that takes the NHL's regular-season crown. Colorado finished with a 52-16-10-4 record.

Joe Sakic

Veteran Stevens Still Shines on D

A surly, snarling rearguard who played as tough at 37 as he did at 18, Scott Stevens finished the 2000-01 NHL season with a plus-40 rating, tops among NHL blue-liners. After 1,434 regular-season NHL games, Stevens—one of the best defensemen never to win the Norris Trophy—owned an almost inconceivable plus-341 career mark. Stevens helped New Jersey amass a conference-high 111 points.

2000-01

• With Alexei Yashin (40-48-88) back in the mix, Ottawa sets a franchise record with 48 wins, taking the Northeast Division.

• Buffalo goalie Dominik Hasek continues to dominate, winning 37 games and guiding the Sabres to a second-place finish.

• Five 20-goal scorers (Gary Roberts, Mats Sundin, Yanic Perreault, Sergei Berezin, and Jonas Hoglund) lead the Leafs to third place in the Northeast.

• Not even a 95-point performance from ace playmaker Jason Allison, or 37 goals from Joe Thornton, can get Boston back into the playoffs.

• For the first time since 1922, the once-proud Canadiens miss the play-offs for a third straight year, their roster decimated by injuries.

• Washington capitalizes on Peter Bondra's 45 goals and takes the Southeast Division with 96 points.

Kings Shock the Wings in First-Round Upset

A well-oiled machine, the Red Wings headed into the 2001 playoffs as the Western Conference's second seed—and prohibitive favorites in their first-round battle against Los Angeles. The Kings, however, pulled off a shocker, winning two over-time games en route to a six-game triumph. Here, L.A. celebrates Adam Dead-marsh's extra-session goal in Game 6 as Larry Murphy slouches off in defeat.

Western Conference Quarterfinals

Western Conference Quarterfinals

Stars Need Three Overtime Wins to Fend Off Oilers

Just two years removed from their 1999 Stanley Cup triumph, the Stars overcame a huge challenge in the opening round of the 2001 playoffs. Their series against sixth-seeded Edmonton and superstar goalie Tommy Salo (pictured) featured four sudden-death overtime games. Dallas won three of the donnybrooks, taking Game 5 on Kirk Muller's OT winner.

• Jeff O'Neill's career-best 41 goals, aided by Ron Francis's 50 assists, pace Carolina to a second-place finish in the Southeast with 88 points.

• Inconsistency continues to mar the Panthers as Pavel Bure nets 59 goals but the club gives up 246. They finish out of the playoffs.

• In its second season, Atlanta boosts its seasonal point total from 39 to 60. Ray Ferraro leads the way with 29 goals.

• Rookie Brad Richards (62 points) is a lone bright spot for Tampa Bay as the team finishes second to last in the Eastern Conference.

• The Eastern Conference playoffs feature three first-round upsets: Toronto over Ottawa, Pittsburgh over the Caps, and Buffalo over Philly. The Devils quiet the Hurricanes.

• In the Western Conference, Colorado, Dallas, and St. Louis win as predicted, but Los Angeles stuns

Eastern Conference Semifinals

Pens Beat Sabres in Game 7 Thriller

Pittsburgh defenseman Darius Kasparaitis (shown hammering Buffalo's Steve Heinze) is known for his rambunctious style and fearless approach to warfare. On May 10, 2001, he became a playoff hero when he tallied only his second career postseason goal. Kasparaitis scored 13:01 into sudden-death to defeat Dominik Hasek and the Sabres in Game 7 of their second-round series.

Devils Whip Pens in Eastern Finals

In 2000-01, the Devils boasted the most potent offense in the NHL, scoring 295 regular-season goals. In the Stanley Cup semifinals, they flexed their muscles, scoring 17 goals in five games, including this one from rugged Randy McKay (behind net). They also got help from goaltender Martin Brodeur, who registered shutouts in Games 3 and 4 in Steeltown. New Jersey won Game 5 of the series 4-2 to eliminate the Penguins and enter the Stanley Cup Finals for the second straight year.

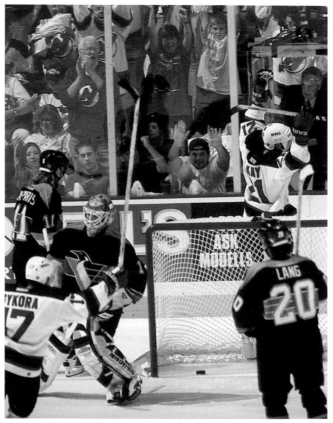

Eastern Conference Finals

2000-01

second-seeded Detroit in six games in the first round.

• Pittsburgh wins two games in OT en route to a dramatic seven-game Eastern semis series win over Buffalo.

• St. Louis has surprisingly little trouble eliminating the favored Stars

in the Western semis, pulling off a four-game sweep.

• In other semifinal action, Colorado crowns the Kings in seven, while New Jersey goes the limit to beat the Leafs.

• Goaltender Martin Brodeur's two shutouts help the Devils defeat Pitts-

burgh in five in the Eastern Conference finals.

• Colorado downs St. Louis in five Western finals games, winning the final two in overtime.

• The Avalanche and Devils split the first six games of the Stanley Cup

Blake Gives Avs the Edge They Need in Finals

In their quest for the Stanley Cup, Colorado acquired defenseman Rob Blake, the 1998 Norris Trophy winner, in February 2001. The deal paid huge dividends, as Blake scored 19 points in the playoffs and helped defuse New Jersey's potent offense. Here, he ties up the Devils' Sergei Brylin in Game 1, in which he tallied a goal and two assists in a 5-0 Avalanche victory.

Stanley Cup Finals

Western Conference Finals

Avs Shoo the Blues in Western Finals

Despite the often heroic play of goalie Roman Turek, St. Louis was dispatched from the 2001 Western Conference finals by Colorado in five games. The Blues fought the good fight, pushing three games to sudden-death. St. Louis won Game 3 on a double-OT goal by Scott Young, but the Avs took the next two in overtime. They clinched the series on a Joe Sakic tally just 24 seconds into the extra session.

Tanguay's the Hero in Cup Finale

It was clear by his composure throughout the 2001 playoffs that nobody had bothered to explain the sophomore jinx to Colorado's Alex Tanguay (right). In Game 7 of the Cup Finals, the second-year star ripped two goals past Martin Brodeur, the second of which is pictured here. Tanguay also assisted on the third goal in the Avs' 3-1 victory. Alex, who had lived in Patrick Roy's basement as a rookie, was born on November 21, 1979, when Ray Bourque's NHL career was 18 games old.

Stanley Cup Finals

Finals. Colorado's Patrick Roy logs shutouts in Games 1 and 6, while New Jersey guts out road victories in Games 2 and 5.

• In Game 7 of the Finals, Alex Tanguay nets the game-winning goal in a 3-1 Avs triumph. Ray Bourque finally hoists the Stanley Cup.

• Patrick Roy becomes the first to win the Conn Smythe Trophy three times.

• Joe Sakic wins the Hart Trophy as well as the Lester B. Pearson Award and the Lady Byng.

• San Jose netminder Evgeni Nabokov is honored with the Calder Trophy.

• Detroit's Nicklas Lidstrom wins his first Norris Trophy.

• Dominik Hasek claims his sixth Vezina Trophy.

• Devil John Madden cops the Frank Selke Trophy, while Philly coach Bill Barber wins the Jack Adams Award.

GRETZKY, MARIO LEAD CANADA TO GOLD MEDAL

Eager to showcase its finest players on the largest stage possible, the NHL once again made a commitment to participate in Olympic competition. Thus, in February 2002, for the second time in four years, the league suspended operations in the midst of the regular season to allow its superstars to compete in the Winter Games—this time held in and around Salt Lake City, Utah.

Despite the enthusiasm of the host nation's team (led by 1980 Olympic coaching hero Herb Brooks) and the strength of such teams as Sweden, Russia, and the Czech Republic, no single country had a more publicly fervent desire to win gold than Team Canada, which last took an Olympic crown in 1952. Their general manager, Wayne Gretzky, became caught up in the heat of competition. At one point, he abandoned his calm, soft-spoken demeanor and angrily lashed out, taking on an us-against-the-world attitude.

The Great One's tactic worked wonders, as his team responded to his diatribe and evolved from early-round doldrums to play brilliantly in the medal round. Like its counterparts, Team Canada featured a panoply of future (and indeed current) Hall of Fame superstars. Captained by

Mario Lemieux, who tallied six points in five games despite a painful hip injury, the Canadians simply would not be denied. Joe Sakic, who was voted by his peers as the best player in the NHL in 2000-01, earned Olympic MVP honors with four goals and seven points in six games.

Sakic's most memorable tally came against the United States in the gold-medal game. With just 1:41 to play in the second period, he converted a power-play setup with Ed Jovanovski and Avalanche teammate Rob Blake to put Team Canada ahead 3-2. While Martin Brodeur subsequently slammed the door shut in goal, Sakic set up a third-period goal by Jarome Iginla (who was in the middle of his own coming-out party as the NHL's leading goal-scorer and overall scoring champion). Sakic then hammered the final nail into the coffin with his second goal of the game to make the final score 5-2.

With many of them shedding tears of joy, the Canadians lined up to accept their gold medals, as 50 years of Olympic frustration came to a spectacular end. "This was a chance of a lifetime," said team captain Lemieux, who has now officially done it all. "Once you're born [in Canada], you're always going to be a Canadian and you always do whatever you can for your country."

Mario and his mates were not the only Canadian heroes at the 2002 Winter Games. The Canadian women's squad, led by Hayley Wickenheiser and Danielle Goyette, defeated the favored American team 3-2 in the gold-medal tilt, avenging their loss at the 1998 Nagano Games. Even a sterling performance by American Cammi Granato (who led her team with 10 points in five games) could not hold back the Canadians.

The double-dip sweep of the Americans by their neighbors to the north served to reignite a friendly rivalry between the adjacent nations. "It's our pastime, it's our game," Sakic said afterward. "With hockey moving toward the United States, it meant a lot more to Canadians to beat the U.S.—especially in the U.S."

2001-02

• At the 2001 NHL Draft, Thrashers selection Ilya Kovalchuk becomes the first Russian ever taken first overall.

• In a blockbuster trade, the Rangers obtain Eric Lindros from the Flyers.

• Six-time Vezina Trophy winner Dominik Hasek is traded from Buffalo

to Detroit for Slava Kozlov. Brett Hull, a recent playoff hero in Dallas, signs to play in Motown.

• Pittsburgh ships scoring ace Jaromir Jagr to Washington.

• For the first time in NHL history, a man of African descent wins the

scoring title. Calgary's Jarome Iginla leads the league with 96 points, followed by Canucks Markus Naslund (90) and Todd Bertuzzi (85).

• Jarome Iginla also wins the NHL's Rocket Richard Trophy with 52 goals. No one else reaches 50.

Captained by Mario Lemieux (third in line behind Theo Fleury and Joe Sakic), Team Canada won the 2002 Olympic hockey gold medal with a dramatic 5-2 win over USA. It was Canada's first Olympic title since 1952. Sakic led his team in points (seven), scored the game-winning goal in the gold-medal game, and was named the tournament MVP.

• Adam Oates, who moves from Washington to Philadelphia at the trade deadline, leads the NHL in helpers (64).

• Colorado's Patrick Roy registers the NHL's best goals-against average (1.94), while Detroit goalie Dominik Hasek leads the NHL in wins (41).

• Red Wing Luc Robitaille scores his 600th goal, then passes Bobby Hull for most career red lights by a left winger.

• On January 30, 2002, speedy center Jeremy Roenick, who left Arizona to play for the Flyers in 2001-02, notches his 1,000th career point.

• Red Wings sniper Brendan Shanahan scores his 500th career goal on March 23, 2002.

• Patrick Roy shuts out Dallas on December 26, 2001, to become the first NHL goalie to win 500 regular-season games.

Eric Lindros, Mark Messier

Ho-Hum: Sakic Leads the Avs to Another Division Title

Leading an Avalanche squad that was missing Peter Forsberg for the entire regular season, Joe Sakic simply went about his business as usual in 2001-02. Sakic topped the Avalanche in goals (26), assists (53), and points (79) and helped them win their eighth consecutive division title, going back to 1994-95, when they were the Quebec Nordiques.

Joe Sakic

Rangers Tip Caps to NYC Firefighters

The horror that befell New York on September 11, 2001, shattered countless lives but also brought a city and a nation closer together. The Rangers, represented by captain Mark Messier and superstar Eric Lindros, celebrated a long, close relationship with the city's firefighters in a pregame ceremony. Messier was presented with the helmet of a fallen firefighter.

Atlanta Boasts Two Dynamic Rooks

The arrival of two budding superstars in 2001-02 turned the Atlanta Thrashers from fledgling expansion hopefuls into an enormously promising squad that could do some serious damage. The dynamic duo of Dany Heatley (left) and Ilya Kovalchuk combined for 55 goals and 118 points and were two of the NHL's top Calder Trophy candidates.

Dany Heatley, Ilya Kovalchuk

- Carolina's Ron Francis collects his 500th goal on January 2, 2002.

- Led by Brendan Shanahan's 37 goals and 75 points and Dominik Hasek's first 40-win season, Detroit finishes atop the Central Division with a league-best 116 points.

- Pavol Demitra ties for seventh in the NHL in scoring (78 points) as the Blues take second in the Central Division.

- The Blackhawks are back in the Stanley Cup playoffs following a 41-win season and a career year from left winger Eric Daze (38 goals).

- The Predators fail to qualify for postseason competition, as center Greg Johnson leads the team with a mere 44 points.

- In its second NHL campaign, Columbus slips from 28 to 22 wins. Veteran journeyman Ray Whitney leads the way with 61 points.

Team Leader Naslund Ranks Second in NHL in Total Points

Vancouver captain Markus Naslund enjoyed a career year in 2001-02, finishing second overall in the NHL scoring race with 90 points (40 goals). Originally drafted by the Penguins in 1991, the slick Swede emerged as a leader on and off the ice in 2000-01, when he filled the shoes of Mark Messier. Naslund reached 40 goals in that season as well.

Todd Bertuzzi

Bertuzzi Emerges With 85 Points

Vancouver's Todd Bertuzzi (shown outmuscling Isles defenseman Kenny Jonsson) used the 2001-02 campaign as a personal coming-out party. En route to a third-place finish in the NHL scoring race, Bertuzzi rang up 36 goals and 85 points. Also amassing 110 penalty minutes, the burly winger carved out a new place among the NHL's most feared power forwards. As for the Canucks, they led the league in goals with 254 and finish with a 42-30-7-3 record. However, that finished earned them only an eighth seed in the Western Conference playoffs and a first-round loss to Detroit.

Markus Naslund

Jarome Iginla

Iginla Breaks Barriers, Tops All Scorers

One of the game's most complete players, Jarome Iginla of the Flames blossomed as a bona fide sniper in 2001-02, winning the Maurice "Rocket" Richard Trophy as the NHL's top goal-scorer (52). The hard-hitting, quick-skating right wing captured the league scoring title with 96 points and became the first man of African descent to win the Art Ross Trophy.

- Thanks to Patrick Roy's goaltending and Joe Sakic's 79 points, the Avalanche win their eighth division title in a row.

- Vancouver finishes second to Colorado in the Northwest Division thanks to scoring aces Markus Naslund and Todd Bertuzzi.

- Despite finishing 10 games over .500, the Oilers fail to qualify for the playoffs, finishing third in the Northwest Division.

- Calgary fades in the second half, wasting Jarome Iginla's first scoring title and a surprising season from center Craig Conroy (75 points).

- The Wild continue to grow, as the playmaking of Andrew Brunette (48 assists) and the scoring of Marian Gaborik (30 goals) thrill fans.

- En route to first place in the Pacific Division, Sharks goalie Evgeni Nabokov sets a new club record for wins (37).

Evgeni Nabokov

Nabokov Breaks Win Record, Scores a Goal

One year after winning the Calder Trophy with a San Jose-record 32 wins, Evgeni Nabokov snubbed his nose at any sophomore jinx talk in 2001-02. He again set the team mark for victories (37) while leading the Sharks to their first division title. Nabby also scored a goal into an empty net in Vancouver on March 10.

Jose Theodore

Theodore Renews Pride in Montreal

The club of legendary Montreal goalies, which includes Georges Vezina, Bill Durnan, Jacques Plante, Ken Dryden, and Patrick Roy, added another member in 2001-02. Jose Theodore was always steady and frequently brilliant, posting a GAA of 2.11. He was the chief reason the Habs not only made the playoffs but were able to shock the Bruins in the first round.

Bill Guerin

Local Guy Guerin Blasts In 41 Goals

Few players epitomized the Bruins' tradition with as much vigor and determination as Wilbraham, Massachusetts, native Bill Guerin. A hard-driving power forward, Guerin possessed a rocket launcher for a shot and a frequently chippy disposition. In 2001-02, he enjoyed his second straight 40-goal season (41) and helped Boston rise to the top spot in the Eastern Conference standings (43-24-6-9).

2001-02

- The Kings surge to a second-place finish in the Pacific on the playmaking genius of center Jason Allison.

- Daniel Briere has a breakout season (32 goals), Daymond Langkow leads in points (62), and goalie Sean Burke is the team MVP as Phoenix finishes third in the Pacific Division.

- Mired in controversy, including the midseason firing of coach Ken Hitchcock, the Stars finish out of the playoff picture despite 90 points.

- Goalie Jean-Sebastien Giguere emerges as a bona fide No. 1 goalie, but the Mighty Ducks finish last in the Pacific Division.

- Boston, the only team with a pair of 40-goal scorers—Bill Guerin and Glen Murray—wins the Eastern Conference title with 101 points.

- Mats Sundin finishes fourth overall in points (80) as the Maple Leafs take second place in the Northeast Division with 43 wins and 100 points.

Ron Francis

Francis Reaches 1,700, Powers Canes

On January 2, 2002, Ron Francis, captain of the Hurricanes, scored the 500th goal of his NHL career, making him one of only five players in NHL history with at least 500 goals and 1,700 points. The wily veteran led Carolina through the first three rounds of the NHL playoffs, then won Game 1 of the Stanley Cup Finals with an overtime goal at Detroit.

Glen Murray

Peca Steers Islanders to the Playoffs

Pound for pound the hardest hitting forward in the NHL, Mike Peca came to the Islanders in 2001-02, assumed the captaincy, and delivered in every way imaginable. On a rebuilding team that missed the postseason for seven straight years, Peca led the way back to the Stanley Cup chase. He tallied 25 goals, including the game-winner in the victory that clinched their playoff berth.

Mike Peca

Murray Scores on Every Sixth Shot

Boston's first-round draft pick in 1991, right winger Glen Murray began his NHL career with the Bruins that fall. After detours in Pittsburgh and L.A., he returned to Beantown nine games into the 2001-02 season—then enjoyed a career year. The power forward stockpiled 41 goals and a team-high 71 points, while his 16.5 shooting percentage made him one of the most accurate snipers in the league.

• Ottawa finishes third in the Northeast on the scoring of Daniel Alfredsson (71 points) and goaltending of Patrick Lalime.

• Montreal ends a three-year playoff drought, riding the brilliant goaltending of Jose Theodore to fourth place in the Northeast Division.

• Buffalo finishes .500 and fails to qualify for the playoffs, wasting a top-20 scoring performance from Miroslav Satan (37 goals, 73 points).

• Led by Jeremy Roenick (67 points) and late-season addition Adam Oates, the Flyers finish atop the Atlantic Division with 97 points.

• Bolstered by the scoring of Alexei Yashin (75 points), the Isles take second in the Atlantic with 96 points.

• Martin Brodeur equals goalie Tony Esposito's NHL record for consecutive 30-win seasons (seven) as the Devils take third place in the Atlantic with 41 victories.

Flyers Gain Edge When J.R. Takes Ice

Philadelphia may be known as the City of Brotherly Love, but Flyers fans leave that sentiment at the gate—as did their newest hero, Jeremy Roenick, in 2001-02. In his first year in black and orange, J.R. led the team in points (not counting March arrival Adam Oates) and plus-minus rating (+32). He also registered 74 PIM, notched the 1,000th point of his NHL career, and led the Flyers to first place in the Atlantic Division with a 42-27-10-3 record.

Wayne Gretzky

Jeremy Roenick

Gretzky Gets Tough with Canadians

Wayne Gretzky in a business suit is hockey's version of a wolf in sheep's clothing. At the 2002 Olympics, the intensity that characterized his brilliant 20-year career in the NHL was on international display. Normally reserved and comparatively low-key, the Great One—serving as executive director of Canada's eventual gold medal squad—was a fiery advocate in his new role. "Nothing short of a gold medal will be acceptable," Gretzky said throughout the competition. His coaches and players got the message.

2001-02

• Despite the courageous comebacks of Eric Lindros (73 points), Theo Fleury, goalie Mike Richter, and defenseman Bryan Berard, the Rangers fail to make the playoffs.

• Pittsburgh misses the playoffs, as Mario Lemieux sits out the second half of the season due to injury. Alexei Kovalev (76 points) is among the few bright spots.

• Ron Francis amasses 77 points as Carolina takes the Southeast Division with 91 points.

• Peter Bondra leads the NHL in power-play goals (17) and Jaromir Jagr ties for fifth overall in scoring (79 points), but the Caps fail to make the playoffs.

• Brad Richards leads Tampa Bay in points (62), and Nikolai Khabibulin regains his status as one of the best goalies in the world, but the Bolts don't make the playoffs.

Columbus Fan Dies After Being Hit by Puck

Tragedy struck the NHL on March 16, 2002, when a slap shot by Blue Jackets forward Espen Knutsen deflected off the stick of Flames defenseman Derek Morris and soared into the stands at Nationwide Arena in Columbus. Thirteen-year-old Brittanie Cecil, whose initials are visible on the back of Knutsen's helmet, was struck by the puck and died from her injuries two days later. Doctors said Cecil died not from the force of the puck, but from snapping her head back, which caused damage to an artery that led to her brain.

Espen Knutsen

Donald Audette

Courageous Habs Stun Bruins in First Round

Montreal's Donald Audette, shown celebrating a goal against the Bruins in the first round of the 2002 playoffs, returned to the Habs in time for the postseason after enduring a severe arm injury. He was joined by Saku Koivu, who missed all but three regular-season games while receiving cancer treatments. Meanwhile, goalie Jose Theodore did his impression of a brick wall as the eighth-seeded Habs shocked top-seeded Boston in six games.

Brendan Shanahan

Shanahan Nets 500th, Powers Wings

On March 23, 2002, Brendan Shanahan (center, with "A" on his jersey) joined an elite fraternity when he scored the 500th goal of his career. The goal was in many ways a "typical" Shanny clutch tally. Assisted by defenseman Nicklas Lidstrom, it was a power-play game-winner that victimized goalie Patrick Roy of the Avalanche. On the season, Shanahan helped lead Detroit to a league-best 51-17-10-4 record. He also scored a key goal in Game 5 of the Stanley Cup Finals.

- Florida, which trades Pavel Bure to the Rangers in March, is led in scoring by a defenseman. Sandis Ozolinsh's 52 points lead the way for the fourth-place Panthers.

- Although the Thrashers have the NHL's fewest points (54), two bright spots are rookies Dany Heatley (67 points) and Ilya Kovalchuk, who scores 29 goals before suffering a season-ending injury.

- Canada wins the Olympic hockey gold medal, defeating USA in the final game 5-2. GM Wayne Gretzky and scoring greats Mario Lemieux and Joe Sakic lead the way.

- The Eastern Conference quarter-finals see eighth-seeded Montreal stun No. 1 Boston in six games and seventh-seeded Ottawa oust the Flyers in five contests.

- Also in the East, Carolina edges New Jersey (4-2) and Toronto nips the Islanders (4-3).

Eastern Conference Quarterfinals

Wings Down Rival Avalanche in West Finals

Considered *the* series of the 2002 playoffs, Colorado faced the Red Wings in the Western Conference Finals. The Avalanche took a 3-2 lead in games before Detroit goalie Dominik Hasek notched shutouts in Games 6 and 7. Avs goalie Patrick Roy, shown yielding a goal to Sergei Fedorov, was pulled during Game 7, which Detroit won 7-0.

Western Conference Finals

Leafs Oust the Senators in Ontario War

In the second round of the 2002 Stanley Cup playoffs, the Maple Leafs, led by tenacious disturber Darcy Tucker (right), took on Chris Phillips (left) and the Senators in a battle for provincial bragging rights. The seesaw series went the distance before Toronto prevailed with a 3-0 win in Game 7. Ottawa had a chance to finish off the Leafs in Game 6, but Toronto won 4-3 on Alexander Mogilny's third-period winner.

Eastern Conference Finals

Tough Canes D Overpowers Maple Leafs

The Cinderella of the 2002 playoffs, Carolina (with the worst record of the NHL's 16 playoff teams) shocked Toronto in the Eastern Conference finals, ousting the injury-plagued Leafs in six games. Goalie Arturs Irbe allowed just 17 goals in his first 13 playoff games, while the Canes' defense, led by Sean Hill (#22), played a patient, often punishing style.

2001-02

- In the Western Conference quarters, all the favorites win. Colorado beats Los Angeles (4-3), San Jose takes Phoenix (4-1), Detroit eliminates Vancouver (4-2), and St. Louis erases Chicago (4-1).

- Second-round action in the Eastern Conference features an epic provincial battle between Toronto and Ottawa, won by the Leafs in seven games. Carolina ousts Montreal in six.

- The Western Conference semifinals see Detroit cruise past St. Louis in five games. The Avalanche go the distance for the second straight series, needing seven games to shed the Sharks.

- The upstart Hurricanes, led by goalie Arturs Irbe, knock off the Maple Leafs in six games in the Eastern Conference finals.

- Detroit and Colorado hook up in a seven-game battle royale in the Western Conference finals. Shutouts by goalie Dominik Hasek in Games 6

Detroit's 3-OT Win Cripples Hurricanes

Saturday night on June 9, 2002, looked to be party time in Raleigh, as the Hurricanes seemed on the verge of winning the first Finals game ever held in the Carolinas. However, after Detroit's Brett Hull scored with 74 seconds left in regulation, 41-year-old Igor Larionov sent Canes fans home dejected. His goal at 14:47 of the third OT ended the third longest Finals game ever—just 26 seconds off the record. Larionov became the oldest NHL player ever to score an OT playoff goal.

Stanley Cup Finals

Stanley Cup Finals

Star-Studded Wings Hoist the Cup

The Red Wings bask in glory after winning the Stanley Cup with a 3-1 triumph over Carolina in Game 5. Owner Mike Ilitch (in suit) had assembled a roster that included eight potential Hall of Famers. Coach Scotty Bowman (front) captured his ninth NHL title, while Brett Hull (behind Bowman) won his second. Veteran superstars Luc Robitaille (to Bowman's left) and Dominik Hasek (to Ilitch's right) sipped from the Cup for the very first time.

and 7 put Detroit in the Stanley Cup Finals.

• In Game 1 of the Cup Finals, the man they call Ronnie Franchise (Ron Francis) scores in the first minute of overtime to give the Hurricanes a stunning 3-2 victory.

• After saving face in Game 2, 3-1, Detroit beats Carolina 3-2 in triple overtime in Game 3. The marathon doesn't end until Igor Larionov scores with 5:13 left in the sixth period.

• Deflated by their Game 3 defeat, the Hurricanes drop the next contest to Detroit 3-0.

• The Red Wings cruise to a 3-1 home-ice victory in Game 5, securing their third Stanley Cup title in six years.

• Detroit defenseman Nicklas Lidstrom, who averaged more than 31 minutes of ice time in the playoffs, wins the Conn Smythe Trophy.

INDEX

INDEX

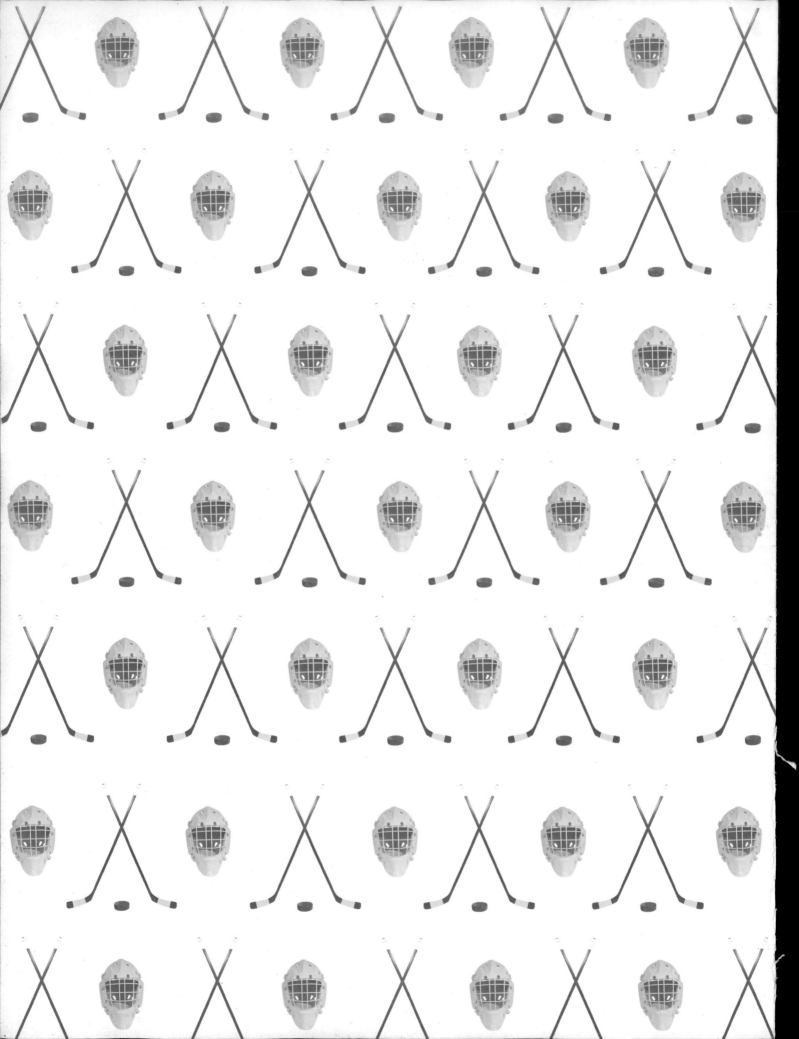